The Lion and the Springbok

The Lion and the Springbok presents a unique account of the dynamics and divergences of the 'uneasy special relationship' between Britain and South Africa. From the bruising experience of the South African War (1899–1902) to South Africa's withdrawal from the Commonwealth in 1961, the authors chart this relationship in all its political, economic, cultural, and geostrategic aspects.

All the major disputes are discussed, including the struggle for the High Commission Territories, the crisis over Seretse Khama's marriage, and the transfer of the Simon's Town naval base. These issues trace, for the most part, a continuing deterioration in relations, as Afrikaner nationalist identity hardened and South African politics slid into the extremes of apartheid. The perceptions each side had of the other after 1948 are examined through representations in the media, and an epilogue considers the reasons for the return of the 'new South Africa' to the Commonwealth in 1994.

RONALD HYAM is Emeritus Reader in British Imperial History, University of Cambridge, and a Fellow and former President of Magdalene College.

PETER HENSHAW is a Research Professor in History at the University of Western Ontario.

Nelson Mandela after admission to an Honorary Fellowship at Magdalene College, Cambridge, 2 May 2001. Left to right: security officer, Dr Mandela, Cheryl Carolus (South African high commissioner), Professor W. R. Cornish (President), Professor Sir John Gurdon (Master), Thabo Makupula (Mandela Magdalene Scholar). *Source*: Magdalene College Archives, P/30/2/10

The Lion and the Springbok

Britain and South Africa since the Boer War

Ronald Hyam and Peter Henshaw

CAMBRIDGE UNIVERSITY PRESS
Cambridge, New York, Melbourne, Madrid, Cape Town, Singapore, São Paulo

Cambridge University Press
The Edinburgh Building, Cambridge CB2 8RU, UK

Published in the United States of America by Cambridge University Press, New York

www.cambridge.org
Information on this title: www.cambridge.org/9780521824538

© Ronald Hyam and Peter Henshaw 2003

This publication is in copyright. Subject to statutory exception
and to the provisions of relevant collective licensing agreements,
no reproduction of any part may take place without the written
permission of Cambridge University Press.

First published 2003
This digitally printed version 2007

A catalogue record for this publication is available from the British Library

ISBN 978-0-521-82453-8 hardback
ISBN 978-0-521-04138-6 paperback

Contents

Frontispiece		*page* ii
List of illustrations		vii
List of tables		ix
Preface		xi
Acknowledgements		xiv
List of abbreviations		xv
1	The uneasy special relationship: dynamics and divergencies	1
2	Breakdown: into war, 1895–1899	37
3	Post-war: the myth of magnanimity, 1905–1907	57
4	African interests and the South Africa Act, 1908–1910	76
5	'Greater South Africa': the struggle for the High Commission Territories, 1910–1961	102
6	The economic dimension: South Africa and the sterling area, 1931–1961	118
7	Britain, the United Nations, and the 'South African disputes', 1946–1961	146
8	The political consequences of Seretse Khama and Ruth, 1948–1952	168
9	Containing Afrikanerdom: the geopolitical origins of the Central African Federation, 1948–1953	198
10	Strategy and the transfer of Simon's Town, 1948–1957	230
11	The parting of the ways: the departure of South Africa from the Commonwealth, 1951–1961	254

12	Enfeebled lion? How South Africans viewed Britain, 1945–1961	273
13	Springbok reviled: some British reactions to apartheid, 1948–1994	307
Epilogue	The relationship restored: the return of the new South Africa to the Commonwealth, 1994	343

Select bibliography 351
Index 372

Illustrations

MAPS

5.1	Plans for a 'Greater South Africa'	*page* 104
5.2	The Tomlinson Commission's threat to the High Commission Territories and the creation of Bantustans, 1955	109
9.1	Central African Federation	199

FIGURES

1.1	The evolution of Afrikaner political parties	20
1.2	The institutional structure of Afrikanerdom	24
6.1	British gold imports, 1931–72	122
6.2	South African gold production by prices realised and quantities, 1931–72	123
6.3	British reserves of gold and convertible currencies, 1931–72	124
6.4	South African imports from and exports to Britain as a percentage of total South African imports and exports of produce (excluding gold), 1931–72	125

ILLUSTRATIONS

Frontispiece: Nelson Mandela in Cambridge, 2001		ii
1.1	Cartoon: *Dienswillig die uwe*: Smuts as 'your willing servant' of Britain (*Die Burger*, 1942)	29
2.1	Boer prisoners in St Helena: (a) Broadbottom Camp and Boer enclosure (b) General Cronje and his officers	55
11.1	Cartoon: Britain aligns with the Asians at the United Nations after South Africa's departure from the Commonwealth (*Die Transvaler*, 1961)	271

viii   List of illustrations

12.1 Cartoon: The 'enfeebled lion' and the riddle of the Sphinx
     (Suez Crisis) (*Rand Daily Mail*, 1957)   295
13.1 Cartoon: Verwoerd: a nation mourns (*Private Eye*, 1966)   324
13.2 Cartoon: The campaign against the Springbok cricket tour
     of 1970 (*New Statesman*, 1 May 1970)   326

Tables

1.1	Trade between Britain and South Africa, 1946–1961	*page* 13
6.1	South African exports to Britain, 1931–1963	119
6.2	External capital investment in South Africa, 1913–1972	120
6.3	The sterling area 'dollar pool', 1946–1956	121
9.1	Immigrants into the Rhodesias, 1946–1950	226

Preface

'A special relationship and its mutual benefits, which history has bound us in' is how Nelson Mandela described relations between Britain and South Africa in the spring of 2001. The tragedy is that for most of the twentieth century this 'special relationship' was compromised, first by jingoistic Britain, then by Afrikaner nationalist South Africa. This book is about that tragedy.

We have worked together, with a shared outlook, over many years, with the long-term intention of producing a study more comprehensive than either of us could have managed to write by ourselves. Since it is based overwhelmingly on fundamental research in British government archives,[1] there are two inevitable limitations. One is that the perspective is mainly, though not exclusively, from the British side – so the book finds its home in the general field of British imperial and Commonwealth history, as well as South African history. The other is that the emphasis is on the period before the departure of South Africa from the Commonwealth in 1961, the British government's 'thirty-year rule of access' – in practice more like thirty-five years – preventing us from tackling the issues after the 1960s with anything like the authority we hope we bring to the period before then.

Our main concern is with inter-governmental relations, and we do not aim to give an account of the long British tradition of radical and liberal criticism of what happened in South Africa. But in conformity with current historical interest in identity-formation and media representation, and since it would otherwise look hopelessly incomplete, we have traced anti-apartheid opinion through to the 1990s (using newspaper evidence). South African perceptions of Britain are also examined. And we have attempted in an epilogue a brief assessment of the return of the new South Africa to the Commonwealth in 1994.

We present a series of studies rather than a connected narrative, but our chapters are not chosen at random. Their selection is dictated by the weight of evidence surviving in the archival record: in other words, they reflect the issues

---

[1] Although many other overseas archives have been trawled, the returns were much less rewarding, not least because the National Party government in South Africa operated a 'fifty-year rule' of access, and in the 1980s and early 1990s imposed a blanket closure on external affairs records.

which excited most attention at the time. There might be objections to this way of proceeding, but it can hardly be said to be unhistorical.

We deal with problems which have always been controversial, and are contested by scholars. We should therefore like to express our thanks to those historians and social scientists with whom we sometimes disagree, since they have provided not merely additional stimulus but also a sense of historiographical purpose. More positively, we wish to thank a number of research students who have contributed enthusiastically to the project over the years, among them more particularly Simon Cardy, Marc Feigen, and Lesley Reeves; and to thank our colleagues Rodney Davenport, Alan Jeeves, John Lonsdale, Bill Nasson, Ian Phimister, Christopher Saunders, and Iain R. Smith, for their friendship and support, though we hasten to add that we do not mean to claim from them any sort of endorsement. Finally, we should say how much we have appreciated the patience and expertise of Andrew Brown and his team at the Cambridge University Press.

R. H.
South Africa Freedom Day, 27 April 2002 P. J. H.

My particular understanding of Anglo-South African relations has been sharpened up over many years by discussions with the late Nicholas Mansergh and R. E. Robinson, with Noel Garson, Ged Martin, and David Throup, and above all with Rodney Davenport. I had the good fortune to have a family home close to the Public Record Office at Kew. My research has been generously supported in Cambridge by Magdalene College, with grants from the Morshead–Salter Fund, and by the Managers of the Smuts Memorial Fund, who enabled me to travel through the heartlands of Afrikanerdom in the darkest days of apartheid, and to visit Swaziland, Lesotho, and Mozambique. I remain grateful for the hospitality and insights of the USPG Fathers of the Community of the Resurrection at their mission houses in Luyengo, Swaziland, and Rosettenville (Sophiatown), Johannesburg.

R. H.
Cambridge

My work on this book began in 1986 as a Cambridge PhD student with Ronald Hyam, continued in Cape Town from 1990 to 1997, and was completed at Queen's University in Kingston, Ontario. It could not have been accomplished without the assistance of a number of individuals and institutions. For their financial support, thanks go to St John's College, the Managers of the Smuts

Memorial Fund, and of the Holland Rose studentship, all in Cambridge; to the National Maritime Museum, Greenwich for the Caird junior research fellowship; and Queen's University, Kingston. I would also like to thank the many librarians and archivists who have assisted my research – especially the librarians at the African Studies Library, the Jagger Library, and the Special Collections Library at the University of Cape Town; Stephen Lees at the Cambridge University Library; and the archivists at the South African National Archives in Pretoria. Doing archival research has almost invariably meant imposing myself for considerable periods on friends and relations. I owe a particular debt of gratitude to Anna Mary Young and her family, whose home in Putney has been a frequent base for my sessions at the Public Record Office; and to Paul Haines and Pauline Graham in Cambridge. Chris and Elaine Dodson provided extended and incomparable hospitality at Woodcroft, KwaZulu-Natal. My parents in Ottawa have always given their unstinting support. Finally, my wife Belinda Dodson deserves special acknowledgement for her intellectual, practical, and personal contributions to this endeavour.

P. J. H.
London, Ontario

Acknowledgements

Ronald Hyam is grateful to the publishers of the following journals and books for permission to reproduce material which first appeared in their pages: the *Historical Journal* (chapters 4, 8, and 9), the *Journal of Imperial and Commonwealth History* (chapter 11), the *Joernaal vir die Eietydse Geskiedenis* (chapter 5), and *Reappraisals in British imperial history*, by R. Hyam and Ged Martin (Macmillan, 1975) (chapter 3). Peter Henshaw is similarly grateful in respect of the *Historical Journal* (chapter 6), the *Journal of Imperial and Commonwealth History* (chapter 10), the *South African Historical Journal* (chapter 7), and *The international impact of the Boer War*, ed. Keith Wilson (Acumen Publishing, Chesham, 2001) (chapter 2).

Quotations from Crown copyright material are used by permission of the Public Record Office under licence from the Controller of Her Majesty's Stationery Office. The photograph of Nelson Mandela is by permission of the Master and Fellows of Magdalene College, Cambridge. Cartoons reproduced by permission of *Die Burger*, *Rand Daily Mail*, *Die Transvaler*, *Private Eye*, and *New Statesman*.

Abbreviations

The following abbreviations are used in the footnotes:

BDEEP	British Documents on the End of Empire Project
CAB	Cabinet Office Records
CO	Colonial Office Records
CRO	Commonwealth Relations Office
DO	Dominions Office/CRO records
FO	Foreign Office
HJ	*Historical Journal*
JAH	*Journal of African History*
JICH	*Journal of Imperial and Commonwealth History*
JSAS	*Journal of Southern African Studies*
PREM	Prime Minister's Office Records
PRO	Public Record Office, Kew
SAHJ	*South African Historical Journal*

1 The uneasy special relationship: dynamics and divergencies

Of all the regions of the world where imperial Britain sought to exert influence, none exhibited more contradictions, and therefore such intractable dilemmas and frustrations, as South Africa. Cape Colony was conquered from the Dutch in 1806 and retained in 1815 because of its strategic importance on the route to India. Control of the hinterland inevitably followed. Britain thus acquired a foreign settler community of some 40,000, who resented a more intrusive government than they were used to and doctrines of race relations which seemed to them wrong-headed. Many Boers trekked into the interior from the 1830s, determined to assert their right to a quiet sweet life (*lekke lewe*) of their own choosing, free from interference, and to preserve what they regarded as 'proper relations between master and servant'.[1] The fundamental constitution (*grondwet*) of the South African Republic (Transvaal) made their intransigent Bantu policy all too plain (clause 9): 'The people will admit no equalising (*gelijkstelling*) between the white and coloured inhabitants whether in church or state' (February 1858). It was not simply that the Boers would not accept or admit black *equality* (for which the word would have been *gelijkheid*), but, more uncompromisingly, no assimilation, no *making equal* or treating *as if equal*.[2] Treks enormously enlarged the area of contact and potential conflict on the highveld with spirited and sometimes highly mobile African chiefdoms determined to resist subjection. In 1879 at Isandhlwana the Zulu inflicted humiliating defeat on a contingent of the British army, although the Zulu were unable to prevent the destruction of their kingdom. The threat of a major African uprising thereafter loomed ominously in the background and further complicated relations between barely compatible white communities. Africans were seen overwhelmingly as 'the Other', but despite this some Africans sought imperial support or protection against local oppression.

Although British settlers had arrived in the Eastern Cape in 1820, South African conditions were not attractive to emigrants in the decades which

---

[1] G. M. Theal, *History of South Africa, from 1828 to 1846* (London, 1904), pp. 266–7 for manifesto of Piet Retief, 22 Jan. 1837; for the latest account, N. Etherington, *The Great Treks: the transformation of Southern Africa, 1815–1854* (London, 2001).
[2] P. Mason, *An essay on racial tension* (London, 1954), p. 85.

followed. Until the discovery of diamonds in 1867 and gold in 1886, South Africa's economic future looked bleak, and even the maintenance of viable European-style states in the interior was in doubt. British policy-makers were always perplexed as to what to do. Withdrawal without first providing some sort of collaborative structure (perhaps through federation) would imperil strategic and humanitarian interests. Gladstone came to the conclusion that South Africa was an insoluble problem. In these circumstances, it is hard not to accept the validity of Jan Smuts's critique of British rule and intervention in South Africa as a perfidious record of duplicity and fraud, violence and vacillation, by an alien, remote, and, in its 'native policy', quite possibly hypocritical government, a record which he summed up in the title of his polemic as *A century of wrong* (1899). Many well-informed English observers agreed with him: men like the Anglican archdeacon Augustus Wirgman, who described the British handling of the Transvaal as 'a series of miserable blunderings and tactless ineptitudes'.[3] There were in fact five formal changes in British relations with the Transvaal in a little over fifty years (six if you include an adjustment made in 1884): recognised as independent in 1852; annexed in 1877 (as a prelude to a projected federal reconstruction of South African states); self-government restored (subject to a notoriously undefined British 'suzerainty') in 1881; annexed again in wartime, 1900; responsible self-government restored again in 1906. Similar patterns of maddening uncertainty can be traced, for example, in relations with the African kingdom of Basutoland, of particular concern to the neighbouring Orange Free State: protection status refused in 1866; granted in 1868, transferred to the Cape government in 1871; resumed in 1884.

British and Boer communities had always sat uneasily together. In 1880 the British blundered into a Transvaal war, and in 1881 the Boers defeated them at the battle of Majuba Hill ('the hill of the doves', beautifully onomatopoeic), and forever thereafter taunted their opponents about it. Relations got worse as the mineral revolution brought in more money-making British immigrants. These thrusting Uitlanders (outsiders, denied the vote), who created Johannesburg and the Witwatersrand mines, gave deep offence to highly conservative, religious Boers, 'whose standards could not be measured by those of Birmingham or Threadneedle Street'.[4] The Boers were essentially unsophisticated Calvinist farmers, who had few schools and no higher education as yet. President Kruger refused to allow postal pillar-boxes in Pretoria on the grounds that town-dwellers should not have facilities denied to those in rural areas – an attitude the British found incomprehensible. Boer trust in imperial government was irretrievably

---

[3] A. T. Wirgman, *Storm and sunshine in South Africa, with some personal and historical reminiscences* (London, 1922), p. 79.
[4] C. W. de Kiewiet, *The anatomy of South African misery* (Oxford, 1956), pp. 10–11, 24.

destroyed by the Jameson Raid of 1895 (an ill-considered incursion into the Transvaal meant to spark off an uprising against Kruger's regime), and the cover-up which followed it.

A land with such a complex history of interaction between Black, Coloured, and Indian communities, and two diverse white groups, was never going to be free of controversial historical interpretation, not least in its external relations with the British overlord, six thousand miles away. And so we begin with an analysis of the modern historiography, and the ways in which this can be challenged.

I

Historiographical approaches

Since the 1960s, the dominant revisionist historiography has written an overall economic determinism (and several varieties of Marxism) into South African history. The distinctiveness of twentieth-century South Africa has been attributed by one of its leading historians to the 'imperatives of South Africa's capitalist development', to a history dominated 'to a very large extent' by the history of mining; and we are invited to believe that 'gold linked South Africa to the British empire'.[5] The fundamental tenet of this type of approach is that British policy towards South Africa was mainly directed to the formation and preservation of a modern industrial infrastructure, in order to maintain vital British economic interests.[6] Even historians who do not subscribe to this version of neo-Marxist analysis are inclined to ascribe governmental action, whether British or South African, to definite material interests, and underestimate the role of non-economic motives.[7]

---

[5] S. Marks, 'Southern Africa' in J. M. Brown and W. R. Louis, eds., *Oxford history of the British empire*, vol. IV (Oxford, 1999), ch. 24, pp. 547 and 550; A. Atmore and S. Marks, 'The imperial factor in South Africa', *JICH* vol. 3 (1974), pp. 105–39. Two articles, S. Marks, 'Scrambling for South Africa: a review article', *JAH* vol. 23 (1982), pp. 97–113, and S. Marks and S. Trapido, 'Lord Milner and the South African state reconsidered' in M. Twaddle, ed., *Imperialism, the state and the Third World* (London, 1992), represent a considerable retreat from the excesses of earlier formulations, as in S. Marks and S. Trapido, 'Lord Milner and the South African state', *History Workshop Journal* vol. 8 (1979), pp. 50–80, but the central contention remains the same: 'focus on the nature of the British economy'.

[6] H. Wolpe, 'Capitalism and cheap labour power in South Africa, from segregation to apartheid', *Economy and Society* vol. 1 (1972), pp. 425–56, partly repr. in W. Beinart and S. Dubow, eds., *Segregation and apartheid in twentieth-century South Africa* (London and New York, 1995), ch. 3, pp. 60–90; F. Johnstone, *Class, race and gold: a study of class relations and racial discrimination in South Africa* (London, 1976).

[7] G. R. Berridge, *Economic power in Anglo-South African diplomacy: Simonstown, Sharpeville and after* (London, 1981) and *South Africa, the colonial powers and 'African Defence': the rise and fall of a white entente, 1948–1960* (London, 1992).

To make a contribution to the challenging of these simplistic propositions is the aim of the present project. It is based on testing them against an intensive exploration of the British archival record. Once this is begun, it becomes immediately obvious that such notions bear little relation to the way governments think, or to the actual preoccupations of British policy-makers. Our alternative approach to the complex and uneasy special relationship between Britain and South Africa provides a place for the economic dimension, whilst widening the perspective to restore political, strategic, geopolitical, diplomatic, ethical, and socio-cultural considerations to their appropriate place. Thus we find ourselves taking issue with two historical approaches: (1) those which are based on economic determinism, but also those which neglect or over-play and thus misinterpret the economic dimension, and (2) those which are based on overly speculative or theory-bound work which neglects essential archive evidence and thus misinterprets the way the British government behaved. We are not attacking methodological diversity, only interpretations which are plainly wrong.

No doubt this stance makes us 'empiricist' historians, a label which is not usually employed in a complimentary sense. But while we are uncommitted to any of the grander theoretical positions, this does not mean that we have any claim to be free of presuppositions or bias. Realistically, no historian can cope simply by hoping high-mindedly to go ideologically unencumbered 'where the evidence leads', since the bits of evidence which get investigated are subjectively selected. It is a complete delusion to suppose 'that any given body of material would suggest all the concepts necessary to interpret it', and it is impossible to expect to ask only such questions as arise *out* of the evidence, since no-one can ever discover what all the evidence is.[8] For no historians is this more true than those working on twentieth-century imperial history and international relations, where the quantity of surviving British evidence is so massive. Accordingly, all any of us can do is to put questions of our own choosing to a part of the evidence, the portion which, speculatively, seems likely to be interesting or significant. Our own particular interest is in issues of 'high policy' at the ministerial level of government, and our theoretical bias is towards a belief in 'the primacy of geopolitics', the importance of strategy and prestige in policy-making and inter-state relations.[9]

Such a position arises, of course, out of our understanding of the nature of British government – perhaps of all government. State decisions are not taken by trends, or abstract phenomena, but by a few individuals acting in very small groups. Governments – whether village elders, oligarchs, politicians, or

---

[8] See the trenchant criticism of G. R. Elton's *The practice of history* by Betty Behrens, *HJ* vol. 12 (1969), pp. 190–3.

[9] R. Hyam, 'The primacy of geopolitics: the dynamics of British imperial policy, 1763–1963', *JICH* vol. 27 (1999), pp. 27–52, repr. in R. D. King and R. W. Kilson, eds., *The statecraft of British imperialism: essays in honour of Wm. Roger Louis* (London and Portland, OR, 1999).

fighting-service chiefs, and their various advisers – are by definition elites. All elites – again, almost by definition – have their own particular 'cosmologies', ways of looking at the world and interpreting their responsibilities within a bureaucratic tradition. In Britain the relevant training of most government ministers for ruling an empire or playing the world stage has always been minimal. The members of the British elite, drawn in part from the aristocracy and upper classes for a long period of time, and mostly with an Oxbridge education mainly classical in emphasis, were amateurs. Many had some experience of large-scale farming and local administration, and Lord Palmerston was not alone in trusting to the simple homely principle that looking after world-wide British interests was merely a problem of estate-management writ large. Mostly this elite understood the basic principles of survival-politics, but not the economic technicalities of say, monetary policy. They were frequently disdainful of business and industrial interests, highly resistant to the attempts of pressure-groups to persuade them. Some government decisions might coincide with what commercial lobbies or mining magnates or 'gentlemanly capitalists' wanted, but this emphatically does not mean that they were genuinely influential, still less instrumental, in bringing those decisions about. (This point has an important bearing on the interpretations of the outbreak of war between Britain and South Africa in 1899, and we shall return to it.)

It is worth reminding ourselves that ministers of the Crown do not think in or talk the language of social science theorists, and are unlikely to know their Foucault from their Weber. It is important not to overestimate the sophistication of their decision-making. J. A. Spender, an astute and well-connected Edwardian journalist, the biographer of two prime ministers, believed that 'the motives of politicians are few and simple, and the action they will and must take in given circumstances can nearly always be deduced with certainty by those who know the rules of the game'.[10]

Unfortunately Spender did not spell out what those 'rules' were. However, we may be sure that government is mostly about response to immediate problems rather than the implementation of preconceived or long-term plans, and in the face of crisis ministers must concentrate on the essentials. Apart from holding on to office, these are primarily concerned with protecting 'the national interest'. This is most obviously interpreted to mean the security of the state against attack or collapse. This is the realm of 'high politics', the most serious preoccupation of ministers, concerning especially their relations with other states, also pursuing their own national interests. The dynamics of this rarefied world – the very essence of what constitutes international relations – are frequently driven by something called prestige. What is prestige? Harold Nicolson, a British writer and diplomat, usefully defined it as 'power based on reputation', an amalgam of

---

[10] J. A. Spender, *Life, journalism and politics* (London, 1927), vol. I, p. 113.

the two, something which has to be acquired by power but can only be retained by reputation; prestige is thus more durable than power alone.[11] Estimates formed by rival states of another's power may determine action taken, and so all governments worry about prestige. This calculation had a particular relevance to the way the South African government evaluated whether from the mid-1950s Britain still had what Bismarck called *Bündnisfähigkeit*, the quality which makes for a worthwhile ally. And while it may at first sight seem implausible to ascribe to an Afrikaner nationalist regime any concern with international reputation, in the end they found they had to concede its imperatives in the face of sanctions and the increasing difficulties experienced in performing its desired role as a regional power (see Epilogue).

Almost all decision-making is a contested business. Advisers seldom agree. There can never be in 'the real world' any automatic application of theoretical solutions. People change their mind. Jockeying for position, personality conflicts or loyal allegiances, gut reactions and private moral belief-systems, can all modify expected outcomes. In 'the real world' the complexity of the various factors and factions to be taken into consideration make clear-cut, overwhelmingly supported conclusions difficult. Even prime ministers find themselves constrained, and with surprisingly little freedom of manoeuvre 'at the top'.[12] One of the most striking features of British Cabinet minutes is the rehearsal (seldom, alas, attributed to the individual ministers) of arguments put 'on the one hand', but 'on the other', or 'as against this'. Conclusions were often reached in the form 'the balance of advantage lies . . .'. Sometimes the Cabinet had to decide between different positions taken up by ministers advised by different government departments. Even when officials agreed, the Cabinet might reject, on strictly political grounds, what had been submitted inter-departmentally as objectively desirable. This happened in May 1950, when recommendations were made for dealing with the South-West Africa dispute at the United Nations (see chapter 7, pp. 156–7).

Ministerial understanding of South African personalities and politics relied heavily on reports from the high commissioner on the spot. When we speak of 'the British government' in respect of South African policy, the high commissioner must be understood as playing an essential role as part of that government. This is true whether we are looking at Sir Alfred Milner and the origins of the South African War, or Sir John Maud and the construction of prime minister Macmillan's 'wind of change' speech sixty years later.[13] The extent to which

[11] H. Nicolson, *The meaning of prestige* (Rede Lecture, Cambridge, 1937). Compare an American secretary of state's definition: 'prestige is the shadow cast by power' (Dean Acheson, *Present at the creation: my years in the State Department*, London, 1969, p. 405).
[12] P. Hennessy, *The prime minister: the office and its holders since 1945* (London, 2000), p. 54.
[13] For a detailed analysis of Maud's contribution to the speech, see R. Hyam and W. R. Louis, eds., *The Conservative government and the end of empire, 1957–1964* (BDEEP, London, 2000) intro., pp. xxxviii–xl.

Dynamics and divergencies 7

a high commissioner might effectively influence the metropolitan government, however, depended largely on the degree of trust reposed in him. A high commissioner appointed by a previous government might be regarded with suspicion by his new political masters, and this might circumscribe his ability to carry his ideas into action. This happened with Lord Selborne from 1906 (see chapter 4). Interestingly, not a single high commissioner was 'captured' by local political society, in the way that successive governors of Kenya were seduced by the settlers; in South Africa there were no proconsular converts to apartheid. The high commissioner was essentially an intermediary, a proconsular link between metropolis and periphery. Before the Union, the high commissioner 'worked as a half-way relay station that could charge up, or scale down, the impulses transmitted in either direction'.[14] Thereafter, with South Africa becoming more and more an Afrikaner state, the high commissioner's role became increasingly restricted to that of an imperial agent.

Any study of government policy must accept the 'human agency' of individuals, and not only consider carefully the input from the high commissioner, but also grapple with the detailed work of Whitehall departments. Disparaging scepticism about the value of studying 'what one clerk said to another' is to be deplored as the product of an unsound historical sense. Understanding the inwardness of a situation or policy in fact depends upon it. The power of the civil service to formulate or frustrate policy was something the National Party in South Africa after 1948 (or the African National Congress after 1994) was acutely aware of, hence the reconstruction of its senior levels. It is vital to study what policy-makers themselves thought they were trying to achieve. Anything else is but idle speculation, however clever or intellectually elegant in itself. No doubt it is tiresome (and at times boring) month after month, year after year, to make the trek to archives remote from home-base or inconveniently situated,[15] to pore for hours over muddled batches of paper, disentangling rusty paper-clips from musty sheets, deciphering bottom-carbon-copies on flimsy paper, or to endure the miseries of churning the microfilm machine. For some scholars, no doubt, archival research is logistically too difficult or temperamentally uncongenial. Such must survive by their theorising, and hope to invent a concept which catches on. But history is too important to be left to the stay-at-home theorisers. Intensive primary research is absolutely essential if history is not to succumb to the dangers of relying on abstract formulations, the prescriptions of theoretical models constructed around purely secondary literature. All too often theoretical analysis assumes that there is a precise set of static 'givens', when in 'the real world' all is fluid and confusing.[16] On the other hand, the

---

[14] J. Benyon, *Proconsul and paramountcy in South Africa: the High Commission, British supremacy and the sub-continent, 1806–1910* (Pietermaritzburg, 1980), p. 335.
[15] An observation which applies with some force to the British Public Record Office at Kew.
[16] As powerfully argued by Dan O'Meara, *Forty lost years: the apartheid state and the politics of the National Party, 1948–1994* (Randburg and Athens, OH, 1996), pp. 429–31.

limitations of the archives have also to be recognised. Empathy with the dilemmas of government must not result in seeing things uncritically only from the government's point of view; nor must it be supposed that the written record will yield all the answers we should like. We have accordingly devoted two chapters (12 and 13) to media opinion and the 'representation' of public attitudes. Nevertheless, in-depth archival research such as we have undertaken is the fundamental, unavoidable, unrivalled, and only safe starting-point for all sustainable historical analysis.

Economic historians have exercised a powerful grip over all branches of history since the Second World War, and nowhere has this been more true than with respect to South Africa. A suspicious and sceptical generation was perhaps bound to look to material self-interest and entrepreneurial conspiracy for explanations in history. Concurrently, too, any alternative approach to empire history through 'geopolitics' – more or less invented by a British historical geographer, Sir Halford Mackinder, in the years before the First World War – had been fatally discredited by its association with Nazi and Fascist expansionist programmes in the 1930s, in which 'geographical imperatives were used to legitimise imperialism'.[17] From the vantage-point of the early twenty-first century, however, it is high time to explore the explanatory potential of 'the primacy of geopolitics'. It is no part of our purpose to replace 'economic determinism' with 'geographical determinism'. Nevertheless, it is worth pointing out that South Africa's history and integration into the wider world has been at least as much shaped by its geographical location as by its Transvaal gold-mines. South Africa stands at the intersection of major global sea-routes, providing a vital link in 'the routes to the east' – which is why the British went there in the first place – and it commands access to two oceans, the Atlantic and the Indian, with an unrivalled surveillance of both, and it was of increasing importance as an air-transport base. These were factors of considerable significance throughout the Cold War, which formed the background to the Afrikaner nationalist regime of 1948 to 1989.[18] Moreover, control of the hinterland, far to the north, has remained a salient geopolitical theme in South African history.

Our approach is both comprehensive and unusual. Most imperial historians since 1945 have not been preoccupied with South Africa, and most historians of South Africa have paid even less attention to the British connection. One notable exception in the latter category has been Shula Marks and her collaborators. We cannot, therefore, avoid commenting upon their interpretation of the relationship between Britain and South Africa. The first thing to say is that they have never succeeded in proving one of Marks's basic original claims: that there was a historically determinant link between the demands of

---

[17] M. Bell, R. Butlin, and M. Heffernan, eds., *Geography and imperialism, 1820–1940* (Manchester, 1995), and G. Parker, *Western geopolitical thought in the twentieth century* (London, 1985).

[18] O'Meara, *Forty lost years*, p. 476.

mining magnates and British policy-making. Magnates might indeed support Sir Alfred Milner in the run-up to the South African War, but they did not in fact manipulate him. He used them, not vice versa. Both Chamberlain and Milner were antipathetic to the magnates, whose concerns they recognised were purely self-interested. They were not a monolithic group of British patriots, not a set of 'ideal prefabricated collaborators', but a cosmopolitan and heterogeneous collection, including many European Jews, who found their funds not just in Britain but throughout Western Europe. In 1906, the biggest group of twenty-six companies, known as 'Corner House' and including Wernher-Beit, held only 17 per cent of their share capital in Britain; perhaps 30 per cent was in France, and 9 per cent in Germany. Some were purely financial speculators, more interested in market operations than in gold production. Essentially they functioned as an international group of developers and speculators. The last thing the mining magnates wanted in 1899 was a war, least of all a war instigated and won by Britain. Their desire for political power was strictly limited. Their political stance was wholly unco-ordinated.[19]

The truth is that some sort of war might well have broken out in 1899 even if gold had never been discovered in the Transvaal in 1886.[20] The historic long-term causes driving the two sides apart pre-dated the discovery of gold. The war was above all a regional geopolitical conflict with international ramifications ('the estimate formed of our power and influence in our Colonies and throughout the world', as Chamberlain expressed it in 1899).[21] These issues are examined in detail in chapter 2.

[19] R. V. Kubicek, *Economic imperialism in theory and practice: the case of South African gold mining finance, 1886–1914* (Duke, NC, 1979), esp. pp. 177–204; A. A. Mawby, review of A. H. Duminy and W. R. Guest, eds., *Fitzpatrick, South African politician: selected papers, 1888–1906* (Johannesburg, 1976) in *JSAS* vol. 5 (1979), p. 257; M. Fraser and A. Jeeves, eds., *All that glittered: selected correspondence of Lionel Phillips, 1890–1924* (Cape Town, 1977); J. Butler, 'The gold mines and labour supply: a review article', *SAHJ* no. 18 (1986), pp. 93–7; R. V. Turrell, '"Finance . . . the governor of the imperial engine": Hobson and the case of Rothschild and Rhodes', *JSAS* vol. 13 (1987), pp. 417–32.

[20] For sound expositions of the 'role of gold' see A. Jeeves, 'Control of migratory labour in the South African gold mines in the era of Kruger and Milner', *JSAS* vol. 2 (1975), pp. 3–29; P. Richardson and J. J. Van-Helten, 'The gold mining industry of the Transvaal, 1886–1899' in P. Warwick, ed., *The South African War, 1899–1902* (London, 1980), ch. 1, pp. 18–36; and J. J. Van-Helten, 'Empire and high finance: South Africa and the international gold standard, 1890–1914', *JAH* vol. 23 (1982), pp. 529–48.

[21] J. S. Marais, *The fall of Kruger's republic* (Oxford, 1961), p. 318. Essential reading on the origins of the war now also includes G. Cuthbertson and A. Jeeves, 'The many-sided struggle for Southern Africa, 1899–1902', *SAHJ* no. 41 (1999), pp. 2–21 (special issue: centennial perspectives on the South African War, 1899–1902); Iain R. Smith, *The origins of the South African War, 1899–1902* (London, 1996); A. N. Porter, 'The South African War (1899–1902): context and motive reconsidered', *JAH* vol. 31 (1990), pp. 43–57, and 'The South African War and the historians', *African Affairs* vol. 99 (2000), pp. 633–48; J. Butler, 'The German factor in Anglo-Transvaal relations' in P. Gifford and W. R. Louis, eds., *Britain and Germany in Africa: imperial rivalry and colonial rule* (New Haven: Yale University Press and London, 1967), pp. 179–214; N. G. Garson, 'British imperialism and the coming of the Anglo-Boer War', *South African Journal of Economics* vol. 30 (1962), pp. 140–53.

Post-war, the basic position remained the same: the British government was not mesmerised by gold, and magnates and governments were frequently at cross-purposes. The Randlords were dependent on government rather than able to dictate to it. The London government, and the Botha–Smuts elite which succeeded it in the Transvaal, both disliked the magnates, and neither was manipulated or intimidated by them. Governments might arrive at some conclusions which suited the mine-owners, but they did so by different routes. Some decisions were fundamentally against the wishes of the mining magnates, such as increases in rates and taxes, and, most important of all, the curtailment in 1907 of the importation of Chinese labour, which had come to represent some 27 per cent of the total work-force in the mines. The reasons for its suspension were exclusively ethical: the taint of slavery. The Liberal government also tackled the problem of mining monopsony, that is, the collective recruiting monopoly, the Witwatersrand Native Labour Association (WNLA), and for no other reason than an ideological objection to monopoly in all its forms. Nevertheless, magnates and politicians had to live together. Any government would be bound to have some working relationship with the leading industry of a country, and no South African government has ever wanted the mining industry to contract. If the British authorities up to 1910 were keen to build up mining, industrial, and commercial development, this was not an end in itself, but rather the means to a larger political objective. Milner needed to increase the revenues of growth industries, especially gold, in order to finance, as he hoped, a massive immigration of British settlers who would numerically swamp the Boers and through demography ensure British supremacy.[22]

The 'Marks-ist' picture of Briton and Boer conspiring through and after the introduction of responsible government in the Transvaal and Orange Free State in 1906 and 1907, in an alliance of 'maize and gold' – enshrined as apparent orthodoxy in the *Cambridge history of Africa* – has to be rejected.[23] Trapido first suggested a commonality of interest between British Rand financiers and Boer farmers now beginning to grow maize for the export market in a big way. He postulated as an essential link in forging this alliance the granting of British government loans. Botha's new Transvaal government received £5 million, half

---

[22] D. Denoon, 'The Transvaal labour crisis, 1901–1906', *JAH* vol. 8 (1967), pp. 481–94, and '"Capitalist influence" and the Transvaal government during the Crown Colony period, 1900–1906', *HJ* vol. 11 (1968), pp. 301–31, and *A grand illusion: the failure of imperial policy in the Transvaal Colony during the period of reconstruction, 1900–1905* (London, 1973); Benyon, *Proconsul and paramountcy in South Africa*, pp. 300–1; A. A. Mawby, 'The political behaviour of the British population of the Transvaal, 1902–1907' (PhD thesis, Witwatersrand, Johannesburg, 1969), and *Gold mining and politics – Johannesburg, 1900–1907: the origins of the old South Africa?* (2 vols., Lampeter, 2000).

[23] S. Trapido, 'Landlord and tenant in a colonial economy: the Transvaal, 1880–1910', *JSAS* vol. 5 (1978), pp. 26–58; S. Marks, 'Southern and Central Africa, 1886–1910' in R. Oliver and G. N. Sanderson, eds., *Cambridge history of Africa* vol. VI: *1870–1905* (Cambridge, 1985), p. 488.

of it to be used for the establishment of a Land Bank, and the rest to be used for rehabilitating farmers, and for improving public works, irrigation, and railways. Yet this is to be properly understood as a British *imperial* government alliance with Boer maize – if you wish to put it in those terms – expressly designed to break the possible link between *local* gold magnates and maize farmers. The chief British aim in making this loan – paid for by British taxpayers, not gold-mining magnates – was to release the new Transvaal government from dependence on the magnates. Without it the credit of the new Transvaal government would otherwise depend on the gold magnates and their goodwill. The British government was determined to secure for the inheritor government complete independence of action *vis-à-vis* the magnates. Nor was this without strings: the deal seems to have been that as a quid pro quo the Boer part of the bargain would be to soft-pedal its discriminatory policies towards Indians. Of course Trapido is right to say that the effect of the loan was useful in calming down the anti-Britishness of the main Afrikaner political party, Het Volk. But he appears completely to have misunderstood its purpose.[24]

A further misreading of the evidence was made in '*Volkskapitalisme*' by Dan O'Meara, who, relying upon the work of Marks and Trapido, argued that in 1906 Smuts proposed to the head of the largest mining house an alliance with the Het Volk party, partly on the grounds that their interests were in many ways identical; and political co-operation between the wealthier farmers and the mine operators is said to have developed from this point.[25] But all that happened was that Smuts suggested action on a specific point: the good sense of getting a uniform labour recruiting system. The upshot was that the renegade J. B. Robinson Group rejoined the Witwatersrand Native Labour Association in January 1908. In no sense did this make Het Volk the 'willing ally of the mining industry' (Marks and Trapido).[26] Magnates had to make their peace with the Botha–Smuts government in 1907.[27] And the Act of Union in 1909 represented the entrenchment of white rural voting power (through a rural percentage variation-weighting of otherwise equal constituencies of voters), and not of mining capital. Only when in the early 1920s Smuts's South African Party absorbed the old true-blue magnates' party, the Unionist Party, can the phrase 'alliance of gold plus maize' be said to have acquired some real meaning.

A more general point may now be made. There is no necessary connection between industrialisation and racial oppression, or between white supremacy and economic growth. It is now increasingly admitted that one of the basic neo-Marxist contentions of the 1970s, that 'apartheid was functional to capitalism',

[24] R. Hyam, *Elgin and Churchill at the Colonial Office, 1905–1908* (London, 1968), pp. 262–8.
[25] D. O'Meara, *'Volkskapitalisme': class, capital and ideology in the development of Afrikaner nationalism, 1934–1948* (Johannesburg & Cambridge, 1983), pp. 166 and 258 n. 4.
[26] Marks and Trapido, in *History Workshop Journal* (1979), p. 70.
[27] Butler, 'The gold mines and labour supply', *SAHJ* (1986), p. 97.

that the two were integrally linked together if not indistinguishable, was an ahistorical suggestion. We now have it on the authority of Dan O'Meara that: 'as its many critics, and indeed some of its own (and erstwhile) protagonists were quick to point out, this approach suffered from a number of theoretical deficiencies, which rendered its ability to explain the demise of apartheid more than somewhat problematic'.[28] It may well equally be the case that 'capitalism' is an inadequate explanation of the origin of apartheid ('apartness'). Throughout the 1950s the bulk of 'capitalists' regularly expressed opposition to apartheid policies, especially the rigid controls in the labour market; even during the black urban uprising of 1984 to 1986 the government obstinately refused the demands of major business groups to dismantle apartheid. There was nothing new in this. In fact for decades, white South African industrialists had put continual pressure on government and white workers' trades unions to be allowed to use more black labour and to get more blacks into skilled jobs. The mining magnates resisted the application of the government's so-called 'civilised labour' policy of 1924 because of what Johnstone has called its 'extreme incompatibility with profit maximisation'.[29] In other words, because it did not pay. Indeed the whole of the 'civilised labour' policy, the replacing of black labour with 'civilised' white workers, was part of a political rescue of the Afrikaner *volk*, the poor white *bywoners*, reversing a tendency to blurring the line between black and white at the working-class level, a policy introduced at the expense of the economy. It simply made no sense economically to have to pay white men more to do an unskilled job, such as railway portering, less well than an African had been doing it.

As for the priorities of the British government, the most recent statement from Shula Marks acknowledges that belief in the strategic importance of the Simon's Town naval base, substantial trade, and the fate of the High Commission Territories were all of 'some significance'. But: 'Far more vital to Britain's pre-eminence in the world, however, was the unimpeded flow of South African gold to the City of London, as was starkly revealed during both world wars'; it was this which made the stability of the region of 'critical concern' to Britain; trusteeship was 'not of the essence'.[30] This formulation completely reverses the priorities as successive British governments would have seen them. We address

---

[28] O'Meara, *Forty lost years*, pp. 424–5; the whole of O'Meara's 'Theoretical appendix: understanding politics in the apartheid state', pp. 419–89, is essential reading. M. Lipton, *Capitalism and apartheid: South Africa, 1910–1985* (Aldershot, 1986) remains a valuable guide, together with C. Saunders, *The making of the South African past: major historians on race and class* (Cape Town and Johannesburg, 1988), esp. pp. 186–91. It is to be hoped that another important statement by O'Meara will be widely noticed: 'I agree that it is essential to avoid the crude reductionism and/or economic determinism of some of the 1970s marxist writings on South Africa' (*Forty lost years*, p. 447).

[29] Johnstone, *Class, race and gold*, p. 71.

[30] Marks, in *Oxford history of the British empire*, vol. IV, p. 546.

Table 1.1. *Trade between Britain and South Africa, 1946–1961*

	British imports from S. Africa %	British exports to S. Africa %	S. African imports from Britain %	S. African exports to Britain %
1946–8	1.4	7.9	30	25
1948–58	2.3	5.7	34.2	27.5
1959–61	2.2	4.2	29.6	28.6

the particular point about gold head-on in chapter 6, and it is surely clear that it is all too easy to fantasise about the importance of gold. Trusteeship for the High Commission Territories is examined in chapters 4 and 5, and found to be, on the contrary, very much 'of the essence'. Criticisms of the thesis in chapter 4 recently offered by Torrance are not found to be of much substance.[31]

II

The dynamics of the relationship

What were the links which tended to bind Britain and South Africa together? The most persistent were the economic connections. The general trade links are indicated in table 1.1.[32]

As an export market, South Africa was important to Britain as a buyer of engineering products, motor cars, and tractors. Britain was South Africa's chief supplier of lorries, trucks, and locomotives. South Africa was usually one of the top five export markets for Britain between 1945 and 1970, and always so until 1961. Before 1955 South Africa was regularly in second or third place. Only about 5 per cent of the total of British exports went to South Africa, however. As to imports, in 1961 South Africa supplied Britain with 10 per cent of its fruit and vegetables, 28 per cent of its wood-pulp, 15 per cent of its asbestos, and 24 per cent of its manganese ore. About a quarter of British diamond imports came from South Africa, especially the industrial variety. Gold imports accounted for 64 per cent of the total in 1960. South Africa was not only the world's largest producer of gold, but dramatically increased her production in the 1960s, so alternative sources were harder to find. Thus although the sum total of British

---

[31] D. Torrance, 'Britain, South Africa and the High Commission Territories: an old controversy revisited', *HJ* vol. 41 (1998), pp. 751–72.

[32] D. J. Geldenhuys, 'The effects of South Africa's racial policy on Anglo-South African relations, 1945–1961' (PhD thesis, Cambridge, 1977), pp. 96 and 446–7; D. Austin, *Britain and South Africa* (Oxford, 1966), pp. 151–4; F. Wilson, 'Southern Africa', table 6.10 in M. Crowder, ed., *Cambridge history of Africa*, vol. VIII: *c. 1940–1975* (Cambridge, 1984), p. 276.

imports from South Africa was not large – an average of about 2 per cent – they contained several items of significance.

If gold is left out of the equation, South Africa consistently ran a huge annual trade deficit with Britain. South Africa always needed to use a substantial part of its gold output to cover this deficit, in other words, to pay for its imports from Britain. This deficit averaged £58m in 1946–8, £62m in 1948–58, and £35m in 1959–61. In normal circumstances Britain would eventually have acquired and accumulated a significant proportion of South African gold production whether or not South African gold was *marketed* in the first instance in London. (This is something which has frequently not been properly understood.) Thus the *accumulation* of South African gold in London did not depend on its being shipped directly from South African ports to London. Moreover, it augmented Britain's hard currency reserve, helping Britain to sustain its own, and a large part of the world's trade on a multilateral basis. Additionally, the *flow* of South African gold through the London gold market greatly assisted the management of sterling as an international currency (see chapter 6).

South Africa received between about 7 per cent and 10 per cent of British investments, which made it as important as the USA, with only Canada and Australia more important. These investments were profitable and yielded returns above the global average return on capital. Even in 1982, 10 per cent of British direct investments were still in South Africa.[33] The figures for British capital as a percentage of the total external capital invested in South Africa were: 91 per cent in 1913, 62 per cent in 1956, and 50 per cent in 1972 (see chapter 6).

Strong economic links had their manifestations in everyday life. South African shops were full of imported British magazines and comics, goods and brand names, with local products, such as Joko tea and Baker's biscuits, very much the exception. But beyond this, there were profound cultural influences at work. As the Foreign Office briefing for the new high commissioner put it in 1963: 'more broadly the two countries, though now foreign to each other, have preserved a special relationship flowing from their historic ties and the existence of a population of British speech, descent, and in some cases nationality, who comprise some 40 per cent of the Republic's three million Europeans'.[34] (The percentage of British South Africans was formerly even higher: 45 per cent in 1911.) The British commanded great wealth, dominated the higher echelons of the military, and they retained very considerable influence on cultural

---

[33] Berridge, *Economic power in Anglo-South African diplomacy, passim*; R. Ovendale, 'The South African policy of the British Labour government, 1947–1951', *International Affairs* vol. 59 (1983), pp. 41–58.

[34] Hyam and Louis, eds., *The Conservative government*, part 2, p. 463, document no. 463, Lord Home to Sir H. Stephenson, despatch, 28 June 1963; John Lambert, 'South African British? Or Dominion South Africans? The evolution of an identity in the 1910s and 1920s', *SAHJ* no. 43 (2000), pp. 197–222, esp. 208–11. See further below, pp. 275–7.

life and ways of doing things. Freemasonry and boy-scouting took root. Civic architecture and organisation followed British models. Parliamentary procedures stuck closely to those of Westminster. Nelson Mandela has declared that for South Africans of all backgrounds and persuasions, Britain is the country outside Africa where they felt most at home and which they could best relate to.[35] The English press in South Africa was much larger and more influential than the Afrikaans press. The *Cape Times*, *Natal Mercury*, and *Pretoria News* actively promoted a sense of British identity. Education was British-orientated at all levels, from primary schooling upwards, especially among black communities, until well into the 1960s. Missionary work throughout southern Africa was almost entirely the preserve of the British churches.

Sporting links were also important. The dissemination of British sports was one of the more conspicuous legacies of British rule and caught the imagination of peoples throughout the globe. Whilst some, notably soccer, became internationalised, others remained distinctively British. Rugby and cricket were in this category, though both became the 'glamour sports' of the countries which played them. Cricket became the 'sporting lingua franca of the entire Commonwealth', except in Canada.[36] Rugby had a narrower appeal, but conquered South Africa. The triangular rugby contests between Britain, South Africa, and New Zealand had great popular significance in those Commonwealth countries. Cricket in South Africa, as the epitome of English empire, became confined at the national level to English-speaking South Africans, although there were plenty of keen schoolboy Afrikaner cricketers, and interested Coloured and South African Indians. The black majority played mainly soccer. Rugby took off in South Africa in the 1880s, but became the Afrikaner's game, although it was played in the Eastern Cape by Coloureds and also some Africans. British teams toured South Africa in 1891, 1896, and 1903. Colonials generally from about 1900 used sport to assert their nationalistic sense of equality with and potential superiority over the old mother country. The Afrikaner choice of rugby for this purpose has a certain irony, since in Britain the 'union' rules game was firmly associated with, and for long restricted to, public-school circles. Afrikaners, however, perceived it as a 'macho' sport, responding to its required physical resilience and collective discipline. The South African rugby team beat the British in 1903, and in the United Kingdom itself in 1906, and again in 1912–13, when the name 'Springbokken' was invented for the British press – who anglicised it to Springboks. From the 1930s the Afrikaners 'co-opted rugby as part of their nationalist project' and as an expression of power in white South Africa. 'Rugby', it has been said, 'is the Afrikaner's second religion'. The

---

[35] Magdalene College Archives, P/30/2, address by Nelson Mandela on the occasion of admission to an honorary fellowship, 2 May 2001.
[36] Hyam and Louis, eds., *The Conservative government*, part 2, pp. 649–50, document no. 535, 'The British Legacy', CRO confidential print, 9 Aug. 1960.

Broederbond made active attempts to gain control of the game, eliminating Britons from management and administration. By the 1950s and 1960s many Springbok captains were members of the National Party and the Broederbond; and nearly all the managers were members of the latter from the 1960s.[37] The loss of rugby internationals, especially with the New Zealand 'All Blacks', as a result of international sanctions against the apartheid regime, was a painful deprivation, which proved to be perhaps the most powerful of the cultural influences on the decision to abandon apartheid.[38] Sporting links were easily reactivated after 1989.

One other common interest between British and South African governments might have been a powerful link after 1945: their mutual concern to combat global communism.[39] Defence co-operation to this end did indeed at one time seem to be on the cards. However, not even a shared anti-communism could deliver an active co-ordination of military and naval effort in Africa beyond South Africa's borders and territorial waters. South Africa's anti-communist laws were so bluntly and broadly drawn that they seemed to buttress apartheid. Indeed, 'communism' seemed idiomatically to be defined as anything seeking change through disturbance and disorder, and a 'communist' was anyone who had ever done so.[40] Thus it came to seem to British politicians that apartheid was itself a cause of communism's becoming attractive to African nationalists. The sub-text of Macmillan's 'wind of change' speech in February 1960 was that South Africa had become an actual liability to the West in the global east–west struggle for men's minds. The South African government urged the formation of an African Defence Organisation, but since they would not agree to countenance the arming of their Africans, the problematics of apartheid were underlined for the British government. For the British it was axiomatic that Africans should defend Africa, and it was equally obvious that a Russian invasion would come via the Middle East. South Africa's equivocal attitude towards Middle East defence was therefore another source of exasperation, giving rise to sarcastic

---

[37] D. R. Black and J. Nauright, *Rugby and the South African nation: sport, culture, politics and power in the old and new South Africas* (Manchester, 1998), pp. 1–29, 60–9, 93; P. van der Schyff, 'Lions versus SA: "The ultimate of Rugby in SA"', SARFU's *Official Guide to 1997 Tour*, pp. 104–9 ('History').

[38] Alongside its rugby-players and dentists, South Africa has also produced a world-class boys' choir, its international emergence being held back by sanctions. Founded in 1967, the Drakensberg Boys' Choir from KwaZulu-Natal has undertaken many international tours since 1981 (though never in Britain), singing a mixture of classical Western choral music and African music. In 1992 it was acclaimed one of the best in the world at the Triennial World Boys' Choirs Festival at Poznan in Poland, and in the following year four boy soloists took top honours in an international competition at Des Moines, Iowa, USA. In 1995 the choir sang at the opening match of the Rugby World Cup in Cape Town.

[39] Berridge, *South Africa, the colonial powers and 'African Defence'*, and review by P. J. Henshaw in *SAHJ* no. 30 (1994), pp. 164–7.

[40] F. Welsh, *A history of South Africa* (London, 1998), p. 444.

observations about South Africa's parochial obsession with 'hedgehogs along the Limpopo'. It had long been the case that Britain wanted South Africa's co-operation in war, but found it difficult and embarrassing to co-operate militarily in peacetime. South Africa was torn between her desire to avoid even the appearance of being a cog in the British war-machine and recognition of the need for British help. The result was that peacetime governmental co-operation between the two was largely restricted to disease control, agricultural marketing, and scientific and technical matters. Anything which signalled South Africa's involvement in political issues elsewhere in Africa was studiously avoided by British planners.[41]

In any analysis of the nature of British governmental concern for its relations with South Africa, the defining statement to be considered is the Cabinet memorandum of 25 September 1950, jointly agreed between the Commonwealth Relations Office, the Colonial Office, and the Foreign Office, and issued under the name of P. C. Gordon Walker, the Labour government secretary of state for Commonwealth relations. This paper set out the fundamentals of British policy as they persisted for at least the next thirty years. Echoes of it were apparent in official papers through into the 1990s. Its conclusions were endorsed by the Cabinet at a meeting on 28 September 1950, one of the most serious discussions of South African policy ever held in Whitehall and Westminster. The preservation of good relations was held to be important for four reasons. (1) From the strategic and defence point of view, the naval base at Simon's Town was of vital importance (it being assumed that the Suez Canal would be closed in war), and other South African ports were indispensable to shipping and as staging-posts for troops. The Union might also contribute military and civilian manpower and uranium, and had already contributed assistance in the Berlin airlift and Korean War. (2) South Africa was an important export market, and several hundred millions of capital were invested there; it was also of 'the utmost importance' to the viability of the sterling area to obtain a substantial part of the country's gold output. (3) The High Commission Territories 'could at any time be economically strangled by the Union Government withholding essential facilities'. (4) Britain had obligations to South Africa as a fellow-member of the Commonwealth; 40 per cent of the white population was of British stock; it was to be hoped South Africa would remain in it, even as a republic.[42]

The Cabinet as a whole was apparently impressed mainly by the strategic argument: the importance of South Africa's support in the struggle against communism. In other words, for most ministers, South African policy had to

[41] PRO, FO 371/70195, no. 37, high commissioner Sir E. Baring to secretary of state, 15 Oct. 1948; A. Seegers, *The military and the making of modern South Africa* (London, 1996).
[42] Hyam, ed., *The Labour government and the end of empire, 1945–1951* (BDEEP, London, 1992), part 4, document nos. 429 and 431.

be attuned to the overall geopolitical imperatives of the Cold War. Maintaining the integrity and prestige of the Commonwealth itself was also a weapon in this struggle. However, the civil servants and Gordon Walker himself were principally concerned with trusteeship obligations and the protection of the High Commission Territories against South African expansionistic tendencies; equally important with maintaining some co-operation was 'containment' – preventing the spread of apartheid northwards, beyond South Africa's boundaries. It was thought that the South Africans could in theory 'march in' at any time to effect incorporation; but short of that they had a whole battery of economic sanctions they could apply, through control of the running of railways, buses, customs, currency and banking facilities, mail and telecommunications, food supplies and job opportunities. Sanctions thus applied to the three Territories would make British administration almost impossible, and maybe only at a financial cost which Britain could not pay. If that happened, the Territories would dissolve into chaos, which would then provide the ideal excuse and opportunity for South Africa to 'march in'. A gloomy scenario indeed.[43]

These considerations formed the background to the conduct by the British government of the biggest issues of the day in its relations with Afrikanerdom: Seretse Khama (chapter 8), the disputes with the UN, including South-West Africa (chapter 7), the formation of the Central African Federation (chapter 9), and the Simon's Town Agreements (chapter 10). Consistent underlying themes run through all of them, and demonstrate that British policy was essentially an ambivalent and paradoxical mixture of containment and co-operation, a policy worked out mainly by civil servants and high commissioners, and endorsed by ministers mainly on the basis of strategic and geopolitical considerations.[44]

III

The Afrikaner Nationalist perspective and identity

The inauguration of a republic in May 1961, after a referendum narrowly voted in its favour, represented the attainment of a historic Afrikaner objective, the resolution of an age-long debate about the British connection.

A sweeping and much quoted generalisation has it that white South African politics from 1910 to 1961 was essentially a debate among Afrikaners about what to do with the South African British. According to one authority, the relationship between the two white communities was in this period 'the principal

---

[43] PRO, DO 119/1172, no. 6, despatch from high commissioner to secretary of state, 8 July 1954, with memorandum, 'The transfer issue: probabilities of retaliatory measures by the Union government'.

[44] *The Labour government and the end of empire*, part 4, document no. 433, pp. 310–15, Cabinet memorandum by P. C. Gordon Walker, 16 Apr. 1951.

Dynamics and divergencies 19

issue of South African politics and the chief determinant of partisan alignments'. Or, as O'Meara puts it: 'The victim mentality of Afrikaner nationalism required a demonised external enemy.' Thus appeals to the British bogeyman helped to mobilise the *volk*, and the vote for the republic (1960), reinforced by departure from the Commonwealth (1961), left a vacuum which revealed just how important this defining focus had been.[45] By 1961 the historic argument between Britain and Afrikanerdom was largely superseded – the popular generalisation runs – by an almost total preoccupation with black racial issues; and white South African politics became a debate among the whites about what to do with the blacks. Wags predicted that one day there would be a third phase: a debate among the blacks about what to do with the whites.

There is thus ample evidence of an Afrikaner preoccupation with 'the British problem'. South African perceptions of Britain are described in chapter 12. Although internal personality conflicts were vicious and endemic, sharp divisions and party splits in Afrikanerdom (fig. 1.1) often sprang from disagreements about relations with Britain. In 1914 a rebellion fundamentally divided the old South African War comrades, with Botha and Smuts in favour of supporting Britain against Germany in war, and De La Rey, Beyers, and De Wet opposed. The rebels considered entry into the war and a campaign against German South-West Africa as a great betrayal. Botha and Smuts put them down without hesitation. But a South African general election in October 1915 indicated an accelerating drift in Afrikaner allegiance into National Party ranks; and one half of all Afrikaners appeared to be opposed to the war. In 1939 prime minister J. B. M. Hertzog took his stand on neutrality, again reviving memories of the South African War: why should Britain (the only power ever to have attacked South Africa) be supported against Germany (who had shown only friendship)? Smuts opted for supporting Britain, rejecting the neutralist argument that participation was a denial of South African independence. The Union parliament divided 80:65 in favour of Smuts and war. This crisis led to the downfall of Hertzog and then his eventual brief reunion with Malan.[46] If Hertzog had preached a two-stream white development, and Smuts 'conciliation' (better regarded as a policy of using the imperial connection for the furtherance of Afrikaner ends), Malan was unequivocally for 'Suid-Afrika Eertse'. This slogan is to be understood idiomatically not simply as 'South Africa First' but as 'Afrikanerdom first and only'. The more extreme Afrikaners under Dr J. F. van Rensburg continued their flirtation with Nazi symbols and trappings.

After 1948 anti-Britishness reached new heights, and in some respects seemed to take precedence over the imperatives of implementing white

[45] N. Stultz, *Afrikaner politics in South Africa, 1934–1948* (California, 1974), p. 2; O'Meara, *Forty lost years*, p. 476.
[46] T. R. H. Davenport, 'The South African rebellion, 1914', *English Historical Review* vol. 78 (1963), pp. 73–94, and *South Africa, a modern history* (4th edn, London, 1991), pp. 295–7.

20   The Lion and the Springbok

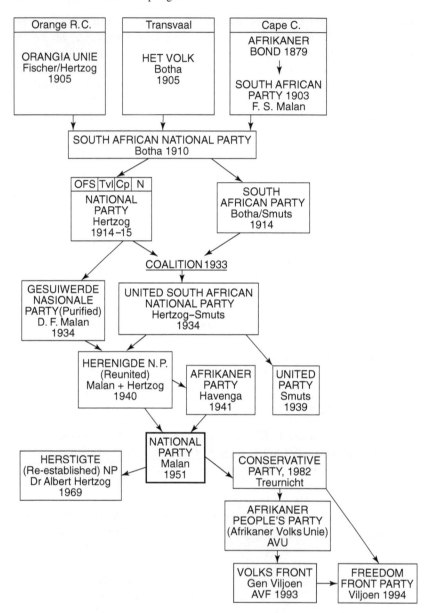

Fig. 1.1 The evolution of Afrikaner political parties.

supremacy. This can be seen in the curtailment of immigrants from Britain, whose numbers plummeted from 25,513 in 1948 to 5,094 in 1950, and further declined to 3,782 in 1959, a mere fifth of the total. By 1960 there was a net loss of 2,823 whites from South Africa.[47] And this at a time when the priority might have been building up the size of the white community. Getting rid of 'the British connection' was the object of the republican movement. The referendum produced a turn-out of 91 per cent. It demonstrated overwhelming Afrikaner support, even if the actual overall majority was only 52 per cent. Like apartheid itself, perhaps, republicanism was designed in part to produce a greater harmony in a white society rent by conflict.[48]

The departure from the Commonwealth did not mean the removal of the British problem. The response of Britain to deepening apartheid, to the implementation of 'grand apartheid' through bantustans or African homelands, and to international calls for sanctions against South Africa, meant that Afrikaners were still compelled to take an attitude towards British 'interference'. This is the subject of chapters 12 and 13.

So, clearly, the debate about the British connection mattered. But from at least the mid-1920s, there were in fact two great simultaneous debates in South African politics, not one: the debate among Afrikaners about what to do with the British, certainly, but also the debate among whites about what to do with the blacks. The two debates interlocked and complicated the situation, embittering it in a fateful way. For example, although the hugely divisive and acrimonious dispute about adopting a new national flag (1926 to 1928) – the most prominent issue of the 1920s – might at first sight look like a straightforward intra-white debate, the wider implications became apparent when Afrikaners started burning the Union flag at public demonstrations, providing a potentially dangerous precedent for black protest.[49] Conversely, the removal of Cape African voters from the common-roll franchise in 1936 – the most significant event of the 1930s – which at first sight seems a simple black/white issue, was probably intended by Hertzog to deal with a white/white problem, by eliminating some 14,000 pro-British voters. The Cape Afrikaners had never accepted the Cape African franchise, resented as 'an incubus saddled upon [them as] a subject people' in 1853 and preserved in the Act of

---

[47] Geldenhuys, 'The effects of South Africa's racial policy on Anglo-South African relations', pp. 146–7, 337; J. Barber, *South Africa's foreign policy, 1945–1970* (Oxford, 1973), p. 51; H. Brotz, *The politics of South Africa: democracy and racial diversity* (Oxford, 1977), p. 78; F. G. Brownell, *British immigration to South Africa, 1946–1970, Argief-Jaarboek vir Suid-Afrikaanse Geskiedenis/Archives Yearbook*, 48th year, vol. I (Pretoria, 1985), pp. 1–192; S. A. Peberdy, 'Selecting immigrants: nationalism and national identity in South Africa's immigration policies, 1910 to 1998' (PhD thesis, Queen's University, Kingston, Ontario, 1999).
[48] A. W. Stadler, 'The Afrikaner in opposition, 1910–1948', *Journal of Commonwealth Political Studies* vol. 7 (1969), p. 209; O'Meara, *Forty lost years*, pp. 105–9.
[49] H. Saker, *The South African flag controversy* (Oxford, 1980).

Union.[50] In elections, too, colour appears to have been a factor in every one since 1915, except perhaps in 1933, and especially salient in 1929, 1938, and 1948. In 1929 and 1948 it was the dominant issue.[51] Dunbar Moodie suggests that references to the black threat in 1938 were usually made in the context of blaming the British bogey for thwarting Afrikaner segregationist policies rather than to express fear of black domination *per se*. The underlying strategy was therefore to mobilise non-National Party supporters by playing the race card in order to bring about greater solidarity among voters. When the National Party was victorious in 1948 the general Afrikaner reaction was 'from today a kaffir is a kaffir again' – a comment within the black/white arena. But Malan's official gloss was rather different, and most revealing: 'for the first time since Union, South Africa is our own' – a commentary upon the predominant debate on the intra-white issues.[52]

Once in power, on a minority of votes, the Afrikaner regime was determined to consolidate its position. From 1938 a systematic programme had been developing, by which Afrikanerdom was entrenched in power for forty years after 1948. Four main strategies were articulated to achieve this: securing the electoral base, organising and politicising a tightly structured but flexible sociological laager, promoting a religious sanction devised by the Dutch Reformed Church, and mobilising state power and authority (legislative and judicial), supported by control of the army, the police, and the bureaucracy.[53]

First, electoral success had rested upon the steady progressive urbanisation of Afrikaners in the previous half century. In 1904 only 6 per cent of Afrikaners lived in towns; by 1960 it was 76 per cent.[54] The National Party holding of key

[50] S. Trapido, 'The origins of the Cape franchise qualifications of 1853', *JAH* vol. 5 (1964), pp. 37–54. See further below, pp. 283–5.
[51] W. K. Hancock, 'Literacy and numeracy and some South African elections', *Australian Journal of Science* vol. 28 (1965), pp. 114–19, and *Smuts*, vol. II: *The fields of force, 1919–1950* (Cambridge, 1968), pp. 497–507; K. A. Heard, *General elections in South Africa, 1943–1970* (Oxford, 1974); W. B. White, 'The United Party and the 1948 general election', *Journal for Contemporary History/Joernaal vir die Eietydse Geskiedenis* (Bloemfontein) vol. 17 (1992), pp. 73–97.
[52] T. Dunbar Moodie, *The rise of Afrikanerdom: power, apartheid and the Afrikaner civil religion* (Berkeley, CA, 1975), p. 247; D. J. Geldenhuys, 'The politics of race: a study of the impact of South Africa's general election of 1948 on Anglo-South African relations', *Journal for Contemporary History/Joernaal vir die Eietydse Geskiedenis* vol. 4 (1979), p. 9; C. and M. Legum, *South Africa: crisis for the West* (London, 1964), p. 19.
[53] Apart from O'Meara, *Forty lost years*, studies essential for understanding Afrikanerdom include: Dunbar Moodie, *The rise of Afrikanerdom*; D. Welsh, 'The politics of white supremacy' in L. M. Thompson and J. Butler, eds., *Change in contemporary South Africa* (Berkeley, CA, 1975), pp. 51–78; D. J. Worrall, 'Afrikaner nationalism' in C. Potholm and R. Dale, eds., *Southern Africa in perspective* (New York, 1972), pp. 19–30; L. Salomon, 'The economic background to the revival of Afrikaner nationalism' in J. Butler, ed., *Boston University Papers in African History*, vol. I (1964), pp. 219–42; and H. Adam and H. Giliomee, *Ethnic power mobilised: can South Africa change?* (New Haven: Yale University Press and London, 1979).
[54] D. Welsh, 'Urbanisation and the solidarity of Afrikaner nationalism', *Journal of Modern African Studies* vol. 7 (1969), pp. 265–76; E. S. Munger, *Afrikaner and African nationalism: South African parallels and parameters* (Oxford, 1967), p. 35.

urban seats increased from four in 1944 to fifteen in 1948 to fifty-five in 1966.[55] They were successful during the 1940s in drawing working-class Afrikaner voters away from the British-dominated South African Labour Party.[56] The electoral grip was further tightened by removing Indian political participation (1948), abolishing the Cape Coloured common roll franchise and substituting white representatives (1956), together with allocating six white seats to South-West Africa (1949), all held by the National Party until 1978.

Secondly, in order to control and counteract the inherently fissiparous tendencies of Afrikanerdom, there was a concerted drive to establish an interlocking apparatus of institutions, covering political, religious, cultural, economic, and educational activities, so as to bring about what sociologists call an 'elite consensus' (fig. 1.2).[57] A key role in this was assigned to the Broederbond ('Brotherhood'), the militant club of the professional elite (mainly civil servants, teachers, educational administrators, and clergy – a grouping which in Islamic society would constitute the *ulema*). Acting as the central custodian of policy-formation, the co-ordinator of specific efforts, the guarantor of like-mindedness, it became the most powerful political instrument of Afrikanerdom. Supporting agencies underpinned all walks of life and formed a huge network of organisations – everything from boy-scouting to an ambulance service (*Noodhulphiga*) – designed to make the Afrikaner national community both self-sufficient and exclusive. This infrastructural drive for effective interconnectedness meant that the same individuals often ended up as office-holding pluralists. H. van Rensberg was leader of the Broederbond and sat on the boards of SANLAM and SANTAM (the investment and insurance agencies); Professor van Rooy was chairman of the FAK (Federation of Afrikaner Cultural Organisations) and the National Institute for Christian Education; Dr Piet Meyer was secretary of the Broederbond and FAK, as well as the OB (*Ossewa Brandwag*) and RDB (*Reddingsdaadbond*).[58] Thus the strategy of *herenigde eenheidsfront* ('reunification as one') was a brilliant success. Remarkably, too, by 1971 the head of the Dutch Reformed Church (DRC), Dr J. D. Vorster, was brother of the prime minister, B. J. Vorster.

Thirdly, a veritable theocratic regime was created. The exact weight to be attached to the religious element in Afrikanerdom is disputed.[59] But it seems

---

[55] M. Wilson and L. M. Thompson, eds., *The Oxford history of South Africa*, vol. II: *South Africa, 1870–1966* (Oxford, 1971), p. 208.
[56] O'Meara, *Forty lost years*, pp. 34–6.
[57] W. H. Vatcher, jr, *White laager: the rise of Afrikaner nationalism* (London, 1965).
[58] O'Meara, *Forty lost years*, pp. 43–8, and 'The Afrikaner Broederbond: class vanguard of Afrikaner nationalism, 1927–1948', *JSAS* vol. 3 (1976), pp. 156–86; Welsh, *A history of South Africa*, pp. 416–18.
[59] S. R. Ritner, 'The Dutch Reformed Church and apartheid', *Journal of Contemporary History* vol. 2 (1967), pp. 17–36; I. Hexham, 'Dutch Calvinism and the development of Afrikaner nationalism', *African Affairs* vol. 79 (1980), pp. 195–208; A du Toit, 'No chosen people: the myth of the Calvinist origins of Afrikaner nationalism and racial ideology', *American Historical Review* vol. 88 (1983), pp. 920–52.

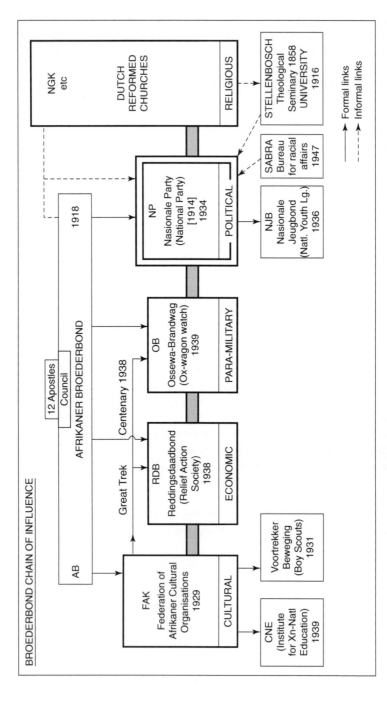

Fig. 1.2 The institutional structure of Afrikanerdom. *Sources*: Hofmeyr Papers, A 1/C.e, Military Intelligence Reports, 1943–1944 [E. G. Malherbe, director]; W. H. Vatcher, jr., *White laager: the rise of Afrikaner nationalism* (London, 1965), p. 84.

incontestable that apartheid was a doctrine principally worked out by the DRC clergy in the 1930s; that most Afrikaners were susceptible to religious direction; and that the withdrawal of religious sanction after 1985 was a major element in precipitating the collapse of the apartheid regime. As prime minister, Dr Malan declared racial differences were 'permanent and not man made', and 'Afrikanerdom is but a creation of God'. The minister for Bantu administration, De Wet Nel, said in May 1959, introducing the so-called 'Promotion of Bantu Self-Government Bill' – the cornerstone of the notorious 'grand apartheid' of 'separate development' in Bantustans or African homelands – that apartheid was 'a divine task which has to be implemented and fulfilled systematically'.[60] This theocratic ethos conveniently placed discriminatory legislation beyond the reach of modern principles of rational criticism.

Finally, there was a significant manipulation of state power for Afrikaner political ends. Abandoning traditional British conceptions of the state as 'the holder of the ring', the Afrikaner regime made it the vehicle for the advancement of a single community. Perhaps no other state has ever used the law so systematically to control its people, most notoriously through the 'pass laws' restricting African movement, at the same time boasting of its respect for legality and expecting to get credit for not being purely arbitrary. Apartheid was enforced by armed police and the army itself, and by the Afrikaner capture of the bureaucracy. Afrikanerisation of the civil service and restructuring of the military proceeded with purges of the senior posts.[61] The number of Afrikaners employed in 'public administration' increased by 98.5 per cent between 1946 and 1960, while 'English' representation fell by 25.2 per cent. The notorious secret police agency, BOSS (Bureau of State Security), was established in 1969.[62,63]

---

[60] G. M. Carter, *The politics of inequality: South Africa since 1948* (London, 1958), p. 370; Dunbar Moodie, *The rise of Afrikanerdom*, p. 265.

[61] T. Dunbar Moodie explains how his investigation into *The rise of Afrikanerdom* arose out of trying to understand the disruption of his father's army career: see the introduction to the paperback edition (Berkeley, CA, 1980), p. x. Similarly, Martin Legassick's radical hostility to the regime traces back in part to his father's dismissal as head of the General Botha Naval Academy because he was English-speaking (C. Saunders, *The making of the South African past*, p. 176).

[62] The reach of BOSS extended even into the Cambridge History Faculty in the mid-1970s, where Dr Hyam's course on South African History was monitored for several years: two big, middle-aged Afrikaner men sat conspicuously at the back, making no notes, bewildered by the jokes; they eventually gave up, presumably concluding that the lecturer was of no real danger to the South African state.

[63] Thompson and Butler, eds., *Change in contemporary South Africa*, esp. ch. by A. Sachs, 'Instruments of domination', pp. 223–49; O'Meara, *Forty lost years*, pp. 61–3; D. Posel, *The making of apartheid, 1948–1961: conflict and compromise* (Oxford, 1991), and 'Does size matter? The apartheid state's power of penetration' in H. Judin and I. Vladislavić, eds., *'blank': architecture, apartheid and after* (Rotterdam, 1998), pp. 237–47.

What the Afrikaners taught in their schools they called 'Christian-National education'. This has been memorably described by Saul Dubow as an eclectic amalgam of neo-Calvinism, neo-Nazism, and pseudo-scientific eugenics, with a dash of hopeless romanticism.[64] This peculiar exclusivist concoction, and apartheid itself,[65] ultimately derived from a complex set of fears – fears bred by history, experience, and misleading racial theories, fears of competition (economic, mainly, though sexual in part), and above all by demographic fears of being swamped by a black majority perceived as alien, an 'Other' of which there was profound ignorance. In 1921 the prediction for 1971 was that African and Coloured population levels would have increased from 5.2 million to between 19 and 24 million, with white population rising from 1.5 million to 4 million. In 1970 the actual totals were 17 million and 3.7 million. J. L. Sadie's 1972 projection for 2002 was 37.3 million and 6.9 million respectively.[66] Rodney Davenport has defined the dominant political dogmas of South African politics since the Union as 'formulae designed by the over-ingenious for the consolation of the under-critical'[67] – one might add, 'and over-anxious'. As Davenport also says, it was a 'society dominated by social engineers', with a mentality which paid much attention to the engine, but too little to the steering-wheel and the brake.[68]

IV

Divergencies and turning-points

In the aftermath of war from 1902 both sides continued to pursue their national interest. If it was expedient for the British government to cloak with an apparent magnanimity its continuing search for some sort of geopolitical supremacy in southern Africa, for the defeated Afrikaners it was equally the case that the

---

[64] S. Dubow, 'Afrikaner nationalism, apartheid and the conceptualisation of race', *JAH* vol. 33 (1992), pp. 209–37.

[65] Studies essential for understanding apartheid include: C. Saunders, 'Historians and apartheid' in J. M. Lonsdale, ed., *South Africa in question* (African Studies Centre, Cambridge, 1988), pp. 13–32; P. Bonner, P. Delius, and D. Posel, eds., *Apartheid's genesis, 1935–1962* (Braamfontein, 1993), esp. introduction, pp. 1–41; Beinart and Dubow, *Segregation and apartheid in twentieth-century South Africa*, esp. introduction, pp. 1–24; S. Dubow, *Racial segregation and the origins of apartheid in South Africa, 1919–1936* (Oxford, 1989); A. du Toit, 'Political control and personal morality' in R. Schrire, ed., *South Africa: public policy perspectives* (Cape Town, 1983), pp. 54–83; and Nelson Mandela, *Long walk to freedom: the autobiography* (London, 1994).

[66] Davenport, *South Africa, a modern history* (4th edn), pp. 370–1 (5th edn, p. 427).

[67] T. R. H. Davenport, 'The tiger in the grass', *SAHJ* no. 9 (1977), pp. 3–12 (presidential address to South African Historical Society, 1977).

[68] T. R. H. Davenport, *Senses in turmoil: an inaugural address at Rhodes University* (Grahamstown, 1977), p. 22.

conciliatory attitudes of the younger and more liberal leaders were conceived as part of the 'high political' strategy for national survival.[69]

Chapter 3 explores these complexities, and perhaps provides clues as to how a convergence on the goal of Union came about. Both sides had an interest in a geopolitical reconstruction and consolidation which would strengthen South Africa, not only internally by eliminating economic friction (especially in tariffs and transport systems), but also externally by preparing it to meet a threat via German-controlled South-West Africa, in the event of an Anglo-German war, already perceived in Whitehall by 1908 as almost inevitable.[70]

It has often been argued that whatever else the settlement of 1906 to 1910 may or may not have achieved, at least it ensured to Britain the support of South Africa in two world wars. The absence of that support both in 1914 to 1918 and in 1939 to 1945 could have had most serious strategic consequences. Anglo-South African relations were indeed at their most intense and productive in wartime. During the First World War it is remarkable that recent enemies fought on the same side, but also that the local war aims of Botha and Smuts were congruent with British geopolitical perceptions and military grand strategy, most notably over the invasion of South-West Africa. An expedition to German East Africa (Tanganyika) was also despatched, though a portion of the troops was withdrawn in late 1916 to join the Western Front, where a 'Native Labour Contingent' was already serving, though in a non-combatant capacity. Altogether 136,070 South Africans volunteered for active service. Smuts sat in the Imperial War Cabinet in London. However (as mentioned above, p. 19), the war also sharpened local differences between British South Africans, with their heightened sense of imperial loyalty, and the Afrikaners, who were themselves split between moderate supporters of a broad 'South African nationalism' in partnership with 'Britishness', and those who looked to a forcible restoration of Boer republicanism, with German help.[71]

---

[69] And very successful they were too. We reject the suggestion that the Union constitution was 'imposed' by Britain; on the contrary, it was accepted by the British government almost entirely on South African terms, as master-minded by Smuts, who understood that the 'Westminster constitution' was essential to confer international credibility.

[70] L. M. Thompson, 'The compromise of Union' in *Oxford History of South Africa*, vol. II, ch. 7, pp. 325–64: P. Lewsen, *The South African constitution: euphoria and rejection* (Raymond Dart Lecture, Johannesburg, 1982), and *John X. Merriman: paradoxical South African statesman* (New Haven: Yale University Press and London, 1982), pp. 283–349.

[71] R. Hyam, *The failure of South African expansion, 1908–1948* (London, 1972), pp. 25–32; R. Holland, 'The British empire and the Great War, 1914–1918' in J. M. Brown and W. R. Louis, eds., *The Oxford history of the British Empire*, vol. IV: *The twentieth century* (Oxford, 1999), ch. 5; N. G. Garson, 'South Africa and World War I' in N. Hillmer and P. Wigley, eds., *The first British Commonwealth: essays in honour of Nicholas Mansergh* (London, 1980, repr. from *JICH* vol. 8), pp. 68–85; B. Nasson, 'War opinion in South Africa in 1914', *JICH* vol. 23 (1995), pp. 248–76.

During the Second World War, in all some 342,692 South Africans (including a considerable number of non-Europeans) volunteered for active service of various kinds. This represented a huge military effort on the part of a country which had a mere 3,353 men serving in the armed forces at the outbreak of war. Most of the fighting was in North Africa. Parallel to this, and even more remarkably, South Africa also turned itself into an important producer of munitions and armament for the allies. Because of the Cape route, South Africa 'was geopolitically necessary and Smuts was politically necessary' to Britain (Hancock). But as in the First World War, Smuts's role was ambivalent. Once again he seized the opportunity to turn South African participation to South Africa's advantage, pursuing expansionist aims. With shocking speed, Smuts immediately tried to force through a transfer of Swaziland to South African administration, but he misjudged the strength of British trusteeship commitment. Despite the stony reception accorded to his overtures in the autumn of 1939, he managed to retain his overall credibility with the British government, both as a Commonwealth statesman and a military expert. He was a staunch supporter of Churchill and friendly with all the top commanders, became a field-marshal in the British army, and helped to shape plans for a post-war United Nations.[72]

When Union was established, the British planners expected, or at least hoped, three things would happen. Their adumbrations of the future rested, first, on an expectation that the old sectionalisms of Britisher and Afrikaner would be buried and that they would merge in a genuine mixed co-operative partnership. Secondly, that the whites, no longer quarrelling among themselves, and grateful for being allowed to run their own affairs, would apply the lessons of do-as-you-had-been-done-by, and treat the African majority better than in the past. And thirdly, that the geographical area of the Union would be enlarged by the transfer to it of Basutoland, Bechuanaland, and Swaziland, together with Southern Rhodesia, to form a 'Greater South Africa', thus relieving Britain finally from its southern and Central African responsibilities. All these expectations failed to materialise, and relations between Britain and South Africa deteriorated steadily as the century wore on.

The unravelling process began dismayingly soon. The Natives Land Act of 1913 set aside existing African reserves as 'scheduled areas', reserved for black ownership and occupation, and prohibited Africans from buying land outside those woefully inadequate reserves. In the delimitation only finalised in 1936

---

[72] Hancock, *Smuts*, vol. II *The fields of force, 1919–1950* (Cambridge, 1968), pp. 315–33, 412; H. J. Martin and N. D. Orpen, *South Africa at war: military and industrial organisation and operations in connection with the conduct of war, 1939–1945* (Cape Town, 1979; vol. VII of *South African forces, World War II*, ed. N. D. Orpen), pp. 346–7; Hyam, *Failure of South African expansion*, pp. 163–71; O. Geyser, *Jan Smuts and his international contemporaries* (Johannesburg, 2001), ch. 5, 'Winston Churchill', pp. 95–113.

Illustration 1.1 *Dienswillig die uwe*: Smuts as 'your willing servant' of Britain. Field-Marshal Jan Smuts polishes the boot of 'British interests', supported by a blinkered South Africa, and gaining nothing from the umbrella of 'British protection'. *Source*: *Die Burger*, 14 March 1942

these reserves covered merely 13 per cent (approximately) of the land area of South Africa. The agrarian effects of the 1913 Act, whether experienced as the dispossession of an emerging African peasantry, or their conversion into servile share-croppers, were harsh and catastrophic. Nothing could have demonstrated more plainly that a South African government could not be trusted to evolve a decent native policy.[73] The Colonial Office was aghast. It could not support a policy of divorcing Africans from land ownership, if only because it ran counter

[73] F. Wilson, 'Farming, 1866–1966' in *Oxford history of South Africa*, vol. II, pp. 104–71; C. Bundy, 'The emergence and decline of a South African peasantry', *African Affairs* vol. 71 (1972), pp. 369–88; C. M. Tatz, *Shadow and substance in South Africa: a study in land and franchise policies affecting Africans, 1910–1960* (Pietermaritzburg: Natal University Press, 1962). More recent reassessments include: H. Feinberg, 'The 1913 Natives Land Act in South Africa: politics, race and segregation in the early twentieth century', *International Journal of African Historical Studies* vol. 26 (1993), pp. 65–109; P. L. Wickens, 'The Natives Land Act of 1913: a cautionary essay on simple explanations of complex change', *South African Journal of Economics* vol. 49 (1981), pp. 105–29; T. Keegan, 'The share-cropping economy: African class formation and the 1913 Natives Land Act in the high veldt maize belt' in S. Marks and R. Rathbone, eds., *Industrialisation and social change in South Africa: African class formation, culture and consciousness, 1870–1930* (London, 1982), pp. 195–211.

to the ideas it was implementing everywhere else, except for special reasons in the highlands of Kenya.

The first turning-point was 1913; the next was 1922, with the decision of the European settlers of Southern Rhodesia in a referendum not to enter the Union. With Afrikaners perhaps only 18 per cent of the total white Rhodesian population of 33,000, any other decision was perhaps always unlikely, and there were many reasons why British Rhodesians did not feel confident that their interests would be respected, let alone promoted, in Pretoria.[74] The Union's unitary constitution acted as a definite deterrent to joining South Africa. With a looser federal constitution the outcome might have been different. At all events the rejection of a South African destiny fatally undermined the grand design for a Greater South Africa. Not only did the decision deny to South African expansionists a crucial geopolitical link for advance northwards and towards Delagoa Bay, it also called in question the whole scheme of transferring the High Commission Territories.[75] We examine this in chapter 5.

From the point of view of Anglo-South African relations, the fall of Smuts in 1924 seemed to be more alarming than would his departure in 1948. J. B. M. Hertzog succeeded to the premiership in 1924, and fifteen years of Hertzog did nothing to re-assure the British government. Regarded as not very clever, as petty, petulant, obstinate, and fumbling, even (in Fabian quarters) as 'a hysterical dunderhead', Hertzog caused offence by making it one of his principal aims to get a greater autonomy for South Africa within the Commonwealth. This seemed to place the continuing loyalty of Afrikaners to the British connection in doubt. That Hertzog also bore heavily on African prospects for improvement and pressed so insensitively for the transfer of the High Commission Territories only made matters worse.[76] Interestingly, Lord Selborne, architect of the terms devised in 1909 under which transfer of the Territories would have taken place, publicly renounced his support for the plan in 1933. Selborne had concluded that Hertzog intended to establish an Afrikaner state 'no more advanced than Elizabethan England', closed off from the outside world, and treating every African as 'the helot of the chosen people'.[77]

---

[74] J. van der Poel, ed., *Selections from the Smuts Papers*, vol. V: *1919–1934* (Cambridge, 1973), pp. 144–54; R. Blake, *A history of Rhodesia* (London, 1977), pp. 179–204; P. R. Warhurst, 'Rhodesian–South African relations, 1900–1923', *SAHJ* no. 3 (1971), pp. 93–108; H. C. Hummel, 'Sir Charles Coghlan: some reflections on his political attitudes and style', *SAHJ* no. 8 (1976), pp. 59–79.

[75] M. Chanock, *Unconsummated Union: Britain, Rhodesia and South Africa, 1900–1945* (Manchester, 1977).

[76] R. Holland, *Britain and the Commonwealth alliance, 1918–1939* (London, 1981), pp. 90–2; Fabian opinion is quoted from *Sydney Olivier: letters and selected writings* (ed. M. Olivier, London, 1948), p. 164. See also Davenport, *South Africa, a modern history* pp. 259–68; Tatz, *Shadow and substance*, pp. 38–91; and J. W. Cell, *The highest stage of white supremacy: the origins of segregation in South Africa and the American South* (Cambridge, 1982), pp. 218–225.

[77] *Parliamentary Debates, House of Lords*, vol. 88, cc. 1128–1129 (26 July 1933), quoted by Torrance, 'Britain, South Africa and the High Commission Territories', pp. 770–1.

Long before 1948 it was thus apparent that the British ability to influence the direction of the South African polity had disappeared. Why was this? Lord Cranborne, as Dominions secretary in 1941, identified one reason: 'the great tragedy of South Africa at the present is that the British . . . abandon the field to the Dutch'. The British South African community became introverted and opted out of public life. Even Natal, the most 'British' of the provinces, had a 'lamentable record' of participation in Union affairs.[78] By 1949 the Commonwealth Relations Office regarded Natal as 'politically the rogue province' which could not be relied on to oppose the National Party and which had applauded its harsh treatment of Indians.[79] In 1951 Gordon Walker reported that British South Africans were arrogant and exclusive; symptomatically and short-sightedly, they refused to learn Afrikaans. In all, he was 'extremely disappointed' with them.[80] But there was a further reason for the erosion of British influence. British policy-makers clung to the charismatic figure of Smuts as some sort of collaborative agent. But Smuts had his own agenda, and in any case he was of dubious value in such a role simply because he was unrepresentative of the Afrikaner community, indeed insensitive to some of its most cherished aspirations. Too Anglophile for the Afrikaners, too much the wily old Afrikaner opportunist for the British South Africans, the white electorate finally rejected him in 1948.[81]

Until the National Party took power, it was above all the deadlock over the High Commission Territories which had driven Britain and South Africa apart. This was the issue right at the heart of their inter-governmental relations.

The South African state was inherently expansionist from its inception (map 5.1).[82] Indeed, Smuts had defined Boer war-aims in 1899 with the slogan, 'from Zambesi to Simon's Bay: Africa for the Africander', and he remained the most

---

[78] PRO, PREM 4/44/1, Lord Harlech to W. S. Churchill, 2 Oct. 1941.
[79] PRO, CAB 134/56, CA(49)1, note by Commonwealth Relations Office on the Durban riots, 24 Jan. 1949.
[80] Hyam, ed., *The Labour government and the end of empire*, part 4, document no. 433, report on visit, 16 Apr. 1951, pp. 305–6.
[81] For recent reassessments of Smuts, see Iain R. Smith, 'Jan Smuts and the South African War', *SAHJ* no. 41 (1999), pp. 172–95; Geyser, *Jan Smuts and his international contemporaries*; R. Hyam, 'South Africa, Cambridge, and Commonwealth history', Smuts Distinguished Lecture on the 50th anniversary of the death of Smuts, delivered Nov. 2000, *The Round Table: The Commonwealth Journal of International Affairs* no. 360 (2001), pp. 401–14; there is an alternative view in S. Marks, 'White masculinity: Jan Smuts, race and the South African War', Raleigh Lecture on History, 2000, *Proceedings of the British Academy*, vol. 111: *Lectures and Memoirs, 2000* (2001), pp. 199–223.
[82] J. Butler, *South Africa: an empire with its colonies at home?*, lecture at Rhodes University, 1974 (Grahamstown, 1975) 33 pp.; S.C. Nolutshungu, *South Africa in Africa: a study of ideology and foreign policy* (Manchester, 1975). The Union inherited the expansionist tendencies of the Transvaal, for which see N. G. Garson, *The Swaziland question and a road to the sea, 1887–1895* (*Argief-Jaarboek vir Suid-Afrikaanse Geskiedenis/Archives Yearbook for South African History*, 20th year, vol. II, part 2 (Pretoria, 1957), pp. 263–434. For map, see p. 104 below.

committed and energetic expansionist of them all.[83] In fact, every prime minister from Botha in 1911 to Verwoerd in 1961 pestered Britain for the transfer of the High Commission Territories. Strangely, this central feature of Afrikaner politics continues to de denied. For example, the sociologist Seiler has dismissed *The failure of South African expansion, 1908–1948* (1972) with the categorical assertion that before the 1950s South Africa's dominant motive was neither steadily nor intermittently expansive, but 'a continuing inward preoccupation with the achievement and consolidation of power'.[84] Fortunately, British authorities at the time were more perceptive and vigilant. 'To despise or ignore the strong and expanding force of South African nationalism', warned high commissioner Sir Evelyn Baring, 'would be as unwise as it was to decry in March 1933 the power of Hitler to do harm'.[85] Every South African government report on land division, including the Tomlinson Report of 1955, assumed the incorporation of the High Commission Territories, and for the simple reason that it would make land division appear more respectable: instead of 13 per cent of the land area for Africans it would look more like 50 per cent. And quite apart from prime ministers, other important politicians like Hofmeyr and Oswald Pirow were expansionists too. Pirow (minister of justice, 1929–33, and minister of railways and mines, 1933–9, the 'führer' of the *Ossewa Brandwag*) feared that, unincorporated, the Territories would become havens for Union dissidents. Moreover, he planned a defence and communications policy on an all-Africa scale in the 1930s – 'railway imperialism' combined with 'an empire of the air'. Pirow used South African Airways as the preferred instrument to challenge British pretensions to control the airspace south of Nairobi. As a result British Airways (Imperial Airways/BOAC) had severely restricted access to South African destinations until the 1980s. On the ground, railways were simultaneously being exploited in a parallel expansionist strategy. South African Railways not merely worked the continuation of the line in Southern Rhodesia up to Bulawayo, but had personnel lent to Kenya, Uganda, Nyasaland, and Mozambique. In 1936 Pirow pulled off a major coup, with an African transport conference with these countries, together with Northern Rhodesia, Tanganyika, Angola, the Belgian Congo, and even Madagascar, which agreed to adopt as standard the South African gauge of 3'6''. In consequence the copper of Katanga flowed out through the South African

---

[83] J. C. Smuts, *Plans for a better world: speeches* (London, 1942), pp. 243–54, 'Greater South Africa'; the South African edition was overtly entitled *Greater South African plans for a better world* (Johannesburg, 1940). See also P. R. Warhurst, 'Smuts and Africa: a study in sub-imperialism', *SAHJ* no. 16 (1984), pp. 82–100.

[84] J. Seiler, 'South African perspectives and responses to external pressure' *Journal of Modern African Studies* vol. 13 (1975), pp. 447–8.

[85] *The Labour government and the end of empire*, part 4, document no. 441, 'Review of affairs, 1944–1951' (25 July 1951), p. 355.

port of East London, and South Africa acquired increasing influence over her neighbours.[86]

High commissioner Baring had concluded as early as April 1945 that 'we should never sacrifice the true interests of Africans to a desire to remain friendly with a United Party government at Pretoria'. He feared that a deal might be done with Smuts, which would transfer Swaziland as a compromise. It was unthinkable this would happen with a National Party administration, and, with Smuts out of the way, Baring was reported to have slept more soundly in his bed.[87] Thus, paradoxically, in the moment of its triumph in winning the election of 1948, the National Party ensured the defeat of the foundation-dream of a Greater South Africa.

The accession of the National Party to power in 1948 was a turning-point in Anglo-South African relations principally in that the cause of continuing British disillusionment shifted publicly to revulsion against apartheid as it became institutionalised. A seismic shift took place in South Africa from pragmatic, occasional, and limited measures of discrimination and separation, to an ideologically driven, unified, and systematic denial of black rights in all spheres of life: something dogmatic, rigorous, and totalising. *Ad hoc* arrangements were superseded by an unmerciful programme, restricting movements, regulating relationships, enforcing educational underdevelopment. It was both lunatic and laughable.

Post-apartheid Afrikaner ideologues would like to fix part of the blame for this on the British government. Now, as to this: it is not in dispute that 'segregation' was the framework within which apartheid developed, nor that the roots of segregation pre-date 1910. After all, the Lagden Report of 1905 reflected Edwardian attitudes, and separate black urban locations were well established in the main South African towns before 1910.[88] However, this needs to be put in perspective. Such arrangements – ethnic quarters, Chinatowns, and so on – seem almost to be a historic and universal principle of urban life. Separate European areas were common throughout the British and French empires.

---

[86] R. L. McCormack, 'Man with a mission: Oswald Pirow and South African Airways, 1933–1939', *JAH* vol. 20 (1979), pp. 543–57, and 'Airlines and empires: Great Britain and the "Scramble for Africa", 1919–1932' *Canadian Journal of African Studies* vol. 10 (1976), pp. 87–106; E. A. Walker, *A history of Southern Africa* (London, 1957 edn), pp. 658, 668–70; see also G. Pirie, *Winged Britannia: civil aviation and British imperialism* (forthcoming).

[87] PRO, DO 35/1172, Y 706/7, Baring to secretary of state, 2 Apr. 1945, quoted in Hyam, *Failure of South African expansion*, p. 178; C. Douglas-Home, *Evelyn Baring: the last proconsul* (London, 1978), p. 171.

[88] M. Legassick, 'British hegemony and the origins of segregation in South Africa, 1901–1914' in Beinart and Dubow, eds., *Segregation and apartheid*, ch. 2, pp. 43–59; M. W. Swanson, 'The sanitation syndrome: bubonic plague and urban native policy in the Cape Colony, 1900–1909', *ibid.* ch. 1, pp. 25–42, repr. from *JAH* vol. 18 (1977), and 'Urban origins of separate development', *Race and Class* vol. 10 (1968), pp. 31–40; R. F. Hudson, 'The British origins of South African segregation' (PhD thesis, Cambridge, 2000).

At the turn of the century the empire's most notorious racial villain was not South Africa but 'white Australia'. What has to be explained is how it came about that segregationist policies held in common around the British empire as the twentieth century began, were gradually repudiated everywhere else, but in South Africa were transmuted and re-invented into something much worse in the 1950s. There is a fundamental difference between segregation and apartheid, and Afrikaners, not the British, must bear the responsibility for the latter.[89]

A very distinct hardening of British government attitudes towards South Africa can be detected for 1949 to 1950, reflected especially in changes of approach to the South-West African dispute, analysed in chapter 7. A further graphic illustration may be deduced from the high-profiled Els case and its aftermath. Adrian Els had in a fit of marital jealousy murdered a European farmer in Swaziland in 1945. His appeal against conviction took fourteen months to come to court in London. This raised the whole question of appropriate appellate jurisdiction for the High Commission Territories. Initially the Labour government seemed inclined to opt for the simplest and cheapest solution, which was to use the Union Court for High Commission Territories appeals. Malan in December 1948 indicated that he was more than willing to offer the necessary facilities, but within the year it had become politically impossible for the British government to go ahead with this solution, and it had to fall back on the more complicated and expensive alternative of judicial decentralisation in regional superior courts.[90] The Seretse Khama case, discussed in chapter 8, altered the whole terms of the Anglo-South African relationship, as geopolitics and gender, race and even class, dramatically intersected.

Throughout the 1950s British policy-makers moved slowly towards a redefinition of official attitudes, reluctant to force a 'parting of ways', but increasingly aware of the damage done by seeming to be too close to the South African government. Macmillan's 'wind of change' speech in Cape Town on 3 February 1960 marked a climactic moment in Anglo-South African relations, with its unequivocal warning that there were aspects of South African policy 'which make it impossible to support you without being false to our own deep convictions about the political destinies of free men, to which in our territories

---

[89] The term 'apartheid' seems to have been invented by the Afrikaner historian P. van Biljon to indicate an 'all-embracing racial policy essential to replace the old notion of segregation' (1935). Historians of sexuality may find parallels here with the invention of the term 'homosexuality' in 1868 by Karl Benkert (or Kertbeny), and the debate as to whether something can 'exist' before it becomes necessary to invent a new concept for it: like homosexuality, apartheid described a total way of life, as opposed to, but incorporating, a pre-existing practice (sodomy/segregation), but transcending it. To conflate segregation and apartheid is as unhistorical as the tendentious claim that 'gay people' existed in ancient Greece or medieval monasteries, though this is not to say there might not be a pre-disposing general culture (homoerotic/racially prejudiced).

[90] Hyam, ed., *The Labour government and the end of empire*, part 1, introduction, pp. lxvi–lxvii.

we are striving to give effect'.[91] The background to this major policy statement is given in chapters 7 and 11; the latter goes on to deal with the departure of South Africa from the Commonwealth in March 1961. The South African side of the 'parting of the ways' is the subject of chapter 12.

Nevertheless, it is by no means the case that South Africa's removal from the Commonwealth represented closure for the tensions between the two governments. True, it definitively removed the last vestigial possibility of a transfer of the High Commission Territories to South Africa, although their vulnerability continued to exercise successive British governments. The problems experienced by the Labour government after 1964 were very familiar to the civil servants who handled them in the previous twenty or thirty years or so. South Africa outside the Commonwealth still had to be treated as half-ally and half-untouchable at the same time.[92] 'Containment' and 'co-operation' continued to be the guiding watchwords.[93] The 'four reasons' for trying to remain on friendly terms *despite apartheid* continued to operate. British governments equivocated on the complicated issues of sanctions, trying to distinguish in arms sales between weapons which might be used for internal repression and those required for external defence, and thus continued to pay a price in domestic and international criticism which they believed to be unavoidable in order to preserve essential higher objectives, the 'national interest' and the best interest of Africans as they saw them.[94] It was still the case that, as Gordon Walker had told the Labour Cabinet in 1951, those who would ostracise South Africa and have nothing to do with it, 'completely fail to understand the realities of the situation'.[95] British high commissioners and civil servants encouraged their government to take the long view. Eventually, they argued, apartheid must

---

[91] Hyam and Louis, eds., *The Conservative government and the end of empire*, part 1, document no. 32, address by Macmillan, Cape Town (3 Feb. 1960), p. 171. See also O. Geyser, *Watershed for South Africa, London 1961* (Durban, 1983); and M. Makin, 'Britain, South Africa and the Commonwealth in 1960: the "winds of change" re-assessed', *Historia (Historiese Genootskap van Suid-Afrika/Historical Association of South Africa)* vol. 41 (Pretoria, 1996), pp. 74–88.

[92] Hyam and Louis, eds., *The Conservative government and the end of empire*, part 2, document nos. 462 (valedictory despatch by Sir J. Maud, 14 May 1963) and 463 (briefing despatch to Sir H. Stephenson, 28 June 1963), pp. 455–68.

[93] J. Barber, '"An historical and persistent interest": Britain and South Africa', *International Affairs* vol. 67 (1991), pp. 723–38; *The United Kingdom's policy towards South Africa and the other states of the region*, House of Commons Foreign Affairs Committee Report, 1990–1991 (London, 1991).

[94] J. W. Young, 'The Wilson government and arms to South Africa, 1964', *Journal of Contemporary British History* vol. 12 (1998), pp. 62–86; T. Bale, '"A deplorable episode": South African arms and the statecraft of British social democracy', *Labour History Review* vol. 62 (1997–8), pp. 22–40.

[95] Hyam, ed., *The Labour government and the end of empire*, part 4, p. 315, report on visit (16 Apr. 1951). Or, as 'Sir Humphrey Appleby' once put it: 'Unfortunately, the interests of Britain usually involve doing deals with people the public think are Baddies' (J. Lynn and A. Jay, eds., *Yes prime minister: the diaries of the Rt Hon James Hacker*, London, 1986, vol. I, p. 176).

collapse, and one day there would almost certainly be a black government in Pretoria. Sir John Maud's advice, therefore, was: 'keep faith' with the African majority, keep a foot in the door (making sure Cold War rivals did not exploit an opening),[96] and meanwhile do not antagonise the National Party government to no good purpose or real effect.[97] It was sound advice, and the return of the new South Africa to the Commonwealth in 1994[98] – discussed in the Epilogue – surely vindicates the essential rightness of this British strategy.

[96] J. E. Spence, 'Southern Africa in the Cold War: ideological and geopolitical factors in the struggle for supremacy', *History Today* vol. 49, 2 (1999), pp. 43–9.

[97] Hyam and Louis, eds., *The Conservative government and the end of empire*, part 2, document no. 451, Sir J. Maud to Sir A. Clutterbuck (13 Apr. 1960), p. 411; and document no. 469, Foreign Office minute by P. M. Foster (13 Sept. 1963), p. 481.

[98] The master-work is O'Meara, *Forty lost years*, but helpful contributions to the emerging history of the new South Africa also include: G. Mills, ed., *From pariah to participant: South Africa's evolving foreign relations, 1990–1994* (Johannesburg, 1994); T. R. H. Davenport, *The birth of a new South Africa* (Toronto and London, 1998), and T. R. H. Davenport, *South Africa, a modern history* (5th edn, with C. Saunders London, 2001), chs. 19 and 20, pp. 550–657; N. Etherington, ed., *Peace, politics and violence in the New South Africa* (London, 1992), pp. 102–20, 'Exploring the death throes of apartheid'. And there are several good general introductions, such as N. Worden, *The making of modern South Africa: conquest, segregation and apartheid* (Blackwell, Oxford, 1994), ch. 6, pp. 121–41; Welsh, *A history of South Africa*, pp. 484–96; J. Barber, *South Africa in the twentieth century: a political history – in search of a nation state* (Blackwell, Oxford, 1999), pp. 207–314; and W. Beinart, *Twentieth-century South Africa* (Oxford, 2nd edn, 2001), pp. 289–347.

2 Breakdown: into war, 1895–1899

After the passage of a century and the appearance of countless publications on the South African War, there remain the most profound differences of opinion about the war's origins. Many of the more recent accounts have emphasised Britain's economic interests in the southern African periphery – principally in the production and supply of gold – and the consequent necessity of removing the administratively backward and economically obstructionist regime of Paul Kruger in Pretoria.[1] Other accounts have stressed the concerns of British government decision-makers at the imperial centre – concerns about British power and prestige, about the necessity of maintaining British paramountcy in southern Africa, and about safeguarding the strategically vital Cape route.[2] Further divisions exist between those accounts which stress the broader

---

This chapter is based on research undertaken while Peter Henshaw was a Caird research fellow at the National Maritime Museum, Greenwich. He would like to thank Iain Smith, Alan Jeeves, and Saul Dubow for their comments on earlier versions of this chapter. It springs from a paper presented both at Shula Marks's Southern Africa seminar and at the University of Cape Town's history department seminar. Thanks are also due to all those who offered questions and insights at these seminars.

[1] See, for example, S. Marks and S. Trapido, 'Lord Milner and the South African state reconsidered', in M. Twaddle (ed.), *Imperialism, the state and the Third World* (London, 1992), pp. 80–94; S. Marks and S. Trapido, 'Lord Milner and the South African state', *History Workshop Journal*, vol. 8 (1979), pp. 50–80; P. J. Cain and A. G. Hopkins, *British imperialism, 1688–2000* (2nd edn, London, 2001), pp. 318–27; and R. Ally, *Gold and empire: the Bank of England and South Africa's gold producers 1886–1926* (Johannesburg, 1994). J. A. Hobson's influence on the economic interpretations of the war's origins is discussed in P. J. Cain, 'British radicalism, the South African crisis, and the origins of the theory of financial imperialism', pp. 173–93; and I. R. Smith, 'Capitalism and the war', pp. 56–75, both in D. Omissi and A. S. Thompson (eds.), *The impact of the South African War* (Basingstoke and New York, 2002); also I. R. Smith, 'A century of controversy over origins' in D. Lowry (ed.), *The South African War reappraised* (Manchester, 2000), pp. 23–49.

[2] I. R. Smith, *The origins of the South African War, 1899–1902* (London, 1996); A. N. Porter, *Origins of the South African War: Joseph Chamberlain and the diplomacy of imperialism, 1895–1899* (Manchester, 1980); J. S. Marais, *The fall of Kruger's republic* (Oxford, 1961); A. N. Porter, 'The South African War (1899–1902): context and motive reconsidered', *Journal of African History*, 31, 1 (1990), pp. 43–5; I. R. Smith, 'The origins of the South African War (1899–1902): a reappraisal', *South African Historical Journal*, 22 (1990), pp. 24–60; and N. G. Garson, 'British imperialism and the coming of the Anglo-Boer War', *South African Journal of Economics*, 30 (1962), pp. 140–53.

structural forces at play and those which give a central role to key individuals such as Sir Alfred Milner (Britain's high commissioner and regional proconsul for southern Africa) or Joseph Chamberlain (the colonial secretary in London).[3] This chapter will attempt to explain the War's origins through an analysis combining the broader economically driven developments in southern Africa; the geopolitical concerns of decision-makers in London; and the influence of Milner as the key 'man on the spot' and intermediary between the periphery and the centre.[4]

This explanation will be based on a model of imperial expansion first proposed by Ronald Hyam.[5] This model presumes that an event such as the South African War cannot be explained except in terms of the *interaction* between the colonial periphery and the imperial centre, interaction in which the influence of the British government's proconsular 'man on the spot' might be crucial. Developments within southern Africa could not by themselves be decisive. Nor could actions solely by decision-makers in London or solely by the British high commissioner. The model further presumes that economic forces and motives had their greatest influence on developments in the periphery, while decisions at the centre were determined by geopolitical calculations relating to Britain's power and prestige in relation to other states. Finally, Hyam's model indicates how individual human agency could shape the course of events, how the action of a man such as Milner operating at the point of 'proconsular interlock' could have disproportionate significance.

The 'two level' 'proconsular interlock' model will be used to tie together several arguments about the origins of the South African War. The first is that the gold-mining industry of the Transvaal – the private and public wealth that it created, and the pressures for economic and political change that it

[3] Thomas Pakenham called the conflict 'Milner's War' in *The Boer War* (London and Johannesburg, 1979). G. H. L le May did likewise in *British supremacy in South Africa, 1899–1907* (Oxford, 1965). D. M. Schreuder called it 'Chamberlain's war' in *The scramble for southern Africa* (Cambridge, 1980), p. 53.

[4] An explanation of the war in terms of the intersection between local economic pressures and the strategic preoccupations of the metropolis has been provided by R. E. Robinson and J. Gallagher, *Africa and the Victorians: the official mind of imperialism* (London, 1961), ch. 14. Two of the best recent discussions of metropolitan and local pressures for war are found in B. Nasson, *The South African War, 1899–1902* (London, 1999), pp. 15–45; and I. Phimister, 'Unscrambling the scramble for Southern Africa: the Jameson Raid and the South African War revisited', *South African Historical Journal*, 28 (1993), pp. 203–20. A further provocative, if brief, discussion of the origins of the war can be found in A. N. Porter, 'The South African War and the historians', *African Affairs*, 99 (2000), pp. 633–48. An excellent discussion of Milner's pivotal proconsular role can be found in J. Benyon, ' "Intermediate" imperialism and the test of empire: Milner's "excentric" high commission in South Africa', in D. Lowry (ed.), *The South African War reappraised*, pp. 84–103.

[5] See R. Hyam, *Britain's imperial century, 1815–1914: a study of empire and expansion*, 1st edn (London, 1976), pp. 373–5; and 2nd or 3rd edn (London, 1993, 2002), pp. 285–90. See also R. Hyam, 'The primacy of geopolitics: the dynamics of British imperial policy, 1763–1963', *Journal of Imperial and Commonwealth History*, 27, 2 (1999), pp. 27–52.

stimulated – produced some of the key local pressures for a showdown with the Kruger regime in the 1890s. Some mining capitalists, concerned about the declining profitability of their investments, saw their salvation in a radical transformation of the Transvaal state, a transformation which would clear the way for the cost-reducing reforms. Some even saw that this could best be achieved by promoting the cause of Uitlander rights (i.e. the rights of foreign white settlers in the Transvaal). This would produce a Transvaal dominated by British settlers rather than Boers, a territory more likely to form part of a larger British dominion of South Africa – a state better adapted to meet the long-term needs of the mining industry. The second argument is that the activities of this gold-mining industry also intensified the pressures felt by decision-makers in London to assert British paramountcy in southern Africa; but that these pressures at the centre were quite different in nature and character from the ones shaping developments at the periphery. The chief fear of the British government in London was that the wealth of the mines would not only enable the Transvaal to assert its independence from Britain, but also enable the Transvaal to dominate the region economically and, eventually, politically. This threatened British ascendancy in the Cape Colony and Natal, damaging enough in terms of London's strategic preoccupation with the protection of the Cape sea route to India and the East. No less importantly and more immediately, though, a strong Transvaal aspiring for independence was a source of grave uncertainty and weakness in Britain's dealings with its European rivals, particularly Germany, but also France and Russia. For the British government, then, the political and economic transformation of the Transvaal was less important as an end in itself than as a *means* of removing this weakness and uncertainty. Indeed, once it became apparent that the Transvaal could use the Delagoa Bay route through Portuguese East Africa to escape from dependence on British ports and railways, it was clear to Milner and the Colonial Office that early intervention on the issue of British settler rights was the only effective means of asserting control over the Transvaal. The third argument is that the interests of the British government and of the mining capitalists, while generally quite different or even conflicting, coincided on the issue of the political transformation of the Transvaal. Both came to see that this could best be brought about through Uitlander enfranchisement. Both were encouraged to adopt this view by Milner who, through his influence at the point of interlock between the centre and the periphery, was able to build up the Uitlander issue and shape events in a way that made war almost inevitable.

I

Though debate persists, most historians would now agree that by the mid-1890s the main source of local pressure for a radical transformation of the Transvaal state came from those mining capitalists who were concerned about the profitability of their long-range mining programmes.[6] These mining capitalists were particularly anxious about the extra and, in their view, unnecessary costs their operations had to bear. Such costs arose because of the inadequate supply and control of cheap labour, because the granting of monopolies for the supply and manufacture of such vital inputs as dynamite significantly raised their price, and because tariffs, customs duties, and railway rates further increased costs of production either directly or indirectly through the higher local cost of living. Such concerns are generally seen as the principal cause of the Jameson Raid – the attempt, led by the mine magnate Cecil Rhodes and tacitly supported by Chamberlain, to overthrow the Kruger regime through the combination of an armed incursion and an Uitlander rebellion on the Rand.[7]

The failure of the Raid in December 1895, and the subsequent steps taken by the Transvaal government to address the grievances of the mine owners and the Uitlanders, may have induced some mining capitalists to work with the Kruger regime rather than to seek its overthrow; but, for the remainder of the 1890s some powerful mining interests continued to agitate for more radical change there. For many mining capitalists the key thing was that the Transvaal should 'modernise' to the benefit of the mining industry. How that modernisation came about, and whether a modernised Transvaal should be inside or outside of the British empire, were entirely secondary. Some mining capitalists would conclude, however, that their interests might be better served by a united British South Africa. The most important of these were associated with the Wernher-Beit & Eckstein group and its allies.[8] By the late 1890s they were particularly powerful by virtue of their extensive control of the English-language press in southern Africa. Moreover, it now seems evident that this group remained seriously concerned about the long-term profitability of their operations in the absence of a major political transformation of the region. They were worried not only about the additional costs arising out of the Transvaal's protectionist and monopolistic policies; but also about the general inefficiency

---

[6] Phimister, 'Unscrambling the scramble for Southern Africa', p. 215; R. Mendelsohn, 'Blainey and the Jameson Raid: the debate renewed', *Journal of Southern African Studies*, 6, 2 (1980), p. 170. Arthur Mawby has argued that the pressure for radical political change generated by the Uitlander reform movement has been seriously under-rated, and should be seen as being more significant than the pressure exerted by mining capitalists in the late 1890s: A. A. Mawby, *Gold mining and politics – Johannesburg, 1900–1907: the origins of the old South Africa?*, vol. I (Lampeter, 2000), pp. 85–154.

[7] I. R. Smith, 'Joseph Chamberlain and the Jameson Raid', p. 99 and R. Mendelsohn, 'Thirty years' debate on the economic origins of the Raid', pp. 55–87, both in E. J. Carruthers, ed., *The Jameson Raid: A centennial retrospective* (Houghton, Johannesburg, 1996).

[8] This was the London partnership of Wernher, Beit Co., and their Johannesburg subsidiary H. Eckstein & Co. See A. Jeeves, 'Hobson's *The War in South Africa*: a reassessment', paper presented at the 'Rethinking the South African War 1899–1902' conference, Pretoria, 1998.

of the Transvaal state, the unpredictability of its politics and policies, and the threat of arbitrarily high and ruinous new taxes.[9] 'There is no law and no appeal against any decision' in the Transvaal, complained one capitalist in November 1898.[10] And, no less importantly, they remained concerned about the supply and control of cheap labour and looked to a united, reformed, and British South Africa to provide the state structures in which their operations might prosper.[11]

This was the context in which some mining interests pressed the case for Uitlander rights in 1898 and 1899, seeing it as the best way of securing the political and economic transformation they desired. Isolation from the Uitlander cause was seen as a real danger. It would play into the hands of the Kruger regime which sought to promote division between Uitlander mine workers and the capitalists. It would also antagonise Milner, who was so evidently trying to promote Uitlander rights. As one capitalist noted, Transvaal 'legislators and other big officials . . . are determined to make as much as they can and squeeze the industry to the utmost. Hence this official campaign carried on by official organs against capitalists. They do all they can to get the poorer classes up in arms against capital.'[12] Moreover, for some mining interests, an alignment with Milner and with the British imperial cause seemed necessary to avoid isolation from the British-dominated regime that looked likely to supplant Kruger's before long. In the view of the Wernher-Beit & Eckstein group, at least, the safest course was to support the Uitlander cause in the hope that any new Transvaal government under Uitlander or British rule would be sympathetic to the gold-mining industry.[13]

A further force for political change and regional integration in southern Africa was exerted by the requirements of railway finance. The governments of the Cape Colony, Natal, the Orange Free State, and the Transvaal were all heavily dependent on the revenues generated either directly or indirectly by the railways. Customs duties, transit duties, and railway receipts were closely inter-linked and were the mainstays of government revenue in the region. A large proportion of the Cape Colony and Natal governments' debts arose from capital expenditure on government-owned railways. These had been built principally to link their

---

[9] Jeeves, 'Hobson's *The War in South Africa*', p. 9.
[10] G. Rouliot to J. Wernher 19 Nov. 1898, quoted in A. Jeeves, 'The Rand capitalists and Transvaal politics, 1892–1899' (unpublished PhD thesis, Queen's University, Kingston, Ontario 1971), p. 326.
[11] Jeeves, 'Hobson's *The War in South Africa*', pp. 6–10.
[12] G. Rouliot to J. Wernher 19 Nov. 1898 quoted in A. Jeeves, 'Rand capitalists and Transvaal politics', p. 327.
[13] A. Jeeves, 'Rand capitalists and the coming of the South African War, 1896–1899', *Historical Papers* (1973), pp. 61–83. Mawby has argued persuasively that some key mining capitalists, notably the Wernher-Beit & Eckstein group – the 'Corner House' – did not instigate pressure for radical political change in the late 1890s, but instead followed the lead of the Uitlander reform movement and of Milner: Mawby, *Gold mining and politics*, vol. I, pp. 155–212.

ports with mineral-producing areas of the interior.[14] The Delagoa Bay route – on which neither the port nor the railway was British controlled – was the shortest link between the Rand and the sea. If properly developed and managed it promised to become the cheapest and the most heavily used. These facts were perfectly apparent at the time, not only to governments in southern Africa but also to decision-makers in London. The latter saw that the Transvaal's largely independent access to the sea through Delagoa Bay gave the Kruger regime an increasing degree of leverage in dealing with other governments in the region, leverage that might lead to political domination. Lord Selborne, the junior minister at the Colonial Office, outlined the problem for Lord Salisbury, the prime minister and foreign secretary. If the Delagoa Bay railway were operated by Transvaal or other hostile interests, they could reduce the governments of the Cape and Natal 'to the verge of bankruptcy, so dependent are they upon their railway revenue. It needs no words to prove what a powerful use could be made of this instrument in squeezing the British South African Colonies into joining a United South African Republic.'[15] It was partly because of the unifying forces of railway geography and finance that the Colonial Office believed that southern Africa would either unite 'into a confederacy on the model of the Dominion of Canada and under the British flag' or 'inevitably amalgamate itself into a United States of South Africa'.[16]

Another economic force encouraging the political unification of southern Africa was the wealth generated by, and the population attracted to the Transvaal's gold-mining industry. As Selborne noted in 1896:

South African politics must revolve around the Transvaal, which will be the only possible market for the agricultural produce or the manufactures of Cape Colony and Natal. The commercial attraction of the Transvaal will be so great that a Union of the South African states with it will be absolutely necessary for their prosperous existence. The only question in my mind is whether that Union will be inside or outside the British Empire.[17]

Within southern Africa, powerful economic forces were not only pushing for a radical transformation of the Transvaal state. They were also tending to draw the region together under the leadership of the local economic powerhouse – the Transvaal. As far as the British government was concerned, the crucial question

---

[14] By the late 1890s, railway revenues had become of dominant importance for the Cape and Natal, with the Cape earning three-fourths of its railway profits in 1897 from through-traffic to the Transvaal. J. van der Poel, *Railway and customs policies in South Africa, 1885–1910* (London, 1933), pp. 46 and 98.

[15] D. G. Boyce, *The crisis of British power: the imperial and naval papers of the Second Earl of Selborne, 1895–1910* (London, 1990), pp. 36–7 (memorandum by Lord Selborne, 26 March 1896).

[16] Boyce, *Crisis of British power*, pp. 36–7 (memorandum by Lord Selborne, 26 March 1896).

[17] Boyce, *Crisis of British power*, p. 44 (Selborne to J. Chamberlain, 18 Oct. 1896).

was whether the Transvaal's transformation and the region's integration would weaken or strengthen Britain's power and prestige locally and in the wider world.

II

Whatever the methods and motives of individuals and groups seeking to influence British policy in southern Africa, government decision-makers in London conceived and justified their southern African policies in terms of national power and prestige. Power in this context meant armed and economic strength in relation to other states. This of course had geographical and territorial dimensions to the extent that political control of key parts of the globe conferred strategic advantage. Strategy – in the official British parlance of the day – related to more than just the projection of, or defence against armed force. It also related to a mercantilist concern to protect the sea-borne trade upon which Britain and the empire depended for their material strength. Prestige related to the perceptions both of Britain's power and of its willingness to defend its interests. It was 'power based on reputation' or the 'shadow cast by power'.[18]

During the 1890s, decision-makers in London became increasingly concerned about the impact of southern African developments on Britain's power and prestige, not only within southern Africa but also in the European and wider international context. The most threatening of these developments arose from the Transvaal's growing ever stronger on the back of the mining industry and ever more anxious to assert its independence from Britain. So long as Britain's control over the region was in doubt, Britain's European rivals could be expected to exploit this uncertainty to Britain's international disadvantage. Indeed, it was the wider international implications of this uncertainty which explains why Salisbury and the Foreign Office were so anxious to force a showdown with the Transvaal on the question of British paramountcy.[19] From London's perspective, the threat posed to British power and prestige by an independent Transvaal could best be removed by forcing Pretoria to accept Britain's supremacy in principle and to implement the political reforms which would ensure Britain's predominance in practice.

The pivotal point in any consideration of British power in southern Africa was the strategic significance of the Cape route. The importance of this route had diminished little, if at all, after the opening of the Suez Canal in 1869. The Admiralty Intelligence Department was clear about this in an 1897 report: 'It is impossible to over-estimate the strategical value of the Cape. In the probable

---

[18] See Hyam, 'Primacy of geopolitics', p. 29, and chapter 1 above, pp. 5–6.
[19] A. N. Porter, 'Lord Salisbury, Mr Chamberlain and South Africa, 1895–1899', *Journal of Imperial and Commonwealth History*, 1, 1 (1972), pp. 3–26.

event of the interruption in time of war of the Suez canal route to the East, the Cape would at once become the most important coaling station of the Empire.' This report also reiterated the accepted wisdom of the 1882 Royal Commission on Defence that the defence of the Cape route was 'essential to the retention by Great Britain of her possessions in India, Mauritius, Ceylon and even Australasia'.[20] The Cape route's defence had three main dimensions. First, the protection of the Royal Navy's main dockyard and repair facility at Simon's Town on the Cape peninsula. Secondly, the protection of the other key British coaling stations in the region – St Helena, Cape Town, Durban, and Mauritius. And, thirdly, the prevention of rival powers' gaining a controlling influence at other ports in the region, ports from which they might threaten British maritime traffic.

By the 1890s, the chief local problem associated with maintaining control of Simon's Town and the other ports in British southern Africa was to ensure that the internally self-governing colonies of the Cape and Natal remained firmly within the British empire. Some decision-makers in London sought to hedge Britain's strategic bets by proceeding on the assumption that in the final resort Britain would always be able to hang on to Simon's Town even if the rest of southern Africa were lost. In fact it was with such an eventuality in mind that the Salisbury Cabinet agreed in 1897 that the expensive new dockyard proposed for the Cape should be built at Simon's Town rather than Cape Town. The alternative view, though, had been stated clearly by Lord Kimberley in 1881 (a statement published in his memoirs in 1898): 'It is an entire delusion to imagine that we could hold Cape Town, abandoning the rest. If we allow our supremacy in South Africa to be taken from us, we shall be ousted before long from that country altogether.'[21] The War Office also assumed that it was 'impossible, for obvious political reasons, to create a Gibraltar out of the Cape Peninsula, and that the permanent retention of this peninsula . . . is dependent upon the maintenance of British ascendancy in all South African Colonies'.[22] But, whatever was thought in London about possible futures in southern Africa, it seems clear that most senior British decision-makers believed that strategically valuable coaling stations, anchorages, and dockyards in southern Africa could best be safeguarded by the establishment of a large united British dominion there.

In addition to the strategic dangers of a gradual drift of the Cape and Natal towards the Transvaal and away from the British empire, there was the more immediate threat that the Transvaal would seek to assert its regional predominance by force of arms. The Transvaal's purchase of huge quantities of arms

---

[20] ADM 231/28, Intelligence Department (No. 494) *British Colonies*, 1897.
[21] D. Schreuder, *Gladstone and Kruger: Liberal government and colonial 'Home Rule', 1880–1885* (London and Toronto, 1969), p. 15 (Kimberley to R. P. Selborne, 11 Oct. 1881).
[22] Schreuder, *Gladstone and Kruger*, p. 503 (War Office memorandum, 1 Oct. 1884).

and ammunition in the 1890s was thought to have completely altered the local strategic situation. One Colonial Office official noted in 1896 that 'it is now quite clear that the Boers have arms and ammunition enough to shoot down all the armies of Europe'.[23] Major Edward Altham, Britain's senior Military Intelligence officer in South Africa, warned in 1898 that the scale of the Transvaal's military preparations pointed:

to the existence of a definite policy which will build up a Dutch Oligarchy in South Africa strong enough to shake off English suzerainty when favourable opportunity offers, and, perhaps, even to carry out the larger dream of a great Dutch independent State reaching from the Zambezi down to the Hottentots Holland Mountains, and with Delagoa Bay as its sea port.[24]

Field-Marshal Lord Wolseley, the commander-in-chief of the British Army, concurred: 'sooner or later we shall have a violent explosion' in South Africa. 'Were we now or at any time in the near future to have any serious trouble with a foreign power, that explosion would take place at once.'[25] European tensions thus intersected with and exacerbated the Transvaal armed threat. Great power rivalries thereby served to increase the British government's determination to assert its ascendancy in southern Africa.

The chief threats posed to the Cape route by rival European powers were all linked to the problem of Britain's uncertain paramountcy in southern Africa. The Cape route could never be secure so long as the Transvaal sought to assert its independence from Britain. This was true whether the Transvaal acted alone or as the leading influence in a United States of South Africa outside of the British empire. In 1896 Selborne recorded that:

So long as the British South African Colonies have not united with the Transvaal into a British Dominion . . . France and Germany will . . . strive only to disintegrate British influence and Empire in South Africa by playing off the different South African states against each other and by helping the Transvaal in its game of attracting British Colonies away from the British Empire.[26]

Once a United States of South Africa was established, France would seek to strengthen its strategic position in Madagascar where its naval base at Diego Suarez had been 'established avowedly as the head-quarters of offence against our commerce passing round the Cape for India'.[27] Moreover, 'The next day after the United States of South Africa had declared her independence Germany would walk into Walfisch Bay', the Cape-controlled port on the coast of German

---

[23] CO 537/130, Note by E. Fairfield, 3 June 1896.
[24] CO 537/134, E. A. Altham to Colonial Office, 17 March 1898.
[25] WO 32/7844, Wolseley to permanent under-secretary, 20 April 1898.
[26] Boyce, *Crisis of British power*, p. 44 (Selborne to J. Chamberlain, 18 Oct. 1896).
[27] CAB 37/50, 36, Cabinet memorandum by Austen Chamberlain, 10 June 1899.

South-West Africa.[28] Hence, even if a United States of South Africa could be induced to keep rival powers out of its own ports and to allow Britain to retain Simon's Town, it was likely that the loss of British paramountcy would allow rival European powers to gain bases in neighbouring territories from which to threaten the Cape route.

And there was a further strategic threat associated with Britain's lack of control over the Transvaal. This was that a rival power might gain a commercial foothold in Portugal's southern African empire and turn this to strategic advantage. Typical of such anxieties was a report by Britain's chief representative in Pretoria in 1897 about the development of a German trading concession at Delagoa Bay to serve a proposed new line of Transvaal steamers. This development might include a coaling station 'under the management of German officers, which might serve in case of need as a naval station; and, as these commercial vessels will be manned by able-bodied German seamen, up to the standard of the Imperial Navy, Germany would thus secure a footing in peace or war in Lourenço Marques'.[29] The Anglo-German Convention of August 1898 was intended to reduce such German threats in southern Africa. But to the horror of the Colonial Office (which was shut out of the British negotiations with Germany) the convention not only permitted the development of port facilities at Delagoa Bay by a German company, it also renounced Britain's previous right of veto over such developments.[30] The strategic threat posed by German or French commercial developments in Portuguese territory would, though, be much reduced if the Transvaal no longer sought to encourage such schemes as a way of reducing its dependence on British-controlled railways and ports.

The strategic significance of southern Africa and of the Cape route more generally was not merely a matter of naval warfare and military transport routes. It also related to trade protection. This fact is crucial to understanding British policy debates in the 1890s, though it has typically been overlooked or misunderstood by historians. The link between strategy and trade could not have been more apparent than in the Admiralty report[31] which formed the basis of the great naval works programme of the 1890s – a programme that included the allocation in 1899 of £2.5m for the construction of a 'first-class dock' at Simon's Town.[32] This report noted that through the East Indies, Cape, and China stations 'lie the great trade routes to the East, whether the Suez canal be blocked or not, and the importance of protecting them will be vital'.[33] This point was

---

[28] Boyce, *Crisis of British power*, p. 35 (Selborne to Salisbury, 30 March 1896).
[29] CO 537/131, C. Greene to Lord Rosmead, 11 Feb. 1897.
[30] P. Henshaw, 'The "key to South Africa" in the 1890s: Delagoa Bay and the origins of the South African War', *Journal of Southern African Studies*, 24, 3 (1998), pp. 538–9.
[31] CAB 37/41, 8, memorandum by the Admiralty Hydrographer, 11 Jan. 1896, forwarded to Cabinet by G. Goschen, 7 Feb. 1896.
[32] CAB 37/48, 36, memorandum by A. Chamberlain on the Naval Works Bill, 10 June 1899.
[33] CAB 37/41, 8, memorandum by the Admiralty Hydrographer, 11 Jan. 1896.

repeated in Cabinet memoranda in 1896, 1898, and 1899.[34] It was also made in the House of Commons by Austen Chamberlain, a junior Admiralty minister, in his defence of the Naval Works Bill: 'The importance of the Cape is patent to everyone. It is a great calling place for our trade in time of peace, and a much larger volume of trade would, probably, pass there in war time.'[35] Even the Admiralty's own assessments of the strategic value of ports were based in considerable measure on the amount of trade that passed through them.[36] To some extent this reflected nothing more than a recognition of the fairly obvious point that Britain's wealth and power were more heavily dependent on sea-borne trade than its great rivals were. It also reflected a recognition that national commercial interests were often, in this period, the basis on which great powers made political or territorial claims in areas controlled by weaker states. It should therefore come as no surprise that the British government concerned itself so much with questions of trade and commercial concessions in this period, and particularly with the threats posed by rival industrial powers to British trade and commerce.

In southern Africa this concern centred on the efforts being made by American, French, but above all German enterprises to secure larger shares of the region's trade and commerce. Colonial and Foreign Office representatives in southern Africa, the Board of Trade, and the inter-departmental Commercial Intelligence Committee in London all paid close attention to such matters in the 1890s. And they gave special attention to reports that Germany and France might be using subsidised shipping rates, preferential customs and railway rates, or monopolistic concessions to secure a larger share of the Transvaal trade.[37] Whatever the private calculations of the German government in this period,[38] there continued to be concerns in Whitehall after the signing of the 1898 Anglo-German Convention that German and Transvaal interests would conspire to increase the German economic stake in southern Africa at Britain's expense.[39] And there were fears of similar conspiracies involving France.[40] But, however worrying these developments may have been economically, it

---

[34] CAB 37/41, 8, 7 Feb. 1896; CAB 37/48, 68, 22 Aug. 1898; and CAB 37/50, 36, 6 June 1899.
[35] H.C. Deb., col. 278, 25 July 1899.
[36] ADM 231/28, Intelligence Department (No. 494) *British Colonies*, 1897.
[37] Henshaw, 'Key to South Africa', pp. 532–3; A. Porter, *Victorian shipping, business, and imperial policy: Donald Currie, the Castle Line, and southern Africa* (Woodbridge, Suffolk, and New York, 1986), pp. 211–16, 231–5; Porter, *Origins of the South African War*, pp. 159–60 and 177–78; Porter, 'Lord Salisbury', p. 4.
[38] M. Seligmann, *Rivalry in Southern Africa, 1893–1899: the transformation of German colonial policy* (London, 1998).
[39] Henshaw, 'Key to South Africa', pp. 538–9; J. Butler, 'The German factor in Anglo-Transvaal relations', in P. Gifford and W. R. Louis, eds., *Britain and Germany in Africa: imperial rivalry and colonial rule* (New Haven, CT, 1967), pp. 179–214.
[40] CO 417/271, notes by Selborne, 1 June, and J. Chamberlain, 2 June 1899.

seems that the principal concern at the senior decision-making level in London was that they all increased the possibility that the Transvaal would succeed in asserting its independence and in becoming the leader of a United States of South Africa.

The British government's concerns about the mining industry and gold sales seem to have been based on similar anxieties about the future of British paramountcy in southern Africa and about the interference by rival powers in free British trade. This may certainly be inferred from a Colonial Office note written in December 1898. Henry Lambert noted that the Transvaal's restrictive economic policies, particularly the granting of monopolies to non-British firms, would in the long run cripple the territory; the immediate result was 'loss to the mining industry run mainly by English capital and the deanglicising of the country by emigration of the English, Australians etc who cannot get work'.[41] If the British Uitlander population declined sufficiently, the British government would lose what seemed to be its best means of asserting control there – i.e. to insist that Pretoria grant full political rights to British subjects in the Transvaal, something which would (it was assumed) lead to the establishment of a pro-British government in Pretoria.

If senior political decision-makers in London were anxious about the production and sale of Transvaal gold itself (and there is still no direct evidence from the late 1890s to demonstrate the existence of such anxieties) it seems likely that they would have had no more than a general concern to ensure that rival European powers did not conspire with the Transvaal to take control of the gold trade away from Britain. There is certainly no reason to suppose that anyone in the Salisbury Cabinet had a clear understanding of Transvaal gold's specific significance for the London gold market or for the Bank of England's management of sterling as an international currency.[42] Such concerns as were expressed by British officials focused on the problem of how gold was shipped from southern Africa and to which destinations. Close attention was paid to the redirection of gold away from British ships departing from Cape Town, to be carried instead by German and French ships sailing from Delagoa Bay.[43] But the concern seems to have been as much about the fact that Britain's European rivals were taking control of this trade as about the fact that less Transvaal gold was flowing directly to London.

---

[41] CO 417/251, note by Lambert, 31 Dec. 1898.

[42] This assertion should not surprise historians. After all, few historians have ever demonstrated an effective understanding of gold's significance. Fewer still have agreed on the subject.

[43] The British consul in Lourenço Marques reported in August 1899 that there was 'every reason to believe that this trade' in gold through Delagoa Bay to Paris would increase 'because of lower shipping costs', *Board of Trade Journal*, 27, 159 (1899), p. 472. See also the similar report from this source in *Board of Trade Journal*, 26, 150 (1898), p. 89.

In the 1890s senior British decision-makers were beset by fears about southern African threats to British power and prestige, threats that arose from the weakness and uncertainty of Britain's position there. The first threat was that most of southern Africa would gradually fall under the control of an independent and anti-British Transvaal. This would not only endanger British control of strategically vital ports in the Cape Colony and Natal. It would also provide an opportunity for Britain's European rivals to gain a foothold in other ports in the region – most dangerously Delagoa Bay and Walfisch Bay – from which to challenge British control of the Cape route. The second threat was that the Transvaal would assert its independence and regional predominance by force of arms the moment that Britain became engaged in a serious military confrontation with another great power. The third was that Britain's European rivals would continually conspire with the Transvaal to undermine British influence in the region, seeking wherever possible either to challenge Britain's local economic and strategic dominance or to exploit Britain's weakness in southern Africa for geopolitical gain elsewhere in the world – as indeed was the German goal in the negotiation of the 1898 Anglo-German Convention.[44] The obvious, and perhaps the only way to defuse these threats was to make clear both to the Transvaal and to rival powers that Britain was the paramount power in southern Africa. To impose order on the region, the British government wished ultimately to unite the Boer republics with the British colonies there. The precursor to this was the establishment of a pro-British regime in Pretoria. And, as it turned out, the most effective way of doing all that in the local, British, and international political circumstances of the late 1890s was to insist that Pretoria recognise the political rights of British Uitlanders. This recognition would, it was thought, transform the Transvaal and the region to the great benefit of Britain's power and prestige, locally and around the world.

III

While economic conditions within southern Africa, and concerns in London about British power and prestige generated converging pressures for a rapid transformation of the Transvaal state and for the political unification of rival colonies in the region, war might not have broken out in 1899 without the intervention of Milner – Britain's determined and influential proconsul. He successfully linked and harnessed the local and metropolitan pressures for change in the Transvaal. He did so by building up the Uitlander issue as the one which could best serve the often divergent interests of the British government and the mining capitalists. And he was able to exert a crucial influence over the course and timing of events by virtue of his position as the 'man on the spot',

---

[44] Seligmann, *Rivalry in Southern Africa*, pp. 113–36.

controlling the lines of communication between the imperial centre and the southern African periphery.[45]

Milner himself recognised clearly what was at stake in southern Africa, at stake economically for the mines and geopolitically for Britain and its empire. From his contacts with mining capitalists he knew all about the problems the mines faced as a result of Kruger's policies. But he was also an imperial visionary who saw the importance for the empire as a whole of a strong, united and *British* South Africa. And he was a realist in international affairs who believed that Britain needed a united empire in order to stand up to its great power rivals. Much of the world was watching British policy in southern Africa. A failure to defend British interests, or the rights of British subjects there, was bound to undermine Britain's prestige in the eyes of many. Furthermore, he hoped that South Africa was going 'not only to federate itself as a free nation like Canada and Australia, but to be one of the means of federating the Empire'.[46]

Milner saw the crucial importance of the Uitlander issue as a means of linking the demands of the mining capitalists for an economic transformation of the Transvaal and the desire of the British government to assert Britain's supremacy in the region. The Uitlander issue was, in itself, of no great moment to either group. For the capitalists, Uitlander rights were a means to an end, an end that might be secured through an accommodation with the Kruger regime rather than through its replacement by an Uitlander-dominated one. By 1899, though, some key mining capitalists (particularly those associated with the Wernher-Beit & Eckstein group and its allies) had become convinced they must support the South African League campaign for Uitlander rights, 'otherwise we should have everyone against us'.[47] Such capitalists feared the consequences of political isolation either from white mine workers or from the British government as represented locally by Milner. By then the Kruger regime was seen by some mining capitalists as being too untrustworthy, corrupt, and inefficient to establish a political and economic framework in which the mines could prosper in the long term. The high commissioner and his local agents, for their part, worked hard to establish close links with the South African League and with some of the leading mining capitalists themselves.[48] Through these links too Milner and the High Commission encouraged the leaders of the League, certain key capitalists, and the newspapers they controlled, to take a strong stand on

---

[45] J. Benyon, *Proconsul and paramountcy in South Africa: the High Commission, British supremacy and the sub-continent, 1806–1910* (Pietermaritzburg, 1980), pp. 260–87; Benyon, '"Intermediate" imperialism and the test of empire', pp. 84–103.

[46] Hyam, *Britain's imperial century*, 2nd or 3rd edn, pp. 244–5.

[47] Georges Rouliot (a partner in Ecksteins) to Julius Wernher, 9 Jan. 1899, quoted in Jeeves, 'Rand capitalists and the coming of the South African War', p. 75.

[48] Benyon, *Proconsul and paramountcy*, pp. 269–74.

the Uitlander issue as the best way of securing the desired transformation of the Transvaal.[49] By May 1899, one associate of the Wernher-Beit & Eckstein group insisted that 'England is our only possible security and Milner the only possible intermediary'.[50]

In London, senior British policy-makers did not hold either the Uitlanders or the capitalists in high regard. Selborne thought that the Kruger regime could have been forced to change by 1897 'had not the pre-eminent Uitlanders been generally so worthless and contemptible'.[51] Milner, too, had his doubts about the Uitlanders. But he saw the importance of building up their cause as a way of persuading the British government to take a strong stand against the Transvaal and, in effect, to force it into a united British South Africa. As Milner noted in January 1899, Chamberlain's support for this aggressive policy 'depends on the amount of external pressure and excitement corresponding to our prodding of him from within. If only the Uitlanders stand firm on the formula of "no rest without reform" ... we shall do the trick yet ... And by the soul of St Jingo they get a fair bucking up from us all one way and another.'[52] Despite Milner's best efforts – through his heated despatches to London and through his influence over press coverage of the issue – some British ministers continued to the end to doubt the wisdom of forcing a showdown with the Transvaal on the issue of Uitlander political rights. The prime minister himself wanted 'to get away from the franchise issue, which will be troublesome in debate'.[53] Salisbury saw, however, that Milner had effectively forced the British government to confront the Transvaal on this issue: 'We have to act upon a moral field prepared for us by him and his jingo supporters. And therefore I see before us the necessity for considerable military effort – and all for people whom we despise, and for territory which will bring no profit and no power to England.'[54] Nevertheless, as Sir Michael Hicks Beach (the chancellor of the Exchequer) saw, 'equality of the white races in the Transvaal would really secure all we can desire, viz. British predominance'.[55]

The Uitlander franchise was the issue which Milner could use most readily 'to work up to a crisis'.[56] It was on this issue that he was able to take a stand and

---

[49] Jeeves, 'Rand capitalists and the coming of the South African War', pp. 61–83.
[50] P. FitzPatrick to J. Wernher, 1 May 1899, quoted in Jeeves, 'Rand capitalists and Transvaal politics', p. 327.
[51] CO 537/129, note by Selborne, 24 March 1897.
[52] E. T. Stokes, 'Milnerism', *Historical Journal*, 5, 1 (1962), p. 54 (Milner to G. Fiddes, 3 Jan. 1899).
[53] Quoted in E. Drus, 'Select documents from the Chamberlain papers concerning Anglo-Transvaal relations, 1896–1899', *Bulletin of the Institute for Historical Research*, 27 (1954), p. 181 (Salisbury to J. Chamberlain, 18 Sept. 1899).
[54] Quoted in Drus, 'Select documents', p. 189 (Salisbury to Lord Lansdowne, 30 Aug. 1899).
[55] Quoted in Drus, 'Select documents', p. 187 (Hicks Beach to J. Chamberlain, 29 Sept. 1899).
[56] Milner quoted in Hyam, *Britain's imperial century*, p. 244.

terminate the Bloemfontein Conference with Kruger in June 1899. The rapid breakdown of these talks annoyed senior decision-makers in London who were less willing than Milner to push the Transvaal to the brink of war at this time. Joseph Chamberlain had wanted Milner to be 'restrained rather than encouraged at the moment'.[57] Milner intervened again in July 1899 to urge a stiffer British line on the franchise question, just when tensions between London and Pretoria seemed to be easing.[58] Milner himself had no doubts about the part he had played prior to the outbreak of hostilities. He had, he admitted in 1900, 'been largely instrumental in bringing about a big war'.[59]

IV

In October 1899 the Transvaal government declared war on Britain and, along with its Orange Free State ally, launched an invasion of Natal and the Cape. For Pretoria it was a fight for freedom and independence. To have met all of Britain's demands, demands backed locally by the mining capitalists and the South African League, would have been to concede political control of the Transvaal. And this the Kruger regime steadfastly refused to do.

Capital's demands for improved returns on southern African investments was an undeniably powerful force for political change in the region. But it did not, by itself, draw Britain into war with the Transvaal. Few mining capitalists were so desperate for a transformation of the Transvaal state that they wished to see a war to bring it about. Many capitalists preferred to seek improved economic conditions through more gradual reforms. Moreover, the unification of the Cape and Natal with the Boer republics and the amalgamation of their railways may have been financially desirable to these British colonial governments and to the holders of their debt; but it was not necessarily to the advantage of capital invested in the Rand. More desirable from the latter's perspective was that the shorter, and potentially cheaper, Delagoa Bay route should predominate – something that might bankrupt the Cape and Natal and place them at the Transvaal's economic mercy. But, under the influence of Milner and the British government, and fearful of an alliance between working-class Uitlanders and the Kruger regime, some key mining capitalists gave their support to the Uitlander and British imperial cause in the belief that this was the best way to secure what they desired.

Some mining capitalists, like some British government decision-makers, were anxious for change in the Transvaal, though neither group was as anxious

---

[57] Porter, 'Lord Salisbury, Mr Chamberlain and South Africa', p. 17.
[58] Benyon, *Proconsul and paramountcy*, p. 276.
[59] J. Benyon, ' "Main show or side-show"? Natal and the South African War', *Journal of Imperial and Commonwealth History* 27, 1 (1999), p. 29 (Milner to Lord Roberts, 21 June 1900).

as Milner. He saw, more clearly than most, that time was on the side of the Kruger regime, particularly after it had become apparent that there would be no 'second Rand' in Rhodesia and that Britain would be unable to get control of Delagoa Bay: 'if we are not to fight and are yet not to be worsted, one of 2 things must happen. Either Rhodesia must develop *very* rapidly, or we must get Delagoa Bay.'[60] By late 1898 it was obvious to Milner that neither of these things was possible and that war might be the only way to assert control over the Transvaal. The alternative was to allow it to grow in strength and independence, gradually drawing the rest of the region under its political sway; this in no small measure because of the inescapable logic of railway geography and finance. Milner, though, had a key role in building up the Uitlander issue as one that could link and serve the interests of both mining capitalists and the British government. In doing this, and in exercising, at the point of 'proconsular interlock', a critical degree of control over the course and timing of events, Milner helped to create a situation in which war was almost inevitable.

Though the Boer republics took the initiative in declaring war on Britain, the British government had nevertheless been well prepared to fight in principle, even if not in effective military practice. It fought not to transform the Transvaal or unite southern Africa for the benefit of the mining capitalists, nor, in truth, to defend the rights of British subjects there. It fought because it seemed to be the best way to place southern Africa – and all that was at stake there for Britain's power and prestige – more firmly under British control. Indeed, it was feared in London that unless Britain asserted its paramountcy, southern Africa would remain a source of grave international uncertainty and of strategic weakness. The Transvaal's position would have become inexorably stronger with its growing wealth, its increasingly free access to the sea through Delagoa Bay, and with its shared interest with European powers in frustrating Britain's regional ambitions. Unless Britain intervened it seemed clear that the Transvaal would eventually become the centre of a United States of South Africa outside of the British empire. It even seemed likely that the Transvaal would seek to assert its independence and regional predominance by force of arms as soon as Britain went to war with another great power. Moreover, Britain's European rivals seemed more than likely to take advantage of any British weakness in southern Africa to gain advantages for themselves at Britain's expense in this region, in Europe, or elsewhere in the world. As Joseph Chamberlain put it so succinctly to his Cabinet colleagues in September 1899: 'What is now at stake is the position of Great Britain in South Africa and with

---

[60] C. Headlam, ed., *The Milner Papers: South Africa*, vol. I: *1897–1899* (London, 1931), p. 267 (Milner to J. Chamberlain, 6 July 1898).

it the estimate of our power and influence in our colonies and throughout the world.'[61]

After the war,[62] Milner remained in charge of reconstruction in the defeated republics. He was not primarily concerned with the conciliation of former enemies, but sought rather to keep the Boer communities quiet until he could engineer a numerically superior British population which would keep them permanently in check. The mining industry had to be developed to finance a programme of imperial land settlement and to stimulate British immigration more generally. This was not a success and only angered the Boers, who saw it as a policy of expropriation and anglicisation.[63] The post-war recovery of Boer morale and assertiveness was above all due to Milner's failure to import sufficient 'loyalist' immigrants and to keep the Transvaal British united. In fact, Milner's long-term legacy was the poisoning of Anglo-South African relations for fifty years.[64]

Milner was succeeded by Lord Selborne in May 1905, Chamberlain having been replaced by Alfred Lyttelton at the Colonial Office in October 1903. Then in December 1905 the Unionist government fell, and the Liberals came into office. Though many of them had been 'pro-Boers', principles of continuity of policy were strongly maintained, and the new government was committed to a continuing search for British supremacy in South Africa. However, they

---

[61] Quoted in Drus, 'Select documents', p. 187 (Chamberlain's memorandum to Cabinet, 6 Sept. 1899). While this chapter's account of the origins of the war resembles that of Robinson's and Gallagher's in various respects, there remain several key differences. First, Robinson and Gallagher misread the consequences of the Anglo-German Convention of August 1898. They mistakenly concluded that it eliminated the multiple threats posed by the development of links between Germany and the Transvaal through Delagoa Bay. And they did not see that, for this reason, the Convention made Milner and the Colonial Office more anxious than ever to force an early showdown with the Kruger regime. Secondly, Robinson and Gallagher underestimated Milner's role both in forcing such a showdown and in building up the Uitlander cause – an underestimation deriving in part, perhaps, from the lack of a theory to account for the proconsul's disproportionate influence. Thirdly, and following from the preceding shortcomings, Robinson and Gallagher overstated the extent to which the Colonial Office and the high commissioner followed the lead of the Uitlanders. As a result, *Africa and the Victorians* over-emphasised the extent to which the British government merely reacted to developments in the Southern African periphery, and underestimated the significance of European rivalries in the British calculations which led to war. See Robinson and Gallagher, *Africa and the Victorians*, pp. 410–61.

[62] See P. Warwick, ed., *The South African War: the Anglo-Boer War, 1899–1902* (London, 1980), part 3: 'Aftermath of war', pp. 333–403, chapters by S. E. Katzenellenbogen, 'Reconstruction in the Transvaal', R. Hyam, 'British imperial policy and South Africa, 1906–1910', and I. Hexham, 'Afrikaner nationalism, 1902–1914'.

[63] M. Streak, *Lord Milner's immigration policy for the Transvaal, 1897–1905* (Johannesburg: Rand Afrikaans University, 1969), pp. 65–6; K. Fedorowich, 'Anglicisation and the politicisation of British immigration to South Africa, 1899–1929', *JICH* vol. 19 (1991), pp. 222–46; A. Grundlingh, 'The War in twentieth-century Afrikaner consciousness', in D. Omissi and A. Thompson, eds., *The impact of the South African War* (Basingstoke and New York, 2002), pp. 23–37.

[64] Benyon, *Proconsul and paramountcy*, pp. 309, 330.

(a)

(b)

Illustration 2.1 Boer prisoners in St Helena: (a) Broadbottom Camp and Boer enclosure. (b) General Cronje and his officers. *Source: Pictorial views of St Helena and illustrations of the military camps and Boer prisoners of war*, by T. Jackson (n.d.).

recognised that Afrikaners must be taken more into account, and South African policy made to 'stand on two legs', one British, one Boer, and not merely on one only, the 'inherent vice' of Milner's approach. The Liberal redefinition of South Africa's role in the empire – with no 'third' black leg – proved to be a project which Milner's principal lieutenants could adapt to.[65]

[65] S. Dubow, 'Colonial nationalism: the Milner Kindergarten and the rise of "South Africanism", 1902–1910', *History Workshop Journal* vol. 43 (1997), pp. 53–85, is an important re-interpretation of the period; also S. Dubow, 'Imagining the new South Africa in the era of reconstruction', in Omissi and Thompson, eds., *The impact of the South African War*, pp. 76–95.

3 Post-war: the myth of magnanimity, 1905–1907

When the British Liberal government in 1906 granted self-government to the Transvaal it is highly unlikely that ministers were moved by genuine magnanimity towards the defeated Afrikaners. It is equally unlikely that the Afrikaner leaders before 1914 felt any genuine sense of reconciliation to the British empire. The Liberal government pretended to be acting magnanimously, while Jan Smuts and Louis Botha pretended to be pursuing a policy of conciliation. Both sides projected these attitudes for purely tactical reasons. Neither trusted the other, but each independently thought that they could attain their objectives by behaving as if they did; and yet out of this unpropitious situation of double deception a workable relationship was in fact hammered out. The key fact is that the Liberals never intended Botha and Smuts to form the first ministry when responsible government was established in the Transvaal, but, turning a failure of planning to good account, gave the clear impression that they *had* intended it; and they thus perhaps began the process of turning Smuts's marriage of convenience to the empire into a love relationship with the Commonwealth.

The idea of magnanimity has proved irresistibly attractive, even to those historians rightly sceptical of the influence of Smuts on this supposed British policy; and to advance such a set of contrary propositions is of course to challenge some of the most treasured orthodoxies enshrined both in imperial history and in the hagiographies of Smuts and the Liberal prime minister Sir Henry Campbell-Bannerman.[1] And we personally wish to take the argument tentatively advanced in *Elgin and Churchill at the Colonial Office* much further – to abandon the equivocal inverted commas which (in an excess of caution) were placed around the word 'magnanimity' in the book, and to follow the logic of the evidence to its ultimate conclusion. In attempting to do so, we are

---

[1] G. H. L. Le May, *British supremacy in South Africa, 1899–1907* (1965), pp. 191, 215; N. Mansergh, *South Africa, 1906–1961: the price of magnanimity* (1962), ch. 1, 'The magnanimous gesture'; L. M. Thompson, 'The policy of conciliation' in L. Thompson and M. Wilson (eds.), *The Oxford History of South Africa*, vol.: II, *1870–1966* (1971), pp. 339–43, 334; W. K. Hancock, *Smuts*, vol. I, *The sanguine years, 1870–1919* (1962); J. Wilson, *CB: a life of Sir Henry Campbell-Bannerman* (London, 1973).

encouraged by interpretations put forward by Donald Denoon and Rodney Davenport. Denoon rejects the idea of magnanimity, though we think for the wrong reasons; while Davenport has convincingly pointed more than once to the purely tactical nature of the Afrikaner policy of conciliation. Moreover, Le May has shown how Botha's energies in the post-war years were primarily devoted to reuniting and reconciling Afrikaner factions.[2] We are now in a position to suggest a historical reinterpretation relevant to British and South African history as well as to biographies of Smuts and Campbell-Bannerman and, ultimately, in the context of the evolution of the Commonwealth, one which throws light on the curious, confused, and slender mechanisms which can sometimes bring about surprising changes in relationships between states, after transfers of power.

In chapter 1 we express scepticism about interpretations of British policy which do not inhabit 'the real world', and argue that considerations of power were fundamental. The case of the Transvaal, even in 1906, suggests that we should doubt whether magnanimous foresight could ever govern imperial affairs. This is not to deny that there are good intentions (and even some happy endings): for example, we shall suggest in chapter 4 that the British government was far more anxious to help black African interests than has usually been supposed. This intention, however, only makes sense in the context of demolishing the myth that the priority of British South African policy between 1905 and 1910 was magnanimity towards the Afrikaners.

I

On 31 March 1905 the Unionist government issued Letters Patent granting to the Transvaal a representative constitution, known almost at once, and to history, as the Lyttelton Constitution. This constitution never came into force. It was abrogated in February 1906 by the new Liberal government, who decided, at a dramatic Cabinet meeting on 8 February, to grant responsible government instead. General J. C. Smuts had come to Britain on a mission to persuade the Liberal government to grant responsible government, and oral tradition for long regarded the Smuts mission as 'the climax in the drama of the South African settlement'; it assumed that Smuts 'convinced' Campbell-Bannerman

---

[2] R. Hyam, *Elgin and Churchill at the Colonial Office, 1905–1908* (1968), ch. 4, hereafter cited as *E&C;* D. Denoon, *A grand illusion: the failure of imperial policy in the Transvaal Colony during the period of reconstruction, 1900–1905* (1973); T. R. H. Davenport, *The Afrikaner Bond: the history of a South African political party, 1880–1911* (1966), and 'The South African Rebellion 1914', *English Historical Review* 78 (1963), pp. 73–94; Le May, *British supremacy in South Africa*, pp. 144, 164, 173–4.

that immediate responsible government should be granted, and that the prime minister then persuaded the Cabinet.[3]

The myth was based largely upon the subsequent recollections of Smuts himself. In his later years, Smuts referred repeatedly to his meetings with the Liberal ministers. The first version of these verbal recollections to be published was the account he provided for his biographer, S. G. Millin:

'I went', says Smuts, 'to see Churchill, Morley, Elgin, Lloyd George and Campbell-Bannerman . . .

'The last man I saw was Campbell-Bannerman. I explained our position to him, and said we were anxious to co-operate with the English. He asked me why, if that were so, we had refused to join Milner's Legislative Council. I answered : What would it have led to but friction? . . . There was only one thing that could make the wheels run: self-government.

'I went on explaining. I could see Campbell-Bannerman was listening sympathetically . . . He told me there was to be a Cabinet meeting next day, and he said: "Smuts, you have convinced me". 'That talk', says Smuts, 'settled the future of South Africa'.[4]

In private conversation with H. U. Willink, minister of health, in 1944, Smuts recalled :

I had been sent over to try to get self-government for [the Transvaal] . . . The Colonial Secretary . . . said it was quite impossible, out of the question . . . The others said the same, but at last I got a long evening with Campbell-Bannerman, and I persuaded him. He said he would raise it with the Cabinet. It was only years afterwards that I learned that he had raised it as his own proposal, and not one member of the Cabinet had spoken in opposition. Leadership![5]

In an account written forty-two years after the event, Smuts wrote:

My mission failed with the rest . . . But with Campbell-Bannerman my mission did not fail . . . I used no set arguments . . . and appealed only to the human aspect. He was a cautious Scot, and said nothing to me, but yet I left that room that night a happy man. My intuition told me that the thing had been done.[6]

Smuts apparently reminded Campbell-Bannerman of his own speeches during the Anglo-Boer War, and put it to him that he had a choice between having another Ireland on his hands or a friendly country within the British empire.[7]

---

[3] See, for example, G. B. Pyrah, *Imperial policy and South Africa, 1902–1910* (1955), pp. 164–5, 171–3. Pyrah was able to see the original Colonial Office records only down to 1902.
[4] S. G. Millin, *General Smuts*, vol. I (1936), p. 214.
[5] Sir Henry Willink, 'Memo. of lunch with Smuts, 22 May 1944', Willink Papers (Churchill College Archives Centre), File IV.
[6] Hancock, *Smuts*, vol. I, p. 215.
[7] Sir John Kennedy, *The business of war* (1957), pp. 316–17, records these remarks by Smuts made on 19 Nov. 1943.

In fact, some weeks before Smuts appeared, the prime minister and the Cabinet committee on the Transvaal constitution had already decided in principle to grant responsible government to the Transvaal. The Cabinet decision on 8 February was, among ministers, a foregone conclusion. Campbell-Bannerman did not have to persuade his colleagues about this: Asquith in 1912 dismissed the story of opposition in the Cabinet as 'a ridiculous fiction', since there was 'never the faintest difference of opinion about it'.

Smuts thus certainly exaggerated the extent of his influence in claiming for the remainder of his life that he had persuaded Campbell-Bannerman to grant immediate responsible government. His recollections are not, in their recorded versions, wholly consistent, and so it is not for example clear whether Campbell-Bannerman said 'Smuts, you have convinced me' or remained silent. But there are in any case good reasons for supposing that his influence was unlikely to have been decisive. Ministers and officials were almost inordinately suspicious of Smuts at this time. Because Smuts later became the very paragon of a loyal Commonwealth statesman, it is all too easy to suppose that in 1906 he was ready to be reconciled, and also to forget that he was regarded by British politicians as the most dangerous of the Afrikaner leaders. Lord Selborne, the high commissioner, telegraphed a warning as soon as Smuts departed for London:

He is a very clever, well-educated man, agreeable to meet, and personally I much like him; but please remember that he is an absolutely unreconciled Afrikander Republican, and that he has an ultimate ideal of a Boer South African Republic always before him, and all that he says or does politically has that ultimate end in view.

Selborne's views were at this stage taken more notice of than they were subsequently. After Smuts had gone, the colonial secretary, Lord Elgin, wrote to Selborne reviewing the decisions taken and the reasons for them, and he referred incidentally to Smuts:

I and many of my colleagues saw him; I am sure he cannot complain of any want of attention; he was as you foretold very pleasant and plausible; but so far as I can judge he did not leave behind him any undue impression.[8]

Smuts argued the case for granting immediate self-government to the Transvaal in a long and elaborate memorandum,[9] nicely calculated to appeal to Liberal sympathies and predilections. This memorandum was not, however, printed until March 1906, a whole month after the Cabinet decision had been taken,

---

[8] Elgin Papers (Broomhall, Dunfermline), Selborne to Elgin, private telegram, 28 Dec. 1905; Elgin to Selborne, private, 22 Feb. 1906; B. B. Gilbert, 'The grant of Responsible Government to the Transvaal: more notes on a myth', *HJ* 10 (1967), pp. 457–9.

[9] CO 879/92, PRO Colonial Office Confidential Print, *African (South)*, no. 837, extensively quoted in Pyrah, *Imperial policy and South Africa*, pp. 165–71, and Hancock, *Smuts*, vol. I, pp. 207–10.

Post-war 61

and so it is not at all certain how many ministers had read it before they took their decision.[10] Over and above this, the very persuasiveness of his argument ought to have put them on their guard against accepting some of its main contentions without corroboration. When this memorandum was eventually printed, it was circulated with a commentary by one of the most senior members of the Colonial Office staff, Sir Fred Graham, head of the South African Department, who warned readers:

> Mr Smuts is a Boer and a lawyer. His Memorandum . . . exhibits all the cunning of his race and calling . . . a new line of argument, which forms the basis of [it], . . . is that, unless the Constitution is framed in accordance with the views of the Boer leaders, the Transvaal will be dominated by the Mining Houses, who will crush every other interest under foot for their own aggrandisement. Until lately the Boer leaders were somewhat indifferent on the subject of Chinese Labour and absolutely indifferent to the interests of the Native population. Now the former is anathema and the latter is a matter which at least merits sympathetic consideration. Is it unreasonable to suppose that this new attitude on the part of the Boer leaders is not genuine, but assumed for the purpose of enlisting the sympathy of those who form so strong a party in the present House of Commons, and in this way influencing His Majesty's Government to give them, what they really desire, a Constitution which will result in a Boer domination?

Graham thought Dr Leyds had been the moving spirit of the 'clever unscrupulous gang' who led Kruger into war, and who were now trying to regain in the political arena what they had lost on the field of battle:

> Let us beware lest Mr Smuts prove to be his natural successor. There is a remarkable similarity between the two. Both are lawyers and very acute. Both are highly educated and of persuasive manners. Neither is to be trusted. There are at least two cases in the published Blue Books in which Mr Smuts appears in a shady light.

For these reasons Graham urged ministers to look suspiciously both on the honesty and the motives of the memorandum.[11]

Although the assumption of the traditional mythology of these proceedings is that Smuts devoted his energies to persuading the Liberals to grant immediate responsible government, it is clear from his memorandum that he was at least as concerned with more specific constitutional points, irrespective of whether the constitution was on the basis of representative or responsible government; in particular, he devoted considerable space to attacking the principle 'one vote one value' in the delimitation of constituencies. The Lyttelton Constitution had adopted this voters basis in preference to the alternative population basis, which it was realised would be to the advantage of the Afrikaners.[12] (On the voters basis the size of constituencies would be calculated proportionately to the actual

---

[10] Smuts certainly sent a copy to Bryce: see Elgin Papers, Bryce to Elgin, 5 Feb. 1906.
[11] CO 879/92, *African (South)*, no. 837 (a), 1 Apr. 1906.
[12] Only *white* voters and populations were of course being considered.

number of voters; on a population basis, the size would be calculated in proportion to the total number of inhabitants, whether voters or not.) Smuts knew the key issue was not the formal status of the constitution but the distribution of electoral power. With a population basis his party would dominate the legislature and practically dictate the terms of full self-government by refusing supply – a probability which the lord chancellor, Loreburn, had foreseen at least a fortnight before the crucial Cabinet meeting. On the other hand, a responsible government constitution with a British majority would be worse than useless to the Afrikaners, and Smuts said they would prefer an indefinite period of Colonial Office rule to the threat of permanent domination by mining magnates. Thus Selborne had no doubt that Smuts would 'make a great effort to induce H.M.G. to depart from the principle "one vote one value" in the delimitation of Transvaal constituencies'. He most earnestly asked Elgin to give no encouragement to such a proposal.[13] Only one record of Smuts's conversations with individual ministers appears to have survived, the one with Winston Churchill, parliamentary under-secretary of state for the colonies, in the Colonial Office on 26 January, and at this meeting, if the brief précis of it may be relied upon, the discussion was largely concentrated upon the 'one vote one value' issue.[14] If Smuts succeeded in making any of the ministers change their mind upon any important point it was certainly not upon the basis for delimiting constituencies. He failed to impose his view on this most important matter, and the Liberals stuck to 'one vote one value' in their constitution.

Smuts found his meetings with Liberal ministers, in contrast to that with the prime minister, disappointing:

I found it very hard to deal with my new masters. I stated my case. Winston said he had never heard anything so preposterous. He said England had conquered South Africa only three years before, and here was I asking for my country back ... I saw all the other ministers, too. I made no great headway. Morley was unsympathetic. He said he agreed with most of what I had said, but that British public opinion would never stand for it.[15]

Smuts's disappointment does not of course prove that ministers were not in favour of immediate responsible government. Their reticence may be explained by the necessity of preserving proper discretion upon a matter so controversial, and upon which even the high commissioner, when he asked for information, was told he must await the Cabinet decision. It is not clear whether Campbell-Bannerman actually gave Smuts a hint of what would be done, but if he did say 'Smuts, you have convinced me', it should be remembered that he alone, within a few hours of the Cabinet which would decide, was perhaps in a position to take Smuts rather more into his confidence. Some of his colleagues when they saw Smuts may have wanted to do the same, but were precluded from doing so;

---

[13] Elgin Papers, Selborne to Elgin, private telegram, 28 Dec. 1905.
[14] Elgin Papers, typed memorandum, 26 Jan. 1906.   [15] Kennedy, *Business of war*, pp. 316–17.

did not Morley, for example, seem to admit as much? Smuts wrote to Margaret Clark on 1 February 1906:

> Kindest of all were C.B. and John Morley. The latter felt very deeply what I told him (and as I left he said, 'I wish I could say what it is in my heart to say to you'. Keep this to yourself).[16]

On the fundamental policy decision, whether or not to grant immediate responsible government, although he could not know it, Smuts had no need to persuade the Liberal ministers. He was in fact preaching to the converted. It was already an agreed policy, and the Cabinet had merely to record it formally. The meeting on 8 February 1906 was remarkable only because Campbell-Bannerman intervened to upset the recommendation of the Cabinet committee to proceed rapidly with responsible government by amending the Lyttelton Constitution. He introduced two new ideas: scrapping the Lyttelton Constitution as the basis, and sending out a commission to ascertain up-to-date facts. His unexpected intervention left his most closely concerned colleagues puzzled and a bit resentful, while he himself went away with the elation of a man who had got his own way.[17] The prime minister had apparently never given a hint previously that he would make these two recommendations, which suggests that if Smuts had any influence on Campbell-Bannerman, it was upon these two procedural points, both of which he had urged in his memorandum. Smuts wrote as follows:

> While the Boers think that responsible government will be the proper and natural remedy for many of the ills under which the new Colonies are at present suffering, and that the time has come when the grant of responsible institutions might fairly and safely be ventured, they wish it to be clearly understood that responsible government granted on the basis of the present Constitution will only make matters worse and is strongly disapproved of by them. Responsible government under such conditions will simply substitute the mine-owners for the Colonial Office in the government of the Transvaal, and the Boers would rather have an indefinite period of Crown Colony administration than see the Transvaal permanently put under the government of the financial magnates... it will simply add a new and most potent source of discord and agitation.

If the British government and people were still apprehensive of the Boers, Smuts suggested that

> it would be better by far to delay the grant of a Constitution until the truth has been fully ascertained, either by an impartial commission, or in any other way, and it has become possible for a policy of trust and reliance on the people to be inaugurated.[18]

---

[16] Hancock, *Smuts*, vol. I, p. 213
[17] *E&C*, pp. 124–52; Wilson, *CB: a life of Campbell-Bannerman*, pp. 478–85, gives a very satisfactory account of the encounter between Smuts and CB and its relationship to the Cabinet decision.
[18] Smuts memorandum, paras. 15 and 16.

Perhaps even at this late moment Campbell-Bannerman had of his own accord come to the same conclusions, independently of Smuts, and then very cleverly had allowed Smuts to gain the impression that he had decisively influenced him, but it may equally well be that Smuts did indeed convert the prime minister to a view about the method of granting immediate responsible government, by suggestions about procedure he had not previously decided upon. Smuts certainly did not convert the prime minister to the principle of responsible government, though he may well have gone away with that impression. If Smuts had any influence at all, either on the principle or the procedure, we still have only Smuts's word for it; there is no corroboration. If Campbell-Bannerman *had* been influenced over procedure he could never admit it, because, in view of the horror in which Smuts was held, to have done so would have been sure to bring fatal opposition to his proposals.

In the end, however, although the Lyttelton Constitution was formally scrapped, and a committee of inquiry (not a commission as suggested by the prime minister) sent out, it made little difference. Campbell-Bannerman did not press his views further, and ministers worked to mitigate the evil effects they believed would result from their adoption. The fundamental features of the Lyttelton Constitution were retained, and Smuts was totally unimpressed by the West Ridgeway Committee, either by its personnel or its procedure; its report he never saw – but it would only have confirmed his worst suspicions that the British object was 'simply to see how little they could give to the Boer without making the latter stand aside'. The terms of the new Transvaal constitution were received without enthusiasm, and perhaps with disappointment. The voters basis was much disliked. And the delay in settling the future of the Orange River Colony was a bitter pill, creating a most unfavourable impression. On 28 November 1906 Smuts wrote privately of self-rule being South Africa's one aim, in order to avoid 'the malevolence of Conservative Government, and the stupidity of the Liberals'.[19]

According to the myth we ought presumably to have found Smuts writing of the 'magnanimity' of the Liberals by the end of 1906. Not so. It was the 'stupidity' of the Liberals he commented upon. If in later years he began to talk of a 'miracle of trust and magnanimity', this was largely because it flattered his own ego to be able to claim that he had himself converted Campbell-Bannerman to such a policy and persuaded him to give what he, Smuts, had asked for. Smuts no more than his followers really regarded the restoration of independence as magnanimous, but saw it as a tardy and imperfect act of repentance for 'A century of wrong'.

---

[19] W. K. Hancock and J. van der Poel, eds., *Selections from the Smuts Papers*, vol. II: *1902–1910* (1966), pp. 247, 318; Ripon Papers, B.L. Add. MSS. 43640, 17, Emily Hobhouse to Ripon, 29 Sept 1906.

II

To come now to the central argument of this analysis. What evidence is there for rejecting the idea of a deliberately magnanimous British policy? Denoon has called it in question by arguing that the project of strengthening the Transvaal as a British colony was doomed to fail by the end of 1905: 'Viewed in this light, the "Magnanimous Gesture", whereby the Liberal Government handed over power in such a way as to facilitate the electoral victory of Afrikaners in 1907, may be regarded as a realistic acknowledgement of defeat, rather than a deliberate and altruistic gesture of recompense.' With an understandable desire to make a neat ending to his own study of the 'reconstruction' period in the Transvaal, and his ability to phrase a striking aphorism, Denoon has unfortunately forgotten his historical sense, and foreclosed the future too finally (though it is true he does not do so without a later qualification).[20] There is no evidence that the Liberals were merely realistically acknowledging defeat. The reverse was true: they were fully determined to secure British interests and continue the search for British supremacy. When the 1907 election results showed that they had made a grave miscalculation, and that they had in effect, as Milner said, 'given South Africa back to the Boers', they sharply tried to turn this mistake to good account by saying, 'yes of course, this is what we always meant to do'.

But was it? Seven points can be made which controvert this interpretation.

First: in origin the Liberal government's decision to scrap the Lyttelton representative constitution instead of to amend it to a responsible government form was not so much a generous gesture as a party-political tactic. This was how it was seen at the time by those who wrote to Campbell-Bannerman. Lloyd George congratulated him 'on the way you saved the government from inevitable disaster', and Lord Carrington remarked: 'The Party would have been up in arms if we had capitulated to Lyttelton and the mine-owners.' They said nothing about magnanimity to the Afrikaners, but simply expressed relief that a means had been found to forestall further serious splitting in the Liberal ranks.[21]

Second: on 15 March 1906 Winston Churchill finished a highly secret memorandum, saying that what people could not know – and what he intended they never should know – was that the government 'are absolutely determined to maintain, in the words of Lord Durham's Report, "a numerical majority of a loyal and English population"'. He poured scorn on the idea the Boers could be relied on:

I would do strict justice to the Boers; but when we remember that 20,000 of their women and children perished in our concentration camps in the year 1901/2, is it wise to count too much upon their good offices in 1906?

---

[20] Denoon, *A grand illusion*, pp. xii, 230.
[21] Campbell-Bannerman Papers, B.L. Add. MSS. 41212, 310 and Add. MSS. 41239, 36; *E&C*, p. 135.

Altogether, Churchill concluded:

> It would be far better to give the country back to the Boers as a great act of renunciation and of justice than to fritter it away piece-meal.

In other words Churchill believed that British policy had in fact become one of piecemeal frittering away by mismanagement and was never intended to be a great act of deliberate justice and magnanimous renunciation.

Churchill later took good care that nobody should ever see what he had written. It was too near the truth for comfort. He removed all copies of this memorandum from all sections of the government archives. When the archives were opened at the end of the 1950s, every appropriate file was found to contain merely a slip stating that all copies of the memorandum were 'removed by Mr Churchill'. Among thousands of files from this period this procedure has no known parallel. However, Winston's son Randolph found the one single remaining copy among his father's private papers, and presented a photocopy to the Public Record Office.[22]

The third point is that colonial secretary Lord Elgin repeatedly insisted in the Cabinet that 'an actual Boer majority in the new parliament is not desirable'. Electoral calculations governed the form of the constitution, and they were designed to secure a small British majority. The Liberals intended Sir Richard Solomon to be the first prime minister under the new Transvaal constitution, and not General Botha, who actually took office. Solomon, virtually prime minister designate, was defeated at the polls. Elgin had found Solomon of considerable assistance in drafting the constitution; Solomon was acting lieutenant-governor of the Transvaal at the time. Elgin had high hopes of his ability and adaptability and of his chances of getting the confidence, to some extent, of both sides.[23] Solomon's political past was not unassailable. He was a hard-faced man who had done well out of the spoils of the Anglo-Boer War; he had worked for Milner and been in favour of Chinese labour; and although he had considerable ability as a lawyer and administrator, he was politically rather naïve.[24] This then was the man to whom the British looked as a prime minister. The Afrikaners looked elsewhere.

The fourth piece of evidence is the Report of the West Ridgeway Committee. Its fundamental premise was as follows:

> We regard British supremacy as vital and essential, and we have also looked upon a British majority at the coming General Election as a desirable outward and visible sign of that supremacy, which should be, if possible, obtained.

---

[22] CAB 37/82, 83, Confidential print by Churchill, *African (South)*, no. 834 'Situation in South Africa', 15 Mar. 1906 (Secret); *E&C*, pp. 140–1.

[23] Cabinet memorandum by Elgin, 6 Mar. 1906; *E&C*, p. 153; Elgin Papers, Elgin to Selborne, 23 Nov. 1906 and 23 Feb. 1907.

[24] F. V. Engelenburg, *General Louis Botha* (1929), pp. 146–7.

It contained a good deal more stuff in the same true-blue vein. This is one of the very few British government reports *never* to have been published because, in that bland official phrase, it would be 'contrary to the public interest'. Why? Because it was unduly revealing and showed that nothing magnanimous was being intended towards the Afrikaners. There was thus deep consternation when John Burns lost his copy of this report; an amateur journalist found it and sold it to the *Evening Standard*. The whole weight of government then descended on the newspaper to prevent its publication even in extract. It was 'not in the public interest'.[25]

The fifth consideration is this: the most important single matter to be settled in the constitution was the basis for the distribution of seats, the method of carving up the constituencies. Was it to be done on a voters basis or a population basis? On a population basis, Churchill believed that : 'the parties will be numerically equal' and Botha would have to be sent for. 'Is this what H.M.G. desire?' Obviously not, since they chose a voters basis, which gave an advantage to the unmarried British men in the mining towns over the large families of Afrikaner farmers in the rural districts. As A. B. Keith, then a clerk in the Colonial Office, wrote: the Boers would not be satisfied with 'one vote one value', and 'indeed however outwardly reasonable that basis, it must be admitted that its real *raison d'être* is to create a British majority'. There was nothing magnanimous, then, in the fundamental and crucial issue to be settled by the Liberals' constitution, since it adhered to Lyttelton's 'one vote one value' principle.[26]

For the sixth point we return to the grant of responsible government to the Orange River Colony in 1907. In *Elgin and Churchill at the Colonial Office* the following comment was offered:

> The decision to grant full responsible government here too was an even more remarkable demonstration than in the Transvaal of the policy of trusting the Boers. For in the Orange River Colony there was no possibility whatever of a British majority, and the Orange River Colony had the reputation of being the most 'disaffected and illiberal' portion of South Africa.

We now repudiate this interpretation. The grant of self-government to the Orange River Colony provides no real clue to the intentions of policy. Once the Transvaal obtained it, the sister colony could not possibly be denied it. Furthermore, the Orange River Colony was regarded as a completely hopeless case from the imperial viewpoint. Self-government was thus granted to it without this being magnanimous. It was unavoidable, and its grant was based on two assumptions. One was that its power for mischief as a centre of Afrikaner

---

[25] *African (South)*, no. 853, 'Report of the Committee appointed to enquire and report upon certain matters concerned with the future constitutions of the Transvaal and Orange River Colony', p. 8; *E&C*, pp. 146–8.

[26] CO 291/97, 10356.

disaffection would be temporarily counterbalanced by British supremacy in the Transvaal, and the other was that its nuisance-potential would eventually be nullified through absorption in a federation or Union of all the South African colonies.[27]

Lastly, by far the strongest piece of evidence is this. It had always been Chamberlain's intention to proceed with constitutional advance in the Orange River Colony before the Transvaal. The Liberals had a different order of priority. Why? The answer lies in their desire to get rid immediately of responsibility for Chinese labour. Elgin publicly admitted that the Orange River Colony had not 'the same urgency in the conditions of labour'. Chinese labour in the Rand mines was to the Liberals a major embarrassment. Some 50,000 Chinese in the womanless compounds took to erotic improvisation enlivened only by occasional boisterous forays into the brothels of Johannesburg. There were several scandalous cases of their being flogged by the British authorities. Because of the success of the 'Chinese slavery' cry in the Liberal election campaign, it was important that a Liberal government should not have to administer the system which lent itself to this charge. Responsible government for the Transvaal, then, was speedily arranged not so much as a magnanimous gesture, but as a means of getting rid of the dangerous liability of Chinese labour. The lord chancellor, Loreburn, urged the necessity of divesting themselves of duties which only placed them in a false position: 'the one question of Chinese Labour makes it necessary that responsible government should be installed in the Transvaal', if possible by the end of July 1906, he wrote in January 1906. One of the most perceptive of the officials, Hartmann Just, noted that the first decision of the Liberal government was to stop further importation of Chinese labourers, but as long as a representative government lasted, responsibility for administering the labour system previously created would be incurred by the British government:

It would therefore be the wish of H.M.G. to escape all responsibility, by advising His Majesty to grant responsible government to the Transvaal at the earliest possible moment.

The foreign secretary Sir Edward Grey explicitly described responsible government in the Transvaal as necessary because it appeared to be 'the only way out of the impasse' over Chinese labour. Churchill, in a memorandum prepared on behalf of Loreburn, Elgin, Ripon, Asquith, and Bryce, warned that the difficulties of the House of Commons situation might be considerable if the government were forced for 'a prolonged or indefinite period to be *responsible* for the day-to-day administration of the Chinese Labour Ordinance', with its 'various objectionable features and possible recurrence of improper incidents'.

---

[27] *E&C*, pp. 177 ff.

Time, they concluded, was therefore a factor which 'must powerfully influence, if indeed it should not govern, Cabinet policy'.[28]

It seems almost certain that Balfour's prediction was right:

> They will be confronted with their dishonest and insincere utterances about Chinese Labour by . . . their followers, and I am convinced that they will extricate themselves from a painful dilemma by granting self-government to the new colonies *sans phrase*.[29]

Where then in all this is the magnanimity? Surely nowhere at all. The clue to Liberal policy was expediency not magnanimity, and it was put into effect by a gamble rather than a gesture. The Liberal ministers did not trust the Afrikaners; they wanted to retain British supremacy. But they were undeterred by the fact that it was impossible to prove the loyalty and reliability of the Afrikaners. Evidence of disloyalty was ruled to be irrelevant. They based themselves on Gladstone's formula: Britain did not give Home Rule because colonies were loyal and friendly but colonies might *become* loyal and friendly because they were given responsible government. Responsible government was the last desperate remaining hope of making the Transvaal loyal. And so they tried it: but this was expediency – it was not magnanimity.

Moreover, contrary to carefully planned expectations, the Afrikaners won the election of 22 February 1907 in the Transvaal. In the distribution of the sixty-nine seats in the legislative assembly, thirty-four seats were given to the Rand, six to Pretoria, and twenty-nine to the rural areas. This, it was expected, would result in a British majority of at least five, and possibly ten, seats. In fact Het Volk took thirty-seven seats, and quickly buttressed its position by a coalition with the moderate British party, the Responsible Government Association, which won six seats. There were two Labour Party members and two independents. Thus the main British party, the Progressives, took only twenty-one seats, and Het Volk obtained a clear majority of five over all other parties. 'We are in for ever', commented Smuts. They have 'given South Africa back to the Boers', growled Milner. Sir Richard Solomon failed to gain election. Botha became prime minister.

Thus it is obvious that the British had miscalculated their electoral arithmetic. As Denoon has remarked, 'with better luck and better electoral management', the Liberals might well have secured the selection of Solomon as prime minister and 'precluded Afrikaners from direct and untrammelled control over the instruments of government'; although there would have been Afrikaner participation, the 'Magnanimous Gesture' would thus, he suggests, in theory have acquired a different complexion from that which it seemed to bear.[30]

---

[28] *E&C*, p. 104 (Grey), p. 109 (Cabinet memo. 4 Feb. 1906), pp. 122–3.
[29] A. Lyttelton to Milner, Apr. 1904 (Edith Lyttelton, *Alfred Lyttelton: an account of his life* (1917) p. 320), reporting Balfour.
[30] Denoon, *A grand illusion*, p. 230.

How is their bad luck and inadequate management to be explained? The root cause was division among the British community. Although the permanent officials in Whitehall realised that the British were 'hopelessly at variance among themselves', knew of the tension between Pretoria and Johannesburg, and expected the British vote to be split between factional splinter parties, the Liberal politicians seem rather to have supposed that the community would behave monolithically in the election. They did not foresee adequately or early enough how some British would vote for Het Volk, including the mining magnate J. B. Robinson, or how Het Volk would pick up five seats on the Rand, or how a sense of 'fair play' would lead to a feeling that it was time to give the 'other side' a chance. Seven English-speaking MPs got in on the Het Volk ticket – and Het Volk thus obtained British money and organisational skills enabling it to campaign effectively in urban districts where it had been assumed it would exert no influence. The Labour Party, regarding other British parties as 'capitalist', allied itself with Het Volk. The proportion of abstentions was large, amounting to almost one-third (32.5 per cent) throughout the Transvaal, but it was especially high in the British dominated urban-areas. Het Volk benefited also from ten uncontested seats. The British community was lulled into believing it could afford the luxury of disunity, and the true-blue Progressives suffered badly from the lack of internal cohesion. As early as 1903 Smuts had realised that the political unity of the Transvaal British was being disrupted, and he determined to take advantage of this. He coordinated the anti-Progressive campaign which led to the victory of Het Volk, while Botha stressed hostility to the mining magnates partly as a means of dividing the British. Both promoted Chinese labour as the major issue, seeing its potential for ruining the Progressive cause. Arthur Mawby has further suggested that Smuts helped to guide the West Ridgeway Committee in its proposed constituency delimitation, and did so in a way which devalued British votes compared with the rural Afrikaner votes. It was expressly part of the committee's informal instructions that it should listen mainly to Afrikaner views, in order to counterbalance the British-orientated information supplied by the high commissioner. The committee apparently found what it heard to be plausible.[31]

III

Smuts's success raises the whole question of how far he and his followers were genuinely following 'a policy of conciliation' after 1902. In 1905 Botha and

---

[31] D. Denoon, '"Capitalist influence" and the Transvaal government, 1900–1906', *HJ* 11 (1968), pp. 301–31, and *A grand illusion: the failure of imperial policy in the Transvaal Colony during the period of reconstruction, 1900–1905* (London, 1973), ch. xvii; N. Garson, 'Het Volk: the Botha–Smuts party in the Transvaal, 1904–1911', *HJ* 9 (1966), p. 116; A. A. Mawby, 'The political behaviour of the British population of the Transvaal 1902–1907' (unpublished PhD thesis, Witwatersrand, Johannesburg 1969), ch. xii. For Smuts's grasp of the situation see *Selections from the Smuts Papers*, vol. II, pp. 94–5, 124, 177, 292.

Smuts made references to being 'bound' to the British flag, and wanting a united South Africa as an Afrikaner goal. Schalk Burger said he wanted an independent flag. General C. F. Beyers predicted a possible new Slachtersnek rebellion.[32] Such remarks occasionally leaked out in unguarded moments in speeches in rural areas before all-Afrikaner audiences.[33]

In 1914 Botha and Smuts took their country into the war against Germany, and did so, it may be suggested, not from any sentimental or loyalist desire to uphold the British empire, but from a hard-headed, calculating belief that it was the best and most expedient way to advance South Africa's own interests. They wanted to get hold of German South-West Africa for themselves. This they felt certain of achieving if they campaigned there. Colonial secretary Harcourt quickly realised what their strategy was:

I warned the Cabinet early in August, when they decided (rather against my inclination) to ask the Union Government to take German South-West Africa, that we could never take the bone out of the dog's mouth. Nor can we, when he gets it.[34]

The South-West campaign caused an Afrikaner rebellion against Botha and Smuts. By far the largest number of rebels came from the Orange Free State, which was severely rocked by it. Hertzog supported Beyers in refusing to fight in South-West Africa. Many of the rebel leaders, like J. H. de la Rey, had been *bittereinders* (those who fought on to the bitter end) in 1902. Some Afrikaners looked uneasily to Botha and Smuts for a lead: Van Rensburg believed they would pronounce in favour of independence when Britain's hands were tied, and others were convinced that if a blow were struck for freedom, General Botha would not fire upon them. General de la Rey planned to call the burghers of Treurfontein together, and march them to Pretoria, where a republic would, he supposed, be established with the full co-operation of Botha and Smuts; Botha persuaded him to abandon this enterprise. An Afrikaner biographer has written of this episode: 'It is worth noting how many Afrikaners, even those in high positions, believed that Botha and Smuts were well-disposed towards the proclaiming of a Republic in South Africa. It was a time of unparalleled confusion.'[35]

To understand this confusion we have to go back to 1902, the year of Afrikaner surrender. In order to obtain the signing of the Peace of Vereeniging, there is a little evidence – though it is inconclusive – that Botha and Smuts and others held out the hope of a future rising to regain independence. President M. T. Steyn alleged that he received a private letter from Smuts in May 1901, saying

---

[32] In 1815, after a Boer farmer was killed resisting arrest for alleged mistreatment of a Hottentot herdsman.
[33] Mawby, 'Political behaviour of the British population of the Transvaal', ch. vii.
[34] Earl of Crewe Papers (ULC), C/10, Harcourt to Crewe, 2 Dec. 1914.
[35] Davenport, 'The South African Rebellion, 1914', *EHR* vol. 78 (1963), p. 88; C. M. van den Heever, *Gen. J. B. M. Hertzog* (1946), pp. 165–72.

that if they gave up now it would be with the intention of fighting again when Britain might be in difficulties. This letter was apparently seized by the British military authorities, but Smuts denied all knowledge of it in 1921. While it may be doubted whether any of the leaders used such an argument formally, it is undoubtedly the case that many Afrikaners believed that their old leaders, including Botha and Smuts, would one day lead them again in the field against Britain in order to regain their republican independence. It is perfectly possible that Botha might have spoken of this informally in private behind the scenes at the time of the Vereeniging negotiations. The peace offer was accepted by fifty-four to six by the commandants, with Hertzog, Steyn, C. R. de Wet, and Beyers among those who wanted to fight on to the bitter end. It is equally certain that the restoration of a republic remained a secret article of faith. Thus in 1914 there were those who felt Botha and Smuts had gone back on their word.[36]

After 1902 official and public expression of the republican ideal was almost non-existent; it was specifically renounced by Botha, Smuts, Schalk Burger, and others. It was to be quietly stored up in the heart. Displays of disaffection had to be suppressed in order to keep the British community divided. But as a result Botha had considerable trouble with his 'extremist' followers. Selborne, touring the eastern Transvaal in February 1906, noted:

> In every district I found a bitter irreconcilable minority, formed of the remains of the corrupt and obscurantist Kruger party, and always clustering around the Hollander and Stellenbosch influence, a minority which is fast transferring to Botha the feelings it has about us.[37]

Davenport argues that 'a campaign for a limited restoration of rights conducted in a mood of conciliation' was the only realistic course open to the Afrikaner leaders:

> Even for Botha and Smuts ... conciliation was probably not in the first instance the fruit of any irrational desire to bury the hatchet, but above all a practical expedient dictated by urgent political necessity – the only available course, perhaps, to men deprived of effective bargaining power.[38]

On the whole the British government was prepared to take the gamble of believing that Botha and Smuts meant what they said about conciliation. They were under no illusions about the other Afrikaner leaders, however. Selborne said that no one outside 'a lunatic asylum [could] believe that ex-President Steyn was reconciled'. In the Colonial Office Graham referred to the 'ample

---

[36] N. J. van der Merwe, *Marthinus Theunis Steyn* (1921), vol. II, p. 75; G. C. A. Arthur, *Life of Lord Kitchener* (1920), vol. II, p. 39; J. Kirstein 'Some foundations of Afrikaner nationalism' (Honours research essay, University of Cape Town, 1956).
[37] Elgin Papers, Selborne to Elgin, 15 Feb. 1906; see also 2 Dec. 1907.
[38] Davenport, *The Afrikaner Bond*, pp. 253–63, 324.

evidence' they had 'of the persistent efforts of the ministers of the Dutch Church and others' to encourage race-hatred between British and Afrikaners 'in the surest way' – through the education of the young. Furthermore, however loyal Botha might be, or however enlightened Smuts was, H. W. Just felt that the 'terrible deadweight' of rank-and-file opinion would 'always be pushing them towards indefensible acts'.[39]

IV

Conventionally, the tragedy of South Africa in the twentieth century has always seemed to be the more poignant because of the presumed magnanimity of 1906. The British, it was argued, held out the hand of partnership to the Afrikaners whom they had previously wronged, and so reconciled the white communities, but the whites as a whole not only never extended the gesture to the black majority but proceeded to do it even greater injustice. It would be naïve to argue that the whites in South Africa were never 'magnanimous' towards the Africans because the Liberal government had in fact never intended to be generous towards the Afrikaners, although there can surely be little doubt that Smuts at least knew how circumscribed was the role of altruism in the business of government. The basic defect in the traditional view was not so much its belief that kind-heartedness was infectious, as its failure fully to recognise that the British government and English-speaking South Africans were two distinct forces, and that the first could only imperfectly rely on the second. Chamberlain and Milner had used the Uitlander franchise issue to prise concessions from the Transvaal before the war, but even then there had been doubts whether British miners would in fact uphold imperial interests. The Liberals did not depart from Chamberlain's grand strategy of securing British predominance: they merely pursued it with something less than his cunning. With hindsight the Liberal government's blunder seems almost incredible. They ought perhaps to have seen the danger-signs of division among the Transvaal British, especially since exactly the same divisions among English-Canadians in the 1840s had then thwarted an attempt to produce a British majority, and the key Liberal ministers professed themselves to be influenced by their study of Canadian experience. At the very least, the rising force of the Labour Party at home might have given them a sixth sense that tensions within the Transvaal British might prove too strong for a common front; but in both Britain and the Transvaal their perception

---

[39] Elgin Papers, Selborne to Elgin, 10 Mar. 1906; CO 48/586, 33366; CO 291/117, 23161. J. D. du Toit of the Dutch Reformed Church declared in 1903 that the people must re-establish all the lines which fixed the boundary between them and all Uitlanders, for the power of Afrikanerdom lay 'in the isolation of our principle': S. R. Ritner, 'The Dutch Reformed Church and apartheid', *Journal of Contemporary History*, vol. 2 (1967).

of the class basis of electoral behaviour was blurred. Yet it is also important to remember that the Afrikaners too were less than monolithic. For Het Volk to win the Transvaal election it was necessary to draw together the *bittereinders, hensoppers* (those who surrendered, hands-up), and those who had fought alongside the British as National Scouts. For Botha and Smuts, conciliation towards the British was part of the more important strategy of reconciliation inside the Afrikaner *volk*. It was necessary to adopt as lowest common denominator the policy of co-operation with the empire favoured by *hensoppers* and National Scouts, while doing nothing to dispel the *bittereinders*' belief that Jannie and Louis would lead them to the republic when the time was right – a double game which crashed in the rising of the irreconcilables in 1914. Vital to this strategy was the winning of some British South African support: it brought added electoral strength; it ensured that white South African divisions were confined to the British community, obscuring British and Afrikaner tensions; and it gave Smuts a weapon with which to contain the wilder spirits of the rural areas. Fundamentally, however, conciliation was never a policy holding much significance for the rank-and-file. What really interested the electors in 1907 was not relations with the empire but, as the *Bloemfontein Post* put it, 'Scab Law and Locust Destruction, Railway rates for farming material and sheep dip, grain rates and stock disease, irrigation problems and wool prices'.[40]

Unfortunately Smuts's political balancing game became harder and harder to play. In 1907 Het Volk virtually absorbed the moderate British on its own terms, but by 1920 Afrikaner nationalism had become so strong that Smuts was obliged to lead his South African Party into junction with Unionists, the old true-blues, and thus limited his freedom of action. Viewed in this perspective, the Chinese labour issue assumes a more sinister aspect than that of a small people struggling against the cynical manipulation of big financial interests. The Afrikaners cared little about the fate of Chinese labourers, but they used the issue to rally their own factions and divide the British. It was a sad precedent: later attacks on the Cape African franchise and on the Indian community in Natal followed the Chinese labour issue in making an alleged threat to white standards out of a non-European group. Far from moving outwards to embrace all South African communities, Smuts accepted attacks on non-whites as a price of appeasing his own followers. Ironically Smuts lost power in 1948 not only because he had failed to satisfy a majority of white South Africans, but also because he repeated the electoral error of his hero (Campbell-Bannerman)'s government. The weighting of the rural electorates which he had unsuccessfully lobbied for in 1906 now enabled the Nationalists to win power on a minority vote. The

---

[40] Davenport, *Afrikaner Bond*, p. 261. Milner declared: 'It is not true that our generosity has made a deep impression on the Boers': Lord Milner, *The nation and the empire: speeches and addresses* (1913), p. 181.

elections of 1907 and 1948 were perhaps both lost mainly as a result of similar psephological misfortunes.[41]

Afterword

As late as 1999, James Barber in *South Africa in the twentieth century: a political history – in search of a nation state* repeated essentially the mythical Smuts version of his 'influence' on Campbell-Bannerman and the 'magnanimity' of the latter (pp. 47–8). Barber does not cite Hyam's work, but instead relies on Hancock's biography and Le May's now superseded book on *British supremacy* (1965). But as Eric Walker pointed out in a review article ('Jan Christiaan Smuts', *Historical Journal*, vol. 11, 1968, pp. 565–81) – his last published work – Hancock most unfortunately 'repeats the traditional account', 'presumably because he had not seen the documents which have only been published since he wrote' (pp. 567–8). Walker then refers to R. Hyam, 'Smuts and the decision of the Liberal government to grant Responsible Government to the Transvaal, January and February, 1906' (*HJ* vol. 8, 1965, pp. 380–98) and Bentley B. Gilbert's endorsement, 'The grant of Responsible Government to the Transvaal: more notes on a myth' (*HJ* vol. 10, 1967, pp. 457–9).

---

[41] The irony was that in 1906 Smuts attacked the British insistence on one vote one value for constituency delimitation in the Transvaal, while in the 1948 election, on a strict one vote one value basis he would have won the straight fight with Dr D. F. Malan by twenty seats, instead of losing it by eight. He had long known that the complex electoral arrangements were damaging to his party. From 1943, however, he had enough parliamentary power to change some of them, and he was pressed to do so. He refused, apparently for entirely honourable reasons. Notice, however, that he also failed to pursue with any tenacity the political gestures and concessions which he was prepared to make to the African community. Smuts was in many ways a dilatory statesman. As Hancock mildly comments on the 1929 election (which Smuts also lost despite obtaining a majority of votes): 'Smuts possibly should have paid more attention to the arithmetic of elections' – and that is precisely our contention about British Liberal policy in 1906. (Hancock, *Smuts*, vol. II: *The fields of force, 1919–1950* (1968), pp. 217, 489, 505–6.)

4 African interests and the South Africa Act, 1908–1910

Whatever the ulterior motives on either side, the policies pursued by British and Afrikaner politicians between 1906 and 1909 did result in an improvement in the general atmosphere. British victory in 1901 had made one thing certain, that the constitutional shape of the future South Africa would have a British-monarchical complexion, tied to the empire, and not a Boer-republican one outside it. Within these parameters there now emerged a considerable convergence on unification as the next goal. Both sides began to feel more optimistic. With Het Volk in power in the Transvaal and Orangia Unie in the Free State, and with the South African Party having ousted Jameson's Progressives from office in the Cape, the Afrikaners began to feel that even if power was not immediately within their grasp, at least time and demography were in their favour. Botha and Smuts quickly won good opinions in London, and British policy-makers were ready to contemplate unification, confident that the British lion would prevail. They believed that a stronger, rationalised, and more grateful South Africa would be in British imperial and strategic interests. A further attraction was that the Union should produce a less parochial regime for Africans in Natal, where Zulu disturbances had been met with a disconcerting degree of panic and unimaginative brutality, thus earning it the Churchillian epithet of 'the hooligan of the British empire'.

The choice of a unitary instead of a federal constitution has often been criticised as misguided, even disastrous, 'the very worst prescription for a multi-racial society', because the concentration of power at the centre played into the hands of an illiberal elite. The reasons for preferring a unitary constitution were simple enough. The white community was not large enough to sustain properly an elaborate and complex federal structure. Federation seemed an expensive solution for a geographical area which was manifestly a single economic unit. Moreover, the federal case became associated with the discredited politicians of Natal. Alternatives were carefully examined. The newly established loose federation of Australia had got off to a shaky start, and hardly seemed an encouraging example, while the more centralised Canadian constitution was promoted, especially by Smuts, as the better model. Nor was Union necessarily the wrong choice. Federations are one of the most difficult forms of government to operate, and there have been many breakdowns and failures. It could be suggested that the Zulu people in Natal were indeed better off for a few decades within the Union; even more definitely, the Shona and Ndebele were protected by its unitary constitution from Southern Rhodesia's absorption as a fifth province.

Many historians have also denounced the Act of Union for endorsing a system which precluded any enlargement of African political participation and restricted the Union parliament to white MPs. Of course, as Bismarck famously said, 'politics is the art of the possible', and it was impossible for Britain to do more for Africans than the local politicians were prepared to accept. Nevertheless, it is hard not to sympathise with contemporary African opinion, such as that expressed glumly in the newspaper *Imvo Zabantsundu* (31 August 1909), 'That cow of Great Britain has now gone dry.'

I

Commenting authoritatively upon the passage of the South Africa Act (1909) L. M. Thompson has written in *The Oxford history of South Africa*: 'In attaining the primary goal of its South African policy, Britain had sacrificed the secondary goal ... The price of [white] unity and conciliation was the institutionalization of white supremacy.' According to Thompson, the British ministers thus coolly 'washed their hands of responsibility for the political rights of Africans, Asians, and Coloured people'.

It has indeed often been argued that British ministers in the years leading up to the Union of South Africa in 1910 were so obsessed with the principle of white self-government that they forgot their obligations to the African majority.[1] The result, it is alleged, was that African interests in general were sacrificed on the altar of Anglo-Afrikaner reconciliation, and in particular betrayed in the South Africa Act. If there is a partial exception allowed – the withholding of Basutoland, Bechuanaland and Swaziland from the Union – then, it is assumed, the credit for this could not possibly be given to the imperial government. An article in the *Journal of African History* in 1969 by Alan R. Booth argued that, in the apparent absence of any actual imperial policy or concern, local African and missionary pressures on the high commissioner were decisive in bringing this about.

---

[1] L. M. Thompson, *The Oxford history of South Africa* (ed. M. Wilson and L. M. Thompson), vol. II: *South Africa 1870–1966* (1971), pp. 358 and 364; see also G. B. Pyrah, *Imperial policy and South Africa, 1902–1910* (1955), ch. 4, p. 105; Lord Hailey, *The Republic of South Africa and the High Commission Territories* (1963), pp. 25–31; Mary Benson, *South Africa: the struggle for a birthright* (1966), pp. 19–20; Alan R. Booth, 'Lord Selborne and the British Protectorates, 1908–1910', *JAH* 10 (1969), pp. 133–48. For an alternative and better-informed interpretation, see N. Mansergh, *South Africa, 1906–1961: the price of magnanimity* (1962), ch. 3.

British government archives can now be studied in full, and two things stand out. The first point is this: they show it to be not in the least true that African interests were overlooked. On the contrary, from the moment the Liberal government came to power in Britain in December 1905 there was constant preoccupation with the problem of trying to safeguard these interests.[2] The problem was probed exhaustively during the drafting of the new Transvaal constitution in 1906; it became clear, however, that little could usefully be done, beyond resisting Afrikaner demands for the return of Swaziland, which had been a Transvaal protectorate before the South African War. Effective power to act, it was concluded, had largely disappeared in self-governing colonies; but where imperial control remained, as in the 'Protectorates' (the High Commission Territories) of Basutoland (Lesotho), Bechuanaland (Botswana), and Swaziland, the Liberals were determined, as if by compensation, to exert themselves to the full. Tremendous care was taken with the preparation of the Schedule dealing with the High Commission Territories which was appended to the South Africa Act, 1909. Moreover – and this is the second point – the decision to withhold them from the Union at the outset, but nevertheless to specify future terms, was in fact a decision taken in Whitehall. The imperial factor cannot be discounted. Local pressures on the high commissioner were purely secondary.

After all the new evidence has been evaluated, it might still be thought that, in all, the British government did not do enough for African interests between 1905 and 1910, but what they did actually achieve should not be underestimated, and it cannot legitimately be alleged that they were unconcerned. It may not be unfair to assess some of their reasoning as misguided, but we cannot dub them knaves who cynically ditched the Africans.

Four preliminary observations may be offered upon the perverse currency of the opinion that British action for African interests was inadequate. First, the racial problem in South Africa before 1910 was not as intense as it became subsequently, and it is unrealistic to expect the British government then to have acted as if South Africa were already the world's greatest racial villain – a notoriety which unquestionably belonged to the southern states of the United States of America. In 1899 the Liberal James Bryce could nowhere in South Africa see 'any cause for present apprehension', and in 1902 it was possible for him to list areas of racial tension without including South Africa, which he knew at first hand.[3]

[2] R. Hyam, *Elgin and Churchill at the Colonial Office, 1905–1908* (1968), where the evidence in support of this statement is set out in chapter 4.

[3] J. Bryce, *Impressions of South Africa* (3rd edn 1899), pp. 361–2, and 'Relations of the advanced and the backward races of mankind' (Romanes Lecture, 1902). The British were perhaps more farsighted than Afrikaners: at any rate, Smuts later admitted that, unlike Selborne, he had not seen the importance of the African problem in 1908–9 (J. C. Smuts, *Wartime speeches: a compilation of public utterances in Gt Britain* (London, 1917), p. 88; W. K. Hancock, *Smuts*, vol. II: *The fields of force, 1919–1950* (Cambridge, 1968), p. 114).

Secondly, much of the argument about apparent unconcern hinges on British failure to promote enfranchisement of Africans. The reasons for this omission were as follows: British Liberals did not consider franchise rights alone to be sufficient to secure adequate attention for African interests, and they decided that for the time being the best way to represent African interests was through 'development of native institutions' (such as the Basutoland *pitso* or national council) 'on native lines', under paternalistic guidance, rather than through a 'hasty admission . . . to political rights for which neither they, nor the whites, are as yet prepared'.[4] (The fact that somewhat similar sentiments subsequently became the apologia and smoke-screen for apartheid does not necessarily detract from the well-intentioned sincerity with which they were held by Edwardian Liberals in Britain.) Uninterest in enfranchising Africans does not prove unwillingness to advance their interests, or even to secure some other form of representation for their views. (And it is, incidentally, quite unhistorical to argue that because the roots of segregation were put down by Cecil Rhodes and Godfrey Lagden, the British were therefore the architects of apartheid. We may be reasonably certain that if the Liberals had been in danger of being involved in such a development, most of them would, like E. H. Brookes in South Africa itself, have recanted their earlier beliefs.)

Thirdly, it is hard to demonstrate that any humanitarian organisation (such as the Aborigines Protection Society) or mission society had any direct influence on the framing of the government's South African policy. There is another misunderstanding here too: they tended to give the impression of ignoring attempts from such bodies to bring pressure to bear, but they did so only in the confident belief that Whitehall itself was the true, rational, and the one effective guardian of the humanitarian tradition, to which outside bodies, with imperfect access to information, could add little or nothing. They continued to respect the power of such bodies to whip up public opinion.

Fourthly, although the Union of South Africa was the overriding British Liberal objective, Union could be regarded as a way of improving the position of Africans. This theory went back to the days of Carnarvon's scheme; the colonial secretary in Gladstone's second ministry, Lord Kimberley, described better treatment for natives as one of the objects of confederation: a federal government, he wrote, might be expected to take larger views and be more impartial.[5] The British wanted Union, and they wanted to protect Africans, but in fact they contrived seldom to see any incompatibility between their desire and their duty, between promoting white self-government and securing African improvements. Indeed, the Liberals saw white self-government and Union,

---

[4] Elgin Papers (Broomhall), Elgin to Crewe, 7 May 1908 (draft).
[5] W. E. Gladstone Papers, B.L. Add. MSS 44225, 176, Kimberley to Gladstone, 25 May 1880. The Colonial Office files for the Carnarvon period (colonial secretary, 1874–8) were turned up in the summer of 1908 – see CO 417/463, 16130, minute by C. P. Lucas, 8 May 1908.

largely on local terms, as perhaps the only effective means to an improvement in the position of the Africans. How, they argued, could Africans hope to be better off while the white overlords were not only divided among themselves, but also apprehensive of a black uprising? They believed the reconciliation of the whites to be the indispensable prerequisite to the elevation of the Africans, and they thought that the Africans would benefit more from the reduction of white fears than anything else. Small, weak, disunited states in a balkanised South Africa seemed inevitably prone to parochial attitudes and panic in the treatment of their African subjects. Self-governing Natal, they argued, amply demonstrated the truth of this proposition, twice declaring martial law, in 1906 and 1907, to cover drastic repression of Zulu disturbances. It was firmly believed that the Zulu would not have been so harshly treated if Natal had been merely a province of the Union and unable to call on imperial aid to rescue her from the penalty of mistakes. Thus African interests seemed actually to require Union, because Union might steady panicky white opinion, giving more confidence, and thus generosity, to white government. A good governor-general might hold things steady. Much might depend on Britain's showing trust in South African capacity for liberal development: hence it was necessary to declare at least long-term willingness to transfer the High Commission Territories. 'In my opinion', declared Lord Crewe, colonial secretary from 1908 to 1910, 'His Majesty's Government are bound to place confidence in Union Government which is supreme.' Whether in fact they genuinely *felt* confidence is another matter.[6]

Now it may well be the case that in all this there were elements of wishful thinking and well-meaning self-delusion. The Colonial Office was prepared to admit (though only to itself) that there was no easy answer to Khama and the Ngwato people when they said: 'We do not know how it is possible for a nation to change the character of its treatment of the native races through the mere fact of union between themselves, nor how it can come to pass that four separate faulty native administrations when joined into one can be anything else than a faulty administration.' But the government, like most groups of politicians, faced with the embarrassing necessity of balancing imperial strategies and humanitarian sentiments, managed to convince themselves that their political main aim (Union) was not inconsistent with their moral obligation (to the Africans). They even made this conviction seem plausible to their opponents.[7]

Despite a considerable area of broad agreement, as on franchise rights, and qualified optimism about future improvement, the British government was far

---

[6] Hyam, *Elgin and Churchill*, ch. 7; CO 417/458, 25076, Selborne to Crewe, 22 Jun. 1908; Earl of Crewe Papers (Cambridge University Library) C/17, R. B. Haldane to Crewe, 25 Dec. 1908.

[7] CO 417/471, 12029, Crewe to Selborne, telegram, 14 Apr. 1909; for Khama's petition, see CO 417/428, 16895.

from happy with particular South African attitudes and native policies as they stood in 1908. Hence their worry over African interests. There were two distinct problems: the interests of Africans within the Union from the beginning, and the interests of those in the High Commission Territories who could be kept out.

As far as the position of the Africans within the future Union was concerned, all hope was placed in the expected good effects of a demonstration of trust in the whites, which might encourage the improvement of attitude which most observers claimed was beginning to take place. The Liberals genuinely believed themselves to be doing the most they could for Africans by establishing a Union grounded more upon a demonstration of trust in the new rulers than upon specific safeguards for the protection of Africans. Partly because of their imperfect knowledge of the local situation in detail, which, in any case, had long ago receded beyond effective imperial control, the Liberals knew only too well the impossibility of enforcing paper provisions for the Union against a determined, entrenched, self-governing white community. As Winston Churchill recognised in 1908 they were not the arbiters of the situation: 'We have great influence; but power has passed.'[8] The Liberal government did not waste time fighting this stubborn fact. They saw no point in hammering the colonials with suggested provisions or contentious declarations, which, while bringing no practical benefit to Africans, would irritate the whites. They concentrated on selected priorities.

As a result, although the Cape native franchise was entrenched in section 35 of the South Africa Act (and thereby in theory better safeguarded than under the existing Cape constitution), there was no provision for its extension. This was partly because, as already mentioned, the British were sceptical about the Cape franchise on its merits. Lord Selborne, the British high commissioner in South Africa from 1905 to 1910, had very little faith in it; he thought many had the franchise in the Cape who were quite unfit for it. British ministers at home were more favourable to it than Selborne, but Lord Elgin, colonial secretary from 1905 to 1908, had doubts about its utility, and at all events, the Liberals did not regard it as the only possible way of securing African representation. Colonel J. E. B. Seely, parliamentary under-secretary for the colonies from 1908 to 1911, officially announced in 1908 that they were not committed to this method. In justifying scepticism about the Cape franchise, the southern states of the United States of America were frequently cited as the classic proof of the dangers of prematurely conceding equal citizenship. When one of the civil servants advocated a franchise without a colour bar, Seely replied that unjust decisions by juries on racial grounds, and lynchings, were in all the

---

[8] Crewe papers, C/7, 7 Churchill to Crewe, 25 Dec. 1908, 'Secret'.

world 'most terribly frequent' precisely in the place where a franchise without a colour bar had been imposed upon an unwilling white population, namely in the southern states of the USA.[9]

II

The South African national convention opened in Durban on 12 October 1908. Close contact was maintained in correspondence between Crewe and Selborne throughout the sittings of the convention. Selborne's role was essentially reduced by the British government to that of an instrument of communication – he was not allowed to act as an independent negotiator. Although Selborne thus privately suggested to delegates the justice and expediency of giving the vote to such Africans as had 'really raised themselves to the level of the white man's civilisation', when the convention proved completely unwilling to consider even a franchise with a formidable civilisation test, Selborne signified acceptance of a policy of merely continuing the *status quo*, which would leave Africans everywhere outside the Cape without the franchise. The Colonial Office was satisfied with this and, indeed, even seemed relieved that the draft constitution did not actually restrict future grants of the franchise. Selborne forwarded the draft bill on 15 February 1909. Officials in the Colonial Office agreed that, as the bill was the result of compromise achieved with difficulty between a number of conflicting views, the essential thing was to alter as little as possible, and in practice they saw nothing vital to alter.[10]

Some members of parliament were not quite so accommodating. In answer to a deputation in May 1909 from five of them – Dilke, Alden, Ramsay MacDonald, Keir Hardie, and Robertson – Crewe said that whilst he shared to a considerable extent some of the views they put forward, more particularly a strong feeling against a colour bar excluding Africans from sitting in parliament, and could say this much in private, the practical question was how far the South Africans could be expected to agree to amendment, especially since Australia maintained a colour bar, and in practice no African had ever as yet sat in parliament.[11] The colonial secretary also saw a 'Coloured' deputation and an African deputation led by W. P. Schreiner (lawyer and former minister of the Cape), together with the Revd Walter Rubusana (a Congregationalist minister) and John Tengo Jabavu (the Mfengu newspaper editor), pleading for fuller formal provision for African interests in the constitution. Schreiner described their two interviews with Crewe in July 1909 as not advancing matters 'beyond the facts of great

---

[9] 4 *Parliamentary Debates (PD) Commons* 188, 13 May 1908, 1248; CO 417/463, 38204, minute, 30 Oct. 1908; see also Crewe, 5 *PD Lords* 2, 3 Aug. 1909, 859–60.
[10] CO 417/459, 41744, Selborne to Crewe, 24 Oct. 1908; CO 417/471, 8099, minutes, Mar. 1909; Crewe papers, C/47, Sir F. Hopwood to Crewe, 16 Aug. 1908.
[11] CO 417/478, 17977, May 1909.

courtesy, real sympathy and earnest attention'.[12] Liberal ministers took much the same line towards the Schreiner mission as John X. Merriman, prime minister of the Cape, recommended to them. Merriman pointed out that the retention of the Cape franchise had been conceded in the convention only after a severe struggle and at the price of a colour disqualification for election to parliament; without this bar, he said, Union undoubtedly would not have been agreed; Schreiner's mission, therefore, must not succeed. If it did, bitter feeling, Merriman predicted, would be caused throughout South Africa, perhaps leading even to an attack on existing African rights, which were strongly supported by a minority only; and delicately growing pride in the superior liberty of the Cape system would be destroyed at a stroke. In any case, Merriman added, Schreiner's mission would have an evil effect on the mind of Africans, who would 'be taught to read into the Act of Union an attack on their rights wholly contrary to the spirit in which the Act is conceived'; far worse, it would make the whites more unfriendly, for they would feel 'that their dearest wishes have been imperilled for the sake of some paper guarantee of an equality which they do not believe in . . . No worse blow could have been struck at the cause of sound relations between the races.' Crewe's comment on Merriman's argument is illuminating – 'Mr Merriman's *apologia* is able and conclusive.'[13] Seely described it as 'extraordinarily well put, and coming from him, the foremost negrophile amongst Cape statesmen, is well nigh unanswerable'. Seely wished to publicise Merriman's views as an effective defence of the British case,[14] which was, essentially, that African interests in the Union were best provided for by not assertively discussing them, and by maintaining the *status quo*.

On the whole the British ministers accepted the Union bill in the form presented to them. Apart from the Schedule, the only Cabinet discussion appears to have been about possible amendments relating to the better protection of Asian, not African, subjects.[15] Native policy should be mainly settled in the Union of Africa itself: this was now the fixed conviction of the Liberal government. Asquith, the prime minister, defended this position in parliament: experience and common sense both showed, he declared, that where difficult racial situations existed, the community must be allowed to adjust itself without outside interference from a distance. British interference was, he said, capricious and spasmodic, often ill-informed and sometimes sentimental, and thus not in the best interests of the Africans themselves. There was no point, he concluded, in wrecking Union by attempting to make changes in favour of Africans.[16]

---

[12] Sir Charles Dilke Papers, B.L. Add. MSS 43921, 181, Schreiner to Dilke, 22 Jul. 1909.
[13] CO 48/602, 22201, enclosure on Sir Walter Hely-Hutchinson (governor of the Cape) to Crewe, 16 Jun. 1909, and minute by Crewe, 12 Jul. 1909; see also L. M. Thompson, *The unification of South Africa, 1902–1910* (Oxford, 1960), pp. 402–3.
[14] CO 417/478, 29845, minute, 4 Aug. 1909. [15] CAB 41, Asquith to the King, 16 Jul. 1909.
[16] 5 *PD Commons* 9, 16 Aug. 1909, 1009–14; Thompson, *Unification of South Africa*, p. 428.

Crewe made an appeal to British willingness to let the South Africans themselves solve problems within their own boundaries as a fact entitling the British government to expect considerate treatment over the problem of the High Commission Territories.[17] All Crewe's positive effort was concentrated on this, since this was a situation over which the imperial government had some real control and, being 'the man in possession', could not be charged so easily with interference. Thus Crewe used his Union policy as a lever to extract better conditions for Africans in the High Commission Territories. He could then proceed to use his 'Protectorates' policy to deflect British critics of his Union policy. Retention of the Territories was partly designed to sugar the pill of handing over the vast majority of Africans to white rule. The imperial factor was dominant in deciding to hold the Territories, but this decision was a partial substitute for pushing African rights in the Union. The reason for this emphasis is not unrelated to the relative strength of the lobbies in favour of the Union and 'Protectorate' Africans. Imperial government was always selective in the distribution of trusteeship benefits. Public opinion could determine the particular issues on which it chose to fight general principles. (This explains, for example, why Chinese labour in the Transvaal was destroyed, while Indian indentured labour in Natal under equally bad conditions was ignored.) The protests of Khama and Letsie, loyal or Christian paramount chiefs, attracted much more sympathy than those of Jabavu and Rubusana, mere journalist and clergyman, suspected of being open to manipulation by 'agitators'.

Selborne discussed the subject of the future of the High Commission Territories in a despatch dated 8 May 1908. Britain's duty towards them was, he wrote, plainly only to transfer responsibility for their good government to the South Africans on fixed conditions embodied in the South Africa Constitution Act. The British obligation to Basutoland and Bechuanaland was 'a very special obligation of honour', for they had volunteered to be ruled by Britain, and had been scrupulously loyal. Equally, however, Selborne was firmly convinced that 'if necessary and proper conditions can be embodied in the Constitution' it was in everybody's interest, whether imperial government, South African Union, or African tribe, for the three territories to be 'absorbed into the new South African political system and not to be left as Imperial administrative islands floating in a South African National sea', causing constantly increasing friction.

Although Crewe was informed that the South Africans probably would not tackle the Territories until after Union was accomplished, he none the less decided to act at once (as Selborne advised), while avoiding the appearance of interfering. If Britain waited until the Union made proposals, he argued,

---

[17] Confidential Print, *African*, no. 933, 'Conference between delegates from South Africa and the secretary of state for the colonies', 20 and 21 Jul. 1909.

permanent retention would be the only alternative to concurrence in the South African plan. Crewe considered this

an objectionable course to take, and there would consequently be little scope for bargaining. Whereas, on the *divide et impera* principle, we are more likely to secure favourable terms for the natives, while the Colonies are still separate, and Union depends on a satisfactory issue devised for this particular problem.

A little while after writing this, Crewe accepted the advice of Seely and the officials to warn Selborne privately that he must not go too fast: 'the less said the better at present'.[18] There was some reason to suppose that certain Afrikaner politicians were trying to shelve the question until they were in a better position for pressing their views. Nevertheless, the policy to be pursued seemed to Crewe as yet obscure.[19] The government accepted the obligation of honour not to hand over the Territories except on terms fulfilling conditions 'which the Chiefs and peoples have a right to expect', and if those conditions were fulfilled 'they would be quite willing to make the transfer'. But when? And should they arrange terms without actual transfer?[20]

In further despatches between May and July 1908 Selborne urged transfer of all the Territories to 'the responsibility of a South African Government on its first coming into existence'. If it did not take place, he envisaged that stock-stealing across frontiers, the straying of native cattle, the spread of cattle disease, and difficulties over prospectors or labour contracts would lead to disputes and deadlock between Whitehall and South Africa. 'A true fulfilment of our trust', he concluded (27 July 1908), compelled an attempt to get fair terms for the transfer of Swaziland and Basutoland, which he was convinced could take place 'at the time of the granting of the Constitution'. African opposition led by Basutoland must not stand in the way:

Greatly superior as the Basutos are to all other tribes, even they must be regarded in such a matter as children; we are their guardians and they are our wards; and it would be cruel to put the responsibility on them of a decision which might be absolutely fatal to their eventual interests.

They would, he believed, certainly protest, but 'they will never take any hostile action unless they are unjustly treated or hopelessly mismanaged'. His advice, therefore, was: eliminate friction by gratifying South African sentiment and transfer the Territories while Britain was still in a strong position to prevent

---

[18] CO 417/458, 19782, minute by Crewe 14 Jun. 1908 on Selborne to Crewe, 8 May 1908; CO 417/455, 22355, minute by Seely, 25 Jun. 1908.
[19] CO 417/458, 25076, Selborne to Crewe, 22 Jun. 1908; W. K. Hancock and J. van der Poel, eds., *Selections from the Smuts Papers*, vol. II: *1902–1910* (Cambridge, 1966), p. 374, Smuts to Merriman, 3 Jan. 1908; CO 417/463, 24605, Crewe to Selborne, 1 Jul. 1908.
[20] CO 417/459, 25754, Crewe to Selborne, telegram, 17 Jul. 1908.

unjust treatment of the Africans. He viewed with misgiving the compromise of arranging terms without actual transfer at the start.[21]

Between July and October 1908 Selborne shifted his ground and resolved to keep the Territories out of the Union for the immediate future. Why did he change his mind? The argument of Alan Booth's paper may be summarised as follows: The key to the change of policy seems to have been Selborne's dealings with the Sotho, who had impressed him on his visits to them in February 1906 and April 1907; he was also influenced by a missionary in Basutoland, the Revd E. Jacottet (of the Paris Evangelical Society), who wrote to him in August and saw him on 21 September 1908, expressing himself against transfer at once; Selborne in his turn persuaded the British Cabinet, which until this moment had been 'consistently heedless' of the interests of the Africans involved; the Colonial Office was 'convinced' by his persistence, partly from fears that he would resign if he were not supported; thus, 'responsibility for the retention . . . lay more with Lord Selborne than with the British government as a whole', and at his insistence the Schedule of transfer was placed in the Act.

Even apart from the incomplete documentary basis (mainly a few pieces of mere Confidential Print), and its doctrinaire determination to exclude the imperial factor, this thesis raises several difficulties. In the first place, why did it take Selborne so long to draw the appropriate conclusion from visits to Basutoland undertaken more than a year earlier? In the second place, how much real weight would he attach to an intense foreign missionary who suddenly presented himself to state the obvious, namely that the Sotho did not want to be transferred:[22] a fact which had also been adequately emphasised already by the Resident Commissioner (but which, as we have seen, failed to impress Selborne)? In the third place, is it at all probable that Selborne would be able to persuade the government to change its mind, when the recent history of his high commissionership had been marked by the consistent rejection of his advice on almost every significant matter? A government which in 1906 had nearly recalled him was not likely to be unduly frightened by the thought of his resignation. Nor were the British ministers predisposed to listen to Selborne. Asquith found him inept at the 'diagnosis and prognosis' of South African affairs, and 'singularly deficient in the larger questions of policy, both in insight and foresight', Lewis Harcourt (First Commissioner of Works, who took over the Colonial Office from Crewe) described Selborne's mind as 'small and not very effective'. Crewe himself regarded him as energetic and loyal but 'rather a dangerous plenipotentiary . . . intensely obsinate, and his ideas run away

---

[21] CO 417/458, 20630, Selborne to Crewe, 18 May 1908 and CO 417/459, 29921, 27 Jul. 1908.

[22] Jacottet wrote several long letters to Bryce (James Bryce Papers (Bodleian Library) C. 2) and two of his letters were printed for the Cabinet committee. Bryce thought him reliable: see Crewe papers, C/3, 20 Jul. 1908.

with him . . . We must not find ourselves in Lord Carnarvon's silly plight.' Tight control was therefore kept over Selborne, and, as explained above, he was retained merely as a channel of communication.[23]

The truth of the matter is, of course, that Selborne changed his mind because he was required and persuaded to do so by his political bosses in London. Reviewing the situation retrospectively in 1909 he sought to excuse his original advocacy of wholesale immediate transfer by saying he had not dared to hope that guarantees could have been obtained in the Act without it. 'Most happily the secretary of state took a different view': and now, before transfer, he agreed they should wait and see what native policy was. This frank admission of a difference of opinion with Crewe in the summer of 1908[24] appears to make it unnecessary to search for local pressures on Selborne, and at the same time (except in the single case of Bechuanaland) to dispose of the possibility that he changed his mind quite independently.

British ministers and officials entertained serious doubts concerning Selborne's original policy, which they may to some extent have misunderstood. At any rate, as they saw it, the policy was one of trying practically to dictate terms and of rushing Britain into handing over the Territories to a South Africa diverging from London ideals of native policy. Seely was quite certain that it would be most unwise for the government to propound any scheme of transfer, especially since Selborne on 23 July 1908 for the first time recommended treating Bechuanaland exceptionally, and keeping it alone *out* of the Union. Thus Selborne, commented Seely, 'had already discovered that his original proposal, which he was so anxious to cram down our throats, won't hold water. (The metaphor is mixed, but the meaning I hope is clear.)' Crewe expressed his doubts in two important private letters to Selborne in the first half of August 1908. These letters show how fully Crewe was aware of his responsibilities for Africans. Taking a different view from the one he supposed Selborne to hold, he felt there was much to be said for deferring the inclusion of the Territories in the Union 'until we see how the new machine works'. Though he was not as mistrustful of the new government as some of those who gave this advice, he did think immediate transfer

would be a leap in the dark. Once the Protectorates are gone, our power of protest has practically disappeared . . .

---

[23] Hyam, *Elgin and Churchill*, pp. 143–4, 530; Herbert Gladstone Papers, B.L.Add.MSS. 45997, 239, Harcourt to Herbert Gladstone, 19 Sept. 1911; Crewe Papers, C/40, Asquith to Crewe 7 Jul. 1908, and C/7, 7, Crewe to W. S. Churchill, 29 Dec. 1908 (copy).

[24] CO 417/471, Selborne to Sir Francis Hopwood, 22 Mar. 1909. Booth's opinion that Selborne was before July 1908 'having reservations' about handing Africans over is not supported by my reading of the despatches; his argument for the 'effect' in London of Selborne's missives rests simply on an unsupported speculation in Pyrah, *Imperial policy and South Africa, 1902–10*, p. 127.

It is scarcely a question of allowing either Basutoland or Swaziland to put a veto on inclusion, but as regards the former, any marked objection on their part would have to be taken into account.

He admitted the force of Selborne's contention that delay was pointless, since if the new Union was unfair and unscrupulous it could put the screw on the Territories to a disagreeable and perhaps calamitous extent, even before they came under its formal control; furthermore, 'if South Africa really considers it an insult not to be entrusted with full government, that is also a strong argument'. But on the other hand, 'if things do not go right after we have parted with the Territories, a terrible responsibility will rest upon us in view of our obligations'. Because it might be difficult to get satisfactory terms, he thought that Britain would be in a stronger position and more likely to obtain proper terms written into the Act if they said in effect, Unify: but these are the conditions for transfer; rather than admitting they might be prejudicing unification altogether by insisting on this or that point in favour of the Africans. It was no use denying that the whole thing was a risk. Current South African attitudes to African rights were not encouraging. He thought Selborne over-sanguine if he expected the mere terms of a constitution permanently to check cupidities and to mitigate sentiment unfavourable to Africans:

> I do not doubt that the present men will keep their word, but we are legislating in permanency. And it will be no more difficult to create the friction later on which will give the excuse for modifying the terms. It is this consideration which makes some of my colleagues, even more than myself, anxious not to part with control of the native Territories until it becomes obviously necessary.

For the sake of argument he was prepared to admit that the necessary moment might be concurrent with the introduction of the new constitution, and that there might be disadvantages for all parties in an intervening period. A decision about this must depend, Crewe felt, on the degree of anxiety which South African statesmen displayed for an immediate inclusion. But, he concluded, he did not intend to 'throw the native Territories at their heads'. He would wait for the moment and watch developments to see how South African politicians thought and behaved. The more liberal the attitude they displayed, the less stringent need be the conditions for transfer.[25]

---

[25] CO 417/458, 25076 and CO 417/459, 26883, minutes by Seely, 17 and 29 Jul.; CAB. 37/94, 110, Crewe to Selborne, private, 1 and 12 Aug. 1908 (copies). In reply Selborne acknowledged the risk, but pointed out that since the risk 'arises from the fact of closer union ... from that risk no policy or plan which we may adopt in respect of the Protectorates will be free'. He advocated transfer 'from the commencement' as the policy which involved the least risk. He was willing to defer transfer, and believed Crewe had misunderstood him in thinking that he, Selborne, would say to South Africa 'You may have the Protectorates' or 'throw the native territories at the heads of the South African statesmen'. To prove this he listed six conditions which he believed Britain was bound to secure for the chiefs and tribes to be included in the future union (CO 417/459, 34176, Selborne to Crewe, telegram, 17 Sept. 1908).

In October 1908, Crewe, for Selborne's guidance, indicated four general policy considerations in the mind of the British government.[26] First, immediate transfer was out of the question; the Territories should be kept in trust, and it would be well to retain control of them as long as was possible without creating friction in South Africa. Second, on the other hand, the Territories must surely be ultimately included in the Union. Third, Britain 'must insist upon insertion in the Constitution of all reasonable specific safeguards for their native inhabitants'; South Africans must understand that

> it would be practically impossible to secure the assent of the House of Commons and the country here to any constitutional Act which failed explicitly to provide for the security of the native population in the Protectorates, so that inclusion of these safeguards must be regarded as a necessary condition.

Finally, above all, nothing must be done to prejudice the movement for Union; therefore the British government could not at this stage formulate an official policy which leading delegates to the convention might reject. (As Crewe explained to Asquith, the government must 'walk warily in order to get what we want or – most of it – without seeming to interfere too directly'.)

III

Selborne originally envisaged entrusting the whole detailed administration of the Territories, when part of the Union, to an executive high commission whose members would have the status and independence of judges of the supreme court.[27] The commission would be controlled, not by the South African parliament, but by the governor-general acting as British high commissioner. The purpose of this administrative separation was to avoid a 'breach of faith' and to obtain better treatment for Africans. Selborne was authorised to discuss the matter confidentially and unofficially with the convention leaders. If such an independent executive commission was quite unacceptable to the convention, Crewe was prepared to subordinate the commission to the governor-general in council.[28] Crewe always agreed with Selborne that in theory an independent commission would have afforded an excellent future government for the Territories; but he could not authorise him to urge it upon the South African premiers even unofficially as the policy preferred by the British government, because such a complete removal of native affairs from the cognisance of the

---

[26] CO 417/459, 34176, Crewe to Selborne, telegram, 16 Oct. 1908, and CO 417/46715, private letter, 17 Oct., quoted in minute by H. W. Just, 24 Dec. 1908; Asquith Papers (Bodleian Library) Dep. 46, Crewe to Asquith, 5 Jan. 1909; see also E. A. Walker, *Lord de Villiers and his times: South Africa, 1842–1914* (London, 1925), p. 456, and Pyrah, *Imperial policy and South Africa*, pp. 127–30.
[27] CO 417/458, no. 20630, Selborne to Crewe, 13 May 1908.
[28] CO 417/459, no. 46715, Crewe to Selborne, 17 Oct. 1908, quoted by Just, 24 Dec. 1908.

South African government would hardly be entertained by them; and 'by asking for so much we might endanger the prospect of getting even our minimum, at least without a collision of opinions which might throw upon us the onus of wrecking altogether the scheme of Union'.[29] By the middle of December the British government, to secure consent, accepted the idea of the commission as an administrative and advisory body, 'with an independent position secured to it', but subordinated in the last resort to the governor-general in council as the legislative authority. Direct legislation for the Territories by a parliament in which their inhabitants were not represented was regarded as inadmissible. This principle had been recognised in the Transkei, where, although power to legislate was possessed by the Cape parliament, legislation was usually left in the hands of the governor in council. The case for following this precedent in the Territories was strong, since Africans did at least have some votes in the Cape.[30] Thus, although the Territories were regarded as geographically part of South Africa, they were to be kept administratively separate in perpetuity. The commission concept was part of a wider attempt to foster administrative entities governed by white experts on African affairs, insulated and protected as much as possible from the pressures of the white electorate. The commission would act as a permanent buffer between Africans and members of parliament. It was felt in some respects to be possibly analogous to the council in London which advised the secretary of state for India.[31]

The proposal was to administer the Territories by three or four commissioners appointed by the governor-general in council. Legislation was to be in the form of proclamations by the governor-general in council on the advice of the commissioners. Further probable conditions of transfer, approved by Crewe, were intimated to convention delegates: African land to be inalienable, the sale of intoxicating liquor to be prohibited, the Territories to receive due share of Union customs dues, and the Basutoland national council to be maintained. While Crewe hoped the South African parliaments would accept the commission, he did not regard it 'as *porro unum necessarium* in the same sense that some inclusion of safeguards in the constitution undoubtedly is'.[32] Sir Henry de Villiers, chief justice of the Cape and chairman of the convention, agreed to proceed on this basis in drafting the Schedule, which, let it be emphasised, provided for transfer of administration to the Union, not incorporation in the Union.

---

[29] Crewe to Selborne, 18 Mar. 1909, private (copy in Confidential Print, 26 Mar 1909).
[30] CO 417/459, 45345, Crewe to Selborne, telegram, 16 Dec. 1908.
[31] 5 *PD Lords*, 2, Crewe, 27 July 1909, 765. Selborne would have liked to treat Zululand in a similar administrative fashion (CO 417/455, 22355, minute by H. C. M. Lambert, Jun. 1908).
[32] CO 417/459, 41072, Selborne to Crewe, telegram, 6 Nov. 1908; Crewe papers C/17, Crewe to Haldane, 27 Dec. 1908 (copy).

The convention discussed the draft Schedule on 17 December. There were frequent divisions. A strong minority did not think the attitude of the British government fair or reasonable. Its conditions, especially participation of the governor-general in choosing commissioners, were thought to display great mistrust of the future South African government in its dealings with Africans. Merriman was very sensitive on this point, and said the whole movement for union could be wrecked over it. Crewe was somewhat disturbed by this reaction, especially since the proposal did indeed imply mistrust. In his uneasiness, Crewe reminded Selborne of the danger of turning semi-official negotiations into the final pronouncement of exact British terms, which had not yet been determined:

Our object has been merely to inform them of the general line of thought with regard to the Protectorates passing through your mind and mine, because it would have been unbusinesslike to keep them wholly in the dark. It must be distinctly understood, on the other hand, that they are expected to make their own propositions for consideration ... If the proposals made by the Convention approximate closely to those which you yourself unofficially outlined, all the better, for the final negotiation here will be much simplified.

Britain must be most careful, he added, not to give the colonial parliaments an opportunity of rejecting the whole scheme of unification on a 'fancied plea' of mistrust and interference, which they might be only too ready to do. It was Selborne's job to elicit workable proposals from the South Africans.[33]

If the proposals of the convention did not reach the Liberal government's minimum, Crewe planned to hold a conference in London, where a South African delegation could be impressed with the strong British parliamentary feeling in favour of African interests.[34]

Meanwhile, Crewe forbade Selborne to put the British view formally in writing to de Villiers: the convention must take the first formal step and make a proposition, in order both to protect the British government from the unfortunate charge of making union harder and to placate the people of Basutoland.[35] The terms of inclusion outlined by Selborne in unofficial conversations with the leading South Africans were accepted somewhat unwillingly by the convention, and it was rumoured that the Schedule would be thrown out by one or more of the local parliaments. In the face of this threat, the British government was forced to try to sort out its priorities. Crewe warned his Cabinet colleagues that the proposed inclusion of terms in the constitutional act might become impossible. It was not, perhaps, the terms themselves which constituted the chief danger, but the device of placing the safeguards on constitutional record. He therefore

---

[33] CO 417/459, 46715, Crewe to Selborne, 23 Dec. 1908; Crewe papers C/47, Hopwood to Crewe, 15 Jan. 1909.

[34] Asquith papers, 46, Crewe to Asquith, 5 Jan. 1909.

[35] CO 417/459, 47952, Crewe to Selborne, 7 Jan. 1909; CO 417/468, 3495, minute by Hopwood, 3 Feb. 1909.

asked the Cabinet seriously to consider whether, in order to prevent the entire scheme of unification breaking down, they would forgo integration of terms within the act, and merely confer power upon the Union to take them in later on terms and conditions to be agreed. But, he added, as Selborne was deeply concerned about African interests, and 'we also feel strongly' about them, if there was to be any disagreement with the high commissioner, 'it must not be on the degree in which the Protectorates are to be safeguarded, but on the methods in which the safeguards are to be recorded, so as to give the protected natives the full benefit of them at the time of transfer to the Union'.[36]

Winston Churchill quickly made up his mind: 'The union of South Africa is the first consideration, and far outweighs the specific terms upon which the Protectorates may be ceded.' The 'Protectorates' question, he wrote, could be postponed. To lay down general principles was premature and academic. Safeguards would be illusory since they had been accepted only reluctantly by the convention. It did not therefore seem worth while to run any serious risk of wrecking the constitutional settlement for the sake of including detailed and specific terms on behalf of Africans. Churchill nevertheless stressed the importance of the British government's retaining an unprejudiced hold on the High Commission Territories. In his view there should be no difficulty for five or six years in resisting transfer upon anything but the most satisfactory terms; meanwhile, Africans would become increasingly better equipped to make their own bargain with, hopefully, an increasingly liberal white South Africa.[37]

The fears which Crewe had so anxiously laid before his Cabinet colleagues proved groundless almost immediately. By the middle of January all the leading South Africans accepted the informally indicated British position on the Territories. The Natal dissentients, in particular, came quite a long way to meet the British government. Crewe reflected:

We cannot yet regard ourselves as quite out of the wood, but we see pretty clear daylight between the trees ... It has been the saving of the situation (if it is saved), that this has been one issue among many, and in the eyes of the South African statesmen, not the paramount issue.[38]

This was indeed an extremely fortunate circumstance. The British government would have been in a grave difficulty if the South Africans had launched a massive campaign for the inclusion of the Territories.

---

[36] CAB 37/97, 4, memorandum by Crewe, 11 Jan. 1909, 'South African unification: Native affairs'.
[37] CAB 37/97, 6, memorandum by W. S. Churchill, 16 Jan. 1909, 'South African unification'. Seely said if it were a question of preventing union from being wrecked he would have no hesitation in deferring the whole matter of the Territories (CO 417/471, 12442, minute, 3 Feb. 1909).
[38] CO 417/471, 2096, minute, 19 Jan. 1909.

Encouraged by this success, Selborne continued to work for further insulation of Africans in the Territories from the Union government. In March 1909 he recommended alterations in the agreed draft Schedule to achieve this end. His new draft made the prime minister president of the commission in order to induce him to look only to the commission for assistance in administration: Selborne was anxious to prevent the Native Affairs department from becoming the office of administration for the Territories. He also wished to strengthen the independent and executive influence of the commission, and to require the concurrence of the colonial secretary in the appointment of its members.[39] These proposals were badly received in London. Crewe realised the impracticability of attempting any marked stiffening of the powers of the commission: 'though we will do our best here, it is useless to run our heads up against a brick wall'.[40] With one minor exception, Seely noted, Selborne's suggestions showed less confidence in the justice of the whites, whereas the South Africans were pleading for any amendments to show greater confidence; as the British government believed in the policy of showing trust in the South Africans, Selborne ought to be disabused at once of opinions irreconcilable with this attitude. Crewe, however, whilst admitting the impossibility of reopening questions of principle, did not want to inform the South African governments that Britain entirely agreed to the Schedule exactly as it stood. He hoped to be able to suggest personally to the South African ministers, when they came to London, some amendments which, though not involving principles, yet could not be called merely drafting amendments.[41]

The Cabinet committee for South Africa confirmed the view that Selborne's proposals represented inadmissible changes in principle.[42] Undeterred, Selborne repeated obsessively one final suggestion, as impossibly ambitious as it was stupidly amateurish. This was to set up the commission as soon as possible, before transfer, and by this ploy to try to render eventual transition less obtrusive: commissioners selected in Whitehall would automatically be taken over by the South African government.[43] Colonial Office officials naturally questioned the latter assumption. They also thought such a course would disturb Africans, by seeming a presage of impending change, and would lead to an

---

[39] CO 417/471, 12442, Selborne to Crewe, 22 Mar. 1909, and to Hopwood.
[40] Crewe to Selborne, private, 18 Mar. 1909 (copy in Confidential Print, 26 Mar. 1909).
[41] CO 417/471, 12442, minutes of 19 and 20 Apr. 1909. Crewe's changes dealt with (i) prohibition of differential railway rates on produce from the Territories entering other parts of the Union, (ii) strengthening the clause on salaries and pension rights of the commissioners, and (iii) stipulations to ensure stringency of curbs on sale of intoxicating liquors. De Villiers persuaded Crewe to drop all these amendments. A verbal ambiguity possibly affecting Basutoland boundaries was spotted by the Basutoland National Council and rectified in time (Lesotho Government Archives, Maseru, S. 3/20/1, 2, and 3).
[42] CO 417/471, 12442, Crewe to Selborne, telegram, 14 May 1909.
[43] CO 417/471, 8100, Selborne to Crewe, 15 Feb. 1909.

earlier demand by South Africa for transfer. They suggested consultation with the new governor-general.[44] Eventually Herbert Gladstone, when appointed to this post, counselled and secured rejection of Selborne's suggestion, since it would create a host of unnecessary difficulties.[45]

IV

As early as March 1908, paramount chief Letsie of Basutoland, feeling that the question of the future status of his people was already urgent, wanted to lead a deputation to London. Selborne regarded this as foolish and 'wholly premature'. Seely, with a surer instinct, took this initiative seriously: 'Don't tell them their fuss is needless because they are well informed and would not believe it.' Crewe was prepared to send them a message indicating how the Colonial Office was 'watching the matter with anxious care on their behalf', but thought it would be better if Selborne reassured the Sotho chiefs by a personal visit.[46]

Next, Khama and other Tswana chiefs let it be known that they felt happy and well treated under the imperial government, and expressed great concern at the prospect of any change, even one postponed for some years. Crewe was not so impressed by Tswana representations – 'If we can get the Basutos fairly contented', he wrote, 'I should hope that there will be no serious difficulty with these people.'[47] In March 1909 copies of letters arrived in the Colonial Office from chiefs Sebele, Linchwe, Baitlotle, and Bathoen. Sebele of the Bakwena instanced examples of South African legislative iniquity, and urged the advisability of seeing how the Union treated Africans before making a decision. Bathoen was blunt: he would never agree to transfer, which would be a breach of trust. He feared an increase in the facilities for procuring the white man's dreaded liquor, and he questioned whether the king's representative would be able to prevail against the Union parliament. Crewe commented drily, 'Bathoen's dialectic is very good.' He fully realised now that while the Schedule did not make consent of chiefs an essential condition of transfer, 'there will obviously be difficulty when the time comes, in carrying out the transfer without their consent or at least their acquiescence'. Bathoen was told not to regard the 1895 settlement (removing them from Company rule) as incapable of alteration, and reminded that, even after transfer, appeal to the king would still be possible.[48]

---

[44] CAB 37/98, 48, memorandum by Crewe, 25 Mar. 1909 on draft bill; CO 417/472, 377, Crewe to Selborne, 26 Mar. 1909, minutes.
[45] CO 417/488, 20749, Herbert Gladstone to Hopwood, private, 20 Jun. 1910; Herbert Gladstone Papers, B.L. Add. MSS. 45996, 63–5, 86, 153; 45997, 85–7.
[46] CO 417/455, 44771, minutes, 15 and 16 Dec. 1908. Selborne paid a visit to Basutoland in March 1909.
[47] CO 417/465, 4385, minute, 16 Feb. 1909.
[48] CO 417/465, 8082, Crewe, minute, 15 Mar. 1909, and 8972, Crewe to Selborne, 30 Apr. 1909.

The Sotho presented a petition in London, stating

a grave anxiety that our national existence will cease, our native laws and customs be cast aside and our whole constitution... will be shattered... We feel that our country is not yet ripe for a great change of ideas and customs and habits which our people could neither understand nor appreciate.[49]

Crewe saw the Sotho deputation on 15 February 1909, and the Resident Commissioners of the Territories, who had spoken with the chiefs, on 19 March. The official reply to the Sotho petition spoke of sympathy, and contained an assurance that no change would take place for some time; transfer some day would, however, be desirable and necessary in their own interest.[50]

It was felt impossible to insert into the Schedule a detailed code of administrative regulations such as the Basutoland national council would have liked. Crewe contented himself with trying to attain two ends, which he defined as follows:

(a) to secure, as far as may be under the new conditions, a continuance of the principles of administration under which Basutoland has prospered, and (b) to embody safeguards in respect of three matters which they regard as essential in the interest of the population, viz, possession of the land, prohibition of liquor, and maintenance of the National Council.

Through the Schedule, he thought, a certain uniform and agreed standard of administration would be obtained; general principles were laid down which might ensure continuity of administration and, above all, avoid uncertainty. The *status quo* was preserved, and an administration would be established which was based upon existing principles, yet was flexible enough to take account of the advancing civilisation of the inhabitants: for this reason, it was decided not to include specific provision for continuing the jurisdiction of chiefs. The villains to be kept out were the drink-seller, the mineral prospector, and the land-speculator; the labour recruiter, however, was not regarded as harmful.[51] There was no attempt to prescribe in detail future policy for African development in the Territories. Selborne nicely expressed the underlying philosophy of the British government when he wrote:

[49] CO 417/468, 3495. [50] CO 417/478, 5596.
[51] CO 417/468, 21210 and 24270, Crewe to Hely-Hutchinson, 31 Jul. and 6 Aug. 1909. Crewe Papers, C/3, Bryce to Crewe, 20 Jul. 1908. Crewe had of course always regarded it as impossible to try to extend African 'privileges' (CO 417/468, 7096, minute, 12 Mar. 1909). In its final form, the Schedule provided for a commission of four, headed by the prime minister, appointed by the governor-general in council; the conditions of transfer were: (i) native land to be inalienable, (ii) sale of intoxicating liquor to be prohibited, (iii) Territories to receive due share of Union customs dues, (iv) Basutoland National Council to be maintained, (v) legislation about the Schedule to be reserved to the Crown for approval. For Sotho reaction to the terms, see Proceedings of the Basutoland National Council, 1910 (Lesotho Government Archives, S. 3/20/1/3).

I have never thought it advisable to attempt to tie the hands of the South African Government in matters of policy. If their native policy is sound, they will not listen to absurd or manifestly unjust suggestions; if it is unsound, no safeguards will make it sound; but the existence of the Commission is the best insurance we can provide against an unsound policy.[52]

During the second reading of the South African bill, Crewe expressed the British government's sense of a 'very solemn duty indeed' towards the High Commission Territories:

We felt bound to regard ourselves as trustees for these bodies of natives, and considering that it does not do for a trustee to hand over his trust to another man, however great his personal confidence may be in him, without a guarantee that the trust itself will be taken over, we decided to ask South Africa to accept the provisions embodied in the Schedule . . . We have no desire, we are in no hurry, to hand over these areas to anyone . . . [but] it does not seem conceivable that for an indefinite future these areas should remain administered from here, . . . Nor do I believe, in view of the varying circumstances of these districts, that it is possible to name a time limit . . . What weighs with me as much as anything is that the natives themselves are not anxious to be transferred, but, admitting that they may be some day transferred, actively desire the incorporation of a charter such as this in the Act itself.

At the committee stage, there was proposed an amendment to provide for transfer 'at the expiration of ten years from the establishment of the Union'. The government fought this on two grounds. First, if they said that no handing over could take place for ten years, the insertion of the Schedule at all would appear to be 'somewhat premature'. An application for Swaziland was extremely probable within ten years, and it could not be said that such a request would be refused. Secondly, and on the other hand, the government feared that the general effect of a fixed time limit would be the reverse of what was intended by the amendment – it might give the impression that having safeguarded the Territories for ten years they would then wash their hands of them, and at once transfer them to South Africans who might reasonably be saying: 'Our time limit is up and we must now be allowed to take over the Protectorates.'[53]

Thus although eventual transfer was undoubtedly contemplated and planned, it was not promised, and Britain was wholly uncommitted to a date. Transfer was essentially conditional, and section 151 of the Act, referring to the Schedule, was purely permissive. Its existence in fact made transfer harder. The British government had no desire to precipitate transfer, especially since the Africans themselves were opposed to it. Before transfer could take place, the wishes of the Africans would be 'most carefully considered', although the imperial

---

[52] CO 417/468, 10717, Selborne to Crewe, 8 Mar. 1909.
[53] 5 *PD Lords* 2, 27 Jul. 1909, 762–5, and 3 Aug., 866–70 (Crewe); *Commons* 9, 19 Aug. 1909 (Seely), 1946.

government did not bind itself to obtain their consent; it retained the right of final decision for itself. Parliament, however, would be consulted: important pledges (to be much quoted in the future) to this effect were given in both houses of parliament. British policy might seem to have been cunningly devised to conciliate both parties without conceding fully the wishes of either. It was hoped that white South Africans would be placated by a clear indication that they had the reversionary interest, Africans by the postponement of transfer. Although the Africans were far from convinced that the Schedule could be 'any permanent safeguard' for their interests, it was they, as it turned out, who really had the better cause to be pleased with the settlement.

V

In the perspective of imperial history, refusal to relinquish imperial control of the Territories at the time when Union was established appears, to some extent, as a departure from the policy which might have been expected, and was indeed expected by the African chiefs, and recommended by Selborne. The normal procedure in the past had been gradually to transfer local Africans to self-governing regimes, and grants of self-government had invariably been associated with such transfers. The Cape Colony was made to look after Basutoland in 1871, British Bechuanaland (between the Molopo and Orange rivers) had been transferred to the Cape in 1895, Zululand and Tongaland were transferred to Natal in 1897, and in 1894 Britain had agreed to a Transvaal protectorate over Swaziland. As far as the future was concerned, Africans in Southern Rhodesia were handed over to the new white self-governing regime when it was established in 1923. The case of the Territories in 1909, then, appears exceptional. How did this exception come about? Refusal to hand over the Territories was certainly not the result of South African indifference or ready acquiescence. As Selborne put it, '*kopjes* of Imperial administration jut[ting] out from the middle of the veld of a self-governing South Africa' were an unwelcome reminder to Afrikaners that they still were not complete masters of their subcontinent.[54] Louis Botha badly wanted Swaziland: he had once mentioned possible boycott of the 1906 Transvaal constitution by his party, Het Volk, if its incorporation was denied.[55] In 1907 at the time of the Colonial Conference Botha stated the case very fully in discussion and memorandum. In 1909, in London once more, as prime minister of the Transvaal, he again specially urged the early transfer of Swaziland. Crewe held out no hope of this.[56] In April 1911, this time as prime minister of the Union, Botha notified his conviction that the time had now come for the

[54] CO 417/459, 29921, Selborne to Crewe, 27 Jul. 1908.
[55] *Selections from the Smuts Papers*, vol. II, p. 307, Merriman to Smuts, 6 Dec. 1906.
[56] Confidential Print, *African*, no. 933.

'incorporation' of Swaziland. Smuts had calculated that altogether, between 1890 and 1899, the South African Republic must have spent £493,540 in Swaziland, hoping to secure its future incorporation. Moreover, Botha pleaded,

> a considerable portion of the land in Swaziland belongs to residents in the Transvaal, many of whom continually trek to and fro ... A very determined effort will now be made by the Union government to eradicate stock diseases – and in view of the constant trekking of farmers ... this aspect of the question alone is of the greatest importance and warrants the immediate incorporation of this territory, which is, by its relation, placed in a very different position to other territories adjoining the Union. Swaziland, too, has a fairly large white population which promises to increase rapidly, and from this point of view it also differs considerably from the other native Protectorates.

This overture came to nothing.[57] In 1913, Botha put forward a claim for Bechuanaland, which was decisively rejected. As for his colleague Smuts, he had always believed the case for the immediate transfer of the Territories to be unanswerable, because the Zoutpansberg in the Transvaal had an African population equal to Basutoland's (the Territory with the largest population), and Zululand in Natal had a population which was larger.[58]

The British government, however, turned a deaf ear to Afrikaner logic. Was this out of tactical expediency or respect for obligations and vital principles? Since there was nothing positive to be gained for British material interests either by putting the Territories into the Union or by putting them on ice, the decision to take the latter course may reasonably be said to have been based on trusteeship grounds, on the concern for African interests which emerges in the correspondence quoted above. Humanitarian opinions expressed in the House of Commons had some background influence. Parliamentary and public opinion was not simply ignored: as Lewis Harcourt wrote as colonial secretary, 'we must recognize the exigencies and prejudices of Parliamentary government' and bow to parliamentary opinion; he acknowledged, moreover, that 'so long as Khama is alive, the bare suggestion of handing him over to the Union would bring the whole missionary world and others upon me at once'.[59] We may reasonably postulate a real revival of the trusteeship conscience in informed and ministerial circles in Britain during the years of Liberal government, although the history of missionary concern for Africans in the Territories was long and continuous. Their retention under Colonial Office rule, even temporarily, was – it could be argued – the course least likely to serve British material interests, partly because these predicated total withdrawal as quickly as possible from Africa

---

[57] CO 417/502, 15689, Botha to high commissioner, 21 Apr. 1911; R. Hyam, *The failure of South African expansion 1908–1948* (1972), pp. 82–91.
[58] *Selections from the Smuts Papers*, vol. II, p. 442, Smuts to J. A. Hobson, 13 Jul. 1908.
[59] CO 417/484, 38728, minute, 16 Jan. 1911; B.L. Add. MSS 46000, 210, Harcourt to Herbert Gladstone, 20 Apr. 1913.

south of the Zambesi, and partly because the government did not wish to upset white South Africans if they could avoid it. The British government, in short, reaffirmed a disinterested pro-African policy advocated in 1897 by a former Liberal colonial secretary, Lord Ripon: Britain, he said, should 'let no more natives come under the management of those [South African] Colonies until we have greater security than now exists, as to how they would be treated'.[60]

It would, however, be misleading to end on this note. The basic guiding principles of the government in the transfer of power to South Africa were determined by their hope that 'for geographical and political reasons' there would ultimately be one white South African authority exercising undisputed power from the Cape to the Zambesi. The Liberals made no attempt to challenge Botha's assertion that 'the Union would never be complete until Rhodesia and all the Protectorates had been included'.[61] The Union which was made was a provisional one. And so the Africans in the Territories received a reprieve from settler clutches which eventually enabled them to procure independent regimes in the 1960s. This was certainly not intended in 1909. The vast majority of Africans south of the Zambesi were less fortunate in both the short and the long term. The greater part of a trusteeship obligation was gambled with (not ignored or callously waved aside) in some confidence (which now seems naïve), and not at all lightly – for the sake of imperial power politics and strategic preoccupations. The first priority of the government was a large South African dominion, loyal to the empire, no longer the weakest link in the imperial chain. Nothing was allowed to threaten attainment of this objective. Fortunately, when the Liberals were conceding so much of a free hand to Botha and Smuts within the Union, they could afford to resist Afrikaner demands for the Territories without jeopardising this priority. Africans in the Territories were *not* staked upon a calculated risk, but the numbers involved were relatively small. The government's policy for the Territories was thus a salve to their consciences and a partial answer to their critics in circumstances where larger numbers were involved; it pleased British parliamentary opinion; it was a real but marginal dividend of trusteeship the value of which only became clear in the resistance to the overtures to secure transfer made by Hertzog in the 1920s and 1930s, and then by all South African prime ministers down to 1961.

Afterword

As the earliest of the studies in this book to take published form (*Historical Journal*, vol. 13, 1970), this chapter has been revised, with some additional material and technical tidying-up. However, the footnotes (though sometimes

[60] Asquith papers, 9, 94–5, Ripon to Asquith, 29 Dec. 1897.
[61] B.L. Add. MSS 46007, 174, Botha to Herbert Gladstone, 7 Nov. 1913.

amplified) have not been re-numbered, nor the argument modified. The article has been subjected to reconsideration by David Torrance in 'Britain, South Africa and the High Commission Territories: an old controversy revisited' (*Historical Journal*, vol. 41, 1998, pp. 751–72). Torrance's principal claim to revisionism is that he has had access to the papers of Lord Selborne, the high commissioner. However, all Selborne's despatches were available in the Public Record Office for the original article, together with the most important of Selborne's letters, in the papers of the colonial secretary, Lord Elgin. And so, in practice, Torrance's revision hinges more on re-interpretation than new material.

Torrance *is* persuaded that the decision to withhold the Territories from the Union at the outset was determined not by Selborne but by Crewe and the Liberal government in London, and that the centrality of trusteeship considerations cannot be denied, given that ministers were indeed deeply mindful of African interests. He accepts the correctness of the factual contentions, but seeks to qualify the argument with two broad modifications. The first is that whilst he acknowledges the way in which the decision proved to be of critical importance to the Africans concerned, he believes the transfer issue was not as central as it later became; in the circumstances of the time what appeared to be more significant were the terms of transfer set out in the schedule. And this schedule was primarily the work of Selborne. Though not without a touch of old-fashioned paternalism, Selborne's proposals 'display a modern enthusiasm for bureaucratic state building'. Secondly, Torrance suggests that although the article recognised the salience of the African factor, the impact of African pressure (bypassing the high commissioner) was understated, when in fact it was both effective and influential.

On the first point, it is certainly reasonable to argue that Hyam approached the whole question too much from the perspective of Liberal ministers, coloured by their adverse perceptions of Selborne, and to that extent might have been unfair to Selborne. As against that, however, Torrance makes excessive claims for Selborne's 'exuberance' as 'an enthusiastic proponent of material progress', with a commitment to 'capital accumulation', and the economic development of the Rand as his foremost objective. He even manages to find in him that elusive Cain and Hopkins archetype, 'a gentleman and a capitalist' (D. E. Torrance, *The strange death of the Liberal empire: Lord Selborne in South Africa*, Liverpool, 1996, pp. 191–5). Such a picture is hard to square with the Selborne who had been First Lord of the Admiralty for five years (1900–5), or the disciple of Milner for whom economic development was essentially a means to a political or geopolitical end (D. George Boyce, ed., *The crisis of British power: the imperial and naval papers of the Second Earl of Selborne, 1895–1910*, London, 1990).

On the second point, it is perfectly possible that the article/chapter underestimates African effectiveness. But much depends on how historians evaluate public opinion. In *general*, our view is that government tends to be disdainful of pressure: remember how later British governments persisted in their predetermined South African policy almost regardless of anti-apartheid protests. In this *particular* case, however, the dispute comes back to the position of Selborne in his role of 'high-commissioner-as-intermediary', at the point of 'proconsular interlock'. What Africans needed was a high commissioner who could 'scale up' indigenous pressures, and Selborne was unable to do this, perhaps even unwilling to do it. Pressure which bypassed him was never going to be an adequate substitute. (See J. Benyon, *Proconsul and paramountcy in South Africa: the High Commission*, Pietermaritzburg, 1980, pp. 312–15.) A close study of the principal metropolitan South African pressure-group of the day has failed to uncover much in the way of a positive role, beyond usefully buttressing the sympathetic approach of colonial secretaries Elgin and Crewe, who were not in need of persuading. (D. R. Edgecombe, 'The influence of the Aborigines Protection Society on British policy towards Black African and Cape Coloured affairs in South Africa, 1886–1910', unpublished Cambridge PhD thesis, 1976.)

In the course of his wider re-examination of Hyam's approach to this question, Torrance argues that the concept embodied in the title *The failure of South African expansion* promotes the wrong emphasis. The *reverse* (obverse?) side of the coin, he concedes, may well be true: namely, that Britain was successful, to the extent that it wanted, in containing South African expansion. Torrance then goes on to suggest – following Jonathan Crush, *The struggle for Swazi labour, 1890–1920* (Kingston, 1987) – that the underlying truth, at least as far as Swaziland is concerned, is that South Africa achieved exactly what it wanted: in the economic sphere, a client state acting as a labour reserve for South African industry. Here again, interpretation boils down to what is seen as more significant: the political or the economic circumstances under which people live. It is, however, a false distinction. Both are important, but it is simplistic to give precedence to economic factors. Labour reservists they might have been, but it was still beneficial for Swazi self-esteem *not* to be part of the Union. Moreover, Swaziland was surely better off as an internationally recognised state than as a Bantustan, especially in terms of its access to overseas markets and to foreign development assistance, both before and after independence. The economic improvements in Swaziland as a 'late colonial state' from the mid-1950s were impressive. (R. Hyam and Wm Roger Louis, eds., *The Conservative government and the end of empire, 1957–1964* (British Documents on the End of Empire, 2000), pt I, p. lxiii, pt II, document nos. 310, 311, 323–6).

5 'Greater South Africa': the struggle for the High Commission Territories, 1910–1961

The Union of South Africa Act had the effect of uniting South Africa but of dividing southern Africa. The partitioning of the whole area, with imperial responsibility retained in the Rhodesias and Nyasaland, and in the High Commission Territories of Basutoland, Bechuanaland, and Swaziland, was not intended to be a permanent arrangement. The Union as formed was expressly regarded both in London and Pretoria as a provisional union. The Act of 1909 laid down a procedure for the incorporation of Rhodesia, and the Schedule prescribed the terms for a possible future transfer of administration in the High Commission Territories. However, the expectations of 1908–10 were not realised, and the formal political expansion of the Union in southern Africa did not materialise.

I

Perhaps the fundamental reason for this 'unconsummated Union' was determined in 1908. The British government's decision to retain control of the High Commission Territories after Union meant that the first setback to dreams of a Greater South Africa were registered even before the Union came into being. This important decision conflicted with the known wishes of the white South African leaders. The general strategy of the British government in 1908–9 was well expressed by Winston Churchill, who had just moved from the Colonial Office to the Board of Trade. He wrote to the colonial secretary, Lord Crewe:

The only securities which the natives have are first of all our power to delay by a variety of methods the handing over of the Protectorates. I have always been in favour of this Fabius Cunctator Game as simple, obvious, safe and practical: and I am still . . . We should assert our intention to hand over the Protectorates, should frame in general terms the necessary adhesion or inclusion clauses – the more S.A. will swallow the better for

---

This chapter has its origin in an invitation from Professor O. Geyser to contribute to the inaugural number of the *Joernaal vir die Eietydse Geskiedenis* published by the Institute for Contemporary History, Bloemfontein (1974). It is based upon R. Hyam, *The failure of South African expansion, 1908–1948* (1972), hereafter cited as *FSAE*. Since the book was published, both the Earl of Crewe Papers and the Smuts Papers have become available in the University Library, Cambridge (the latter on microfilm), and account has been taken of this newer material in preparing this chapter.

'Greater South Africa'   103

House of Commons – and should then play steadily for time with all the cards in our hand. There is only one way to steer this question through that assembly . . . Confront parliament with a complete scheme – majestic, beneficent, far-reaching. Prove to them that you have done your best for the native. Console them by assurances that you have no immediate intention of handing over the Protectorates – on the contrary that you intend to wait and watch. Invite them to ratify or reject – and they will acclaim your settlement.[1]

Crewe did not wish to seem to be applying pressure to the South African governments, but he insisted absolutely on dealing with the High Commission Territories before the Union was created. He did not share Churchill's view of letting the South Africans settle everything for themselves 'for good or ill in South Africa for South Africa'. He agreed with Sir Francis Hopwood, permanent under-secretary of the Colonial Office: 'It would be pleasant to allow them to go their own way but there are obvious reasons why they must treat with us for our own.'[2] Pre-eminently these reasons involved meeting some pressure upon the government to do something for African interests, a pressure which coincided with their own predilections. Thus, during the passage of the Union bill through parliament, the government gave pledges (which proved to be central to subsequent discussion) that both Africans and the British parliament would be consulted before transfer took place. But if British concern was with trusteeship, South African policy was much more self-interested.

Smuts repeatedly from 1895 declared for South African expansion – doubling the area to form a united state stretching from Simon's Town to the Zambesi and possibly to the Equator, and including South-West Africa and at least southern Mozambique. With Rhodesia, Mozambique, and the High Commission Territories absorbed, Pretoria would be the true geographical capital of a Greater South Africa. Smuts was thus an expansionist, an empire-builder, on the grandest scale: 'I like to browse on hopes for the future', he wrote, after six weeks' motoring in Central Africa in 1930. But dreams were matched by some large-scale concrete proposals. His territorial designs on South-West Africa and Mozambique need to be emphasised. These will not, however, be discussed here (since this is a study in Commonwealth relations), but they form an essential part of the context of his plans for imperially controlled British territory. Although immediate objectives were bounded by the Zambesi, Smuts also looked beyond it to an economic and political hegemony in the equatorial north, which nature linked to South Africa by what he called a 'broad backbone' of mountainous plateau. This euphoric geopolitical interpretation of the map led him to take a great interest in Kenya and Tanganyika in the 1920s.

---

[1] See chapter 4 above; Crewe papers, C/7, 7, W. S. Churchill to Crewe, 3 Jan. 1909.
[2] Crewe papers, C/47, F. Hopwood to Crewe, 29 Dec. 1908, and C/26, Crewe to Sir W. Hely-Hutchinson, 17 Oct. 1908 (copy).

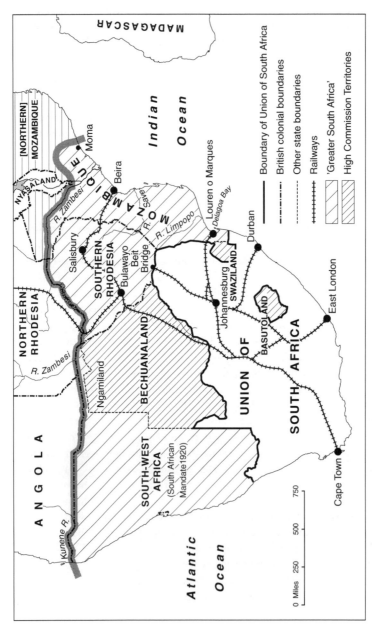

Map 5.1 Plans for a 'Greater South Africa'. The heavy northern line represents the limit of Smuts's abortive 'immediate' aim from 1916 to 1919, with a plan to remove Portugal from southern Mozambique (with possible compensation in south-east Tanganyika), either at Moma, or at the exit of the Zambesi (or alternatively at the exit of the Save, with Southern Rhodesia taking the area between the two rivers and the port of Beira). *Source*: S. E. Katzenellenbogen, *South Africa and Southern Mozambique* (1982), p. 123, 'Smuts's expansionist aims'.

He refused to accept 'the stupid [1930] White Paper on paramountcy' of African interests in East Africa. He was impressed by the settlers: they were, he wrote, of an 'extraordinarily good type'. He was anxious to help East Africa in every way he could. In 1922 he sent a small delegation to examine the region from a commercial point of view, 'to see how we can assist its development and at the same time help our own industries'. He also sent two senior officials for East African railways. In 1928 he wrote to Philip Kerr:

If sufficient land is reserved for elbow-room for white expansion and civilisation on this continent, we may have the makings of something very big in future south of the Equator. There is land enough for white and black, but I am afraid that with the somewhat negrophilistic temper which is about today, due regard will not be given to these larger points of view, and to the necessity of keeping the widest door possible open for the future white settlement over all the highlands of South Africa.

In 1924 he sent E. F. C. Lane to look around Kenya and bring him first-hand information. There was a danger, he thought, of its becoming 'a purely Native state' with an Indian trading aristocracy in charge. Yet the whole area could, he believed, 'be made into a great European state or system of states during the next three or four generations':

It is one of the richest parts of the world and only wants white brains and capital to become enormously productive. But the present tendencies seem all in favour of the Native and the Indian, and the danger is that one of the greatest chances in our history will be missed. The cry should be 'the highlands for the whites' and a resolute white policy should be pursued. The fruits of such a policy will be a white state in time more important than Australia . . . a chain of white states which will in the end become one from the Union to Kenya.

Looking then, to 'grandiose dreams' of creating 'one of the greatest future Dominions of the Empire', which would take 'a high place with Canada and Australia', Smuts was constantly working upon L. S. Amery as the man who might give a lead in Britain to this project, perhaps the 'next great phase of Empire development'. Amery was not uninterested. He agreed that South Africa should keep the development of the eastern plateau in view, because whatever the future arrangements of those states, 'the interest of each part in its neighbours will grow increasingly stronger', especially as air communications developed.[3]

To turn from plans to proposals: Smuts worked hard to bring Southern Rhodesia into the Union in 1921, and continually involved himself in negotiations for

---

[3] J. C. Smuts, *Greater South African plans for a better world: speeches* (1940); W. K. Hancock and J. van der Poel, eds., *Selections from the Smuts Papers*, vol. V: *1919–1934* (1973), pp. 170, 237–9 (Smuts to L. S. Amery, 20 Nov. 1924), and pp. 251, 347–8, 380–1, 506; Smuts papers (microfilm), vol. 22, no. 271, vol. 37, no. 8 (L. S. Amery to Smuts, 30 Mar. 1927), and vol. 40, no. 177 (to P. Kerr, 23 May 1928); W. K. Hancock, *Smuts*, vol. II: *The fields of force, 1919–1950* (1968), pp. 223–9.

the transfer of High Commission Territories. These efforts failed. It is apparently necessary to justify the telling of this story at all. The neo-Marxist revisionist historians have attacked the very concept of a 'failure of South African expansion', of its drive for political and territorial extension between 1908 and 1961. Being primarily concerned to uncover the roots of the white supremacist system, it is a theme which holds only marginal interest for them. What really mattered, they say, was the success of informal economic and cultural influence in southern and Central Africa, especially after 1961: and therefore that the real history of the earlier period ought to hinge upon tracing the crucial origins of that success story. Now whilst we do not deny that uncovering the origins of these informal ties is indeed an important exercise, the fact still remains that what South Africans *at the time* wanted, and primarily sought during the period down to the end of the 1950s, was formal political control of neighbouring territories, and that they failed to achieve this. Although Smuts was in a far-sighted way trying to explore an alternative method, this should in no way detract from the historical importance of studying the abortive diplomatic negotiations for a Greater South Africa, and of exploring the containment of her political ambitions by the imperial power. 'Status' and 'prestige' should not be dismissed merely as elitist abstractions or 'quasi-psychological' explanations.[4]

II

For fifty years there were nearly continuous unofficial discussions between the Union and British governments about the possibility of transferring the three High Commission Territories. The only breaks were between 1914 and 1918 and 1940 and 1949, as a result of war, together with a gap from 1927 to 1932 as a result of L. S. Amery's insistence on postponement for a while. Every South African premier from Botha to Strijdom initiated informal discussions. Despite misunderstandings and the National Party's electoral propaganda in the 1929 election, there is no reason to suppose that Hertzog was much less interested in some sort of South African expansion than Smuts was; indeed he moved with extraordinary speed to start discussions after becoming prime minister in 1924, and the strategy of northward influence worked out by his lieutenant Oswald Pirow bore strong resemblances to the views of Smuts and Hofmeyr.[5] Unlike

---

[4] See reviews of *FSAE* by M. Legassick in *African Affairs* vol. 72 (1973), pp. 458–9, and S. Marks in *History* vol. 59 (1974), pp. 313–14; for alternative (and less ideologically blinkered) assessments, see C. W. de Kiewiet in *Journal of Modern African Studies* vol. 12 (1974), pp. 512–13; J. E. Spence in *JAH* vol. 14 (1973), pp. 522–3; A. Sillery in *English Historical Review* vol. 89 (1974), p. 464; and T. R. H. Davenport, in *SAHJ* no. 5 (1973). From an Afrikaner perspective, the book inevitably appeared to be flawed by bias and outspokenness: J. L. Hattingh and H. O. Terblanche, 'Suid-Afrikaanse kroniek, 1971–1972', *SAHJ* no. 9 (1977), p. 92.

[5] See *FSAE*, pp. 37–40; O. Pirow, 'How far is the Union interested in the continent of Africa?' *Journal of the Royal African Society* vol. 144 (1937), pp. 317–20: J. H. Hofmeyr, *South Africa* (1931), chs. x and xiv.

Smuts, who thought expansion might be undertaken as part of an imperially agreed plan, Hertzog insisted on it as an act of indemnity. But although they had motives which sometimes differed, and they might disagree about timing, their fundamental objectives were not dissimilar. The most spectacular of the South African overtures was made by Smuts alone just after war broke out in 1939, when in order to strengthen his hand against the Nationalists, he mistakenly tried to take advantage of Britain's supposed preoccupation with the war in order to prise at least one of the High Commission Territories out of its control. He hoped that faced with a demand for all three Territories, Britain might transfer Swaziland as a compromise. He met with a sharp and displeased rebuff. The British government made it clear to him that they could make no such bargain:

It would be a grave mistake to underrate the public interest in this matter at the present time. Nothing could make a worse impression than if we were to appear to hand over these Territories in time of war when we were fighting for the interests of small nations.[6]

Britain was caught between its intentions, constitutionally provided for, to transfer, and the pledge not to do so without paying some attention to African wishes, which were plainly hostile throughout. In this situation it was able to take refuge in the doctrine of the Unripe Time and, from 1933, to point to a strong (though not unanimous) body of public opinion in England as evidence of this. Margery Perham led opposition to transfer; Lionel Curtis and *The Round Table* disagreed with her. Nor was British official opinion of one mind. Two high commissioners, Lord Gladstone in 1913 and Lord Harlech in 1943, were ready to negotiate a deal with the South Africans, and Sir William Clark was tending towards that conclusion in 1940, at least in respect of Swaziland. On the other hand, high commissioners Lord Buxton (1914–20), Lord Athlone (1924–30), Sir Herbert Stanley (1931–5), and Sir Evelyn Baring (1944–51) took their stand on delay. Secretaries of state Lord Milner, L. S. Amery, and Malcolm MacDonald were inclined to be more sympathetic towards Union policies than Lewis Harcourt and J. H. Thomas. But one of the most interesting conclusions to emerge from the British archives is that the permanent officials of the Colonial and Dominions Offices upheld trusteeship doctrines and were consistently opposed to taking any initiative to alter the *status quo* in the control of the Territories. The most they were ever prepared to consider was an experimental transfer of Swaziland, but they were less willing to entertain even that compromise after 1925. Thus, as South African irritation and pressure mounted in the 1930s, the lines were all set to make this question a major problem of Commonwealth relations. It became exceedingly troublesome to British politicians, second only to Ireland as the major Dominions Office headache in

---

[6] DO 35/903, no. 352; *FSAE*, pp. 163 ff.

Commonwealth affairs, and second to none in its intractability. The peak of discussions was reached in 1935–7, by which time references to the British Cabinet had become frequent.

The reasons for this South African pressure arose out of desire for land, concern about administrative convenience, and above all considerations of status. The attraction of the Territories, particularly Swaziland's pastures, for land-hungry South African farmers is obvious. But there was also interest in the north of Bechuanaland, where it was hoped Ngamiland might, through irrigation, be able to support a large surplus population from the Union. In the House of Assembly in 1946, Mr J. M. Conradie outlined 'very great possibilities' if they could incorporate Bechuanaland: 'We could then develop the waters of the mighty Okovango River and, as it were, create a new province of South Africa out of the desert-like Kalahari.'[7] But there were fears also. Increasing alarm was felt about soil erosion caused by rivers. There was worry lest Basutoland should be half washed away before South Africa could acquire it. Farmers in border districts were also alarmed about stock diseases: Mr P. J. du Plessis MP called Bechuanaland a 'hot-house hatchery of disease and vermin' in 1934.[8] Other reasons were advanced too, such as the necessity of comprehensive planning of native policy and land legislation in 1913, and again after the Tomlinson Report of 1955 [1956] – which assumed the incorporation of the three Territories (see map 5.2) – or the implications of railway development in the early 1920s, or the hopes of speculative mining concerns in the 1930s, or problems of strategic defence from the 1950s. All of these interests were advanced to justify South African demands. Yet, essentially, South African interest in the Territories was more political than economic, and much more than the desire to make the desert rejoice and blossom like a rose. Prestige loomed prominently throughout. Deep-seated within this motive there was a historic grievance about British imperial presence in southern Africa. It was openly admitted that the Territories would be an economic burden, but the 'manifest absurdity' and humiliation of their being administered from London rankled with the Nationalists, who saw this continuing British presence as a possible obstacle to the attainment of a republic. The chief interest was thus negative: not so much a positive desire for the Territories, as a determination to get rid of an intolerable reminder that the Nationalists were still not entirely masters in their subcontinent. Eventually prestige became tied up with the question in another form. By 1939 South African ministers were clearly smarting under the realisation that Britain thought them incapable of a humane native policy. William Clark (high commissioner 1935–40) observed: 'The Territories are not a vital concern to them except in so far as refusal to hand over becomes part

---

[7] South Africa, *House of Assembly Debates*, vol. 56, cc. 4000–4001, 21 Mar. 1946.
[8] South Africa, *House of Assembly Debates*, vol. 23, c. 2757, 25 Apr. 1934.

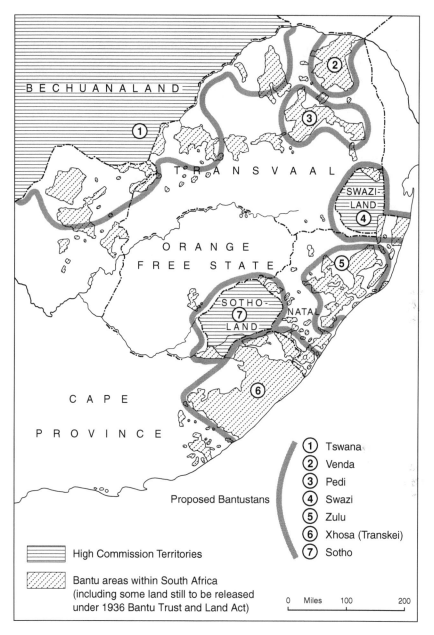

Map 5.2 The Tomlinson Commission's threat to the High Commission Territories and the creation of Bantustans, 1955. *Source*: Tomlinson Commission, *Summary of the report* (Pretoria, 1955), map 63. The Tomlinson Report was completed in 1954. The *Summary* was printed and dated in 1955, but not published until 1956. The maps were then dated 1956.

of the British attitude of reprobation on Union native policy generally, about which they are extremely sensitive.'[9]

What caused the British government to seek to hold up implementation of the intentions of 1910? The turning-point was in the early 1920s. Up till that moment Smuts's Greater South Africa policy was viewed sympathetically by the British government. Britain found Smuts's local war aims by no means incompatible with her own, and would have been happy to see him realise his surprisingly large territorial objectives in South-West Africa and Mozambique.[10] The British government's bias was 'a little in favour' of Rhodesia's joining the Union in the 1921 Referendum: but it wished to keep its options open, despite pressure from Smuts for a clearer British lead.[11] Ministers were seriously prepared to consider transferring the administration of Swaziland to Smuts. But this favourable disposition was altered by two events: the Rhodesian decision to run its own internally responsible self-government, and the accession to power of Hertzog in 1924.

The Rhodesian decision altered the whole prospect of British planning in southern and Central Africa. From the imperial point of view, Rhodesia's function was to act as a counterpoise to Afrikanerdom, preferably inside the Union, but if not, then outside it. The decision cast doubt upon the future of the High Commission Territories. The Union's terms of incorporation for Rhodesia involved the purchase of railways through Bechuanaland and the acquisition of British South Africa Company rights there. Acceptance must have made the transfer of Bechuanaland a matter of practical politics. The Rhodesian decision to stay outside the Union meant that the chief ground for assuming the inevitable destiny of Bechuanaland must be transfer to the Union disappeared. By 1931 the high commissioner (Stanley) was writing:

it seems to me quite essential, on grounds of high policy, that we should hold on to the Bechuanaland Protectorate. The Protectorate may very likely become the key to a satisfactory solution of the problem of building up a strong British state or group of states in Central Africa.[12]

The configurations of a possible future Central African Federation were only vaguely perceived, but Southern Rhodesia laid claim to at least part of Bechuanaland, and British policy-makers felt they could not make plans without

---

[9] DO 35/901, no. 58, Clark to E. G. Machtig, 24 July 1937; *FSAE*, p. 75.
[10] Earl Buxton papers (Newtimber Place, Hassocks, Sussex) and Lewis Harcourt papers (Bodleian Library, Oxford), correspondence between Buxton and Harcourt, Sept. 1914 to May 1915; and Buxton to Lord Milner, 10 July 1919. See also S. E. Katzenellenbogen, *South Africa and Southern Mozambique: labour, railways and trade in the making of a relationship* (Manchester, 1982); and W. G. Martin, 'South versus Southern Africa in the inter-war period', *JSAS*, vol. 16 (1990), pp. 112–38; P. G. Eidelberg, 'The breakdown of the 1922 Lourenço Marques port and railway negotiations', *SAHJ* no. 8 (1976), pp. 104–18.
[11] CAB 23/27; *FSAE*, pp. 64–5. [12] DO 35/392, 9 Dec. 1931; *FSAE*, p. 132.

allowing for this aspiration, and were increasingly glad of an excuse to move Bechuanaland gradually out of the South African orbit.

On the South African side, the Rhodesian decision was a great disappointment to Smuts. His desire to incorporate it has to be seen in the wider context of plans for South Africa's northern expansion. Sir Lewis Michell, resident director of the British South Africa Company, wrote to the Company president, Lyttelton Gell, as follow:

Between ourselves his ambitions are not small. He desires to freeze out Portugal and with our railways in his hands he would have a great pull. The disappearance of the Imperial factor is part of his scheme.

Smuts himself described the Rhodesian decision as 'a mistake . . . made in a fit of local patriotism'. Rhodesia had 'gone wrong' and it was 'a great blow' to him, although he realised that in seeking through its incorporation to 'round off the South African state with borders far flung into the heart of this continent', he was probably trying to move too fast. If Rhodesia had come in, he felt that he could immediately have manipulated Mozambique and Nyasaland to his grand design:

I confess the result is a great disappointment as there were even bigger issues at stake than the incorporation of Rhodesia in the Union.

We should have had no difficulty in dealing with the Portuguese over Delagoa Bay if the result in Rhodesia had been in our favour, because they would have seen that with the Union in possession of Beira, it would be folly to stand out about Delagoa Bay.

At the time, Smuts was negotiating with Lisbon about the running of the Lourenço Marques docks, a section of which he wanted to place under Union government management. He also hoped to extend the influence of the Union to Nyasaland through the agency of the Nyasaland Company. This would have added, he thought, 'immensely to the importance of South Africa as a market'. A 'favourable' decision in Rhodesia would have meant, he wrote, 'a tremendous thing in the development of Southern Africa'.[13] It would also have given him a bridge to the north – he was watching developments in Kenya closely. The continuing difficulty of getting a foothold at Lourenço Marques meant that Smuts's immediate interest in Swaziland, and a railway through it from the coalfields of the eastern Transvaal, was diminished. Whilst he continued to regard the adhesion of Rhodesia as eventually inevitable, he made no further positive efforts to forward it, being content to leave it to natural processes. The Rhodesians must in the end surely see their community of interest with South Africa, for their

---

[13] *Selections from the Smuts Papers*, vol. V, pp. 136, 151–4; Smuts papers, vol. 22, no. 271, Smuts to F. Holt, 20 Nov. 1922, and no. 272, to A. Hunt, 20 Nov. 1922.

position was ultimately untenable, and 'in the long run this subcontinent has only one destiny, and it may be delayed, but cannot be prevented'.[14]

Only three years after the Rhodesian decision, Smuts fell from power. In retrospect the 1924 election can be seen as a major, perhaps crucial, turning-point. If Smuts had won that election, a transfer of Swaziland might well have followed. But the British did not trust Hertzog and had no 'special relationship' with him. He was entrenched in power for fifteen years, and his promotion of Afrikaner Nationalist objectives was distasteful to the British government. The British increasingly found his approach to negotiations about the Territories petulant, humourless, ill-informed, and blundering. His lack of diplomatic finesse, and disposition to introduce a note of acrimonious wrangling, together with his inaccurate public statements, press leakages, and misrepresentations, were ruinous to the presentation of the South African case, as Smuts himself was well aware. His domestic policy – new flag, 'native' bills, Havenga's search for a more independent economic policy, and Afrikanerisation of the civil service – also made the British government less willing to meet South African demands. Hertzog's government did not seem to be maintaining the spirit of Union as understood in 1910. If South Africa moved further away from Britain, was it reasonable, Britain argued, that she should exert herself to meet South African wishes on the Territories? In fact, Hertzog's policy tended to promote a reassertion of the imperial factor as the shortest cut to the old goal of a great *British* South Africa – through the strengthening of Southern Rhodesia and the maintenance of imperial control in the Territories. Capt. Bede Clifford (imperial secretary and representative of the British government in South Africa from 1924 to 1931) argued that since Britain's hold on South Africa was weakening, and as the Nationalists looked more and more to 'independence', Britain should dig her heels into every foothold and nurse all 'the meagre "interests" we still possess'. Of these the Africans were important as 'one of our biggest allies in the country'. Everything possible should be done to retain their loyalty and confidence, 'as a buffer against the process of secession by attrition which is going on now'. When the Territories went, he added, direct imperial interest in South Africa would cease, and 'an important bridgehead' would be lost.[15] These views were powerfully taken up by L. S. Amery as Dominions secretary. In 1927 he concluded that

---

[14] *Selections from the Smuts Papers*, vol. V, pp. 136–54, and vol. VI: *1934–1945* (1973), p. 41; Smuts Papers, vol. 95, no. 164, Smuts to Sir E. Guest, 2 Mar. 1950. See generally on the Rhodesian decision, *FSAE*, ch. 3; P. R. Warhurst, 'Rhodesian–South African relations, 1900–1923', *SAHJ*, no. 3 (1971), pp. 93–108; M. L. Chanock, *Unconsummated Union: Britain, Rhodesia and South Africa, 1900–1945* (Manchester, 1977); Hancock, *Smuts*, vol. II, p. 154; see also M. A. G. Davies, *Incorporation in the Union of South Africa or self-government? Southern Rhodesia's choice, 1922* (University of South Africa, communication C.58, Pretoria, 1965), pp. 36–56.

[15] DO 9/1, no. 3717, and DO 9/4, no. 2508, Bede Clifford to C. T. Davies, 18 and 26 Mar. 1926; *FSAE*, p. 116.

the Protectorates are an undeveloped asset of the first importance . . . The more we do for the development of the Protectorates the greater the prize that is dangled before the eyes of the Union and the greater the influence in keeping the Union straight.

The key to his whole policy was to delay transfer in order to build up British settlement in Swaziland, making it 'effectively British before it goes into the Union'. He saw in the Territories a 'by no means negligible opportunity for influencing the future political development of South Africa as a whole'. His view was cogently argued, even if it did not allow sufficiently for the difficulty of persuading fresh settlers into the area:

In the present close balance of forces making for Imperial unity in South Africa, and those which would keep South Africa in sentiment and action, if not formally, outside the Empire, . . . to create . . . centres of progress and British sentiment east and west of the Transvaal in Swaziland and in such parts of Bechuanaland as may be available to white settlement, . . . is something that may still make a very valuable contribution to the whole future of South Africa.

A policy of elevating the Africans in the Territories might provide 'a potent influence in shaping South African native policy on sounder lines', thereby enabling Britain to 'give a lead to the whole of South Africa as well as help to keep the British uppermost'.[16]

Amery achieved a delay, but five years later Hertzog began to renew his challenge. The Dominions Office worked out a three-point policy: it sought to postpone transfer again, to find a compensating conciliatory political gesture (a *détente* achieved in the conclusion of the Hertzog–Thomas concordat of 1935), together with means of diminishing through co-operation the risk of South African economic pressure on the Territories. This policy was successful, partly because Hertzog's ineptitude played into British hands.

III

Britain's continuing desire to temporise on transfer stemmed mainly from an unwillingness to withdraw the imperial factor in the face of the growth of the Afrikaner national movement. As de Kiewiet observes, 'it was not that those in Downing Street loved the natives more, but that they loved the Afrikaners less'. Britain did, however, also increasingly come to respect African opposition to transfer. This opposition had been consistently maintained from 1908, and from the early thirties it was given focus by the able exertions of Tshekedi Khama of Bechuanaland. The Basutoland National Council also periodically reiterated its

---

[16] DO 9/8, no. 10918, L. S. Amery to S. Baldwin, 24 Sept. 1927; DO 9/8, no. 10867, memo by Amery, 5 Oct. 1927; *FSAE*, pp. 119–21.

opposition.[17] The attitude of King Sobhuza in Swaziland was apparently more equivocal, particularly in 1937–9, since his country (with two-thirds of the land alienated to Europeans) had less to lose, and possibly something to gain, by coming under South African administration on agreed terms. But the opinion of the African masses everywhere was strongly against transfer, disliking the obvious trend of Union policy, and especially being influenced by the Natives Land Act of 1913, and by fear of a republic. From 1933 public opinion in Britain became more vocal on the African side. This opinion weighed with successive British governments because it cut across normal party lines: the Left mistrusted Union native policy and the Right disliked handing over any territory. The passing of the Statute of Westminster had some bearing on this renewed public interest in the Territories, because it was realised that, as a result, the Schedule to the South Africa Act could no longer be relied upon as a legal safeguard. The most that could be hoped for was that the South African government would continue to regard it as morally binding. Nevertheless the relevance of Union native policy was thought to be greatly increased for the Territories.

At the same time even J. H. Thomas (Dominions secretary 1930–5) realised the stern political implications of the problem:

I do not disguise ... my absolute horror of handing over any natives to the Union unless there is a radical change in the South African policy towards the native ... but ... whatever may be the future, except with the goodwill and co-operation of South Africa we shall never make a success of it.

Therefore, he concluded (this was in 1934) that it was in the best interests of Britain and of the Africans to carry the South African government 'with us rather than antagonise them'. It was in this cautious spirit that he arranged the 1935 concordat with Hertzog under which the two governments tried to work more closely together in the administration of the Territories.[18]

There was also a basic restraint in the presentation of the South African case. In many ways, of course, it was expedient to allow the *status quo* to continue, since South Africa reaped the advantages of an informal control without its costs and liabilities, especially that of ruling unwilling African populations. Moreover, they were also reluctant to risk a head-on clash with the British government. This consideration weighed heavily with Smuts (but was not confined to him). Smuts wrote to Amery in 1937:

---

[17] Lesotho Government Archives (Maseru), S 3/20/1/1–50, Proceedings of the Basutoland National Council, 1908–1958, *passim*; De Kiewiet in *Journal of Modern African Studies*, vol. 12, p. 513.

[18] DO 35/393, no. 192; also DO 35/904 (1939–1940), nos. 356 and 358; J. E. Spence, 'British policy towards the High Commission Territories', *Journal of Modern African Studies* vol. 2 (1964), pp. 221–46; Cmd 8707: *Basutoland, the Bechuanaland Protectorate and Swaziland: a history of discussions with the Union of South Africa, 1909–1939* (HMSO, 1952), pp. 59–63.

Relations between us and Great Britain are very good, but there is this small fly in the ointment, and the sooner it is got rid of the better. As a wholehearted supporter of what is called the British connection, I take a very grave view of this matter, which, however trifling in itself, may yet become an occasion and the cause of very far-reaching misunderstandings . . . this apparently small issue may very soon become one of first-class importance.[19]

Smuts had been advised by Sir Roderick Jones of Reuters that if friction was to be avoided, South Africa must approach the question with the 'utmost caution and moderation', with patient and reasoned arguments temperately and judicially presented; he pointed out that British opinion regarded the Territories as more a moral responsibility than as a territorial question; that Exeter Hall sentiments were not dead in a substantial and politically very potent section of British opinion, and that unless this opinion was handled with the utmost circumspection there might easily arise 'a red-hot controversy' between Britain and the Union, dangerous to the whole imperial relationship generally. The problem, he concluded, undoubtedly did contain the seeds of mischief, and he was 'burningly anxious' to see South Africa present her case so as to 'disarm, and perhaps win over, the critics and opponents of Transfer'.[20] Smuts needed little persuading to such tactics. He believed that it was not only valuable for South Africa to have Commonwealth friendship, but also for the good of the world that the empire should hold together and provide a solid nucleus in a fluid and chaotic international situation. His sudden and rather rash attempt to persuade Britain into a transfer in October 1939 is not really inconsistent with this wider consideration, since he appears to have felt that a transfer would greatly strengthen his hands domestically, by cutting the ground from under the feet of his Nationalist opponents, who were increasingly looking towards a republic, and who could argue Britain's recalcitrance over the Territories as a cogent reason for seeking it. Furthermore, he became genuinely convinced that unless *something* was done, a serious 'running sore' would develop between the two governments.[21] In addition, he was always attracted by the prospects of informal economic expansion to the north. In 1942–3 he was working on a plan for 'squaring a pan-African policy' (embracing states right up to the Equator, including the Portuguese colonies and the Belgian and French Congos) 'with the linking up of British territories in any form of closer union they may desire': they 'may yet be in the net . . . After all, the days for these pygmy units are passed' – Hitler proved that. But it seemed impossible to make his countrymen grasp this 'prospect of future expansion and security'. Strongly advocating 'a policy of friendship and political rapprochement with the young British states

---

[19] *Selections from the Smuts Papers*, vol. VI, p. 113, Smuts to Amery, 9 Dec. 1937.
[20] Smuts papers, vol. 53, no. 90, Sir Roderick Jones to Smuts, 3 Apr. 1935.
[21] *FSAE*, ch. 7; Smuts papers, vol. 55, no. 148, Smuts to Amery, 20 Aug. 1937; *Selections from the Smuts Papers*, vol. VI, p. 195, Smuts to Amery, 11 Oct. 1939.

to our north which are our real industrial and political hinterland', it was increasingly an aim with him to coax them 'as junior members of the family' into partnership with a dominant South Africa.[22] This policy also prompted the necessity of keeping on good terms with Britain.

By the 1940s, however, official British dislike of Afrikaner National Party policies was generally so great that British policy-makers were reluctant to conciliate South Africa over the Territories, as they felt unable to trust any government which might supersede Smuts's. Moreover, their sense of obligation to the Africans was now so strong that, as Baring put it in 1945, despite the increasing strategic imperial importance of South Africa, 'we should never sacrifice the true interests of Africans to a desire to remain friendly with a United Party Government at Pretoria'.[23] Britain was even less likely to sacrifice these interests to a National Party government. Thus, when Smuts lost the 1948 election to Malan, the vestigial hope of a negotiated transfer of any of the Territories finally disappeared. In winning the election the Nationalists ensured the defeat of South African formal territorial expansion. The continuing British refusal of transfer thereafter was no mere procrastination (though it was good politics for Britain to make it seem to be so), but part of a renewed positive policy of containing Afrikanerdom, of which the setting up of the Central African Federation was but another aspect. The defeat of Smuts thus promoted a further reassertion of the imperial factor. Dr Malan became very disheartened about failure to achieve transfer, and as De Kiewiet points out, 'Afrikaner disillusionment and outrage reached their climax' after 1948 as a result of what were considered to be broken promises and bureaucratic evasiveness; the rise of the homelands policy meant 'the acceptance of the failure of expansion and integration'. Thus, from the late 1950s, as Nationalists realised that Britain had no intention of handing the Territories over – indeed was preparing them for independence (achieved 1966–1968) – they came to see that the Territories could be regarded as virtual Bantustans. They also realised that Smuts's vision of informal expansion to the north, in a co-prosperity area embracing all Africa south of the Congo, held out much better prospects. By the time that the withdrawal of South Africa from the Commonwealth in 1961 brought a natural term to all possibility of transfer of the Territories, the South African government was already launched onto this alternative project of trying to develop diplomatic and economic influences northward.[24]

---

[22] Speech at Pretoria, 30 Apr. 1929: *Selections from the Smuts Papers*, vol. VI, p. 401; see also pp. 241 and 347, letters to M. C. Gillett, 24 June 1940 and 31 Jan. 1942; Smuts papers, vol. 70, no. 2.
[23] DO 35/1172, no. 7, Sir E. Baring to secretary of state, 2 Apr. 1945; *FSAE*, p. 178.
[24] R. Davies and D. O'Meara, 'Total strategy in Southern Africa: South African regional policy since 1978', *JSAS* vol. 11 (1985), pp. 183–211; C. Saunders, 'The history of South Africa's foreign policy', *SAHJ* no. 23 (1990), pp. 147–54.

Nevertheless, defeat over the High Commission Territories was a major blow to Afrikanerdom. The struggle for their control was the principal contest between the British and South African governments for more than half a century. The outcome was a victory for trusteeship exercised at the expense of British imperial political advantage. British governments refused to buy the favour and co-operation of South Africa's rulers, which economic and strategic interests required, by relinquishing the Territories, which were a drain rather than an asset, in no sense valuable as showpieces of empire. It was feared that any development of their resources would only make them more attractive to the Union, so they were largely left alone as backwaters almost to the end of colonial rule. That was the price exacted by the moral imperative. But the essential point is this. In dealing with the evil of apartheid, containment of the boundaries of the South African state was the most effective contribution Britain could possibly have made.[25]

---

[25] R. Hyam, 'Bureaucracy and "Trusteeship" in the colonial empire', in J. M. Brown and W. R. Louis, eds., *The Oxford history of the British empire*, vol. IV: *The twentieth century* (Oxford, 1999), ch. 11, pp. 255–79. For more detail on the situation in the 1950s, see below, pp. 255–60.

6 The economic dimension: South Africa and the sterling area, 1931–1961

South Africa's long and loyal membership of the sterling area is one of the most remarkable features of that country's relations with Britain in the twentieth century (tables 6.1–6.3; figs. 6.1–6.4). Membership of the area signified a commitment to sustain a world-wide monetary and trading system that was the economic counterpart to and underpinning of the British empire and Commonwealth. Yet for the Afrikaner nationalists who dominated the South African government between 1924 and 1933, and again after 1948, there was no higher ambition than to free their country from subordination to Britain. What, then, induced successive South African governments to tie the value of the country's currency to sterling, conduct the bulk of its international business in sterling, and adopt measures which protected Anglo-South African trade from outside competition when, as the world's leading gold producer, South Africa could dig out of the ground what was for much of the century the most prized medium of international exchange?[1]

The sterling area first took recognisable shape in 1931 when Britain's abandonment of the gold standard forced other countries, including autonomous members of the Commonwealth such as South Africa, to choose between aligning their currencies with sterling or fixing them on some other basis. The overseas dominions, with their long-standing political and economic ties with Britain, may have seemed natural candidates for membership of the sterling area, since in many ways the area merely preserved an existing system of international economic relations. Indeed in Australia and New Zealand (where, unlike South Africa, there was neither an effective central bank nor significant external reserves other than sterling deposits in London), a break with sterling

---

[1] For an account of the pre-war sterling area see: I. M. Drummond, *The floating pound and the sterling area, 1931–1939* (Cambridge, 1981); and P. J. Cain and A. J. Hopkins, *British imperialism, 1688–1990* (2 vols., London, 1993), vol. II, ch. 5. For wartime developments: R. S. Sayers, *Financial policy, 1939–1945* (London, 1956). For the post-war years see S. Strange, *Sterling and British policy: a political study of an international currency in decline* (London, 1971); G. Krozewski, 'Sterling, the "minor" territories, and the end of formal empire, 1939–1958', *Economic History Review*, 46, 2 (1993), pp. 239–65; Cain and Hopkins, *British imperialism*, vol. II, pp. 281–5; and R. Hyam, ed., *The Labour government and the end of empire, 1945–1951* (4 parts, BDEEP, London, 1992), pt. II, doc. nos. 95–8.

Table 6.1. *South African exports to Britain of animal, agricultural, and pastoral products and foodstuffs, 1931–1963*[a]

	1931	1933	1935	1937	1939	1941	1943	1945	1947	1949	1951	1953	1955	1957	1959	1961	1963
Class I[b]																	
exports to Britain, £m.	6.0	7.5	8.8	10.6	9.7	4.8	4.2	7.7	14.5	23.8	45.4	49.9	61.7	64.5	64.1	65.5	79.4
As a percentage of total Class I exports	47	44	43	37	47	50	45	84	31	34	33	37	40	36	39	35	34
Foodstuffs[c]																	
exports to Britain, £m.	3.4	3.7	5.5	7.3	7.1	3.7	2.8	2.7	6.3	9.1	17.9	22.2	33.6	37.6	36.6	44.6	55.4
As a percentage of total foodstuffs exports	69	67	70	64	73	66	49	37	46	42	45	53	49	45	50	44	41
Wool[d]																	
exports to Britain, £m.	1.7	2.6	2.0	1.9	1.0	—	—	3.1	4.0	8.5	14.9	14.8	12.4	11.0	10.3	7.6	6.5
As a percentage of total wool exports	31	31	22	16	15	—	—	33	22	30	25	27	26	20	25	16	14
Jam[e]																	
exports to Britain, £000	2	3	3	3	25	634	768	872	1,452	1,045	1,059	470	415	729	348	746	1,454
As a percentage of total jam exports	41	80	13	18	55	91	81	43	76	70	60	41	52	59	41	44	56

Notes:

[a] All amounts are in South African pounds at prices current at the time. Amounts for 1961 and 1963 have been converted into pounds at the rate of two rand per pound. From 1955 exports from South-West Africa are included.

[b] The South African department of customs and excise defined Class I as animal, agricultural, and pastoral products and foodstuffs.

[c] Foodstuffs (Class Id) as defined by the South African department of customs and excise.

[d] Wool defined by the South African department of customs and excise as item 44: sheeps' wool 'in the grease'. (The definition was subject to minor change over time.)

[e] Jam defined by the South African department of customs and excise as item 162: jams, jellies, and marmalade. (The definition was subject to minor change over time.)

Sources: South Africa, department of customs and excise, *Annual statement of the Union of South Africa and the territory of South West Africa*, 1931–54; *Annual statement of trade and shipping of the Union of South Africa*, 1955–60; *Foreign trade statistics*, 1961–3 (Pretoria, 1932–64).

Table 6.2. *External capital investment in South Africa, 1913–1972*

	1913	1936	1956	1966	1972
Total British capital invested in South Africa (SA £m.)	320	—[a]	866	1,095	1,950[b]
Total external capital invested in South Africa (SA £m.)	350	523	1,396	1,883	3,896
British capital as a percentage of total	91	—	62	58	50

Notes: Amounts shown in South African pounds at prices current at the time. Those for 1966 and 1972 were converted from rand at the rate of two rand per pound.
[a] Frankel offered no estimate.
[b] Author's estimate based on the assumption that the ratio of British investment to total sterling area investment in South Africa was the same in 1972 as it was in 1966 (the last year in which British investment was distinguished from the other sterling investment).
Sources: S. H. Frankel, *Capital investment in Africa: its course and effects* (London, 1938), pp. 150–1. South African Reserve Bank, *Quarterly Bulletin of Statistics*, supplement to no. 50 (1958); no. 86 (1967), pp. S-58 and S-59; no. 115 (1975), pp. S-64 and S-65.

was hardly considered. But in Canada, where the government was inclined to follow sterling, it was decided that the country was too closely tied to the United States for this to be workable. In South Africa a predominantly Afrikaner nationalist government was at first determined to remain on the gold standard, partly as a matter of economic principle, though above all as a demonstration of independence from Britain. A rising economic and political crisis eventually forced the South African government to abandon gold, devalue, and tie the South African pound to sterling, where it would remain fixed for the next thirty-four years in defiance of Afrikaner nationalist attacks on almost every other facet of the British connection.[2]

The explanation for South Africa's adherence to the sterling area from 1933 until the area itself disintegrated in the 1970s is to be found first in South Africa's dependence on Britain both as a source of capital and as a market for agricultural exports; and secondly in Britain's determination to sustain the sterling area not merely for economic reasons, but for wider political and strategic reasons as well. The highly capital-intensive gold-mining industry in particular, and the South African economy in general, could not be developed without substantial overseas investment.[3] The need to attract such investment, especially from

---

[2] I. M. Drummond, *The gold standard and the international monetary system, 1900–1939* (London, 1987), p. 42; and *Floating pound*, chs. 3–5.

[3] In 1956, according to the South African census of that year, £454 million of external capital was invested in South African mines, including £308 million invested in gold mines. Frankel calculated that the accumulated capital of gold mines existing at the end of 1965 was £639 million. South African Reserve Bank, 'The foreign liabilities and assets of the Union of South Africa: final results of the 1956 census', supplement to the *Quarterly Bulletin of Statistics*, no. 50 (1958), table 1. S. H. Frankel, *Investment and the return to equity capital in the South African gold mining industry, 1887–1965: an international comparison* (Oxford, 1967), p. 17.

Table 6.3. *Net contributions to and drawings from the sterling area 'dollar pool', 1946–1956*[a]

	1946	1947	1948	1949	1950	1951	1952	1953	1954	1955	1956[c]
United Kingdom	−5	1,276	−189	151	872	−1,303	−385	48	−42	−571	−319
UK colonies	158	62	233	229	436	487	385	283	302	137	143
Other sterling area (excluding South Africa)	−199	−858	−284	−301	139	−118	−257	−39	−112	188	221
South Africa	82	−94	335	47	179	137	176	218	272	263	283
Other[b]	183	−1,004	−317	−293	−14	−167	−407	162	−176	−658	−314
Total (change in gold and dollar reserves)	220	−617	−223	−168	1,612	−965	−489	672	244	−641	14

Notes:

[a] All amounts are in United States dollars at prices current at the time.

[b] This represents transactions (on behalf of the sterling area as a whole) with non-dollar and non-sterling countries, and with non-territorial organisations. The largest of these transactions were of two types: first, gold payments made to continental Europe; and secondly, contributions to and drawings from the International Monetary Fund.

[c] The amounts shown for 1956 were subsequently revised. The revised figures are not shown here because they do not distinguish between British colonies and other sterling area countries.

Sources: The figures shown for South Africa were not published and were taken from DO 35/26721, DO 119/1167, DO 35/5717, and T 236/4246. Other figures were published in British Parliamentary Papers, *United Kingdom balance of payments, 1946 to 1956*, Cmnd 122 (1957) and *United Kingdom balance of payments, 1955 to 1957*, Cmnd 399 (1958).

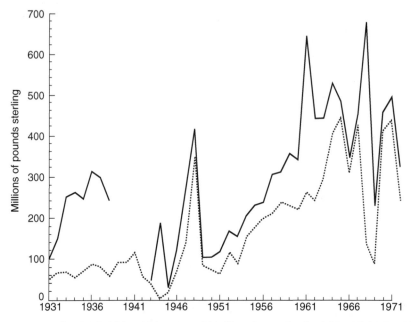

Fig. 6.1 British gold imports, 1931–72 (prices at the time). Total British gold imports —; gold imports from South Africa ·····. *Note*: Figure shows year-end totals. Amounts are in pounds sterling. Full details of British gold imports were not published for the years 1939–43. The figures for South African gold exports to Britain for those years were estimated by the South African Reserve Bank. *Sources*: Parliamentary Papers, *Accounts relating to the trade and navigation of the United Kingdom for each month of the year* (1931–9). Britain, commissioners of H.M. customs and excise, *Annual statement of the trade of the United Kingdom* [various titles] (1947–72). South African Reserve Bank, *Quarterly Bulletin of Statistics*, 4 (1947), 14–15.

London, was a leading consideration in the determination of South Africa's exchange policy. But in the peculiar circumstances of South African electoral geography, where white farmers were disproportionately influential, the need to protect earnings from agricultural exports was an even more important consideration, even though such earnings never amounted to more than a small fraction of the earnings from mineral exports.[4] For the British government, the attractions of keeping the world's leading gold producer in the sterling area

---

[4] The value of agricultural exports is shown in table 6.1; the value of gold exports can be judged from figure 6.2. In the years 1932/3 to 1938/9, the average value of gold exports accounted for over 70 per cent of the value of all exports, with agricultural exports accounting for just over 20 per cent of all exports. S. H. Frankel and H. Herzfeld, 'An analysis of the growth of the national income of the Union in the period of prosperity before the war', *South African Journal of Economics*, 12, 2 (1944), p. 124.

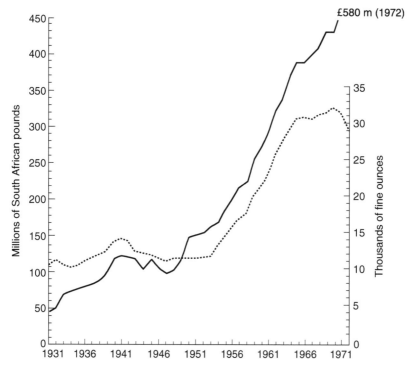

Fig. 6.2 South African gold production by prices realised and quantities, 1931–72. Gold production at prices realised —; gold production in fine ounces ⋯. *Note*: Figure shows year-end totals. Prices are in South African pounds. Amounts published in rand (1961 onwards) were converted into pounds at the rate of two rand per pound. *Sources*: South Africa, Bureau of census and statistics, *Union statistics for fifty years: 1910–1960, Jubilee issue* (Pretoria, 1960), pp. K-4 and K-5. South Africa, Department of Mines, *Mining statistics: summary of the data submitted to the government mining engineer by mines and works as defined by the Mines and Works Act, No. 27 of 1956* (1973), table 8.

seemed clear enough. The flow of South African gold to the London market facilitated the Bank of England's international operations (especially its management of sterling's value) and helped to sustain both the image of the City of London as the world's pre-eminent financial centre and confidence in sterling as an international currency.[5] Membership facilitated the free and profitable

---

[5] While sterling was convertible (or at least partially so), the Bank of England's intervention in the London gold market was one of the principal means by which it managed the sterling price of gold (which was in effect the sterling–dollar exchange rate). The London gold market was, to a remarkable extent, based on the sale of South African gold. See fig. 6.1.

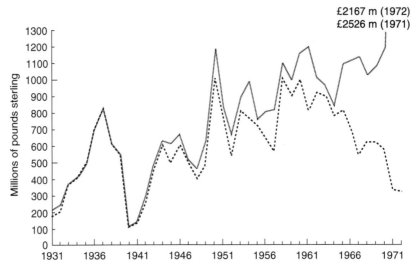

Fig. 6.3 British reserves of gold and convertible currencies, 1931–72 (prices at the time). Gold ····, gold and convertible currencies —. *Note*: Figure shows year-end totals. Amounts are in pounds sterling. *Sources*: Parliamentary Papers, *Reserves and liabilities, 1931–1945*, Cmd 8354 (1951). Bank of England, *Statistical abstract*, no. 1 (1970), table 27; no. 2 (1975), table 21.

participation of British capital in South African development, particularly of the mining industry. And the area protected a pattern of trade which both assisted the balancing of British trade on a multilateral basis and strengthened Anglo-South African political ties. After 1933, Afrikaner nationalist pressure for South Africa to extricate itself from Britain's economic orbit would be held in check by an inescapable reliance on Britain as a customer and financier, a reliance actively fostered by British governments anxious to sustain Britain's world-wide power.[6]

I

The sterling area, as it emerged in 1931, was an unplanned by-product of actions taken by the British government in response to a currency crisis – a crisis arising

---

[6] G. H. de Kock, *A history of the South African Reserve Bank* (Pretoria, 1954), chs. 14, 17, and 18. T. Gregory, *Ernest Oppenheimer and the economic development of southern Africa* (Cape Town, 1962), ch. 8. The inter-relationship of Britain's world-wide economic and political influence was acknowledged publicly and explicitly by the Radcliffe committee, which did not think it possible to dissociate sterling area arrangements 'either from the long-standing trading relationships that lie behind them or from the political and other links by which most members of the area are joined in the Commonwealth'. British Parliamentary Papers, committee on the working of the monetary system [Radcliffe committee], *Report*, Cmnd 827 (1959), p. 240.

Fig. 6.4 South African imports from and exports to Britain as a percentage of total South African imports and exports of produce (excluding gold), 1931–72. Imports ····; exports —. *Source*: South Africa, department of customs and excise, *Annual statement of trade and shipping* [title varies] (1931–72).

out of problems which would plague the British economy for at least the next four decades: a shortage of gold and convertible currency reserves and a weak current-account balance. Sterling was taken off the gold standard and allowed to float downwards by about 30 per cent in relation to gold, thereby encouraging British exports to, and discouraging imports from, those countries that adhered to gold. The dependent empire and some parts of Britain's informal empire in the Middle East had no choice but to follow. The British government seems not to have put pressure on the dominions to leave the gold standard and peg their currencies to sterling. To have done so was to run the risk not only of entanglement in bitter local political controversy with damaging repercussions for the Commonwealth connection but, even worse, of being saddled with the financial responsibility for the local currency policy. The dominions and independent foreign governments were left to make their own decisions, and by December 1931 a sterling area had emerged that included the dependent empire, the Pacific dominions, as well as Egypt, Iraq, and Portugal. It did not yet include South Africa.[7]

For South Africa, as a gold producer with its own central bank, substantial gold reserves, and a government dominated by Afrikaner nationalists anxious to assert their independence from Britain, the choice of whether or not to follow sterling at first seemed obvious. Maintenance of the gold standard was genuinely believed to be economically and morally correct. Moreover, many Afrikaner nationalists regarded the maintenance of the gold standard as a demonstration of economic independence worthy of South Africa's newly asserted constitutional equality with Britain. Thus in 1931, Nicholaas Havenga, the minister of finance in the Hertzog government, had little difficulty in justifying his declaration that South Africa would never follow Britain in leaving the gold standard.[8]

Pressure to change this policy was exerted most powerfully first by farmers and then by mining interests. South African manufacturers also called for an abandonment of the gold standard, arguing among other things that devaluation was essential if South African manufactured goods were to regain a share of the important Rhodesian market. But, in South African politics, what mattered more was the opinion of farmers who were already suffering from depressed local and international prices. After Britain left the gold standard, they saw their incomes drop even further as the sterling prices of their exports to the British market failed to rise to compensate for sterling's depreciation. After some hesitation, the opposition South African Party under the leadership of former prime minister Jan Smuts took up the cry that farmers' interests were being sacrificed on the altar of the gold standard. Some members of the South African Party also spoke on behalf of gold-mining interests, arguing that the devaluation of the South African pound would (by raising the price of gold in terms of the domestic currency) increase the industry's profitability, extend the life of existing mines, open up vast new areas to exploitation by allowing a lower average grade of ore to be worked, and stimulate the investment of new capital which was essential for future development. The gold producers' committee of the Transvaal chamber of mines informed the parliamentary select committee on the gold standard that it was 'difficult to exaggerate the importance to the mines of the increased facilities to obtain working capital which would follow devaluation'. Not only would new capital flow into the country, but the large

---

[7] Britain's (and the sterling area's) central reserves of convertible external exchange are shown in fig. 6.3. This figure also shows that these reserves were, until the late 1960s, held mainly in gold. Drummond, *Gold standard*, pp. 39–42; and *Floating pound*, ch. 1.

[8] Drummond, *Floating pound*, ch. 4.

amounts of capital that had fled would return. The vast sums of capital associated with gold-mining development made South Africa particularly vulnerable to the speculative outflows of capital which would eventually force South Africa off the gold standard. Nevertheless, the final decisive flight of capital would be sparked by a belief that devaluation was inevitable not because mining interests wanted it but because white farmers and their spokesmen were prepared to force a change of government to secure it.[9]

The National Party, the party of Afrikanerdom, was split by the crisis over exchange policy. D. F. Malan led the more extreme Afrikaner nationalists into a new 'purified' National Party. Hertzog stayed in power by means of a coalition with Smuts and most of his followers. Havenga, who stayed on as minister of finance, accepted the necessity of the link with sterling, initially doing so with little enthusiasm.[10]

South Africa's entry into the nascent sterling area had not been the result of inter-governmental bargaining or of economic pressure exerted by the British government. Britain's dominance as a customer for South African agricultural goods and as a supplier of capital had, through the political influence of farmers and mining interests in South Africa, forced the country into the area. And by joining the area, South Africa had in effect concluded a wide-ranging bargain in which South African farmers gained higher prices for their exports; gold mines enjoyed a higher domestic price for their output as well as a new wave of investment and development; and the South African government regained the confidence of investors and reduced the difficulties of managing a currency no longer on the gold standard. On the other side of this bargain, British customers continued to acquire South African agricultural goods at stable prices; British capital gained a stable and more profitable field of investment; and sterling's prestige was enhanced.[11]

For most of the rest of the 1930s, South Africa would be held in the sterling area by this bargain, a bargain sustained by the operation of British markets for agricultural produce, gold, and capital. In some cases these markets were relatively free. In others they were significantly shaped by policies designed to favour trade and investment within the empire for political as well as economic reasons. In particular, the preferential tariff regime negotiated in Ottawa by

---

[9] In presenting their case before the select committee on the gold standard, representatives of the South African federated chamber of industries put forward three reasons for a return to parity with sterling. First, this would be the quickest way of drawing capital back into the country. Secondly, devaluation would remove the price advantage gained by imported manufactured goods. Finally, 'there would be every opportunity to recover the trade with Rhodesia which has practically ceased to exist in many cases'. South African Parliamentary Papers, *Report of the select committee on the gold standard* (Cape Town, 1932), pp. 665–8. For the views of the gold producers' committee of the Transvaal chamber of mines see ibid. pp. 468–543.
[10] T. R. H. Davenport, *South Africa: a modern history* (London, 3rd edn, 1987), pp. 302–8.
[11] Drummond, *Floating pound*, ch. 4.

British and empire representatives in 1932 entrenched the dependence of many South African agricultural producers on the British market. Furthermore, the British policy of discriminating in favour of empire borrowers in the London capital market ensured that a whole range of South African government authorities and industries would continue to rely on British capital.[12]

As war approached, the British and dominion governments recognised that they would have to take more direct and concerted action to sustain the mutual benefits of the sterling area system. The British government's wish to sustain sterling as an international currency, and London as a hub of international trade and finance, led it to devise a system of exchange controls which would manage transactions with hard currency countries, and check any outward flight of capital, while freely permitting transactions with as many as possible of the countries which used sterling as their principal medium of external exchange. The wartime sterling area would therefore include only those countries willing to impose exchange controls in parallel with those in Britain. The only countries to do this at the outset of war were Britain, the dependent empire, Egypt, Iraq, and those dominions which had already linked their currencies to sterling – Eire, Australia, New Zealand, and South Africa.[13]

II

Although the crisis over South Africa's declaration of war against Germany brought Smuts to power and forced Hertzog and Havenga into opposition, the country's inclusion in the sterling area was by no means simply the product of Smuts's devotion to the British connection. Hertzog and Havenga may in fact have envisaged the imposition of the necessary exchange controls while preserving South Africa's neutrality, as the government of Eire would do. In any case, the Smuts government would not have agreed to sterling area membership if membership had not had evident economic advantages. Membership could have become a dangerous political liability for Smuts if Afrikaner nationalists could show that South Africa would be better off following Canada's lead in remaining outside the sterling area. As it was, membership ensured first, and

---

[12] I. M. Drummond, *British economic policy and the empire* (London, 1972), chs. 1–3. So entrenched became the dependence of South African fruit growers on the British market that the chairman of the South African deciduous fruit board said, in 1960, that 'One of the most important factors contributing to the economic welfare of the South African fruit farmer were the preferences which the Union received through its membership of the Commonwealth.' H. M. Robertson, 'Can industry afford to break the economic link?', *Optima* 10, 3 (1960), p. 128.

[13] R. S. Sayers, *The Bank of England, 1891–1944* (2 vols., Cambridge, 1976), vol. II, p. 568. Sayers, *Financial policy*, chs. 8–10.

most importantly, that South African agricultural exports and applications for capital funds and goods were treated at least as favourably in British markets as those from any other part of the world; and secondly that South Africa could continue to conduct most of its trade in sterling, finance it in London, retain access to the London money market, and settle external accounts through the Bank of England. These benefits of membership were the South African side of bargains which, as government controls became increasingly pervasive, came to be mediated more through inter-governmental negotiations than through the mechanisms of international markets.[14]

The principal objectives which the British government aimed to secure through these bargains were threefold: to gain assured sources of supply; to maximise the amount of hard currency available for the empire–Commonwealth war effort; and to sustain confidence in sterling. This last objective was crucial, for upon it rested not only sterling's future as an international currency, but also the willingness of governments inside and outside the sterling area to build up sterling balances – or in effect to extend credit to Britain repayable in sterling. But as direct British government involvement in the bargains holding independent members of the Commonwealth such as South Africa in the sterling area increased, so these bargains became more distorted by a wider British concern: to foster collaboration which safeguarded British strategic, economic, and geopolitical interests which were themselves intertwined with the maintenance of the Commonwealth connection.[15]

One of the first economic bargains struck after South Africa included itself in the wartime sterling area was the Smuts government's agreement to make any external sales of gold through the Bank of England. The advantage for South Africa was that South African accounts in London could be regularly credited for the sale of gold at an assured price even if the gold remained in South Africa, ready for shipment from South African ports. High wartime shipping and insurance costs could in this way be avoided. Nevertheless, the agreement had little bearing on the extent to which South African gold accumulated in the sterling area's central reserves.[16]

This accumulation depended on the size of three things. First, Britain's trade surplus with South Africa. Secondly, South Africa's own hard currency expenditure. And finally, South Africa's reserve holdings of sterling. (For Britain, beset as it was for most of this period by a chronic shortage of dollars, the crucial consideration was South Africa's net contribution to the sterling area's

---

[14] Sayers, *Financial policy*, pp. 306–20. J. A. Henry, *The first hundred years of the Standard Bank* (London, 1963), pp. 261–9.
[15] K. Wright, 'Dollar pooling and the sterling area, 1939–52', *American Economic Review*, 44 (1954), p. 560.
[16] De Kock, *History of S.A.R.B.*, pp. 241–4. Henry, *Standard Bank*, p. 261.

central reserves of gold and convertible currency – the so-called 'dollar pool'.)[17] If the acquisition of South African gold had been the British government's sole and over-riding objective, it would have maximised sterling area exports to, and minimised imports from, South Africa while restricting South Africa's access to the area's central reserves of hard currency. In that way, South Africa would have had to cover a large sterling deficit by selling gold to the Bank of England. But while the British government would do what it could to sustain exports to South Africa, it could not afford to discriminate against South African imports, because of the political ramifications of doing so. Nor could it risk the break-up of the sterling area by restricting access to the central reserves by independent members. Except for its ability to control wartime shipping and supply, there was little the British government on its own could do to control South Africa's hard currency expenditure except exhort the South African government to restrict consumption of hard-currency goods. Of all the dominion governments which had declared war, South Africa's was the least willing to strain its electoral support by extending austerity and controls in the interests of the Commonwealth war effort. Yet, in the absence of such measures, or of an undertaking to hold more reserves in sterling rather than in gold, South African gold could be of only limited value to Britain and the sterling area.[18]

The British government sought to make the sterling area connection with South Africa more profitable to itself through a series of wartime and post-war bargains in which Britain's willingness to purchase South African agricultural goods and to allocate scarce capital goods to the gold-mining industry were used as British bargaining counters. As a result of these bargains, the Smuts government agreed to increase the amount of gold at Britain's disposal by a variety of means. British investments were repatriated in exchange for gold. Fixed annual sales of gold were made with the intention of accumulating sterling in London. South Africa agreed to carry a larger share of the cost of maintaining South African forces in north Africa and Italy. Finally, and least directly, South Africa imposed import controls which reduced the amount of gold expended on hard-currency imports and increased the amount available for sterling imports. Although these arrangements were often negotiated separately from one another, the common factors in each bargain were Britain's tacit or explicit agreement to purchase agricultural goods and supply the needs of the gold mines and Britain's reliance on the personal intervention of Smuts to secure a

[17] For South Africa's relative significance as a contributor to the post-war 'dollar pool' see fig. 6.3. The figures shown for South Africa were not published, though they were guessed at. The British government, conscious of the political dangers of advertising which independent members of the sterling area were net drawers from the 'pool', refused to reveal publicly the full details of drawings and contributions by countries such as South Africa.
[18] Sayers, *Financial policy*, pp. 313–15.

deal. But although the British government would never find a South African leader more amenable to collaboration than Smuts, these bargains usually fell well short of what the British government hoped could be achieved, largely due to the British fear of weakening Smuts's hold on power and hence South Africa's attachment to the Commonwealth.[19]

During the war, South Africa's gold production had benefited no country more than South Africa itself. Its gold reserves rose throughout the war, increasing by £150 million between 1939 and 1945; overseas debt was reduced by over £70 million; and sterling balances grew by £30 million – all of this at a time when South Africa's domestic consumption was less restricted than that of almost any other part of the Commonwealth.[20]

After the war, the Smuts government's unwillingness to constrain South Africa's import policy in Britain's interests led to a crisis which threatened South Africa's membership of the sterling area. This crisis was resolved through a bargain once again based on South Africa's need for agricultural markets and capital. In 1947, such large amounts of capital were flowing into South Africa (where it was being used to finance hard currency instead of sterling imports) that a frantic British Treasury called for the flow to be stopped by immediately excluding South Africa from the sterling area. (One Treasury official warned that 'every day we wait ... may be costing us up to a million dollars'.)[21] Although Britain was desperately short of hard currency (the result of the attempt to make sterling freely convertible into other currencies) the Bank of England could not believe that such a drastic step was really necessary. Its governor, Lord Catto, questioned whether the evidence called for

such a far-reaching corrective when South African controls have been effectively and loyally maintained largely in our own interest. I should regard the exclusion of South Africa from the sterling area as an act of self-mutilation on our part and I feel sure they would regard such an action as inflicting unnecessary damage on the South African economy.[22]

British capital must, thought Lord Catto, continue to participate in South African development; 'Our paramount interest in the gold mining industry must be

---

[19] N. N. Franklin, 'South Africa's balance of payments and the sterling area, 1939–1950', *Economic Journal*, 61 (1951), p. 305. London, Public Record Office (PRO), Dominions Office (after July 1947, Commonwealth Relations Office) papers DO 35/1220, WT 670/4/6, note of conversation between Harlech and Wood, 1 July 1943. D. Moggridge (ed.), *The collected writings of John Maynard Keynes* (30 vols., Cambridge, 1979–89), vol. XXIII, pp. 121–2 and vol. XXIV, p. 532. Pretoria, Transvaal Archive, Smuts papers, A1/160, Cranborne to high commissioner, 15 Feb. 1945.

[20] Sayers, *Financial policy*, pp. 319–20.

[21] PRO, Treasury papers, T 236/2268, note by A. T. K. Grant, 25 June 1947; T 236/2269, Eady to Playfair, 16 Aug. 1947 and Bridges to Catto, 22 Aug. 1947.

[22] T 236/2269, Catto to Bridges, 23 Aug. 1947.

protected.' The real problem was the extent of South Africa's hard-currency imports.[23]

Attlee consequently informed Smuts that 'urgent discussions' about financial relations were required. At stake was Britain's willingness to continue supplying capital and purchasing agricultural goods. The result was an agreement in which the South African government undertook to make a loan of £80 million of gold. In return, the British government agreed to restrict neither the export of capital goods nor the legitimate flow of capital to South Africa and to buy £12 million of specified agricultural goods each year for three years.[24] Finally, in place of agreements which had been in place during and for the first two years after the war to sell fixed quantities of gold to the Bank of England, South Africa would directly cover hard currency drawings from the central reserves by sales of the equivalent amount of gold.[25]

But, as British Treasury officials rightly complained, South Africa had managed to secure the best of both the hard currency and the sterling worlds. On the one hand, the Smuts government gained priority for imports of capital goods by arguing that they would be paid for in gold.[26] On the other, it claimed the full benefits of sterling area membership, thereby escaping controls on the movement of British capital, limits on drawings from the central reserves, or discrimination against exports to Britain and British dependencies. This was so despite the fact that South Africa, unlike other sterling area members, did not place the bulk of its convertible currency reserves in the sterling area 'dollar pool'. But calls from the British Treasury to exclude South Africa from the area met with an immediate and irrefutable objection: such a step would be 'just what General Smuts's political adversaries were waiting for'. Britain's economic bargaining power, constrained in dealings with all of the dominions by the desire to sustain the Commonwealth and sterling systems, was particularly limited in dealings with South Africa where strategic and geopolitical concerns were so great, and the forces of exclusivist nationalism so strong. The paradoxical result was that the presence of Smuts (continually criticised by Afrikaner nationalists as being

---

[23] T 236/2269, Catto to Bridges, 23 Aug. 1947 and note by Bank of England, 25 Aug. 1947.

[24] DO 35/3518, Attlee to Smuts, 27 Aug. 1947. The South African government's concern about capital goods had been expressed by Hofmeyr. He had been 'informed by Oppenheimer that all gold mining machinery for new Free State mines must come from United Kingdom and he had some fears lest deliveries of machinery from United Kingdom to Union might suffer through priority being given to United Kingdom to manufacture for export to hard-currency countries'. T 236/2269, Baring to Machtig, 25 Aug. 1947.

[25] T 236/2270, Herbert to Fisher, 26 Sept. 1947. T 236/2271, note of meeting, 10 Sept. 1947. Johannesburg, William Cullin library, Hofmeyr papers, A1/D1 1/2, Holloway to Hofmeyr, 1 Oct. 1947.

[26] A few months after Smuts's defeat a British Treasury official complained that 'South Africa is getting 9% of our total exports of capital goods; the only country getting a higher proportion is India with 10%.' T 236/1514, R. Burns to J. J. S. Garner, 1 Sept. 1948.

the 'tool of British imperialism') may have produced economic bargains more advantageous to South Africa than those which might have been secured by a National Party government.[27]

III

Although the avoidance of actions which might undermine Smuts's electoral position had been elevated to the point of being perhaps the paramount principle of British policy in relation to South Africa, Smuts's United Party went down to electoral defeat all the same in 1948. Into power came Malan's National Party which, with the support of Havenga's Afrikaner Party, formed the first Cabinet in the history of the Union of South Africa from which English-speaking South Africans were entirely excluded. National Party rhetoric seemed to commit the new government to breaking down the British connection whenever and wherever possible. As indeed it would do, the Malan government was expected to seek out alternative customers and sources of supply as a means of reducing dependence on Britain. Havenga, who returned to his position as minister of finance, had already made one attempt to chart an independent monetary course and might have been expected to take advantage of Britain's post-war financial weakness to try again. Furthermore, compared to some of their Cabinet colleagues, Malan and Havenga were the moderates. Who could tell how reckless a journey towards economic independence the extremists would wish to take?[28]

Ironically, the strength of Afrikaner nationalist opposition to participation in the war probably reduced South Africa's capacity to free itself from economic dependence on Britain. The unwillingness of the Smuts government to impose greater austerity or higher levels of taxation on a deeply divided electorate meant that the levels of exchange reserves, domestic savings, and even industrial development were perhaps less than they might have been had the electorate been more committed to the war.[29]

In 1948, officials in Whitehall and Threadneedle Street thought that Britain's objective should be to allow South Africa's reserves to be exhausted as rapidly as possible. The South African government would have to 'wake up one day to

---

[27] T 236/2272, note by A. T. K. Grant, 2 April 1948. DO 35/3518, Baring to Machtig, 27 Oct. 1947. T 236/2269, Treasury note, 15 Sept. 1947.

[28] D. J. Geldenhuys, 'The effects of South Africa's racial policy on Anglo-South African relations, 1945–61' (unpublished PhD thesis, Cambridge University, 1977), pp. 99, 103, 111, and 117–18.

[29] Sayers, *Financial policy*, pp. 319–20. De Kock, *History of the S.A.R.B.*, p. 241. B. Kantor, 'The evolution of monetary policy in South Africa', in M. Kooy, ed., *Studies in economics and economic history: essays in honour of Professor H. M. Robertson* (London, 1972), p. 79.

the difficult position it would soon be in'. Capital had been fleeing South Africa since Smuts's fall. American capital was not available on acceptable terms. The London capital market was proving difficult. The mining houses were worried about finding sufficient capital to open up the Orange Free State gold fields. British officials felt sure that 'the whole of South Africa's Development Programme was in jeopardy'.[30]

The idea of waiting until the Malan government itself sought assistance had to be abandoned in 1949 as Britain slid inexorably into its second post-war balance of payments crisis. Havenga's 'entirely objective' attitude at a July meeting of Commonwealth finance ministers did not fill British representatives with confidence, but by then they knew that South Africa was 'desperately short' of sterling, that the gold loan had almost been repaid, and that £1 million of capital was fleeing South Africa each week. The British government alone was in a position to help. It could grant authority to borrow in the London market and make a bulk purchase of 'non-essential' goods such as fruit and wine. Furthermore, the benefits of sterling area membership were sustained at Britain's discretion. The British Treasury wanted to extract a guarantee that Britain would acquire £50 million of gold each year: 'surely we owe it to ourselves *and to the other members of the sterling area* to demand a guarantee while we are holding so strong a hand'.[31]

Hugh Gaitskell, the British minister of fuel and power, proposed in discussions with Havenga that South Africa should sell gold to Britain and pay for 'essential' imports from whatever source in gold to an extent that would guarantee Britain's acquisition of 50 per cent of South Africa's gold output. In return, South Africa would be granted access to the London capital market and the British government would agree to continue the annual purchase of £12 million of less essential South African agricultural goods.[32] It was a measure of the weakness of South Africa's position that the agreement eventually signed by Gaitskell and Havenga followed the British proposal, except that Britain would be assured of obtaining only 25 per cent of South Africa's gold output while being given a fair chance to earn an additional 25 per cent. In order to avoid a formal treaty (which would have to be registered with the United Nations thereby

---

[30] T 236/2274, note of Treasury and Bank of England meeting, 24 Nov. 1948.
[31] T 236/2275, notes by H. G. C. and Flett, 28 June 1949. T 236/2276, note by L. P., 26 July 1949.
[32] The political importance of seemingly insignificant agricultural exports should not be underrated. A good example is jam which, if compared to wool, was of no consequence from a balance-of-payments perspective (see table 6.1). Jam was, nonetheless, vital in certain parliamentary constituencies, including those of two long-serving Nationalist cabinet ministers: Eric Louw and Eben Dönges. In 1948, Louw made direct personal appeals to British ministers in his efforts to encourage greater British jam imports from South Africa. Dönges was known to be similarly concerned about the scale of these imports. T 236/1514, McNeil's report on talk with Louw, 11 Oct. 1948; note of conversation between Cripps and Louw, 15 Oct. 1948; Baring to CRO, 25 Oct. 1948.

publicising the intention to contravene the rules of the International Monetary Fund and the General Agreement on Tariffs and Trade), the agreement became known as the 'Memorandum of Understanding'.[33]

The crucial feature of the Understanding was that South Africa should administer an import licensing system in a way that discriminated in favour of sterling imports. Details of this system were left to be settled by British officials sent to South Africa for this purpose. They had not been there long before they encountered strong resistance to the Understanding's implementation. The problem was not Havenga, but Eric Louw, the minister of economic affairs, and Eben Dönges, the minister of mines and internal affairs who for a time was also acting minister of finance. These two emerged as the irreconcilables. They seized upon sterling's devaluation in September 1949 as a justification for abandoning the less attractive features of the Understanding.[34]

In contrast to 1931, the National Party government had not hesitated to devalue the South African pound in line with sterling. Moreover, as in 1933, devaluation immediately increased the profitability of the gold mines, stimulating a new wave of investment. With this strengthening of South Africa's economic position, its government must have felt confident that it could hold out for a new and less onerous arrangement.[35]

The Malan government's reluctance to adhere to the Understanding provoked more than mild consternation in Whitehall. Sir Evelyn Baring, the British high commissioner to South Africa, was instructed to press for South Africa's adherence to the Understanding's original terms. The limiting factor was the need to avoid undermining the political position of Havenga who was regarded, in the absence of Smuts, as the most effective agent of collaboration. With this in mind, Baring judged that some compromise was needed. But he could not recommend the agreement that emerged out of renewed negotiations. It departed from the original in 'both letter and spirit'.[36]

Baring saw four options. First, the changes proposed by South Africa could be accepted. Secondly, a British ministerial approach to secure a new agreement could be made. Thirdly, South Africa could simply be pressed to return to the original scheme. Finally, Britain could 'wave the big stick'. Baring thought that his government would wish to consider carefully whether it

would in fact be prepared to impose economic sanctions of any kind against South Africa. The political consequences of sanctions would be so serious to the United Kingdom as well as to South Africa that my personal view is that we should avoid taking such a step

[33] Pretoria, Central Archives Depot, Holloway papers, A80/8, Holloway to Steyn, 28 July 1949; A 80/10, Steyn to Holloway, 5 Aug. 1949.
[34] A 80/10, Steyn to Holloway, 1 Sept. 1949. DO 35/3520, note by Pickard, 14 Oct. 1949.
[35] DO 35/3520, note by Pickard, 14 Oct. 1949. Gregory, *Oppenheimer*, p. 566.
[36] DO 35/3520, Baring to CRO, 20 Oct. 1949 and 16 Nov. 1949.

at almost any cost, especially when there will in any case be trouble with the Union government over the High Commission Territories.[37]

If there were any illusions in Whitehall about Britain's ability to use the 'big stick', M. T. Flett in the Treasury did his best to dispel them. The stick had two 'knobs' on it: cutting off 'non-essential' imports from South Africa and refusing access to the London capital market. The first, by reducing South African exports of fruit and wine, would 'undoubtedly hit the South African Government disproportionately hard'. But the second was the 'real crux of the matter': 'If we could do it, it would hurt South Africa very hard indeed.' Unfortunately, it would 'almost certainly hurt us considerably'. South Africa held a 'valuable hostage' in the form of British gold-mining investments. Furthermore, the Bank of England believed that real control over the flow of capital would involve exclusion from the sterling area. This 'might also mean departure of South Africa from the Commonwealth with all of the political and strategic results of such a step'.[38]

Although sanctions were ruled out, the British government insisted that South Africa adhere to the original Understanding. This insistence paid off. When pressed, Havenga stood by the agreement which he had signed in London.[39]

By 1953, the essential features of the Memorandum of Understanding were still intact despite the revisions made to it each year after it was signed. But by then, the Malan government had become insistent that South African discrimination against dollar imports must soon be brought to an end. Discrimination was distorting South Africa's price structure and was embarrassing in relation to GATT. Moreover, how could a National Party government justify the protection of Britain's industry when South Africa was exposed to international competition?[40]

The start of limited sterling convertibility and the re-opening of the London gold market in 1954 would, in any case, have necessitated major changes to the Understanding. The guaranteed annual sale of £50 million of gold to the Bank of England was overtaken by sales in this market. There was no compulsion to sell there. South Africa would do so to obtain the best prices. The special arrangements for covering hard currency payments made on South Africa's behalf were no longer needed because under convertibility all non-sterling currencies were equally hard. The British and South African governments agreed that, in these circumstances, the Memorandum of Understanding, which had with various modifications governed financial relations between the two countries

---

[37] DO 35/3520, Baring to CRO, 16 Nov. 1949.   [38] T 236/2277, note by Flett, 18 Nov. 1949.
[39] DO 35/3520, note of meeting, 28 Nov. 1949.
[40] T 236/2642, note by Flett, 30 June 1950. T 236/2914, Thompson-McCausland to Brittain, 24 Sept. 1951. T 236/3272, note by Flett, 28 Nov. 1952 and note by Rowan, 10 June 1953.

since 1949, need not apply after the end of 1954. To a great extent, a return had finally been made to the pre-war situation in which Britain's gold earnings were determined by the extent of British exports to South Africa.[41]

Fears that an Afrikaner nationalist government would steer South Africa away from the sterling area had not, at the end of 1954, been borne out by events. South Africa's need for agricultural markets and capital, and Britain's need for gold, provided the economic basis for bargains which held South Africa in the area, bargains that the Malan government had felt compelled to reaffirm. Afrikaner nationalists had not forgotten the political consequences of the attempt to break with sterling in the early 1930s. As Baring reported, these nationalists 'have very long memories. Only once in the past have they been in as strong a position as they are now.' They lost that position owing to the crisis over the gold standard. In practice, Havenga had proved to be as valuable in fostering economic collaboration after 1948 as Smuts had been before. When, in 1953, the *Economist* claimed that Havenga was waiting for the first opportunity to take South Africa out of the area, the long-serving minister of finance was gravely offended: he protested that he had been a 'staunch partner' and had brought the whole of the Cabinet round to his point of view.[42]

But in December 1954, after the extremists in the National Party declared that they would contest Malan's designation of Havenga as the next prime minister, Havenga followed Malan into retirement. Their departure would thus coincide with the end of the Memorandum of Understanding and the start of a new phase in South Africa's relationship to the sterling area. Markets would henceforth play a larger role than explicit inter-governmental bargains in determining this relationship: South Africa's willingness to sell its gold in Britain would depend upon the attractions of the London market; Britain's ability to *earn* a share of that gold would depend less on discriminatory import restrictions than on the competitiveness of British goods and services in the South African market. South African agricultural exporters would rely not on inter-governmental bulk-purchases but on the preferences of British consumers; and South Africa's acquisition of capital goods would be governed less by the priorities set by the British government than by the prices South Africans were willing to pay. All of this was just as well for the British government, because the minister of finance in the Strijdom government was none other than Eric Louw, whose aggressive tactics in dealing with other governments were already notorious.[43]

---

[41] Holloway papers, A 80/12, message to Cobbold, 16 March 1954. T 236/4083, note by Halley, 13 Dec. 1954. For the rise in sales of South African gold in Britain after the reopening of the London market see fig. 6.1.

[42] PRO, prime minister's papers, PREM 11/539, note of meeting between Havenga and Swinton, 12 June 1953. DO 119/1167, note of meeting between Havenga and Butler, 12 June 1953.

[43] DO 35/5632, biographical notes on Louw, undated.

IV

However much the Strijdom government may have wanted either to assert South Africa's economic independence from Britain or to secure political ends through economic threats, the realities of international markets for capital and agricultural goods in the late 1950s tended to hold South Africa in the sterling area, making such threats seem unconvincing. While the overall importance of the British market was in decline, Britain was still the single largest market for South African exports and it remained a vital customer for South African agricultural exports.[44] Furthermore, the South African government wanted to retain access to the London capital market at a time when the drive for Afrikaner ascendancy was frightening away existing and prospective investment. The precarious state of the sterling area system meant that the British government too was constrained by the need to sustain the bargains underpinning South Africa's sterling area membership. Neither the British nor the South African government would prove willing to endanger these bargains in pursuit of political ends.[45]

Louw nevertheless tried to use his position as minister of both finance and external affairs to bully Britain into joining a proposed 'Pan African Conference' of 'white' powers in Africa. In a confrontation with Lord Home, the secretary of state for Commonwealth relations, Louw emphasised that his government had given Britain 'the fullest possible co-operation over defence, over finance, and over economic issues generally'. If Britain would not participate in the Conference or join an African Defence Organisation, Louw claimed that his government would take their country 'into isolation'.[46] The CRO was not unduly alarmed.

> We do not wish to have a first class row with the South Africans at present in view of the difficult questions coming up over the expansion of Commonwealth membership and the vulnerable position of the territories, particularly Basutoland. Economically, South African trade, particularly gold and uranium, is also important to us, though equally to them.[47]

Home took a firm line, telling Louw to make do with what his government had already been offered – a conference on logistics and communications to be attended by Britain and other colonial powers in Africa. In the end, not even this conference took place, emphasising the failure of Louw's tactics. His threats could not be taken seriously while South Africa remained so dependent on Britain economically.[48]

---

[44] For Britain's significance as a market for agricultural goods see table 6.1. For Britain's overall significance as a customer and as a supplier see fig. 6.4.
[45] S. Jones and A. Muller, *The South African economy, 1910–1990* (London, 1992), p. 223.
[46] DO 35/7139, note by Home, 13 July 1955.
[47] DO 35/7139, Laithwaite to Home, 13 July 1955.
[48] DO 35/7139, note by Home, 18 July 1955.

The crude use of economic threats was short-lived, partly, it would seem, because South Africa's own economic position became weaker. Two separate forces caused the flow of capital into South Africa (which had averaged £88 million per annum in the years 1947 to 1954) to decline sharply in 1955 and then to go into reverse. First, British interest rates were raised in 1955 and 1956, making deposits in London more attractive. Secondly, and perhaps equally importantly, the controversy surrounding the removal of 'Coloured' voters from the common roll by the government's riding roughshod over the constitution profoundly shook investor confidence. In February 1956, the Strijdom government resorted to the imposition of exchange control on the movement of capital within the sterling area by South African residents. Stricter controls were applied in 1958, but so great became the need to find new capital that the South African government made an approach to raise a loan in London for the first time since 1949.[49]

Under the terms of the Memorandum of Understanding, there was an outstanding commitment to allow South Africa to raise £5 million. Dönges, who had become minister of finance in the new Verwoerd government, argued that this commitment and his government's desire to 'preserve close financial relations between London and South Africa' justified the request to borrow £10 million of new money and to deal with £5 million of maturing stock.[50]

Whitehall had already debated the wisdom of trying to influence political developments in South Africa by controlling access to British capital. In 1954, British Treasury officials could imagine 'nothing more injurious' to British interests 'than for us to attempt to apply political criteria to proposals for investment in South Africa'. Dönges was told that South Africa could borrow £10 million in 1959.[51]

The British and South African governments seem to have recognised not only their own, but also the other's dependence on the economic bargains that bound them together. While each was in practice reluctant to threaten those bargains in a serious way in pursuit of non-economic ends, each also saw that its own political initiatives were unlikely to meet with economic retaliation. The continuing validity of these bargains thus tended to insulate economic affairs from political disputes occasioned by South Africa's expansionist ambitions, devotion to repugnant racial policies, or advance towards a republic.

This tendency was apparent at the end of 1959 and early in 1960 as the British government considered the effects of distancing itself from South Africa at the United Nations. Shortly after Harold Macmillan returned from his 'wind of change' tour of Africa, the chancellor of the Exchequer warned that if 'our

[49] Jones and Muller, *South African economy*, p. 223.
[50] T 236/4877, Heathcoat Amory to Dönges, 18 Dec. 1958.
[51] T 236/4083, note by Hillis, 15 Feb. 1954. T 236/4877, Heathcoat Amory to Dönges, 18 Dec. 1958.

relations with the Union were to deteriorate to the point where South Africans considered leaving both the Commonwealth and the sterling area, the financial and economic consequences must be very serious for us'. The chancellor, Derick Heathcoat Amory, was not arguing against the change of policy at the United Nations being proposed by the CRO. Such a change would not, he hoped, have 'such untoward consequences'.[52]

These consequences, explained in a note prepared by the Treasury and the Bank of England, so impressed Macmillan that he ordered that the note be circulated to Cabinet before any decision was taken on UN policy. This note, while acknowledging the scale of British exports to and investment in South Africa, emphasised the value of South Africa's inclusion in the sterling area. The Treasury and the Bank accepted that 'a purely technical case could perhaps be made out for saying that, if South Africa were to leave the Sterling Area, it would not make a big practical difference'. South Africa might cease to use sterling for payments to non-sterling countries or to hold reserves in sterling, both of which would hurt Britain to a limited degree. But this was far from being the whole story. As the Bank had been at pains to stress, South Africa's departure from the sterling area would be regarded as 'a major crack in the Sterling Area system'. Furthermore, South Africa might sell its gold somewhere other than London, with damaging effects for the City's position as an international financial centre. This was, however, merely a forecast of the worst that could be expected. No-one in the Treasury or even the Bank expected the proposed shift in policy at the UN to produce such a reaction, not least because South Africa's economy would be harmed as much if not more than Britain's.[53]

The Macmillan Cabinet was still waiting to make a final decision on its policy for the next session of the UN General Assembly when the Sharpeville massacre intervened to force an immediate decision. Verwoerd urged the British government to oppose discussion of the South African situation by an emergency meeting of the Security Council on the grounds that all matters of domestic jurisdiction were outside the competence of the UN. In the Cabinet's

---

[52] T 236/4873, Heathcoat Amory to Macmillan, and Treasury note, 17 Feb. 1960. The Radcliffe committee (which studied the problems of British monetary policy over a period of almost two years) concluded in August 1959 that 'Although there have been occasions when the functioning of the sterling area has thrown an added strain on the reserves and when the capital requirements of the area have added to the total load on the reserves of the United Kingdom, we are satisfied that it is in the interest of this country to maintain existing arrangements.' Radcliffe committee, *Report*, p. 240.

[53] T 236/4873, Heathcoat Amory to Macmillan, and Treasury note, 17 Feb. 1960. T 236/4874, note by Pliatsky, 30 Dec. 1959. The sterling area may, as Krozewski argues, have become less valuable 'when the dollar gap closed, and after convertibility was re-established in 1958'. But there is nothing in the evidence available in connection with South Africa to suggest that the British government itself viewed the sterling area as having diminished in importance prior to the end of 1960 at least. Krozewski, 'Sterling, the "minor" territories, and the end of formal empire', p. 241.

discussion of this question, Home brought the CRO's well-rehearsed arguments to bear. 'The continued adherence of South Africa to the Sterling Area was a matter of great importance' but the South African government was unlikely to leave the Commonwealth or the sterling area because Britain did not veto discussion of Sharpeville. Moreover, as the Foreign, Colonial, and Commonwealth Relations Offices saw, Britain needed to avoid either undermining its own authority in British dependent territories or alienating newly independent countries, especially those in the Commonwealth. Cabinet accepted this reasoning, agreeing that, despite South Africa's objections, Britain could afford to veto neither discussion of Sharpeville nor the resulting Security Council resolution.[54]

Economic considerations had not been paramount in these British decisions. The British government recognised that the Verwoerd government was unlikely to undo mutually beneficial economic bargains unless white South Africa was provoked into uniting against Britain. The British concern to contain Afrikanerdom, safeguard strategic interests, protect the High Commission Territories, and hold South Africa in the Commonwealth was undoubtedly sufficient to ensure that such provocation would be avoided at almost any cost.[55]

Where British policy was shaped by economic dependence on South Africa was in regard to that country's ability to reap the economic benefits of Commonwealth membership after the Verwoerd government had taken South Africa out of the Commonwealth. The principal benefits were the right to preferential access to British markets and capital. In the run-up to white South Africa's referendum for a republic, the British government would neither confirm nor deny that these economic advantages would continue if the Commonwealth connection were severed. South African opponents of the republican constitution argued that these advantages would soon be lost once the first step towards departure from the Commonwealth was taken by declaring a republic. But the potency of this, their leading argument, was drastically diminished by National Party claims that South Africa would stay in the Commonwealth as a republic and that even if it left, any economic benefits could be retained. If Britain had been less dependent on South Africa economically, the Macmillan government might have declared openly that this would not be so. In those circumstances, South Africa's continued economic dependence on Britain might, even as late as 1960, still have assured the preservation of the Commonwealth connection. As it was, the Verwoerd government probably calculated that the British

[54] PRO, Cabinet papers, CAB 128/34, CC 21(60)3, 29 March 1960, and CC 22(60)3, 1 April 1960; repr. in R. Hyam and W. R. Louis, eds., *The Conservative government and the end of empire, 1957–1964* (BDEEP, London, 2000), part I, doc. nos. 447 and 448.

[55] See chapter 8 below. R. Ovendale, 'The South African policy of the British Labour government, 1947–1951', *International Affairs*, 59 (1983), pp. 41–58.

government could not afford to withdraw South Africa's preferential access to British markets and capital.[56]

Although South Africa remained surprisingly dependent on Britain as a customer and supplier in 1960, the British government was (due to Britain's own peculiar economic dependence on South Africa) in no position to use economic means to force a change of political course in South Africa. And while the prospect of large-scale capital flight was still viewed with concern by the South African government, the threat posed by such a development had diminished considerably since the 1930s. Gold production was set to increase steadily in the 1960s without substantial new injections of capital. Industrial development had somewhat reduced both the relative importance of the mining industry and the need to hold the South African economy fully open to external investment. The growth of Afrikaner-dominated business indirectly brought more of the economy under what was equivalent to government control. Furthermore, South Africa had, after 1955, developed an effective money (i.e. short-term capital) market, thereby lessening the country's dependence on the London market. Finally, the growing power and efficiency of the South African state had increased the government's ability to control economic affairs (including the problem of capital flight) almost as thoroughly as affairs in any other sphere of South African life.[57]

National Party governments could thus continue to benefit from long-standing economic bargains while pursuing political policies increasingly at odds with international opinion. In the 1930s, the British government refused to interfere in South Africa's relationship to sterling in order to avoid either incurring financial liabilities or damaging the British connection by making it a subject of political controversy; South Africa had, nonetheless, been forced into line by economic pressures. Similar pressures might have forced the Verwoerd government to change course if the British government had felt able to use the economic power theoretically at its disposal, or if capital had been as free to move in and out of South Africa as it had been in the 1930s. As it was, the Verwoerd government was far less vulnerable than any of its predecessors to the sort of economic pressure that had transformed the South African political scene in 1933.

Unlike Hertzog's government, Verwoerd's was able to resist pressure for political change applied indirectly by domestic and overseas holders of capital. The Verwoerd government stemmed the flight of capital (which began with Sharpeville and continued as the country moved towards a republic and departure from the Commonwealth) by applying, for the first time, strict controls on any movement of capital out of South Africa, including capital owned by

---

[56] Geldenhuys, 'The effects of South Africa's racial policy', ch. 4.
[57] Jones and Muller, *South African economy*, p. 210.

other sterling area residents. These controls, imposed less than three weeks after South Africa left the Commonwealth, brought to an end the free flow of funds between Britain and South Africa that had been more or less uninterrupted since the formation of the Union. The South African government succeeded with a policy that seemed to cut off the country from future external investment, partly because direct overseas investment in South African industry was already so large that when South Africa embarked on a programme of import substitution, overseas companies were forced to invest more in the 1960s to protect their existing commitments. This, the rising output of the gold mines during the 1960s, and the fortuitous increases in the gold price when output ceased to rise, would put off for another twenty-five years the day when white South Africa really began to suffer economically as a result of its government's policies.[58]

After 1961, as before, South Africa's currency remained fixed in value relative to sterling. The majority of South African external accounts were still settled in sterling through the Bank of England, and a portion of South African external reserves continued to be held in sterling. While revulsion against apartheid forced an intransigent South Africa out of the Commonwealth, there seems to have been no corresponding move to oust South Africa from the sterling area. In the 1960s, all of the area's members had too much to lose from the shock to the sterling system which would have inevitably followed South Africa's exclusion. By the 1970s, when pressure for such an exclusion might have begun to build, the area had collapsed under the strain of Britain's own economic under-performance and chronic balance-of-payments deficits.[59]

The equivalent in economic affairs of 31 May 1961 – the date of South Africa's declaration of a republic and departure from the Commonwealth – is not definite, nor even obvious, but so far as South Africa was concerned, the final and effective end of the sterling area came in 1972 when both the flow of British capital to South Africa was officially restricted and South Africa's currency was pegged to the United States dollar.[60]

V

When the sterling area emerged in 1931, the Afrikaner nationalist government then ruling South Africa resolved that the country should stand apart. South Africa's (and particularly the gold-mining industry's) dependence on the London capital market, the country's resulting vulnerability to speculative outflows of funds, and its dependence on British markets for agricultural products (which in the politics of South Africa was, and would continue to be, a major

[58] Jones and Muller, *South African economy*, pp. 223–4, 352–7.
[59] Y. Bangura, *Britain and Commonwealth Africa: the politics of economic relations, 1951–1975* (Manchester, 1983), pp. 77–8.
[60] Bangura, *Britain and Commonwealth Africa*, p. 113.

concern) forced the abandonment of the gold standard, the devaluation of the South African pound, and adherence to sterling.

If the Second World War enabled the National Party to regroup in opposition to South Africa's active alliance with Britain, the war's disruptions to international trade and the strength of National Party opposition had the effect of entrenching South Africa's economic dependence on Britain. The British government was prepared to concede almost anything economically to keep South Africa in the war. South Africa, instead of having to adjust to the loss of external agricultural markets by expanding domestic markets or shifting into alternative economic activities, found Britain willing to pay assured prices for almost all of the primary products that South Africa could produce. And instead of painfully adjusting to international shortages of capital funds and goods by accepting that mining output must fall and other industries should be more rapidly developed, the Smuts government found that the threat of a National Party victory was enough to convince Britain and the United States to channel scarce resources into gold production. Moreover, the lightness of South African austerity during and after the war left the country with fewer reserves and domestic savings with which to meet development needs. The availability of large quantities of external capital remained as essential as ever after the war.

Whatever the Malan government's anti-British inclinations, continued dependence on Britain as a customer, supplier, and financier forced it to reaffirm the bargains that held South Africa in the sterling orbit. Any desire by post-war National Party governments to break away from the sterling area seems to have been held in check by the fear of precipitating an economic crisis of the sort that had split the party in 1933. Questions of economic independence were left quietly on one side while the government promoted Afrikaner political ascendancy and Afrikaner economic advancement within South Africa.[61]

An ironic result of South Africa's continued devotion to the sterling area was that by the time the Verwoerd government prepared to crown Afrikanerdom's domestic dominance with the establishment of a republic, the country was still such an essential part of the area that Verwoerd could confidently assert that no economic advantages would be lost if South Africa abandoned the monarchy

---

[61] The conclusions drawn by this chapter thus accord with those accounts which have emphasised both the many continuities of South African government policy which were unbroken by the advent of National Party rule and the pragmatism of Nationalist governments supposedly bent from the outset on implementing a 'grand plan' of apartheid. For an early expression of this view see R. Hyam, 'The myth of the "magnanimous gesture": the Liberal government, Smuts and conciliation, 1906', in R. Hyam and G. Martin, *Reappraisals in British imperial history* (London, 1975), p. 184: 'If the Nationalist government brought a new feature to the South African scene it lay ... in their efficiency in securing their electoral base.' Such views have been the subject of considerable debate but they have recently gained more widespread acceptance: see I. R. Phimister, 'Secondary industrialisation in southern Africa: the 1948 customs agreement between Southern Rhodesia and South Africa', *Journal of Southern African Studies*, 17, 3 (1991), pp. 430–42.

and left the Commonwealth. South Africa would retain the economic substance of the Commonwealth connection even if it had so clearly rejected the spirit of the multi-racial association.

From beginning to end, the sterling area was a grouping of those countries most securely tied into a world-wide economic system centred on Britain – a bastion where sterling retained its formerly global pre-eminence. The attractions of bargains based on South Africa's need to sustain agricultural exports and capital imports, and on Britain's need for a steady supply of gold, underpinned not only South Africa's presence in the sterling area, but also the wider strategic, economic, and political connections which bound Britain and South Africa so closely together. Defence and economic connections outlived the Commonwealth tie, although by 1972 the sterling area relationship had collapsed and by 1975 formal defence co-operation had come to an end. Some economic connections lasted longer still, with the Thatcher government demonstrating the value it attached to them and to strategic considerations by resisting to the end the tide of domestic and international pressure for economic sanctions. Perhaps the South African remnant of the British economic world system was so durable, or the vision of a post-apartheid South Africa allied to the West so alluring, that the British government could not bring itself finally to terminate the remains of economic connections which had endured since the nineteenth century.[62]

---

[62] J. Barber and J. Barratt, *South Africa's foreign policy: the search for status and security, 1945–1988* (Cambridge, 1990), pp. 157–60, 327–31.

7 Britain, the United Nations, and the 'South African disputes', 1946–1961

The British alignment with South Africa at the United Nations in the years 1946 to 1960 seems simple enough to explain. A British government preoccupied with protecting its economic and strategic interests in South Africa (or even just its economic interests there) supported South Africa in this international forum until the domestic and international reaction against apartheid forced a limited change of British policy; and though in 1961 the British government joined the majority of nations represented in the General Assembly in admonishing South Africa, it continued to resist Assembly initiatives which threatened those same economic and strategic interests for many years to come. This is a familiar explanation of Anglo-South African relations at the United Nations (UN), though a far from accurate one.[1]

For the first fifteen years after the Second World War, the British government was indeed South Africa's leading ally on the issues that most directly concerned South Africa at the UN: the future of South-West Africa (Namibia), the treatment of 'Indians' in South Africa and the 'race conflict' there. The British government backed the Smuts government's initial attempt to incorporate South-West Africa within the Union of South Africa and supported the South African contention that the UN could intervene in the administration of South-West Africa only with the agreement of the South African government itself. In these years, the British government also supported the South African government's claims that its treatment of South Africans of Indian origin, and its racial policies more generally, were matters of essentially domestic concern, therefore not issues in which the General Assembly could legitimately intervene. Obviously, then, there were potent reasons for a policy which forced

---

[1] According to Andrew Young, American ambassador to the United Nations during the Carter administration, '[t]here was always a desire on the part of Britain to avoid any confrontation with South Africa because of economic connections': quoted in H. Hunke, *Namibia: the strength of the powerless* (Rome, 1980), p. 17. For further expressions of the view that economic, or economic and strategic, considerations were decisive, see G. R. Berridge, *Economic power in Anglo-South African diplomacy: Simonstown, Sharpeville and after* (London, 1981); J. Mayall, 'The South African crisis: the major external factors', in S. Johnson, ed., *South Africa: no turning back* (London, 1988), p. 304; H. Bull, 'Implications for the West', in R. Rotberg and J. Barratt, eds., *Conflict and compromise in South Africa* (Cape Town, 1980), pp. 175–7.

Britain's UN delegation into narrowing and increasingly disreputable company on the South African disputes. But these reasons were not exclusively or decisively economic (or even economic and strategic) in nature.[2]

The British government never simply judged that the moral and material advantages of an anti-South African stance at the UN (advantages for Britain's position as a colonial power no less than for its leadership of an expanding multiracial Commonwealth) were outweighed by the economic and strategic need to preserve close relations with South Africa. British policy was based on calculations altogether more complex. Not only did British interests in South Africa extend far beyond the purely economic or strategic. British interests there were also inextricably entwined with, and formed a crucial part of, a vast structure of world-wide power and responsibilities – Britain's inescapable imperial inheritance. The British government wished to defend not only the Commonwealth connection with South Africa and Britain's strategic and economic interests there, but also Britain's own direct authority elsewhere in Africa – in the High Commission Territories (Basutoland, Bechuanaland, and Swaziland), in the areas of white settlement (the Rhodesias and Kenya) and elsewhere. Everywhere in Africa, Britain's primary objective in relation to the UN was the same: to resist UN interference which threatened to stimulate nationalist forces antagonistic to Britain – whether those nationalists be black or white, nominally loyal to the Crown or anti-British. The South African government's devotion to 'totally repugnant' racial policies brought the contradictions inherent in the pursuit of this objective into sharp relief at the UN. As this chapter will show, British policy on the South African disputes at the UN was the product not just of the British government's desire to preserve close relations with the South African government (for reasons of strategy, economics, geopolitics, and prestige) but also, crucially, of the British determination to resist UN interference in the British empire or Commonwealth – interference that was as real a threat to British interests in South Africa as it was to British authority in the dependent empire.[3]

I

The problems that would bedevil Anglo-South African relations at the UN did not emerge gradually as the product of a steadily growing international reaction against South African racial policies; nor were they merely a post-1948

[2] *Yearbook of the United Nations*, 1946–61; *Official records of the General Assembly* (hereafter GAOR) 1946–61.

[3] R. Hyam, ed., British Documents on the End of Empire Project (hereafter BDEEP), *The Labour government and the end of empire, 1945–1951*, 4 parts (London, 1992); R. Hyam, 'Africa and the Labour government', *Journal of Imperial and Commonwealth History*, 16, 3 (1988), pp. 148–72; J. Barber and J. Barratt, *South Africa's foreign policy: the search for status and security, 1945–1988* (Cambridge, 1990), pp. 13–62.

phenomenon, a response to the National Party government's intransigence and rigid racial assumptions. They took stark and unavoidable form at the General Assembly's first session when the international standing of South Africa (and more particularly of its prime minister, J. C. Smuts) was at its height. South Africa had been part of the victorious 'grand alliance' against fascism, a founding member of the UN. Smuts was one of the Commonwealth's most widely admired leaders, a veteran of the Paris Peace Conference and elder statesman of the successor to the League of Nations. But neither South Africa's prestige nor Smuts's personal appearance at the General Assembly were sufficient to counteract the widespread antipathy for South African racial policies – antipathy which was stimulated by the government of India's complaints about the treatment of 'Indians' in South Africa and which would be the main cause of South Africa's failure to incorporate South-West Africa.[4]

Incorporation had been the South African government's ambition from the time that South African troops invaded German South-West Africa in the First World War. This ambition had been held in check by the insistence of the founders of the League that the territory be administered under a League of Nations mandate. The South African government never regarded this as a permanent arrangement (it held up South-West Africa's designation as a 'C' class mandate as proof that incorporation was the agreed ultimate destiny of the territory) and saw the final dissolution of the League at the end of the Second World War as an opportunity to annex the territory.[5]

Before the first part of the Assembly's first session began in London, the Smuts government knew that its plans for South-West Africa might encounter substantial opposition. Even among the other old dominions, seemingly South Africa's most likely allies, there were committed advocates of the proposals not only for the compulsory transfer of all League mandates to UN trusteeship, but also for UN supervision of all non-self-governing territories. The British government's steadfast opposition to both these proposals left the way open for South-West Africa's incorporation, though it in no way ensured British support for incorporation.[6]

As it was, the British Labour government was even more reluctant to offer such support than the South African government supposed. George Hall, the colonial secretary and veteran trade-unionist, rejected the view (accepted officially by his own department) that Britain could support incorporation. He

---

[4] J. Barber, *South Africa's foreign policy, 1945–1970* (Oxford, 1973), pp. 24–31; W. K. Hancock, *Smuts*, vol. II: *The fields of force, 1919–1950* (Cambridge, 1968), pp. 467–71.

[5] S. Pienaar, *South Africa and international relations between the two world wars: the League of Nations dimension* (Johannesburg, 1987), pp. 111–56.

[6] Pretoria, Central Archives Depot, Smuts papers (hereafter SP), A1/91, minutes of Commonwealth prime ministers meeting, BCM(45)12; SP, A1/163, G. Heaton Nicholls to J. Smuts, 15 Dec. 1945.

recommended that the government restrict itself to an undertaking not to oppose incorporation. An alarmed Dominions Office warned that failure to support incorporation would inevitably be interpreted as a demonstration of dissent, removing any chance of success for South Africa's territorial ambitions. This, officials there predicted, was likely to alienate not only the Smuts government but also the public opinion of the 'whole European population of the Union'.[7]

Lord Addison, the Dominions secretary, argued along these lines in Cabinet. Against this, Hall noted that South Africa had already been much criticised at the UN, New Zealand's prime minister being among the critics; that a considerable body of British opinion opposed incorporation; and that support for South Africa might both negate the credit Britain hoped to gain by supporting the principle of trusteeship and lead France to incorporate its own mandates, leaving Britain as the only power with any significant territories under UN trusteeship. Other ministers wondered why incorporation could not be supported if the consent of South-West Africa's inhabitants was sought and obtained by methods agreeable to the UN. The arguments were thought to be 'nicely balanced'. A decision was deferred until the question had been discussed personally with Smuts.[8]

Smuts was already scheduled to attend a meeting of Commonwealth prime ministers in London. The effect of his personal intervention was immediate. In 1946 he still seemed to be the key to the maintenance of the Commonwealth connection with South Africa, the indispensable agent in almost every sphere of Anglo-South African collaboration – political, strategic, or economic. His talks with British ministers (which ranged from the disposal of South African uranium to the future of the Italian colonies) tipped the balance in favour of support for incorporation, though not to the extent desired by Smuts or the Dominions Office. Cabinet agreed that incorporation would be supported but only if the inhabitants' consent had been sought and obtained by methods agreeable to the UN.[9]

Cabinet also considered whether to allow Tshekedi Khama, regent of the Bangwato in Bechuanaland (one of the three High Commission Territories bordering on and long-coveted by South Africa), to travel to London and New York to voice his opposition to South-West Africa's incorporation. In the British and South African reactions to Tshekedi's request can be seen striking parallels with the crisis over the marriage of Tshekedi's nephew Seretse Khama (heir to the chieftainship) to a white woman. Smuts, in no uncertain terms, gave the British government notice that Tshekedi's appearance at the UN 'might easily serve to inflame opinion in the Union', sparking agitation

---

[7] London, Public Record Office (hereafter PRO), Dominions Office (later Commonwealth Relations Office) papers, DO 35/1934, note by F. E. Cumming-Bruce, 16 Apr. 1946.
[8] PRO, Cabinet memoranda, CAB 129/9, CP(46)157, 15 Apr. 1946 and CP(46)158, 16 Apr. 1946; Cabinet minutes, CAB 128/5, CM 37(46)3, 24 Apr. 1946.
[9] CAB 128/5, CM 45(46)8, 13 May 1946; Hyam, BDEEP: *Labour government*, doc. 412.

for the transfer of the Territories; and because transfer was bound to be opposed in Britain (as well as in the Territories themselves) the resulting crisis might wreck the Commonwealth connection with South Africa and all that went with it.[10]

Faced with warnings from Smuts that failure to offer unconditional support for incorporation would cause much mischief in South Africa and increase pressure there for the immediate transfer of the Territories, Addison urged Cabinet to approve South Africa's methods. South-West Africa's black population had been consulted not as individuals but grouped together in 'tribes', with the consultation left exclusively in the hands of South African 'native commissioners'. The result was a large majority in favour of incorporation: 208,850 opposed by only 33,520. No less an authority than Lord Hailey declared himself satisfied with South Africa's methods. But some British ministers still expressed serious doubts. The acceptance of consultation undertaken without international supervision would set an 'embarrassing precedent' and might increase the difficulties of negotiating trusteeship agreements for Britain's own mandated territories. Cabinet once again deferred its decision until ministers could speak directly to Smuts.[11]

As it had five months previously, the balance of opinion in the British Cabinet tipped in Smuts's favour after his talks with British ministers. Despite the strong doubts expressed by some British officials about the validity of the consultations in South-West Africa, Cabinet agreed that the long-awaited statement of British policy would include the declaration that the British government was 'satisfied as to the steps taken by the South African government to ascertain the wishes of the inhabitants'.[12]

By the time this decision was taken, a debate was already well under way in Whitehall about the second major South African issue confronting Britain at the United Nations – the government of India's complaint about the treatment of 'Indians' in South Africa. Discrimination against the quarter million or so people of Indian descent within South Africa had long been a source of tension, having led to the 'Cape Town agreements' of 1927 and 1932 in which the governments of India and South Africa settled their differences, temporarily at least, over the rights and status of these people. But tensions remained and

---

[10] DO 35/1935, note dictated by D. D. Forsyth, 24 May 1946 and note by Lord Addison, 28 May 1946; R. Hyam, 'The political consequences of Seretse Khama: Britain, the Bangwato and South Africa, 1948–1952', *Historical Journal*, 29, 4 (1986), pp. 921–47 (chapter 8 below); M. Crowder, 'Tshekedi Khama, Smuts, and South West Africa', *Journal of Modern African Studies* 25, 1 (1987), pp. 25–42.

[11] SP, A1/166, J. Smuts to G. Heaton Nicholls, 7 Oct. 1946; CAB 129/13, CP(46)371, 8 Oct. 1946; CAB 128/6, CM 85(46)5, 10 Oct. 1946; Hyam, BDEEP: *Labour government*, doc. 413.

[12] For the doubts of officials see DO 35/1214, WR213/9/16, A. H. Poynton to C. W. Dixon, 18 Sep. 1946; CAB 128/6, CM 88(46), 18 Oct. 1946.

were exacerbated by segregationist legislation enacted in South Africa during and after the Second World War. In 1946 the immediate cause of complaint was the Asiatic Land Tenure and Indian Representation Act which, though regarded by many white South Africans as unacceptably liberal, was rejected by South African 'Indians' as placing unacceptable limitations on their rights to acquire and occupy property and on their rights to political representation. The government of India, responding to appeals from South African 'Indian' leaders, took the issue to the UN.[13]

Within the British government the 'Indian complaint' provoked deep divisions in Cabinet and further rare ministerial rejections of official advice, again because of the international ramifications of the proposed policy. A note prepared in the Foreign Office (and agreed at official level by the India, Dominions and Colonial Offices) recommended that the British government declare the subject of the complaint to be a matter of domestic jurisdiction and seek to secure UN acceptance of this view. To do otherwise was to invite UN interference in British dependent territories.[14]

Lord Pethick-Lawrence, the secretary of state for India, took the strongest exception to this recommendation. He believed that such a policy could seriously damage future relations with India: British actions in this 'very delicate situation' could determine whether India would seek to remain in the Commonwealth (an issue much in doubt and agonised over) or would turn to the Soviet Union. The British delegation should, he thought, make its neutrality at the UN absolute, by stating that since the dispute lay between two members of the Commonwealth, Britain would take no part in discussions of it.[15]

His views would not prevail. Cabinet, acting on the advice of the Foreign Office (backed by the Dominions and Colonial Offices), agreed that although the British delegation should avoid expressing any views on the merits of the dispute, it must insist that the subject was a matter of South Africa's domestic jurisdiction. Cabinet shared the Foreign Office belief that 'it would be impossible for the United Kingdom Government, as one of the leading members of the UN, to dissociate themselves from all discussion of this matter in the Assembly'. Furthermore, this line, the one least likely to give offence to either side, would safeguard 'the interests of the administration of the British colonial Empire'.[16]

---

[13] B. Pachai, *The international aspects of the South African Indian question, 1860–1971* (Cape Town, 1971); L. Lloyd, '"A family quarrel": the development of the dispute over Indians in South Africa', *Historical Journal* 34, 3 (1991), pp. 703–25.
[14] DO 35/1293, note by H. N. Tait, 10 Oct. 1948.
[15] N. Mansergh and P. Moon, eds., *Transfer of power in India*, vol. VIII (London, 1979), p. 859.
[16] CAB 129/13, CP(46)394, 21 Oct. 1946 and CP(46)397, 23 Oct. 1946; CAB 128/6, CM 91(46), 25 Oct. 1946.

As instructed, the British delegation joined South Africa in opposing an Indian-backed resolution, because it assumed the Assembly's competence to intervene in the dispute. As predicted, the resolution gained the required majority all the same. According to the British delegation, the tide had turned against South Africa not so much because of the charges made by the Indian delegation as because of the statements made by South Africans in their own defence: in making it reasonably clear that South African 'Indians' were not maltreated, they made it obvious that the basis of the governmental order in South Africa was racial discrimination.[17]

The Indian criticism followed South Africa into the debates on South-West Africa, galvanising international resistance to incorporation. Smuts and his Cabinet had known that their chances of success at the Assembly were slender but their view was that to hesitate 'would put us in a worse position next year' and expose the government to criticism from the National Party opposition. Britain's delegation (the only one to support South Africa actively) felt that although South Africa's tactical handling of the issue was poor, this had not affected the ultimate fate of the South African plans, which were thought to have been doomed once United States opposition became known. And while 'anti-colonial prejudices', 'sympathy for India', and suspicion of 'imperialism' all played a part in engendering opposition to incorporation, the predominant factors operating against South Africa were the antagonism generated by the Indian complaint and 'the rising tide of nationalism amongst the races of Asia' which rallied the 'coloured states' against a government 'avowing a policy of white supremacy'.[18]

The first session of the General Assembly (the first part in London, the second in New York) cast British policy in a form which would remain, in its essentials, virtually unchanged for almost fifteen years in respect of the Indian complaint, twenty-nine years in respect of South-West Africa. For better or worse, the British government had declared, first, that the subject of the government of India's complaint was a matter of South Africa's domestic jurisdiction; secondly, that it approved the consultations with South-West Africa's inhabitants; and, thirdly, that South Africa was under no legal or moral obligation to place South-West Africa under UN trusteeship. The second declaration was largely the product of the British government's concern not to alienate or undermine Smuts, whose goodwill and hold on power were thought to be vital for the protection of British interests in South Africa. The first and third declarations were the product not just of this concern but also (and just as vitally) of the

---

[17] DO 35/1214 and DO 35/1295. L. Lloyd, ' "A most auspicious beginning": the 1946 General Assembly and the question of the treatment of Indians in South Africa', *Review of International Studies* 16, 2 (1990), pp. 131–53.

[18] SP, A1/165, G. Heaton Nicholls to D. D. Forsyth, Aug. 1946; PRO, Colonial Office Papers, CO 537/2073.

determination to resist UN interference in South African or South-West African affairs – something which would inevitably open the door to such interference in British dependencies.[19]

II

From the beginning, the British government's stand on the South African disputes attracted considerable criticism, both in Britain and abroad. And though some British officials would express their reservations about the wisdom of this stand, the British external affairs departments continued to agree (at the official level at least) that this stand was necessary. Ministers, especially while Labour remained in power, were less certain of its necessity. They became considerably less so after the South African government, under National Party rule, began to revel in its defiance of international opinion and to implement its policies of apartheid. The official view of the external affairs departments would be directly challenged, even temporarily overturned, before the Labour Cabinet would agree that this stand must continue.

The British government could, of course, have escaped much of the criticism that its policy on the South African disputes attracted if the disputes themselves had been headed towards a definite solution. But though Smuts was still in power, there seemed little prospect of that. Lord Listowel, the new (and last) secretary of state for India, thought that acceptance of the government of India's demands for a round-table conference to negotiate the reduction of discrimination against South African 'Indians' would mean 'political suicide for Smuts': the United Party had lost an important by-election 'mainly because of Smuts's alleged liberal attitude towards Indians'; if he went any further to conciliate Indian opinion, 'his fall in the 1948 election in the Union seems certain'. The story, with respect to South-West Africa, was much the same: Sir Eric Machtig, permanent under-secretary at the newly established Commonwealth Relations Office (successor to the Dominions and India Offices) pointed out that white South African opinion was 'almost unanimously opposed to trusteeship' for South-West Africa; to propose it was 'politically out of the question' for Smuts. Thus it was hardly surprising that at the Assembly's second session no progress was made towards a solution of these disputes.[20]

This proved to be the Assembly's last session before the advent of National Party rule in South Africa. If a government composed exclusively of Afrikaner nationalists had come to power two years earlier, Britain's initial course at the UN might well have been different. In Smuts's absence, the British government

---

[19] P. J. Henshaw, 'South Africa's external relations with Britain and the Commonwealth, 1945–1956' (PhD thesis, Cambridge University, 1989), 17–32.

[20] Mansergh and Moon, eds., *Transfer of power in India*, vol. XII, p. 253.

would probably not have *supported* incorporation publicly; it might not have *supported* South Africa against India. But neither would it have *opposed* South Africa in these disputes unless it could have done so without either antagonising the whole of white South Africa or exposing British dependencies to UN interference. As long as the British government was preoccupied with preserving its world-wide power, it would remain as concerned with preserving close relations with autonomous governments of the British Commonwealth such as South Africa as it was with maintaining British authority in the empire's dependent territories – neither concern would ever take complete precedence over the other.

As it was, British policy at the UN would be constrained not only by the desire to establish a fruitful relationship with Smuts's successors but also by the stance it had adopted at the UN while Smuts was in power. In Paris, at the Assembly's third session, the British delegation was once again called upon to be as helpful as possible to the representatives of the South African government, now under the premiership of D. F. Malan.[21]

The British delegation's supportive attitude did not pass unnoticed at home. Objections to it were forcibly expressed to British ministers by a high-profile deputation led by Tom Driberg, a back-bench Labour member of parliament who took a close interest in southern Africa throughout his time in the House. The questions Driberg put to Philip Noel-Baker (the secretary of state for Commonwealth Relations) and Gordon Walker (the parliamentary secretary) were blunt: 'Can you not afford to get a bit tougher with the Malan Government?' 'If our attitude to the Union Government is based on economic and strategic considerations, is it not true at least that they need us at least as much as we need them?' In response Noel-Baker asserted that British policy 'is not in the slightest degree influenced by economic or financial or strategic considerations, not at all'. Policy was, he argued, influenced by the concern to avoid 'an all out quarrel with another member of the Commonwealth in the creation of whose self-government we still take a considerable national pride'.[22]

In fact, despite Noel-Baker's claims to the contrary, British policy was not shaped solely by the desire to maintain the Commonwealth connection with South Africa; there were also economic and strategic considerations as well as the concern to protect the High Commission Territories. In any case, the problem facing the British government was the same. As an official of the Commonwealth Relations Office (CRO) noted, Britain had 'no real political hold' which would force the South African government to change its policy. Representations without this advantage 'might do more damage than they were

---

[21] CO 537/3478, note by P. Gordon Walker, 12 Nov. 1948; PRO, Treasury Papers, T 236/2271, H. McNeil to E. Bevin, 24 Sep. 1948.
[22] CO 537/4596, note of meeting on 3 Mar. 1949.

worth'. A public statement of disapproval would 'only increase the influence of the hotheads among the Nationalist Party' and drive the Union to 'further extremes of isolationism and defiance'. Unfortunately, these arguments could not be developed in public. Consequently the public defence of British policy had to be based on legal considerations – a far from simple matter, as the referral of the South-West African dispute to the International Court of Justice would show.[23]

This referral presented the British government with a new and pressing problem: should it intervene at the Court to protect Britain's own colonial interests or should it let South Africa fend for itself? Unfortunately, British intervention might be misinterpreted as a demonstration of support for the South African government at a time when revulsion against apartheid, and the desire to chart a far different course in British Africa, was hardening British opinion against South Africa.[24]

Once again, a South African issue provoked sharp divisions between ministers and officials in Whitehall. The Colonial, Foreign, and Commonwealth Relations Offices favoured (at the official level at least) British intervention at the Court. Issues raised there would have 'a direct and most important bearing upon the Colonial Empire'. A ruling to the effect that the General Assembly was entitled to a say in the constitutional development of non-self-governing territories 'would be nothing short of disastrous'. Some ministers agreed. Others thought intervention itself to be the greater danger. Two junior ministers took the lead in questioning the official view. In the Foreign Office, Hector McNeil (through his attendance at the General Assembly, personally acquainted with the international implications of siding with South Africa) noted that the British government was already under fire for its opposition to Michael Scott's appearance in the Trusteeship Committee of the UN. (Scott, who championed the cause of South-West Africa's black inhabitants at the UN, would long prove to be a thorn in the side both of the South African government, which was incensed by Scott's attacks on South African racial policies, and of the British government, which feared that Scott's activities would lead to appearances at the UN by disaffected residents of British dependencies.) In the Colonial Office, John Dugdale emphasised the domestic political dangers, insisting that British representation at the Court would be 'most unwise politically' since 'we shall in fact, whether we like it or not', appear to be defending South Africa: 'We are already in enough difficulty with the Seretse case without putting our head into a noose' by intervening at the Court – a reference to the furore that had

---

[23] DO 35/3811, note by R. C. Ormerod, 3 May 1949.
[24] Hyam, 'Africa and the Labour government', pp. 165–7. Intervention meant, in effect, that British legal experts would help South Africa present the case against compulsory UN Trusteeship for South-West Africa.

erupted after Gordon Walker announced the government's decision to withhold recognition of Seretse Khama as chief and exclude him from Bechuanaland.[25]

The Labour government, nursing its slender majority after the February 1950 general election and wary of exposing itself to further attacks on its policies in southern Africa, repeatedly put off a decision until the deadline for intervention at the Court forced one upon them. Kenneth Younger, the minister of state for foreign affairs, Patrick Gordon Walker, the Commonwealth Relations secretary, and James Griffiths, the colonial secretary, presented jointly a memorandum which was the product of five months of inter-departmental deliberation. All three ministers favoured intervention. Other members of Cabinet were more concerned about the domestic and international dangers of appearing to support South Africa and of inviting the Court to pronounce on issues of concern to Britain 'in a context most unfavourable to our case'. The arguments, as they had been in the 1946 deliberations on South-West Africa, were described as 'nicely balanced'. But in 1950, Cabinet was no longer worried about sustaining Smuts's hold on power; and in the wake of the Seretse Khama affair it was acutely aware of the domestic reaction against South Africa's racial policies. Intervention was rejected.[26]

If Cabinet were willing to over-rule departmental advice and abandon South Africa at the International Court of Justice, what might it not do in determining British policy in the General Assembly? The prospect of another, if still rare, rejection of official advice was undoubtedly viewed with alarm in Whitehall. And nowhere more so than in the CRO where, over several months and in consultation with the Foreign and Colonial Offices, officials prepared a memorandum setting out the reasons for preserving close relations with South Africa and, more particularly, for Britain's aligning itself with South Africa at the UN.

The memorandum, after acknowledging the contradictory requirements of British policy, the domestic and international dangers, set out the four reasons why Britain should preserve close relations with South Africa. First, the Cape shipping route, South Africa's industrial and military potential, and its possession of uranium were important strategically. Secondly, South Africa was valuable as a market for British goods and as a destination for British capital; its gold was of the 'utmost importance' for the viability of the sterling area. Thirdly, South Africa's co-operation was essential if Britain were to retain control of the High Commission Territories. And finally, there was the desire to maintain the Commonwealth connection with South Africa, that powerful source of British prestige and symbol of Anglo-South African solidarity. Despite doubts

---

[25] CO 537/5708, note by A. N. Galsworthy, 19 Dec. 1949; notes by J. Dugdale, 10 and 15 Mar. 1950; FO 371/88560, note by H. McNeil, 3 Jan. 1950; Hyam, 'Political consequences of Seretse Khama', pp. 921–47 (chapter 8 below).
[26] CAB 129/39, CP(50)88; CAB 128/17, CM 28(50)3, 4 May 1950; Hyam, BDEEP: *Labour government*, doc. 427.

expressed by James Griffiths and Aneurin Bevan, Cabinet agreed that Britain should, in concert with other countries, seek to exercise a moderating influence in the UN disputes involving South Africa, and 'do all it could to retain South Africa as a member of the Commonwealth'.[27]

Although Britain would remain anxious to offer what help it could to South Africa behind the scenes at the UN, by 1950 it would not vote with South Africa (or speak in South Africa's defence) unless some principle thought vital to the protection of Britain's own interests was at stake. By then, moreover, the British delegation (encouraged by domestic and international criticism of its stance at the UN) had lost its reluctance to vote against South Africa on what in British eyes appeared to be reasonable resolutions. This tendency to allow South Africa to isolate itself at the UN was perhaps one of the reasons why, in 1951, Gordon Walker re-emphasised the importance of Britain's supporting South Africa at the UN. He did this in the second major Cabinet memorandum on South Africa in less than a year, this one drafted by himself, the product of his own six-week tour of southern Africa. The memorandum, which would set the course of British policy in the region for three decades or more to come, defined the dual aim of British policy: to co-operate with South Africa (for the 'four reasons') but, equally, to contain South Africa's influence in Africa. At the UN this meant giving South Africa 'what help and guidance we decently can'.[28]

III

Had Labour remained in power after the October 1951 general election, the official predisposition in Whitehall to stand by South Africa at the UN (a predisposition that Gordon Walker's memorandum reinforced) might well have been challenged in the early 1950s. And even if the policy favoured by the civil servants had not been overturned, it might at least have been so modified as to leave the British delegation less closely aligned with South Africa than it would be while the Conservative Party was in office. As it was, the period of Conservative rule was notable for the absence of ministerial challenges to official advice on the South African disputes.

And if any Conservative ministers had been inclined to favour offering greater support to South Africa at the UN, developments there provided little opportunity for this to be done: the South African government's belated and grudging

---

[27] CAB 129/42, CP(50)214; CAB 128/18, CM 62(50)4, 28 Sep. 1950; Hyam, BDEEP: *Labour government*, doc. 431; R. Ovendale, 'The South African policy of the British Labour government, 1947–51', *International Affairs* 59 (1983), pp. 41–58.

[28] *UN Yearbook*, 1950, 807–22; *General Assembly Official Record*, 5th sess., 322nd plenary meeting, 629 and 631; CAB 129/45, CP(51)109, 16 Apr. 1951; Hyam, BDEEP: *Labour government*, doc. 433, and introduction, pp. lxiv–lxvi.

concessions on South-West Africa fell short of the minimum requirements for a solution to this dispute; and its ruthless implementation of racial policies, widely regarded as a symbol of oppression, ensured that the Indian government would persist with its complaint. Moreover, new British ministers were no less concerned than their predecessors about the effect that Britain's stand on the South African issues might have on British prestige and moral leadership at the UN. British policy would thus be constrained by the same contradictory requirements as before, and ever more tightly so as repugnance for apartheid and the strength of anti-colonial forces at the UN grew.[29]

The Churchill Cabinet did not turn its attention to the South African disputes until after the sixth session of the General Assembly had ended and the Indian government had announced that it would place a new item on the agenda – the race conflict in South Africa resulting from the policies of apartheid. Yet another lengthy Cabinet memorandum on relations with South Africa at the UN emerged in Whitehall – representing, once again, the thinking of officials in the Commonwealth Relations, Colonial, and Foreign Offices. South Africa was, the paper advised, likely to be 'severely attacked' not only on the treatment of Indians and South-West Africa issues, but also on its general racial policies. British policy had, however, to have regard for three basic (and contradictory) factors: first, 'we must preserve our rights as a Colonial Power vis-à-vis the United Nations'; secondly, 'we have a reputation to maintain as a champion of liberal western civilization'; and thirdly, 'we must do all we can to preserve and strengthen our relations with South Africa'. Existing policy should, the paper argued, be maintained. The race-conflict issue would be regarded as a more obvious infringement of South Africa's domestic jurisdiction, its inclusion on the agenda vigorously opposed.[30]

This official advice seems to have encountered no ministerial dissent. The Churchill Cabinet accepted the memorandum's recommendations without qualification, agreeing to a policy which would in its essentials remain unchanged for the rest of the decade. The British delegation would refrain from public condemnation of South African policies (though not from expressing its commitment to different racial policies); would vote with South Africa if principles vital to British interests were clearly at stake; or would abstain if to do otherwise would be too damaging to Britain's relations with either South Africa or its antagonists.[31]

---

[29] Henshaw, 'South Africa's external relations', pp. 193–218, 269–79.

[30] At a separate meeting Cabinet agreed that the British delegation should threaten to withdraw, and if necessary actually withdraw, from any UN proceedings that threatened to establish the principle that colonial powers were accountable to the General Assembly. CAB 129/55, C(52)323, 24 Sep. 1952; CAB 128/25, CC 75(52)7, 26 Sep. 1952; D. Goldsworthy, 'Britain and the international critics of British colonialism, 1951–1956', *Journal of Commonwealth and Comparative Politics* 29, 1 (1991), pp. 1–24.

[31] CAB 128/25, CC 81(52)7, 26 Sep. 1952.

In the years 1952 to 1959, the seventh to fourteenth sessions of the Assembly, the British delegation opposed or at least abstained on resolutions that assumed the race-conflict issue to be a matter of legitimate UN concern. Before the eleventh session, the British delegation could usually vote in fairly respectable company that included, among others, the other old dominions. But after the Suez crisis of 1956, the company Britain kept on these votes narrowed somewhat, often being confined to the handful of colonial and trusteeship powers which shared Britain's determination to resist UN interference.[32]

The story with respect to the 'treatment of Indians' issue was much the same except that the British delegation had generally abstained, arguing that the dispute (from which UN involvement was not so clearly precluded) lay between two members of the Commonwealth. Although the company in which the British delegation voted shrank more slowly here, its position eventually became just as unfavourable. The turning-point was 1958 when Britain was left stranded in the company of a few colonial powers after Canada and New Zealand 'defected' by joining the overwhelming majority of countries voting for a resolution appealing to South Africa to enter negotiations with India and Pakistan.[33]

On the South-West Africa issue the deterioration of Britain's position at first seemed less pronounced and less inevitable than it did with respect to the 'race conflict' and 'treatment of Indians' issues. This was due mainly to the belief that this was the most readily soluble of the South African disputes, that it could be resolved if only the right atmosphere were created for the South African government to make the few concessions needed to bring any settlement into line with the International Court's ruling. But the emergence of H. F. Verwoerd as J. G. Strijdom's successor in 1958 (leading a government thoroughly preoccupied with the advancement of Afrikanerdom, seeing the *volk*'s salvation in grandiose schemes of social engineering) dimmed the prospect of a real solution to any of the South African disputes. And by 1959, the British delegation was as isolated on South-West Africa as on any other dispute.[34]

Before then, the extent of Britain's isolation was to some degree masked by the desire on the part of the other old members of the Commonwealth, as well as of the United States, to avoid provoking South Africa into a permanent withdrawal from the UN. Under the abrasive leadership of Eric Louw, the minister of external affairs in the Strijdom and Verwoerd governments, the

---

[32] *UN Yearbook*, 1952–9; *GAOR*, 1952–9.

[33] Canada, *Canada and the United Nations* (Ottawa, 1959), 32–4; DO 35/10724, T. W. Keeble to H. G. M. Bass, 19 Dec. 1958.

[34] A settlement at this time did not necessarily depend on South Africa's placing South-West Africa under UN Trusteeship. An agreement might have been struck whereby Britain, France, and the United States would act as a surrogate for the Permanent Mandates Commission of the League of Nations. The chief problem was South Africa's refusal to concede that this surrogate must report to the UN. *UN Yearbook*, 1952–9; *GAOR*, 1952–9.

South African delegation was recalled from the General Assembly in 1955 in protest at the passage of a resolution on apartheid. This prompted the delegations from the old Commonwealth and from the United States to work against the passage of any further resolutions that might cause South Africa to stay away from the next session of the Assembly. Governments of the old Commonwealth were also anxious to avoid a clash with South Africa just at the time when the delicate issue of the Gold Coast's admission to the Commonwealth was under consideration. Keeping South Africa in the Commonwealth and in the UN were thought to be inter-related problems, with membership being seen as valuable in promoting the reform of South African racial policies. The British desire to maintain the UN and Commonwealth bridges with South Africa seems to have been more important than any particular concern about defence or economic relations which at that time rested on the relatively firm foundations of the Simon's Town Agreements and of various sterling area understandings respectively. The old Commonwealth (and to a limited extent even the new Commonwealth) rallied to the cause of keeping South Africa in the UN both in 1956, when Louw once more withdrew South Africa's delegation, and in 1957, when the debates on the South African disputes were toned down sufficiently to convince the South African government that its delegation should return to full participation in the Assembly in 1958.[35]

The British delegation's isolation on the South African disputes had been attracting growing attention in the British parliament since 1956. From that year onwards the House of Commons witnessed a small but steady stream of questions relating to these disputes, with many focusing on the narrowing company in which the British delegation found itself. But in 1958, the stream turned into a relative torrent leading to what was before then an event rare for the post-war period – a parliamentary debate on British policy towards South Africa. In 1959, British public and parliamentary criticism of South African racial policies and of British policy at the UN became even more intense, with plans being laid for boycotts of South African goods and another debate on South African racial policies taking place in the House of Commons.[36]

---

[35] *UN Yearbook*, 1955, pp. 70–1; 1956, p. 143; 1957, pp. 99–104 and 307–14; Canada, Department of External Affairs, file 5600-40-8; DO 35/5058, Sir G. Laithwaite to Lord Fairfax, 19 Oct. 1955; P. Henshaw, 'The transfer of Simonstown: Afrikaner Nationalism, South African strategic dependence, and British global power', *Journal of Imperial and Commonwealth History* 20, 3 (1992), pp. 419–44; P. Henshaw, 'Britain, South Africa and the sterling area: gold production, capital investment, and agricultural markets, 1931–61', *Historical Journal* 3, 2 (1995) (see chapter 10 below and chapter 6 above).

[36] Britain, *House of Commons Debates*, vol. 582, 382; vol. 594, 610–11; vol. 594, 70; vol. 595, 30, 39, 839–42, and 1130; vol. 596, 334–7; vol. 613, 389 and 1131–2; vol. 614, 90; vol. 615, 6. For the debate on 24 Nov. 1958, see vol. 595, 181–90. For the debate on 7 Dec. 1959 see vol. 615, 107–78. See also D. Geldenhuys. 'The effects of South Africa's racial policy on Anglo-South African relations, 1945–61' (PhD thesis, Cambridge University, 1977), pp. 350, 433 and 470.

Even so, before the Assembly's eighteenth session, late in 1959, there was little dissent in Whitehall from the view that Britain's existing policy on the South African disputes must be maintained. Public and parliamentary criticism was uncomfortable but still bearable. And though British representatives at the UN were unhappy at their isolation in 1958, at worst they were voting with four other countries: France, Portugal, Belgium, and Australia – which together with Britain became known as the 'famous five'. But in 1959, 'the five' were reduced to 'the three' after Australia and Belgium abandoned ship. And with French decolonisation gathering pace 'the three' looked set to become 'the two'. Such isolation was bad enough in itself. But it had serious implications for an ever more pressing British problem: how to keep those countries about to emerge from British colonial rule within the Commonwealth when Britain's moral leadership at the UN was being cast so gravely into doubt by the British stand on the South African disputes. Before the eighteenth session had ended, Lord Home, the secretary of state for Commonwealth relations (led, as ever, by his officials in the CRO) had decided that Britain's stance on the South African disputes must be changed.[37]

IV

How far Britain could afford to go in distancing itself from South Africa was not yet clear. The chief problem was that the South African disputes were still inextricably enmeshed with Britain's colonial problems in Africa, Britain's influence in South Africa (no less than in Britain's African dependencies) seeming to depend on the continued exclusion of UN interference. And throughout British territories in Africa, great changes were under way. Everywhere the timetables for constitutional change were being revised, developments to have taken decades compressed into a few years. Progress towards independence, instead of being geared to local political development, accelerated under the influence of political changes elsewhere. And with each further grant of independence in Africa or Asia, international pressure on the colonial powers, instead of being eased, intensified as the ranks of the newly independent nations swelled at the UN. Throughout Commonwealth Africa, UN interference threatened to stimulate nationalists antagonistic to the British connection. Paradoxically, as major constitutional change became imminent (whether this change marked the end of British sovereignty or, as in South Africa, the severance of the link with the Crown), the British government became more determined both to resist UN interference in the empire–Commonwealth and to maintain a high standing in

[37] DO 35/10725, H. G. M. Bass to L. E. T. Storar, 4 Nov. 1958; DO 35/10621, L. E. T. Storar to W. A. W. Clark, 2 Apr. 1959; Lord Home to Sir G. Laithwaite, 13 Aug. 1959; W. A. W. Clark to Sir A. Clutterbuck, 11 Dec. 1959; note by Lord Home on draft Cabinet paper, undated [11 Dec. 1959].

the General Assembly. Policy on the South African disputes had to be changed, but within tight constraints.[38]

The initiative for this change came from the CRO – formerly the leading advocate of support for South Africa at the UN. Lord Home circulated a minute (written, in the main, by his officials) which emphasised that the 'goodwill and confidence of the emerging masses of Asia and Africa are of vital and increasing importance to us, and there is no doubt that our support of South Africa tends to damage that confidence'. 'We can perhaps discount to some extent Parliamentary difficulties', noted Home, but British voting on the South African items at the UN 'is undoubtedly doing us harm'. Britain's wider international interests and relations with the new African states (especially Nigeria) were at stake. The time had therefore come to warn South Africa that 'unless she can be more forthcoming at the U.N., we may be compelled to abstain on a number of issues on which we have hitherto supported the Union case'. Selwyn Lloyd and Iain Macleod, the foreign and colonial secretaries, both supported this view. Lloyd thought that in the UN 'more harm is being done to our reputation as a Colonial Power by our attitude on these South African items, than is being done by any troubles that may occur in the Colonies themselves'. 'Our reputation for being progressive is going to be increasingly necessary as, while various territories achieve independence, the United Nations spotlight is more and more focussed on those which continue to be British colonies.' Macleod, similarly exercised by the problem of avoiding a clash with the UN on the administration of British dependencies, pointed out that the British delegation's task in the Trusteeship Committee (where South-West Africa was habitually discussed) was 'becoming increasingly difficult with the increasing number of African members, but Tanganyika's problems and next year's delicate questions about the British Cameroons make it particularly important that we should not get at odds with this Committee'. The preservation of British influence, both before and after British territories gained independence, demanded the change.[39]

Macmillan's 'wind of change' speech, delivered to the South African parliament in February 1960 at the end of his African tour, was taken by many white South Africans to be a warning that British support at the UN might not be so forthcoming in future. But while Macmillan's speech and his private talks with Verwoerd prepared the ground for a change of British policy, the British government, when Macmillan returned to London, had still not decided what distance, if any, it could afford to go in dissociating itself from South Africa at the UN.[40]

---

[38] H. Macmillan, *Memoirs*, vol. V: *Pointing the way, 1959–1961* (London, 1972), pp. 116–77.
[39] DO 35/10621, Lord Home to H. Macmillan, 17 Dec. 1959; S. Lloyd to Macmillan, 2 Jan. 1960; I. Macleod to Macmillan, 5 Jan. 1960. R. Hyam and W. R. Louis, eds., BDEEP: *The Conservative government and the end of empire, 1957–1964* (London, 2000), pt II, pp. 384–8 (docs. 439–41).
[40] DO 35/10728, R. W. D. Fowler to R. H. Belcher, 2 Mar. 1960. PRO, Treasury papers, T 236/4873, H. Macmillan's marginal comment dated 21 Feb. on D. Heathcoat Amory's note of 17 Feb. 1960.

The United Nations

Within the British government, the South African question had lost none of its power to divide opinion. In the Treasury and Bank of England there were widely divergent views about the probable economic effects of a severe rift between Britain and South Africa. The initial reaction in the Treasury was that the British government had little to fear. The Governor of the Bank of England was, by contrast, highly alarmed. A rift with South Africa might, he argued, have 'very untoward consequences' for South Africa's membership both of the sterling area and of the Commonwealth. The Treasury was persuaded to agree that South Africa's departure from the former would be 'a major crack in the sterling area system', though the Treasury and Bank agreed that failure to support South Africa at the UN need not have this effect. Macmillan himself was less certain. He wanted Cabinet to consider carefully a joint Treasury–Bank memorandum on this subject in advance of any change of policy.[41]

Before it could do so, the police massacre of black demonstrators at Sharpeville and Langa diverted the British government's attention to a new and more pressing problem at the UN. Twenty-eight African and Asian delegations requested 'an urgent meeting of the Security Council' to consider the situation in South Africa. In the Council Britain's problems would be much the same as they had been at the Assembly except that the spotlight of world opinion would shine even more brightly on British policy in the Council.[42]

British ministers recognised that a failure to veto the Security Council's discussion of the South African situation would damage relations with South Africa and open the door to UN interference in British territories. According to the British high commissioner, South Africa would 'feel betrayed by the last of their friends'. Home was 'quite sure . . . that we have too much at stake (the obvious case that comes to mind is Nyasaland and the Federation) to do otherwise' than exercise the British veto. Macleod, who happened to be in the Central African Federation at the time, cabled his agreement.[43] Selwyn Lloyd and Sir Pierson Dixon (the latter, the leader of Britain's permanent mission to the UN) took an entirely contrary view. They believed

> that it would be a serious error to challenge inscription. We should be badly beaten . . . There would be widespread indignation at home. That we can bear, but more important, the position of our friends in black Africa would be sorely affected. The issue for all except the lawyers and a few purists is, 'are you for South Africa on the shootings or against her?'[44]

Macmillan was less concerned about UN interference and the domestic pressure than about the future of the Commonwealth – which, remarkably enough,

---

[41] T 236/4873, note by A. W. Taylor, 5 Jan. 1960; M. H. Parsons to Sir D. Rickett, 7 Jan. 1960; A. W. Taylor to F. Lee, 8 Jan. 1960; D. Heathcoat Amory to H. Macmillan, 17 Feb. 1960.
[42] DO 35/10730, W. A. W. Clark to G. E. B. Shannon, 24 Mar. 1960.
[43] DO 35/10730, Sir J. Maud to CRO, 27 Mar. 1960; Lord Home to S. Lloyd, 25 Mar. 1960.
[44] PRO, prime minister's papers, PREM 11/3109, S. Lloyd to H. Macmillan, 25 Mar. 1960.

seems to have lost none of its significance in ministerial eyes, despite the growing concern with gaining entry into the European Economic Community. 'In the long run', commented the prime minister, 'it is much more important to preserve the Commonwealth and keep the Union in it, than to avoid some temporary unpopularity or misunderstanding. Once the Commonwealth begins to disintegrate I feel it is really finished.' The problem, as Macmillan judged it, was to balance 'the danger of South Africa leaving the Commonwealth (never to be put back) against the danger of other people getting very tiresome'.[45]

The solution, British ministers believed, lay in avoiding a vote on inscription and working for a moderate resolution on which the British delegation could abstain. The foreign, Commonwealth, and colonial secretaries judged that if this line were followed, South Africa would not leave the Commonwealth. The alternative of vetoing all discussion 'would not only be futile but would create the most adverse reaction here and elsewhere in Africa', having very serious effects on Ghana, Nigeria, and perhaps some Asian powers.[46]

As was hoped, the Security Council agreed to discuss the issue without voting on whether to do so. But there were grave British objections to the resolution that emerged there. Although Home and Lloyd were convinced that the British delegation should express its objections by abstaining, at least one other member of Cabinet, Sir David Eccles – the minister of education – was certain that Britain should support the resolution. Other ministers suggested that UN interference threatened Britain's relationship not only with its dependencies but also with newly independent countries: it was not in the best interests of the latter that they should be subject to international interference 'at a critical time when turmoil, often racial in character, was likely'. International and domestic pressures were insufficient to deflect the British government from its preoccupation with protecting colonial and Commonwealth ties from the UN's disruptive influence. The British delegation was instructed to abstain.[47]

This proved to be the last significant vote at the UN in which the British government declared South African racial policies to be a matter of essentially domestic concern. The British government had persisted in declaring them so not only because of the 'four reasons', but also because it wished to exclude UN interference everywhere in the empire–Commonwealth. But if one of the four reasons can be singled out as being of particular importance, it must have been the desire to protect the Commonwealth connection with South Africa, for within three weeks of Verwoerd's withdrawal of South Africa's application to

---

[45] PREM 11/3109, H. Macmillan to S. Lloyd, 25 Mar. 1960; note of H. Macmillan's telephone conversation with T. Bligh, 26 Mar. 1960.
[46] PREM 11/3109, R. A. Butler to H. Macmillan, 28 Mar. 1960.
[47] CAB 128/34, CC 21(60)3, 29 Mar. 1960 and CC 22(60)3, 1 Apr. 1960; BDEEP, *Conservative government*, doc. 448.

retain membership of the Commonwealth, Britain's representative in the General Assembly declared apartheid to be so exceptional as to be an issue in which UN intervention was legitimate. Within a month, Britain's vote in the General Assembly had, in striking contrast with previous policy, been cast in favour of a resolution deploring South African racial policies and declaring them to be a flagrant violation of the UN Charter; in favour too of a resolution regretting South Africa's failure to reply to communications from India and Pakistan regarding the 'treatment of Indians'. The end of South Africa's Commonwealth membership was the end of a crucial reason for Britain's sheltering South Africa at the UN.[48]

Of course the other reasons remained and would, in the years to come, often lead Britain into isolation on the South African disputes. The strategic and economic relationship with South Africa was left largely untouched by the demise of the Commonwealth connection. The problem for Britain was not so much salvaging the material ties from the Commonwealth wreckage – the Verwoerd government was all in favour of maintaining the material *status quo* and favoured a special relationship with Britain along Irish lines. Rather it was one of preventing South Africa from holding on to all the benefits of the Commonwealth association without actually being a member. The Macmillan government was relieved at the smooth continuation both of close defence ties under the auspices of the Simon's Town agreements and of effective economic collaboration within the sterling area. But it was relief not untinged with embarrassment at the failure to penalise South Africa more for the intransigence which led to exclusion from the Commonwealth. In the event, Britain's shift of policy at the UN was one of the few immediate and obvious results of Verwoerd's effective withdrawal from the association.[49]

On 28 November 1961, less than six months after South Africa formally severed its link with the British Crown, the Commonwealth was for the first time united in support of a resolution condemning South Africa's racial policies. Commonwealth delegations, by now numbering eleven, also voted as one in support of a resolution urging South Africa to enter negotiations with India and Pakistan on the treatment of 'Indians' in South Africa. But on the thorny South-West Africa issue, the British delegation remained as isolated as ever. The problem was that UN intervention in South Africa's racial policies could more readily be regarded as exceptional, not setting a precedent for intervention in British dependencies, than could UN intervention in South-West Africa. Moreover, the South-West Africa issue impinged more directly than did the other South African disputes on the problem of protecting the High

---

[48] CO 936/602, note by J. G. Tahourdin, 6 Apr. 1961. *UN Yearbook*, 1960, pp. 147–53.
[49] CAB 134/2493–2496, 'Committee on Future Relations with South Africa', 1961–2. PREM 11/3994, D. Sandys to H. Macmillan, 19 May 1961.

Commission Territories and, through that, to the continuing concern to preserve close relations with South Africa for strategic and economic reasons.[50]

The British government's concern about the Territories was no less important than its concern about its economic and strategic interests in shaping its attitude towards sanctions. (And judging by subsequent South African governments' cavalier attitude towards the sovereignty of neighbouring states, the British government had good reason to be anxious about the Territories.) When, in 1960, the not-yet-independent government of British Guiana wished to introduce economic sanctions against South Africa, the leading British concern was not that the South African government would retaliate by doing anything so dramatic, and self-destructive, as leaving the sterling area but that it might cut off the Territories economically – a move which, though minor in itself, might easily lead to a major crisis in Anglo-South African relations. Even without the Territories to consider, the imposition of economic sanctions against South Africa was thought to be highly undesirable and not only because of the British economic interests that would be put at risk. The task of encouraging positive political change in South Africa would not, it was felt, be furthered by sanctions: these would only unite white South Africans against Britain and the world. Indeed, British resistance to sanctions would, after 1974 (when the British government at last conceded that South Africa's occupation of South-West Africa was not legal), become the one thing that precluded a lasting escape from isolation on the South African disputes. By the 1970s, Britain's formal colonial responsibilities in Africa had ended, and the relative importance of the Commonwealth declined, so that by the late 1970s and 1980s British policy on these disputes may well have been dominated by strategic and economic concerns.[51]

V

But it had not always been so. Britain formerly had wider reasons for wishing to preserve close relations with South Africa – reasons of geopolitics and prestige, not just of strategy and economics. Moreover, from the General Assembly's first session to the time of South Africa's effective withdrawal from the Commonwealth, British policy on the South African disputes was conditioned above all by the desire to defend British authority and influence in the empire–Commonwealth by resisting UN interference wherever that

---

[50] *UN Yearbook*, 1961, pp. 108–17 and 455–69. The British decision in July 1961 to block the visit to Bechuanaland of the UN Committee on South-West Africa was based above all on the fear that a clash between the Committee and South African authorities on the South-West Africa/Bechuanaland border might provoke a crisis over British authority in the Territories: CAB 128/35, CC 39(60)8, 6 July 1960.

[51] CAB 128/34, CC 34(60)3, 2 June 1960. *UN Yearbook*, 1961–90.

interference was directed – at South Africa or at British dependencies. In either case, the central British concern was the same: to prevent the structures through which Britain exercised its world-wide influence from being directly usurped or from being destabilised by foreign intervention which might stimulate nationalist forces antagonistic to the British connection, whether those nationalists were Africans or Afrikaners, communists, or conservatives.

The British government's preoccupation with preserving its world-wide prestige and influence seems to have been diminished not at all by the apparent scramble out of empire and into Europe: holding the former empire (including South Africa) together in the Commonwealth remained, even in 1960–1, a leading British objective. Still, the underlying structure of Anglo-South African relations was not completely transformed by South Africa's exit from the Commonwealth and neither was the basis of British policy on the South African disputes. There remained potent reasons – again, not just of strategy or economics – not only for preserving close relations with South Africa, but also for defending Britain's influence throughout its former African empire.

So does the political transformation in South Africa in the early 1990s demonstrate the success or ultimate failure of British policy towards South Africa at the UN? To the extent that positive change in Namibia and South Africa was the product of sanctions and other aggressive tactics resisted by Britain at the UN, British policy must be judged a failure. Yet however large this failure seems when viewed from atop the ruins of apartheid, it is not difficult to imagine that southern Africa as a whole would have suffered worse calamities had the British government from an early date challenged South Africa's racial policies, and its hold on South-West Africa, more forcefully and directly. An early show-down with South Africa might have shocked white South Africa into reforming its racial policies. It could just as easily have led to a more pervasive and insidious extension of white South African influence or even direct control in southern Africa (particularly in the High Commission Territories) and to the intensification and spread of racial conflict throughout the areas of white settlement in central and East Africa. As it was, the British government never had the luxury of considering its policy towards South Africa in isolation from its world-wide concerns and responsibilities. The vindication, if there needs to be one, of British policy towards South Africa at the UN in the years 1946 to 1961 perhaps lies in its contribution to Britain's comparative success in guiding former dependencies to independence without, in general, allowing them to descend into immediate economic and political chaos.

8 The political consequences of Seretse Khama and Ruth, 1948–1952

Ruth Williams was not a typist. She was apt to be put out when the newspapers called her that. In fact she was a secretary, a confidential clerk, with a firm of Lloyds' underwriters in London. On 30 September 1948, at a register office in Kensington, she married Seretse Khama, heir to the chieftaincy of the Bangwato in the Bechuanaland Protectorate. No-one knew whether the Bangwato would accept a white consort. British newspapers ran features headed 'Shall typist be a Queen?' (*Sunday Dispatch*, 28 November 1948), and 'This girl can upset the peace of Africa' (*Sunday Express*, 10 July 1949). White opinion in South Africa was aghast: the marriage was condemned as 'distasteful and disturbing' (*Johannesburg Star*, 28 June 1949), as 'striking at the root of white supremacy' (*Natal Witness*, 2 July 1949). Ruth's parents opposed the marriage and did not attend the ceremony. Her father, George Williams, was a retired Indian army officer, working as a commercial traveller. Ruth was born in 1923, and brought up in Blackheath and Lewisham. She attended Eltham High School, took polytechnic classes in cookery, and served for four years in the war as a corporal-driver with the WAAF (Women's Auxiliary Air Force). Together with her sister Muriel, she was a churchgoer, keenly interested in the African work of the London Missionary Society (LMS). They were constant visitors to the colonial students' hostel at Nutford Place in Bayswater. It was at an LMS meeting in 1947 that she met Seretse, a quiet, friendly, relaxed, and thoroughly Anglicised law student of twenty-seven, with an alert mind and honest manner. The sexual attraction between them was apparently strong. But there was also in their decision to marry a challenging element of anti-apartheid zeal. Ruth abhorred the colour bar, and felt she could do at least as much good in Bechuanaland as missionary wives had done.[1]

---

[1] The principal research source is the Commonwealth Relations Office (CRO) papers, especially files Y 3480/1–54 (1948–52), Public Record Office (PRO), DO 35 series; these files alone contain well over a thousand documents. J. Redfern, *Ruth and Seretse: 'a very disreputable transaction'* (London, 1955) remains a useful introduction. The best older account of British policy towards Seretse is C. Douglas-Home, *Evelyn Baring: the last proconsul* (London, 1978), pp. 172–95. For officials' assessments of Ruth, see DO 35/4116, 9 and DO 35/4131, 119, and Foreign Office political papers, PRO, FO 371/91171.

I

Ironically, a marriage which shook the empire might never have been possible but for the incompetence of an Oxford professor of imperial history, Sir Reginald Coupland, holder of the Beit Chair. Seretse was a graduate of Fort Hare College in South Africa, and old enough (b. 1921) to be installed as chief. But his uncle Tshekedi (who had been acting as regent for him since 1925) and the other elders agreed that Seretse should first equip himself with a British legal training. When Seretse arrived at Balliol College, however, Professor Coupland unsuccessfully pressed him to read PPE (Philosophy, Politics, and Economics) instead of law, and then insisted on devising a compromise course. Seretse embarked on this, but unfortunately it proved to be ineligible for a degree. After a year of frustration (and playing rugby), Seretse decided he would be better off in London, studying for the Bar at the Inns of Court. Coupland, who liked him, opposed this. His dismay was complete when he learned of Seretse's London marriage. 'It will be a miracle if the marriage turns out happily', he wrote, 'It's a real tragedy.'[2]

Since he had firmly made up his mind, Seretse felt it would be wiser not to seek advance permission to marry from his regent-uncle, but he did give Tshekedi a little notice of his intention:

I realise that this matter will not please you because the tribe will not like it as the person I am marrying is a white woman. I do not know what the people will say when they hear of this ... I realise that it was my duty to have asked your consent before I had done this thing but I know you would refuse and it would be difficult for me to disregard your advice ... Please forgive me ... Please don't try to stop me.

But of course Tshekedi did try to stop him. Receiving this letter on 20 September 1948, he at once telegraphed his London lawyer, J. N. Buchanan, who got in touch with Dr R. Pilkington of the LMS, asking him, as a friend of the Khamas, to intervene. Pilkington tried to talk Seretse out of it, telling him that his behaviour was 'cowardly and unworthy'; it was the end of their friendship. Pilkington persuaded the bishop of London to require a postponement of the special licence while he approached the Colonial Office and Commonwealth Relations Office (CRO). The civil servants wondered if unofficial pressure could be brought to bear by Coupland, and asked him if he had any influence with Seretse. Coupland had to explain that he no longer had. Official action against the marriage was regarded in the CRO as impossible, while any further moralising by parents or clergy (or their wives) was simply likely to be counter-productive. But the whole thing was 'a sorry mess'. The clergyman who was to have married them, the Revd. L. Patterson, took the line that since there was no legal or moral impediment he could not refuse to marry Seretse and Ruth just because the union

---

[2] DO 35/4113, Sir R. Coupland to C. G. L. Syers, 27 Sept., 1 and 5 Oct. 1948.

was inadvisable. Nevertheless he had harangued Seretse with his misgivings. The initial assumption of almost everyone – clergy, missionaries, lawyers, and civil servants alike, to say nothing of the Bangwato people themselves – was that it was a simple case of 'the prince and the showgirl': Ruth would not last, and Seretse would soon look elsewhere. But Seretse was no playboy, and no Kenyatta either (Kenyatta had an English wife and two concurrent African ones). And Ruth, far from 'getting into a scrape', had made a genuine commitment. All who met her were quickly surprised to discover how 'nice and respectable' she was, with more intelligence and determination than expected; but this meant that 'unfortunately money won't talk as it would with a chorus-girl' (Buchanan).[3]

There were ample reasons why the marriage seemed ill-advised to everyone but the contracting parties themselves (and the bride's sister). Even Seretse himself initially assumed he ought to have got permission, though it later turned out that this was not an inescapable duty, and his own father had not bothered about it. If he was not the first Mongwato to marry a white woman, he was probably the second. British administrators in Bechuanaland, as indeed throughout the empire, were bound by the ruling of Crewe's circular (1909), which forbade liaisons with black women. Tshekedi was a puritan in sexual matters. He had fallen out with his half-brother Sekgoma (Seretse's father) partly because of Sekgoma's addiction to the flesh-pots. Tshekedi had first come to the notice of the British public in 1933 when he ordered the flogging of some young white traders, Phean McIntosh and two companions, for promiscuous conduct with Mongwato women and for assaulting one of their protesting boyfriends. Although he had no legal jurisdiction over Europeans, and was accordingly threatened with as near an approach to gunboat diplomacy as the Kalahari would permit, Tshekedi's hard moralistic line was in the end officially vindicated by the British government. Since then he had repeatedly been the scourge of the 'Mahalapye women', the prostitutes of the railway township. Tshekedi was thus not the man to take kindly to any but the most conventional form of marriage in his own family. In Britain in 1948, not only was the 1933 incident recalled, but memories of the abdication of Edward VIII in 1936 were still fresh in everyone's mind, tending to reinforce high expectations of public responsibility in the matter of 'royal' marriages. Moreover, there was plenty of British prejudice against black people. In South Africa the marriage would have been illegal in terms of the Prohibition of Mixed Marriages Act (1949). (Extra-marital sexual intercourse between black men and white women had been punishable since 1927 under the Immorality Act.) The debates on the Mixed Marriages Bill showed unequivocally that even all the opposition leaders (Smuts, Sir de Villiers Graaff, J. G. N. Strauss) regarded mixed marriages as an 'unmitigated

---

[3] DO 35/4113, especially no. 45.

evil' with tragic social consequences. They believed this was the universally held opinion among whites in South Africa, supported too by overwhelming majorities in other races. 'If there is one thing on which all South Africans are agreed', declared Smuts, 'it is this, that racial blood mixture is an evil.' There were fewer than a hundred such marriages a year during the mid-1940s.[4]

Apart from a few 'bright young things', who rather liked the idea, the Bangwato were at first shaken to the core by the marriage. They were against it, and indeed opposed to Seretse's succession and installation while he stuck to it – but they confidently expected him to ditch his white wife before long. Seretse therefore returned home alone to Serowe, the capital of Gammangwato, three weeks after the wedding, to explain himself to the people. Two gatherings of the traditional tribal assembly or *kgotla* were held. The upshot of the first *kgotla* (15–21 November 1948) was that Seretse was told he must choose between the chieftaincy and his wife. He refused to make such a choice. The second *kgotla*, 28–29 December, produced much the same deadlocked result. Seretse insisted that the Bangwato must accept Ruth if he was to be their chief. No-one opposed Seretse's claim to the chieftaincy – which was hardly surprising, granted a clear rule of primogeniture, and the paucity of legitimate male Khamas. But Tshekedi campaigned bitterly against Ruth, and argued that she should be prohibited from entering Gammangwato. As early as February 1949 he began making allegations personally unfavourable to Seretse, saying he would disregard Bangwato custom, lacked integrity, and was drinking strong liquor, contrary to strict family tradition.

Meanwhile in Britain, the CRO hoped Seretse would renounce his claim (following the precedent of the duke of Windsor), and quietly live in London. The secretary of state for Commonwealth relations, Philip Noel-Baker, was particularly reluctant to see the Bangwato quarrel develop in such a way as to lead to the loss of Tshekedi's services, for he had been for a decade now an indispensable collaborator in ruling Bechuanaland. Early in January 1949 Seretse returned to Ruth in London, intending to complete his Bar examination in May, and pondering the position in the meantime. Not surprisingly, the examination went badly. He then went back to Bechuanaland in June 1949. The third *kgotla* was held from 20 to 24 June. It produced an astounding turn in the wheel of fortune. The *kgotla* reversed its previous attitude, a majority now being prepared to accept Seretse as chief, while leaving the question of

---

[4] R. Hyam, 'Concubinage and the colonial service: the Crewe circular (1909)', *Journal of Imperial and Commonwealth History*, 14, 3 (1986), pp. 170–86; DO 35/4149, 4 and 5; DO 35/4135, 607; DO 35/4137, minute by W. A. W. Clark, 2 Jan. 1952. For South African debates on the Mixed Marriages Bill, see *House of Assembly Debates*, vol. 68 (Cape Town, 1949), cc. 6164–6206, 6344–6359, 6367–6463, 6471–6511 (19, 23, 24 and 25 May 1949); vol. 69, cc. 9065–9071 (24 June 1949); see also A. du Toit, 'Political control and personal morality', in R. Schrire (ed.), *South Africa: public policy perspectives* (Cape Town, 1983), pp. 54–83.

the status of his wife, and any future children, rather obscure. Tshekedi, having thus catastrophically overestimated the strength of his position and significantly lost control of Bangwato opinion, announced his intention to resign as regent, together with his determination to fight the marriage to the bitter end. Because Bangwato tradition allowed for no formal opposition, he went into voluntary exile in neighbouring Bakwena territory. We can gloss this as the Tswana equivalent of the fall of a government on a vote of no confidence. On the very same day as the *kgotla* closed (24 June), in the South African House of Assembly, the Mixed Marriages Bill passed its third reading by 71 votes to 51. The Bangwato crisis was thus well and truly launched.[5]

What had caused this startling *volte face* in the attitude of the third *kgotla*? It would be agreeable to suggest that brave, red-headed Ruth had won all hearts. But, although she would one day do so, Ruth had not yet even arrived in Bechuanaland, and the truth was more complex. Tshekedi believed that the third decision was 'more anti-Tshekedi than pro-Mrs Khama'. Most observers agreed that it was indeed mainly a reaction against the regency. As regent for twenty-three years, Tshekedi had established himself as outstanding among African rulers, admired by the British for his formidable political talents and intelligence, his real executive drive, and energetic administrative ability.[6] He had developed into a tenacious tyrant, albeit a charming one. People tended either to like or dislike him strongly. To the Bangwato he was a hard taskmaster. He had ruled firmly and well, but not altogether wisely. He had become increasingly puritanical, obstinate, high-handed, vindictive, and rude. Ambitious now for continuation in power, he would not have been, perhaps, altogether averse to Seretse's 'abdication'. And he was being cast more and more in the role of a wicked uncle who was opposing a handover to his nephew in order to preserve his own position. Thus a small pro-marriage faction began to emerge as a rallying-point for all who disliked Tshekedi. Nor was that all. Historic faction-struggles were also being catalysed by the marriage; the old feud between the Khama and Sekgoma factions was brought to the surface. Sekgoma II, Seretse's father, who ruled for only two years (1923–5), was the controversial eldest son of Khama III, alienated both from his father and Tshekedi. During Tshekedi's regency, the supporters of Sekgoma had had a long time out in the cold. Now they looked to Seretse to bring them the sweets of office. They began to see that his marriage was made in heaven, as far as they were concerned, simply because it was opposed by Tshekedi. A contested succession suited the Sekgoma faction well, since they hoped to exact from Seretse a high price for their support against Tshekedi in fraught circumstances. The marriage thus provided

---

[5] DO 35/4113, especially the views of G. E. Nettelton (no. 37), A. Sillery (nos. 67 and 73), and V. F. Ellenberger (no. 100).

[6] M. Crowder, 'Tshekedi Khama and opposition to the British administration of the Bechuanaland Protectorate, 1926–1936', *Journal of African History* 26 (1985), pp. 193–214; M. Benson, *Tshekedi Khama* (London, 1960); for Clark's assessment of Tshekedi, see DO 35/3883, 157.

them with the long-awaited chance to get rid of Tshekedi, as the obstacle to a legitimate succession. Beyond all that, there was undoubtedly a widespread popular desire for achieving the legitimate succession, and, since Seretse was adamant about not giving up his wife, the third *kgotla* deliberately took a decision which was at least in part positively in favour of Seretse. Moreover, Seretse handled the third *kgotla* astutely. By seizing the initiative and employing a display of eloquence, he challenged the assembly with an emotional appeal: 'Stand up those of you who will not accept my wife.' This produced an acclamation in his favour, although the constitutional propriety of demanding a head-count in this way was doubtful.

The Bangwato had thus signified their willingness to instal Seretse as chief, but his formal designation was subject to recognition by the British high commissioner and confirmation by the secretary of state. Accordingly, the South African government began immediate lobbying to prevent this. In London, their own high commissioner, Mr Egeland, requested a meeting with Noel-Baker. This took place at the end of June 1949. Egeland said he was instructed by Dr Malan to represent urgently the grave view which the Union government took about Seretse and Ruth, and to make an earnest request that Seretse should not be recognised as chief. The British record of the conversation described this as an unofficial/semi-official/private representation. Egeland offered three arguments against recognition. One, that all races in the Union would think the marriage, thus condoned, a grave infringement of a basic principle. Two, that it would be disastrous for the Bangwato by breaking up the basis of their tradition and by losing them the services of Tshekedi. Three, that Ruth's future would be sombre if not hopeless: she would be lonely, isolated, and ostracised, and she probably would not last six months.[7] Noel-Baker did not want to take these arguments very seriously, but in Pretoria, D. Forsyth, secretary of the department of external affairs, worked much more effectively on Sir Evelyn Baring, the British high commissioner, whose immediate presupposition after the third *kgotla* was that Seretse would now be confirmed as chief.

Baring's view of the Seretse affair crucially hardened as a result of Forsyth's representations on 7 July. Seretse in retrospect rightly detected a change of policy towards him at about that time. In a private letter to Percivale Liesching, the formidable permanent under-secretary at the CRO, Baring described the question of Seretse's recognition as the gravest issue in relations with South Africa since he became high commissioner in 1944. The political consequences would be far more serious than he had hitherto realised. There was a most invidious choice of evils. They must either provoke the Union into applying sanctions against the High Commission Territories (Basutoland, Swaziland,

---

[7] DO 35/4113, 115, secretary of state to high commissioner, 2 July 1949. British recognition of the chief was provided for under Proclamation no. 74 of 1943 (see I. Schapera, *A handbook of Tswana law and custom* (2nd edn, Oxford, 1955), p. 87).

and the Bechuanaland Protectorate), or antagonise the Bangwato, together with a large body of non-European opinion throughout the Commonwealth. Refusal to recognise would bring accusations of surrendering to the prejudices of South Africa and flouting the wishes of an African people. But prompt recognition would lead to a disastrous and dangerous head-on collision with the Union 'at the worst possible time and for the worst possible reason'. He reluctantly concluded that this case was the one exception to his general rule of never sacrificing African interests to the maintenance of good relations with the Union – though in fact he did not think that the interests of the Bangwato would be served by recognising Seretse, since it would give a 'great impetus to the demand for the transfer of the High Commission Territories'. But there was an even worse implication. The Commonwealth itself was at stake. The more extreme Nationalists in South Africa would argue

> that our action demonstrates the folly of allowing the existence side by side in Southern Africa of two systems of Native administration diametrically opposed to one another ... and they will make Seretse's recognition the occasion of an appeal to the country for the establishment of a republic, and not only of a republic, but of a republic outside the Commonwealth. Dr Malan is desperately worried and feels that he could not successfully oppose an extremist offensive on these lines ... They [the 'extremists'] believe that Seretse's recognition would enable them to exploit colour feeling in order to sever the tie with Great Britain without exasperating English-speaking South Africans ... They would thus fight the battle for a secessionist republic with the ideal war-cry and at the ideal time.

Baring realised that 'to argue that this incident on the edge of the Kalahari might lead to the complete secession of South Africa from the Commonwealth may seem far-fetched', but he was convinced that the threat was real. Dr Malan's own distress and anxiety indicated that there was something even more radical and vital at stake than a campaign for the High Commission Territories, namely the future of South Africa's connection with the Commonwealth.[8]

Liesching accepted this analysis as 'most significant'. Moreover, he too was lobbied, by General Beyers, who told the permanent under-secretary that Seretse's recognition would 'light a fire through the British Colonial Territories in Africa which would not soon be quenched': all white settlements, dependent on keeping white women inviolable, would rise up in protest. And so to Baring's spectre of a threatened Commonwealth, Liesching was convinced they must add the possibility of South Africa's whipping up trouble in Southern Rhodesia, Kenya, and Tanganyika. Southern Rhodesia was in any case likely (he said) to react violently; there had long been 'a rather unholy alliance' between South Africans and Kenyan settlers on racial issues; and Tanganyika

---

[8] DO 35/4114, 34, Baring to Liesching, 11 July 1949, extensively quoted in Douglas-Home, *Baring*, pp. 182–5.

could easily be infected. 'In short there may be a very bitter harvest here.' To the CRO Seretse now seemed indeed irresponsible, because he was imperilling relations with South Africa. They now believed that the Bangwato in the third *kgotla* had made an ill-considered decision. They agreed with the high commissioner that the best thing to do was to play for time. The issue was complicated, and they feared that by a false move they might damage not only the British case for retaining the High Commission Territories, but also the cause of all Africans in South Africa.

Patrick Gordon Walker, parliamentary under-secretary for Commonwealth relations, minuted: 'This is an extremely grave matter and can involve us in historic calamities if we are not careful.' He wanted serious thought given to the possibility of declaring that a chief could not have a white wife, and facing the inevitable uproar which would result. At any rate he was convinced Seretse could not be recognised. Unmistakable alarm signals were sent up to Noel-Baker, with Liesching urging upon him urgent study of the case, 'as I find it difficult to think of any other current topic which is likely to cause more trouble than this unless we handle it successfully'. Noel-Baker accepted that there were 'great issues at stake' in the general structure of African policy. Officials certainly did not think it journalistic exaggeration when the *Manchester Guardian* commented: 'This is on its lesser scale a crisis comparable with the abdication of Edward VIII, and its possible implications are almost unlimited.'[9]

The high commissioner recommended holding a judicial inquiry. He did not think 'the three *kgotla*s' had been fully representative, attracting as they did mainly the large urban population of Serowe, where they were held. He felt they were vague in their outcome, and this increased the danger of a split among the Bangwato. Moreover, Tshekedi was demanding an inquiry to clarify the position of the wife and children. Confronted with Baring's representation, the British government felt it particularly needed to know two things: whether the Bangwato really wanted Seretse, and whether his failure to consult over his marriage had unfitted him for the chieftaincy. Liesching believed they would have to refuse recognition of Seretse, but to do so at once would place the whole emphasis on the racial issue and divide the Bangwato. Arthur Creech Jones (secretary of state for the colonies) agreed that an inquiry would be the right way to proceed. 'Immediate refusal to recognize Seretse would be likely to have serious repercussions, and, from the Colonial Office point of view, is the worst possible course.' His chief advisers were R. S. Hudson (formerly secretary of native affairs, Northern Rhodesia) and the ubiquitous Andrew Cohen (head of the African department). Hudson believed it right and normal where there was doubt about African opinion to hold an inquiry into the suitability of a

---

[9] DO 35/4114, especially minutes by Gordon Walker (15 July 1949) and Liesching (14 and 15 July 1949).

chief. Immediate recognition would disrupt the Bangwato, and there was 'great merit in a delay.' Cohen, in a characteristically incisive and comprehensive minute, defined three possible courses of action: (i) to recognise Seretse, (ii) to declare immediately no recognition, or (iii) to hold a judicial inquiry. Immediate recognition might adversely affect relations with the Union. Non-recognition would provoke most unfavourable reactions in African dependent territories, where it would be widely said they were giving way to South African colour prejudice. But an inquiry 'might do good, and would be unlikely to do harm'.[10]

The issue was now put to the Cabinet. Noel-Baker's CRO memorandum largely reiterated Baring's arguments, but expressed them even more forcibly. The threat to the Commonwealth must be taken 'extremely seriously', because Malan was 'desperately worried' and showing 'extreme anxiety'. Armed South African incursion into the Territories was a possibility. Even if the government were to recognise Seretse they should not rush into it. An inquiry would provide clearer material for a decision, and demonstrate to South Africa and Southern Rhodesia that Britain was mindful of the gravity of the issues involved. The Cabinet itself felt the recognition of Seretse would not provide a satisfactory or lasting solution. It was 'not a question of mixed marriages as such', and general issues of race must be firmly excluded from the terms of reference to the inquiry. Nevertheless, a white wife for a chief might have consequences 'gravely prejudicial to good government' and to the stability of the local Native Administration. Tactically, ministers did not want a hasty decision. A judicial inquiry would allow time for reflection all round. The Cabinet also headed off Noel-Baker's proposal to try to get Seretse to relinquish his claim voluntarily, being persuaded by Creech Jones's argument that this would not only be widely criticised as interference in response to South African pressure, but also give rise to hostile propaganda. It would be most embarrassing if it failed.[11]

The decision to hold a judicial inquiry was announced on 30 July 1949. Tshekedi immediately agreed to continue as regent pending its findings. Ruth Khama arrived in Gammangwato on 20 August. She at once made efforts to improve social mixing in Serowe and started to learn Setswana. Eight days later the South African government declared the Khamas to be prohibited immigrants. This was not just a gesture: since the protectorate's administrative headquarters was anomalously still located in Mafeking in northern Cape Province, the ban could present a genuine obstacle to the conduct of business. Seretse was consolidating his position in the autumn, and his popularity was growing. The judicial inquiry commenced its sittings at Serowe on 1 November, under Sir Walter Harragin, Chief Justice of the High Commission Territories, a blunt but patient

[10] Colonial Office papers, supplementary correspondence, PRO, CO 537/4714, minute by A. B. Cohen, 20 July 1949.
[11] Cabinet Office papers, PRO, CAB 129/36, CP(49)155, memo 19 July 1949; CAB 128/16, CM 47(49)8, conclusions 21 July 1949.

old-timer. Much of the time was taken up with hearing what Tshekedi had to say. Repeated reference was made to the works of Professor Isaac Schapera for clarification about Tswana custom. Tshekedi did not challenge Seretse's claim as heir apparent, but argued that failing to get the consent of the elders had disqualified him as a fit and proper chief. In all he listed thirteen reasons against Seretse's fitness, including his 'taste for drink'. He objected also to the steps Seretse was taking to get himself proclaimed chief and Ruth queen. He cast doubt on whether Ruth as a European could ever be accepted socially.

The report of the Harragin inquiry was dated 1 December 1949. It found that the third *kgotla* was properly conducted, and that the desire for Seretse was genuine. Modest drinking did not make Seretse 'unfit', and he was not corrupt. Indeed, the 'unfortunate marriage' apart, his prospects of success as a chief were 'as bright as any Native we know'. Moreover, if his people forgave him, 'who are we to insist on punishment?' Nevertheless the report found Seretse 'not fit in present circumstances', though he should not be disinherited for ever. A period of direct rule was required to heal dissension and to reform the tribal administration. Tshekedi's disappearance need not be regretted: he had 'outstayed his welcome'. The report gave three reasons why Seretse could be pronounced unsuitable: (i) he would be a prohibited immigrant in Mafeking, and so he could not be an efficient chief; (ii) friendly co-operation with South Africa and Southern Rhodesia was essential, and opinion in both was against him; (iii) it would undoubtedly lead to internal disorder.[12]

Most of Whitehall would have agreed with Creech Jones's verdict: the report came to the 'right conclusions by use of the wrong arguments', but it would be 'a formidable thing' to reject the wishes of the Bangwato. The reasons given for non-recognition were thin and likely to prove a serious public embarrassment. The first reason seemed preposterous, because the administrative difficulties over Mafeking could always be got round somehow if necessary. The second reason would seem like appeasement, and was impossible to justify publicly. The third reason was not actually given much weight by Harragin, and, to support it, would need more evidence than the report provided. Nor did officials like the emphasis on forecasts of what might happen, as opposed to basing the case on what had actually occurred already. Some officials would have preferred a simple statement that Seretse's handling of his marriage was a disqualifying irresponsibility. On the other hand, Hudson argued that if Seretse's degree of irresponsibility unfitted him, then half the chiefs in Africa would not be recognised. To hold up hands in horror at an African putting his marriage before his people was going too far, he argued, as many of them did this.

---

[12] DO 35/4116; DO 35/4123, official record of proceedings of judicial inquiry at Serowe 1949 under Sir Walter Harragin; report, 1 Dec. 1949; see also DO 119/1152 (high commissioner's correspondence).

'The act of irresponsibility alone would be condoned', he added, but for its 'effect on neighbouring states'. Other officials were disappointed that a 'reasonable compromise' had not been suggested. It was known that 'moderate' opinion in Bechuanaland favoured a 'morganatic' solution – that is to say, Ruth should be a 'private' wife only, and not an official consort. The report also contained inconsistencies, for example, as to whether Seretse would or would not choose advisers sensibly. Some of the evidence favoured recognition. There appeared to be a direct incitement to divorce in the hint that recognition could follow upon changed circumstances. From another perspective, the language of the report was objectionable: the Bangwato were referred to as 'comparatively primitive and unlearned', though Harragin magnanimously conceded that Seretse was not the sort of African to be satisfied 'with a mud-and-wattle hut and crude sanitary conveniences'. In short, the report was to be written off as 'inflammatory and embarrassing' (Noel-Baker) and 'lamentable and explosive' (Gordon Walker). Curiously, Baring found it 'exceedingly clear and useful',[13] but that was before the civil servants had used all their arts to discredit it.

Noel-Baker now put the position to the prime minister, underlining his 'very real anxiety'. The government's decision, he wrote, must consider not only the best, long-term interests of the Bangwato, but also the general interests of Africans throughout southern Africa. Many 'representative Africans' were against recognition, but non-recognition might unfortunately seem to be dictated by South Africa. Noel-Baker gave Attlee a poor opinion of Seretse. 'His character and his attainments so far are not of the first order . . . His irresponsible conduct in connection with his marriage does not inspire confidence in his judgement, or in his care for the interests of the tribe.' (Privately Noel-Baker even thought the government might draw attention to Seretse's failure in the Bar examinations to imply that he had not benefited much from his opportunities; his officials, however, persuaded him that this would be unfair.)[14]

Attlee replied that they must not be precipitate over this. He would read the report before deciding about its wider circulation. About a month later he minuted in his careful hand:

This matter must come to Cabinet. The document is most disturbing. In effect we are invited to go contrary to the desires of the great majority of the Bamangwato tribe, solely because of the attitude of the governments of the Union of South Africa and Southern Rhodesia. It is as if we had been obliged to agree to Edward VIII's abdication so as not to annoy the Irish Free State and the United States of America.[15]

[13] DO 35/4118; CO 537/5927.
[14] CRO, private office files, DO 121/23, Noel-Baker to prime minister, 21 Dec. 1949; DO 35/4118, minute by G. H. Baxter, 7 Jan. 1950.
[15] Prime Minister's Office papers, PRO, PREM 8/1308, minutes by Attlee, 21 Dec. 1949 and 22 Jan. 1950.

Gordon Walker felt this missed the point. Moreover, by the end of January 1950 he had discovered new elements of urgency. Ruth was pregnant. Malan seemed to be on the verge of demanding the transfer of the Territories. If non-recognition of Seretse were to follow this, it would appear to be a consequence of the criticism of Britain in the Union which would go with the demand. Such criticism would be all the more virulent if the British government delayed making up its mind much longer. And the longer the decision was delayed, Gordon Walker argued, the more opportunity Seretse would have to establish himself, with the possibility of minor disturbances meanwhile.

As the divergence of opinion between Gordon Walker and Attlee indicates, it was a real decision which the Cabinet had to make. The Cabinet paper put up by the CRO (and in which Gordon Walker's hand is strongly evident) contained the key phrase that a decision to recognise might 'unite and inflame' opinion in South Africa. This would lead to greater support for Malan if he demanded the transfer of the Territories, or applied economic pressure to them. Thus, the argument ran, Seretse's recognition 'would therefore play directly into Dr Malan's hand', while an early announcement against it might possibly deflect the demand for transfer altogether. At the Cabinet meeting on 31 January 1950 Noel-Baker presented three main reasons for refusing recognition, quite deliberately distancing himself from the trilogy offered by the Harragin report. In the first place, he believed the inquiry had underestimated the risks of disruption among the Bangwato. Because of fear of Tshekedi, the third *kgotla* should not be regarded as an endorsement of Seretse's claims. In the second place, Seretse had shown himself 'utterly unmindful' of his public duty by his marriage, but he had also displayed irresponsibility in other matters, 'which made it doubtful whether he could safely be entrusted with the duties and responsibilities of Chief'. Finally, he believed 'liberal European opinion generally' was against recognition, and so was a strong body of African opinion in South Africa. In Noel-Baker's view, these three reasons alone would justify a decision not to recognise, but it 'would not be wholly realistic' to ignore the South African dimension. 'From the point of view of African interests the paramount need was to safeguard the position of the High Commission Territories.' He proposed to invite Seretse and Ruth to London and make an attempt to get him to relinquish his claim voluntarily. African government in the reserve should gradually be made more representative. With all this Creech Jones agreed generally: 'The decisive consideration was that the recognition of Seretse would undoubtedly endanger the stability and well-being of the Bamangwato tribe.' Although (following Cohen's brief) he thought African opinion in southern Africa was divided, it was clear that a substantial body of it was opposed to recognition. In the general discussion which followed, ministers agreed that it was impossible for the government to endorse the inquiry's reasons, and there were passages in the report likely to arouse damaging controversy. But Seretse's marriage had introduced among the Bangwato a 'persisting element of controversy and unsettlement which would be further aggravated if he should have children'. The Cabinet now thought there might be a chance of getting Seretse to step down, since he might be aware of the risks to the Bangwato which his continuing presence would involve. He could be offered an allowance and other appropriate forms of help. If they could persuade him not to return to Bechuanaland they might avoid publishing the controversial report.

The Cabinet was, however, getting into dangerous waters. It did not need any great perspicacity on the part of the Cabinet secretary (Brook) to observe afterwards that a strong case against Seretse had not actually been made out, at least not if the racial prejudices of the Union were ignored, as they would be for purposes of public presentation. Surely, therefore, it would be a mistake to issue a White Paper attempting to prove that Seretse was unfit to serve as chief, since in fact 'the main ground for the decision is the need to avoid continuing friction with the Union'?[16]

Seretse arrived in Britain on 14 February 1950 at the government's request. He did not bring Ruth with him as the government had hoped he might. His advisers said it was too risky, as the British authorities would not guarantee her return. She was in any case determined to have her baby in Serowe in May. A series of meetings in the CRO followed. Noel-Baker saw Seretse on 16 February, and told him they did not want to impose a decision. If, he explained, Seretse would voluntarily relinquish his claim, and live in Britain, he would receive an allowance of £1,100 a year (£800 net). He would also be free to take a job (perhaps in overseas student welfare). The government was planning a period of direct administration for the Bangwato, so he could be assured that Tshekedi would not return either, and Seretse himself might eventually be allowed back. Seretse commented: it appears the government 'thought it better to annoy the tribe than to annoy Dr Malan'. Direct rule would be unpopular, he thought, and, if he accepted the government's offer, the Bangwato would think he had deserted them for money. He complained that the government was not being entirely frank with him. For instance, why would they not tell him what Harragin's findings were? Seretse made it perfectly plain that he was not going to expose himself to the charge of selling his birthright for a mess of potage. He must consult his people. It was for them to decide. Seretse made a good impression. He showed a grasp of the situation as acute as it was polite. Even Noel-Baker had to admit he was 'a gentleman'. Indeed, he saw this as 'our best hope', but it was hard to deal with him properly without a frank discussion of race relations in the Union. Could they risk this? His officials did not think they could. Matters were left inconclusively, pending the result of the British general

---

[16] DO 35/4118; CAB 129/38, CP(50)13, memo 26 Jan. 1950; CAB 128/17, CM 3(50)1, conclusions 31 Jan. 1950.

election on 23 February. Because of this Seretse remained in England until the end of March, getting more and more bored and depressed. Meanwhile Baring kept up the pressure for non-recognition.[17]

The Labour government was returned to power with a much reduced majority. In the Cabinet reconstruction which followed, Attlee replaced Noel-Baker as secretary of state by Gordon Walker, the under-secretary since October 1947. Attlee had lost confidence in Noel-Baker. Gordon Walker, on the other hand, impressed him as having 'exceptional ability'.[18] The newly promoted minister was more than acceptable to his officials, but his bleak manner did not endear him to Seretse.

At the second CRO meeting on 3 March, Gordon Walker began by asking Seretse if he would resign voluntarily. Seretse replied: 'how can my resigning be in the interests of the tribe when they want me?' He was told that since he would not agree to relinquish the chieftaincy, a Cabinet decision would be imposed on him. What Gordon Walker had in mind, as his own plan, was to postpone a decision – for five years – as to whether Seretse could be installed. This suspension would be on the understanding that meanwhile he remained outside Bechuanaland; an allowance could then be paid (which might attract Seretse, as he was hard up). Such a suspension would cause considerable, but not, he thought, insuperable difficulties within Gammangwato. Essentially, of course, it was a compromise solution, perhaps the unavoidable and only acceptable one. The high commissioner was not at all keen on it, but since the objections were mainly because of the problems it would create for internal administration, he could not pretend they were overwhelming – provided Ruth also remained outside the protectorate for the full period. Baring hoped ministers fully understood that the dangers of recognition would certainly be no less in five years, if Ruth was still married to Seretse, than they were now. The Cabinet agreed to Gordon Walker's plan on 3 March, no doubt calculating that (because of their poor electoral prospects) substantial postponement might well mean the Conservatives would be landed with the final decision in five years' time, though the Cabinet did not wish to specify an exact period. Three days later, however, Gordon Walker got them to accept postponement for not less than five years: 'Otherwise the Bangwato would never settle down', and in Britain there might be continuous pressure to reconsider. To make the decision more palatable and enforceable, Tshekedi must be controlled on a more or less equal footing with Seretse. He could not be allowed back into the reserve to take advantage of Seretse's absence. (If they said they could trust Tshekedi, criticism of their attitude towards Seretse would be further intensified.)

[17] DO 35/4119.
[18] Attlee papers, Churchill College Archives Centre, ATLE 1/17, draft autobiography, ch. XVII; Gordon Walker papers, Churchill College Archives Centre, GNWR 1/7, especially Attlee to Gordon Walker, 30 Apr. 1949.

At the third meeting on 8 March Seretse was confronted with the Cabinet decision. He took it badly, complaining of exclusion on 'vague grounds of tribal interest'. He felt he had been tricked into leaving Gammangwato, since he would not now be allowed back. Gordon Walker impressed on Seretse the need to remain silent until the decision could be announced simultaneously in London and in Serowe on 13 March. However, in his anger, Seretse (who had hitherto been very wary of journalists) went straight from the meeting to leak the result to the press. At a consequent fourth meeting Gordon Walker told him he had thus forfeited any right to be treated with any particular consideration.[19]

There followed a parliamentary storm. In his first appearance in the House of Commons as the responsible minister, Gordon Walker made a statement on 8 March 1950. Recognition would be withheld for not less than five years. Seretse would be excluded from the protectorate; Tshekedi from the reserve. The district commissioner would exercise the functions of Native Authority as a temporary expedient, and some of the duties of the Native Authority would be transferred to a small council of leading persons. In the transitional period the government hoped to make the Native Authority more representative in character, 'in line with more direct and full participation of Africans in their own affairs'. He denied any communication with the Union government: they had not taken into account South African feeling on mixed marriages as such. (Political obfuscation indeed!) Winston Churchill questioned whether Seretse was being treated fairly 'as between man and man'; it seemed to him 'a very disreputable transaction'. In the parliamentary debate on 28 March, Quintin Hogg (later Lord Hailsham) sagely observed that it was a grave decision, which might be necessary, but the government had failed to justify it, and offered virtually no case. 'Our long-run future', he added, 'depends on the confidence with which we are regarded by Africans. The future of our civilization and our religion very largely depend upon the extent to which we can carry these people with us in the fight against Communism.' Fenner Brockway, in a sentence which has also stood the test of time, suggested that they should have welcomed the tribal acceptance of a white wife as an advance towards racial equality. Asked why the government was not publishing the Harragin report, Gordon Walker put the point that it contained unacceptable arguments which would be inconveniently used for misrepresentation against the government. He denied that the Bangwato people had incontrovertibly accepted the marriage. He emphasised the sheer difficulty of the decision he had to make: 'the issue is whether a person can, as

---

[19] DO 35/4119, and 4120; CAB 128/17, CM 7(50)1, conclusions 3 Mar. 1950; CM 11(50)7, conclusions 1 Mar. 1950. Although nobody challenged it, CRO ministers later realised that the suspension of Seretse was almost certainly illegal, owing to defective wording of the proclamation: there were some scathing remarks about the 'useless' legal advice given by 'cocksure and careless' legal officers: see DO 35/4129.

public head of a community or people, do things which it is his undoubted right to do as a private individual'. Seven Labour MPs voted with the Conservatives – the only instance of cross-voting by Labour MPs on an imperial issue during the life of the Labour government. Other Labour members registered a protest by absenting themselves from the vote. It was a turning-point. The Left thereafter began to take a closer interest in imperial questions. Many politicians were bewildered by the weakness of the government case (which was, as we now know, the result of their refusal to admit the South African factor). Fenner Brockway recalled: 'I have rarely been made more angry . . . It was beyond my belief that such a thing could happen under a Labour government, and I caused a scene by my hot words.' He became the main spokesman of the critics.[20]

'A melancholy and distressing episode', was the verdict of *The Times* (17 March 1950). Could South Africa best be met by appeasement at the cost of personal justice? No good could come of a 'compromise which does injustice to individuals', if its aim was 'to blur the outline of the truth', which was that a tragic conflict existed with South Africa on colour, and could not be for ever evaded. Margery Perham urged readers of *The Times* to recoil (as with the Hoare–Laval Pact) from a decision which 'affects the moral foundations of the Commonwealth'. Dingle Foot, writing in the *Sunday Times* (12 March 1950), saw it as an issue precisely calculated to present world Communism with a great opportunity to attract African support against Britain and the West. The distinguished West Indian economist, Professor W. A. Lewis, resigned in protest from the Colonial Economic Development Council, writing to the *Manchester Guardian* (16 March): 'I consider the Socialist Government's action . . . to be dishonest in suppressing the report; cowardly in surrendering to South African policies which are certain to cause the disintegration of the Empire; and insulting to the 400 million coloured subjects of the Empire.' The Seretse Khama Fighting Committee was set up: its most famous member was the cricketer Leary Constantine. It accused the government of racial prejudice and arbitrary, myopic conduct: 'the only parallels for such deplorable conduct are in relations between Hitler and . . . Central and East Europe'. In its view, by evading the issue of black/white relations the government 'forfeits the confidence of African peoples everywhere'. Krishna Menon made protests on behalf of the government of India. In America, black opinion was strongly behind Seretse, but white American opinion was much more divided. (After all, thirty out of the forty-eight states in the USA had legislation prohibiting mixed

---

[20] *House of Commons debates*, 5th series, vol. 472, cc. 285–97 (8 Mar. 1950); vol. 473, cc. 334–58 (28 Mar. 1950). See also Fenner Brockway, *Towards tomorrow: an autobiography* (London, 1977), p. 161; D. Goldsworthy, *Colonial issues in British politics, 1945–1961* (Oxford, 1971), pp. 157–62, 241; M. Kahler, *Decolonization in Britain and France: the domestic consequences of international relations* (Princeton, NJ, 1984), pp. 238–9.

marriages.) As to the situation in Gammangwato itself, when Baring travelled a thousand miles to Serowe to explain the decision, his *kgotla* was ostentatiously boycotted.[21]

Gordon Walker wondered to himself how long the name of Seretse Khama would be remembered. For longer than his own, he suspected. In a lengthy and reflective diary entry in April 1950 he wrote:

All along I was convinced that he could not be recognized. I had been impressed by Baring's dictum that we could only hold the High Commission Territories from the Union so long as white opinion there was divided and cool (as it now is): if it became inflamed and united we would be helpless . . .

We would certainly lose the High Commission Territories to the Union. This would not directly affect our interests, but it would subject two million Africans to oppression. It would probably drive the Union out of the Commonwealth and inestimably weaken us in any war with Russia. South Africa not only can provide important forces, but holds an immensely important strategic position. Besides this, there was impressive evidence from Liberals in the Union and from Africans that Seretse's recognition would weaken and split the tribe and damage the position of Africans in the Union.

However, he felt he had made a bad mistake in telling Seretse in advance what he proposed to do. Seretse thus 'got 48 hours start on me and it took me several weeks to catch up'. The stir in the press was 'tremendous', but very much less among the public at large. The general impression got about that Seretse was being treated badly in his private capacity, so a concession had to be made, letting Seretse return temporarily to the protectorate. Aneurin Bevan was 'hostile throughout', and 'probably egged on the dissidents in the Party'. Attlee, Morrison, and McNeil stood firm, but Addison wobbled on the issue of exclusion from the protectorate.

The repercussions were altogether bigger than I had expected – though not nearly as big as the papers made out. Unfortunately the thing is news as a personal story. There is clearly a powerful world negro opinion – not as rich or well organized as the Zionists – but similar . . . From all this I have learned to stand up to much abuse and publicity . . . There is something to be said for having oneself talked about, whatever the cause.

Fortunately Baring was pleased with his parliamentary performance: 'a major disaster has been avoided and the effect on relations with the Union Government has been admirable'.[22]

The government was also fortunate in that Churchill did not pursue his criticism. This was because Churchill had asked Smuts for his views, and Smuts had warned him that the issue was 'full of dynamite'. 'It would be a mistake',

---

[21] DO 35/4125, 13; *The Times*, 7, 9, 17, and 18 Mar. 1950; Noel-Baker papers, Churchill College Archives Centre, NBKR 4/39; CO 847/45/2, 2 (Africa, original correspondence). Krishna Menon's representations are in DO 121/121. See also below, p. 311, press reactions.

[22] Gordon Walker papers, GNWR 1/9, diary 2 Apr. 1950; DO 35/4120, 216, Baring to Gordon Walker, 10 Mar. 1950.

he telegraphed, 'to exploit British feeling in favour of Seretse to an extent which may damage the relations of South Africa to the Commonwealth and the Commonwealth itself.' The questions of Seretse's marriage, the transfer of the Territories, and the demand for a republic were all linked together.[23]

Gordon Walker nevertheless felt the situation remained 'full of explosive possibilities of several different kinds'. The most criticised aspect of government policy had been the decision to exclude Seretse from the entire Bechuanaland Protectorate. Critics said this was unnecessarily inhuman, harsh, and oppressive. Gordon Walker asked Baring: 'Is there a possibility that we have gone too far?' Parliamentary and public opinion could not be ignored, he felt, if only because it represented a means through which Seretse, or those agitating for him, could cause trouble. Seretse was therefore allowed to visit Lobatsi in April, and the reserve in July, in order to sort out his business and family affairs. But the government was not at all happy about the way Seretse then behaved, and in any case his very presence was awkwardly being interpreted (not least in South Africa) as implying eventual recognition. Baring reported that he seemed to make himself as much of a nuisance as possible without overstepping the mark.[24] He was convinced that Seretse was stimulating resistance to the government and that unless quickly removed he would become a focus of discontent for other Tswana peoples. Historically, he argued, banished chiefs – he cited Cetewayo, Dinizulu, and Lobengula – continued to exercise great influence. Seretse and Ruth, he added, were bound to seek European company, and, given Ruth's acid remarks against racial prejudice, this could give rise to 'unfortunate incidents', arousing unwelcome press interest. Ruth must be excluded too, for she would become a tool of Seretse's followers, and what if her sister joined her and also married an African? Gordon Walker at the end of June accordingly took the matter back to the Cabinet and persuaded them that it would, after all, be inexpedient to allow the Khamas to remain in Bechuanaland much longer. In the last resort the government should be prepared to remove them by force, and face the fierce (but perhaps not prolonged) public criticism this would produce. Ruth, he thought, would be more difficult than Seretse. 'Unpredictable, astute and ruthless', she could feign illness and refuse to move. (In the event, force was not needed.) He hoped that both Seretse and Tshekedi could be induced to reside elsewhere than in either Bechuanaland or Britain.[25]

Gordon Walker's long memorandum of June 1950 was described by the Cabinet secretary as 'exhausting', but perhaps he meant to say exhaustive. It

---

[23] Smuts papers (microfilm), Cambridge University Library, SP 95/180, Smuts to W. S. Churchill, 16 Mar. 1950; see also DO 35/4018, 92 for what Smuts told Baring.

[24] DO 35/4120, and 4121, and 4122.

[25] DO 35/4121, 484, memo by Baring, June 1950; CAB 128/17, CM 40(50)6, conclusions 29 June 1950. Cohen, for the Colonial Office, reluctantly agreed there was no effective alternative to excluding Seretse from Bechuanaland (CO 537/5926, minute 28 June 1950).

presented 'conclusive grounds in terms of local administration' for adhering to the original 6 March decision to exclude Seretse and Tshekedi. Disturbances were occurring, tax collection was impossible in Serowe and negligible outside it, the elaborate system of native courts had practically ceased to function, and no-one would come forward to help in administration for fear of being treated as an enemy by Seretse. The government was, in short, faced with systematic Bangwato non-cooperation and the threat of complete administrative collapse. If the government seemed to weaken now they would get the worst of both worlds: it would stiffen Seretse in his defiant opposition, throw Tshekedi and his followers against Britain, and leave them without any support at all. That was the obvious internal dimension, but it was not the underlying one, which was external:

I am bound to draw attention to the grave effects on our vital interests in southern Africa which a contrary decision would have. Our major concern, in the interests of the African inhabitants of the three Territories, is to preserve the Territories from the Union: this is even more important than the case of Seretse. We must also do our utmost to keep the Union in the Commonwealth.

Britain had some strong cards in her hand to deter South Africa from taking 'extreme action to incorporate the Territories'. South Africa knew she must stand with Britain against the Russian threat and not get strategically isolated. Economically, South Africa needed the labour of the Territories, and the meat of Bechuanaland. But,

if all white opinion in the Union were to become both united and inflamed our deterrents would cease to be effective . . . The Seretse case represents perhaps the one set of circumstances that could unite – and inflame – all white opinion in the Union against us . . . and can drive South Africa into completely irrational attitudes and actions . . . [in] an outburst of uncontrollable emotion and anger . . . A failure to adhere to our original decision to exclude Seretse and Ruth would have much the same effect.

It would, he concluded, be extremely foolhardy and short-sighted to run this risk (by 'giving the official seal and blessing of H.M.G. to the principle of mixed marriage', in the midst of what South Africans saw as their national territory), 'for the sake of a man who has not even succeeded in evoking any significant support among the African populations' outside Gammangwato.[26]

---

[26] CAB 129/38, CP(50)138, memo 26 June 1950; CAB 129/46, CP(51)173, memo 22 June 1951. Both Noel-Baker and Gordon Walker, relying on Baring's impressions, tended to exaggerate African opposition to Seretse. Baxter of the CRO was aware of this, while Cohen said it plainly was not right to suggest that Africans outside southern Africa would welcome non-recognition. A number of southern African black leaders were, however, certainly against recognition, perhaps because the marriage was seen as a bad example ('what the lion does the jackal will copy'): notably S. Thema (editor of the widely circulating *Bantu World*), Dr A. B. Xuma (president of the African National Congress), and Sobhuza II of Swaziland. Sobhuza privately felt Seretse should 'abdicate', because the end result (if a son should also marry a European) would be a white chief, but he also keenly realised that a violent South African reaction would endanger the

Gordon Walker thus put the geopolitical implications more strongly than ever before, though the Cabinet previously had preferred to look at the problem more upon the less controversial basis of effective administration and Bangwato domestic interests. If the Cabinet were now to take any account of South African views (wrote Cabinet secretary Brook), they should admit in public discussion that they *had* allowed these considerations to influence them. Ministers did not agree.

This issue was prominent in discussion of the contents of the White Paper which Gordon Walker insisted was necessary to explain the government's position, since they were refusing to publish the Harragin report. Advised by Liesching and Baxter of the CRO, he disagreed with Brook and Baring (who was backed by W. A. W. Clark and A. Sillery, the Resident Commissioner) about including a reference to the 'geographical position and economic weakness' of the Territories. Such a statement might win over their critics, but it would be too dangerous to admit their vulnerability before South Africa. Attlee agreed that evasiveness was safer, and the White Paper as published on 22 March 1950 was actually at pains to deny the influence of the governments of the Union and Southern Rhodesia. In parliament Gordon Walker seems to have come perilously close to lying (albeit for highest 'reasons of state'), claiming categorically that 'no representations' had been received from South Africa. This contention relied on a unilateral interpretation of Egeland's interview with Noel-Baker in June 1949 as merely unofficial. The South African government itself was 'surprised' that HMG took this line, but in view of the extent to which the secretary of state had committed himself, they agreed, in the interests of not embarrassing Gordon Walker, not to press their view. (Indeed, the Union prime minister blandly stalled a question on the subject in the House of Assembly.) In a yet further re-jigging of the trilogy of reasons for not recognising Seretse, the White Paper argued: (i) that a split among the Bangwato would be caused, (ii) that Seretse was unmindful of the true interests of his people and of his public duty, and (iii) that the uncertain status of his children would become a cause of serious dispute.[27]

High Commission Territories as a whole; nevertheless, Sobhuza disliked the idea of overruling *kgotla*. The Bangwaketse chief Bathoen II was quoted as opposed to recognition, but it was not explained that he was a life-long friend of Tshekedi's. Baring tended to argue that the absence of editorial comment in *Imvo Zabantsundu* indicated a lack of Zulu and Xhosa interest. African opinion in Southern Rhodesia, he claimed vaguely, was 'swinging against Seretse'. But generally African opinion was decidedly mixed in southern Africa, and those who supported non-recognition did so reluctantly. Evidence that white 'liberals' were often against recognition was also exaggerated: D. Rheinallt Jones and Q. Whyte (director of the South African Institute of Race Relations) were only against recognition on balance. (See DO 35/4114, 47, and 4118, 5 and 13, and 4131, 121, and 4133, 324; CO 537/5927.)

[27] PREM 8/1308, minute by N. Brook, 28 June 1950; CAB 129/38, CP(50)36, memo 14 Mar. 1950, and draft White Paper; DO 35/4115; *House of Assembly debates*, vol. 71, cc. 3619–20 (24 Mar. 1950). The White Paper was published as Cmd 7913: *Parliamentary Papers* (1950), XIX. See also A. Sillery, *Botswana, a short political history* (London, 1974), p. 149.

By the autumn of 1950 the crisis was beginning to subside for the moment. The White Paper seemed to remove the heat from a dangerous situation. Seretse, Ruth, and their baby daughter, were in England. Tshekedi had resigned the regency, and was now living in Bakwena territory. Progress was however slow in setting up the representative district councils linked to a central council. Tshekedi seems to have realised that the councils would consolidate the break-up of his own power, and so he prevented his followers from taking part. Seretse's men, on the other hand, saw the councils as only another potential instrument for Tshekedi's domination, and became increasingly apathetic about making them work. It was becoming more and more obvious that what people really wanted was the institution of chieftaincy.

To sum up the position as it appeared to Whitehall officials by the end of 1950: they hoped they could 'play it long', but realised this would critically depend on public opinion and the protagonists. Although an open mind would be kept on the question of Seretse's eventual recognition (bearing in mind that circumstances might change), the whole tenor of current thinking was that there was no real prospect of recognition at any time. Despite the distracting and unpropitious local situation, the most hopeful line of constructive action still appeared to be one of associating the Bangwato people more closely with their own government, and getting the moderate followers of both Seretse and Tshekedi into a central council. At the same time, exceptionally energetic steps ought to be taken to find some possible useful employment for Seretse and Tshekedi: both had good qualities, which ought not to be allowed to 'go sour from frustration'. Seretse might be found a colonial service post in West Africa, where 'quite a number of professional Africans had European wives'. Tshekedi might like to play an advisory role in the administration of the Territories as a whole. At any rate, officials realised that Tshekedi could do a lot of damage if permanently antagonised. It would be a considerable gain, they thought, if he could be made to relax and co-operate without residing in Gammangwato, but with facilities to keep an eye on his cows. Government could not just ignore the hardships he was experiencing as the largest cattle-rancher in Bechuanaland (with 20,000 scattered head).[28]

The wider geopolitical implications of southern African policy were comprehensively examined in the autumn of 1950 and the spring of 1951. Gordon Walker himself made a thorough tour of the whole area between 18 January and 3 March 1951. As a result, it was decided that although apartheid could not possibly be supported, co-operation with South Africa was to remain a prime object of British policy.[29] Moreover, Gordon Walker returned more than ever

---

[28] DO 35/4011, 5, and 4131.
[29] CAB 129/42, CP(50)214, memo 25 Sept. 1950; CAB 129/45, CP(51)109, memo 16 Apr. 1951; PREM 8/1284, minute by Syers, 22 Aug. 1950. See also DO 35/3839; CO 537/5710;

convinced that 'our decision about Seretse was the right one'. The main problem now seemed to be what to do with Tshekedi.[30] In Serowe, Gordon Walker found the demand to exclude him more strongly expressed than the desire to have Seretse back. There seemed to be 'overwhelming evidence of Tshekedi's extreme unpopularity'. He was satisfied that the Bangwato were ready to accept Seretse's exclusion, but they were fearful that if Tshekedi were returned to power he would punish them for their opposition. 'We must therefore drop Tshekedi.' His unconditional return would increase the danger of disorder and retard progress with the representative councils, the setting up of which might deflect some of the criticism. Liesching agreed that a hard line against Tshekedi must be maintained: any impression that British policy was wobbling would indeed be 'quite fatal'.[31] Nevertheless, with Tshekedi in London between March and July 1951 (assiduously and effectively promoting his cause), and with a government majority of only six in the House of Commons, the position was 'extremely delicate and involved'. Any appearance of injustice or persecution must be avoided. The CRO was notably patient with Tshekedi's tiresome legalism. Gordon Walker was genuinely prepared to offer him the 'greatest possible concessions' over his private rights as a farmer, on condition that he simply visited his cattle-posts and stayed out of politics and administration. Tshekedi refused these terms. Accordingly, his exclusion was confirmed at the end of May.[32]

Gordon Walker was satisfied that they had an integrated and defensible policy. Attlee agreed. Tshekedi and Seretse must both be excluded, and there could be no compromise of letting one of them back. The Cabinet felt some concession to back-bench feeling was required, however, and James Griffiths (by now secretary of state for the colonies) suggested sending out independent observers to report. The civil servants were 'displeased' (i.e. furious) at this ministerial initiative, the outcome of which could not be wholly predicted.[33] Nevertheless, it was a useful political gesture, which, together with some private lobbying and deft debating by Attlee – and some Conservative votes – enabled the government to survive the opposition confidence motion on 26 June. Attlee skilfully

FO 371/88560 and 91171; DO 35/3140, 55, high commissioner to secretary of state, 30 June 1951; R. Ovendale, 'The South African policy of the British Labour government, 1947–51', *International Affairs*, 59 (1983), pp. 51–8.

[30] The main CRO file on Tshekedi was Y 3480/37, parts I–VII; DO 35/4132–4138. See also Benson, *Tshekedi Khama*, pp. 173–272.

[31] DO 35/4132, 12, Gordon Walker (Cape Town) to Liesching, 7 Feb. 1951; DO 35/4133, minutes by Liesching (6 Apr. 1951) and Gordon Walker (6 Apr. and 15 June 1951); CAB 129/45, CP(51)103, memo 9 Apr. 1951, and CP(51)109, memo 16 Apr. 1951, and CP(51)145, memo 28 May 1951.

[32] DO 35/4133.

[33] CAB 129/46, CP(51)173, memo 22 June 1951, and CP(51)177, memo 24 June 1951; CAB 128/19, CM 45(51)2, conclusions 21 June 1951, and CM 46(51)4, conclusions 25 June 1951; CAB 128/20, CM 51(51)3, conclusions 12 July 1951; DO 35/4134.

denounced the motion (calling for Tshekedi's 'summary banishment' to be rescinded) as seeking to force Tshekedi on the Bangwato people against their will. (Less effectively, perhaps, he compared Tshekedi with Aristides: 'we all remember the case of ostracism in Athens'.)[34] At the end of August the returning 'observers' confirmed the government's view: Bangwato majority opinion was strongly against Tshekedi.[35] There matters rested for the moment.

II

After the election of 25 October 1951, the incoming Conservative regime was fed the official doctrine that Seretse's recognition was the 'one thing that might unite and inflame' South Africa against Britain. If he got back, 'all our relations with the Union would simultaneously be prejudiced, e.g. trade, gold, Middle East defence, etc.' (Clark). Conservative politicians in power were thus forced to adopt a policy they had attacked in opposition. But the change of government also provided the opportunity for a radical reappraisal of how that policy was to be implemented, an opportunity which the civil servants were quick to exploit, vigorously pushing their ideas of how to clear up this intractable problem. Within five months, the Conservative government had taken two main decisions. They arranged a 'new deal' for Tshekedi, and they confirmed the non-recognition of Seretse as permanent.

To plan the eventual return of Tshekedi in his private capacity was a sharp change of tactics, not thought feasible by Gordon Walker and the 'observers', or by Sir John Le Rougetel (the new high commissioner) and many of the local administrators. But the CRO officials, led by W. A. W. Clark, had for some time been determined to move in this direction. (Arthur Clark had recently taken charge of the Territories' department, returning from South Africa after two years as chief secretary to the high commissioner.) Clark was convinced that insufficient account was being taken of Tshekedi's formidable capacity to hit back against his banishment. It was impossible to expect him to lie down quietly under his yoke, and he might, by a tactical reconciliation with Seretse, demolish a principal argument for the latter's exclusion. The local British administration

[34] *House of Commons debates*, 5th series, vol. 489, cc. 1190–1318 (26 June 1951); see also *House of Lords debates*, vol. 172, cc. 380–448 (27 June 1951). The government was defeated in the Lords.
[35] Since the opposition parties declined to nominate back-bench MPs, the observers were independent 'individuals of standing' chosen by the government: Prof. W. M. Macmillan (director of colonial studies at St Andrews), H. L. Bullock (General and Municipal Workers' Union, past president of the TUC, and a widely travelled man), and D. L. Lipson (a Gloucestershire county councillor, former headmaster and ex-Independent-MP for Cheltenham). It was said of this ill-assorted trio that 'they came, they saw, they quarrelled'. See DO 35/4135, and 4140; CAB 129/46, CP(51)198, memo 11 July 1951; CAB 129/47, CP(51)250, memo 22 Sept. 1951, with annexes; CAB 128/20, CM 60(51)8, conclusions 27 Sept. 1951; PREM 8/1308, part II.

had, he argued, by supporting the anti-Tshekedi faction, been buying short-term peace at the expense of good government. This must be stopped.[36]

The reappraisal of policy, as it evolved in the CRO, involved five propositions. One, the exclusion of Seretse must be made permanent, because of the South African factor. This was not to be seen as the appeasement of the Union, but rather as Britain's denying to her opponent her best potential weapon. Two, the reconciliation of Tshekedi was essential. The resented stigma of his exclusion must be removed, but he for his part must also clearly renounce any claim to the chieftaincy, in order to quieten Bangwato fears. Three, the government should get tough with the ascendant Seretse/Sekgoma faction, and peg its members back before they became unmanageable by monopolising the administrative posts. Since their main demand (the return of Seretse) could not be met, it was no good appeasing them. Four, Tshekedi's followers, who were the ablest administrators available, must be boldly brought forward again. Without them, there would be continuing administrative chaos. Five, the institution of chieftaincy had to be accepted as indispensable. The councils policy simply had not worked, and direct rule by European officers had proved an unhappy expedient. Rasebolai Kgamane (a great-nephew of Khama III, and Tshekedi's principal lieutenant) should be groomed as a legitimate prospective chief. It seemed eminently possible that he might prove to be 'the ace in the hole'.[37]

Such were the recommendations laid before the new minister at the CRO, Lord Ismay, whose brief tenure of the office was dominated by the Bangwato issue. He fully accepted Clark's basic assumption that the five-year suspension of Seretse was a bad compromise, giving everyone the worst of all worlds. The Bangwato were in turmoil and entertaining false hopes; the uncertainties were unfair on Seretse and on any potential alternative chief; and the British government was being accused of shilly-shallying.[38] He proposed to the Cabinet a comprehensive solution, approached gradually in three stages. The first and crucial step would be an agreement with Tshekedi. Next, Rasebolai's popularity should be promoted, enabling him to become a rallying-point, alternative to Seretse. The final act, after an interval, would be the permanent exclusion of Seretse, thus permanently removing from the Union a potentially powerful weapon in its campaign for the transfer of the Territories, which (Ismay reaffirmed) Britain had to resist.

The Cabinet endorsed this general policy on 22 and 27 November 1951. No announcement about Seretse would be made until the government's plans for the projected Central African Federation were secure. African opposition

[36] DO 35/4136, especially no. 712, Liesching to Sir J. Le Rougetel, 28 Sept. 1951, and replies thereto, 22 Oct. 1951 (nos. 718, 727); no. 729, note on Bangwato affairs [by Clark, 29 Oct. 1951]; DO 121/148, 45.

[37] DO 35/4135, especially no. 590, draft note [by Clark], 20 Aug. 1951; DO 35/4136, 733 A.

[38] DO 121/148, 37 and 40, notes by Lord Ismay, 4 and 22 Nov. 1951.

to that must not be compounded at a critical moment by complaints from the Bangwato that their wishes were also being flouted.[39] The 'new deal' was, however, successfully sold to Tshekedi by Ismay early in December, on the basis that he could be helped as a farmer but not as a possible chief. Tshekedi promised full co-operation. Clark then recommended the removal of officers too closely associated with the anti-Tshekedi dispensation, notably E. B. Beetham (the resident commissioner) and J. D. A. Germond (the district commissioner at Serowe).[40]

As for Seretse, ministers accepted the officials' argument that, unlike Tshekedi, he could not be allowed back as a private individual, because Bangwato sentiment and dynastic leanings would ensure his being treated as *de facto* chief, thus making administration impossible and upsetting South Africa. In mid-March 1952, Ismay and Lord Salisbury (his successor) told prime minister Churchill that the moment had come to grasp the nettle and abandon the Labour government's 'indecisive line' on Seretse. Otherwise there would be three more years of unhappiness and discord, trouble and criticism. As Salisbury put it, only when the Bangwato had been definitely told Seretse could never come back would they settle down and look at other alternatives. A parliamentary row had to be faced some time, and in three-and-a-half years' time 'we are likely to have to take the same decision on the very eve of a General Election here, which will be even more embarrassing'.[41]

There appeared to be a chance that Seretse might now consider 'alternative employment' if the institution of chieftaincy were assured. Ismay therefore set great store upon the offer of a job to Seretse as perhaps the key to a satisfactory settlement, and Sir Hugh Foot, governor of Jamaica, was willing to help. If Seretse would step down voluntarily, it would get the government off the hook of having to impose an unpalatable decision. Together with Lord Salisbury, Ismay saw Seretse and Ruth on 24 and 26 March 1952. In as friendly a way as possible, Ismay urged him to follow the example of the duke of Windsor's 'supreme self-sacrifice' by 'abdicating' and taking the offer of a government post in the West Indies. A job in Jamaica should provide an agreeable fresh start and solve his financial worries; it would also give him a chance to use his 'inherited talents', while Mrs Khama would have 'opportunities for service'; and it would ease the path for an alternative chief. Seretse was bitterly disappointed. He replied that he could not desert his people in this way, particularly since they now so

---

[39] CAB 129/48, C(51)21, memo 19 Nov. 1951, and C(51)49, memo 17 Dec. 1951 (Transfer of the High Commission Territories); CAB 128/23, CC 10(51)5, conclusions 22 Nov. 1951, and CC 11(51)4, conclusions 27 Nov. 1951, and CC 18(51)6 and 7, conclusions 19 Dec. 1951.

[40] DO 35/4137. Three assistant district officers made representations to the secretary of state, asking him to reconsider the policy of letting Tshekedi return to the reserve. They were reprimanded for their 'presumption and partisan blindness' and then transferred. See DO 35/4138, 970.

[41] DO 35/4138, 1058, Ismay to Churchill, 14 Mar. 1952, and no. 1065 A, Lord Salisbury to Churchill, 18 Mar. 1952.

demonstrably wanted him. He was sure he could use his 'inherited position' to resolve the Bangwato problem peacefully. He was prepared to renounce his claim, but he must have full liberty to take part in political life. He could not understand why Tshekedi should get preferential treatment.[42]

Unmoved, the government announced its decision on 27 March 1952. Ministers argued that their predecessors, having quite rightly concluded that Seretse was 'not a fit and proper person' to be chief, had then been guilty of 'a classic example of procrastination in public affairs'. Peace was hardly likely to be achieved by continuing uncertainty; 'temporary exclusion' must therefore now be turned into permanent non-recognition. This was a line of argument the Labour opposition found hard to rebut.[43]

The Bangwato received the news sullenly rather than violently, although there was a quite serious riot in Serowe early in June 1952. In Britain, press reaction was mixed: 'statesmanlike' (*The Times*), 'courageous' (*Daily Telegraph*), 'inevitable' (*Liverpool Post*), 'vindictive' (*Daily Express*), 'wise' (*Daily Graphic*), 'bad' (*Birmingham Post*). The *Manchester Guardian* made perhaps the liveliest comment: the permanent ban redoubled the injustice done to Seretse, and would give mortal offence to millions of Africans; it would grievously impair the chances of securing African acceptance of the Central African Federation; and it was hard to believe it was a right or final answer to a difficult problem.[44]

III

The four-year Khama controversy was significant at several different levels. In terms of Bangwato administration, it suggests an intense British difficulty within the 'politics of collaboration' of deciding which faction to support. In particular, should Tshekedi be dropped or not? The older local officials tended to think not, but the younger ones seemed to prefer Seretse. Labour ministers were on the whole against Tshekedi, while Conservative ministers favoured him. In 1950 the resident commissioner, Anthony Sillery, was sacked because 'he could not handle Tshekedi' firmly enough; in 1952 several officers were transferred for being too unsympathetic towards Tshekedi's return. In terms of African policy, attempts to side-step traditional rulership altogether, and move towards a more modern system approaching self-government, fractured

---

[42] CAB 129/50, C(52)76, memo 13 Mar. 1952; CO 537/7776; DO 121/151.
[43] CAB 128/24, CC 34(52)1, conclusions 27 Mar. 1952; CAB 129/50, C(52)76, memo 13 Mar. 1952; *House of Commons debates*, vol. 498, cc. 896–960 (27 Mar. 1952), and vol. 499, cc. 1615–26 (30 Apr. 1952); *House of Lords debates*, vol. 175, cc. 1099–1166 (31 Mar. 1952).
[44] About 150 letters (most, but not all, of them protesting about the government's policy) were received in the CRO, together with formal representations, which, in the case of the Labour Party, were usually in the form of composite resolutions condemning both the policies for Seretse and for the Central African Federation. See DO 121/151; DO 35/4144, and 4145, and 4146, and 4147, and 4149; FO 371/96649.

on the rocks of Bangwato angry non-cooperation and innate conservatism. In terms of British public opinion, the crisis provided a seminal awakening to the implications of South African apartheid, gave the Left a new distrust of government, and led to the formation of the Africa Bureau. At the personal level, Baring could never be welcomed by Africans as governor of Kenya, his next assignment; while the controversy did Gordon Walker's reputation no good, and strangely prefigured the shattering of his career as Wilson's first foreign secretary. (In a malign inversion, his rapid double humiliation at the hands of the electors of Smethwick (1964) and Leyton (1965) turned upon racial issues.) In terms of British government, the episode throws much light on the crucial role of civil servants (notably Liesching and Clark) in forming policy, and especially on the way in which they could take advantage of a change of government to drive their own solutions through.[45] At the Cabinet level, the pre-eminent concern with pragmatic issues of strategy and prestige can be clearly demonstrated. Co-operation with the Union government was to be a basic aim of Britain's South African policy. For most ministers this was because it must conform to the context and imperatives of the Cold War. For the departmental ministers most concerned, and the civil servants, however, the primary reason for co-operation with South Africa was the vulnerability of the High Commission Territories, a geopolitical fact strongly underlined by the consequences of Seretse's marriage. The resulting controversy intersected with criticism over the formation of the Central African Federation in the teeth of African protest.

Seretse lost the chieftaincy because he precipitately married a white woman. The deposition of African chiefs normally required stronger grounds than this. As Hudson of the Colonial Office said: 'The act of irresponsibility alone would be condoned [but for] its effect on neighbouring states.' Government consistently refused to reveal the real reason for its sacrifice of Seretse (and, to a lesser extent, of Tshekedi), namely, that it regarded the rights (not altogether undoubted) of two individuals as less important than risking the liberties of nearly two million Africans, who might otherwise end up under South African rule. Since this could not or would not be publicly admitted, successive governments rested their case on the supposed requirements of internal order among the Bangwato. Although there were occasional hints off the record, and a groping in public discussion for an 'undisclosed factor' which might provide a more convincing justification for British policy, government never at any time admitted to anyone (not even to Margery Perham) that its fundamental concern

---

[45] R. Wingate, *Lord Ismay, a biography* (London, 1970), p. 188, grossly over-estimates the minister's influence on policy-making. An altogether safer general guide is J. Lynn and A. Jay, *The complete 'Yes, minister': the diaries of a Cabinet minister, by Rt. Hon. James Hacker, M.P.* (London, 1984), especially pp. 336–7. See also A. Seldon, *Churchill's Indian summer: the Conservative government, 1951–1955* (London, 1981), p. 337.

was the South African threat to the High Commission Territories.[46] (Of course some expert observers guessed it was so.) British policy was to do nothing which might help Malan to press his claim for the transfer of the Territories, nothing which might *unite and inflame* white South African opinion solidly behind him. But even if this vital South African factor had been disclosed, it is unlikely that all criticism would have been dispelled. To Tom Driberg and Fenner Brockway and others it was 'naked appeasement', and that was all there was to be said.

From a historical perspective, however, 'appeasement' often seems to be more of a strategic imperative than a dirty word. The principal historical judgement to be made about the Seretse affair is therefore this: did the British government exaggerate the South African threat to the Territories? Geographically they were embedded in South Africa. Economically, South Africa held them in a stranglehold. Constitutionally, the South Africa Act (1909) provided in principle for their eventual transfer to the Union. All South African prime ministers had demanded their transfer. If Malan was less pressing than most, it was because he doubted whether the Labour government of 1950–1, and even its Conservative successor, were stable and strong enough to handle so momentous a negotiation. The possibility of South Africa's actually invading one or more of the Territories in force was no doubt remote. Meanwhile, they depended on South African co-operation for their customs, defence, transport, and postal facilities. They also needed South Africa's goods, food, and labour opportunities. Any change in this precarious situation would involve Britain in much unwanted difficulty and vast expense. Any money poured in might well be wasted. Revision of the Customs Agreement would result in serious revenue losses; its termination would mean Britain's stepping in to finance complex customs and frontier arrangements of her own. Although economic sanctions against the Territories would also to some extent hurt South Africa herself, and although she might think twice for international reasons about quarrelling with Britain, the British authorities did not believe these deterrents would in the last resort be decisive: the Nationalists were perfectly capable of cutting off their nose to spite their face. Moreover, a more sinister possibility might be the use by South Africa of indirect political intimidation. Basutoland could be starved into submission as an alleged 'hotbed of Communism'. Swaziland might be made ungovernable by stirring up violent agitation among the Afrikaner settler community in the south. Bechuanaland also had groups of discontented European settlers open to political exploitation.

---

[46] Sillery, *Botswana*, p.150, ascribes the government's 'timid fear' of confessing the South African factor to the role of the high commissioner. This is wrong: it was Cabinet, both in 1950 and in 1952, which insisted on silence, *against* the advice of the high commissioner, and, in 1952, against the advice of the departmental minister as well. See CAB 128/24, CC 31(52)4, conclusions 18 Mar. 1952, and CC 33(52)7, conclusions 25 Mar. 1952; CAB 129/50, C(52)76, memo 13 Mar. 1952, and C(52)81, memo 21 Mar. 1952.

All in all, therefore, the British government probably did not exaggerate the threat to the High Commission Territories from South Africa.[47] To that extent its sacrifice of Seretse, against the wishes of the Bangwato, can be broadly vindicated on geopolitical grounds.[48]

Afterword

The argument of this chapter, first published in 1986 (*Historical Journal*, vol. 29), has not, it seems, proved sufficiently persuasive for Seretse's principal biographers. The otherwise admirable study of *Seretse Khama, 1921–1980* by Thomas Tlou, Neil Parsons, and Willie Henderson (Macmillan Boleswa/South Africa, Braamfontein, 1995) is marred by the difficulty the authors have had in detaching themselves from Seretse's own enduring resentment at the treatment his marriage crisis received from Gordon Walker and the British government. The complex imperial dilemmas are not given much sympathy: the British government is carelessly described as simply 'bamboozled' into a 'craven' policy of 'appeasement' because of a supposed 'cosy official relationship between Britain and South Africa' (pp. 75–96, 139). A more reliable and objective account of British policy on this issue was called for. Most unfortunately too, credence is given to Michael Dutfield's quite tentative speculation – about which Dutfield himself was sceptical – that ministers were influenced by the need to secure uranium supplies from South Africa (p. 88) and the delays in July 1949 in concluding an agreement, which the South African government may have imposed because of the Seretse affair: see M. J. Dutfield, *A marriage of inconvenience: the persecution of Ruth and Seretse Khama* (London, 1990), pp. 100–4, Dutfield's own conclusion being that 'there was no indication that the two events were directly related'. Dutfield's book is a readable if journalistic narrative, which tends to interpret everything in terms of racial prejudice; it is based on some Public Record Office material and newspapers, but there are no

---

[47] CAB 129/46, CP(51)173, memo 22 June 1951; DO 35/4018, 60; DO 119/1172, high commissioner to secretary of state, memo and despatch, 8 July 1954. The events of January 1986 in Lesotho, when South African pressure toppled the government of Chief Jonathan and installed a more compliant regime, suggest that British fears were by no means fantasies.

[48] Tshekedi returned to the reserve in October 1952. Rasebolai in May 1953 was appointed African Authority 'without prejudice', but failed to secure designation as chief. Tshekedi and Seretse became reconciled. Seretse was allowed to return as a private individual in the autumn of 1956. Rasebolai then chaired the tribal advisory council, Seretse acted as vice-chairman, and Tshekedi as secretary (until his death in 1959). Seretse founded the Bechuanaland Democratic Party in 1962, became prime minister in 1965, and first president of Botswana in 1966. Ruth and Seretse had four children. Seretse Khama Ian Khama, the eldest son, became chief of the Bangwato in 1979. Seretse died in 1980. For a tribute to his statesmanship, see J. Redcliffe-Maud, *Experiences of an optimist: memoirs* (London, 1981), pp. 187–90, 'Sir Seretse Khama: memorial address in Westminster Abbey' (7 Aug. 1980).

references at all, and little evidence of much in the way of secondary reading; he was unaware of Hyam's article on the subject.

Michael Crowder's essay, 'Professor Macmillan goes on safari: the British government observer team and the crisis over the Seretse Khama marriage, 1951', is more important and wide-ranging than its title might suggest; but he too was unaware of Hyam's contribution: see Hugh Macmillan and Shula Marks, eds., *Africa and empire: W. M. Macmillan, historian and social critic* (Aldershot, 1989: ICS Commonwealth Papers no. 25), chapter 12, pp. 254–78. R. D. Pearce gives a sound account as editor of *Patrick Gordon Walker: political diaries, 1932–1971* (London, 1991), pp. 23–7 (see pp. 187–9 for the important diary entry of 2 April 1950).

9 Containing Afrikanerdom: the geopolitical origins of the Central African Federation, 1948–1953

The Central African Federation (1953–63) was the most controversial large-scale imperial exercise in constructive state-building ever undertaken by the British government. It appears now as a quite extraordinary mistake, an aberration of history ('like the Crusader Kingdom of Jerusalem'), a deviation from the inevitable historical trend of decolonisation. Paradoxically, one of its principal architects, Andrew Cohen (head of the African department of the Colonial Office) is also credited with having set the course for planned African decolonisation as a whole. There have already been several attempts to explain how an error so interesting and surprising, so large and portentous, came to be made.[1] No-one, however, has yet presented an analysis based on British government archives, and the authoritative evidence that they alone can provide.

Several historical reference-points constitute the background. Foremost among them, perhaps, was the famous British propensity to look to the 'federal panacea' as a solution for the perennial imperial problem of governing big intractable areas, of establishing more viable units, to whom power could be safely transferred. Some successes had been initiated in the white dominions in the past, at least when the situation was sufficiently dynamic, the local elite

---

The main research sources used are the Colonial Office and Commonwealth Relations Office files in the Public Record Office (PRO), principally DO 35/3585–3613 (1949–52), R.2000/18–70; CO 1015/51–158 (1951–2) and 746–798 (1952–3); together with CO 537/3608, 4687–4691, 5884–5886, 7201–7205 (1948–51).

[1] J. R. T. Wood, *The Welensky papers: a history of the Federation of Rhodesia and Nyasaland* (Durban, 1983), with an introduction by Lord Blake (from which the quotation is taken); R. Blake, *A history of Rhodesia* (London, 1977), pp. 243–69; C. Leys and C. Pratt (eds.), *A new deal in Central Africa* (London, 1960), pp. 1–58; R. I. Rotberg, *The rise of nationalism in Central Africa: the making of Malawi and Zambia, 1873–1964* (Harvard, 1966), pp. 214–52; L. H. Gann and M. Gelfand, *Huggins of Rhodesia: the man and his country* (London, 1964), pp. 208–29; L. H. Gann, *A history of Northern Rhodesia: early days to 1953* (London, 1964), pp. 405–33; C. Palley, *The constitutional history and law of Southern Rhodesia, 1888–1965, with special reference to imperial control* (Oxford, 1966), pp. 333–44; P. Gifford, 'Misconceived dominion: the creation and disintegration of the Federation of British Central Africa', in P. Gifford and W. R. Louis (eds.), *The transfer of power in Africa: decolonisation, 1940–1960* (Yale, 1982), pp. 387–416. For Andrew Cohen see R. E. Robinson, 'Sir Andrew Cohen: proconsul of African nationalism (1909–68)', in L. H. Gann and P. Duignan (eds.), *African proconsuls: European governors in Africa* (Stanford, 1978), pp. 353–64.

Map 9.1 Central African Federation: the Federation of Rhodesia and Nyasaland, 1953–1963, marked with heavy boundary line.

keenly committed, the imperial government tactfully supportive, and where an external threat imparted an expediting sense of urgency.[2] Canadian confederation was actually completed in 1949 by the accession of Newfoundland, a

[2] G. W. Martin, 'Launching Canadian Confederation: means to ends, 1836–64', *Historical Journal*, 27 (1984), pp. 575–602, and 'An imperial idea and its friends', in G. Martel (ed.), *Studies in British imperial history: essays in honour of A. P. Thornton* (London, 1986), pp. 49–94, and 'The Canadian analogy in South African Union', *South African Historical Journal* 8 (1976), pp. 40–59; R. L. Watts, *New federations: experiments in the Commonwealth* (Oxford, 1966).

consummation strongly promoted by prime minister Clement Attlee. (According to a Foreign Office official, this was an achievement 'shining like a good deed in a depressing and naughty world'.)[3] Then there was the doctrine of trusteeship, a steady Colonial Office tradition of trying to provide protection for African interests against the vociferous and importunate demands of white settlers. The trusteeship doctrine consistently and successfully refused white Rhodesians the amalgamation (unitary state) they desired in Central Africa. It was indeed one of the principal victories of trusteeship in the 1920s and 1930s.[4] There was also a long history, albeit of an intermittent character, of trying to find a counterpoise to the expansion of Afrikaner nationalism north of the Limpopo (but not only north of it): the policy of 'keeping the Rhodesians out of the Union . . . to balance the Union' (as L. S. Amery put it), of trying to build up Southern Rhodesia as the nucleus of a pro-British buffer-state between South Africa and the Colonial Office African territories, dedicated to different principles of native administration. The outlines of some new geopolitical configuration in Central Africa, a 'British bloc', had begun to be explored by some administrators almost immediately after the 1922 referendum which denied Southern Rhodesia her destiny in the Union and set her on the path to internal self-government. Smuts was an ardent expansionist, particularly interested in Southern Rhodesia; but so also was the Nationalist leader Oswald Pirow. The Colonial Office in 1941 was well aware of the way in which the extension of Union influence northwards under the exigencies of war might be creating a 'problem of first-class significance', and alerted Lord Harlech (the new high commissioner) to the dangers.[5]

In 1948, however, none of these strands of inherited historiography – neither federal panacea, nor African trusteeship, nor Afrikaner counterpoise – was sufficiently to the fore in Central Africa to suggest that a major constructive

---

[3] PRO, FO 371/70191; PREM 8/1043.
[4] R. E. Robinson, 'The Trust in British Central African policy, 1889–1939' (unpublished Cambridge PhD thesis, 1950), and 'The moral disarmament of African empire, 1919–47', *Journal of Imperial and Commonwealth History* 8 (1979), reprinted in N. Hillmer and P. Wigley (eds.), *The first British Commonwealth: essays in honour of Nicholas Mansergh* (London, 1980), pp. 86–104; R. Hyam, 'African interests and the South Africa Act, 1908–10', *Historical Journal* 13 (1970), pp. 85–105 (see chapter 4 above); H. I. Wetherell, 'The Rhodesias and amalgamation: settler sub-imperialism and the imperial response, 1914–1948' (unpublished PhD thesis, University of Rhodesia, 1977), and 'British and Rhodesian expansionism: imperial collusion or empirical carelessness?', *Rhodesian History*, 8 (Salisbury, 1977), pp. 115–28, and 'Settler expansionism in Central Africa: the imperial response of 1931 and subsequent implications', *African Affairs* 78 (1979), pp. 210–27; R. I. Rotberg, 'The federal movement in East and Central Africa, 1889–1953', *Journal of Commonwealth Political Studies* 2 (1964), pp. 141–60. See also K. Robinson, *The dilemmas of trusteeship: aspects of British colonial policy between the wars* (Oxford, 1965).
[5] M. Chanock, *Unconsummated Union: Britain, Rhodesia and South Africa, 1900–1945* (Manchester, 1977); R. Hyam, *The failure of South African expansion, 1908–1948* (London, 1972); PRO, CO 847/23, 47173. For L. S. Amery's view see N. Mansergh *et al.* (eds.), *Transfer of power in India*, V (London, 1974), p. 591 (Amery to Wavell, 28 Feb. 1945).

exertion of imperial power was about to take place. A Central African Council had been set up in 1945 to provide some administrative co-ordination, and that was as far as Whitehall wished to go. In the genesis of the Central African Federation the historical reference-points, analogies, and inherited continuities in the minds of policy-makers were decidedly weak. (Nor did plans for an emerging Caribbean federation exert any influence.) They did what they did largely in response to immediate Rhodesian initiatives, and for pragmatic reasons dictated by the situation as it expressly confronted them at the time, although they certainly believed themselves to be acting within the tradition of securing the interests of Africans,[6] and their decisions were taken in the context of the larger issues of east and southern African policy as a whole, of which the most important were calculations about the relative value to British interests of having white settler or African collaborators, of being friendly or unco-operative towards South Africa.[7] For more than twenty-five years British policy in Central Africa had been to block amalgamation. But when the Rhodesians decided to opt for federation (a second-best as far as they were concerned), British civil servants and politicians were forced to reconstruct their static Rhodesian policy, a process which ineluctably led them into becoming convinced that federation in Central Africa was an urgent geopolitical necessity.

I

It was in July 1948 that the Northern Rhodesian settler leader Roy Welensky decided to go for federation not amalgamation. The ever-perceptive Cohen at once fastened upon this as a 'very important development'. Personally, he wrote, he had for some time believed that federation of the three territories (Northern and Southern Rhodesia, and Nyasaland) 'should be the ultimate aim of policy'. Hitherto he had believed that federation must wait until Africans in Northern Rhodesia and Nyasaland had developed politically and were able to take both an 'intelligent decision on the question and to play an effective part in the federal arrangements'. But he was now increasingly beginning to wonder 'whether we are really right not to attempt a step forward towards federation (perhaps on the lines of the East African High Commission) in the fairly near future'. There were plenty of practical difficulties. The crux of the problem was keeping ultimate responsibility for Northern Rhodesia and Nyasaland without infringing Southern Rhodesia's position as a self-governing regime. The problem should

---

[6] Thus far we accept the argument of Wood, *Welensky papers*, p. 35.
[7] D. W. Throup, 'The origins of Mau-Mau', *African Affairs* 84 (1985), p. 410; D. M. Anderson and D. W. Throup, 'Africans and agricultural production in colonial Kenya', *Journal of African History*, 26 (1985), p. 344; R. Ovendale, 'The South African policy of the British Labour government, 1947–1951', *International Affairs* 59 (1983), pp. 41–58.

not, however, be regarded as insoluble or insuperable constitutionally. The main difficulty would be the probable opposition of African opinion.[8]

The Labour government's enigmatic secretary of state for the colonies, Arthur Creech Jones, accepted that certain changes had occurred in the situation since the war, making 'some revaluation of the existing arrangements' desirable: 'our strategic needs in Africa, the importance of more thorough-going development, the desirability of certain common services and regional approach – suggest the need of a closer association of the three territories'. Some loose form of federation might be within the realms of possibility, he thought. But the 'political stuff is dynamite and must be handled with great care'. It was not for Britain to take the initiative. Everything must be vague at first in discussions with the Rhodesians, 'but I am certain we must not advance an inch if it involves us in any surrender of African rights'. He agreed to see Welensky unofficially, but proposed to 'go slow with such discussions'. The main point he made to Welensky was that although Welensky himself must get things going as he thought best, 'no scheme that failed completely to satisfy African interests or win African approval had the slightest chance of success'.[9]

By the spring of 1949 Welensky had, after a conference of Rhodesian unofficials at Victoria Falls in February, produced a far-reaching scheme for Central Africa which was regarded in Whitehall as utterly unrealistic. It was little short of amalgamation, and therefore unthinkable. Cohen described Welensky as having overplayed his hand: the general impression was that the federal proposals were a political device to make Central Africa safe for white settler predominance. Nevertheless, they could not just sweep the whole matter aside: Cohen thought it extremely doubtful whether they could successfully handle the situation unless they themselves were prepared to propose the adoption of 'some effective and substantial alternative proposition'. Constitutional development was 'not a process which can stand still'. To stick with the Central African Council 'would alienate European opinion in Northern Rhodesia, and a large section of opinion in Southern Rhodesia'. Much could be gained by creating a strong Central African bloc, which would resist Union pressure and prevent the spread of Afrikaner ideas northwards.[10]

The initial reaction of CRO officials to Welensky's proposals was even more dismissive. They did not see how federation could possibly be regarded as a live issue. Secretary of state Philip Noel-Baker agreed: 'The crucial point is Native

---

[8] CO 537/3608, 24 and minutes by Cohen, 16 and 21 July and 12 Oct. 1948. It seems that Col. Stanley, the former Conservative secretary of state for the colonies, suggested to Welensky that he should substitute federation for amalgamation, though Welensky subsequently seems to have muddled him up with Creech Jones: see R. Welensky, *Welensky's 4000 days: the life and death of the Federation of Rhodesia and Nyasaland* (London, 1964), pp. 24 and 43, and Wood, *Welensky papers*, pp. 122–3.

[9] CO 537/3608, minutes by Creech Jones, 8, 21, and 28 Oct. 1948.

[10] CO 537/4687, minutes by Cohen, 7 and 23 Mar. 1949.

policy; I don't believe in any development which means self-government by a very small minority of Europeans, ruling a very large number of Africans.' However, his more able parliamentary under-secretary, Patrick Gordon Walker, minuted presciently: 'The difficulties are very great: but the advantages of some sort of federation would be immense. One day we should give our minds to seeing whether the difficulties could not be overcome'. Britain, he added, might have to take the initiative some time, because 'great strategic and economic issues are involved'.[11]

Creech Jones paid a visit to Central Africa in April 1949. The settlers found him suspicious and abrasive. Everywhere he found African opinion not only opposed to the idea of federation but actively hostile, speaking against it with 'fierce antagonism'. He was unconvinced of the soundness of Southern Rhodesian race relations policy, which he described as 'mid-way between South Africa's and our own'. He told Welensky his mind was not closed to the argument for change. Privately however, he felt 'great scepticism whether a central authority will ever be realised in Central Africa, except in form of a federation completely unacceptable to H.M.G.'. Creech Jones still believed the most promising line of advance was to build upon the Central African Council; at any rate, natural growth from below was preferable to artificial constitutions. In general his policy directive was 'wait and see'.[12]

The CRO accepted that for the moment. Let the initiative remain with the Rhodesians. If they cared to put forward agreed concrete proposals for improving inter-territorial co-operation, these would be 'studied with an open mind'. Sir Percivale Liesching, the permanent under-secretary, commented in September 1949: 'we should lie low for the present'. Noel-Baker never wavered from the line that 'we must not encourage hopes which have no future': 'federation is not desirable in itself; and it is not practical politics, either in Central Africa or in Westminster' – because of African and parliamentary opposition. He did not believe the difficulties could be overcome, and he repeatedly insisted that they should not even imply that 'closer union' was an accepted objective or even 'the next step'. Like Creech Jones, he hoped that closer economic co-operation might be achieved through the Central African Council. This was the main message in fact given to Rhodesian representatives at the end of November 1949. Hints that Southern Rhodesia might be driven into the Union were received in the CRO as yet with scepticism.[13]

The tide was thus undoubtedly running very strongly against the prospects of federation as the year 1949 closed. Four serious obstacles were clearly apparent: major differences in native policies between Northern and Southern Rhodesia

---

[11] DO 35/3585, minutes by Liesching and Gordon Walker, 28 Jan. and Noel-Baker, 10 Feb. 1949; DO 35/3586, minute by Gordon Walker, 3 Oct. 1949.
[12] DO 35/3586, 3 and 8, Creech Jones to prime minister, 19 Apr. and May 1949.
[13] DO 35/3586, minutes by Liesching, 29 Sept. and Noel-Baker, 11 July, 12 Nov., and 9 Dec. 1949.

(with a colour-bar in some areas), and the British government's responsibilities to Africans in the northern territories; wide differences in the constitutional structures; differences of opinion about the political machinery needed to represent all sections of the population; and above all fierce African opposition. But if federation were impossible, Cohen argued, 'some form of association' was essential, because 'isolation would be disastrous' for Southern Rhodesia. Herbert Baxter (an assistant under-secretary in the CRO) was even more inclined to question the orthodoxy of 'wait and see'. Early in November 1949 he quietly suggested to Cohen that they might consider whether 'we need retain our entirely passive attitude'. Should they not indicate what steps and stages would be required subsequent to the arrival at agreed proposals? But he had no authority to proceed.[14]

II

The sense of deadlock remained in Whitehall as the year 1950 opened, and indeed was compounded when, early in January, Godfrey Huggins, the Southern Rhodesian premier, rather rudely gave notice of his intention to quit the Central African Council by the end of the year. Nor could any fresh policy be adopted, as a British general election was pending. Officials early in February decided to put together a briefing file which would be ready to lay before new ministers after the general election on 28 February. In the Cabinet reshuffle following Labour's return to power (with a much reduced majority), Gordon Walker was promoted to run the CRO, while James Griffiths replaced Creech Jones at the Colonial Office; this, in Attlee's view, put two strong administrators in place of weak, if devoted ones.

Cohen's brief for the new ministers (incorporating amendments suggested by Baxter) rehearsed the pros and cons, and suggested three principles for future policy. One: on practical grounds, much would be gained by some form of closer association. Two: the scheme must be capable of wholehearted recommendation by the British government to Africans, as safeguarding African interests in the north and not prejudicing their advancement. Three: Britain should not give the impression that there was no hope of agreement. This would only encourage the tendency to settler isolation and the danger of leading Southern Rhodesia eventually in the direction of a closer association with the Union. He proposed that officials of the four governments should hold a conference in London and recommend a solution. It was time to act. For eighteen months the British government had deliberately refrained from taking the initiative. The results had been negative, and merely produced the half-baked Victoria Falls proposals, which any British official could have told the Rhodesians were a non-starter.

---

[14] DO 35/3586, 51 and minute by Baxter, 4 Nov. 1949.

There were thus good grounds, Cohen thought, for taking command of the situation, 'but this must be done in such a way as to safeguard African interests and to avoid alarming African opinion'.[15]

In April 1950 Welensky submitted revised federal proposals which were received with as much scorn as his earlier ones. (He was coming to be regarded as a prima donna desperate for the limelight.) Baxter immediately wrote them off as likely to result in an expensive, extravagant, and top-heavy form of executive, to say nothing of causing much apprehension among Africans. Nevertheless, he felt that at this juncture 'the adoption of a purely negative and destructive attitude might have ill-consequences which it would be difficult to overtake ... If we can hold out any prospect of advance this seems to be the time to do it.' He believed that it would be better to take the initiative in the immediate future, rather than 'wait upon the pressure which would inevitably be put upon us from Central Africa'. Cohen supported him. A positive line of action to relieve the frustration and deadlock ought to be taken. The most obvious course was to hold an officials' conference as already proposed.[16]

Ministers were however reluctant to move as Cohen and Baxter suggested. Griffiths said it would in any case be essential to make it clear before a conference that African interests must be safeguarded, and changes in the protection of Africans were a Cabinet matter. Gordon Walker did not think any action was necessary for the moment, and wanted to proceed slowly. The first thing, he thought, was to try to reorganise the Central African Council and make it work efficiently. Then they could look at the question of federation again. A rejuvenated Council went as far as he believed practicable, and it would usefully test the local capacity to work together. Since the goal of policy was as yet no better defined, Gordon Walker could see no point in an officials' conference (though he did not think it would do any harm). Although he did not forbid it, the effect of these remarks was to squash the idea for the time being.[17] As a result Baxter described the omens in the summer of 1950 as 'not very propitious'.[18]

The next step came in the shape of a formal request from Huggins in August 1950 – deliberately suggested to him – that an officials' conference should take place. Supported by A. E. T. Benson, chief secretary of the Central African Council now under sentence of death, this could not be met with a flat refusal. In September 1950 the secretaries of state therefore authorised the preparation of a joint Colonial Office–CRO memorandum for submission to the prime minister, to obtain authority for an officials' conference. The aim of this conference

---

[15] DO 35/3587, 26; CO 537/5884, 34. For Attlee's opinion of his ministers, see Churchill College Archives Centre: Attlee papers, ATLE 1/17.
[16] DO 35/3588, minute by Baxter, 22 Apr. and memo by Cohen, 9 May 1950 (no. 58).
[17] DO 35/3588, minutes by Gordon Walker, 27 Apr., 11 and 21 May 1950, and Baxter, 10 May; CO 537/5884, minute by C. E. Lambert, 28 Apr. 1950.
[18] DO 35/3588, 70.

would be to try to evolve a 'reasonably practical scheme' such as the settlers, left to themselves, had not been able to devise. It would be a means of breaking out of the 'vicious circle' in which concrete, realistic proposals were awaited from Southern Rhodesia but were not forthcoming. The British government, officials argued, ought to meet the criticisms made of it for its 'lack of sympathy' and refusal to take any initiative, its 'indifference' and merely destructive comment. It ought to show it was seeking a solution and not just stonewalling. The conference would also perform an educative function: Rhodesians must be brought to realise the limitations imposed by the facts of the situation. Without a conference, the agitation for federation or amalgamation would not go away, and some means would have to be found of dealing with it. Approving the draft submission, Gordon Walker wrote:

This seems generally O.K. One of our aims must be to keep Southern Rhodesia out of the Union. Another is to watch the infiltration of Afrikaners. Possibly immigration should be one of the central subjects. We should not hanker after federation or imitations of it. What we want is a limited union of governments. Anything else will be dangerous.

He regarded federation in existing circumstances as not only dangerous but impossible. Nevertheless, he agreed that they could not exclude it from the officials' discussions. (Baxter was highly emphatic on this point: it would be an impossible handicap if certain avenues of approach were ruled out in advance. This could only make the officials' work 'infructuous'.) The submission explained to Attlee the 'very real' danger that Southern Rhodesia might turn to the Union. Attlee approved the proposal, and in due course there was a parliamentary statement (8 November 1950) announcing the officials' conference. It would be exploratory and non-committal, and bound to pay particular regard to the African responsibilities of the British government. Privately Griffiths stressed that consultation with African opinion about possible changes in their interests was '**for us absolutely essential**'.[19]

It is often argued that the accession to power of Gordon Walker and Griffiths was an immediate and vital 'breakthrough' for the federal cause, and that the formidable Cohen 'converted' these supposedly more malleable ministers to the need for an officials' conference.[20] This is not at all how it looks in

---

[19] DO 35/3588, 85 and minute by Gordon Walker, 16 Sept. 1950; no. 91, minute to the prime minister, 5 Oct. 1950; PREM 8/1307; double underlining in CO 537/5885, minute by Griffiths, 20 Oct. 1950.

[20] Blake, *History of Rhodesia*, p. 249; Wood, *Welensky papers*, p. 149; D. Goldsworthy, *Colonial issues in British politics, 1945–1961* (Oxford, 1971), p. 48; R. F. Holland, *European decolonisation, 1918–1981: an introductory survey* (London, 1985), p. 141; A. J. Hanna, *The story of the Rhodesias and Nyasaland* (London, 1960), pp. 252–3. The initiative for the officials' conference has been variously ascribed: to G. H. Baxter (Gann, *History of Northern Rhodesia*, p. 410; Palley, *Constitutional history and law of Southern Rhodesia*, p. 335), to Cohen (Rotberg, *Rise of nationalism*, p. 231, n. 37; Goldsworthy, *Colonial issues*, p. 216), and, rather naïvely, to Huggins (Blake, *History of Rhodesia*, p. 249; Wood, *Welensky papers*, p. 168). Clearly the idea did not

the record. Gordon Walker was at the end of 1950 still essentially holding back, and ruling out full federation as impracticable. The assent of Griffiths and himself to the officials' conference was held up for six months, and then given cautiously and unenthusiastically. Gordon Walker was still thinking in terms of a union of sovereign governments who would reach agreement on action only in specific fields. The model might be on the lines of the OEEC (Organisation for European Economic Co-operation) or Atlantic Council. Even Baxter throughout 1950 found the future obscure, and continued to think in terms of a closer association of certain common services, 'some sort of embryonic federation' which would not prejudice African interests; the aim anyway was to find a solution which would head off a wider scheme of federation or amalgamation. Cohen himself advocated the 'league system': a 'functional confederation' like the East African High Commission, based on joint administration of common services run by an inter-territorial organisation parallel to existing state governments, 'on the precedent of the Hanseatic League'. For Cohen too, full federation was impracticable. During preparations for the conference, officials were thus mainly interested in collating material on *non-federal* associations between independent states, such as the East African High Commission, and the OEEC and other embryonic European groupings.[21]

Cohen suggested that Baxter should lead the British delegation. Baxter thus became chairman of the conference, which sat from 5 to 31 March 1951. Professor K. C. Wheare was the academic constitutional adviser, winning good opinions. According to the indispensable folklore, the conference only really got off the ground after Cohen had been persuaded to leave his influenza sick-bed and instil some realism into the Rhodesian delegates. The officials' conference was undoubtedly a turning-point, but a major reason for this was that its conclusions dovetailed in with those Gordon Walker brought back from an on-the-spot investigation.[22]

---

originate with Huggins: he merely put forward the formal request, which had been suggested to him. Liesching reminded Huggins that the 'first initiative' came from the CRO (DO 35/3609, 39 A, 17 June 1952). In all probability both Baxter and Cohen had the same idea independently. What is certain is that they consulted closely at every stage, and thought along similar lines. It is equally clear that Baxter's influence in promoting federation was just as significant as Cohen's, perhaps more so. Baxter recalled in 1956: 'It suddenly came to me, almost with the force of a conversion, that the change had to be brought about ... The politicians had had their whack, and I worked to see whether the officials from both sides could put their heads together and achieve something. Rather surprisingly, we were allowed to have a try.' He later became secretary of the Rhodesia and Nyasaland Committee and a leading publicist for the federal government in London. (Leys and Pratt, *New deal in Central Africa*, pp. 20 and 47, n. 3.)

[21] CO 537/5885, minutes by Cohen, 14 and 19 Sept. 1950; DO 35/3588, 100, Gordon Walker, 20 Sept. 1950. For the East African High Commission see C. Leys and P. Robson (eds.), *Federation in East Africa: opportunities and problems* (Nairobi, 1965).

[22] CO 537/7201, minute by Cohen, 12 Jan. 1951; DO 35/3591, minute by Baxter, 26 Jan. 1951; DO 35/3592, minute by Baxter, 6 Feb. 1951; Wood, *Welensky papers*, pp. 180–1.

III

Gordon Walker's visit to central and southern Africa lasted for six weeks, from 18 January to 3 March 1951. The effect on crystallising policy was profound, and his tour was thus the most important single event in stepping up the commitment of the British government to federation. In Salisbury on 23 January he recorded his surprise at the extent of pro-Union feeling. The governor, Sir John Kennedy, and more than one minister, urged on him the necessity of acting boldly, otherwise the tendency to Union absorption would increase in Southern Rhodesia, and the Europeans in Northern Rhodesia (and later in Kenya) might revolt against Colonial Office control. This analysis formed the basic theme of Gordon Walker's masterly memorandum reporting his reflections to the Cabinet. This memorandum (dated 16 April 1951) is, without question, the most important and intelligent memorandum ever written by a British minister on the problem of British policy towards southern Africa, rivalled for its clarity and insight only by Winston Churchill's 1906 memoranda on the Transvaal constitution, but distinguished from them by being more comprehensive in scope and more influential on long-term policy. A substantial part of it was about the Rhodesian problem.[23]

In many ways the Southern Rhodesian government seemed to him like an enlarged county council. The general level of ministers, civil servants, and businessmen was not high. Huggins was outstandingly the ablest. Some of them had views indistinguishable from South African apartheid, but they were not the majority, who generally took simply an attitude of kindly superiority towards the blacks (as opposed to treating them as permanent children). There *was* a difference between the two native policies, he believed, and the atmosphere in Salisbury was much more relaxed than in Johannesburg. The gravest problem was the pull of South Africa, 'a problem as old as Rhodesia itself'. Perhaps a third of the Europeans would vote for incorporation in the Union, some of them for economic reasons, some to strengthen the pro-British element in South Africa, some out of genuine approval of the Union, and some from dislike of the Colonial Office. Not every Afrikaner immigrant was bad, and most of them came for uncomplicated economic reasons, but there *was* an element of political immigration from South Africa. No one could tell him how large it was, though.

So much for his general impressions. At the heart of his memorandum was the contention that South Africa had dangerous plans for expansion northwards, and Britain could not rely on internal tensions in the Union mounting high enough and soon enough to prevent it. South Africa was strongly placed as

---

[23] DO 35/3591, 51; PRO, CAB 129/45, CP(51)109; Ovendale, 'South African policy', pp. 51–4. For Churchill's 1906 memoranda see R. Hyam, *Elgin and Churchill at the Colonial Office, 1905–1908* (London, 1968), pp. 115–17.

infinitely the most powerful state in Africa, with rapidly increasing economic (and therefore military) strength, which she might use to bring under her political leadership and protection the settler populations of central and East Africa. Thus, he concluded:

> One of our prime aims must be to *contain* South Africa . . . prevent the spread of its influence and territorial sovereignty northwards . . . This would mean that we do not regard as our sole objective the emancipation and political advancement of the African in all our African colonies. That must of course remain a major objective, but we must not subordinate all else to it.

'Containment' did not mean being hostile to the Union; on the contrary, British government must be friendly (as the Cabinet had already agreed the previous autumn);[24] but it would mean being more conciliatory towards settler communities, and adopting a new, positive policy, because Britain could not count on white loyalty alone and for ever. There was, he continued, a very real danger that, to avoid domination by Africans (through the British policy of political advancement for them), the white communities would in the end throw in their lot with the Union. Out of this line of reasoning Gordon Walker articulated a striking new dimension to the discussion of federation in Central Africa:

> We must in our long-term African policies reckon this as a grave danger to be set alongside the danger of some African (and Indian) discontent. Should we, intentionally or by default, throw British communities in East and Central Africa into the arms of the Union, our whole work in Africa would be undone. The policies that we detest in the Union would be established far to the North and in the heart of this part of our Colonial Empire. Millions of Africans would be subjected to oppression. Terrible wars might even be fought between a white-ruled Eastern Africa and a black-ruled Western Africa.

Gordon Walker developed his apocalyptic scenario by pointing out that in the last resort the British government had no real power to control their settler communities. As these grew in numbers and wealth, so they would become 'potential American colonies – very loyal, but very determined to have their own way'. If Britain were eventually faced by defiance in the Rhodesias or Kenya, 'there will in effect be nothing that we can do about it'. Certainly Britain's power on the spot would be found inferior to South Africa's. This dreadful prospect would arise if Britain allowed the impression to be given that she was committed to a policy of subordinating whites to Africans. 'Rather than face that, the whites will in the end revolt.' Britain's well-intentioned policies for Africans would be thwarted, and 'tens of millions of Africans', for whom she was responsible, would be 'calamitously worse off'. Southern Rhodesia would be the test case. The day was not far off when it could defy Britain

---

[24] CAB 129/42, CP(50)214, memo 25 Sept. 1950; CAB 128/18, CM 62(50), conclusions, 28 Sept. 1950. See above, p. 17.

with impunity. The whole fate of British policy in southern Africa thus turned on whether Southern Rhodesia was drawn northwards or southwards. One or other was inevitable, because she was not large enough to stand on her own as a separate unit without access to the sea. Therefore, he argued, Britain must adopt a deliberate policy of attracting Southern Rhodesia to the north:

If we do not, we will fail to contain South Africa and in the end all our good work and all our influence will be ruined.

I would therefore propose that it should become one of our cardinal policies to keep Southern Rhodesia out of the Union. This is a key-stone of the policy of containing South Africa. This should be a policy of *equal* weight and importance in our eyes with the political advancement of the Africans in our Central and East African colonies. It should not be a secondary or a subordinate policy, but an equal one.

A policy of greater accommodation towards Rhodesian settlers would not be popular or easy to put across, and they could expect abuse for adopting it. But the stakes were too high not to adopt it. If they insisted on treating Southern Rhodesian native policy as identical with South African native policy, 'we shall in the end succeed in making it so':

By driving Southern Rhodesia into the Union we would allow a fatal shift of the balance of power and immensely increase the attractive power of the Union's policy for white communities in neighbouring colonies. By listening to the protests of Africans and others against any truck with Southern Rhodesia we would in the end betray our trust to the Africans by being unable effectively to protect them against South African Native policy.

Thus they would have to contend not only with South African expansion, but 'the will of our own white communities'. If Britain failed to grapple with the current opposition to closer union, the result might be that Southern Rhodesia finally lost hope in any possibility of closer association with her northern neighbours. Moreover, were Britain at some later time to attempt 'some sort of Central African Union', they would certainly find African opinion even more strongly against it. The need was for immediate action.

Before completing this analysis, Gordon Walker already had in his hands the persuasive report of the officials' conference (the Baxter report, 31 March 1951), together with an appendix, the all-important confidential minute by Baxter and Cohen about the South African factor, which could not be published for fear of offending the Union.[25] The crucial argument of the minute was that the expansion of South Africa constituted 'a serious and imminent threat to the independent existence' of the Rhodesias, undermining their 'British way of life', gravely prejudicing race relations, and sooner or later leading to their

---

[25] CAB 129/45, CP(51)122, annex 1, confidential minute on the conference on closer association in Central Africa, by G. H. Baxter and A. B. Cohen, 31 Mar. 1951; see also Wood, *Welensky papers*, pp. 193–4.

absorption in the Union. Although Afrikaner immigration was the immediate and most easily identified problem, a linked danger was the uncomfortable geopolitical susceptibility of the Rhodesians to economic pressure from the Union. The overall situation was therefore grave, and the building up of a strong British state (the report concluded) was essential in order to withstand external pressures. The supreme advantage of such a state appeared to be that it could enforce a common immigration policy for all three territories, and control Afrikaner influx without the embarrassment which the United Kingdom government would experience in acting against it in terms of Commonwealth relations. The congruence of the conclusions of the Baxter report with Gordon Walker's memorandum is striking, and it proved decisive. The interlocking of independent ministerial and unanimous civil service thinking, so powerfully developed, was enough to convince Griffiths.

Accordingly, Griffiths and Gordon Walker were now able to present a joint memorandum (drafted for them by Baxter and Cohen) to the Cabinet. In it they emphasised their belief that closer union was 'urgently desirable in the interests of the territories (including those of the African inhabitants) and of the Commonwealth'. Essentially this was because of the need to counter South African pressure. Afrikaner immigrants on the Copper Belt formed 'a base for the extension of Nationalist South African influence'. The government's principal aim should be to persuade those who were concerned for the welfare of Africans that if they did nothing – 'with the consequence of driving Southern Rhodesians into the Union' – they were likely to expose the welfare of Africans to much greater dangers 'than any that arise from the pursuit of closer association', especially if the new constitution embodied the important safeguards proposed by the officials' conference.[26]

Afrikaner immigration was the main factor which precipitated the British government's commitment to federation. Why did they believe the only effective control of immigration was through a single centralised system? The unreliability of local territorial governments in this matter had already been demonstrated by Northern Rhodesia's refusal of the British government's request to check South African immigration. The Northern Rhodesian government probably had not the strength and political authority required to operate a long-term effective control system. There were several reasons for this. The Copper Belt relied on white South Africans, because Britain could not supply comparably qualified workers, and it was not thought practicable to replace whites with Africans, except over a considerable period of time. Then again, the already considerable South African population in Northern Rhodesia was itself strongly resistant to the imposition of controls. Finally, though the Europeans were nervous about Afrikaner immigration, they tended to stick

[26] DO 35/3594, 11, briefs by Baxter, 21 Apr. 1951; CAB 129/45, CP(51)122, memo 3 May 1951.

together as a colonial community, and were unwilling to risk a serious split with the South African elements among them on an issue of this kind.[27]

Though the immigration question was central, Cohen believed their confidential appendix had not laid enough emphasis on the more informal aspects of South African expansion, on the pressure of ideas disseminated in the press and elsewhere and, more important still, on the powerful economic pressure the Union could exert because of its geographical position and much more advanced development. Above all, there was 'the pressure of the stronger neighbour against the relatively weak'. Britain was at a great disadvantage in any ideological clash with the Union because of the lack of proximity to Rhodesia. Northern Rhodesia was in a particularly weak position. African opinion there was 'immature and unorganized politically' and no use as a 'counter' to South Africa; many of the settlers were from South Africa. Britain could not enforce the ideal policy she would like for African advancement, because she had to act with the European community. Nor could she take a 'strong and vigorous positive line' against Union influence generally, 'in view of our own relations with the Union', which predicated friendliness. If South African ideas gained ground in Southern Rhodesia, it would then be 'immeasurably more difficult to hold Northern Rhodesia', or even develop liberal ideas there. In view of this gloomy picture he thought Baxter was right: now was the 'psychological moment' at which to act.[28]

What then were the officials proposing as a result of their conference? Amalgamation was impossible because the Africans would never agree, and the British government insisted it must be ruled out. Partial amalgamation of the Copper Belt and Southern Rhodesia would be a vivisection unacceptable to Northern Rhodesia. A confederal league of states, co-operating without surrendering sovereignty, might not work, and would probably be a source of weakness rather than of strength; Southern Rhodesia would oppose it. It thus became clear that the only thing all parties might agree upon would be federation – the 'highest common factor of agreement', as Baxter called it. British officials came round to it partly because it seemed the most likely way of providing adequate safeguards for African interests. Cohen defined three aims in relation to these interests. One: to keep the services intimately affecting African life away from the federal authority. Two: to provide federal safeguards for African interests at their present stage of development. Three: to secure the representation of African interests in the legislature immediately. There could be some African MPs. The two main 'safeguards' envisaged were an African Affairs Board, and a minister for African interests. The former would check legislation, the latter the executive action. The Board would include an African member from each territory, promote liaison between them, and have the duty of scrutinising all

[27] CO 537/7203, 7; CO 537/5896. [28] CO 537/7203, 7, note by Cohen, 18 Apr. 1951.

projected federal legislation. If the Board considered legislation to be detrimental to African interests it could not be brought into force without the approval of the United Kingdom government. This would have amounted to a definite power of veto, going beyond the powers Whitehall already held in Southern Rhodesia – in other words, Southern Rhodesian Africans would acquire (federal) safeguards they did not previously have. The lynchpin of the whole system would be a minister for African interests, acting as chairman of the African Affairs Board, but also sitting in the Cabinet. He would be an MP, but outside the ordinary political field, a non-party man without a departmental portfolio. He would be appointed with the approval of the United Kingdom government, to whom he would be ultimately responsible. This proposal was obviously anomalous and unusual, but regarded as essential. Cohen described it as an entirely new kind of safeguard, greatly increasing 'both the range and force of H.M.G.'s reserve powers': 'a very important step forward in breaking down the purely European character of institutions in Southern Rhodesia'. It was 'essential' in order to get parliamentary acceptance of federation, which the report, glossing over the difficulties, strongly and unanimously recommended.[29]

Sir Thomas Lloyd, permanent under-secretary of the Colonial Office, regarded the officials' case as 'clear and convincing'; if it was not accepted, Southern Rhodesia was 'virtually certain' to turn to the Union. Gordon Walker believed there was no compromise position, and he was for the Baxter report. Griffiths agreed with him that they should now 'go for federation', if it was possible to get it. He accepted that this would mean facing some degree of African opposition. He suggested that he and Gordon Walker could best cope with this by going to a ministerial conference in Central Africa. Gordon Walker felt this was a good idea, and likely to be more effective than a ministers' meeting in London. Together they recommended to the Cabinet that the Baxter report should be published. 'The scheme put forward appears to us to be constructive and workable; whether it can be brought into force will depend on the reactions to it of European and African opinion in the territories.' Vocal African opinion was a serious obstacle, but it might be withdrawn if the terms were right.[30]

The Cabinet were not so easy to convince. At the meeting on 7 May 1951 several ministers complained that they had not been given enough time to study the officials' report. How, they asked, was such a small European population going to man effectively the rather complicated machinery of government envisaged? Would it not be embarrassing for the Cabinet to give 'broad approval' to proposals which might not be acceptable? Objections were countered with

---

[29] CAB 129/45, CP(51)122; DO 35/3598,16; DO 35/3594, 9: the Indian constitution of 1937 provided a precedent for the minister for African interests, it was claimed. See also Wood, *Welensky papers*, p. 185.

[30] CO 537/7203, minute by Lloyd, 9 Apr. 1951; DO 35/3594, 3, and minute by Gordon Walker, 25 Apr. 1951.

the single overriding argument that Southern Rhodesia would be drawn to closer association with South Africa if denied the opportunity of association with the north. At a further meeting of the Cabinet on 31 May Griffiths argued that there would be many advantages in going ahead, including economic ones. The northward expansion of the Union through immigration could be checked. The proposals of the report, if workable, would afford adequate safeguards for African interests. However, 'no plan on these lines could succeed unless the Africans could be convinced that it would offer them effective protection'. The government should thus go no further than commending the report as a constructive approach deserving careful consideration. They should not commit themselves to it, 'until we could gauge the effect of the proposals on African public opinion'. Gordon Walker expressed his agreement. Shinwell, minister of defence, reported the chiefs of staff's opinion that there were advantages from the defence point of view. In the discussion, some ministers still thought the provisions too complicated to work smoothly in practice, but the Cabinet agreed generally that the plan was worthy of careful consideration.[31] Accordingly, a white paper was published in June, but the government did not seek positively to promote acceptance of the proposals.

IV

In September 1951, for the second time in a year, Gordon Walker found himself back in Southern Rhodesia, this time for the ministerial conference on the officials' proposals. From Salisbury he reported to the CRO on 15 September that he had completed his meetings with Africans there, and had found them 'rather fun and instructive'. Africans were just like his constituents in England: wearing to talk to. Native commissioners advised him that politically minded urban Africans in Southern Rhodesia were almost unanimously and uncompromisingly opposed to federation. ('Our experience teaches', they said, 'that political promises and assurances are not like cabbage seed, which when you plant you expect to get cabbage: they are controlled by circumstances.') Most of the more educated rural Africans were worried about it, and also against it. The vast conservative majority, perhaps 90 per cent, were said to be fearful of any change of status. Some of them, however, reluctantly admitted there might be an argument of strength through unity ('you don't hunt lion alone'). Gordon Walker's position was now definite: 'we cannot stand still'. Changes would be forced on Africans by the 'danger of Krugerism' and an economic depression. He believed there would be no difficulty in carrying African opinion in Southern Rhodesia if a firm decision were taken for federation. But he did not expect

---

[31] CAB 128/19, CM 34(51)4, conclusions 7 May 1951, and CM 39(51)3, conclusions 31 May 1951.

federation to be agreed. He went to the Victoria Falls conference with little hope. The Rhodesians were 'sticky and obstinate' in protesting about safeguards. He was more alarmed than ever that they would 'go to the Union'.[32]

Meanwhile Griffiths had been for three weeks assessing the situation in Northern Rhodesia and Nyasaland. He held over eighty meetings. His task, he believed, was to get the Africans to look at the Baxter report objectively. He found it difficult. Africans, he reported, had only one word for 'joining together', and it often took an interpreter ten minutes to explain the crucial difference between federation and amalgamation. He found African opposition in the north was not simply confined to the educated or Congress-organised groups, but was common to all Africans who had considered it. They had real fears. Britain could not force it on them, but did not want to abandon it. The key to the whole problem, therefore, was to find means of allaying African fears and suspicions, and of weakening African opposition. This would need full co-operation from Southern Rhodesia, and there surely were a number of things she could do to show goodwill to Africans.[33]

The Victoria Falls conference was not a success. Huggins complained that it degenerated into 'a native benefit society meeting'. Griffiths and Welensky in particular did not get on together, despite the fact that they had both been trade-unionists. Welensky thought Griffiths had 'leaned over backwards trying to placate the African representatives'; Griffiths seemed 'emotional' – he was probably exhausted. Welensky found Gordon Walker less curt and more helpful, shrewd and realistic. For their part, Griffiths and Gordon Walker found Welensky rigid and tactless, and Huggins something of a petulant *enfant terrible*, behaving with a mercurial gusto which was tiresome. The conference was fatally disrupted by news (on the second day) of Attlee's announcement of a British general election, which threw everything into the melting-pot, much to Welensky's fury. The conference finalised nothing. Nevertheless Baxter thought it was only 'a comparative fiasco', and found some gains to count. Representatives of the northern Africans went away less unyielding, he thought. Southern Rhodesian representatives agreed finally that amalgamation was impossible. The British secretaries of state declared themselves for the first time favourable to the principle of federation. And all concerned subscribed to the principle of economic and political 'partnership' between Europeans and Africans, and agreed this was the only policy.[34] What was far less satisfactory to Baxter was Griffiths's insistence that ministers and not administrative officers should be responsible for selling the idea. District officers, he ordered, must be neutral;

---

[32] DO 35/3598, 4, 7 A and 9; DO 35/3599.
[33] DO 121/140; CO 1015/51, minute by Griffiths, 9 Aug. 1951; CO 1015/52, 151; DO 35/3598, 12.
[34] DO 35/3598, 24, minutes by Baxter, 4, 5 and 13 Oct. 1951; DO 35/3600, 51; CO 1015/202, 4. See also Wood, *Welensky papers*, pp. 216–22.

they were to explain but not to advocate. This was contrary to normal practice, and became a major reason for continuing African suspicions.

In the dying days of the Labour government, Attlee called for the preparation of a Cabinet paper to leave on record. This paper was circulated but not discussed before the election on 25 October 1951. In it the two secretaries of state said they were prepared to commend the federal scheme as in the best interests of Africans as well as the other inhabitants of Central Africa. The economic case was unanswerable. The political arguments were even stronger; a political vacuum would develop without it, opening the way to more powerful South African infiltration. The real danger was Afrikaner pressure; there was 'definite evidence' that immigration was being officially inspired. Early action was thus urgent. But Griffiths and Gordon Walker said they would be strongly opposed to any attempt to force the federation proposals through in the face of the present solid, general, and deeply felt African opposition. This opposition might diminish, however. Northern Rhodesian Africans were prepared to reconsider, provided their own local political future was assured. And in Nysasland the governor thought there was a distinct chance, given six to nine months, of persuading Africans to take a less negative line – provided the British government positively supported federation.

It seems probable that the Labour government would, despite some dissenters, have endorsed this carefully thought-out policy, with its vital qualification about not enforcing federation against strong African opposition. In the event, a Labour Cabinet might well have concluded that African opposition was too strong to proceed; Gordon Walker would have been overruled, and the federal proposals would have lapsed. But Labour lost the election. Their Conservative successors became committed to an imperfect scheme in a way that Attlee would never have allowed.[35]

V

Two of the major issues of imperial policy inherited by the incoming Conservative regime in October 1951 concerned southern Africa: the future of Seretse Khama, and the proposed central African federation. One of the most striking features of the Seretse Khama affair was the way in which civil servants used the change of government to push through their own preferred solution.[36] Exactly the same process can now be shown to have been at work in the genesis of central African federation. With new and inexperienced but sympathetic ministers in office – Lord Ismay at the CRO and Oliver Lyttelton at the Colonial

---

[35] CAB 129/47, CP(51) 265, memo 12 Oct. 1951; DO 35/3600, 2.
[36] Chapter 8 above; see also A. Seldon, *Churchill's Indian summer: the Conservative government, 1951–1955* (London, 1981), p. 432.

Office – officials came into their own, pressing unashamedly for an early positive decision. Baxter and others had a major complaint against the Labour government's handling of the issue. As Baxter saw it: 'The fact that further progress was not made at the Victoria Falls Conference was largely due to the failure of the late government to take a more definite line in favour of closer association last June when the report was published.' Government had lost the initiative (a cardinal sin in civil service eyes). And it had fatally refused to allow district officers to commend the scheme. The lost momentum might be hard to recover, but Baxter believed the situation could best be retrieved by the new government's making a public statement in favour of federation on the lines recommended by Griffiths and Gordon Walker. The civil servants decided which papers should be seen by the incoming departmental ministers; they chose the confidential appendix to the Baxter report, and (having cleared it with the two former secretaries of state and the Cabinet Office) the Cabinet paper of 12 October. In addition, they prepared a Cabinet submission, carefully putting the gist of the issue on to a single page, 'so that the prime minister, for example, may be able at once to see the nature of the proposals and the reasons for them, and their urgency' (Baxter). On 7 November Ismay and Lyttelton agreed to propose an early declaration in favour of federation, and to issue a positive statement, as the first step in a campaign of persuading Africans to accept the scheme. Baxter realised there was no certainty that the new Cabinet would approve, but a statement on these lines 'would transform the situation'. The Cabinet paper unmistakably stressed that no solution had yet been arrived at, because 'the last government failed to give a lead to opinion'. Moreover, the strength of African opposition was 'partly due to the lack of a lead from the last government, which allowed the opponents of the proposals to misrepresent them'. Mindful of the Churchillian demand for brevity, the memorandum was only thirty lines long, yet the need for a firm lead was stated no fewer than three times. An appendix added that the danger to British interests assailing Central Africa 'could not be too strongly emphasized'; a decision should be reached 'without delay'; African interests were 'fully secured', but Africans had to be persuaded of this, because any attempt to force federation through would meet with bitter and possibly violent opposition.[37]

Conservative Cabinet ministers approved this policy at their meeting on 15 November 1951, apparently without significant discussion, let alone dissent. Ismay was briefed well by Liesching, and presented the case for 'not missing the tide', since there was now a prospect of success. Ismay dismissed the 'disadvantages' of proceeding as 'mere inconveniences'. True, the far Left

---

[37] DO 35/3600, minutes by Baxter, 30 Oct. and 7 Nov. 1951, and no. 5, Baxter to I. Maclennan, 23 Oct. 1951; CO 1015/65, 115; CAB 129/48, C(51)11, memo 9 Nov. 1951; see also Seldon, *Churchill's Indian summer*, p. 361.

regarded any association with Southern Rhodesia as dangerous to African interests, while South Africa might dislike federation as 'a frustration of its expansionist dreams'. These were not, however, reasons for abandoning the scheme. To do nothing would 'probably kill for ever the possibility of linking the territories together'. But it was of course axiomatic, he added, that they could not force the scheme through if Africans were solidly opposed.[38]

However, no sooner had the civil servants thus registered success in getting Conservative ministers to give the lead they wanted, than a severe blow was dealt them out of Southern Rhodesia. In the midst of all their anxiety about squaring the opposition of Africans (bringing them round 'to a true realization of their own interests', as Cohen put it), they had tended to forget that the scheme would also need the approval of Rhodesian whites. By the end of December 1951 it seemed doubtful if this would be forthcoming. The outlook was 'disheartening and discouraging'. Some officials undoubtedly held 'defeatist' views, especially when the governor of Nyasaland wanted to pull out. Matters were in fact at a fatal turning-point. Above all others, Baxter held firm to the federal faith. He began to consider how they could keep Southern Rhodesian white opinion behind federation. Having invested so much in the scheme, and achieved such a lot in bringing the whites this far – little short of reconciling the irreconcilable, as it seemed to them – officials were desperate not to see the whole thing collapse. The most 'stubborn problem' was the minister for African interests, since the Southern Rhodesian white politicians resented this proposal so much. Undemocratic and contrary to collective responsibility, they said; a 'cuckoo in the nest', Huggins called it. Early in January Baxter and Liesching asked if they absolutely had to keep this particular safeguard. Would it not be ineffective in practice if so much objected to? Would it not become more illusory than real? Perhaps it really was a constitutional nonsense? Maybe it would be easier for a more isolated chairman of the African Affairs Board, reporting direct to the governor-general, to be a more objective guardian of African interests than a political member of the federal Cabinet, in daily contact with his colleagues? If they got rid of the minister, African opposition would hardly increase, since it could not be any greater than it was already. Lyttelton shared these revisionist doubts. He decided he was not going to defend this unorthodox proposal. And he told Huggins and the northern governors as much at the London talks in January 1952, which went all too cosily as a result. There were of course some misgivings about throwing the minister for African interests overboard, but these related chiefly to matters of political presentation. The Cabinet accepted that the original proposal was 'constitutionally unsound'. Nevertheless, Ismay stressed that there was a limit to the concessions they could make to Southern Rhodesia, not only because of British responsibility for the two northern

---

[38] CAB 128/23, CC 7(51)5, conclusions 15 Nov. 1951; DO 121/138, notes for Cabinet discussion; see also Seldon, *Churchill's Indian summer*, p. 361.

territories, but still more because of 'the need to satisfy parliament here'. The settler politicians for their part must also do something to reduce African suspicions. All in all, he felt, it was 'a tremendous and complex operation'.[39]

In order to try to recover the momentum, the planned resumption of the ministerial conference was brought forward by four months. The Lancaster House conference thus opened on 23 April 1952. The British objective was to dispel misunderstanding and rally the waverers by getting out a comprehensive draft scheme as soon as possible. As expected, the conference abolished the proposed minister for African interests. Consequently, the chairman of the African Affairs Board was instead to be a private individual appointed by the federal governor-general. The number of other members of the Board was reduced from nine to six, and their powers trimmed somewhat. Civil servants were only too aware that the safeguards for Africans had thus been undoubtedly weakened. The adjustments made to the Baxter report had nearly all been in the direction desired by Southern Rhodesian settler leaders. Essentially what had been yielded was the re-imposition of a measure of London control over Southern Rhodesian native policy. Baxter believed enough had been conceded to make it easier for Southern Rhodesian ministers successfully to put the scheme across locally. Many of the compromises were not, he knew, perfect, but the scheme was 'acceptable'. (He had surely hoped for more than this.) Liesching was worried about the extent of the concessions, but asked what option they had. To drop the whole thing 'would surely be disastrous, for the compelling reasons for action still remain', and federation in the long run might be 'the only hope of ensuring that British ideas and ideals shall prevail in some part of Africa'. Cohen, too, believed it was politically important not to abandon the field to black nationalists, which would have 'disastrous consequences'. As far as W. L. Gorell Barnes was concerned, 'there can be no turning back, since a failure on our part to take the fence would have a shattering effect on our prestige', and might lead to 'racial strife and bloodshed' in Northern Rhodesia, if Welensky demanded self-government. A 'now or never' mentality was clearly emerging in Whitehall. The job must be done before Huggins retired, while Malan was unpopular, and when African opinion was less vociferous than it would become.[40]

---

[39] DO 35/3601, 153, 158, 162, and 172, and minutes by Baxter, 27 Nov. 1951; DO 35/3605, 74, Ismay to Kennedy, 12 Mar. 1952; DO 35/3607 and 3608; CO 1015/59, minute by Cohen, 31 Oct. 1951. In February 1952 Ismay wrote: 'I would still lay a shade of odds on bringing off Closer Association, but we are going to have an awful lot of trouble from the failure of many people of all parties to realise that the average Northern Rhodesian African is of the mental calibre of a British child of ten, and that if we are to do our job of Nannie and Governess properly, we have got to give him better food, and better education before we even think of full political emancipation' (DO 121/146, to Kennedy, 9 Feb. 1952).

[40] DO 35/3601, 104, telegram from Cohen to G. Colby, 3 Dec. 1951; DO 35/3604, 33; DO 35/3613, 39 A, Liesching to Huggins, 17 June 1952; CO 866/77, minutes by Lambert, 24 Mar., and Lloyd, 28 Mar. 1952; CO 1015/120, minute by Gorell Barnes, 18 July 1952.

From the end of March 1952 such views were reinforced by the new minister at the CRO, Lord Salisbury, who was more inclined than Ismay had been to override African wishes. 'African extremists' would claim abandonment of federation as a victory, and this would, he feared, increase their prestige and make them more uncompromising. Moderates on both sides would fade away. The result might be great, and possibly successful, pressure for the old unacceptable dream of amalgamation on the basis of European domination. Better to push a multi-racial federation through in 'the highest interests of all three territories'.[41]

VI

Throughout 1952 the issue was regarded as in the balance. The final constitutional conference was therefore postponed from October 1952 to January 1953. This would give time for opinion at home to calm down after the end of bi-partisan policy in March 1952, and to digest the White Paper of June 1952. It would also allow a more vigorous effort to be made to persuade Africans of the virtues of *chigwirizano* (literally the 'bridge'), and for the government to try to arrive at a more definitely focused 'African opinion', against the obstacles of 'ignorance, irrelevance and intimidation'. The minister of state at the Colonial Office, Henry Hopkinson, went out to Central Africa in August 1952 to get the latest impressions, and to offset the tactics of Congress in Northern Rhodesia.[42]

Hopkinson held sixty-eight meetings in Northern Rhodesia and Nyasaland, together with informal chats in markets and stores. Africans everywhere were unimpressed by 'safeguards'. But his general conclusion was that 90 per cent of Africans cared little about it and would accept the lead of chiefs, who in turn would accept the lead of the British government, if clearly enough given. There was less specific opposition than he expected. In Northern Rhodesia, the emotional rejection of federation seemed to him mainly because it was seen as the death-blow to hopes of black self-government, a 'Gold Coast solution', which Congress was calling for within five years. Opposition frequently had no direct connection with the federal proposals, but caught up and catalysed other grievances, such as the industrial colour-bar in the Copper Belt. In Nyasaland, too, latent discontent was activated by 'nascent nationalism having its inspiration from events in West Africa and elsewhere': postponing federation would 'only act as a tonic to it'. (Nkrumah's election victory in February 1951 sharpened African expectations everywhere.) As far as Southern Rhodesia was concerned, Hopkinson reported that African opposition was slight, with a large amount of shadow-boxing. He himself was convinced a multi-racial federation

---

[41] DO 121/146, 'Bobbety' Salisbury to Kennedy, 24 Sept. 1952, and Kennedy to Ismay, 30 Nov. 1951; CO 1015/65, 178.
[42] DO 35/3613, minutes, and nos. 81 and 101; DO 35/3597, 13; CO 537/5886.

would be beneficial. A wise, moderate, and useful report, commented Salisbury. (Accurate but unimaginative might be a better judgement.) Hopkinson's main conclusions were supported by the independent impressions of R. S. Hudson of the Colonial Office, who toured Central Africa in July 1952. He suspected African politicians of 'knavish tricks'. With one or two exceptions, European officers told him, 'with some passion', that their position would become intolerable if federation did not go through, because Congress would gain enormously in prestige and power. District officers reported a lot of indifference, or willingness to acquiesce in federation, even if there was little hope of getting more active support.[43]

Attlee also visited Central Africa in the summer of 1952. He too regarded many of the Congress claims as extravagant and extraneous. He tried hard to get objective discussion going and moderate opinion mobilised. Attlee could *in principle* see a strong case for federation, but in the end he voted against federation because it would start 'under bad auspices and with bad feelings'. He believed it rested on a fatal flaw: it froze the pace of African political advancement by making it dependent on European concurrence, and in the long run it might turn African nationalism sour by denying it sufficient outlet. Gorell Barnes accepted this as a genuine objection. But federation would not go ahead if Britain reserved to itself the right to increase African representation in the federal parliament at any time, 'and surely it is right to go forward and not be stopped by this unavoidable element of rigidity?' Though they could not say so, if and when the Africans really became ready for further political advancement, and got it territorially, it was probable Europeans at the centre would not be able to resist a similar advance at the federal level even if they wished. By such tendentious hopes were government doubts resolved, and Attlee's superior judgement set aside.[44]

A major Cabinet paper, designed to juggle away the risks, was put before ministers in mid-December 1952, by Salisbury, Swinton, and Lyttelton. (Swinton had now taken over from Salisbury at the CRO – it was the year of the three ministers there.) Here, they said, was 'a decision which may be vital to the

---

[43] CO 1015/144, 33 (Hopkinson's report, 23 Sept. 1952) and 34; CO 1015/120, 14, 17 and 25 (Hudson's reports), and 48; see also Gann, *History of Northern Rhodesia*, p. 428. As in East Africa, the field administration was reluctant to face up to the long-term necessity of abandoning the settlers: see Anderson and Throup, 'Africans and agricultural production', p. 344.

[44] CO 1015/770, especially no. 43, and minute by Gorell Barnes, 26 Aug. 1952. The Colonial Office paid Attlee the compliment of having no qualms about his visit to Central Africa at Welensky's invitation: 'Mr Attlee is surely far too statesmanlike to cause any difficulty intentionally, and too shrewd to do so inadvertently.' But he did discomfit some of the African leaders: he lectured Harry Nkumbula (president of the Northern Rhodesian African congress) on 'no short cuts to political maturity': politics 'could not all be learned from a textbook': CO 1015/107, minute by J. E. Marnham, 5 June 1952. See also *House of Commons debates*, 5th series, vol. 515, c 425 (6 May 1953).

whole future of Africa'. They were strongly in favour of going ahead with federation, and believed the balance of advantage was clearly in favour of doing so. The disadvantages of abandoning it would 'far outweigh those of proceeding', despite the lack of African acquiescence: 'moderate African resistance to extremists will collapse, loss of confidence in the government will be accelerated, racial tensions will get worse, and unrest will be delayed but not prevented', and create even more lasting antagonism. Southern Rhodesia would become soured and isolated, and be drawn more and more into the orbit of the Union. Abandonment would give marked general encouragement to African nationalists even in East Africa, whereas the introduction of federation would have a stabilising effect. The three ministers dismissed arguments that imposing the federation would lead to a more justified South African demand for the High Commission Territories (a fear certainly felt both in their CRO department and in the Territories themselves):[45] the two cases 'were entirely different', because the British government would remain effectively responsible for Africans in the federation, in a way it would not if the High Commission Territories were handed over. Opposition within Central Africa itself need not worry them unduly: protest would be of short duration. As for opposition in Britain, the Labour Party would fight it, but that must be faced. The 'more emotional elements' – Church of Scotland missions, the Africa Bureau, the Fabians – were 'hardly open to argument'; the only way of convincing them was 'to implement the scheme and to show that it worked successfully and to nobody's detriment'. The paper itself did not have much to say about 'partnership', though Swinton in supporting it at the Cabinet described the scheme as 'possibly the last opportunity for adopting in Africa a progressive policy based on the ideal of co-operation between the races'. If Britain were now to retreat on this issue, he added, 'the days of British administration in Africa would be numbered and there was every likelihood that Southern Rhodesia would join the Union of South Africa'. Discussion as usual was closed with that sobering and overriding thought. The Cabinet minutes were laconic. They merely recorded that there was 'general support' for memorandum C(52)445, and that its proposals were approved.[46]

[45] Lesotho Government Archives (Maseru): Basutoland National Council proceedings, 49th session (1953), speech by councillor Nchocho Seaja: Nyasaland and Northern Rhodesia, countries in a similar situation to themselves, 'are no longer under protection': this was a warning to their own much smaller country, because it showed promises could be broken, and 'what can stop the British government transferring us' to South Africa? (S.3/20/1/46, 56–9); DO 35/3602, 185, minute by W. A. W. Clark, 14 Jan. 1952.

[46] CAB 129/57, C(52)445, memo 16 Dec. 1952; see also CO 1015/787, which shows how little impressed the Colonial Office was by British opposition. A deputation in March 1953 was said to consist of some 'very respectable university names' (e.g. Margery Perham), but also some of the bitterest opponents of federation (Professors W. A. Lewis and K. Little); there were the 'usual ecclesiastical cranks' (? Canon Raven), the Left Book Club, and the 'hardy annuals of medicine' (Alex Comfort).

The final constitutional conference was held in London at Carlton House in January 1953. Its principal significance lay in the British government's agreement, under Southern Rhodesian pressure, to a yet further weakening of the safeguards. The African Affairs Board was made a select committee of the African parliamentary representatives. Southern Rhodesian leaders had complained that it would otherwise have been an extra-parliamentary body anomalously entitled to interfere in the decisions of the federal parliament. Constitutional lawyers regarded the new arrangement as an improvement, but this does not alter the fact that safeguards originally held to be valuable and necessary had been whittled away. This of course made a crucial difference to the attitude of the Labour Party. The voting on the second reading of the federation bill was 247 for and 221 against (6 May 1953). On 9 April the scheme easily survived its other remaining hurdle, the referendum in Southern Rhodesia (25,570 for and 14,729 against). And so the Central African Federation came into being on 1 August 1953.[47]

The change of government in October 1951 was thus essential to the establishment of the federation. It enabled its civil service architects to seize the initiative. Federation was in fact a higher priority to the Conservatives than it had been for their Labour predecessors. This was so for perhaps one special reason. Fundamentally the Conservatives were more inclined as a general policy to want to be friendly towards South Africa. Paradoxically this meant that federation assumed greater importance as the surrogate agent which would carry out the unfriendly work of controlling South African immigration. Labour ministers, not being so concerned to keep relations with South Africa smooth at any price – and a definite hardening of their attitude on South-West Africa can be observed in 1950[48] – would no doubt, in the face of continuing African opposition, have been prepared to act directly to deal with immigration, thus removing the principal geopolitical purpose of the proposed federation.

VII

One of the most obvious conclusions to be drawn from studying the British archival record is to underline the lack of emphasis on economic motives for federation. There is a striking discrepancy between Oliver Lyttelton's published and unpublished recollections. In his *Memoirs* the economic arguments appear as the unchallenged first cause; privately, he admitted that 'fear of South Africa was Number One for me'.[49] The economic arguments were never fully

---

[47] CAB 133/97; James Griffiths, *Pages from memory* (London, 1969), pp. 113–18; Churchill College Archives Centre: Noel-Baker papers, NBKR 4/9 (cuttings on Central African Federation).
[48] CAB 128/17, CM 28(50)3, conclusions 4 May 1950. See above, p. 156.
[49] O. Lyttelton, *The memoirs of Lord Chandos* (London, 1962), pp. 385–7; Churchill College Archives Centre: Chandos papers, CHAN II/4/15/i, 52–53, Lyttelton to R. A. Butler, 6 Dec. 1971,

articulated by the government, and they carried little technical conviction. Hilton Poynton commented: the economic arguments were not *against* federation; though they were not in themselves sufficient to justify it, they operated in its favour. Baxter expressly said the issue would not depend 'on such banausic considerations' as coal supplies for the copper industry.[50]

If the economic argument was only secondary and inessential, defence considerations were purely supportive and even more removed from the central motivation. The ministry of defence complained that it was not consulted; in general, no significant reference was made to the Cold War context. There is no support for the more specific speculation of P. S. Gupta that a motive was to protect Southern Rhodesian sources of chromium for nuclear engineering. Nor was the hope that 'partnership' might modify settler attitudes an original motive for promoting federation. 'Partnership' appealed more to Conservative than Labour politicians, mainly as a means of trying to win over opinion in its favour, or justifying the gamble being taken. Conservative ministers, especially Swinton, invested quite a lot of ill-thought-out idealism in the project. But trying to influence Southern Rhodesian policies through federation was not seriously regarded as a realistic aim.[51]

In truth, the explanation for setting up the Central African Federation is as nearly monocausal as any historical explanation can ever be. The motive was to erect a counterpoise to the expansion of South Africa, especially by checking Afrikaner immigration. This threat, far from being 'over-emphasized by

---

and 4/16/iii, 28–30, interview with Max Beloff, 22 Feb. 1970 (Oxford Colonial/Development Records Project); see also R. A. Butler, *The art of the possible: the memoirs of Lord Butler* (London, 1971), p. 208: 'The arguments for the Federation were primarily economic.'

[50] CO 1015/65, 137; DO 35/3594, 11; see also A. Hazlewood, 'Economics of federation and dissolution in Central Africa', in A. Hazlewood (ed.), *African integration and disintegration: case studies in economic and political union* (Oxford, 1967), pp. 188–95. The 'economic case' as discussed in Whitehall rested mainly on the following propositions: the present units were too small for the vast water-control and hydro-electric schemes required ('the Zambesi should be a centre, not a frontier'), and common action to develop the river system might result; transport improvements might be better planned; industry would develop better if it had a large area to serve; pooled resources would iron out shortages of food; more revenue would be generated for social and economic services (especially for Africans); the flow of Southern Rhodesian coal to the Copper Belt would be improved (to the benefit of Northern Rhodesia generally and of British defence requirements); a federation would face a world recession more strongly, and prevent Barotseland and Nyasaland degenerating into bankrupt isolated backwaters. (See CAB 129/47, CP(51)265 and 48, C(51)11, appendix II; CO 1015/786; DO 35/3592, 45; DO 121/138, minute by Baxter, 13 Nov. 1951.)

[51] The accounts in P. S. Gupta, *Imperialism and the British labour movement, 1914–1964* (London, 1975), p. 340, Holland, *European decolonisation*, p. 141, and Gifford, 'Misconceived dominion', p. 399, all seem to need qualification. For discussion of the Federation in a wide framework of reference, see Gupta's fine essay, 'Imperialism and the Labour government of 1945–1951', in J. Winter (ed.), *The working class in modern British history: essays in honour of Henry Pelling* (Cambridge, 1983), pp. 115–20. For Swinton's commitment to 'partnership', see Churchill College Archives Centre: Swinton papers, SWIN II/6, 19 (speeches, 1953).

post-federation analysts',[52] was in fact even more important than historians have hitherto realised. The Central African Federation was a geopolitical construct designed to place the first line of defence against South African expansion on the Limpopo not the Zambesi, and to prevent an anticipated settlers' revolt linking itself up with the Union. The theory was that such a bloc, opposed to apartheid and republicanism, might be of great value in encouraging a 'proper development' of all British African territories.

The principal historical question to be asked about British policy is therefore this: did the British government exaggerate the threat to the Rhodesias from South Africa? (Or, as Sir Thomas Lloyd put it in the critical spring of 1951, was the Union threat 'so great that some plan for federation, as the answer to that threat, ought to be evolved, even if it must in present circumstances fall short of what is ideally desirable to safeguard African interests?') He and other key officials, both in the CRO and the Colonial Office, thought it was. (Others, like D. Williams and W. A. W. Clark, did not.) Moreover, virtually all British representatives on the spot believed the threat could not be ignored (and to some of them it was both real and dangerous). This is true not only of the high commissioners in South Africa, Sir Evelyn Baring and Sir John Le Rougetel,[53] but also of the governor of Southern Rhodesia (Sir John Kennedy),[54] the governor of Nyasaland (Sir Geoffrey Colby, though he was opposed to the federal solution),[55] and the chief secretary of the Central African Council (A. E. T. Benson),[56] together with the Southern Rhodesian high commissioner in London (K. M. Goodenough).[57] All of them in varying degrees feared their territories' being turned into 'Malanite appendages in a few years', especially if Afrikaners became a majority of the European population in Northern Rhodesia, and if Southern Rhodesia suffered an economic depression; Nyasaland would be dragged in their wake.

Their fears were mainly for the future. Though there was a lot of sympathy in Southern Rhodesia for looking to the south for a solution, especially among the legal fraternity, this was more than balanced by doubts, and a desire for independence. A majority of whites certainly did not want incorporation as an immediate prospect. But if the United Party were returned to power in South Africa, if there was an economic recession, and if anxieties about being swamped by African nationalism grew (was the Colonial Office planning a 'second Liberia in the north', and was Attlee really more of a bogey-man than

---

[52] M. Boucher, review of Wood, *Welensky papers*, in *South African Historical Journal* 17 (1985), p. 131.
[53] CO 537/4691; CO 537/7203, minute by Lloyd, 9 Apr. 1951; DO 35/4019; DO 35/3605,96.
[54] DO 121/146, Kennedy to 'Bobbety' Salisbury, 14 Sept. 1952; DO 35/3586, 21 (16 July 1949).
[55] CO 537/5884, 26 (Colby to Cohen, 10 Feb. 1950); CO 537/7201, 52 (Colby to Cohen, 24 Feb. 1951); CO 1015/65, 165 (memo by Colby, 19 Mar. 1952).
[56] CO 537/4689, 158; CO 537/5885.   [57] DO 35/3587, 28, notes 6 Mar. 1950.

Table 9.1. *Immigrants into the Rhodesias, 1946–1950*

	1946		1947		1948		1949		1950 (Jan.–Oct.)	
	Southern Rhodesia	Northern Rhodesia	Southern Rhodesia	Northern Rhodesia	Southern Rhodesia	Northern Rhodesia	Southern Rhodesia	Northern Rhodesia	Southern Rhodesia	Northern Rhodesia
From Britain	3,582	974	6,320	1,446	8,574	1,990	5,908	2,197	3,959	1,929
From S. Africa	4,654	2,221	5,104	2,361	4,410	2,392	5,173	3,146	7,041	3,360

Source: CAB 129/45, CP(51)122, appendix to annex I.

Malan?), then pro-Union feeling might intensify. Smuts had always regarded the incorporation of Southern Rhodesia as merely a matter of time, and by 1951 the Nationalists were coming to the same conclusion. Strijdom had already said it was Nationalist policy to spread apartheid beyond South Africa's borders. On the whole Nationalists disliked the Central African Federation, because it foreclosed an option on their northward expansion. The links between Southern Rhodesia and the Union were certainly close: social, business, family, entertainment, and sporting ties were strong. Individual white Rhodesians regularly played in South African test teams, and, it was said, 'for cricket and rugby union, Rhodesia and South Africa become one and the same'. Southern Rhodesia was yoked to the South African Customs Agreement. All the banks, and most of the press, the large merchant houses and commercial firms, were Union subsidiaries. The co-operation of South African Railways was vital for marketing and transit. The Union had long given favourable economic treatment to Southern Rhodesia. The Broederbond had branches there. A shadowy militant Afrikaner Nationalist Party was set up some time after 1948; it became the Democratic Party, with incorporation as its main plank. The Dutch Reformed Church demanded that Afrikaans be taught as of right in Southern Rhodesian schools, and threatened to influence its congregations in the Rhodesias to strive for the Union. Advocates of incorporation were active in the press (especially in *Die Volksgenoot*) and Afrikaans societies. Such activities may or may not have had the backing of the Union government. What worried the British government above all things, however, was the political threat posed by South African immigration to the future of Central Africa. Afrikaners by 1951 already made up 13.5 per cent of the total white population in Southern Rhodesia, and perhaps a quarter of the rural elements; the proportion was considerably higher in Northern Rhodesia, though perhaps not quite as high as the estimated 30 per cent.[58] In Northern Rhodesia since the war, in every year, South African immigrants exceeded those from Britain, and in 1946 and 1950 also exceeded British immigration in Southern Rhodesia as well (table 9.1). Speaking in the House of Commons in the spring of 1952, Griffiths put it like this: for every one hundred Britons emigrating to Northern Rhodesia in these years, there were 174 South Africans, a large proportion of whom were Afrikaners. In September 1951 it was forecast that, at this rate, within eighteen months it was quite possible that Afrikaner Nationalists might obtain half the elected seats in the legislative council. In Southern Rhodesia in 1949,

[58] DO 121/138; DO 35/3591, 51; DO 35/3594, 7; DO 35/3598, 1; Wood, *Welensky papers*, pp. 150–1; Hyam, *Failure of South African expansion*, p. 187; C. Fortune, *MCC in South Africa, 1964–1965* (London, 1965), p. 31; C. Leys, *European politics in Southern Rhodesia* (Oxford, 1959), p. 94.

47 per cent of immigrants came from South Africa, and in 1950 it was set to become 64 per cent.[59]

To meet this kind of quantifiable threat – much more significant than the threatening remarks of Rhodesian politicians – Conservative ministers and, even more so, their advisers, took large risks with their eyes open. At the most fundamental level, a counterpoise based on fear of South Africa and apartheid might (they were warned by W. A. W. Clark) actually be counter-productive, for building an overt bulwark against the Union might be the surest way of driving her out of the Commonwealth and making her policies more intransigent; while an imposed federation might alienate Africans everywhere. Were the risks justified?

Territorial aggression by the Union could be completely discounted. Rhodesians were strong enough to withstand Union economic pressure. Other means could have been found – and probably would have been found by a Labour government – of checking Afrikaner immigration, stepping up British emigration to the Rhodesias, and recruiting suitable people for the copper industry. The spread of South African ideas could have been countered by more determined and imaginative propaganda. The case for overriding African wishes was very different from that simultaneously operating in the High Commission Territories over the Seretse affair. The High Commission Territories were genuinely vulnerable (see pp. 166, 194–6). Unlike them, the Rhodesias did not figure on Tomlinson's Bantustan maps (see pp. 108–9). It should not have been assumed that South African interests in Southern Rhodesia were anything more than 'informal', or indeed any greater than they were in Mozambique, Angola, the Congo, or even Kenya. Intense suspicion of South Africa was entertained in all these places, putting distinct limits on what South Africa might achieve in expansionist penetration. Moreover, even if Southern Rhodesian whites had asked for incorporation in the Union they would probably have been refused. It is inconceivable that the Nationalist government would have wished to add more British votes to the Union electorate at a time when their own political future was in the electoral balance and, as a result, they were drastically, even wilfully, trying to put a stop to British immigration.[60]

Federation might have been 'desirable', but it was not essential. Whereas we might reasonably argue that for geopolitical reasons the sacrifice of Seretse could be justified as calculated the better to preserve the interests of Africans in

---

[59] CAB 129/45, CP(51)122, appendix to annex 1, memo 3 May 1951; Griffiths, *Pages from memory*, p. 113; Griffiths, speech in *House of Commons debates*, 5th series, vol. 497, c 211 (4 Mar. 1952). Out of 30,000 emigrants from South Africa in 1950 and 1951, 24,000 went to the Rhodesias: F. G. Brownell, *British immigration to South Africa, 1946–1970*, Argief-Jaarboek vir Suid-Afrikaanse Geskiedenis/Archives Yearbook, 48th year, vol. I (Pretoria 1985), p. 95.

[60] DO 35/3602, 185; CO 537/4691. For South African immigration policies see D. Geldenhuys, 'The effects of South Africa's racial policy on Anglo-South African relations, 1945–61' (unpublished Cambridge PhD thesis, 1977), pp. 146–7.

the High Commission Territories against absorption in the Union, there was no such tangible threat in the Rhodesias, and certainly no danger so immediate or so definite as to justify imposing federation on six million Africans in Central Africa against their unequivocally expressed wishes. That a British government was induced to do this – not least by its own civil servants – is powerful testimony to the multiple fears floating around Whitehall: fears of South Africa's 'totally repugnant' apartheid,[61] fears of demographic and geopolitical expansionist forces, fears of the machinations of obstreperous and untrustworthy settlers getting out of control, fears of 'selfish and extremist' African nationalists wanting to go too fast with political advancement, fears of revolt and racial wars. It demonstrates, too, how politicians and bureaucrats can be dominated by their instinctive urges to maintain prestige, retain the initiative, and occasionally to achieve some constructive action, almost for action's sake; and how, as a result, some of them at least, became committed to a highly dubious scheme beyond the point at which they could pull out without consequences too depressing and damaging to contemplate.

Afterword

Some of the main documentation for this and the previous chapter can now be studied in the 'British Documents on the End of Empire Project' volume on *The Labour government and the end of empire, 1945–1951* (London, 1992: ed. R. Hyam), part IV, chapter 8, section 3, pp. 239–374, 'Southern African issues: relations with the Union government'. Further documents, and perhaps re-interpretation, will be made available in the forthcoming 'British Documents' volume, series B on *Central and Southern Africa*: part I, *Central Africa* edited by P. Murphy, and part II, *The High Commission Territories* edited by P. Henshaw. Ashley Jackson has exploited the Tshekedi Khama Papers in Serowe: see 'Tshekedi, Bechuanaland, and the Central African Federation', *SAHJ* no. 40 (1999), pp. 202–22.

[61] CO 537/5896, 25, Griffiths to G. Rennie, 7 Nov. 1950.

10 Strategy and the transfer of Simon's Town, 1948–1957

Various explanations have been put forward for the 1955 agreement to transfer the Simon's Town naval base from British to South African control: the base had lost its utility in the nuclear age; the British government wished to deflect South African economic pressure, to appease an expansionist Afrikaner nationalism, to effect a financial saving, or to muster a South African commitment to Middle East defence. Yet none of these, either singly or in combination, accurately explains the transfer.[1] Rather, Simon's Town's transfer was conceded above all because, in the face of an increasingly strident Afrikaner nationalism, this was seen as the best and perhaps the last chance to strike a bargain ensuring both access to the base and effective naval collaboration.[2]

This view represents a radical departure from some recent accounts. Geoffrey Berridge, mesmerised by South Africa's possession of gold and uranium, determined to prove an hypothesis about the role of 'economic power' in intergovernmental relations and, relying mainly on secondary sources, asserted that, contrary to the accepted wisdom, the agreements were 'wholly in the Union Government's favour' and derived from circumstances forced upon Britain by South Africa's economic might. British gains were merely 'cosmetic embellishments'. The grant of availability to Britain and her allies in any war, and the expansion of the South African navy with purchases from British yards,

---

[1] We must thank Marc Feigen who started the research ball rolling with his 1985 Cambridge MPhil dissertation on Simon's Town. Although many writers have commented upon the Simon's Town agreements, relatively few have tried to explain British motives. The notable exceptions are: G. R. Berridge, *Economic power in Anglo-South African diplomacy: Simonstown, Sharpeville and after* (London, 1981); M. A. Feigen, 'The power of Proteus: Great Britain, South Africa, and the Simonstown Agreements, 1948–1955' (unpublished Cambridge MPhil dissertation, 1985); G. R. Berridge and J. E. Spence, 'South Africa and the Simonstown Agreements', in J. W. Young (ed.), *The foreign policy of Churchill's peacetime administration, 1951–1955* (Leicester, 1988), pp. 181–205. A brief explanation is provided by E. A. Walker, *A history of Southern Africa* (3rd edn, London, 1968), p. 911.

[2] British control over the naval base at Simon's Town did not, as some writers have assumed, derive from British sovereignty. This error was committed by Berridge, *Economic power in Anglo-South African diplomacy*; and by J. Barber and J. Barratt, *South Africa's foreign policy: the search for status and security, 1945–1988* (Cambridge, 1990), p. 55. The correct position has been described by C. J. R. Dugard, 'The Simonstown Agreement: South Africa, Britain and the United Nations', *South African Law Journal* 85, 2 (1968), pp. 142–56.

were discounted as being 'already assured' by the pressures of the cold war and by a Commonwealth military association that was 'already close'. Although the National Party, while in opposition, had argued fervently and repeatedly for an end to British control of Simon's Town because it undermined South Africa's right of neutrality, Berridge suggests that the National Party government in 1955 wished South Africa's neutrality to be compromised, actively seeking the guarantee of South African security implicit in the agreements as 'a good second-best solution' to their search for a multilateral defence agreement. Furthermore, the British government was supposedly led by a combination of South African pressure and Eden's supposed lack of sympathy for Black Africa to support plans for an African Defence Organisation, conceding that its establishment would be a precondition of any South African commitment to Middle East defence. The British government was also induced (against, we are told, Britain's own best interests) to confirm the strategic importance of the Cape route. Having thus tried to demonstrate how the Simon's Town agreements were 'a very one-sided affair', Berridge proceeded to show how this 'diplomatic triumph' was achieved. Taking as his premise that the British government, left to itself, felt no need either to return the base or to foster closer defence ties with South Africa, he deduced that the reasons for transfer must have been political or economic. The British government was, he argued, unlikely to have been motivated significantly either by a desire to protect the High Commission Territories or by an affection for British 'kith and kin' in South Africa. Having thus disposed of political considerations, Berridge concluded (through a 'process of elimination') that South Africa's 'economic grip' upon Britain was the 'decisive factor'.[3]

Berridge assumed that in British eyes Anglo-South African defence relations would have been regarded as entirely satisfactory once a South African commitment to Middle East defence had been made. He overlooked British distrust of Afrikaner nationalists, a distrust not quelled by South Africa's continued membership of the Commonwealth or commitment to the Cold War. He did not see that for financial reasons the British government was more than willing to transfer Simon's Town, but only into trusted hands – a government where political forces devoted to close collaboration were firmly in the ascendant. In South Africa they were not, and never had been. In such circumstances, transfer would be conceded with the greatest reluctance and only if British interests were protected by formal undertakings.

Unfortunately for Berridge, even if his assumptions about the state of Anglo-South African relations had been correct, much of the rest of his case is at odds with official British records. Nevertheless, continuing his rather theoretical revisionist approach, Berridge in conjunction with Jack Spence (one of

---

[3] Berridge, *Economic power*, pp. 93, 92, 85, 90, and 87.

the chief targets of Berridge's earlier attacks) has renewed the assault on the 'orthodox' interpretation, squeezing new evidence into much the same framework in order to shore up part of the conclusion – that South Africa 'secured the base in return for relatively little by way of concessions to Britain'.[4] Flaws in the orthodox interpretation are taken as proof that its basic contention (that the balance of advantage lay with Britain) was faulty.[5] Berridge and Spence reassert, against abundant evidence to the contrary, that the promise of unqualified availability 'was not a major South African concession', bolstering this with a new assertion (one equally dubious) that the British government did not attach especial importance to such a promise. They also seem to have misunderstood the significance of South African naval expansion (incidentally ignoring altogether the British success in securing a leading role in the development of that navy). They claim, in direct contradiction of the evidence, that the British Admiralty regarded Simon's Town as a 'distant outpost' whose costs it could no longer justify, and discount both the South African failure to advance an African Defence Organisation and British success in resisting it. Finally, they make the unsustainable assertion that a commitment of South African forces to Middle East defence was 'the one great prize which Britain had consistently sought throughout the negotiations from 1949 onwards'.[6]

Though apparently unwilling to say so directly, Berridge and Spence have conceded that transfer was not forced upon Britain primarily by economic

---

[4] 'South Africa and the Simonstown agreements' was evidently written by Berridge and Spence before they had seen one of the most important files on the subject in the Public Record Office, Kew: PREM 11/1765. Spence and Berridge, 'Simonstown', *Contemporary Record* 2, 3 (1988), pp. 35–6, takes account of this file but the article is only about 1,500 words in length. An identical version of this appeared, unsigned, in the Cape Town *Argus*, 31 Oct. 1987, under the title 'Why Simon's Town takeover was a piece of cake'. Yet another version of the Berridge–Spence thesis has appeared as: 'The Simonstown Agreements, 1955', in S. Marks (ed.), *The societies of Southern Africa in the nineteenth and twentieth centuries*, vol. XV, Collected Seminar Papers, 38 (London, 1990), pp. 195–202. The Spence monograph with which Berridge had earlier taken issue was *The strategic significance of Southern Africa* (London, 1978).

[5] According to Berridge and Spence, the principal exponents of this interpretation are: J. Barber, *South Africa's foreign policy, 1945–70* (Oxford, 1973), and W. C. B. Tunstall, *The Commonwealth and regional defence* (London, 1959). Berridge's earlier list included Spence's monograph (though they later granted this revisionist status) and Dugard, 'The Simonstown Agreement'. If one describes as orthodox any interpretation which sees the balance of advantage lying with Britain, the following should be added to the list: D. J. Geldenhuys, *South Africa's search for status and security since the Second World War*, Occasional Paper, South African Institute of International Affairs, (Braamfontein, 1978) – 'transfer provisions were weighed heavily in Britain's favour and gave it a handsome bargain'; G. G. Lawrie, 'The Simonstown Agreement: South Africa, Britain and the Commonwealth', *South African Law Journal* 85, 2 (1968), pp. 157–77 – part of the agreement was 'astonishingly favourable to the Royal Navy'; and N. L. Dodd, 'This is what it is all about!', *Paratus*, 26, 8 (1975), p. 25 – 'Never in the history of the British Empire can such a one-sided agreement have been signed between independent partners without any duress.'

[6] Spence and Berridge, 'Simonstown', p. 36.

pressure from South Africa. Instead they point first to the Admiralty's wish to avoid the continuing expense of Simon's Town's operation and recognition that it would be useless without South African goodwill; and second to the diminished importance of the transfer's '*symbolic cost* to the Empire and to the relative political strength of English-speakers in the Union'. Outweighing these, they suggest, was the need to protect Britain's other interests in South Africa, 'especially gold and uranium'. Finally, we are assured that the transfer was primarily the product of a failed attempt to use Simon's Town as bait to secure a South African commitment to Middle East defence – the fish apparently devouring a substantial meal without being hooked.[7] In fact, as official records show, neither their explanation of British motives in transferring Simon's Town nor their contention that South Africa conceded relatively little in obtaining control can be upheld. As this chapter will argue, the British government was principally concerned to safeguard Britain's strategic interests; moreover, the South African government upheld those self-same interests, propelled into doing so by a paradoxical combination of Afrikaner nationalist exclusivism and fear of strategic isolation.

I

The British governments involved in negotiations over Simon's Town, Labour and Conservative, were determined first and foremost to ensure the availability of a naval base in South Africa in time of war. Attlee, no less than Churchill, was certain that the Cape route was vital strategically. It was particularly so in the Labour prime minister's radical thinking, for he advocated a shift to routine reliance on working round the Cape instead of through the Middle East with its intractable problems.[8] Those two prime ministers ensured that a hard line was taken on the protection of British interests at Simon's Town even in the face of dissent from the Ministry of Defence and the Commonwealth Relations Office (CRO). Officials in those two departments, their ministers, and British men on the spot were at times inclined to have greater faith in South African intentions, and favour transfer on less stringent terms, arguing that the South African government could not be expected to concede what British or other Commonwealth governments would not. The Admiralty (the other key department involved), wary of Ministry of Defence reappraisals downgrading the value of naval communications, convinced of the need for an effective wartime base, and conscious of transfer's practical implications, favoured retention of control at Simon's Town until South Africa had, under British

[7] Berridge and Spence, 'South Africa and the Simonstown Agreements', pp. 201–2.
[8] R. Hyam, 'Africa and the Labour government, 1945–1951', *JICH* 16, 3 (1988), pp. 158–9.

guidance, established a properly organised and reasonably sized naval service. In the vigorous internal debates on this issue, an even stiffer line was taken by the Attlee, Churchill, and Eden Cabinets. They insisted on full and precise guarantees regarding access to the base and the operation of the dockyard. This stemmed not only from Simon's Town's strategic significance, but also from doubts about an Afrikaner nationalist government's attitude in the event of war, and fears of apartheid's disastrous impact on the dockyard – points emphasised in the British press and parliament prior to the conclusion of the agreement. It was one thing to entrust a strategic asset to a loyal member of the Commonwealth with a similar political outlook; quite another to do so where devotion to the Commonwealth was so tenuous and racial policies so repugnant.[9]

In consequence, National Party ministers, anxious to assert South Africa's independence and remove the 'annoying relics' of the colonial past, were asked to accept what they themselves, had they been in opposition, would have vilified as perpetuating subordination to Britain. D. F. Malan, as prime minister after Smuts's fall in 1948, conceded Britain's right to use Simon's Town even in a war in which South Africa wished to remain neutral. In the 1930s he had led the 'Purified' National Party's attacks on the Royal Navy's right to operate from Simon's Town in any circumstances and on South Africa's obligation to defend this 'essential link in the naval communications of the Empire', arguing that both were incompatible with South Africa's newly acknowledged constitutional equality with Britain and made nonsense of the country's right of neutrality. F. C. Erasmus, as Minister of Defence, negotiated the 1955 agreements confirming, and in some ways even extending, Britain's essential rights at Simon's Town. Before the Second World War he joined Malan in the political wilderness and railed against the 1921 Simon's Town agreements reached between the prime minister of the day (that great champion of the Commonwealth connection, Jan Smuts) and the British colonial secretary (a defender of the empire long involved in South African affairs, Winston Churchill). Malan's more extreme successor as prime minister, J. G. Strijdom, presided over the conclusion of the 1955 agreements; he had also been among those in the 1930s who argued that South Africa must have the right to exclude the Royal Navy from the base. Despite leading an aggressive assault on the rights of non-whites, Strijdom accepted that apartheid would not be applied in the Simon's Town dockyard – this despite calls from National Party activists for an end to British authority at naval installations in South Africa precisely because of its bad influence, producing as it did the 'unhealthy state of affairs' of different races working

---

[9] Britain, H.C. Deb., 531 (27 Oct. 1954), 1905–6; H.L. Deb., 190 (26 Jan. 1955), 723, and 191 (2 March 1955), 653. See also Lord Warminster's letter to the *Daily Telegraph* as reported in the *Cape Times*, 31 Jan. 1955.

side-by-side. How did the architects of apartheid and antagonists of the British connection come to make such concessions?[10]

The largest part of the explanation must lie in white South Africa's sense of vulnerability, particularly to the Communist threat, and the recognition that Britain was the country's one certain ally. The National Party government actively sought a wider alliance of colonial powers in an African Defence Organisation, but neither a NATO-style arrangement giving South Africa greater involvement in the defence of colonial Africa nor any form of security guarantee from another Western power materialised. This being so, the United Party Opposition, proponents of the British connection, were sure to derive political capital from any National Party policy that drove away the only guarantor of the country's security. Transfer, even on terms favourable to Britain, none the less satisfied the Afrikaner nationalist urge (which surfaced from time to time in the press and at party congresses) to have control over Simon's Town.[11]

Afrikaner nationalism was not the only source of pressure for transfer. Britain's chronic financial weakness after the Second World War provoked, more than once, proposals to shift the control as well as the expense of Simon's Town to South Africa. Such an act might, it was hoped, stimulate South African naval expansion, further reducing the burden of imperial defence. Moreover, transfer would, in the short term at least, promote good Anglo-South African relations. Whitehall's reasons for fostering the latter were fourfold. First was South Africa's strategic importance: manpower, industrial potential, minerals (including uranium), and ports from which domination of shipping round the Cape could be imposed. Second was her value as a market, a destination for British capital and source of supply, particularly of gold which was indispensable both in the operation of the world-wide trading and financial system centred on London and in the struggle to regain financial independence from the United States. Third was the desire to protect the High Commission Territories, control over which was sought by every South African government from Botha to Strijdom. (At stake here was not only the principle of trusteeship and Britain's moral authority to rule in Africa, but also British influence over settler communities in Central and East Africa, susceptible as they were to the spread of South African racial dogma and an Afrikaner nationalist outlook hostile to the British connection.) Finally, there was the desire to preserve the integrity and authority of the Commonwealth. While each of these considerations was put forward in British deliberations over Simon's Town, the principal doubt which returned again and again to block plans for transfer was that it might lead to

---

[10] *Die Burger* editorial, 6 Aug. 1951, and the translation in *Cape Times*, 7 Aug. 1951. *Natal Mercury*, 7 Aug. 1951. South Africa, H.A. Deb., 23 (23 April 1934), 2568–9; 24 (28 Jan. 1935), 722–3, 728, 731–3; and 24 (30 Jan. 1935), 812–13. *Cape Times*, 31 Jan. 1955.

[11] *Rand Daily Mail*, 10 Aug. 1951; *The Times*, 24 Sept. 1954; *Cape Times*, 17 Aug. 1954 and 22 Oct. 1954; *Natal Witness*, 6 July 1955; *Natal Mercury*, 6 July 1955.

the loss not only of a wartime base but, more importantly, of an active ally (by at once reducing British prestige, a dominion's sense of dependence, and the obstacles to strict neutrality, as had been the case with the British naval bases in the Irish Free State).[12]

II

After the Second World War inter-governmental discussion of Simon's Town began almost by accident. It sprang from the Labour government's preoccupation with convincing the dominions to carry their fair share of the Commonwealth defence burden.[13] In 1949 the British government was seeking contributions to Middle East defence (which, despite an eighteen-month struggle by Attlee to revise the accepted wisdom of the Chiefs of Staff, had been confirmed as a strategic priority).[14] In a bid to secure South African involvement there, minister of defence A.V. Alexander held out the prize of Simon's Town's transfer. By making this offer to Erasmus, Alexander ignored the specific instructions of Philip Noel-Baker, the secretary of state for Commonwealth Relations.[15] Not surprisingly, the CRO was appalled that the Simon's Town issue had been revived in so ill-considered a manner.[16]

The ensuing debate within Whitehall followed the same pattern that it had in the 1920s. Some ministers and officials would argue that South Africa's constitutional status made it impossible to refuse transfer; others that to transfer the base was to risk that it would by unavailable to Britain in war. In 1921 the British government was unwilling to take that risk even though it might have strengthened Smuts's hold on power.[17] Twenty-eight years later, with Smuts in opposition, there was even less enthusiasm to hand over Simon's Town. Transfer would be a 'tremendous feather in the cap for the Nationalists and might greatly strengthen them against Smuts'.[18] It was a measure of the financial difficulties facing the British government (grappling in the summer of 1949 with the country's second post-war balance of payments crisis) that Attlee initially thought that for 'economy reasons' transfer should be considered, provided that Britain's rights of perpetual user could be ensured. The CRO argument that

---

[12] R. Hyam, 'The politics of partition in southern Africa, 1908–1961' in Hyam and G. Martin, *Reappraisals in British imperial history* (London, 1975), p. 190 (see chapter 5 above). Hyam, *The failure of South African expansion, 1908–1948* (London, 1972). Hyam, 'Africa and the Labour government', p. 165.
[13] DO 35/2277, note by James, 2 Nov. 1949, and CRO memorandum, 29 Nov. 1949.
[14] Hyam, 'Africa and the Labour government', p. 158.
[15] DO 35/2368, Noel-Baker to Alexander, 18 July 1949.
[16] DO 35/2368, note by Liesching, 19 July 1949.
[17] ADM 116/3158, S. H. Wilson to B. E. Domvile, 27 Jan. 1921, and L. S. Amery to Lord Lee, 26 April 1921.
[18] DO 35/2368, note by C. G. L. Syers, 19 July 1949.

transfer would undermine the most powerful agent of Anglo-South African collaboration and leave Simon's Town in uncertain hands persuaded Attlee otherwise. Alexander was told to recant. He accordingly informed Erasmus that the matter was not ripe for further active consideration. The CRO was pleased at this effort to retrieve the situation; but there was no altering the fact that Pandora's box had been opened.[19]

The British government hoped to promote defence collaboration with South Africa (and, more specifically, convince South Africa to mobilise forces for the Middle East) without disturbing the *status quo* at Simon's Town. One problem was that the South African government was preoccupied with sub-Saharan Africa and sought a concert of African colonial powers through which South Africa could both align itself with the West militarily and extend its influence northwards.[20] But proposals for such schemes were from the beginning greeted with much scepticism and considerable alarm in Whitehall. For one thing, noted a Foreign Office official, 'it would hardly seem to have a *raison d'être*'. A pact exclusively between European colonial powers and the United States seemed 'bound to arouse the hostility of Middle Eastern countries not to mention India'. There were, furthermore, 'grave political objections in African territories to such a pact' – a point emphasised by the Colonial Office. Scientific and technical matters were practically the only subjects in which co-operation with South Africa in African affairs was acceptable. Political as well as strategic considerations argued for focusing South African attention on the Middle East, though it was far from clear how to make the South African government a full partner in the defence of that region while at the same time resisting the spread of its influence elsewhere in Africa and treating it as a subordinate in naval affairs.[21]

In an effort to encourage the formation of a South African expeditionary force for the Middle East, Erasmus was invited to London for talks in July 1950 (with the optimistic assumption that he would have forgotten all about Simon's Town). He was persuaded to state that an armoured division and air units would be available for the defence of Africa including the Middle East. Naturally enough, he strove to ensure that the defence of sub-Saharan Africa was not neglected, but the conference sought by him (held at Nairobi in 1951) would, at British insistence, be confined to technical items, such as road and rail facilities, signal communications, and the use of ports. Although the South

---

[19] DO 35/2368, note by J. Garner, 22 July 1949, note by Syers, 26 July 1949, note by Garner, 28 July 1949, and note by Gordon Walker, 3 Aug. 1949.

[20] Central Archives Depot, Pretoria, Smuts Papers, A 1/171, Heaton Nicholls to Smuts, 'Foreign affairs report', 12 Nov. 1947. Central Archives Depot, Pretoria, Te Water Papers, A 78/4, 'Commonwealth defence questions', Oct. 1948.

[21] FO 371/76351, note by G. W. Furlonge, 7 April 1949; DO 35/2752, Denning to Syers, 14 April 1949, note of inter-departmental meeting, 21 April 1949, and note by Noel-Baker, 27 April 1949; CO 537/5929, A(49)2, 5 July 1949; CAB 134/1, A1(49)2, 8 July 1949.

African government would later go as far as to make a public declaration of its commitment to Middle East defence, it was less willing actually to take concrete steps (such as paying for equipment) to put this into effect, especially while Britain's own position there remained so unsettled.[22] But, as the CRO feared, Erasmus took the initiative in raising Simon's Town while he was in London. Although there had already been considerable debate on Simon's Town within Whitehall, he was told that transfer could not be discussed at such short notice.[23]

Before Patrick Gordon Walker, by then the secretary of state for Commonwealth Relations, left on his 1951 tour of southern Africa – the outcome of which was a memorandum which would crystallise a dual policy of co-operating with and containing South Africa[24] – briefs were prepared in the expectation that Simon's Town would be discussed when he reached South Africa. Erasmus was unable, however, to present his proposals until the day before Gordon Walker reached Cape Town, forcing the South African side once again to concede that it had given the British government insufficient time to consider the matter.[25]

Erasmus, back in London during June 1951 for a meeting of Commonwealth defence ministers (aimed primarily at promoting commitments to the Middle East), pressed for an early decision on Simon's Town.[26] Gordon Walker, following his own advice that ostracism would only weaken Britain's power to deter South Africa from 'foolhardy acts' (such as seizing the High Commission Territories), advised that it would be a mistake to adopt a purely negative attitude on Simon's Town, since this might provoke pressure which might otherwise be avoided. Accordingly, British ministers explained frankly to Erasmus the four main conditions of transfer – unrestricted availability, maintenance of the existing level of efficiency, safeguards for 'Coloured' workers, and assumption of control by a gradual process. Instead of balking at their severity, Erasmus showed a surprising willingness to accept them all. But after he left Britain it soon became apparent that his government was unwilling to concede Britain's right to use the base in any war, including one in which South Africa wished to remain neutral.[27]

---

[22] DO 35/2277, note for minister of defence, 26 July 1950; DO 35/2671, Rumbold to Gordon Walker, 8 Sept. 1950, and notes for defence talks, Sept. 1950; CAB 131/9, D(50)82, 12 Oct. 1950; WO 216/499, Brownjohn to DMO, 12 Jan. 1951.
[23] PREM 8/1361, note by Gordon Walker, 27 Sept. 1950.
[24] CAB 129/45, CP(51)109, 16 April 1951; Hyam, 'Africa and the Labour government', pp. 167–8; R. Ovendale, 'The South African policy of the British Labour government', *International Affairs* 59 (1983), pp. 54–7. See above, pp. 208–10.
[25] DO 35/2671, Gordon Walker to Liesching, 9 Feb. 1951.
[26] Pretoria had been considered as the venue for this meeting but doubts were cast upon this by, among other things, 'our current difficulties with Dr. Malan's government over the Gold Coast, the High Commission Territories, &c.' CAB 131/11, DO(51)24, 6 March 1951.
[27] CAB 129/45, CP(51)109, 16 April 1951; PREM 8/1361, Gordon Walker to Attlee, 21 June 1951; CAB 131/11, DO(51)96, 28 July 1951.

Simon's Town 239

The British government had thus to consider whether it should resist transfer until this requirement were met. Within the Admiralty officials agreed that it was 'essential that the facilities of Simon's Town and Durban be available to the R.N. in war'. They also pointed out that in 1949, when faced with Canadian protests that a guarantee of availability (precisely of the sort sought in connection with Simon's Town) was an unacceptable derogation of Canadian sovereignty, the British government had retreated, accepting instead a vague assurance that the St John's or another suitable base would be available to Britain in war.[28] James Callaghan took up the argument that South Africa must be granted the same treatment as the other dominions. (He was then a junior Admiralty minister but as foreign secretary twenty-four years later it was he who announced the termination of the Simon's Town agreements.) As he put it:

Sooner or later, we shall have to face the fact that SIMONSTOWN will eventually be as much a South African Base as SYDNEY is Australian and HALIFAX Canadian . . . I feel, therefore, that the most that we can expect in the long term is the form of words used originally by Mr Erasmus that SIMONSTOWN shall be available to OUR (i.e. South Africa's) allies in war.[29]

The British government would, he added, 'gain in goodwill (and that will be the final factor in determining our mutual relations, again in the long term), if we accept this form of words at this juncture'. Lord Pakenham, the First Lord of the Admiralty, was not convinced. He had less confidence in South Africa's intentions in a future war than in Canada's.[30]

The CRO was also wary of accepting assurances that fell short of Britain's full requirements. Sir Percivale Liesching, the permanent head of that department, pointed to the Malan government's recent attempts to overturn the provisions, entrenched in the constitution, protecting 'Coloured' voting rights. British public opinion was 'deeply suspicious of the South African Government and would not be satisfied unless it was clear that the United Kingdom had got everything that we needed'. Furthermore, the Malan government might renew pressure to transfer the High Commission Territories and in that context any substantial move about Simon's Town might well be denounced by British public opinion. At least, concluded Liesching, it would be necessary to have an unequivocal assurance recorded as formally and solemnly as the existing agreement.[31]

Emanuel Shinwell's arrival as minister of defence transformed this department's view. He could not share Alexander's belief that access to the base

[28] ADM 116/5979, note by R. Watson, 22 Feb. 1951; ADM 1/22734, note by G. Moses, 13 Aug. 1951; DO 35/3463, Hall to Attlee, 21 Nov. 1949; DO 127/98, Clutterbuck to Noel-Baker, 3 Dec. 1949.
[29] ADM 1/22734, note by Callaghan, 17 July 1951.
[30] Ibid. and note approved by Pakenham, 16 Aug. 1951.
[31] DO 35/2369, Liesching to Gordon Walker, 27 July 1951.

was best assured by a forthcoming British attitude. Shinwell, Pakenham, and Gordon Walker together rejected the idea of reliance on South African goodwill. They recommended that if, and only if, the South African government gave an unambiguous assurance of availability in both peace and war, the British government would enter into discussion on transfer. For Attlee, the 'outstanding point' was that the base should be available in peace and war, not just a war against Communism as had been implied by Erasmus. It was precisely on the point emphasised by Attlee that the Defence Committee agreed to make a stand; there, too, that progress towards transfer would stall.[32]

Consideration of this question by the Labour government did not end there. H. A. F. Rumbold, the acting high commissioner in Pretoria, reported that the new, more stridently nationalist South African Chief of the General Staff had warned of a 'row' if Simon's Town were not transferred. Christiaan Ludolph de Wet du Toit added that a guarantee of availability in *any* war would be a 'noose round our necks'. As if to heighten British unease, *Die Burger*, the mouthpiece of the National Party, called for the removal of this 'annoying relic of the days of South Africa's dependence'. According to Rumbold, the National Party might think that its best chance of winning the next election would be on an anti-British, pro-republican platform, the chief planks of which would be the High Commission Territories, British policy in the Gold Coast, and British press criticism of South Africa. A grievance about Simon's Town might be a valuable addition. 'The possibility that they have this sort of thing in mind represents the most serious threat to our relations with South Africa at present.'[33]

Faced with these warnings, Gordon Walker's mind began moving towards dispensing altogether with a formula on availability. Shinwell (an unflinching critic on the opposition benches during the war) took a tough stand and refused to shrink in the face of such dangers. The question of availability was 'one on which Parliamentary and public opinion will at once fasten, having regard particularly to our experience over the Irish ports, and neither the present form of words nor any alternative form of words likely, as I see it, to be acceptable to the Union Government would stand up to this criticism'. The British government should, thought Shinwell, be prepared to see discussions broken off forthwith.[34] The Defence Committee concurred. It decided, moreover, that the objective of British policy should be to ensure that South Africa did not remain neutral in a war in which Britain was involved (the use of port facilities at Durban and Cape Town being as desirable as those at Simon's Town). Attlee himself summed up the Committee's views on 10 September 1951: no reply should be made to

---

[32] CAB 131/11, DO(51)96, 28 July 1951; PREM 8/1361, DO 21(51)3, 31 July 1951.
[33] DO 35/2369, Rumbold to Pritchard, 15 Aug. 1951.
[34] PREM 8/1361, Holmes to Attlee, 7 Sept. 1951; CAB 131/11, DO(51)100, 6 Sept. 1951.

Erasmus's latest letter and 'we should delay dealing with this problem for as long as possible'.[35]

III

Until South African records can be studied, the Malan government's precise intentions will remain obscure; not that they were entirely clear to South African representatives at the time. At the end of 1951 Albertus Geyer, the high commissioner in London, complained bitterly of having been left in the dark on Simon's Town. The problem was, he recorded, that external affairs were in the hands of the prime minister, who had neither the time nor the inclination to take an active role in this sphere, while the senior official in that department knew nothing about diplomacy. When Malan did exert his influence, it was to rule in 1952 that Churchill should not be approached on Simon's Town and the High Commission Territories at the same time. If the British prime minister were going to 'scratch his head' over these two matters, it was best that he begin with the more important one of the Territories.[36]

The pressure of business faced by the incoming Churchill government, and the absence of any new South African initiative, meant that six months would pass before Simon's Town again came before the Defence Committee. The CRO had, in the meantime, prepared a comprehensive examination of the question, drawing heavily on the background information provided by their man on the spot – Rumbold. General Lord Ismay, Churchill's chief staff officer during the war and briefly the new secretary of state for Commonwealth relations, accepted without modification his department's view that the South African government would never undertake to make the base available to Britain in all wars. He agreed that the British government ought to 'show willing' by taking the initiative to reopen negotiations.[37]

The 'ball' may, as CRO stated, have been resting with Britain, but neither Churchill nor J. P. L. Thomas, the First Lord of the Admiralty, was convinced of the need to resume play. Moreover, if, under South African pressure, negotiations did resume, Churchill made it clear that he would resist transfer without an unqualified assurance that facilities would be available to Britain in both peace and war. But far from being 'almost single-handedly responsible for sabotaging the progress made by the Attlee government', Churchill in effect merely reaffirmed Labour policy.[38]

---

[35] CAB 131/10, DO 22(51)1, 10 Sept. 1951.
[36] State Archives, Cape Town, Geyer Papers, A 1890/5, diary, 20 Dec. 1951; A 1890/1, Erasmus to Geyer, 12 Feb. 1952.
[37] DO 35/2369, Pritchard to Rumbold, 8 Oct. 1951, and note by Ismay, 15 Dec. 1951; PREM 11/1765, D(51)4, 18 Dec. 1951.
[38] CAB 131/12, D1(52)1, 12 March 1952; Spence and Berridge, 'Simonstown', p. 35.

The result of Malan's preoccupation with the High Commission Territories and Churchill's refusal to take any action on the naval base was that little more was heard in Whitehall about Simon's Town until late in 1953, when financial constraints led (just as they had in 1949) to suggestions from the Ministry of Defence for a major change at Simon's Town. Lord Swinton, the third secretary of state for Commonwealth relations in the Churchill government, was 'horrified' at the proposal to close the base. It would be a 'tragedy' to hand Simon's Town over to Erasmus and Du Toit when they were 'well on the way to ruining the South African Air Force by getting rid of the best English-speaking officers and some good fighting Afrikaners as well who have been the making of the service'. Though blamed in Whitehall for proposing the cuts, the Admiralty was responsible for neither originating nor advocating the reductions at Simon's Town. Berridge and Spence have perpetuated a false version of events, omitting to acknowledge a letter written by Sir Rhoderick McGrigor, the Chief of the Naval Staff. In this, McGrigor complained of a situation 'in which the Prime Minister and presumably other members of the Cabinet are allowed to think that the Admiralty are advocating measures which they have consistently proclaimed as unsound'. The proposal had in fact come from the minister of defence's directive that 'these outlying bases were of the lowest priority in the conditions laid down in the Radical Review'. The Admiralty had 'consistently protested against this directive' and had 'no wish whatsoever to abandon either Simonstown or Trincomalee'.[39]

The desire to leave the Simon's Town issue 'lying happily dormant' led the Churchill government to avoid approaching Erasmus in 1952 or 1953, even though some action was needed to stem the disastrous impact of 'Afrikanerisation' on the South African armed services.[40] In 1954 Erasmus himself suggested a ministerial meeting in London. (He had apparently been encouraged to do so by South African air force and naval authorities anxious to improve the 'present deplorable state of their services'.) CRO officials, always anxious to promote collaboration in less contentious spheres, argued that a 'prompt and forthcoming response by us to Mr. Erasmus's approach would be a useful counterweight to the very negative line we have had to adopt over the High Commission Territories'. Moreover, there seemed little doubt that Simon's Town would be raised in the near future. This being so, it was better to deal with the matter privately than risk the sort of public declaration to which Malan had resorted with regard to the Territories. The British government, recognising that it could hope for 'no worthwhile military contribution' until South Africa 'put her fighting forces

---

[39] PREM 11/1765, Swinton to Alexander, 21 Dec. 1953; ADM 116/6050, McGrigor to Thomas, 22 Dec. 1953.
[40] CAB 131/12, D(52)24, 21 May 1952; PREM 11/274, Jacob to Churchill, 1 July 1952, and D 7(52)2, 2 July 1952.

into proper shape', invited Erasmus to defence talks, with no mention made of Simon's Town.[41]

As feared, Erasmus raised Simon's Town after he reached London. Unexpectedly, he conceded what his government had hitherto resisted – that the base would be available to Britain in any war. Churchill was unmoved. He was 'reluctant to contemplate any transaction which would be presented as yet another surrender of rights and responsibilities'. This was not simply (as Berridge and Spence suggest) a product of Churchill's own intransigence.[42] A meeting of Admiralty officials and the parliamentary secretary had on the same day agreed that it would be 'dangerous to agree in principle at this stage to transfer even if all the conditions desired by the Admiralty were fulfilled'. There were 'many possible sources of complication in the practical implementation of such a decision'. Admiralty Military Branch 'felt sure' that when ministers had read the confidential report by British officials engaged in detailed discussions, they would be unable to share the optimism which pervaded the minute recommending transfer submitted by the minister of defence, Field-Marshal Lord Alexander (another of Churchill's generals brought into Cabinet). It had been 'only too apparent that the South African representatives have sought to avoid precise definitions of their guarantees of availability and efficiency, and to construe these guarantees in a sense contrary to what M. Branch regards as the interests of the Royal Navy'.[43]

Even so, there is no doubt that Churchill was the most strident opponent of transfer, the most determined to stand firm on Britain's existing rights. Why, he asked, should the South African government attach so much importance to the change of status of Simon's Town? It was obviously only because it was 'a step to the final severance of South Africa from the British Crown and Commonwealth'. Transfer would be taken as, and was meant to be, 'a symbol of Britain's decline and fall'. Churchill drew Whitehall's attention to calls in the press by English-speaking South Africans for continued British control at Simon's Town. (He nursed fantasies that Natal, the loyal 'Ulster of South Africa', would secede from republican South Africa and provide an alternative base at Durban; but such views found no support in Whitehall.) Admiralty doubts about the South African government's readiness to honour its commitments merely confirmed Churchill's more deeply seated resistance to transfer. Cabinet ruled that Erasmus should be left under no misapprehension that the British government was in any way committed to transfer. For the South African minister of defence, who had

[41] DEFE 7/178, Garner to Parker, 24 June 1954, and draft minute to Churchill from Alexander and Swinton, 28 April 1954.
[42] CAB 131/14, D(54)30, 21 July 1954; CAB 128/27, CC 57(54)4, 27 Aug. 1954, and CC 58(54)2, 1 Sept. 1954; Spence and Berridge, 'Simonstown', p. 35, and Berridge and Spence, 'South Africa and the Simonstown Agreements', pp. 190–2.
[43] ADM 116/5979, note by Hockaday, 7 Sept. 1954.

arrived armed with his government's startling concession, this was a bitter pill to swallow.[44]

Erasmus had little more success in London in pursuit of his other ambition – the establishment of an African Defence Organisation. Initially, Swinton was not unreceptive to the idea, particularly when the moderate N. C. Havenga appeared likely to succeed Malan as prime minister. In resisting pressure to transfer the High Commission Territories, 'we have', wrote Swinton, 'emphasized the much greater importance and mutual interest in Defence and Economic'; 'The most important thing is to get South Africa . . . firmly committed to fighting in the Grand Alliance.' If South Africa were allied to France, Portugal, and Belgium as well as Britain, there would be less risk of her pulling out 'if they got at loggerheads with a Socialist Government here later on'. Moreover, a National Party government would find it easier to accept an international obligation rather than a Commonwealth one, and be more inclined to commit forces north of the equator. An African Defence Organisation, a South African commitment to Middle East defence, and the transfer of Simon's Town should, concluded Swinton, 'be a "Package" deal' with 'no commitments on either side till we can agree the whole as a fully worked out arrangement'.[45]

This ambitious assessment was not accepted throughout Whitehall. But despite Colonial Office emphasis on the 'unfortunate repercussions in our colonial territories', Foreign Office warnings of likely criticism from Middle Eastern countries, and Ministry of Defence suggestions that 'because of its probable untoward effects in colonial territories it might almost have positive military disadvantage', a meeting of officials from those three departments, as well as the CRO and Chiefs of Staff Secretariat, agreed that an African pact 'should not be rejected out of hand'. 'Provided that it was clearly subsidiary to Middle East defence (the sound organisation of which must come first), a lot could be said for a supporting organisation in Africa concerned with communications, logistics, etc.' At the ministerial level, Anthony Eden, the foreign secretary, took the lead in warning of a pact's damaging implications. The Cabinet agreed with his suggestion that Britain should 'temporise'. Thus a fully blown African Defence Organisation – one of the key elements of a package deal – was in effect ruled out.[46]

Even Simon's Town transfer, the starting point for any larger deal involving Middle East defence, was not without its uncertainties. C. J. Jarrett, the Admiralty official who led the mission to South Africa entrusted with formulating a detailed plan of transfer, reminded ministers that transfer remained 'very much

[44] PREM 11/1765, Churchill's minutes, 25 Aug., 30 Aug., and 6 Sept. 1954; CAB 128/27, CC 59(54)11, 8 Sept. 1954; CAB 129/70, C(54)291, 15 Sept. 1954.
[45] FO 371/108148, 1197, Swinton to Alexander, n.d. [6 Sept. 1954]; Swinton to Eden, 6 Sept. 1954.
[46] FO 371/108148, 1197, note by Eden, 9 Sept. 1954, and note by Hayman, 10 Sept. 1954.

of a gamble'. The base might, or might not, be so run as to make a reality of the promises of availability. Nevertheless, there were, as Jarrett pointed out, 'serious objections to the maintenance of the status quo for any length of time'. The expansion, and indeed the whole future existence, of the South African navy might be jeopardised. Refusal to transfer could be used to generate anti-British feeling at any time that suited the National Party. Above all, there was the argument that Swinton himself found most persuasive. If Afrikaner nationalism

> remains in the ascendant, we shall not secure the naval collaboration of the Union Government by a policy of hanging on to our present position at Simonstown. We may not secure the effective co-operation even if we follow the opposite policy, but at least this would seem to offer an opportunity of gradually accustoming the South African Navy to the habit of working with the Royal Navy and looking to the Admiralty for guidance, and this in the long run might lead to a fruitful relationship which could conceivably make all the difference between sullen neutrality and genuine collaboration by the Union in a future war.[47]

Such reasoning must have played a part in wearing down Churchill's resistance to transfer. In December 1954 he approved a further round of talks with Erasmus which seemed likely to produce an agreement. But despite the feeling that the British government was 'unlikely to get better terms or a greater measure of goodwill in future', there remained doubts about the timing of a settlement.[48]

Strijdom's elbowing aside of Havenga to become prime minister on 30 November 1954 seemed to complicate matters. The British high commissioner, Sir John Le Rougetel, thought that an agreement on Simon's Town might create the impression that 'we will yield to extremists more readily than to their moderate predecessors'. British tactics should, Le Rougetel advised, 'be to play the Simonstown issue long – at any rate for the next few months'.[49] At the Admiralty, Thomas favoured an even longer period of delay. Junior ministers there were sure that there was going to be a 'hell of a row' in parliament over Simon's Town. The issue had already attracted attention in the House of Commons, where former Labour ministers seemed to be gearing up for a major confrontation, asking whether British strategic interests were being jeopardised merely to placate Afrikaner nationalist agitation, or bartered away as part of some general agreement on defence. If the British government would be seriously embarrassed by having to reach an agreement on Simon's Town within a year or so, thought Thomas, 'the wiser course would seem to be to turn down Mr Erasmus's request for an early resumption of talks – with or without a frank

---

[47] ADM 116/6027, Jarrett to Admiralty Secretary, Nov. 1954, and note by Swinton, 9 Dec. 1954.
[48] PREM 11/1765, minute by Thomas, Macmillan, and Swinton, 23 Dec. 1954, and Churchill's approval, 31 Dec. 1954; ADM 116/6027, E. S. J. Morgan, n.d. [Sept. 1954].
[49] ADM 116/6027, Le Rougetel to Liesching, 24 Dec. 1954.

explanation of our difficulties'.[50] Swinton believed that it would be 'absolutely irresponsible' to put off further discussions for a year. Within Britain's grasp was 'a new partnership which is not only vital to the Commonwealth defence and communications but may hold the Union fast within the Empire in spite of apartheid and all that'.[51]

The arguments against a substantial delay would prevail, but not before yet another Cabinet paper on Simon's Town was prepared and presented. In arguing the case for proceeding towards transfer, a joint Admiralty, CRO, and Ministry of Defence memorandum made no claims about Britain's ability to construct a package deal, though there was a repetition of Field-Marshal Alexander's and Swinton's warning that rejection of the agreement in prospect would 'jeopardize the whole range of South African co-operation with us'. Thomas, Swinton, and Alexander argued that in the interests of defence, South African co-operation, and Commonwealth communications, 'the agreement we can make is so satisfactory that we should unhesitatingly recommend it to cabinet'. A meeting of the Defence Committee (one of Churchill's last before Eden finally took over as prime minister) agreed that Erasmus should be invited to resume discussions on defence later that year. Churchill was not recorded as saying anything on any subject at this meeting. He must by then have resigned himself to the inevitable. As he later told Eden after transfer had been agreed, he did not see what else could be done, since 'we live in days when neither South Africa nor Naval defence stand on their foundations of a few years ago'.[52]

IV

To the Eden government was left the task of negotiating a transfer agreement and securing a South African commitment to Middle East defence. There remained hopes of concluding a package deal, but it had become apparent that, with regard to African defence (the third component of the package), the British government could never go far enough to satisfy the South African expectations. Indeed, the British stance on an African Defence Organisation was recognised as a liability, one that the South African government would not readily tolerate. Conscious of this, Harold Macmillan, as minister of defence, asked if the new plan for naval command 'could not be dressed up in some way to look like a regional organisation of the kind for which the South Africans hanker'. The Admiralty, however, was strongly opposed to anything in the nature of a 'fully

---

[50] Britain, H.C. Deb., 531 (27 Oct. 1954), 1905–6; 532 (10 Nov. 1954), question 92, 138; 533 (17 Nov. 1954), 389–90; 533 (24 Nov. 1954), 1225–6 and question 79, 132; and 535 (6 Dec. 1954), question 57, 18. ADM 116/6027, K. T. Nash to H. Smedly, 22 Dec. 1954.
[51] ADM 116/6027, Swinton to Thomas, 22 Dec. 1954.
[52] CAB 131/14, D(55)14, 11 March 1955; CAB 131/15, D 3(55)5, 15 March 1955; PREM 11/1765, Churchill to Eden, 4 July 1955.

Simon's Town 247

integrated NATO-like naval structure', believing it to be absurdly top-heavy and extravagant for the naval purposes involved. Loose naval collaboration with other powers was almost as far as the British government would go (and this not without reluctance) to satisfy the South African urge for a wider alliance. While some in Whitehall urged that control over Simon's Town should be maintained until a South African commitment to Middle East defence materialised, others saw that transfer might be needed to offset South African disappointment over African defence.[53]

Even more objectionable in British eyes than Erasmus's African Defence Organisation was Eric Louw's 'horrifying' plan for a Pan-African Conference. Louw, the combative minister of external affairs, was seeking a meeting of colonial powers to act as a counterpoise to the forthcoming Afro-Asian conference at Bandung. Liesching, by then high commissioner to South Africa, warned that if such proposals for defence co-operation continued to be turned down, there was a real danger of South Africa's 'lapsing into isolationism'. The Defence Committee was not convinced by the CRO's arguments for a more positive response to Erasmus's African defence proposal. It went no further than to accept the possibility of another conference along the lines of those held at Nairobi and Dakar.[54]

Rather than use Erasmus's determination to secure Simon's Town's transfer as a lever to extract a firm commitment to Middle East defence, the Defence Committee chose, as Eden himself preferred, to use it to obtain a more satisfactory transfer settlement. Royal Navy staff were anxious that an agreement, sound on naval grounds, should not be jeopardised. They, along with the Defence Committee, wished to see effective safeguards for 'Coloured' dockyard workers – perhaps the most ambitious of all British objectives.[55] The CRO, backed by unequivocal advice from British representatives on the spot, had all along taken the line that to expect a National Party government to safeguard the position of non-whites was entirely unrealistic. (In considering, at the end of 1954, the points upon which transfer might continue to be withheld, Le Rougetel hoped that 'we shall firmly resist any temptation' to take a stand on the future status of these workers: 'we could not do worse than ventilate an issue such as this'.)[56] The Admiralty concern for the efficiency of the base,

---

[53] ADM 116/6049, Macmillan to Swinton, 10 March 1955; DEFE 7/178, James to Powell, 17 May 1955; FO 371/113481, 1193, Powell to Clarke, 1 April 1955.
[54] DO 35/7139, Swinton to Macmillan, 21 March 1955, note by Snelling, 16 March 1955, and Liesching to Swinton, 28 March 1955; FO 371/113481, 1193, Reading to Howe, 18 April 1955; CAB 131/16, DC(55)10, 7 June 1955; FO 371/113482, 1193, note by A. E. Bromley, 9 June 1955; DEFE 7/1787, Powell to Selwyn Lloyd, 3 June 1955; CAB 131/6, DC 3(55)1, 10 June 1955.
[55] CAB 131/16, DC 3(55)1, 10 June 1955. On the significance of the safeguards for 'Coloured' workers, see M. Lipton, 'British arms for South Africa', *The World Today* 26 (1970), p. 429.
[56] ADM 116/6027, Le Rougetel to Liesching, 24 Dec. 1954.

and the ministerial desire 'to protect ourselves from the criticism that we were conniving at discrimination against coloured people', led the Defence Committee to conclude that, however much the South African government disliked this interference in its racial policies, the British government must insist on full safeguards for dockyard workers. South Africa's potential military contribution to the Middle East was less important than the protection of British interests at Simon's Town.[57]

This is not to say that efforts to secure a South African commitment to Middle East defence were abandoned, but the British government would not delay the conclusion of a transfer settlement in order to obtain it. Faced with the South African refusal to make a 'respectable' commitment there until a Middle East Defence Organisation was established or, at very least, a conference of all powers with interests there had been held, Cabinet chose to conclude an agreement on Simon's Town and naval collaboration, and to be content with a promise of South African participation in military staff talks on the Middle East.[58]

Overall, the British government was notably successful. This was especially so with respect to what was a crucial objective: that South Africa should, *under British guidance*, develop an efficient naval service free from the sort of blind Afrikanerisation that had all but ruined the army and air force, and undermined Anglo-South African defence collaboration in the process. In a vindication of Eden's and the Admiralty's determination to protect the position of 'Coloured' workers, the South African government made the quite astonishing concession that there would be no bar to their recruitment and employment. British negotiators ensured that South African authorities could not easily discriminate against personnel (including those on loan from the Royal Navy) who did not speak Afrikaans. (Securing these last two objectives had been 'extremely tough going' since they drove 'a cart and horse through the Nationalists' favourite devices for preventing coloured men doing skilled work and for getting nationally-minded Afrikaners into the best positions'.)[59] By pointing to the NATO model, a new naval command structure was secured, enabling the British Commander-in-Chief South Atlantic to act in many ways as though he were head of the South African navy. Through him, the South African navy would have direct access to the South African minister of defence – an objective that South African naval officers had themselves failed to obtain even with the threat of mass resignations early in the Second World War.[60] Under the new arrangement, the British

[57] CAB 131/16, D(55)14, annex, and DC 3(55)1, 10 June 1955.
[58] DEFE 7/1788, note for oral statement to Cabinet, n.d. [16 June 1955]; PREM 11/1765, note by Pitblado, 22 June 1955; CAB 128/29, CM 17(55)8, 23 June 1955.
[59] DO 35/2369, Rumbold to Pritchard, 15 Aug. 1951.
[60] University of Cape Town Archives, Harry Lawrence Papers, BC 640, E3.45, 'Situation in regard to South African Naval Forces', n.d. [1939]; E3.41, memorandum by Van der Byl, 3 Nov. 1939.

Commander-in-Chief would be responsible for the combined training of South African and Royal Navy ships, all of which would come under his command in war. Moreover, the South African intention of placing orders for ships in British yards was confirmed. This, as Eden emphasised, 'would have the effect of linking the South African Navy to the Royal Navy for many years to come'. The financial burden of running the dockyard, reckoned in 1949 to be about £600,000 per year, was shifted to the South African government, which agreed to pay £750,000 for British assets there. Finally, there was South Africa's agreement to make the base available to Britain even in war in which South Africa wished to remain neutral. As both sides recognised, this would, by compromising South Africa's neutrality, increase the likelihood of the country's following Britain into war. While the pledges on availability and the rights of 'Coloured' workers stand out as the most striking British achievements, the underlying value of the agreements lay in their contribution to ensuring that South Africa was an active ally in war.[61]

V

The central thrust of British defence policy in connection with South Africa (one which Berridge and Spence have not made plain) was to establish a pattern of collaboration which would safeguard British strategic interests. In no sense did the Admiralty 'regard Simonstown as a "distant outpost" whose cost it could no longer justify', as those two writers have claimed. Until its transfer, the Admiralty could, and did, justify the cost not only of retaining the base but also of maintaining a higher level of activity there than it would have preferred. Such activity was needed to deny South Africa the argument that the Royal Navy no longer used or required the base. To ensure access to the base in war meant maintaining a reasonably sized presence there in peace.[62] Berridge and Spence have not recognised that the reluctance to see Simon's Town transferred both because of its symbolic value, and for fear of undermining the pro-British opposition in South Africa, was to a large extent a manifestation of a deeper concern upon which there was no serious disagreement in Whitehall – the preservation of access to naval bases in South Africa in wartime. The British presence at Simon's Town was a symbol not only of Britain's world-wide power but also of South Africa's strategic dependence. South Africa's following Britain

---

[61] CAB 128/29, CM 17(65)8, 23 June 1955; ADM 167/134, 'Future of Simonstown Dockyard', 7 Nov. 1949. *Exchange of Letters on defence matters between the Governments of the United Kingdom and the Union of South Africa*, June 1955 (Cmd 9520).

[62] Spence and Berridge, 'Simonstown', p. 35. The Admiralty Board rejected in 1949 a proposal to withdraw from the Cape and place Simon's Town on 'care and maintenance' status on the ground that 'once Simonstown had gone out of operation, it would probably be lost to the R.N. for good'. ADM 167/134, 'Future of Simonstown Dockyard', 7 Nov. 1949, and Board minutes, 10 Nov. 1949.

into war – the highest British strategic ambition in relation to South Africa – and the balance of domestic political forces which would bring this about, depended among other things on symbols, perceptions, and the relative strength of Afrikaner nationalism in a way that gave Simon's Town disproportionate significance.

As indeed the key documentation could hardly fail to make plain, Berridge and Spence were right to point to economic considerations, concern for the High Commission Territories, and the desire to preserve the Commonwealth association as reasons for wishing to maintain close relations with South Africa. But these were always present, never proving sufficient cause either to transfer Simon's Town or to accept greater South African involvement in African defence, though the latter would have greatly facilitated a South African contribution to the defence of one of Britain's chief strategic concerns – the Middle East. Such a contribution was not 'the one great prize which Britain had consistently sought throughout the negotiations' on Simon's Town.[63] For the most part, both Labour and Conservative governments tried to deal separately with the transfer and Middle East defence questions, preferring to avoid the former question completely. In each case after A.V. Alexander's initial indiscretion in 1949, Simon's Town was discussed at South Africa's insistence. The proposal for a package deal linking the two only emerged in 1954 when the trusted Havenga was expected to become prime minister and the South African government appeared willing to fulfil all of the conditions upon which transfer had previously been resisted. It was put forward by Swinton, who thought that an African Defence Organisation would provide an added attraction. In fact, an organisation that might satisfy South African ambitions was never a realistic possibility. Recognition of this, and of the need to counteract South African disappointment over African defence, encouraged the British government to settle Simon's Town promptly and accept the involvement of other powers in the defence of the sea routes around the Cape – the latter being a South African achievement that has yet gone unremarked by historians.[64]

This begs a question, perhaps crucial, unasked by Berridge or Spence: why, if control over Simon's Town left the South African government 'with more to impress its white electorate than has hitherto been acknowledged', did it not press far harder for transfer?[65] Considering the attention devoted by the National Party to attacking Britain's position at Simon's Town before 1948, the Malan government was slow to present formally a proposal for transfer – waiting almost three years after coming to power. South African preoccupation with securing control of the High Commission Territories provides part of

---

[63] Spence and Berridge, 'Simonstown', p. 36.
[64] DO 35/7139, Liesching to Swinton, 28 March 1955.
[65] Spence and Berridge, 'Simonstown', p. 36.

the explanation, being directly responsible for the Malan government's three-year delay in raising Simon's Town with the Churchill government. Unlike the Territories, on which the British government endured a barrage of initiatives – from high-level approaches by Malan and Havenga to resolutions tabled in the House of Assembly[66] – Simon's Town was handled almost exclusively by a relatively low-ranking Cabinet minister and was the subject of fewer public pronouncements. There were undoubtedly other reasons for the slow and disorganised South African start on Simon's Town, not least being that the South African government faced financial constraints of its own. There seems little doubt that Havenga, far more interested himself in a sound economy than in dismantling the country's British inheritance, was reluctant to see substantial defence expenditure of any sort, let alone that undertaken primarily for reasons of nationalist pride.[67]

With the failure of the Malan government's initiatives on the High Commission Territories apparent by mid-1954, South African attention shifted to Simon's Town. Even then, their approach was less aggressive than that employed with respect to the Territories. The difference was that most of the South African electorate believed that Britain had a moral obligation to hand over the Territories which would in any case, they believed, be better off under their administration. The same could not so easily be said about Simon's Town, since even with the creation of an effective navy, a Royal Navy presence would still be welcome, if not essential. Moreover, an aggressive approach on Simon's Town might have prejudiced the ambition – advanced in the guise of Malan's African Charter, Erasmus's African Defence Organisation and Louw's Pan-African Conference – of exerting some influence over developments to the north and thus strengthening South African security. The domestic political dimension of these aims cannot have escaped the attention of the National Party. A failure to find a place in a Western defence alliance, or the alienation of South Africa's one certain ally, would have exposed a National Party government at one of their most vulnerable points – to the charge that they were incapable of safeguarding South Africa's external interests.[68]

---

[66] Hyam, *Failure of South African expansion*, pp. 188–92; CAB 128/27, CC 17(54)7, 10 March 1954; CC 24(54)2, 31 March 1954; CC 27(54)4, 7 April 1954; CC 46(54)1, 6 July 1954; and CC 50(54)6, 13 July 1954. See below, pp. 257–8.

[67] For financial reasons the Malan government chose not to tamper with the British position at the armaments depots near Durban and at Ganspan, north of Kimberley – British status at the latter being similar to that at Simon's Town. The future of the strategic reserve of naval mines at Ganspan, described in 1948 as 'by far the most important question now outstanding', was not finally settled until 1958. ADM 116/5741, note by G. Moses, 23 July 1948; DO 35/2264, R. R. Sedgwick to E. L. Sykes, 13 Oct. 1948; J. C. Goosen, *South Africa's Navy: the first fifty years* (Cape Town, 1973), p. 146.

[68] *Natal Witness*, 10 Aug. 1951; *Cape Times*, 26 Oct. 1954; Johannesburg *Star* editorial reported in *The Times*, 3 June 1955.

Here might indeed be the most potent demonstration that South Africa in the mid-1950s remained inescapably enmeshed in a British world system. The Berridge and Spence conclusion that a 'new period of military co-operation between partners of equal status' began in 1955 flies in the face of the historical truth.[69] In reality, a South African government agreed to a pattern of collaboration that would not have looked out of place during the 1920s in Canada or Australia. The National Party government had failed utterly to find either alternatives to Britain as a guarantor of South African security or, during the 1950s at least, to sustain armed forces large enough to maintain even the pretence of strategic self-sufficiency.

Short of reoccupying the Cape or Natal, and fighting another Anglo-Boer war, how could the British government have done more to assure access to South African bases in wartime – the desirability of which was repeatedly affirmed in Whitehall? Some saw that Britain held no other bases in the old dominions and believed that generosity in transfer would be reciprocated by not only a continuation of the unwritten Commonwealth alliance but also South Africa's assumption of greater peacetime defence burdens. Others looked back to the experience of the Irish treaty ports, saw the dangers inherent in entrusting strategic assets to doubtful allies, and recognised that the British government must either stand fast on its position or seek unambiguous guarantees, constructing a framework in which South Africans amenable to intimate defence collaboration might multiply and thrive.

A fear that extreme Afrikaner nationalists would gain ascendancy, and a profound distrust of their intentions, meant that even before Smuts's fall there prevailed in Whitehall a determination to protect British interests by not tampering with existing arrangements at Simon's Town. Financial constraints (but also a firm belief that transfer was the best means of assuring access in future) led A.V. Alexander to challenge these assumptions. After careful consideration, the Attlee government concluded that transfer to a National Party government was best avoided, or to be accepted only under the most stringent conditions. The Churchill government upheld this line, rejecting the advice of CRO officials and British representatives in South Africa (who were, incidentally, the strongest proponents of transferring Simon's Town as a means of offsetting pressure on the High Commission Territories) to consider transfer without unequivocal assurances of either availability or the rights of 'Coloured' workers. When the South African government proved willing to meet almost every condition of transfer dreamed up by the British side, Churchill and his Cabinet conceded that transfer could not be denied indefinitely. This concession was based above all on the calculation that a point had been reached where only by relinquishing direct control would there be any chance of protecting British interests there

---

[69] Spence and Berridge, 'Simonstown', p. 36.

in the long run. All of this serves to show how strong was the desire to preserve the structure of British world-wide power even as Britain appeared to be withdrawing from a world role.

The real end of Simon's Town as strategic outpost in the British world system (by then subsumed in a more open, American-dominated one) came not in 1957 but in 1975 with the termination of the Simon's Town agreements. International and domestic revulsion against apartheid had, by the 1970s, made both naval collaboration and the supply of arms (the latter regarded by South Africa as essential to the bargain) politically impossible for the British government. This termination was for Afrikaner nationalists a source of disappointment, yet also of perverse pride – one of the few real defence ties with the West had been lost, but the imperial legacy had finally been shed in matters of defence. That the South African government had paid a high price for the agreements was made clear by P. W. Botha (who later took on Kruger's mantle as executive state president, erasing one reminder of Britain's former ascendancy). In 1975, while still minister of defence, he proclaimed that South Africa would not enter into another one-sided agreement again.[70]

Paradoxically, for reasons of both nationalist pride and reluctance to undermine the substance of the imperial relationship, the South African government agreed to co-operate with Britain in protecting what had long been a key British strategic asset. The South African government was driven by a desire both to escape the appearance of subordination to Britain and to replace British authority in southern Africa with its own. It also faced the hard fact of strategic dependence on Britain. For its part, the British government would not, in the 1950s, permit its position at the Cape to degenerate into uncertainty or even chaos in which an Afrikaner nationalist government, with no navy to speak of, could use a continuing refusal to transfer Simon's Town to whip up anti-British sentiment or make the Royal Navy's position there untenable by withholding services to the dockyard. Wide-ranging interests would be endangered. A base and, more vitally, a wartime ally would be lost. In the end, the British government relinquished direct control of a base at the Cape for the same reasons that it had assumed control there during the Napoleonic wars: because to do so seemed the best way of safeguarding Britain's strategic interests.

---

[70] South Africa, H.A. Deb., 59 (17 June 1975), 8582; *Keesings Contemporary Archives*, 2742B. See also *Die Burger*, 17 June 1975, and *Die Transvaler*, 19 June 1975, as noted by Geldenhuys in *South Africa's search for status and security*, pp. 2–3.

11 The parting of the ways: the departure of South Africa from the Commonwealth, 1951–1961

Since the autumn of 1950 British ministers and civil servants had contemplated the possibility that they might have to choose between their relationship with South Africa and their relationships with the rest of Africa and the world at large. It seemed increasingly obvious that British embarrassment, combined with South Africa's growing disenchantment, might at any time precipitate a 'parting of the ways'. A Conservative government was faced with precisely that choice in March 1961 at the Commonwealth Prime Ministers' Meeting. Yet more than ten years earlier a significant hardening of attitude towards South Africa had taken place under a Labour government.[1] The Commonwealth Relations secretary, Patrick Gordon Walker, had laid it down that containment of the Union of South Africa was a policy equally important with political advancement for Africans. James Griffiths (as secretary of state for the colonies) had declared apartheid to be 'totally repugnant' and, supported by Aneurin Bevan, had foreseen a time when 'the United Kingdom might have to consider whether she lost more than she gained by her present association with the Union government'.[2] The joint deputy under-secretary at the Colonial Office, Sir Charles Jeffries, was clear before the end of 1952 that Britain was 'committed to the policy of a particoloured Commonwealth', and if a choice had to be made, would side with it against South Africa.[3] The high commissioner in South Africa, Sir Percivale Liesching (1955–8), wrote in 1957 that in the longer term the Union's continued membership of the Commonwealth was an open question. 'On our side', he believed, 'it may be that we are moving towards a situation in which we might ourselves be content to see her outside.' When Sir John Maud took over from Liesching, one of the first things he did was to ask for an assessment of the

---

[1] See generally on the Labour government, R. Ovendale, 'The South African policy of the British Labour government, 1947–1951', *International Affairs* vol. 59 (1983), pp. 41–58; more specifically, chapter 7 above, especially pp. 156–7.
[2] R. Hyam, ed., *The Labour government and the end of empire, 1945–1951* (BDEEP, London, 1992), introd., pp. lxiv–lxviii.
[3] D. Goldsworthy, ed., *The Conservative government and the end of empire, 1951–1957* (BDEEP, London, 1994), part II, p. 174; more generally on South Africa, pt I, pp. 350–79.

economic factors which would influence a South African decision to leave the Commonwealth.[4]

South Africa's departure was more easily contemplated in theory than in practice, and in the meantime the dilemma for the British government was acute. On the one hand, Britain needed good relations with the Union not only because of their mutually beneficial and close economic connections, but also because of British defence requirements and the prestige of the Commonwealth – both important in the context of the Cold War. Good relations were also essential because of the vulnerability of the High Commission Territories, for which Britain remained responsible. So enmeshed were they in the South African orbit, in terms of geography and infrastructure, that Basutoland was regarded as completely dependent on South African goodwill, Swaziland as semi-dependent, and only Bechuanaland as semi-independent. On the other hand, it was vital to contain the expansion of the apartheid state northwards, and Britain needed a decent reputation as an enlightened colonial power who upheld racial equality. Any policy which could be represented as condoning apartheid put its relations with Afro-Asian states in jeopardy. Finding the right balance between co-operation and containment, between the demands of international reputation and national interests, was difficult. To suggest that some risks were undoubtedly taken in the hope that South Africa would see the usefulness of the Commonwealth connection perhaps understates the agony of the tightrope British ministers walked.[5]

I

The incoming Conservative government in October 1951 inherited authoritative advice from Sir Evelyn Baring, retiring after seven years as high commissioner. The three essential measures Britain had to take were, he wrote: to counteract the impact of the new Afrikaner nationalism in the territories north of the Limpopo; to protect and develop the High Commission Territories; and to maintain 'reasonably friendly relations' with the Union government.[6] The Conservatives also inherited three major pieces of unfinished business involving South African policy: what to do with Seretse Khama, whether or not to set up the Central African Federation, and how to settle the future of the Simon's Town naval base. They decided to make the exclusion of Seretse from the Bangwato chieftainship permanent (1952). They determined to bring the Federation of the Rhodesias and Nyasaland into being (1953). They concluded an agreement

---

[4] DO 35/6281, no. 3A, Sir P. Liesching to H. J. B. Lintott, 14 Mar. 1957; DO 35/8712, no. 7, CRO to Sir J. Maud, 19 Dec. 1958.
[5] FO 371/167136, minutes, Sept. 1963.
[6] Hyam, ed., *Labour government and the end of empire*, part IV, pp. 355–6.

over Simon's Town (1955). It is frequently argued that all these policies were mistaken. There is a persistent belief that Seretse was sacrificed to appease the racial prejudices of South Africa.[7] This is not how the government (whether Labour or Conservative) saw it: to them, depriving him of the chieftainship was not appeasement, but a denial of a dangerous weapon to an unpredictable opponent. To recognise Seretse could provide South Africa with an excuse to make a determined push to take over the High Commission Territories in accordance with an administrative reversion provided for in the schedule to the South Africa Act (1909). It might of course be argued that Britain should have called South Africa's bluff, since the risks of the Union government's marching in militarily were negligible – but then people said the same thing about Argentina and the Falkland Islands. Be that as it may, the South African government could still make life in the Territories desperately difficult by economic sanctions and non-cooperation in the provision of services. The risk was real and Britain did not, in our judgement, exaggerate the threat to the Territories from the expansionist Union.[8] On the other hand, Central Africa was a different matter, and the Conservative government probably did over-react to the Afrikaner expansionist threat there. At any rate, the threat to the Rhodesias was not so serious as to justify imposing a highly artificial federal construct against the clearly expressed wishes of the African inhabitants.[9] As far as Simon's Town is concerned, did the government put too high an estimate on getting South African defence co-operation and concede too much? – as has been repeatedly argued by G. R. Berridge, who speaks of 'a form of appeasement'. This interpretation has, however, been challenged by Henshaw, who has shown that the balance of advantage was very far from being all on the South African side. In fact the Union was forced into two most significant concessions: guaranteed availability of the base in a war in which South Africa was neutral, and inapplicability of the colour bar at Simon's Town.[10]

None of these three issues was handled in such a way as seriously to upset the South African government. So what drove the National Party and the Conservative government further apart? Three things. First, it needs to be stressed that above all else it was the policy of apartheid, which British ministers and their advisers without exception thought was utterly wrong and retrograde. The Afrikaner state, commented Sir John Maud, had somehow managed to miss the spirit of the century: 'To a Western European, it seems to owe more to the

---

[7] The biography by T. Tlou, N. Parsons, and W. Henderson, *Seretse Khama, 1921–1980* (Braamfontein, 1995), pp. 97–121, is unregenerate on this issue. See above, p. 196.

[8] See chapter 8 above.

[9] See chapter 9 above.

[10] G. R. Berridge, *Economic power in Anglo-South African diplomacy: Simonstown, Sharpeville and after* (London, 1981), and 'South Africa and the Simonstown Agreements' (with J. E. Spence) in J. W. Young, ed., *The foreign policy of Churchill's peacetime adminstration, 1951–1955* (Leicester/London, 1988), pp. 181–205; and see chapter 10 above.

seventeenth century than to the twentieth century – though there is an ominous Hitlerian smell about it.'[11] Secondly, there were problems caused by Britain's African policy. Indeed, the principal cause of post-war alienation – the new factor in Anglo-South African relations – was Britain's readiness to lead African territories towards self-government. As Sir John Le Rougetel (high commissioner, 1951–5) realised: 'They think our African policy is the most important factor in relations with them.' Malan reacted, he reported in 1951, with rage and terror to Britain's Gold Coast policy: it caused bitter opposition, a 'severe jolt', and led to a profound resurgence of anti-British feeling. To Malan, decolonisation was 'a virus, at least as great a menace as communism', and Britain's Gold Coast policy 'signifies nothing less than undermining the foundations of the Commonwealth and its gradual liquidation'.[12] Strijdom (Malan's successor) was perhaps more pragmatic, and in the event he accepted an unpalatable inevitability and congratulated Ghana on its independence. However, this was not before he had complained bitterly to prime minister Eden that he had not been asked for his views on Ghanaian membership of the Commonwealth: he protested about being 'presented with a fait accompli' – to which he might consent, even though thinking it was 'premature and unwise'. Eden thought the draft official reply was too feeble: 'Strijdom sent me an offensive letter, even an insulting one – we require no lesson from him in how to treat blacks. We must send a firmer reply. We shall not be respected by these bullies if we do not.' Strijdom nevertheless repeated his complaint. Eden commented: 'still obstinate, rude and purblind'.[13] Thirdly, Britain and South Africa were driven apart by the friction caused by the continuing deadlock over the transfer of the High Commission Territories.

Within months of taking office, the Conservative government had decided that it would take no initiative over the transfer issue, but sit tight and wait for Malan to make the first move. He seemed in no hurry to do so. Towards the end of his premiership, however, Malan at last in 1954 signified his long-awaited intention of making a formal request for transfer. He was persuaded not to do this, the British Cabinet appealing to him not to disturb their existing reasonably co-operative contacts. Instead, Malan simply called for the resumption of negotiations where they had been left in 1939. Reply to this was given at once in the form of a statement by prime minister Churchill (in answer to a parliamentary question), expressing the hope that the Union would not 'needlessly press an issue on which we could not fall in with their views without failing in our trust', since there could be no question of agreeing at the present to transfer. It

---

[11] CAB 129/114, C(63)102, Cabinet memo, despatch from Maud to Lord Home, 14 May 1963.
[12] DO 35/4019, no. 204, Sir J. Le Rougetel to CRO, despatch, 28 Dec. 1951; Hyam, ed., *Labour government and the end of empire*, part IV, p. 297.
[13] PREM 11/1367, minutes by Sir A. Eden, July–Aug., 1956; see also DO 35/5058, and Goldsworthy, ed., *Conservative government and the end of empire*, doc. nos. 147, 151–3.

was the strongest and most uncompromising statement on the subject yet made by a British government. A written response to Malan was issued on 21 May 1954 stating that it would be futile to start negotiations because they would yield no practical result except to cause harm to Anglo-South African relations. Malan reacted in a threatening and most intemperate fashion, accusing Britain of finally closing the door on negotiations and repudiating its moral obligations to South Africa. The Cabinet decided it had to be made clear to Malan that it was the current native policy of his government which had fundamentally changed the situation since 1939, but the point 'should not be made too directly or too hard'. It was important they should not say definitively that Britain would *never* transfer the Territories, because that would only precipitate a crisis. Equally, they could not say that *consent* of the inhabitants was essential, though that was certainly the view of at least some Conservative ministers. Another accusatory memorandum was received from Malan in August 1954. It was ignored.[14]

Thereafter the transfer question was more or less dormant until the middle of 1958, when British proposals for constitutional reform in Basutoland prompted the new prime minister, Dr Verwoerd, to ask questions about the wider implications. He made public statements on the Territories in September and November, but these were fairly moderate. High commissioner Liesching defined the British task as comparable to that 'of persuading a weary and exasperated traveller that a constantly receding horizon is the boundary of the Promised Land'.[15] The vulnerability of the Territories was re-examined, and found if anything to have increased.

II

Meanwhile there was the perennial problem of what degree of alignment to afford South Africa at the United Nations. Britain had reasons of its own as a colonial power for not wishing to encourage United Nations interference in the domestic concerns of African states. This explains much of Britain's apparent support for South Africa when the Union's policies were under attack. As British representative on the Trusteeship Council, Sir Andrew Cohen in 1959 was urging the need to put a greater distance between the British and South African positions. The Foreign Office supported him on this, but the Commonwealth Relations Office was anxious not to push South Africa to the 'parting of the ways'. The impending visit of Macmillan to South Africa, however, enabled a more radical position to be adopted. By November 1959 it was clear to the civil servants that the balance was not right between maintaining relations with

---

[14] CAB 128/27/1, CC 17(54)7, Cabinet conclusions, and CAB 128/27/2, CC 46(54); CAB 129/69, C(54)115, 119, 135, 165, 216, Cabinet memoranda by Lord Swinton, Mar.–Aug. 1954; *Parliamentary Debates (Commons)* vol. 526, cc. 966–968, 13 Apr. 1954.
[15] DO 35/7181, no. 20, Liesching to CRO, 14 May 1958.

the Union and securing international reputation. The prime minister would have to take this up with Verwoerd and make a public declaration of the new policy, even if it led to 'the parting of the ways'. Macmillan accepted that there was 'a very strong demand' for him to criticise apartheid. The crucial document in preparing the case originated as a draft Cabinet memorandum, but the Commonwealth Relations secretary, Lord Home, turned it into a personal minute to Macmillan. Its most striking proposition was that the Commonwealth 'would undoubtedly be happier and closer-knit were the ugly duckling out of the nest'. South African membership was described as an embarrassment, an anomaly, and a source of weakness. At the United Nations the British position was increasingly exposed, and voting against all resolutions on South African apartheid was harmful, upsetting the Americans, and damaging the Western cause in the Cold War. 'In the wider context of the battle against Communism for men's minds in the uncommitted countries, South Africa is a liability to the West.' Confidence in Britain was compromised and the sincerity of British thinking and purposes, especially about race, was called into question. However, if there was even a remote hope of a future South African state emerging with a different and happier complexion, it would be 'sad to destroy bridges now which may be invaluable later on'. But the central question remained: 'how long can we afford to support South Africa as much as we do?' Small changes in British voting procedures at the United Nations were proposed, but these were likely to be bitterly resented in South Africa as indicating that the Union could no longer count on Britain over issues regarded as vital to the maintenance of white supremacy. 'The parting of the ways' was thus almost certainly at hand. Home's conclusion was clear: 'our wider international interests and our relations with the new African states (especially Nigeria) are at stake', and it was therefore time to warn South Africa that Britain was going to start abstaining on issues where previously support had been given.[16]

Several senior ministers were asked to comment on Home's minute. The foreign secretary, Selwyn Lloyd, agreed that a change of some sort was required: 'our reputation for being progressive is going to be increasingly necessary as, while various territories achieve independence, the United Nations spotlight is more and more focused on those which continue to be British colonies'. Without a change of policy, British prestige would be further damaged and Britain would be regarded as standing amongst the retrograde. Iain Macleod for the Colonial Office lent his support, while Heathcoat Amory at the Treasury thought that despite the risks it was right to go ahead on these lines.[17]

---

[16] DO 35/10621, no. 39, Home to Macmillan, 17 Dec. 1959. See above, pp. 161–2.
[17] FO 373/145291, no. 16, Selwyn Lloyd to Macmillan, 2 Jan. 1960; T 236/4873, D. Heathcoat Amory to Macmillan, 17 Feb. 1960; see also R. Hyam and W. R. Louis, eds., *The Conservative government and the end of empire, 1957–1964* (BDEEP), part II, docs. 439–42, and 445, for the ministerial discussions, Dec. 1959–Feb. 1960, and part I, introd., pp. xxxviii–xl for an analysis of the genesis and significance of Macmillan's Cape Town speech.

Thus fortified, the speech-writers finalised the text of the speech Macmillan was to deliver in Cape Town on 3 February 1960. The key passage was not about 'the wind of change' but a declaration candidly rejecting 'the idea of any inherent superiority of one race over another': 'there are some aspects of your policies which make it impossible [to support you] without being false to our own deep convictions about the political destinies of free men, to which in our territories we are trying to give effect'. Coming to terms with nationalism was part of the all-important battle against communism: 'the struggle is joined and it is a struggle for the minds of men'. The speech was badly received by Afrikaners. Not only did Macmillan not mouth the expected platitudes, but he radically shifted the British position. One Dutch Reformed Church clergyman (G. J. J. Boshoff) denounced Macmillan as 'the Herod of England', who had said to Black Africa 'ask what you will', and when Black Africa demanded the head of White Man John, Macmillan replied with 'a note of sorrow in his voice as he apologetically agreed to the beheading'.[18]

In his private meetings with Verwoerd, Macmillan failed to establish any sort of rapport, and indeed he could not have been expected to do so. Sir John Maud had frequently warned that Verwoerd was an arrogant and ruthless intellectual, an authoritarian, enigmatic, doctrinaire fanatic of 'impregnable insularity', formidable, and 'frighteningly self-righteous'. Macmillan several times wrote the word 'depressing' on these reports. Once in South Africa, Macmillan was annoyed at being prevented from meeting any African National Congress leaders. He refused to be drawn into saying that a republic would make no difference to Commonwealth membership, carefully confining himself to describing the Commonwealth 'not as the setting sun of British imperialism, but as the dawn of an entirely new concept', one in which he hoped South Africa would be fully involved. He played 'a dead bat' on Verwoerd's representations over the High Commission Territories, giving no recorded undertaking even to consider the matter further. He made it absolutely clear that the Union could not have any kind of veto on constitutional advancement in the Territories.[19]

Some six weeks later came the horror of the Sharpeville police shootings, leaving sixty-nine dead. The United Nations Security Council immediately took

---

[18] DO 35/10570, no. 45, for newspaper report, *Die Burger*, 23 Feb. 1960. See also R. Ovendale, 'Macmillan and the wind of change in Africa, 1957–1960', *HJ* vol. 38 (1995), pp. 455–77. M. Makin, 'Britain, South Africa and the Commonwealth in 1960: the "winds of change" reassessed', *Historia (Historiese Genootskap van Suid-Afrika / Historical Association of South Africa)*, vol. 41 (Pretoria, 1996), pp. 74–88, uses the PRO files of the high commissioner in DO 119/1206, and argues that the speech 'was more of a gentle warning to Verwoerd than a British threat of possible withdrawal of support for white South Africa' (p. 74) – which seems to be taking its 'diplomatic language' too much at face value. And see below, p. 299.

[19] PREM 11/3070, note of discussion between Macmillan and Verwoerd, 4 Feb. 1960; DO 35/10559, no. 169, Maud to CRO, despatch, 12 Mar. 1959; DO 35/7181, no. 86, Maud to Sir A. Clutterbuck, 15 Feb. 1960.

up the issue of censuring South Africa and calling for an end to apartheid. A special Cabinet 'General' committee considered the dilemma this posed for Britain (objection to interference in domestic matters as against legitimate humanitarian protest). After two full discussions the Cabinet decided that Britain would abstain from and not oppose the Security Council resolution. However, in April a General Assembly resolution condemning South Africa was passed, with Britain voting *for* it. The precise reason for this major shift of policy is unclear, as records of the two further meetings of the 'General' committee remain closed for fifty years, but the American government had led the way by voting for the Security Council resolution, and the pressure of world revulsion was becoming stronger all the time. Sharpeville and its aftermath thus greatly increased the significance of the impending meeting of Commonwealth prime ministers.[20]

Following an assassination attempt on 9 April 1960, which he was lucky to survive, Verwoerd was not well enough to attend the Commonwealth Prime Ministers' Meeting in London in May 1960. Sir John Maud regarded this as deeply unfortunate, since it meant that Eric Louw (the foreign minister) attended in his stead. Maud regarded Louw as unfitted to the delicate task of retaining Commonwealth goodwill; he was embittered, spiteful, pedantic, self-righteous, vane, and dreary, an 'unpopular, unprepossessing and neurotic figure, so disturbingly reminiscent of Dr Goebbels'.[21] Macmillan and Home tried to dissuade Louw from raising the question of whether South Africa could expect to remain in the Commonwealth if it adopted a republican form of constitution, as it seemed unlikely there would be a favourable answer. Louw nevertheless not only put the question specifically but also most ineptly asked an additional question as to whether South Africa in its present form was still welcome. This only irritated the prime ministers, although Macmillan was able to say that as far as Britain was concerned they hoped South Africa would remain, it being in the interests of the Commonwealth to keep united. The difficulty about giving an assurance over continuing membership, however, was that it was hypothetical, since they had no idea what the result of the South African referendum might be. The prime ministers agreed that such an assurance would amount to 'interference in an issue of domestic constitutional policy' and they unanimously refused to give it. In their view, a republic was not a nationally agreed policy in South Africa, but opposed by the official Opposition, quite apart from the fact that the majority adult population was excluded from the decision.[22]

[20] CAB 130/173, no. 1, GEN 711, 28 Mar. 1960, minutes of Cabinet committee meeting; CAB 128/34, CC 21(60)3, and CC 22(60)3, Cabinet conclusions, 29 Mar. and 1 Apr. 1960.
[21] FO 371/146499, no. 4, Maud to CRO, despatch, 28 Apr. 1960 (CRO confidential print, 4 May 1960).
[22] DO 119/1206, no. 41A, PMM 8(60)3, extract from minutes of Commonwealth Prime Ministers' Meeting, 10 May 1960. Alistair Horne, *Macmillan*, vol. II: *1957–1986* (London, 1989), p. 204,

In August 1960 Macmillan warned Verwoerd that it had become clear that South Africa's continuing membership as a republic would be opposed by some Commonwealth prime ministers. At best there would be a painful division along racial lines. Could the referendum not be deferred? 'Taking a long-term view, would it not serve your interests better to postpone it until times in Africa are calmer? To secure a breathing-space amid all these fast-flowing developments would be very valuable.' Verwoerd was unmoved.[23]

Although Abubakar Tafawa Balewa of Nigeria had made it plain he hoped to see South Africa 'squeezed out of the Commonwealth' (in order to strengthen it), Macmillan was more alarmed by reports that the Canadian prime minister, John Diefenbaker, might withdraw his support. Diefenbaker was under domestic pressure to make a stand against apartheid, and he felt personally resentful of the abusive treatment he had received from Louw at the previous meeting. Macmillan urged Diefenbaker not to take up any definite position in advance. All prime ministers, he argued, should come to the discussions uncommitted, and alive to the fateful effect on the majority population if South Africa were expelled: 'we can do more to influence the future of these people if they are within the framework of the Commonwealth than if they are outside it'. With a decision about a republic out of the way, Macmillan hoped there might be an opportunity for a resurgence of liberal thought within South Africa, encouraged by the Commonwealth. But to turn South Africa out would condemn the country to ever-growing apartheid bitterness. Moreover, expulsion of South Africa could create a dangerous precedent for the Commonwealth.[24] Six weeks later a similar letter was despatched to Nehru, making even more strongly the point that 'there is a real danger to the whole Commonwealth structure and the beginning of a break-up now'.[25]

Assessments of the likely effects of South African departure occupied officials from the summer of 1960. The Commonwealth Relations Office's brief for the prime minister stressed that bearing in mind the continuing need for good relations with South Africa, it was essential 'to leave Dr Verwoerd convinced that we have done our utmost to keep South Africa in, and we should therefore argue to the last in favour of South Africa'. If the general sense of

---

quotes Macmillan's diary during the conference: 'If we *do nothing*, the Commonwealth will seem to have no faith and no purpose. If we *do too much*, South Africa will secede and this may mean the beginning of a general break up.' J. D. B. Miller, *Survey of Commonwealth affairs: problems of expansion and attrition, 1953–1969* (Oxford, 1974), pp. 142–9, remains a valuable account of the 1960 conference. A good Afrikaner-historical perspective is provided for both the 1960 and 1961 conferences by O. Geyser, *Watershed for South Africa: London, 1961* (Durban, 1983), pp. 54–100, which draws on the Verwoerd Collection at the Institute for Contemporary History at Bloemfontein; Geyser's final chapter is entitled 'The parting of the ways'.

[23] DO 119/1206, no. 62, telegram from Macmillan to Verwoerd (via CRO to Maud), 2 Aug. 1960.
[24] PREM 11/3537, T 698/60, letter from Macmillan to Diefenbaker, 18 Nov. 1960: see Hyam and Louis, eds., *The Conservative government*, part II, doc. no. 452.
[25] PREM 11/3393, T 8/61, letter from Macmillan to Nehru, 6 Jan. 1961.

the Commonwealth meeting was against keeping South Africa in, 'we should, though still with every show of reluctance, be prepared to acquiesce'; not to do so would put at risk the cohesion of the Commonwealth and its significance as a multi-racial association. The departmental advisers were fairly certain no Commonwealth prime minister would want to take the initiative towards expelling South Africa and each would probably accept a majority decision to keep the country in. But no African state could afford to show itself as more accommodating than Diefenbaker, and so his role might become crucial. Officials seemed to agree that membership of the Commonwealth as such was not something to die in the last ditch for. Britain's more fundamental concerns were its economic links and its responsibility for the High Commission Territories. South Africa's membership of the sterling area was more important than membership of the Commonwealth. Most Treasury officials did not think that technically the withdrawal of South Africa even from the sterling area need matter too much, certainly less than it would have done ten years earlier. However, the Commonwealth Relations Office and the Bank of England were much more worried about prestige and the psychological impact of South Africa's withdrawal as 'a major crack' in the sterling area system, wondering whether it might not have a deleterious effect on the international position of the City of London as a financial centre if South Africa stopped selling through it the bulk of its gold.[26]

High commissioner Sir John Maud's advice was consistently on the side of making maximum efforts to retain South Africa in the Commonwealth. Patience and forbearance were required, he thought. He was deeply concerned to uphold the interests of the disenfranchised majority, anxious not to damage the prospects of co-operation with a future *African* government of South Africa. They had to believe in the possibility of 'the Union's eventual redemption'. Retaining South Africa within the Commonwealth would give some chance of influencing it and laying foundations for the future, thus keeping faith with half the whites and all the non-Europeans, who might otherwise look for help elsewhere when their emancipation eventually came. Maud also warned that Verwoerd could well wish to be free of the moral pressures of membership; therefore, to expel South Africa might be playing his own game. He urged that Britain would have to sit it out with South Africa against the day of the collapse of the apartheid regime, just as Britain sat it out with the Russians in the Cold War. The National Party could not be in power for ever, since it was 'inconceivable that in this multi-racial state the criterion of advancement will forever remain the colour of your skin'. 'Verwoerdism' must eventually

---

[26] DO 35/10621, CRO minutes, 13 Aug.–16 Dec. 1959, and T 236/4873, Treasury minutes, 5 Jan.–12 Feb. 1960, repr. in *The Conservative government*, part II, doc. nos. 438, 442; FO 371/152123, no. 71, inter-departmental study. See also chapter 6 above.

collapse, 'for the simple reason that it is not only evil but cannot be made to fit the facts: it is a policy for putting back in their shells eggs which were broken long ago when South Africa first began to become industrialised'. Maud's predictions were proved right: 'in the end the policy will have to be modified in the interests of economic good sense . . . it is likely to be bread and butter considerations which will win the day'. Equally perceptive was his insight that Christianity 'is a much more serious long-term threat than Communism to white supremacy'.[27]

III

As the Commonwealth prime ministers assembled in London for their decisive 1961 Meeting, Macmillan had a long talk with Verwoerd on 7 March. Verwoerd confirmed that South Africa hoped to remain in the Commonwealth, but recognised that discussion of racial policy was unavoidable.[28] There were fifteen conference sessions held between 8 and 17 March, the two dominant issues being South Africa and disarmament.[29] Discussions on South Africa began at the sixth session, on the morning of 13 March. Verwoerd made a short statement requesting acceptance of the wish of the Union government to continue as a member of the Commonwealth after the inauguration of the republic on 31 May. From the chair, Macmillan suggested that, treated purely as a constitutional matter, the issue should not present any great difficulty, since the precedents (India, Pakistan, Ghana, and – potentially – Ceylon) were clearly positive. But it would be disingenuous not to recognise that widespread anxiety about South Africa's racial policy would be a relevant consideration.

By prior arrangement, Nehru then opened the discussion, arguing for a clear declaration against racial discrimination and segregation, 'without which the Commonwealth association would be imperilled': there could be no effective co-operation between countries which did not recognise the validity of the concept of the multi-racial Commonwealth. After Nehru, each of the prime ministers made a prepared statement. Diefenbaker agreed that some public recognition of the multi-racial character of the Commonwealth was needed if

---

[27] DO 35/10559, no. 233, Maud to CRO, despatch, 12 Oct. 1960; DO 35/8712, no. 11, Maud to CRO, despatch, 22 Jan. 1960; CAB 129/114, C(63)102, memorandum, 14 May 1963, Maud's valedictory despatch (extract repr. in *The Conservative government*, doc. no. 462); DO 119/1206, no. 59, CRO briefing, July 1960.

[28] PREM 11/3535, note for the record, meeting between Macmillan and Verwoerd, 7 Mar. 1961 (*The Conservative government*, doc. no. 455).

[29] South African Government Archives, Pretoria, BLO 449; CAB 133/251, PMM 6–10 and 12(61), minutes of Commonwealth Prime Ministers' Meeting, 13–15 Mar. 1961; the entire record is reprinted in *The Conservative government*, part II, pp. 425–51, doc. no. 457. See also National Archives of Canada, MG 30, E163, vol. 18, file 18/1, a commentary sent to Norman Robertson of the Canadian External Affairs Dept, telegrams, 13–15 Mar. 1961.

the association were to be preserved. It might be necessary to identify some fundamental principles on which continuing association could be based. South Africa's racial policy could no longer be treated as a purely internal affair, since it had international repercussions and attracted such close and widespread concern: to accept South Africa's present request would be construed as approval of, or at least acquiescence in, South Africa's racial policy. President Ayub Khan of Pakistan supported the first two speakers, going on to express his country's sense of disillusion that the Commonwealth was an inadequate instrument of conciliation, for example in Kashmir. If it could not now even support the concept of racial equality, there would be further disillusionment about its value: 'the reputation and future influence of the Commonwealth, which it was necessary to maintain if emerging nations were not to fall prey to Communist influences, were at stake'. Next, Australia's Menzies said that it was wrong to link a discussion of South Africa's racial policy with continued membership of the Commonwealth. He opposed drawing up a declaration of basic principles, as this would destroy the character of the present association. Nkrumah, prime minister of Ghana, spoke after Menzies, delivering the shortest of all the statements, surprisingly moderate in tone. In his view, the principle of racial equality did not have to be formally declared, but members ought to subscribe to it as an underlying principle which could only grow in importance. Then Tunku Abdul Rahman, prime minister of Malaya, criticised South Africa for doing so little to help other Commonwealth countries, even refusing to accept accredited diplomatic representatives. South Africa appeared to him as wanting to remain in the Commonwealth because of the material advantage which it gave, but at the same time to pursue racial discrimination without modification, 'a policy which only strengthened the hands of Communists and other ill-wishers against the Commonwealth'. Did such a policy 'not offend the whole moral basis of the Commonwealth?' K. J. Holyoake of New Zealand believed South Africa would have been well advised to re-examine its 'intransigent' policy, but he counselled moderation in taking any irrevocable step which would deprive millions of people of the Commonwealth connection. Mrs S. R. D. Bandaranaike of Ceylon took up the reference to the battle for the minds of African peoples, for 'it was this that was at stake when considering apartheid'. The survival of the Commonwealth would depend on whether it was to become a truly multi-racial association based on equality; if these principles were compromised in order to retain South Africa in it, this could only encourage more extreme racialism in the Union. It was, she continued, being argued that expulsion of South Africa would split the Commonwealth, but 'equally there was the risk of a split if she remained'. They should make a stand and resolve to exclude South Africa unless its government undertook to make a change in racial policy. Finally, Sir Abubakar Tafawa Balewa, the newcomer to the circle, made play with the fact that Nigeria had just become a member in the belief that the Commonwealth stood for equality of the individual, regardless of race, colour, or creed. South Africa offended against this principle, and any arrangement by which it remained in the Commonwealth would merely be an encouragement to persist in its racial policies – something to be avoided at all costs.

At the afternoon session on 13 March, Verwoerd made a long defence of his position and the theory and practice of apartheid. He protested about 'unfriendly attitudes'. After Verwoerd parried a couple of needling questions, Nkrumah then took the initiative, declaring that the essential point appeared to have been missed: 'the Meeting should not waste time in mutual recrimination; the real issue was the whole future character of the Commonwealth'. Abubakar agreed: if members could not publicly subscribe to the principle of racial equality 'their association would be meaningless'. Chairman Macmillan then offered an interim summing-up, but he wanted mainly to emphasise that as this was a Commonwealth of nations, not of governments – which might come and go – the interests of the great population of South Africa, whether European or African, must not be neglected. He hoped they might agree upon a formula which would accept South Africa's continuing membership but also reaffirm the strong feeling of all other members against racial discrimination. The reaction to this appears to have been generally that it was possible but unrealistic, because its two halves seemed incompatible. This was plainly the moment for someone to sharpen the issue, and it was Nehru who did so: 'the eyes of the world were on this Meeting and the Commonwealth Prime Ministers should make it absolutely clear where they stood'. Nevertheless, Holyoake said he thought Macmillan had suggested the only practical course, and after a brief further discussion the proceedings were adjourned.

At the end of the first day it was uncertain what the outcome might be. Only Mrs Bandaranaike had so far used language which appeared to commit her to refusing consent to South Africa's continuing membership. The others had all stopped just short of such a commitment. That evening Macmillan sent a personal message to Verwoerd asking him, after 'a difficult day for us all', if he could not 'make a gesture' by agreeing to exchange high commissioners with other Commonwealth countries – the point raised by Abdul Rahman. This might be 'a small thing, but I think it might have great significance', since it really did not seem possible to maintain a Commonwealth where the prime ministers could only meet in London and were not prepared to receive each other's representatives in their capitals. He understood that Verwoerd based his policies 'upon a theoretical thesis which is very fundamental to you'; however, 'men are not ruled entirely by logic, but often by sentiment'. Verwoerd declined to be moved by this appeal, on several grounds: that it was unwarranted interference, attempting to lay down conditions of membership, when Ghana and Malaya had been admitted without conditions; that he had no particular reason to exchange representatives with New Zealand, Cyprus, or Sierra Leone; and

Parting of the ways 267

that he was not prepared to make a friendly move towards countries which were actively hostile – Ghana, India, Malaya, Tanganyika, and Nigeria.[30]

On the following day Macmillan's draft communiqué was discussed. Verwoerd at once admitted there was much in it he could not accept. Menzies disliked the way it 'constituted in effect notice to South Africa to quit'. Diefenbaker disputed this: 'it was rather a statement of the abiding principles to which the Commonwealth adhered'. Nehru insisted there should be no equivocation in stating that the Commonwealth could only hold together on the basis of racial equality: 'failure to do so would injure the Commonwealth irretrievably'. Discussion, he added, had revealed the true extent of divergence between the South African government and the rest. Nkrumah now made another moderate intervention, suggesting that perhaps the question of South Africa's membership should be postponed to give it time to reconsider its policies. Inevitably that provoked dissent, with Ayub Khan objecting. After a short break, Macmillan launched into a typically reflective excursus on the historical background and the value of the Commonwealth. Let them take a long view and not merely think in terms of an immediate solution. He would be reluctant to contemplate any change in their relationship with all the peoples of different race in South Africa. He realised nevertheless that all the prime ministers were subject to the pressure of public opinion on racial equality, and 'it was of great importance to make clear to the peoples of the Commonwealth and of the world where we stood on this issue'. Macmillan concluded this personal oration by offering to redraft their statement into two separate documents, constitutional and racial, during the lunch interval.

When discussion resumed on the afternoon of 14 March, Macmillan explained that the redrafted documents were intended to show that while the constitutional change did not provide any ground on which South Africa's application could properly be rejected, the other prime ministers still adhered to their objections to South Africa's racial policy. A communiqué would affirm a commitment by all members to build structures of society offering equality of opportunity for all. Nehru accepted that the documents fairly represented the course of discussion but they did not arrive at a reconciled conclusion. And what did Verwoerd think of them? Verwoerd replied tartly that the concept of the Commonwealth had changed in the course of the previous ten months, and it seemed that the intention was to lay down certain rules which might later be used to expel a member; the communiqué read to him as a deliberate motion of censure. Nkrumah underlined the difficulty for the rest of them: the communiqué must indicate that they had not changed their views in any

[30] PREM 11/3535, letters between Macmillan and Verwoerd, 13 and 14 Mar. 1961. A draft communiqué was intensively discussed by Macmillan's advisers, notably Cabinet Secretary Sir Norman Brook, who rejected suggestions by Menzies for greater openness in setting forth the issues and the 'fundamental and vigorous criticism of South Africa'.

way. To this Verwoerd responded that he would be prepared to consider a form of announcement which stated that whatever the views of individual prime ministers on South Africa's racial policies, it was the collective decision of the Meeting that South Africa would remain a member. Nkrumah's comment was that it would be difficult to accept this; the communiqué must contain a statement about agreeing that South Africa's racial policies were inconsistent with the ideals of the Commonwealth. Further redrafting was then considered, but as Nehru observed, the more they discussed the matter the more obvious was the difference of opinion. The session concluded with a powerful statement from Mrs Bandaranaike which reflected the day's hardening of attitudes:

In her view, Dr Verwoerd had made it quite plain that he did not intend to change his racial policy. The question before the Prime Ministers therefore was whether they were prepared to compromise on an issue affecting human rights. She thought that most Prime Ministers would be unable to do this. She considered that the drafts circulated by Mr Macmillan had failed to bring out the salient point of the discussions which had taken place over the last two days. The real question was whether South Africa could be permitted to remain within the Commonwealth while her racial policy remained unchanged.

Nevertheless, the overall position now was that South Africa was confronted with the proposition that its membership would probably be continued if Verwoerd would accept the issue of a declaration by other members (to which he would not be expected to subscribe) recording their detestation of apartheid and affirming the principle of non-discrimination as basic to the multi-racial Commonwealth. Verwoerd, not unnaturally, found that hard to swallow. He asked to be allowed to consider his position overnight.

Next morning, after a private meeting with Macmillan, Verwoerd announced that he would accept such a formula and draft communiqué, provided he was given an opportunity to set out a summary of the arguments justifying his government's policy. Further redrafting was accordingly attempted, as Macmillan proposed. When these revisions were considered on the afternoon of 15 March, Diefenbaker and Nehru both complained that the revised communiqué gave too much emphasis to Verwoerd's views. But it was Abubakar who focused the crux of the debate: there was no indication that the South African government intended to modify its policies in any way, and in these circumstances he would have to consider whether Nigeria should remain a member of the Commonwealth if South Africa stayed in. Nehru seized on this leverage to speak again, insisting that the new draft was unbalanced, and giving notice that India would at the earliest opportunity raise the question of South African membership if her racial policy remained unchanged. Nkrumah now joined in with his hammer-blow, reserving the right also to raise formally at a later stage the expulsion of South Africa; alternatively Ghana would have to reconsider its own membership.[31] Whereupon Verwoerd retorted that he in turn must reserve the right to propose the expulsion of Ghana, since Nkrumah's policy was not in accordance with the principles of democracy. He also took exception to Nehru's remarks, and concluded, 'South Africa could not continue as a member-country if she was under the continual threat of expulsion': he must know that South Africa was welcome to remain, and if the present formula was merely a device to enable an unwelcome member to remain, then he would have to reconsider their position. Presumably there was then a moment of climactic silence, eventually broken by Macmillan, who merely said that his draft had been intended to settle the immediate issue, but if this called in question the continued adherence of several prime ministers to the Commonwealth association, they would all have to reconsider their positions during a short adjournment. After this tea-break, Verwoerd formally withdrew his request for South Africa to remain a member after 31 May 1961. He was, he said, 'amazed and shocked by the spirit of hostility and in this last meeting even of vindictiveness shown towards South Africa . . . the character of the Commonwealth has apparently changed completely during the last year'. There was no further recorded discussion or comment. Macmillan immediately produced a brief communiqué for publication forthwith, which was quickly approved. It was just three sentences long, little more than a simple statement that the prime minister of South Africa had withdrawn his application 'in the light of the views expressed on behalf of other member-governments and the indications of their future intentions regarding the racial policy of the Union Government'.

Later that evening, a highly despondent Macmillan chewed over the result with 'Rab' Butler and his chief whip, Martin Redmayne. He felt that a decisive factor had been the position of Abubakar, who might not politically have survived putting his name to a document agreeing to South Africa's continuing membership; at best he would have had to put down a formal motion (at the next Prime Ministers' Meeting) for South Africa's expulsion. All this meant that their present deliberations would have settled nothing finally, and they would 'get only the shadow and not the reality'. He was worried how the Conservative Party would take the news.[32] Lord Home was well aware of Macmillan's anguish and wrote him a sympathetic note:

---

[31] According to Macmillan's adviser on public relations (press secretary), 'strong, if not angry, words began to be used' at this session, and there were 'raised voices': Harold Evans, *Downing Street diary: the Macmillan years, 1957–1963* (London, 1981), pp. 141–3, which provides a well-informed account.

[32] PREM 11/3535, note for the record, 15 Mar. 1961.

This is a very sad day for you and all of us but I don't see how with emotion overcoming reason it was possible to get a different result. Certainly you must not reproach yourself as you did everything which was humanly possible to keep South Africa in. I could see this morning when I talked to Ayub that the only alternative was the breakaway of all the Asian and African members. That could not be faced.[33]

Home completely accepted Macmillan's own interpretation: the issue had been handled with restraint and if Verwoerd had only made 'one millimetre of concession the result might have been different'. This was the official gloss on the account immediately supplied to high commissioners. Ten days later, however, Duncan Sandys as Commonwealth Relations secretary sent them a more positive interpretation: South Africa's departure made 'bridge building' easier, and provided the psychological climate for a new step forward in Commonwealth co-operation. 'The removal of any doubt about the acceptance of the principle of multi-racialism should enhance the prestige of the Commonwealth in the world as well as its own solidarity.'[34] The prime minister found it personally much harder to put such a brave face on events.

IV

Macmillan's memoirs deployed emotive adjectives in describing the departure of South Africa from the Commonwealth: unhappy, painful, very sad, tragic, disastrous. He harped upon his sense of 'grief and foreboding': 'I felt almost a sense of despair' – was every problem to be met with such rigidity, incomprehension, and lack of compromise as Verwoerd had displayed?[35] Part of Macmillan's unhappiness was a realisation that his own 'wind of change' speech had played its part in the outcome. To right-wing colleagues such as Lord Kilmuir, it was indeed Macmillan's fault, 'a direct consequence of one unguarded phrase in a single speech', though Macmillan had 'no conception of the mine he had unwittingly exploded'.[36] What Kilmuir could not know was that Macmillan had himself confided to Sir John Maud: 'The wind of change has blown us away.'[37] Macmillan never found it easy to forgive Diefenbaker (that 'woolly tub-thumper') for his 'holier than thou' attitude, but it is apparent

---

[33] Ibid., Home to Macmillan, 15 Mar. 1961 (repr. in Hyam and Louis, eds., *The Conservative government*, doc. no. 459).

[34] PREM 11/3535, CRO telegram to high commissioners, 16 Mar. 1961; CAB 129/104, C(61)40, Sandys to high commissioners, 27 Mar. 1961 (Cabinet memorandum).

[35] Harold Macmillan, *Memoirs*, vol. V: *Pointing the way, 1959–1961* (London, 1972), pp. 285–305. P. C. Gordon Walker, formerly the Labour government's secretary of state for Commonwealth relations, took a more robust view: the long, anxious, historic discussions had demonstrated the 'sense of reality and integrity of the Commonwealth', and given dramatic expression to the continuing will to keep it going: *The Commonwealth* (London, 1962), p. 379.

[36] Earl of Kilmuir, *Political adventure: memoirs* (London, 1962), p. 315.

[37] Macmillan, *Pointing the way*, p. 302 (diary, 21 Mar. 1961).

Parting of the ways

Illustration 11.1 *Sluit aan by die meerderheid. Saam met drie Asiatiese ledestate van die Statebond het Engeland in die V. V. O. kant gekies teen Suid-Afrika.* Britain aligns with the Asians at the United Nations after South Africa's departure from the Commonwealth. 'Join the majority': John Bull, shouting 'Wait: I want to pull too', rushes to join the lynching of 'Whites in Africa'. 'With these three Asian members of the Commonwealth, England chose sides against South Africa at the U.N.O.' The figures on the left are Nehru, Mrs Bandaranaike, and Tunku Abdul Rahman. *Source: Die Transvaler*, 6 April 1961.

from the record that it is unnecessary to invoke him as the prime mover of events.[38]

In any case, taking a wider perspective, it would be wrong to conclude that South Africa's departure arose simply out of pressure from the prime ministers. Verwoerd had more than sufficient reasons of his own for not particularly wanting to remain a member any longer. The Suez Crisis had shaken his confidence in Britain's capacity for independent action and military effectiveness.

---

[38] Horne, *Macmillan*, vol. II, p. 204. F. Hayes, 'South Africa's departure from the Commonwealth, 1960–1961', *International History Review* vol. 2 (1980) pp. 453–84, overestimates Diefenbaker's role.

Decolonisation made Britain less and less valuable to South Africa as an African 'ally'. Louw's cherished project for a joint African defence pact had definitively collapsed by 1960, and British automatic alignment behind South Africa at the United Nations had already gone. South Africa had very little interest in any other Commonwealth members apart from Britain itself. Verwoerd could reasonably expect that South Africa's economic links with Britain would remain intact.[39]

Those economic connections certainly persisted, although the Cabinet determined at the outset of departure that 'it would be important to avoid giving the impression that after her withdrawal South Africa was to remain a member of the Commonwealth in all but name'. 'Commonwealth treatment' would not be given unless it was clearly in British interest to do so.[40] Nevertheless, the old imperatives to keep on terms with South Africa, *despite apartheid*, in a reasonable working relationship, remained. After the parting of the ways, the British government had to treat South Africa as half-ally and half-untouchable at the same time, equivocating on sanctions, and continuing to try to preserve its essential interests: arms supply for the strategic requirements of the Cape searoute, discharge of its trusteeship for the High Commission Territories, and the promotion of trading interests which would encourage South Africa to remain in the sterling area. Geopolitics, long-term calculations, and moral obligations combined to ensure that it would continue to be British policy to 'keep a foot in this important door', as Sir John Maud put it, not only because if Britain withdrew entirely 'an enemy or rival would take her place', but because the British government wanted to 'keep faith' with the black majority which would surely one day form an African government.[41]

---

[39] P. J. Henshaw, 'South Africa's external relations with Britain and the Commonwealth, 1945–1956' (unpublished PhD dissertation, Cambridge, 1989), ch. 5, 'Relations with the Commonwealth association, 1945–1961'. For the African Defence Pact plan, see G. R. Berridge, *South Africa, the colonial powers and 'African Defence': the rise and fall of a white entente, 1948–1960* (London, 1992), and Henshaw's review in *SAHJ* no. 30 (1994) pp. 164–7.

[40] CAB 128/35/1, CC 15(61)7, Cabinet conclusions, 21 Mar. 1961; see also PREM 11/3994.

[41] DO 119/1206, no. 76, Maud to CRO, telegram, 13 Aug. 1960, repr. in *The Conservative government*, doc. no. 451. For an important summary of British policy towards South Africa in 1963, see the briefing despatch to Maud's successor, Sir Hugh Stephenson, 28 June 1963, CAB 129/114, C(63)109, repr. in *The Conservative government*, doc. no. 463.

12 Enfeebled lion? How South Africans viewed Britain, 1945–1961

How did South Africans view Britain in the period 1945 to 1961? While perceptions were as diverse as the identities of South Africans themselves, there was nevertheless a general perception that Britain and the British connection mattered far less in 1961 than they ever had before. It might be thought that this was an inevitable consequence of Britain's economic and strategic eclipse as a great power during the Second World War. The war certainly left Britain far behind the United States and the Soviet Union militarily. It also weakened Britain financially, and undermined its hold on its Asian empire. Britain's decline in the eyes of white South Africans seemed to be demonstrated by the fall in 1948 of the strongly pro-British government of Jan Smuts and by the advent of an Afrikaner nationalist government overtly hostile to the British connection. Britain's decline was further suggested by the tendency of African nationalists to turn away from Britain as a source of support in their struggle against racial oppression within South Africa. The establishment of a republic in South Africa and its exit from the Commonwealth in 1961 also seemed to confirm Britain's collapse. Historians have hitherto given little direct attention to South African perceptions of Britain in this period, perhaps because the British connection did not seem to matter much after 1945; or perhaps because the British government seemed to play little positive part in the struggle against apartheid. Yet, however far Britain's significance may have declined in South African eyes by 1945, and however much further it fell in the subsequent decade and a half, there can be little doubt that the British connection still remained crucially important for many South Africans even as late as 1960.[1]

This chapter is based on a paper presented in its conceptual stage at the Canadian Research Consortium on Southern Africa (CRCSA) conference at Queen's University in 1998. More developed versions of the paper were presented at the North-East Workshop on Southern Africa (NEWSA) conference in Burlington, Vermont, in 2000, and at the 'British World' conference in London in 2001. Peter Henshaw wishes to thank all those present at these conferences for their comments, and particularly Dan O'Meara and Dunbar Moodie.

[1] There is, of course, an extensive literature on South African politics and society in this period, much of which engages tangentially with the subject of South African perceptions of Britain. Some of the most important works are: D. O'Meara, *Forty lost years: the apartheid state and the politics of the National Party, 1948–1994* (Randburg and Athens, OH, 1996); T. Dunbar Moodie,

This was true not merely with respect to South Africa's external material relations; it was also true in terms of the ways South Africans viewed themselves culturally and organised themselves politically. Throughout the years 1945 to 1961, Britain remained disproportionately significant strategically, economically, and geopolitically. As Afrikaner nationalists discovered after taking power, there was simply no Western alternative to Britain as military and economic partner in this period. Furthermore, four of South Africa's immediate neighbours, and other more distant ones in Africa, were territories under British jurisdiction. Virtually all South Africans recognised that political developments in these British territories would have a major impact on their own country. Culturally, despite competition from the United States and elsewhere, Britain retained a predominant influence. The British connection still strongly shaped the ways many South Africans behaved or identified themselves as individuals or groups; shaped, too, their systems of government, law and education, their forms of religion, and their types of entertainment. As should be no surprise, then, the British connection remained central to competing projects to organise political alliances across class divisions and along ethnic, multi-ethnic, or even multi-racial lines. 'Nationalist' movements in South Africa – be they Afrikaner, 'Coloured', Indian, African, or multi-racial – often tried in these years to use antagonism to 'British imperialism' to unite their supporters. Other South African political movements – again of almost any ethnic or racial combination – also tried to use loyalty to the British connection as an alternative rallying cry. With British influences so widespread and pervasive, and the British connection still so important, it was natural that many South Africans continued to have strong views about them.

This chapter will attempt to outline Britain's external and internal significance for different groups of South Africans; to explain how some of these external and internal aspects of the British connection interacted in South Africa; and, not least, to show how South African perceptions of Britain shifted in the years between 1945 and 1961. It will do so by looking at popular reactions to such events within South Africa as the British royal visit; the introduction and implementation of various pieces of apartheid legislation; the British Lions rugby tour of 1955; Harold Macmillan's 'wind of change' visit in 1960; and, finally, the establishment of a republic and South Africa's consequent exit from the Commonwealth in 1961. The chapter will also look at South African responses

The rise of Afrikanerdom: power, apartheid, and the Afrikaner civil religion (Berkeley, CA, 1975, 1980); T. Karis and G. M. Carter, *From protest to challenge: a documentary history of African politics in South Africa*, vols. II and III (Stanford, 1973 and 1977); G. M. Carter, *The politics of inequality: South Africa since 1948* (New York, 1958). There is also a growing literature on culture and identity in South Africa: see, for example, R. Nixon, *Homelands, Harlem and Hollywood: South African culture and the world beyond* (London, 1994), and R. Thornton, 'The potentials of boundaries in South Africa: steps towards a theory of social edge', in R. Werbner and T. Ranger (eds.), *Post-colonial identities in Africa* (London, 1996), pp. 136–61.

to British public attitudes and government policies, particularly British policy in Africa. In the course of this analysis, several things should stand out. First, throughout this period, the British connection was subjected to sustained attacks and criticisms by various groups of nationalists, most tellingly by Afrikaners and the National Party government. These attacks steadily undermined the significance of the British connection for many South Africans even if they simultaneously reinforced it in the short term for some others. Secondly, Britain's retreat from colonial rule generated a marked shift in South African attitudes towards Britain, but most particularly at the very end of this period. This had the contradictory effect of reducing Britain's and the Commonwealth's prestige in the eyes of some South Africans, while increasing it in others. And, finally, while the importance of the British connection undoubtedly did decline in this period, this decline was not as steady or drastic as might be supposed. Indeed, for many white South Africans, Britain's standing revived in the 1950s, only to decline rapidly and drastically from 1960 onward. The British connection remained remarkably important even as late as 1960 – a reflection of Britain's continued material significance and pervasive cultural influence, but also of the British connection's utility as a domestic-political rallying cry.

I

In 1945 the legacy of British colonial rule was inescapable in South Africa. It was embedded in South Africa's politics and economics, in southern Africa's defence and geopolitics, and in its peoples' culture and identity. The Union of South Africa had come into being as an internally self-governing 'dominion' of the British empire only thirty-five years earlier. It was an amalgamation of four predominantly black but white-ruled settler colonies. Two of these were historically British (the Cape and Natal), while two were formerly independent Boer republics (the Transvaal and Orange Free State). This dominion had inherited many of its political, bureaucratic, and legal structures from Britain and other parts of the empire-Commonwealth. Like Canada, the Union was bilingual. Its official languages were English and Afrikaans, even if the Union's civil and armed services – all organised along British lines – still operated predominantly in English. The Union parliament was modelled on Westminster. South Africa's highest court of appeal was the Judicial Committee of the Privy Council in London (the supreme court of the British empire and Commonwealth overseas). Its constitution was partly written, in the shape of the South Africa Act, a British act of parliament; and partly unwritten, in the form of British parliamentary convention. In the British monarch, South Africans shared a common head of state with the rest of the formal British empire. In recognising themselves as British subjects, South Africans shared a measure of common imperial citizenship. And in their continued use of the Union Jack and 'God Save the King', they shared a common flag and anthem. South Africa's autonomy after the passage of the Statute of Westminster in 1931 may have been clear to a few legally minded South African politicians but, for most South Africans, the Union seemed as firmly a part of the British empire in 1945 as it had been in 1910.[2]

Economically, South Africa was no less firmly tied to Britain. South Africa's most important trading partner, source of external capital, and provider of financial services was Britain. Many of South Africa's leading businesses and banks were headquartered in London. A large proportion of the capital invested in the mines was British. The mines also looked to British capital to fund future development, particularly of the new Free State gold fields. Virtually all of South Africa's gold was marketed through London. South Africa was a member of the sterling area, a multilateral currency and payments system centred on Britain and administered by the Bank of England. Finally, and by no means least significantly in terms of public perceptions, South Africa used the pound as its domestic currency.[3]

Defence ties were also intimate. The last of the British Army's garrison had left South Africa in 1914 but the Royal Navy was still firmly in place at the British-controlled dockyard at Simon's Town, on the Cape peninsula. This naval presence contributed to the widespread South African perception that their country needed Britain's protection from external enemies and that it would be difficult, if not impossible, for South Africa to remain neutral if Britain were involved in major war. The South African armed services seemed, in terms of organisation, training, equipment, uniforms, rank, and insignia, to be branches of the equivalent British services. The free movement of personnel between British and South African units reinforced this impression, as did Smuts's acceptance of the title Field-Marshal – the highest rank in the British Army. Indeed for many South Africans, either black or white, there was no sharp distinction between serving the king in a South African unit or serving him in a British one.[4]

Geopolitically, many South Africans felt that their futures might be significantly affected by developments in neighbouring or more distant British territories in Africa. Many South African nationalists wished to see an early end to British rule there: many white South Africans because they wished to extend their own influence or control, many blacks and others because they wanted to see an end to 'colonial' rule throughout the continent. Some other South

---

[2] Carter, *Politics of inequality*, pp. 13–47.
[3] S. Jones and A. Muller, *The South African economy, 1910–1990* (London, 1992); P. Henshaw, 'Britain, South Africa and the sterling area: gold production, capital investment and agricultural markets, 1931–61', *HJ* 39, 1 (1996), pp. 197–223 (see chapter 6 above).
[4] A. Seegers, *The military and the making of modern South Africa* (London, 1996), pp. 46–79. P. Henshaw, 'Transfer of Simonstown: Afrikaner nationalism, South African strategic dependence and British global power', *Journal of Imperial and Commonwealth History* 20, 3 (1992), pp. 419–44 (see chapter 10 above).

Africans hoped, instead, that Britain would retain control in order to defend white rule or provide a model for multi-racial development.[5]

Culturally, Britain remained an important influence. In 1946, South Africa had a population of 11.4 million of which roughly 21 per cent were white; 8 per cent were 'Coloured' (or mixed race); 3 per cent were of Asian origin (mainly from British India); and 69 per cent were African (or indigenous blacks). Of the whites, roughly 40 per cent were linked by birth or ancestry to Britain. The majority of formally educated South Africans spoke English, even if their first language was Afrikaans or an African language. Many South Africans modelled their daily behaviour, their form of speech, their style of dress, and their social interaction on British patterns. This arose partly from direct interaction between Britain and South Africa, but also from the movement of people between the two countries, and from South African exposure to British radio, print media, and popular entertainments – not least sport. But there were also the indirect and institutionalised influences exerted through schools, churches, missions, clubs, societies, and sport – all of which could have strong British links. Many English-language schools, for example, derived their organisation and syllabus from Britain. Almost all African schooling was still in the hands of churches and missions, the most important of which were British-based with many of the instructors still, in the 1940s, being British-born and trained. As for sport, the British games of rugby and cricket were the centres of attention, partly because of British influence in the schools and news media. Indeed it was the very predominance of British cultural influences which made the adoption of American styles so attractive for those South Africans who wished to reject the white cultural norms that pervaded their country.[6]

The wide-ranging significance of the British connection at the outset of this period helps to explain why so many South Africans should have devoted so much attention either to attacking or defending Britain, and why the British connection should have been so central to competing South African political movements. Support for the British connection had long been central to the attempt to unite English and Afrikaans-speaking South Africans – urban and rural, working and middle class – in one political party backed by the country's main industrial and financial interests. By the 1940s this had taken the shape of Smuts's United Party. Smuts and other backers of the Anglo-Afrikaner national project portrayed the British connection as being essential to South Africa both materially and ideologically. This was why they emphasised the importance both of South Africa's Commonwealth connection and of Britain's military and economic strength. This was also why they emphasised the inclusiveness of the globe-spanning, cosmoplastic British political system – as being sufficiently

---

[5] R. Hyam, *The failure of South African expansion, 1908–1948* (London, 1972), pp. 163–98.
[6] W. Beinart, *Twentieth-century South Africa* (Oxford, 1994, 2001).

open to accommodate Afrikaners and other 'civilised' groups or individuals, but not so open that it overturned white rule in Africa. Opposition to the British connection had been equally central to the Afrikaner nationalist struggle to unite working and middle-class Afrikaners in an ethnically exclusive political movement. These nationalists emphasised the wrongs suffered by Afrikaners at the hands of British 'imperialism': from the devastation wrought by military conquest and the concentration camps to exploitation by British-Jewish capitalists, from attacks on Afrikaans language and culture to denigration at the hands of British liberals. By the 1940s, other nationalists – African, Indian, and 'Coloured' – had also turned increasingly to attacks on the British connection as a way of mobilising mass opposition to white rule, something that they portrayed as springing from and being defended by Britain. For these nationalists, as for Afrikaner nationalists, this was a way of undermining the approach of an older, more conservative leadership who preferred to advance 'national' aspirations within a British imperial framework. Thus South African attitudes towards Britain not only cut across lines of ethnicity, race, and class; they were also central to the competing projects to mobilise political or class alliances along ethnic or multi-ethnic lines.[7]

The conflicting and contradictory attitudes of South Africans towards Britain were evident throughout the years 1945 to 1948, and never more so than in South Africa's response to the British royal family's visit in 1947. For the South African and British governments the royal visit had several purposes, not all of them complementary. One was to boost the prestige of Britain itself, important both for the British government and for a South African government that had staked so much of its reputation on the continuing value of the British connection. To demonstrate Britain's material strength, the royal family arrived in the Royal Navy's most powerful battleship, HMS *Vanguard*. And they were transported within southern Africa in the British-made carriages of the White Train, in British-made automobiles, or in some of the Royal Air Force's latest transport aircraft. Another purpose was to boost South Africa's prestige by emphasising the country's prosperity and hospitality. However, in so doing, the visit could not but draw attention to the comparative austerity of British life which sprang from Britain's post-war financial weakness. A further shared purpose was to strengthen local attachment to the Crown and, by extension, to Britain and the Commonwealth. A more specifically South African purpose was to give recognition, through the presence in the country of the 'King of South Africa', to South Africa's autonomous *status* as Britain's constitutional equal and to South Africa's *stature* as a leading and separate Allied power. A

---

[7] For Afrikaner nationalism and white politics more generally see O'Meara, *Forty lost years*, and Dunbar Moodie, *Rise of Afrikanerdom*. For the broad political scene in the 1940s and 1950s see Carter, *Politics of inequality*, as well as Karis and Carter, *From protest to challenge*, vols. II and III.

more specifically British purpose was to acknowledge the war service of all southern Africans, both black and white. This was applauded by the Springbok Legion – the left-leaning and staunchly multi-racial South African servicemen's organisation. But it was less welcome to the many white South Africans who thought that active black participation in the war was a dangerous mistake. This aspect of the tour was not therefore calculated to strengthen the largely white Anglo-Afrikaner nation-building project. In admiring the royal family, though, most white South Africans could find validation for an Edwardian way of British life – of style and comfort, of masters and servants – to which many of them aspired. The king (a warrior, hunter, and churchman) with his dutiful and devoted wife and daughters (always fashionably and 'femininely' dressed by leading designers) were for many South Africans a model family, one affirming traditional gender roles. The royal family was also admired by some because it confirmed the validity and utility of hereditary rule – something that was particularly attractive to local defenders of rural, hierarchical, and patriarchal African society. The widespread interest of South Africans in the tour suggests that it served these and other purposes to a notable extent. Of course some of this interest would have attended any well-publicised and lavishly organised spectacle. But some of it, at least, must have reflected and generated genuine enthusiasm for the king and the British connection more generally; reflected and generated, too, an affinity on the part of South Africans for many things British – material and social.[8]

This enthusiasm was further demonstrated by the failure of the boycotts advocated by African and Indian nationalist leaders. Leaders of predominantly black nationalist movements such as the African National Congress (ANC) and Indian National Congress had long advocated the abandonment of loyalty to Britain as a strategy to advance black interests. But amongst many blacks there remained a powerful belief that such loyalty might secure support for black political advancement from the British government and from South Africans of British descent. This is at least one of the conclusions to be drawn from the enthusiastic welcome given to the royal visitors by African, Indian, and 'Coloured' South Africans. The ANC boycott proved to be 'almost invisible'.[9] Rural and urban Africans turned out in large numbers to see the royals pass. Alfred Xuma, the ANC's president, could not resist travelling to Zululand to see the king.[10] Nelson Mandela, with his own 'chiefly background', thought that the British monarchy should be respected as a 'long-lasting institution'.[11] If the Bantu Press is to be believed, when the White Train slowed to a stop in

---

[8] For a general description of the royal visit see D. Morrah, *The royal family in Africa* (London, 1947). For the views of the Springbok Legion see *Fighting Talk*, Feb.–May 1947.
[9] Karis and Carter, *Protest to challenge*, vol. II, p. 91.
[10] A. Sampson, *Mandela: the authorised biography* (London, 1999), p. 50.
[11] Sampson, *Mandela*, p. 51.

predominantly African areas, 'almost invariably the melodious sounds of Nkosi Sikelel' iAfrika were sung by the assembled Africans' – a reflection perhaps of the link in African minds between loyalty to the king, this mission hymn, and African advancement.[12] Perhaps the younger radicals amongst the ANC leadership were less in tune with popular African opinion than were such conservative leaders as James Calata, who continually emphasised his debt to his missionary education and Christian upbringing. In 1948 he could still say that 'we love the people of British descent because of what we owe them'.[13] The Natal Indian Congress was possibly even less successful in its attempt to organise a boycott. It encountered not just passive resistance to its boycott proposal but active hostility. Many Indians actively repudiated the Congress leadership on this issue by turning out in large numbers to greet the royal visitors.[14] Even the pro-Congress press described it as a 'tumultuous welcome'.[15] 'Coloured' South Africans were no less enthusiastic. As the white English-language *Johannesburg Star* reported, the 'non-European demonstration of affection for the royal family has exceeded all expectations'.[16] Such demonstrations of enthusiasm by African, Indian, and 'Coloured' South Africans suggest that loyalty to the king was still widely seen as a means of, first, demonstrating their loyalty to South Africa, the king, and the British connection; secondly, proving their entitlement to the rights that white British subjects enjoyed in the country; thirdly, emphasising their rejection of the republicanism and *herrenvolk* mentality of the more extreme Afrikaner nationalists; and, finally, making a plea for British support in their struggle.

Afrikaner nationalists were somewhat more successful in their protests against the tour, no doubt because Britain was more firmly entrenched as the enemy in the history of the Afrikaner *volk*. Hendrik Verwoerd's staunchly republican *Die Transvaler*, alone amongst Afrikaans-language newspapers, studiously ignored the tour. Oswald Pirow's more extreme nationalist newspaper, the *O.B.* (*Ossewa Brandwag*), covered the tour but in an aggressively hostile fashion: 'in the name of this monarchy 27,000 Boer women and children were murdered for the sake of gold and their fatherland'. The *O.B.* concluded that 'for a member of a freedom movement like the Ossewa Brandwag, it is unthinkable that he should pay homage by his presence to what is for our volk a symbol of deepest humiliation'.[17] Malan and his followers in the National Party adopted a more equivocal stance, boycotting some royal events and attending others. But

---

[12] Bantu Press, *Loyalty and royalty: a pictorial record of the royal family's meetings with the Bantu people of South Africa* (Johannesburg, 1947).
[13] Karis and Carter, *Protest to challenge*, vol. II, p. 83.
[14] E. Reddy and F. Meer, *Passive resistance, 1946: a selection of documents* (Durban, 1996), pp. 240–9.
[15] *Leader*, 22 March 1947, quoted in Reddy and Meer, *Passive resistance*, p. 248.
[16] *Johannesburg Star*, 27 Feb. 1947.
[17] *O.B.* 12 Feb. 1947, in South African Jewish Board of Deputies, *Press Digest* [hereafter *PD*].

despite the admonitions of nationalist leaders and newspapers, many Afrikaners were keen participants in tour events. Conscious of this, and conscious also of the need to attract electoral support from Afrikaners and English-speaking whites who were not so antagonistic towards the British connection, the moderate nationalist press gave the tour wide coverage and congratulated Afrikaners on the polite reception they gave the royal visitors.[18]

Overall, then, the South African response to the royal visit suggests that large numbers of South Africans of all races regarded the British connection as having considerable significance in 1947. For some it was a welcome link to a country that was home to living relations or ancestors, their closest material or cultural ally; or to an empowering ideology, though that could be anything from the liberal doctrine of racial equality to the conservative one of white stewardship and trusteeship. For other South Africans the visit emphasised their country's unwelcome ties to a materially and culturally oppressive imperial power, a connection which had to be shaken off before true national freedom could be attained in a republic, whether white or black ruled. Either way, the British connection was not something that could be ignored in terms of domestic politics or in terms of external affairs.

No South African political movement had more success in using the British connection to rally its supporters after 1945 than Afrikaner nationalists. African, Indian, and 'Coloured' nationalist movements all criticised Britain for imperial exploitation. But such criticism lost much of its force as long as the proponents of apartheid were making similar attacks and while support for the cause of multi-racial democracy continued to emanate from a variety of British sources. Afrikaner nationalist success seems surprising in view of the continued strength both materially and culturally of the British connection. But to some degree, it was precisely because of this strength that the attack on it had such resonance amongst Afrikaners. Afrikaners could be readily persuaded that they were victims of British interference or exploitation precisely because British influences remained so pervasive in the 1940s and 1950s. The British connection could again have led South Africa into a distant war as happened in 1914 and 1939. Exploitation at the hands of British-Jewish capital (as characterised and epitomised by the fictional 'Hoggenheimer') seemed a plausible danger while British and Jewish business leaders remained so prominent in South Africa. Unwelcome British interference in South African affairs remained a threat so long as Britain retained control of neighbouring territories, especially the High Commission Territories – the eventual terms of any South African control of which had been provided for in 1910. The dominance of British and English-language culture also loomed over Afrikaners. But, in the 1940s and 1950s the British threat which drew special attention from Afrikaner nationalists was the threat

[18] *PD*, Feb.–April 1947.

posed to white ascendancy by British liberal doctrines of racial equality both within South Africa and throughout Britain's African dependencies.

Although Afrikaner nationalist attacks on the British connection became somewhat guarded by the mid-1940s in the interests of attracting English-speaking voters, the attack was nonetheless an important theme of nationalist political discourse prior to the 1948 election. The National Party repeatedly emphasised Britain's military and economic weakness, and the consequent dangers for South Africa. In parliament it was pointed out that 'It is not England and South Africa who have won this war, but it is Russia'; Britain had been 'practically ruined by the war'.[19] Smuts's government was attacked for insisting that 'the economic interests of South Africa should be made subservient to those of the British empire'.[20] *Die Transvaler* demanded to know if South Africa was being 'sold for the pot of lentil soup of pretended protection' and argued that 'a country as exhausted as Britain is economically can scarcely remain the centre of a great empire'.[21] Finally, the National Party explicitly linked the racial policies of Britain with those of the Smuts government, suggesting that Smuts and his followers were charting a more liberal course out of deference to Britain: Smuts's 'native policy' was 'nothing more than an imitation of the Imperial policy followed by England ... the policy of equality'.[22]

The precise part played in the 1948 election by South African perceptions of Britain is difficult to discern. Smuts's United Party of course insisted that if it were returned to power, South Africa 'would continue to keep the friendship of her trusted friends within the British Commonwealth. A nationalist Government would mean isolation and secession'.[23] The National Party adopted a calculatedly equivocal stance, arguing on the one hand that they would not endanger any of the material benefits thought to accrue from close relations with Britain; but on the other that South Africa was suffering because of British ideological influence in, or material demands on South Africa. The National Party emphasised the threat posed to whites by the United Party's more liberal racial policies, policies which conceded too much to the 'British imperialist policy of equality between black and white'.[24] The National Party also attacked Smuts for devoting too much of his attention to the affairs of the British empire;[25] for allowing too many British migrants to enter South Africa thereby increasing competition for jobs and housing;[26] and for placing undue restrictions on South African consumers in order to assist Britain. The unavailability of white bread

---

[19] South Africa, *House of Assembly Debates* [hereafter H.A. Deb.] (25 Jan. 1946), col. 285 and (28 Jan. 1946), col. 560.
[20] H.A. Deb. (28 Jan. 1946), col. 559.
[21] *Die Transvaler*, 26 April 1947 in *PD* and *Die Transvaler* 28 Feb. 1947 in *Star*.
[22] H.A. Deb. (13 Feb. 1946), col. 1593.   [23] *PD* (May 1948), 125.
[24] *Die Burger*, 2 Feb. 1946 in *PD*.   [25] *Die Transvaler*, 16 Aug. 1946 in *PD*.
[26] *PD*, 22 August 1946.

in South Africa was seen as just such an issue, with the National Party asking why Britons could buy whiter bread than South Africans.[27] Smuts, by posing as the defender of the British connection, may have ensured that he would win the votes of most English-speaking voters; but he may also have lost Afrikaner votes to the extent that the United Party was seen as too subservient to Britain.[28]

II

While the external realities of relations with Britain changed relatively little in the years 1945 to 1951, the place of the British connection in South African domestic politics was transformed by the National Party's unexpected victory in 1948. Black and white opponents of the Smuts government may have shared a dislike for 'British imperialism' and for South Africa's links with it, but there was never any question that African, Indian, or 'Coloured' nationalists might join forces with Afrikaner nationalists. After 1948, though, there was at least a possibility that black and white opponents of National Party rule might use the British connection to unite against the government. One obstacle to such unity was the republican and anti-imperial sentiments of black nationalists themselves, not least the communists among them.[29] The more fundamental obstacle was white fear of black rule. Even so, Afrikaner nationalists themselves helped to keep the possibility of such unity alive by continually characterising the alternatives to apartheid as being inspired or imposed by Britain. Moreover, in the course of implementing apartheid and of strengthening its hold on power, D. F. Malan's government continually attacked various internal aspects of the British connection. This government also criticised, at times, the policies of the British Labour government, particularly its colonial policy, even while Pretoria carefully sustained the substance of external material ties with Britain.

Conveniently for the Malan government, the assertion of independence from Britain frequently provided a cover for advancing policies designed both to entrench Afrikaner ascendancy and to change the ways in which South Africans would perceive the British connection. Stopping, within South Africa, the radio broadcasts of the British Broadcasting Corporation news was one such policy. These broadcasts had long been resented by Afrikaner nationalists as being unwelcome sources of pro-British propaganda: 'This London news service has interfered in internal Union politics in a direct way for years.' Their termination in 1949, and their replacement by South African Broadcasting Corporation

---

[27] *Friend*, 11 May 1948 in *PD*.
[28] For a more detailed discussion of the 1948 election see O'Meara, *Forty lost years*, pp. 20–37. See also K. A. Heard, *General elections in South Africa, 1943–1970* (Oxford, 1974); and Carter, *Politics of inequality*, pp. 36–7.
[29] See, for example, the anti-imperial view expressed by Z. K. Matthews in P. Lewsen (ed.), *Voices of protest: from segregation to apartheid* (Craighall, 1988), pp. 92–6.

news, was justified as being a natural part of the country's national development: 'In what other country would this state of affairs be permitted?'[30] The South African Citizenship Act of 1949 had a similar motivation. Its purpose was to break the link between South African nationality and trans-imperial British nationality. It was justified as being a natural consequence of South Africa's independent sovereign status. Prior to the passage of this Act, any British subject permanently resident in South Africa automatically became a South African national. This made it easy for British immigrants to gain the right to vote. It had also made it easier for non-white British subjects from other parts of the British empire such as India to claim South African nationality. The new Citizenship Act gave the government power to deny citizenship to whom it chose. The Act also extended, from two to five years, the period in which white British immigrants were denied the vote.[31] The government was sufficiently worried about the electoral impact of British immigrants that it also sharply curtailed the flow from Britain by a series of administrative controls. The elimination in 1950 of the Judicial Council of the Privy Council in London as South Africa's highest court of appeal had a similar justification and purpose. This, like other attacks on the British connection, was portrayed as being a natural step in the country's constitutional evolution.[32]

But it was also intended to assist the government's efforts to take away the voting rights of 'Coloured' voters in the Cape (and thereby break their anti-National Party influence) by overturning the entrenched clauses of South Africa's constitution. At first, the Malan government argued that to deny its right to remove 'Coloured' voters from the Cape's common roll by a simple majority was to assert that South Africa was still subservient to a British act of parliament. It also argued throughout its time in office that the non-racial Cape franchise had, from the first, been an unwelcome British imposition and that the need for a two-thirds majority to alter this franchise had only been entrenched in the South Africa Act at Britain's insistence. In 1950 Malan himself, in an argument that would be repeated *ad nauseam* over the next six years, insisted that 'the entrenchment of those sections took place against the will and voice of South Africa . . . it came from the British government'.[33] In such ways, Afrikaner nationalists hoped to encourage white South Africans to shift their attitudes towards Britain: to stop regarding South Africa and South African identity as being inseparable from Britain and from a trans-imperial British identity; to stop thinking of South Africa as being dependent on British approval

---

[30] *Die Transvaler*, 7 July 1948 in *PD*.
[31] Carter, *Politics of inequality*, pp. 51–60. E. A. Walker, *A history of Southern Africa*, 3rd edn (London, 1959), pp. 786–7; S. A. Peberdy, 'Selecting immigrants: nationalism and national identity in South Africa's immigration policies, 1910 to 1998' (unpublished PhD thesis, Queen's University, Kingston, Ontario, 1999), pp. 221–3.
[32] H.A. Deb. (8 Feb. 1950), cols. 916–42.   [33] H.A. Deb. (27 Jan. 1950), col. 251.

or protection; and to start viewing apartheid as being truly South African, its egalitarian alternatives being unwanted British impositions.[34]

To some extent, though, the linking of apartheid both to Afrikaner nationalist advance and to the elimination of the legacies of British colonial rule merely intensified the link some South Africans saw between British influences and opposition to the National Party. Some defenders of 'Coloured' voting rights and of the 1909 constitution, of English-language rights and of the monarchy, coalesced in an uneasy and unstable opposition movement led by war-veterans in the 'Torch Commando'. Defence of the British connection could not, however, provide an effective unifying force for a movement that included so many Afrikaners and others who were not committed to the monarchy. Neither could the defence of British liberal ideals (as expressed in the Cape franchise) provide this when so many white members of the movement did not believe in them.[35] For some English-speaking whites, such as the separatists in Natal, defence of the British connection was merely a vehicle for preserving their local ascendancy.[36] The National Party's own republicanism and nationalism certainly encouraged some of its opponents to use the British connection as a vehicle for resistance; but the defence of this connection was insufficiently universal in its appeal, and its defenders insufficiently united in their ultimate political purpose, to stop the advance of Afrikaner nationalism. The strength of these defenders did, however, encourage the Malan government to move only slowly towards a republic and to insist that it preferred a republic inside the Commonwealth.[37]

South African attitudes towards Britain shifted in response not only to various initiatives of the Malan government, but also to political developments within Britain and the British empire. By the late 1940s many South Africans recognised that British public attitudes, as well as the attitude of the British government under Labour, had become more critical of South African racial policy. This was partly in consequence of a general wartime and post-war shift in British attitudes on colonial and racial questions. After 1948 it was also reflected a public reaction against the racial policies of a party associated during the war with strong anti-British and pro-Fascist sentiments. Sarah Gertrude Millin, a South African commentator predisposed to be sympathetic towards the British connection, noted publicly in 1950 that 'Practically any South African visiting Britain today must surely resent the general attitude abroad towards the Union'; 'It is dramatic and most unjustified.'[38]

---

[34] For a discussion of the introduction of early apartheid legislation see Carter, *Politics of inequality*, pp. 75–118.
[35] T. R. H. Davenport, *South Africa: a modern history*, 3rd edn (London, 1987), p. 365.
[36] P. Thompson, *Natalians first: separatism in South Africa, 1909–1961* (Johannesburg, 1990).
[37] O'Meara, *Forty lost years*, pp. 86–9. For the Torch Commando see Carter, *Politics of inequality*, pp. 302–39.
[38] *Sunday Times*, 17 Dec. 1950 in *PD*.

South African and particularly Afrikaner nationalist attitudes towards the British connection also changed in response to the Commonwealth's transformation in 1949 to accommodate republics. Prior to April 1949 no member could become a republic without automatically excluding itself from the Commonwealth. While this system prevailed, it was impossible for the National Party to advocate a republic without also advocating a complete break with the Commonwealth. Under the new system, actively endorsed by Malan at the 1949 Commonwealth prime ministers' meeting, it suddenly became possible for Afrikaner nationalists to reconcile their republican ideals with the electorally prudent desire to remain in the Commonwealth. The Commonwealth connection therefore ceased to be a focus of attack by the mainstream of the National Party, particularly while Malan remained as prime minister. The Malan government, and to a lesser extent its successors, were thus able to declare their general satisfaction with the Commonwealth even while they strove to displace all symbols of the British connection within South Africa itself.[39]

The colonial policies of the British Labour government brought about further changes in South African attitudes. Unsurprisingly, every move towards Asian and African independence within the British empire lowered British esteem in the eyes of many whites in South Africa while simultaneously raising it, though to a lesser extent, in the eyes of many blacks there. British policy in Africa was a particular concern. Many white South Africans viewed with deepest apprehension both the moves towards black self-government in West Africa, and the tendency to promote black advancement at the expense of white settler control in East and Central Africa. Malan expressed a common white sentiment when he noted in 1950 that the 'British policy of equal rights and equal franchise for all had already yielded Britain bitter fruits in Africa, for example in Nigeria and on the Gold Coast'.[40] White South Africans were more divided in their attitude towards British efforts to unite Nyasaland and Northern and Southern Rhodesia in a Central African Federation. The failure of initial efforts towards this federation in 1951 had the Afrikaner nationalist press 'chuckling gleefully' because they recognised it as an attempt to limit the expansion of Afrikaner influence to the north. Black nationalists in South Africa also opposed this federation but on the grounds that it might entrench and extend settler control. Other South African opponents of the National Party looked more favourably upon the federation, seeing it as a local bastion of British influence, one that might provide an example of a middle way between apartheid and black domination. South African attitudes towards Britain's continued control of the High Commission Territories were similarly mixed. The Malan government began applying pressure for transfer soon after taking office, arguing that British control was an

[39] P. J. Henshaw, 'South Africa's external relations with Britain and the Commonwealth, 1945–1956' (PhD thesis, Cambridge, 1989), pp. 343–64.
[40] South African Press Association (SAPA) report, 15 April 1950 in *PD*.

affront to South Africa's national sovereignty and a source of unwelcome influences amongst the Territories' African populations. But while most white South Africans agreed that the Territories should one day be incorporated in the Union according to the schedule laid out in the South Africa Act, the National Party's opponents nevertheless saw that continued British control could be depicted as being a consequence of the government's own apartheid policies. South Africans watched closely Britain's own policies in the Territories. These were generally criticised by Afrikaner nationalists as being too liberal. There were occasions, though, when most white South Africans applauded British policy. The most notable and dramatic example of this was the reaction to Britain's banishment of Seretse Khama (the designated chief of the Bangwato) from Bechuanaland after he had married a white woman. *Die Burger* (the mouthpiece of the Cape National Party) claimed that '99 out of every 100 whites, not only in South Africa, but also in British Africa ... heartily approve ... of the decision of the British government ... But to judge by the reaction in Britain, it is apparently just as correct to say that the ratio there is exactly the reverse.'[41] *Die Transvaler* noted approvingly that 'although Britain still supports liberalism verbally, in practice it nevertheless gives in to the demands of apartheid'.[42] While leaders of black nationalist movements condemned this British action, the conservative *Bantu World* claimed that 'Neither black nor white desire inter-marriage because they have pride in their own race. That is the hard fact at the present time.'[43] Most whites, though, were still happy to see the end of Labour Party rule in October 1951. The white hope and the black fear was that Winston Churchill's new Conservative government would pursue policies in Africa more sympathetic to white interests throughout the continent.

III

Churchill's victory marked the start of a period of generally increased white and decreased black confidence in Britain as an African power. *Burger* thought that the 'Conservative Party has a more realistic understanding of questions in Africa'.[44] *Transvaler* suggested that the new government would handle African affairs 'more carefully than the Attlee Government had done, with its Creech Joneses, Griffithses, and Dugdales and their blundering tours through Africa'.[45] The *Rand Daily Mail* expected Britain to hold more tightly to its colonial territories and that 'there were not likely to be many more "Gold Coasts" in the near future'.[46] The British government's own representatives in South Africa

---

[41] *Die Burger*, 10 March 1950 in *PD*.   [42] *Die Transvaler*, 10 March 1950 in *PD*.
[43] *Bantu World*, 25 March 1950 in *PD*.   [44] *Die Burger*, 29 Oct. 1951 in *PD*.
[45] *Die Transvaler*, 27 Oct. 1951 in *PD*. A. Creech Jones and J. Griffiths were colonial secretaries; J. Dugdale a minister of state at the CO.
[46] *Rand Daily Mail*, 27 Oct. 1951 in *PD*.

concluded in 1953 that for many white South Africans, the advent of Conservative Party rule had marked the beginning of the reversal of the 'abdication spirit of the Labour Party'.[47]

The Churchill government's apparent determination to hang on to Britain's African possessions tended to impress and encourage white South Africans. But not always. Its refusal to take any step towards transferring the High Commission Territories infuriated Afrikaner nationalists and many other whites but encouraged the government's opponents. Britain's refusal to transfer control of the Simon's Town naval base was no less infuriating, even if this issue was much less widely discussed in public. White South Africans tended, however, to applaud British policy elsewhere in Africa, such as Britain's firm response to the Mau Mau uprising in Kenya, the apparent slowing of constitutional advance in West Africa, and in 1953 the establishment of the Central African Federation despite strong African protest.

The reaction to the Central African Federation showed, though, the complexity of South African attitudes towards Britain at this time. While most whites welcomed the Federation as a sign of Britain's continued commitment to the region, many Afrikaner nationalists saw that the Federation was designed both to exclude Afrikaner influence and to encourage the development of an alternative to apartheid. On the other hand, many South African opponents of apartheid welcomed federation precisely because the successful development of multi-racial 'partnership' there could undermine support for apartheid. The *Natal Mercury* saw that it would have several advantages: 'A strong federal British state in Central Africa would control . . . Asiatic immigration. It would halt the republican ambitions at the Limpopo. It would guide the developing African by a just and generous policy of race relations to a partnership.'[48] Many black nationalists and advocates of majority rule were, for their part, shocked that African opposition to federation had been ignored by the British government. *Fighting Talk* warned that 'the new federation will be a white-dominated state in which the Africans will exchange the rule of Whitehall for the rule of local settlers'. Black nationalists emphasised the similarities rather than the differences between apartheid and 'partnership': 'We cannot welcome the prospect of our neighbours setting out on the same disastrous road we are now travelling.'[49] If nothing else, the Central African Federation showed all South Africans that Britain remained determined to exert a powerful, if not necessarily welcome influence in the region.

British prestige in the eyes of many white South Africans was enhanced in other ways while Churchill was prime minister. At the UN Britain remained South Africa's strongest ally, despite the growth of international criticism both

---

[47] London, PRO, CRO papers, DO 35/5199, A. W. Snelling to H. F. C. Crookshank, 6 Nov. 1953.
[48] *Natal Mercury*, 3 Nov. 1951 in *PD*.   [49] *Fighting Talk*, Dec. 1952.

of apartheid and of South Africa's administration of South-West Africa. The recovery of the British domestic economy and of sterling as an international currency were seen positively by many South Africans and suggested that Britain would retain its value as a market and as a source of goods, services and capital. In the years 1951 to 1955, the British government also demonstrated its commitment to resist communist expansion and defend British interests around the world by maintaining large armed forces. This was also evident in its participation in various multilateral defence pacts with and without the United States, and in the development of its own nuclear weapons. Yet however important these things may have been, the British government itself believed that British policy *in Africa* remained the 'most important factor, in the minds of South Africans, affecting their relations with us'. In January 1954 it was thought that white South Africans had 'a renewed and growing confidence in us and believe that we are not now afraid to govern'.[50]

While Churchill was in office, successive National Party governments continually stimulated the British public reaction against South Africa by their aggressive implementation of apartheid and by the accompanying attacks on British influences within South Africa. These influences were thought not only to underpin the constitutional rights of 'Coloured' voters but also to have a remarkable and continuing influence on African education. The Malan government's introduction of the Bantu Education Act in 1953 was ostensibly designed to 'improve' the schooling of African children by taking control away from churches and mission societies in favour of the Department of Native Affairs. Above all, though, it was intended to eliminate the enormous influence of British-based religious organisations. As one prominent National Party MP emphasised in parliament, the Anglicans, Methodists, and Wesleyans controlled 90 per cent of the schools for Africans.[51] At the time of the Act roughly 900,000 Africans attended more than 5,000 schools run by religious organisations with the assistance of state subsidies. Afrikaner nationalists argued that the liberal ideas promoted through these schools 'were responsible for the growing discontent which now prevailed throughout Africa'. Moreover, much of this dangerous influence was propagated in South Africa by people who were from Britain and who were thus not true South Africans. *Die Transvaler* complained that 'more than 800 of the 1200 or so white mission workers among the Bantu in the Union were not born in South Africa. The Anglican mission workers were almost without exception born and bred in England.'[52] *Volksblad* believed that the 'Anglican viewpoint ... "is pure liberalist politics" '.[53] In less guarded moments the Afrikaner nationalist press itself admitted that 'One of

---

[50] DO 35/4019, no 204, Sir John Le Rougetel to CRO, 28 Dec. 1951; DO 35/5199, A. W. Snelling to Lord Swinton, 11 Jan. 1954.
[51] H.A. Deb. (23 Sept. 1953) 4058, speech by Albert Hertzog.
[52] *Die Transvaler*, 27 Oct. 1954 in *PD*.   [53] *Volksblad*, 25 Oct. 1954 in *PD*.

the main purposes of the Bantu Education Act was to remove the influence of the English Churches from Native Education.'[54]

South African perceptions of Britain were sharpened by the strong reaction of British-based churches to the Malan government's education policies and its plans to remove Africans forcibly from certain areas of Johannesburg. For many whites it confirmed that Britain was a source both of dangerously liberal ideology and of unwelcome and unwarranted criticism. These negative perceptions were only reinforced by black and left-wing South African expressions of admiration for the stand taken by British church men and women. Nelson Mandela for one thought that the Anglicans had been the 'most fearless and consistent critics' of the Bantu Education Act. The pronouncements of Anglicans such as Trevor Huddleston (a British mission worker in Sophiatown), Ambrose Reeves (the Bishop of Johannesburg), and John Collins (a Canon from St Paul's, London), attracted special attention from proponents and opponents of apartheid alike.[55]

One consequence of the Bantu Education Act was the extension of the number, size, and strength of South African private schools where British influences predominated. Rather than either give control of their African schools to the government or close them, some churches and missions chose to operate some of these schools as private educational institutions. This increased the already considerable number of English-language private schools. Many of the private white schools were sustained by the reaction against the increasingly Afrikanerised state system with its 'Christian National' syllabus. More than a few were explicitly intended to reinforce British influence in South Africa, with some modelling themselves directly on British 'public schools'. Later government attacks on university freedom had a similar ideological purpose and provoked a similar response. And the more determined the National Party became to impose its ideology through government schools and through the universities, the more determined the English-language private schools and public universities became to retain their autonomy, British traditions, and liberal ideals.[56]

By the time Churchill finally retired in April 1955, Britain's material strength in relation to South Africa and its prestige in the eyes of white South Africans was probably at its post-war peak, despite the growth of British public criticism of South Africa. The implementation of apartheid and the concomitant nationalist attacks on the British connection were, however, weakening the internal strands of that connection just as Britain's position elsewhere in Africa was about to undergo a radical transformation. Within six years Britain's

---

[54] See *PD* Nov. 1954. See also Carter, *Politics of inequality*, pp. 100–12.
[55] *Rand Daily Mail*, 22 July 1954 in *PD*. Carter, *Politics of inequality*, pp. 90–1.
[56] See P. Randall, *Little England on the veld: the private school system in South Africa* (Johannesburg, 1982) and J. F. Burnet and L. W. Taylor, eds., *Public and Prepatory Schools Year Book* (London, 1948 and 1961).

Enfeebled lion? 291

importance for many South Africans would erode dramatically, a consequence of developments both internal and external to South Africa.

IV

The years 1955 to 1958 witnessed a significant wave of attacks on the symbols of the British connection by the new and more aggressively nationalist government of Johannes Strijdom. These years also saw developments in Africa which undermined white confidence in Britain as an African power. In many ways, though, the material basis of South Africa's links with Britain remained strong. So did the cultural basis of these links. And, as was demonstrated by such events as the British Lions' rugby tour of South Africa in 1955, the British connection remained a key rallying point in South African domestic political confrontations.

After a protracted battle in parliament and in the courts, the Strijdom government finally succeeded in 1956 in removing 'Coloured' voters from the Cape's common roll, thereby eliminating what was portrayed to the end as an unwelcome British imposition. In the debates on the South Africa Act Amendment Bill, Strijdom himself argued that 'this non-European franchise in South Africa was forced upon us from the outside'.[57] The Afrikaner nationalist view was that the British connection with the Cape in the nineteenth century had been 'safeguarded by granting the franchise to as many non-Europeans as possible' in order to prevent 'the power to govern the country from passing into the hands of the Afrikaners by reason of their numerical superiority'. Britain had insisted on entrenching non-white voting rights in the South Africa Act for the same reason. British 'imperialism' had 'always tried to use the non-white political franchise as a means of combating the national ideal'.[58] It was said that 'the struggle which is now drawing to a close . . . has been the characteristic of the political history of our country . . . It was and it is the struggle between South African nationalism and British liberalism.'[59] In this view, then, breaking free from the British connection and the implementation of apartheid were inextricably linked.

Strijdom also eliminated what many Afrikaner nationalists had long regarded as some of the most blatant symbols of subordination to Britain. First, Strijdom's government secured Britain's agreement to transfer the Simon's Town naval base to South African control. On this question many Afrikaners would have shared the view of F. C. Erasmus, the minister of defence: 'what a day it will be when the Union Jack is slowly hauled down and the South African Flag

[57] Jt Sitting Deb. (15 Feb. 1956), col. 34.
[58] Jt Sitting Deb., S. P. le Roux (21 Feb. 1956), col. 467.
[59] Jt Sitting Deb., H. G. Luttig (23 Feb. 1956), cols. 736–7. See also Carter, *Politics of inequality*, pp. 119–44.

slowly hoisted in its place – it will be a day of rejoicing from the Cape to the Limpopo!'[60] Most of the white English-language press tried to put a favourable light on transfer by emphasising the Royal Navy's continued presence at Simon's Town, and rights to use the base in peace and war. But there is no doubt that transfer was seen, and was meant to be seen, as the end of an imperial era. Many white South Africans took heart from those parts of the agreement that seemed to ensure further close defence ties with Britain both in maritime defence and in the defence of Africa. Opponents of apartheid were encouraged by the condition of transfer which stipulated that there should be no racial discrimination amongst the dockyard's multi-racial workforce, though the Cape *Sun* wondered how long Simon's Town could remain 'the only oasis of liberalism, justice and fairplay' once South Africa took control.[61] This stipulation was a small but significant sign to all South Africans that Britain was prepared to stand up for the principle of non-racialism.

The use of the Union Jack as a national flag, and God Save the Queen as a national anthem for South Africa was ended in the same month as the ceremonial transfer of the Simon's Town dockyard. Afrikaner nationalists had long sought to reduce the status of this flag and anthem. But they had been thwarted in the past by the fierce resistance of South African defenders of the British connection. The compromise of flying two national flags and singing two national anthems reflected a deep division of white opinion on this issue. By the mid-1950s, however, no major political party was prepared to take a strong stand in defence of these dualities. By 1957, the majority of white South Africans probably agreed with T. E. Dönges, the minister of the interior, when he said that the use of two flags and two anthems was 'an anachronism – unreasonable and intolerable and humiliating for a sovereign independent country'.[62] Other more minor symbolic changes were also made in 1957. The Crown ceased to be used as a symbol of rank and identification in the South African armed and police services. And the government insisted that school atlases should cease to indicate South Africa 'in the same colour as even the most insignificant British possession'.[63] The lack of substantial opposition to any of these changes indicates that the British connection had definitely lost some of its former potency as a political rallying cry. Although the immediate impact was no doubt small, they each nonetheless played a part in moving white South Africans towards acceptance of the National Party's most prized constitutional goal – the establishment of a republic outside, or if need be, inside the Commonwealth.

South African perceptions of Britain also continued to shift in response to the unfolding of British policy in Africa and to developments within Britain itself.

---

[60] H.A. Deb. (22 March 1956), col. 2994.   [61] *Sun*, 8 July 1955 in *PD*.
[62] *Daily Despatch*, 26 Oct. 1956 in *PD*.   [63] *Die Transvaler*, 16 April 1957 in *PD*.

The progress of the Gold Coast and Nigeria towards independence had, since the 1940s, been feared by whites as much as it had been welcomed by blacks in South Africa. By 1955 it became clear to the South African government that it could do nothing to delay political advance in British West Africa. Strijdom therefore decided to make a virtue of a necessity by declaring that his policy was 'to maintain and foster good relations with other states in Africa, including the Gold Coast and Nigeria'.[64] Hendrik Verwoerd, then the minister of native affairs, could even depict the independence of black African states as confirming the wisdom of apartheid.[65] But, however much white South Africans were encouraged to welcome the Gold Coast's independence, there can be no doubt that most of them were highly alarmed by the prospect of black African states gaining independence and full membership of the Commonwealth. A National Party MP expressed this sense of alarm clearly in 1956: 'when Britain granted political autonomy to the Black man in the Gold Coast ... it took ... a premature step'. This MP, J. C. Greyling, was no less alarmed by developments in East and Central Africa: 'What is going on in Kenya is nothing but a disintegration of the authority of the White man.' He added: 'Step by step that policy of partnership in Rhodesia will bring the White man to the point where the numbers of the Black man will gain the upper hand'; 'It is this multi-racial political idea of the new British liberalism which is swamping Africa in a floodtide and is casting a shadow over the continent.'[66] Though many black nationalists wished for more rapid progress to majority rule throughout British Africa, liberal gradualists continued to be encouraged by the British policy of 'partnership'. Senator William Ballinger, for example, noted that in Northern Rhodesia 'they are following the logic of British colonial policy in bringing on their non-white charges as fast as possible. Southern Rhodesia is doing something similar and is making an advance which makes it almost impossible to have an alliance with those countries.'[67] In the High Commission Territories too, British policy was viewed by Afrikaner nationalists with displeasure. *Die Transvaler* complained that the formation of a tribal advisory council in Bechuanaland was 'a form of Western democratic control which completely departs from tribal tradition'.[68] At the same time, black nationalists could, with some justification, complain that 'in Bechuanaland we have a colour bar as sharp as in the Union'.[69] As was so often the case, British policies in Africa which encouraged one group of South Africans almost invariably discouraged others.

The South African impact of Britain's misadventure at Suez was another matter. By attempting to regain control of the Suez Canal by force of arms, by doing

---

[64] *Die Burger*, 18 Jan. 1956 in *PD*.   [65] Jt Sitting Deb. (23 Feb. 1956), col. 711.
[66] Jt Sitting Deb., J. C. Greyling (20 Feb. 1956), cols. 447–9.
[67] Jt Sitting Deb. (21 Feb. 1956), col. 496.   [68] *Die Transvaler*, 27 Oct. 1956 in *PD*.
[69] *Fighting Talk*, Jan. 1956.

so without consulting its Commonwealth or American allies, and by failing even to achieve its own objectives, Anthony Eden's government provoked a common response from across the entire South African political spectrum. It was a singular achievement. Most South African newspapers criticised some aspect of British policy at Suez. 'We cannot free ourselves of a feeling of great disaster' (*Die Burger*).[70] The ' "British imperial structure" had received its most serious blow since England had to leave India' (*Vaderland*).[71] The South African Indian press was also critical: 'South African people were shocked particularly at the aggressive war waged by Israel, Britain, and France in Egypt' (*Graphic*).[72] In a press statement the African National Congress, the Indian Congress, the Congress of Democrats, the Federation of South African Women, the Coloured People's Organisation, and the Congress of Trade Unions said that the invasion by the Israeli Army and the decision of the British and French governments to re-occupy the Suez Canal 'constituted a serious act of aggression against Egypt'.[73] The English-language white press put the bravest face on the disaster, but it too was critical of Britain's policy, particularly its failure to consult South Africa about the operation. One young United Party MP was quoted in the press as saying that 'Britain's intervention in the Middle East without reference to other Commonwealth countries had come as a shock to those who set great store by Commonwealth solidarity.'[74] Confidence in Britain was shaken by the Suez debacle whether South Africans regarded Britain as a great power ally, a Commonwealth partner, an exponent of principled international conduct, a force for stability in Africa, or as an agent of progressive change there.

Shifts in British attitudes towards South Africa around this time produced a more varied response from South Africans. The strong criticism in evidence at the British Labour Party's annual conference drew particular South African attention in 1956. *Die Burger* warned that 'South Africa will have to consider the possibility of a British government which, unlike the present one, may leave her in the lurch internationally and may even stab her in the back.'[75] The United Party-supporting Cape *Argus* was only slightly more pleased with Labour's attitude, seeing it as an attack not only on apartheid but also on 'partnership': 'Mr. Gaitskell's policy of "one man, one vote" is certainly not going to solve anything at all in multi-racial states.'[76] *Die Transvaler* reminded its readers that British criticism was nothing new: 'for a long time now but especially since the Nationalist Party's assumption of power, Britain has been an impressive sounding board for denigratory propaganda against the white man. In the bosom

[70] 1 Nov. 1956 in *PD*.
[71] As reported by Britain's high commissioner, DO 35/6339, P. Liesching to CRO, 29 Nov. 1956.
[72] 10 Nov. 1956 in *PD*. [73] *Star*, 3 Nov. 1956 in *PD*.
[74] Zac de Beer reported in *Daily News*, 6 Nov. 1956 in *PD*.
[75] *Die Burger*, 5 Oct. 1956 in *PD*. [76] *Argus*, 5 Oct. 1956 in *PD*.

Enfeebled lion?

RIDDLE

Illustration 12.1 The 'enfeebled lion' and the riddle of the Sphinx. After the Suez debacle, a battered British lion, with the features of prime minister Anthony Eden, comments ruefully to the Sphinx with the features of Colonel Abdul Nasser, the Egyptian leader; a bemused Dr Verwoerd looks on. *Source*: *Rand Daily Mail*, January 1957.

of that people lurk the Collinses and Huddlestons, the Labour Party with its Blackpool resolutions.'[77] *Argus* also saw that Labour's position was undermining the position of the white defenders of the British connection: 'the British Labour Party should find some satisfaction in the knowledge that Nationalists

---

[77] *Die Transvaler*, 21 Aug. 1956 in *PD*.

in South Africa look forward to their advent to power as the time when republicanism will bloom'.[78] Black nationalists welcomed Labour's attitude because it forced white South Africans to recognise how unpopular any policy of white supremacy had become internationally: 'White South Africa has for the past 50 years allowed itself to turn away from the truth. In their selfishness they have closed their eyes to reality and clung to an ideology that has become very unpopular in the free world.'[79] White South Africans may have resented British criticism and feared a Labour victory. But they still believed that a significant body of British opinion supported white rule throughout the areas of British settlement in Africa, South Africa included.

Such belief was grounded in part on the strength of cultural links, strength that was evident in the South African response to the British Lions' rugby tour against the Springboks. The tour by a team of the best rugby players from England, Scotland, Ireland, and Wales was a major event in South Africa in 1955. As was to be expected, rugby was popular amongst South Africans of British descent. It was also popular amongst many black South Africans, no doubt as a consequence of British influence in South African schools. Most surprising was the popularity of rugby amongst Afrikaners. Ironically, they had come to regard this, the quintessential game of the English public school, as their 'national' sport. Indeed it was a source of considerable Afrikaner nationalist pride that Afrikaners should predominate amongst the Springboks' players and coaches. The rough, aggressive, and 'masculine' nature of the game appealed to many South Africans. In 1955, as they would be until the 1990s, the Springboks were all white, something that both reflected and affirmed white political supremacy, especially when the Springboks were victorious. As a mixture of English and Afrikaans speakers, the Springboks were for the supporters of the Anglo-Afrikaner national ideal a symbol of and a metaphor for the great nation-building experiment launched by Britain under the guidance of Louis Botha and Jan Smuts. Afrikaner nationalists, on the other hand, openly looked forward to the day when the Springboks might be exclusively Afrikaner. For many black South Africans the composition of the Springboks was no less symbolic. But it was a symbol of oppression, a demonstration of the inequity of South African society in which privileges and opportunities were bestowed on the basis of race, not talent. Not surprisingly, then, the Lions' tour became an occasion for South Africans to express widely divergent attitudes both about their own country and about Britain.[80]

---

[78] *Argus*, 5 Oct. 1956 in *PD*.   [79] *Sun*, 27 July 1956 in *PD*.
[80] D. R. Black and J. Nauright, *Rugby and the South African nation: sport, culture, politics and power in the old and new South Africas* (Manchester, 1998); J. Nauright, *Sport, culture and identities in South Africa* (London, 1997); A. Grundlingh, A. Odendaal, and B. Spies, *Beyond the tryline: rugby and South African society* (Johannesburg, 1995).

The tour was charged with a high degree of political significance from the start. In part, perhaps, this was because the British connection had been so central to South African political debates in the 1950s. The Strijdom government itself magnified this significance by the attendance at the first test of the prime minister and nearly all the Cabinet. For these men it was a chance to see the sporting pride of the *volk* in action. It was also a chance to bask in the reflected glory of a tour which disproved the claim that apartheid was forcing South Africa into international isolation. But the most notable political event of the tour was the vociferous support given to the Lions by black South Africans in Johannesburg, Cape Town, Durban, and Port Elizabeth. The Johannesburg test was apparently the first time that a significant number of South Africans supported a touring side against the Springboks. But the even larger support given to the Lions by 'Coloured' supporters in Cape Town attracted the most attention of the public and press. Many white South Africans complained about this unpatriotic behaviour. In response, one Cape newspaper pointed out that 'White South Africans cannot expect continually to ram its apartheid policy down the throats of non-Europeans without the latter showing some resentment towards it.'[81] Black and particularly 'Coloured' support of the Lions was hardly surprising when the Strijdom government was at that very time engaged in the final assault on 'Coloured' voting rights. Such support continued in Durban and Port Elizabeth. Bloemfontein city council prevented it by banning blacks altogether from the match there. Some black South Africans would have supported any opponent of the Springboks in the 1950s. *Imvo Zabantsundu* welcomed the victory of the New Zealand All Blacks over the Springboks in 1956, seeing it as proof that 'Selecting players according to their merits and not their colour is the secret of success of those countries who have a cosmopolitan population.'[82] But a measure, at least, of support for the Lions would have been given because Britain was still viewed as being the home of liberal values continually criticised and attacked by the apartheid regime.

The Lions tour was another one of those South African situations, like the royal visit, when expressions of opinion about Britain had more to do with the desire of South Africans to make a statement about their own country than about Britain itself. A cheer for the Springboks could imply support for an exclusive Afrikaner or for a more inclusive Anglo-Afrikaner nationalism. A shout for the Lions could signify support for British liberal values or merely opposition to white or Afrikaner rule in South Africa. Attendance at a match could be an opportunity to find affirmation for sporting values of fair play, or for the patriarchal and racist norms which pervaded the game. At any event, though, the tour's reception demonstrated that the British connection still mattered enormously to

---

[81] *Sun*, 2 Sept. 1955 in *PD*.   [82] 15 Sept. 1956 in *PD*.

many South Africans culturally or politically, positively or negatively. Finally, whether South Africans viewed Britain as an old ally or old enemy, the tour was, like so many other things in South Africa, a contest contained within a framework of largely British inspiration.

V

The most important shift in post-war South African perceptions of Britain began in the years 1958 to 1961. While the underlying cultural significance of the British connection changed relatively little in this period, key symbolic links with Britain were transformed. Moreover, British criticism of apartheid intensified in this period while Britain's external standing as an African power entered into a phase of renewed decline. It would be a mistake, though, to imagine that Britain was seen merely as an opponent of white rule, or that it had ceased to matter as an African power, by the time that Harold Macmillan delivered his 'wind of change' warning to South Africa in February 1960. Despite continual Afrikaner nationalist criticism of post-war British policy in Africa as being too liberal and too willing to concede to the demands of African nationalism, most South Africans (Afrikaners included) did not believe at the end of the 1950s that Britain's complete withdrawal from direct rule in Africa was imminent. Faced with the alternative of majority-rule throughout the rest of Africa, Afrikaner nationalists even begrudgingly welcomed Britain's continued presence as an African power. But, such sentiments merely intensified the impact of Macmillan's message, particularly on the many white South Africans who had hitherto believed that a British Conservative government would, in the final resort, defend white rule in southern and Central Africa.

As Macmillan approached South Africa on his 'wind of change' tour of the continent, the Afrikaner nationalist press reminded its readers that 'Britain was a loyal friend in the U.N., who repeatedly did not shrink from embarrassment in order to stand by us';[83] that 'Macmillan is the embodiment of the best in his party . . . He will bring to Africa . . . clear-headedness about its problems and people';[84] and that both Britain and South Africa were 'striving mightily . . . to make a contribution to the maintenance of the Western white way of life'.[85] The white English-language press was similarly complimentary and was encouraged by Macmillan's statement of policy when he was in the Central African Federation: it welcomed his suggestion that 'the protecting hand of Britain' would continue to support 'partnership' there.[86] Most of the white press also downplayed the significance of the planned boycott of South African goods by British consumers: 'All the boycott talk is little more than chaff in the wind even if the British Labour Party and the British Trades Union

[83] *Dagbreek en Songdagnuus*, 10 Jan. 1960 in *PD*.   [84] *Volksblad*, 5 Jan. 1960 in *PD*.
[85] *Vaderland*, 27 Jan. 1960 in *PD*.   [86] *Johannesburg Star*, 20 Jan. 1960 in *PD*.

Congress is behind it.'[87] The *Rand Daily Mail*, noting the lack of enthusiasm for the boycott in Britain, declared that 'the British people remain sensible and friendly'.[88] Liberals and black nationalists, on the other hand, supported the British boycott and feared that Macmillan's visit would (like an earlier one by Field-Marshal Montgomery) merely validate and consolidate the National Party's hold on power. The leaders of the South African Liberal Party, the ANC, and the South African Indian Congress all appealed to Macmillan not to support apartheid when he visited South Africa, no doubt because they expected him to continue his government's generally supportive stance.[89]

It was therefore with surprise or profound shock that many white South Africans received Macmillan's warning that Britain could not continue to support South Africa 'without being false to our own deep convictions about the political destinies of free men'. *Die Burger* took the lead 'in an almost hysterical Nationalist reaction to the speech'. It was the 'end of an illusion . . . that Pax Britannica still forms a wall between us and the outside world', 'evidence that everywhere in Africa the West was abandoning the White man for its own selfish interests'.[90] And: 'White South Africa is now standing back to the wall . . . it can count on no support from outside.'[91] The English-language, and traditionally United Party-supporting Cape *Argus* noted that there was 'no longer any room for doubt about what Britain's Africa policy really is. She takes the side of African nationalism and African self-government.'[92] Reactions in South Africa's parliament ranged 'from the fantastic to the funereal'. Some believed that 'the death knell of White rule in southern Africa is now being sounded. Others assert that Macmillan's address will harden lukewarm apartheid adherents, particularly among the English-speaking.'[93] Proponents of democratic reform were overjoyed at Macmillan's speech, seeing it as an endorsement of their views and as having 'killed, once and for all, the comfortable Nationalist theory that criticism of South Africa's policies came only from Left wing cranks and an irresponsible press, while the sensible majority of Britons were really on our side'.[94] The black press and black nationalists were also encouraged by Macmillan's 'morale booster': 'Africans cannot but be heartened by his declaration on racialism'.[95] Mandela called it 'a terrific speech' and never forgot Macmillan's courage in delivering it.[96]

---

[87] *Oosterlig*, 20 Jan. 1960 in *PD*.   [88] 7 Jan. 1960 in *PD*.
[89] *Rand Daily Mail*, 7 Jan. 1960 in *PD*.
[90] Reported in *Forum*, March 1960 and *PD*, 10 Feb. 1960. The CRO kept a fat file of press-cuttings about the Cape Town speech: DO 35/10570.
[91] *Volksblad*, 10 Feb. 1960 in *PD*.   [92] *Argus*, 4 Feb. 1960 in *PD*.
[93] *Argus*, 12 Feb. 1960 in *PD*.   [94] *Cape Times* in *PD*, 12 Feb. 1960 and *Forum*, March 1960.
[95] *Imvo Zabantsundu*, 20 Feb. 1960 in *PD*.
[96] Sampson, *Mandela*, p. 129. Mandela recalled his admiration for the speech, both in September 1994 and July 1996 in London. For a fuller treatment of Macmillan's visit see R. Hyam, 'The parting of the ways: Britain and South Africa's departure from the Commonwealth, 1951–1961', *Journal of Imperial and Commonwealth History* 26, 2 (1998), pp. 161–3 (see chapter 11 above).

In these circumstances, the remarkable thing about the October 1960 referendum for a republic is not that the National Party should have won. It is that they should so very nearly have lost. In the end, despite lowering the voting age to eighteen, denying all non-whites the vote, allowing whites in South-West Africa to vote, and calling out the lame and the sick, the republic was secured by a slim margin – only 52 per cent of the votes cast. The result, however, was not simply a consequence of Britain's declining external standing in the eyes of white South Africans. Even after the 'wind of change' speech, most white South Africans still believed that Britain remained their best international friend. Verwoerd's government pushed ahead with its attack on the internal dimensions of South Africa's British connection, despite the strength of Britain's external standing, not because of its weakness. The attack was propelled by the National Party's desire to consolidate its hold on power. It wished not only to realise its long-cherished republican vision. It also wished to destroy, once and for all, the utility of the British connection as a rallying-cry for its political opponents. But it would do all this under the cover of the argument that external relations with Britain would be unaffected by constitutional change in South Africa.

The British connection was central to the referendum, and not merely in terms of the common link with the Crown. Much debated was the threat posed by republican status to South Africa's continued membership of the Commonwealth and to the material benefits which seemed to depend on that membership. This was the 'question that mattered most'.[97] Opponents of the republic pointed out the dangers. Declaration of a republic might lead to the country's exclusion from the Commonwealth. This would put various things at risk: close defence relations with Britain, preferential access to Britain as a customer for South African agricultural products and as a source of capital, together with useful relations with South Africa's closest international partner.[98] The anti-republicans were a diverse group, ranging from the racially and politically conservative United Party to the more liberal Progressive Party, and from English-speaking mining and business interests to English and Afrikaans-speaking agricultural exporters. Even the leading black nationalist organisations campaigned against the republic. The nature of this alliance merely confirmed the fear of some Afrikaner nationalists that they were once again facing the old threat posed by British-linked financial interests operating in conjunction with the forces of liberalism. In this view opposition to the republic was part of the effort to dislodge Afrikaner nationalists from power by any means possible, including

---

[97] *Forum*, July 1960.
[98] See the special edition of *Optima*, the Anglo-American Corporation's mouthpiece, Sept. 1960.

the abandonment of white rule.[99] The pro-republican campaign, for its part, emphasised the value of the republic in promoting white unity. One of the National Party's more prominent slogans was 'Vote Yes for a White Republic'. But, amongst Afrikaans speakers, the National Party also tried to whip up narrower nationalist sentiment by linking their campaign to the old anti-British struggle. Platteland posters showed women in Voortrekker costumes and Boer commandos on rearing horses, with an injunction to 'Saddle-up'.[100] Generally, though, the republicans downplayed the anti-British aspects of the republic in the interests of undermining their opponents. The National Party insisted (astutely but disingenuously) that it was anxious to keep the republic inside the Commonwealth and that relations with Britain might even improve after white South Africans resolved their constitutional differences. It was nevertheless clear to many South Africans that the struggle for the republic was a showdown between two rival political and racial ideologies: what Afrikaner nationalists insisted were the truly South African policies of white supremacy, segregation, and republicanism on the one hand, as against the foreign, British-inspired policies of liberalism, equality, and monarchism on the other.[101]

Black South African opinion about the republic was contradictory. Most black nationalist leaders had long espoused republican ideals of their own. 'What the African wants', declared the *Star*, 'is a truly non-racial democratic republic.'[102] It was therefore difficult to oppose Verwoerd's republic except as a way of delivering the apartheid regime a political setback. *Imvo Zabantsundu* thought it was 'doubtful if Africans had any great interest in the matter'.[103] Even so, a considerable number of black South Africans did oppose the republic through demonstrations prior to the referendum, a continuation perhaps of the sentiments that lay behind black support of the royal tour. Black attitudes towards the republic were recorded by the press as being 'generally hostile' in the months before the referendum.[104] Black nationalists encouraged this opposition, with leaders such as 'Monty' Naicker declaring that 'More oppressive rule must be expected under the heavy boot of republicanism.'[105] *Fighting Talk* insisted that there is only one answer to a Verwoerd republic: 'No to Verwoerd rule – Yes to a Multi-Racial Democracy.'[106] The ANC's attempt to use widespread white and black South African opposition to the republic to advance the cause of

---

[99] Cape Town, Cape Archives, Dönges papers, W. C. du Plessis to T. E. Dönges, 12 April 1960. Du Plessis believed that the fight for a referendum was a 'battle of the bulls' and that the anti-republicans were 'not simply emotional monarchists – their opinions are precisely the same as those that caused the Anglo-Boer War and are strongly based on economic and financial considerations'.
[100] *Fighting Talk*, Oct. 1960.   [101] O'Meara, *Forty lost years*, pp. 105–6.
[102] 25 Jan. 1960 in *PD*.   [103] *Imvo Zabantsundu*, 22 Oct. 1960 in *PD*.   [104] *PD*, July 1960.
[105] *Natal Daily News*, 22 Jan. 1960 in *PD*.   [106] *Fighting Talk*, Oct. 1960.

non-racial democracy would, however, be confounded by the Congress's own contradictory stance on the monarchy and Commonwealth membership.

Black nationalists, despite their generally favourable disposition towards Commonwealth membership, aggressively campaigned for South Africa's exclusion from the association. Operating together as the 'United Front', exiled leaders of the ANC, Pan-Africanist Congress (PAC), South African Indian Congress, and Coloured People's Organisation worked with British anti-apartheid groups in lobbying other Commonwealth governments to refuse South Africa's application to retain its membership as a republic. Such lobbying may well have encouraged the strong stand against apartheid taken by some Commonwealth prime ministers in March 1961. Whatever its causes, this stand impelled Verwoerd to withdraw from the Commonwealth rather than compromise his apartheid principles. *Drum* spoke for many black nationalists when it hailed Verwoerd's walkout as the 'United Front's Biggest Victory'.[107]

While many white South Africans were shocked and dismayed by the walkout, Afrikaner nationalists were jubilant that complete independence had been thrust upon the country.[108] Verwoerd declared, upon returning to a hero's welcome in Cape Town, that 'What happened is nothing short of a miracle. So many nations have had to get their complete freedom only by armed struggle.'[109] *Kerkblad* called it 'a dispensation from God'.[110] The Afrikaner nationalist press placed the blame for South Africa's exclusion on the sanctimonious and hypocritical stand of other Commonwealth governments. It also argued that this move proved that the Commonwealth had lost its utility and that relations with Britain would actually be better if South Africa were outside the association. For some Afrikaner nationalists, though, it was a sign of Britain's decline, South Africa's exit being the 'completion of a process which started when Britain emerged from the war as a "second-rate power"'.[111] And it was a sign, too, of the South African government's strength in resisting external pressure to embrace 'the British Africa policy of increasing political rights for non-whites'.[112] The white opposition press noted the 'shock, anger and disbelief' of the defenders of the British connection and expressed fears about the material implications of South Africa's exit, including 'speculation about whether Springboks can play official test matches in future'.[113] Harry Oppenheimer, the chairman of the economically dominant Anglo-American Corporation, called Verwoerd's withdrawal a 'grave, unmitigated misfortune to South Africa – economically, politically and militarily'.[114] South Africa's exit forced many English-speaking whites to reassess their commitment to the Commonwealth. The *Daily Despatch* noted

---

[107] *Drum*, April 1960. [108] *Cape Times*, 16 March 1961.
[109] *Cape Times*, 21 March 1961. [110] *Kerkblad*, 29 March 1961 in *PD*.
[111] *Die Transvaler* reported in *Cape Times*, 16 March 1961.
[112] *Volksblad*, 23 March 1961 in *PD*. [113] *Cape Times*, 16 March 1960.
[114] *Cape Times*, 27 March 1961.

that the 'real tragedy of the position that has developed was that the British Commonwealth of Nations is no longer British'.[115] 'What has tempered some of the genuine anger and regret in many quarters', noted the *Star*, 'is the recognition that Commonwealth membership is umbilically tied to a partial shedding of the colour bar.'[116] Thus while the elimination of the monarchy and the end of the Commonwealth connection deeply divided many white South Africans, it also helped to stimulate a significant reassessment of the British connection, particularly on the part of English-speaking whites.

Undeterred by white reassessments of the Commonwealth, the ANC tried to use the still widespread white disappointment at the loss of South Africa's British connections as a springboard for a truly democratic constitutional transformation. The ANC called for a 'National Convention' to 'decide a new Non-Racial Democratic Constitution' before the actual establishment of a republic (and the country's consequent exclusion from the Commonwealth) on 31 May 1961.[117] It also called for a three-day 'Stay-at-Home' in protest against the republic. And though there was no explicit attempt to draw on South African attachment to the British connection, this attachment may nevertheless have played a small part in encouraging support for the 'Stay-at-Home'. Black support for the protest fell short of the ANC's expectations. But it did have some success despite mass arrests, the 'continuous show of strength by the Police and Army', the banning of virtually all gatherings, a government news campaign to deny its effectiveness, and PAC calls to ignore this 'white man's issue'.[118] In Johannesburg, Durban, and Port Elizabeth up to 50 per cent of black workers stayed away from work. But while the ANC was certainly right in thinking that a significant number of South Africans of all races opposed the republic, it was probably wrong in thinking that the defence of the British and Commonwealth connection would in 1961 rally significant white forces to the cause of democratic transformation. The motives of diverse groups of South Africans in defending this connection were simply too different and too contradictory, especially when so many white supporters of the British connection were committed to white rule and when so many black nationalists were avowedly republican and had campaigned for South Africa's exclusion from the Commonwealth.[119]

The extent of white opposition to the republic at the time of the referendum, and the absence of more widespread white opposition to the republic's actual establishment seven months later, together suggest that the result of the referendum was less the consequence of a major shift in South African attitudes towards Britain than the cause of one. The loss of the monarchy, the subsequent exit from the Commonwealth, and the gradual revelation that there would be

---

[115] *Daily Despatch*, 18 March 1960 in *PD*.   [116] *Johannesburg Star*, 23 March 1961 in *PD*.
[117] Johannesburg, Wm Cullin Library, South African Institute for Race Relations papers, 13.1.2, 'Prepare for Action at the End of May!'
[118] *Drum*, July 1961.   [119] Sampson, *Mandela*, pp. 146–8.

few consequent material changes to relations with Britain seem to have done much to alter the way white South Africans viewed Britain. So did various actions of the British government itself after Verwoerd's withdrawal. First, Britain almost immediately changed its stance at the UN, joining for the first time the large majority there in openly criticising apartheid and South Africa's administration of South-West Africa.[120] Britain's condemnation of apartheid at the UN in April 1961 made 'a particularly deep impression' in South Africa.[121] The leader of the United Party called Britain's vote 'a shock'.[122] *Die Burger* wrote of the 'debacle' at the UN, of Verwoerd's 'diplomatic Sharpevilles', and of Britain 'abandoning one of its most loyal and strategic allies'.[123] Later in 1961 Britain applied to gain entry into the European Common Market, something which stunned white South Africans with British trading or financial interests. Furthermore, by 1962 it was apparent that British support for 'partnership', as opposed to black majority rule, in Central Africa was largely finished. Indeed white South African attitudes towards Britain and the Commonwealth had shifted so far by July 1962 that Harry Oppenheimer could tell a white Rhodesian audience that the Commonwealth was dead and that Rhodesians should look instead to Europe. From this *Die Burger* concluded that the Commonwealth 'can be written off in everything but name, even by people who cannot be accused of being anti-British'.[124] This generally negative attitude towards Britain and the Commonwealth was further reinforced by Britain's continued retreat from African colonial rule, by the dissolution of the Central African Federation in 1963, by Labour's electoral victory in Britain in October 1964; and by the start of the serious confrontation with settler-ruled Rhodesia in 1965. Between 1960 and 1965, then, white South African attitudes towards Britain undoubtedly changed more substantially than in all the years from 1945 to 1959. This generally negative white South African attitude towards the Commonwealth and towards the British political Left would persist well into the 1990s; but so too would an admiration (grudging or otherwise) for certain British values and institutions – especially sport.

Partially but never fully compensating for Britain's decline in the eyes of many white South Africans, was its rise in the eyes of apartheid's South African opponents. Regardless of British government policy, Britain was always a key centre of external resistance to apartheid. Many political, union, church and other civic organisations there threw their weight behind the struggle, encouraged by and giving support to an increasingly important South African exile community. Nelson Mandela, for one, admired Britain more than ever by the

---

[120] P. J. Henshaw, 'Britain and South Africa at the United Nations: "South West Africa", "treatment of Indians" and "race conflict", 1946–1961', *South African Historical Journal* 31 (1994), pp. 99–100 (see chapter 7 above).
[121] *PD*, 6 April 1961.   [122] *Johannesburg Star*, 6 April 1961 in *PD*.
[123] 7 May 1961 in *PD*, and *Forum*, May 1961.   [124] Reported in *Cape Times*, 6 July 1962.

1960s. He was full of praise for Britain in his Rivonia trial statement in 1964: 'in London I was received with great sympathy by political leaders... I have the greatest respect for British political institutions and for the country's system of justice.'[125] For the opponents of apartheid, though, Britain's standing declined as successive British governments revealed their unwillingness to take more aggressive action to end white domination either in South Africa or Rhodesia. The nadir was the period of Margaret Thatcher's leadership. This, while seeing the emergence of a democratic Zimbabwe, was throughout a time of the most reactionary and retrograde British policy in southern Africa since the end of the Second World War. And it made Mandela's highly favourable attitude towards Britain after he emerged in 1990 from twenty-seven years in prison seem all the more remarkable and magnanimous. Speaking to a South African newspaper in April 1993 Mandela explained that 'I have not discarded the influence which Britain and British history and culture have exercised on us... You must remember I was brought up in a British school and at the time Britain was the home of everything that was best in the world.'[126]

VI

At the start of the twenty-first century Britain seems in many ways to matter little to South Africans compared with its significance during the years 1945 to 1961. The decline of Britain's military strength, South Africa's detachment from any lingering elements of the imperial defence system, and the end of the Cold War mean that few South Africans today regard British defence ties as having much consequence. Indeed, few South Africans can now imagine why their ancestors would ever have wished to fight at Britain's side in two world wars. Economically too, Britain has become less important, partly as a consequence of its relative decline, but also because British economic policy has become subject to the demands of its protectionist European partners. Britain's formal geopolitical significance had already waned dramatically by the 1960s and completely by 1980, even if it retained some residual influence in southern Africa through the Commonwealth. Partly as a consequence of these material changes, the significance of British opinions and policies has also declined in South Africa. And, hardly less important in this regard has been the virtual disappearance of the British connection as a vehicle for ethnic or political mobilisation within South Africa, even if die-hard Afrikaner nationalists still invoked the Great Trek and the Boer War concentration camps to rally the *volk* in the 1990s.

---

[125] Mandela's trial statement, 20 April 1964, in Karis and Carter, *From protest to challenge*, vol. III, pp. 781–90.
[126] *Argus*, 30 April 1993.

Still, it would be wrong to see the transformation of South African perceptions of Britain as being the consequence of a long, steady post-war British decline. As this chapter has tried to show, Britain and the British connection remained remarkably important for many South Africans even in 1960. And this was despite the long Afrikaner nationalist assault on the internal dimensions of the British connection, an assault that had removed all overt symbols of that connection (including the elimination of the pound in favour of the Rand as the country's currency) by 1961. Material links were still remarkably strong at the beginning of the 1960s, partly and ironically as a result of the National Party government's own defence and economic policies; and a result, also, of the international isolation engendered by apartheid itself. Paradoxically, the white South African desire to preserve close external relations with Britain increased in the 1950s even as British public criticism of apartheid intensified and as South African republican sentiment grew. Part of the explanation lies in the fact that the movement towards a republic and a more separate national identity had an internal dynamic of its own. This dynamic was largely independent of the material realities of links with Britain, and it was energised by the National Party's gradual elimination of the symbols of colonial subordination. A further part of the explanation lies in the fact that while Britain was home to some of apartheid's harshest critics (most notably the opposition Labour Party and its supporters), it was also home to some of the strongest international supporters of white interests in Africa. The more significant transformation of South African attitudes took place after 1960, not before.

For a variety of interconnected internal and external reasons, British prestige in many white eyes plummeted in the 1960s and never really recovered. It rose at the same time in the eyes of many apartheid opponents, though only in partial compensation. Still, even the casual observer would recognise that Britain remains disproportionately significant in the thinking and behaviour of South Africans today. This undoubtedly has less to do with obvious or direct material links, than with Britain's still-powerful cultural legacy. British influences still permeate South African society through shared language and literature, education and religion, British goods and name-brand products, sport and music, political and bureaucratic structures, historical experience, and through shared identities shaped by race, class, and gender. Britain will never again have the significance it held in South Africa throughout the 1950s. But many South Africans will continue to look to and be influenced by Britain, even if those influences sometimes owe more to Edwardian England than to New Labour's 'Cool Britannia'.

13 Springbok reviled: some British reactions to apartheid, 1948–1994

During the years 1948 to 1994, the British reaction against apartheid did not simply grow steadily in response to a gradually increasing consciousness of apartheid's repugnant realities. Nor was British opinion always neatly divided between antagonism towards apartheid by a progressive Left, and tolerance of apartheid by a racist Right. Indeed, the most striking things about the pattern of British attitudes towards apartheid are the intensity of British criticism of apartheid by both the Right and the Left during the 1950s and early 1960s; the speed with which the unity of British opinion dissolved in the late 1960s and early 1970s; and the extent to which British attitudes had intensified and diverged by the 1980s. Overall, the pattern of the British public reaction against apartheid was one of rise, ebb, and resurgence.

To a certain extent, the pattern of British attitudes does correspond to the pattern of repression and resistance in South Africa, with the periods of greatest unrest – first in the 1950s and early 1960s, and then in the late 1970s and 1980s – stimulating the growth of British criticism. Likewise, the relative quiescence of the years 1962 to 1975 coincided with British tolerance or indifference. Yet this does not fully explain either the strength and unity of the early British response to apartheid, or the deep divisions in British opinion that emerged subsequently. A further important part of the explanation must be sought in the wider transformation of the South African, British, and international context. Starting in the 1960s, British attitudes towards apartheid changed as apartheid came to be seen as an entrenched policy broadly supported by white South Africa, rather than as a temporary aberration promoted principally by anti-British Afrikaner nationalists. These attitudes changed, at the same time, in response both to Britain's retreat from empire and disillusionment with the Commonwealth, as well as to the rise of racial tensions within Britain itself. Attitudes changed further as South Africa's stability and prosperity contrasted more sharply with the disorder and poverty of many newly independent African states. Beginning in

This chapter was presented in 2002 at the 'British World' conference in Cape Town and at the Canadian Association of African Studies conference in Toronto. Peter Henshaw would like to thank the participants in both conferences for their comments.

the mid-1960s, these changes stirred the development of new-found tolerance of apartheid by the British Right. Other sections of British opinion, meanwhile, became more determined than ever to take positive action against apartheid. The result was the emergence of deeply divided British attitudes towards South Africa, a divide which would be exacerbated by British party politics, and which would persist into the 1990s. There would be no simple evolution of the Springbok from being the symbol of a respected part of the British empire, to being the symbol of oppression in a foreign land.

I

What is surprising about the 1940s or 1950s is not the division of British public opinion on apartheid but its remarkable unity. Indeed, at no stage in these decades was there significant British public sympathy for apartheid. The character of South African race relations may not have been well known in Britain in the 1940s, but it was understood that apartheid was the racial doctrine of Jan Smuts's political foes, and that Smuts had been a great wartime leader, friend of Britain, and proponent of the Commonwealth. It was also understood that his foes were Afrikaner nationalists who had openly sympathised with Nazi Germany during the Second World War, and who had made no secret of their antipathy towards South Africa's British links – its British institutions and substantial 'British' population,[1] as well as its external ties to Britain. Much of what the British public knew about apartheid in the early years of its implementation was learned from the broad range of sources in Britain which were fundamentally hostile to the Nationalist regime in South Africa – sources from across the full spectrum of political opinion and including many religious bodies in Britain, and a long tradition of liberal and radical sympathy for black South Africans. The same cultural and historical connections which made South Africa seem part of a greater Britain overseas, also helped to inform Britain of the injustices and iniquities of apartheid. Many of South Africa's harshest and most effective critics in Britain were British emigrants to, or returnees from South Africa, English-speaking South Africans resident in Britain, or members of British churches and missions. In the 1940s and 1950s, British press reports steadily reinforced the impression that apartheid was an ideology antithetical to British values and ideals, one that threatened to be a thoroughly disruptive force in the British empire and Commonwealth.[2]

---

[1] In 1946, South Africa's total population was about 11.4 million, of which 2.3 million were white, including roughly 1 million English-speaking whites. Most of this last group were of British origin.

[2] For alternative accounts of British attitudes towards apartheid in this period see: H. Griffiths, 'A study of British opinion on the problems and policies of the Union of South Africa from the end of the Second World War until South Africa's withdrawal from the Commonwealth'

The 1948 election which brought the Nationalists to power attracted an unusual degree of attention in Britain, even before the shocking news of Smuts's fall was revealed. It was widely reported that the National Party posed a real threat to Smuts's hold on power; that race relations were a source of sharp tensions within South Africa; and that South African racial policies had already been severely criticised internationally, not least by India. Underlying this interest was a general British sense that the empire and the old dominions like South Africa were more important to Britain than ever, particularly since Britain had emerged from the war so weakened financially, yet with undiminished world-wide strategic, economic, and political responsibilities. The result was that considerable British attention focused on the policies of the victorious National Party, above all on apartheid.[3]

The advent of a government espousing the policies and ideology of apartheid was regarded in Britain as a major setback, if not a disaster for South Africa itself, for Britain, and for the empire and Commonwealth. The *Manchester Guardian* expressed a widely held view when it noted that the elections had 'gone as badly as they could', and described apartheid as a 'neurotic fantasy'.[4] *The Times* argued that apartheid would 'not merely arrest the policy of emancipation at its present stage but would revoke what had already been conceded'.[5] Apartheid was also 'a denial of the first principle of British imperialism' and an undoubted 'setback for the ideas on which the Commonwealth is founded'.[6] According to the left-wing *Tribune*: 'Racialism no less vicious than that preached by Hitler himself is in the saddle in a Dominion of the British Empire.'[7] Also detested was the more general ideological character of D. F. Malan's National Party and of its coalition partner, N. C. Havenga's Afrikaner Party. The

---

(unpublished MSc thesis, University of London, 1962); D. Geldenhuys, 'The effects of South Africa's racial policy on Anglo-South African relations, 1945–1961' (unpublished PhD thesis, Cambridge University, 1977); P. Rich, 'The impact of South African segregationist and apartheid ideology on British racial thought', *New Community* 13, 1 (1986), pp. 1–17; and H. Smith, '*Apartheid*, Sharpeville and "impartiality": the reporting of South Africa on BBC television, 1948–1961', *Historical Journal of Film, Radio and Television* 13, 3 (1993), pp. 251–98. See also S. Howe, *Anticolonialism in British politics: the Left and the end of empire* (Oxford, 1993), chaps. 5 and 6.

[3] The main British periodicals surveyed for this study were: *New Statesman, Guardian, Spectator*, and *The Times*. We have assumed that these publications generally reflected a broad spectrum of British opinion ranging from the *New Statesman* on the Left to *The Times* on the Right. The comparative South African expertise and claims of these and other leading organs to represent the spectrum of British public opinion is usefully sketched in J. Sanders, *South Africa and the international media, 1972–1979: a struggle for representation* (London, 2000), pp. 29–35. British House of Commons debates were also consulted, though it should be noted that, by convention, Britain's parliament generally deferred from debating the internal policies of other Commonwealth countries, as South Africa was until 1961.

[4] *Manchester Guardian*, 29 May 1948.   [5] *The Times*, 26 May 1948.
[6] *The Times*, 29 May 1948.
[7] *Tribune*, 4 June 1948, quoted in Griffiths, 'British opinion on the problems and policies of the Union of South Africa', p. 46.

former was thought to be a party of 'backveld reactionaries';[8] the latter, 'still more reactionary' shading off into 'scarcely veiled Fascism'.[9] Most of the younger members of National Party were thought to be 'steeped in Nazi ideology whose *Herrenvolkism* and anti-Communism has made a lasting impact on their outlook'.[10] British interests would, it was widely believed, inevitably be damaged. *The Times* thought that the 'history of the Nationalist and Afrikaner parties is too much bound up with antipathy to this country and to the gold mining industry';[11] the *Manchester Guardian* that it 'may become distinctly harder for the British Government to secure South African co-operation in economic matters';[12] the *New Statesman* that the 'anti-English, anti-Empire feeling amongst large sections is very real';[13] and the *Observer* that the Nationalist victory 'does weaken the Commonwealth as a factor in world affairs' and 'render the future of the Commonwealth less secure'.[14] The gloomy British outlook on the election result was lightened only by the thoughts that the National Party's opponents had secured a larger share of the popular vote, and that Smuts, with the support of loyal Afrikaners and English-speaking whites, might soon regain power.

The attractiveness of Smuts and his United Party made the National Party's policies and ideology seem all the more odious. This was especially so when the Malan government's actions could so quickly and plausibly be labelled Nazi or anti-British. By October 1948, there were warnings in the British press of the 'Nazifying' of South Africa: 'the Nationalists have already begun to press their policy of race repression to the full'. Not only were the rights of black South Africans being attacked, but 'The English-speaking South African is . . . by no means safe'.[15] The Citizenship Bill of 1949 was seen in Britain, by the Left as well as by the Right, as an early confirmation of the worst fears about the Malan government's intentions. Under the front page headline 'South African Fascism', the *New Statesman and Nation* stated that the Bill was 'a convenient way of disenfranchising' British immigrants, and that Dr Malan intended to 'exclude from the polling booths anyone who opposes the overtly Nazi designs of the present Government'.[16] The *Manchester Guardian* called the Bill an 'abrogation of the rule of law in favour of arbitrary personal rule' and 'another step in the direction of making Great Britain a foreign country'.[17] According to the *Spectator*, 'All the worst features of Afrikaner nationalism are coming to the surface': 'It becomes clearer every day that the Nationalist Government

---

[8] *Sunday Times*, 30 May 1948, quoted in Geldenhuys, 'South Africa's racial policy', p. 113.
[9] *Manchester Guardian*, 29 May 1948, in Geldenhuys, 'South Africa's racial policy', p. 113.
[10] *New Statesman*, 19 June 1948.
[11] *The Times*, 29 May 1948, in Geldenhuys, 'South Africa's racial policy', p. 111.
[12] *Manchester Guardian*, 29 May 1948, in Geldenhuys, 'South Africa's racial policy', p. 111.
[13] *New Statesman*, 19 June 1948.
[14] *Observer*, 30 May 1948, in Geldenhuys, 'South Africa's racial policy', p. 112.
[15] *New Statesman*, 2 Oct. 1948.   [16] *New Statesman*, 18 June 1949.
[17] *Manchester Guardian*, 15 June 1949.

of Dr. Malan has decided to drop even the pretence of moderation.'[18] *The Times* called the Bill 'harsh and arbitrary'. In the British House of Commons, John Platts-Mills (Labour independent) complained that the Act was a 'gross manifestation of nationalism and racialism'.[19] From early on, then, there was a close association in many British minds between the National Party's attacks on the British connection and the implementation of apartheid.

From the outset, apartheid ideology and policies were also seen as threats to British rule in colonial Africa, particularly in territories neighbouring South Africa. Britain was responsible for the rule and protection of Basutoland, Bechuanaland, and Swaziland – known collectively as the 'High Commission Territories' or 'Protectorates' – all predominantly African territories which South Africa felt entitled to control. This responsibility focused additional British attention on apartheid and on the contrast with Britain's own racial policies in Africa. For this reason alone, it was thought impossible for Britain to ignore 'the antagonism between Africans and Europeans created by the present South African Government's native policy'.[20] Increased British awareness and criticism of apartheid was one consequence of the considerable public controversy surrounding the Attlee government's decision to ban Seretse Khama from Bechuanaland after Seretse's marriage to a white woman – a highly unpopular decision widely assumed to have been made in deference to the views of the South African government. It was, as a consequence, widely decried as 'appeasement'.[21] In the British press discussion of the Seretse affair, the *New Statesman* noted that South African policy had 'intensified its *Herrenvolk* nature since Dr. Malan took office'.[22] The *Manchester Guardian* believed that the British public reaction to Seretse's case had made clear 'that almost everyone here detests the sort of attitude towards Africans in particular which is the guiding principle of South African Nationalists'.[23] The *Spectator* commented that the South African government had 'committed itself to a native policy inconsistent with the principles of Christianity or even humanity'.[24] *The Times* thought that the case revealed a 'tragic' conflict between a state that 'believes in the colour bar' and one 'pledged before the nations to respect the equal rights

---

[18] *Spectator*, 24 June 1949.
[19] Britain, House of Commons Debates [HoC Deb.], vol. 466, 1493–4, 30 June 1949, quoted in Geldenhuys, 'South Africa's racial policy', p. 191.
[20] *Spectator*, 17 Feb. 1950.
[21] The charge of appeasement was made by, among others, the *Manchester Guardian*, 17 March 1950; *The Times*, 17 March 1950; *New Statesman*, 18 March 1950. See also N. Parsons, 'The impact of Seretse Khama on British public opinion, 1948–1956 and 1978', *Immigrants and Minorities* 12, 3 (1993), pp. 195–219. Protests about government policy in 1950 were filed in CO 847/45/3. Press reactions to the Conservative government's exclusion of Seretse were gathered by the CRO and filed in DO 121/151, 28 Mar. 1952; about eighty letters from the public (mostly protesting at the government's decision) were registered in DO 35/4145.
[22] Rita Hinden in *New Statesman*, 1 April 1950.   [23] *Manchester Guardian*, 17 March 1950.
[24] *Spectator*, 10 March 1950.

of all races'.[25] The British government's responsibility for the areas of white settlement in Central and East Africa, and its attempt to promote multi-racial 'partnership' there as an alternative to apartheid, was a further reason for people in Britain to examine South African racial policies closely and critically from an early date.[26] Finally, of course, the introduction of each new piece of apartheid legislation intensified the British reaction against apartheid. The object of the Group Areas Bill of 1950 – segregating residential and business areas – was, according to the *Spectator*, 'manifestly the repression of non-white inhabitants of the Union'. Malan was, it was thought, 'laying up unimagined trouble for the Union', with the 'gulf between the British government's attitude towards Africans and the South African Government's . . . getting wider every year'.[27]

In the eyes of many in Britain, the most damnable action of the Malan government in the early 1950s was the long-drawn-out assault on the rights of 'Coloured' South African voters. This assault began in 1951 and attracted considerable British attention then and in the years that followed. British concerns were expressed about its being a fundamental subversion of South Africa's constitution, the country's British-approved foundation. British interest in, and sympathy for 'Coloured' rights was increased by the mass protests of South African war veterans led by Battle of Britain ace, Group Captain 'Sailor' Malan. This South African struggle thus re-emphasised South Africa's close association with Britain at a defining moment of the twentieth century, as well as the National Party's woeful war record. In 1952, the struggle became a real focus of British concern, as can be gauged from the *Spectator's* string of increasingly alarming headlines that year: 'African Unrest' (11 April); 'South Africa's Danger' (18 April); 'Crisis at Cape Town' (25 April); 'Hitlerism in South Africa (30 May); 'South African Whirlwind' (29 August).[28] The *New Statesman* also gave this issue extensive and prominent coverage, including a front page warning that 'Dr. Malan's government has shown that it is bent on destroying the whole fabric of political democracy in South Africa.'[29] *The Times* published seven leading articles about this issue in 1952. These included warnings that the Malan government was, in its attack on the constitution, taking 'a long step towards totalitarian revolution'; that its aim was 'thorough-going Afrikaner domination over other white people and over all non-white people';[30] and that it was 'playing with fire'.[31] The reaction both in Britain and in the colonial empire to this 'constitutional crisis' prompted a

[25] *The Times*, 9 March 1950.
[26] Rich, 'The impact of South African segregationist and apartheid ideology on British racial thought', p. 9.
[27] *Spectator*, 28 April. 1950.
[28] These are some of the headlines of *Spectator* editorials on the crisis over 'Coloured' voting rights. There were nine such editorials in 1952.
[29] *New Statesman*, 31 May 1952.   [30] *The Times*, 25 April 1950, and 29 March 1950.
[31] *The Times*, 28 June 1950.

statement in parliament dissociating the British government from apartheid. In the House of Lords, Lord Salisbury declared that the aim of British policy in Africa was 'the advancement of all communities without discrimination on the grounds of race, colour or creed. Progress must, in our view, be based on partnership between the races, not on domination by any.'[32] In the years that followed – as the Nationalist government went to ever more extreme and convoluted lengths to remove 'Coloured' voters from the common roll – British criticism of apartheid only increased.

Developments within South Africa in 1953 merely confirmed widespread British fears that a bad situation was set to worsen. Early that year, the introduction of additional repressive legislation further darkened the picture. The Criminal Law Amendment Bill was labelled by the *Spectator* as 'a negation of justice': 'it is incredible to think that the Government of any country even nominally within it [the British Commonwealth] can seriously propose to make it an offence for anyone to protest against any law whatsoever'.[33] *The Times* called it 'draconic legislation'.[34] The *New Statesman* labelled it 'a work of thorough-going and ruthless suppression'. Worse still was the National Party's return to power with an increased majority later that year. This was seen as a triumph for Afrikaner nationalism which further threatened the rights not only of black South Africans, but also those of British origin. The *New Statesman* thought the results showed that 'the "gentlemanly racialism" of the United party will never be a match for the natural Fascist product'.[35] The future of South Africa was, according to the *Manchester Guardian*, 'overshadowed by thunderclouds as dark as have been seen since its birth'.[36] The *Spectator* had a similar outlook: 'The white population of South Africa has voted for the continuing subjugation of the black'; 'the first desire of the Nationalists is to remove the Cape Coloureds . . . from the common voters' rolls. The next stage could quite possibly be the dismissal of English from its constitutional position of equality.'[37] *The Times* thought that 'tension in race relations, already severe, is now most unlikely to be relaxed'.[38] The *Economist* concluded that 'the ways of the English-speaking world are to be finally rejected'.[39] Worst of all, though, the election dashed British hopes for an early return to power by the United Party, a return which would (it was assumed) have put South Africa back on a more sensible, liberal, and above all British course.

[32] Britain, House of Lords Debates, vol. 179, cols. 313–14. This statement by the secretary of state for Commonwealth relations was deliberately made without fanfare in order to avoid provoking an 'explosion from Dr Malan or his wilder Ministers': DO 35/2220, P. Liesching to T. Lloyd, 25 Oct. 1952.
[33] *Spectator*, 6 Feb. 1953.   [34] *The Times*, 21 Feb. 1953.
[35] *New Statesman*, 18 April 1953.   [36] *Manchester Guardian*, 17 April 1953.
[37] *Spectator*, 24 April 1953.   [38] *The Times*, 17 April 1953.
[39] *Economist*, 25 April 1953, quoted in Griffiths, 'British opinion on the problems and policies of the Union of South Africa', p. 81.

In the years 1948 to 1954, British opinion was sharply critical of apartheid. Many British people were predisposed to reject apartheid, and to sympathise with apartheid's opponents, because the National Party was seen as being anti-British, its policies as being at odds with British ideals, and its aims as being threats to British interests. By its own anti-British rhetoric and actions, the National Party itself reinforced this predisposition. So did the National Party's indelible wartime association with Nazism. The result was a widespread British rejection of apartheid in this period – by those on the Left who were appalled by the racism and Fascism of the Malan government; by those on the Right who were aghast at its anti-British tendencies; and by those from across the political spectrum who regarded the theory and practice of apartheid as being both contrary to British ideals and values, and a threat to the empire and Commonwealth.

II

The years 1955 to 1961 witnessed a continuation and intensification of British antipathy towards Afrikaner nationalism, and anxiety about the local and external impact of apartheid. All the same, strong British affinities with South Africa persisted. Many British people continued to identify closely with South Africans of British origin – not least because the latter's rights and interests seemed to be at risk, as well as those of loyal Afrikaners – whose war service was not forgotten. Some British people also took a closer interest in the rights of black South Africans, in part because British churches and missions were directly responsible for the education and welfare of so many of them. Close cultural links, and the ready exchange of people and information between the two countries, stimulated and sustained British interest in South Africa.[40] And, as before, the implementation of apartheid policies themselves provoked further British concern. Indeed, such were British concerns about developments within South Africa, and about their impact on Britain's position in Africa and the world, that there emerged by the late 1950s a surprisingly strong British movement for a more forthright stand against apartheid – a movement led by the Left, though not without significant support from all quarters in Britain.

During the remainder of the 1950s, apartheid policies regularly drew strong comments in the British press. The South African decision to ban black spectators from the rugby test match in September 1955 between the Springboks and the British Lions provoked a reaction from *The Times* typifying a general British tendency to despair at the excesses of apartheid, while maintaining a strong sympathy for white South Africa. *The Times* hoped that 'No sportsman – and there are no better sportsmen than those who learn the game on the playing

[40] Smith, '*Apartheid*, Sharpeville and "impartiality"', pp. 251–98.

fields of Stellenbosch, Pretoria and Bloemfontein – can defend it [the ban] in his heart. It is the negation of sportsmanship.' *The Times* could not believe that the average Afrikaner approved 'of going to such extremes of petty and insulting segregation. If they do, then the future outlook for the Union is bleak indeed.'[41] This combination of despair and guarded optimism, linked with an underlying cultural affinity with whites, remained a common feature of British attitudes towards South Africa for many years to come.

For much of the 1950s, though, the leading news from South Africa mainly encouraged British despair. The implementation of the Bantu Education Act and the forced removal of Africans from areas of Johannesburg such as Sophiatown attracted particular British concern.[42] One reason was that they involved a major head-on collision with British churches, missions, and schools in South Africa. The impact of these measures became widely known in Britain thanks to the efforts of people like Father Trevor Huddleston. His graphic portrayal of the realities of apartheid was widely disseminated in his best-selling book, *Naught for your comfort*. In 1956, the London *Sunday Times* described it as 'the most influential book this year'.[43] The protracted attack on 'Coloured' voting rights contributed in no small way to what the *Spectator* saw in 1955 as the 'progressive destruction of constitutional government'.[44] *The Times* commented that 'Every trick of politics is being used to reduce to permanent impotence every element, whether of race or of party, which disputes the ascendancy of the faction now in power.'[45] In this context, *The Times* also noted that the Nationalist claim that its political programme represented 'the will of the people, has been the starting point of every totalitarian revolution'.[46] The arrest 'in authentic Gestapo manner',[47] and subsequent 'Treason Trial' of 156 South Africans, reaffirmed the growing British impression that South Africa's entire justice system had been twisted and subverted by the Nationalists. The trial was universally condemned in Britain. It was labelled 'ill-famed',[48] 'a mockery of Western Freedom',[49] 'a strange and, at points, farcical exercise',[50] and 'a charade' with 'an insidious Alice-in-Wonderland quality'.[51] The South African government attracted further British attention to apartheid with its continued demands for control of the High Commission Territories; through its assertion of control in 1957 of the British naval base at Simon's Town with its multi-racial work force; through the elimination of the Union Jack and 'God Save the

---

[41] *The Times*, 2 Sept. 1955.
[42] *The Times*, 12 Jan. 1955. See also Geldenhuys, 'South Africa's racial policy', p. 213.
[43] T. Huddleston, *Naught for your comfort* (London, 1956). The book was first published in 1956 and reprinted regularly for years afterwards. The *Sunday Times* was quoted inside the cover of the 1960 Fontana edition of the book.
[44] *Spectator*, 1 April 1955.   [45] *The Times*, 14 May 1955.   [46] *The Times*, 20 May 1955.
[47] James Morris, *South African winter* (London, 1958), p. 26.   [48] *Spectator*, 17 Oct. 1958.
[49] *Spectator*, 17 Oct. 1958.   [50] *The Times*, 5 Aug. 1959.
[51] Morris, *South African winter*, p. 28.

Queen' as a South African national flag and anthem, again in 1957; and through its continual pressure for a republic, perhaps outside the Commonwealth.[52]

British objections at this time to the National Party's discriminatory policies did not, however, imply British support for full political equality between black and white in South Africa. In the late 1950s, it was still generally supposed in Britain that some form of white rule should persist in South Africa – as in British East and Central Africa – for decades, if not generations. James Morris probably expressed a common British view, when, in 1957, he wrote:

> I think it obvious that if universal adult franchise were granted to the Bantu, and if a black Government were the consequence – any time during the next half century – then many of the accepted standards of South African life would collapse . . . The whole flavour of the country would alter and many of the services and institutions created by white capital would rot and languish.[53]

Morris could, at this time, see no ready solution to South Africa's racial problems: 'We can hope for a change of heart among the rigid Afrikaner zealots, the shock troops of racialism; . . . but if we feel like praying about it all, we must be frank with the Almighty and ask for a miracle.' Even so, Morris remained convinced that apartheid was 'the wrong solution' – a view undoubtedly shared by many in Britain, on the Right as well as on the Left.[54] The British Right was even more strongly opposed to black rule in South Africa, though no less critical of apartheid. A striking example of this contradictory British attitude was provided by Harold Nicolson. He recorded his own, and Vita Sackville-West's reaction to South Africa during their trip there in January 1960:

> I cannot describe to you the horrors of Apartheid. It is far worse than anything that I had supposed . . . You know how I hate niggers and how Tory Vita is. But I do hate injustice more than I hate niggers, and Vita screams with rage. She says it is like Hitler all over again.[55]

The strength and breadth of the British reaction against apartheid in the 1950s stemmed far more from a rejection of apartheid and of Afrikaner Nationalist rule, than from any perception that white minority rule in Africa was inherently unjust.

By 1959, the apartheid regime's standing had fallen far in Britain. The opposition Labour Party made criticism of Britain's 'disgraceful'[56] stance at the UN on South Africa and on 'the evil policies of *apartheid*'[57] a key part of its attack

---

[52] For Simon's Town see *The Times*, 5 July 1955 and 3 April 1957. For the flag see *The Times*, 6 April 1957.
[53] *Manchester Guardian*, 17 Aug. 1957.   [54] Morris, *South African winter*, p. 15.
[55] H. Nicolson to P. and N. Nicolson, 24 Jan. 1960, in H. Nicolson, *Diaries and letters, 1930–1964* (London and New York, 1980), pp. 393–4.
[56] Fenner Brockway's description in HoC Deb., vol. 613, 1132, 18 Nov. 1959.
[57] John Stonehouse's description in HoC Deb., vol. 614, 1003, 1 Dec. 1959.

on the Macmillan government. The Macmillan government finally admitted (privately at least) the need to distance itself more clearly from apartheid.[58] To judge from British press coverage of, and parliamentary debates on South African affairs, British public interest in South Africa grew substantially in 1959 and 1960.[59] Such interest encouraged the Labour Party to declare 1960 the 'Year of Africa'.[60] British interest was sustained into early 1960 by the acceleration of political change in British Africa, by the calls by such organisations as Christian Action and the Trades Union Congress for a consumer boycott of South African goods,[61] by Macmillan's 'wind of change' tour of South Africa.[62] Proponents of the boycotts recognised, however, that widespread British dislike of apartheid could not readily be turned into positive action: 'The number of Conservative supporters . . . will be small. Nor is it likely that hardcore Labour voters are going to pay any attention to the campaign: most of them supported Suez, and care very little what happens to a bunch of wogs. The apolitical centre care even less.'[63] This view was, however, expressed before the Sharpeville massacre (21 March 1960), an event that crystallised the general British dislike of apartheid which had already become so evident by 1959.

Sharpeville seared into the British public imagination the link between apartheid and brutal state repression. The massacre was condemned unreservedly in the British press. Horrific pictures of dead protesters were given wide and repeated circulation in newspapers and on television.[64] *The Times*, after initially complaining about the British Left's over-reaction, had soon condemned Pretoria for its 'suicidal policies', its 'reign of terror', for having 'wantonly used unnecessary force', and for its 'terrorist authorities' who took severe action not only against blacks, but also against whites 'for not being slavish supporters of the dictatorship'.[65] The *New Statesman* wrote of the 'mass murder of unarmed Africans by white soldiers equipped with machine guns', all part of

---

[58] R. Hyam and W. R. Louis (eds.), BDEEP, series A, vol. 4, *The Conservative government and the end of empire, 1957–1964* (London, 2000), part II, docs. 439–42; H. Macmillan, *Memoirs, V: Pointing the way, 1959–1961* (London, 1972), pp. 116–77.

[59] Commentary on South Africa in the *Spectator*, for example, grew considerably in 1959, particularly towards the end of the year. For the other discussions of Britain's stance at the UN on the 'South African disputes' see: HoC Deb., vol. 613, 389, 11 Nov. 1959; vol. 614, 90, 30 Nov. 1959; and vol. 615, 6 and 107–78, 7 Dec. 1959.

[60] C. Gurney, 'When the boycott began to bite', *History Today* 49, 6 (June 1999), p. 33.

[61] Gurney, 'When the boycott began to bite', pp. 32–4. *Spectator*, 1 Jan. 1960. *New Statesman*, 2 Jan. 1960.

[62] For the BBC television coverage of the 'wind of change' tour see: Smith, '*Apartheid*, Sharpeville and "impartiality"', pp. 258–9. For Macmillan's 'wind of change' speech see Hyam and Louis, *The Conservative government*, part I, doc. 32, pp. 167–74, and introd., pp. xxxviii–xl.

[63] *Spectator*, 26 Feb. 1960.

[64] For television coverage see: Smith, '*Apartheid*, Sharpeville and "impartiality"', pp. 259–60.

[65] *The Times*, 26 March, 6 April, and 22 April 1960, quoted in Geldenhuys, 'South Africa's racial policy', p. 375.

Verwoerd's 'slave state'.[66] The *Mail* argued that 'a country held together by violence must be expected to explode in murder, riot and sudden death'.[67] A Gallup poll conducted a few days after the massacre reported an unprecedented British awareness of the event: 99 per cent had read or heard about the shooting, and 80 per cent of British people opposed apartheid.[68] Sharpeville also prompted a debate in the British House of Commons in which 'every speaker, on both sides of the House, has condemned the system of apartheid'.[69] In this debate South Africa was labelled an 'insane military dictatorship',[70] and 'a police state'.[71] Apartheid was described as an 'evil doctrine',[72] 'a wholly unworkable and repugnant system',[73] and as 'thinly disguised slavery'.[74] The House was reminded that some members of the Verwoerd government had 'sympathised with the Nazis during the war', though one MP preferred 'to remember the South Africans who fought with us and who . . . represent the true South Africa'.[75] As this last comment suggests, Sharpeville was generally regarded in Britain as an indictment not of white South Africa but of Afrikaner Nationalist rule. While British opinion was largely united in condemning apartheid after Sharpeville, it became more divided on the question of whether there should be a boycott either of South African goods or of the Springbok cricket tour of England, scheduled for that summer.[76]

South Africa's exit from the Commonwealth further revealed the contradictory British desires to condemn apartheid and yet preserve links with the 'true South Africa' – the loyal, cricket-playing, and more predominantly British country not represented by the National Party. This exit also showed the extent to which the Commonwealth was still regarded as being vital to the preservation of Britain's world role. Belief in the Commonwealth was thought at this time to be an important reason why the British Conservative Party and its supporters were so forthright in their condemnation of apartheid polices: 'Tories now see that these policies, if persisted with, are likely to shatter the Commonwealth dream and deny Britain the right even of pretending to speak for the Africans, Indians and Asians whose representatives still put in an appearance at conferences of Commonwealth Prime Ministers.'[77] This assessment was confirmed by the broad British acceptance of the inevitability of South Africa's exit from

---

[66] *New Statesman*, 26 March 1960.   [67] *Mail* quoted in *New Statesman*, 2 April 1960.
[68] Geldenhuys, 'South Africa's racial policy', p. 376.
[69] HoC Deb., vol. 621, 811, Fenner Brockway, 8 April 1960.
[70] HoC Deb., vol. 621, 779, John Stonehouse, 8 April 1960.
[71] HoC Deb., vol. 621, 842, John Dugdale, 8 April 1960.
[72] HoC Deb., vol. 621, 775, John Stonehouse, 8 April 1960.
[73] HoC Deb., vol. 621, 788, Jo Grimond, 8 April 1960.
[74] HoC Deb., vol. 621, 775, John Stonehouse, 8 April 1960.
[75] HoC Deb., vol. 621, 840, Bernard Braine, 8 April 1960.
[76] For the cricket boycott see HoC Deb., vol. 621, 795, Cyril Osborne; 795, Brockway; and 801, Michael Stewart, 8 April 1960. See also *Spectator*, 6 Nov. 1959.
[77] *New Statesman*, 16 April 1960.

the Commonwealth, even if some commentators on the Right spoke of it as a 'tragedy'.[78] The *Economist* considered that 'something worth saving had been saved',[79] the *Spectator* that 'the Commonwealth became a sweeter and cleaner community'.[80] In the House of Commons, Harold Macmillan explained that South Africa's membership 'was even threatening to damage the concept of the Commonwealth itself as a multiracial association',[81] and that whole episode was 'a demonstration of the vitality of the Commonwealth'.[82] But, however important the Commonwealth may have seemed in Britain at that time, most people there would have agreed with Macmillan's judgement that 'this is a very sad event; sad because of what seems to us a tragically misguided and perverse philosophy which lies at the root of *apartheid*; . . . sad because it is the end of a fifty-year connection which began with a decision then hailed as an outstanding example of magnanimity after victory'.[83] Most British people would also have agreed with the widely expressed desire to welcome South Africa back in the future: 'she will receive a heartfelt welcome back when, purged of Dr. Verwoerd and those who agree with his policies, she applies for readmission'.[84] South Africa's exit was thus seen in Britain as yet another damaging consequence of apartheid and of intransigent Afrikaner Nationalist rule – a rule that steadily eroded links between Britain and South Africa, links that so many British people wished to sustain.

Throughout the late 1950s and early 1960s, Nationalist policies and ideology turned British opinion strongly against apartheid. In 1960, after Sharpeville, apartheid was condemned more vigorously and widely than ever before. This condemnation sprang from the topmost ministerial levels downwards and across the British political spectrum. For Macmillan personally, white supremacy was 'clearly wrong'. His Commonwealth relations secretary, Lord Home, had concluded by the end of 1959 that the Commonwealth 'would undoubtedly be happier and closer-knit' with the South African 'ugly duckling out of the nest'. By the end of 1963, Home, now prime minister, lectured the South African ambassador to the effect that Bantustans 'just would not work, either economically or politically'. High commissioner Sir John Maud scathingly dismissed Verwoerd's Bantustanisation programme as 'essentially a design for the perpetuation of a conquest'. His successor Sir Hugh Stephenson was warned not to give the impression that the British government had any sympathy with Verwoerd's policies: ministers 'have repeatedly made clear both publicly and through diplomatic channels their condemnation of apartheid which they regard as not only misconceived in the interests of South Africa itself but dangerous to the

---

[78] Geldenhuys, 'South Africa's racial policy', p. 421.
[79] *Economist*, 16 March 1961 quoted in Geldenhuys, 'South Africa's racial policy', p. 421.
[80] *Spectator*, 17 March 1961.   [81] HoC Deb., vol. 637, 442, Macmillan, 22 March 1961.
[82] HoC Deb., vol. 637, 449, Macmillan, 22 March 1961.
[83] HoC Deb., vol. 637, 449, Macmillan, 22 March 1961.   [84] *Spectator*, 17 March 1961.

interests of the West in Africa as a whole . . . [and] contrary to the whole liberal tradition of our colonial policy and to the multi-racial character and principles of the Commonwealth' (June 1963).[85]

The unity of the British Left and Right on the question of South Africa would not, however, persist beyond the early 1960s. The result was that British antagonism towards apartheid was perhaps as intense *and united* in 1960 as it would ever be. But, even in the immediate wake of Sharpeville, at the time of this early peak in British antagonism, Pretoria's chief sins in British eyes did not necessarily include the denial of full political rights to blacks. In 1961, it was still widely supposed in Britain that some form of white rule should continue in South Africa (as in British Central Africa) for many years to come. Far worse sins were Pretoria's authoritarian and repressive rule, its commitment to a repugnant racial ideology, its antipathy towards South Africa's British institutions and population, its disruption of the Commonwealth, and, more generally, its provocation of unrest and disorder that threatened to spread into British Africa.

III

The first decade and a half after South Africa's exit from the Commonwealth saw a considerable shift in, and polarisation of British attitudes towards apartheid. Several things produced these changes. Many people in Britain, particularly on the Right, began to view apartheid with less hostility. The relative stability and prosperity of South Africa, especially in comparison with several black-ruled African states, made apartheid seem less objectionable – less a source of disorder than of stability, less a threat to Britain's strategic and economic interests than a safeguard of them. Britain's economic weakness and Cold War strategic imperatives merely reinforced this tendency. British antipathy towards apartheid also eased as the National Party softened its anti-British rhetoric, and gained new support from white English-speaking South Africans. The failure of multi-racial 'partnership' in British Central Africa – a failure driven home by Rhodesia's Unilateral Declaration of Independence in 1965 – meant that apartheid came to be seen more as the only alternative to black domination in South Africa. The desire to reject apartheid in the interests of sustaining British moral authority in the empire and Commonwealth also diminished as a consequence of decolonisation and disenchantment with the Commonwealth. Finally, growing tolerance of apartheid was in some cases linked to the spread of racial tensions and intolerance within Britain itself. At the same time, however, entirely contrary trends were also evident in Britain. Some there were, not least amongst the Left, who became more actively antagonistic towards apartheid.

[85] Hyam and Louis, *The Conservative government*, part II, docs. 439, 462, 463, 485.

Taking positive action against apartheid rule came to be regarded by growing numbers in Britain as a moral or religious imperative. For some it was a way of taking a stand in favour of democracy and humanity in Africa, or against racism in Britain. For a few it was a way of challenging the capitalist system that was thought to have spawned apartheid. For others it was a reaction against the British Right's tolerance of apartheid and opposition to sanctions. Much opinion divided along party lines. Controversy over the question of arms sales to, and sporting contacts with South Africa intensified the division between the Labour and Conservative Parties. The net effect of these conflicting British attitudes was an overall decline of British antagonism towards apartheid in the decade prior to the Soweto uprising.

Despite the growing division of British opinion on South Africa, apartheid itself – as a philosophy and as a set of policies – continued in the 1960s to be widely criticised in Britain. At the end of 1962, the South African 'Information Department' (i.e. propaganda ministry) reported, after surveying British press attitudes, that 'opposition to apartheid . . . is still 100 per cent'.[86] Not until 1963 did the Information Department get 'the break we have been awaiting for years' when Peregrine Worsthorne 'wrote a reasoned piece supporting apartheid in a reasonable and well-read newspaper', the *Sunday Telegraph*.[87] Generally, however, opinion on both Left and Right in Britain agreed in the 1960s that apartheid should be condemned. The chief disagreements arose over what British response should be made to it.

This broadly critical attitude towards apartheid was evident in the extensive British coverage of the 'Rivonia trial'. The trial focused British attention on Nelson Mandela, who had been charged with high treason and sabotage after he had embarked on an armed struggle against apartheid. The *New Statesman* wrote of 'the almost universal anger which has been aroused over the Mandela case'.[88] The *Guardian* insisted that it was 'of the evil essence of the Afrikaner state' that there was no place for the convicted trialists 'but in its prisons'.[89] The *Observer* noted how much goodwill still existed among African leaders for a genuine multi-racial society, and warned that it was 'extremely doubtful that this goodwill would survive the execution of Mandela and his fellow-accused'.[90] The British press on the other side of the political spectrum took a similar line. The *Daily Telegraph* reported that 'It is the tragedy of the republic that it provides no way but violence for such a man to influence its fortunes.'[91] *The Times*, too, was sympathetic to Mandela and impressed by his defence speech: 'Such sincere, outspoken testimonies against tyranny are . . . proofs

---

[86] Pretoria, South African National Archive, Department of Information (London), ILN, PRO 20, 'The British Press vs. South Africa in 1962'.
[87] ILN, PRO 20, 'Annual Report', 1963.   [88] *New Statesman*, 19 June 1964.
[89] *Guardian*, 13 June 1964.   [90] *Observer* quoted in ILN, PRO 20, 'April Report', 1964.
[91] *Daily Telegraph* in ILN, PRO 20, 'April Report', 1964.

that the government behind the prosecution must share in equity a grave burden of guilt.'[92] Rivonia was, it concluded, 'a landmark in the course of worsening race relations'.[93] Such expressions of British sympathy for the opponents of apartheid would persist in the 1960s, though they would not translate into general support for boycotts or sanctions against South Africa.

The year 1964 was one of transition in British attitudes towards South Africa. The year saw the emergence of new British uncertainty about apartheid. It also saw deeper divisions of opinion about what should be done to promote change in South Africa. As the *Spectator* noted in June 1964: 'A disarming number of people and journals are now on record as admitting they "don't know" about South Africa . . . To move in with sanctions . . . would be to forestall any possibility of peaceful reformation.'[94] Consumer boycotts had proved to be largely ineffective: 'All attempts at organising boycotts of this or that product have broken down miserably before the torpid indifference of the consumer and of the market.'[95] Comprehensive, internationally agreed sanctions might, by contrast, have a decisive impact. But, concerns were expressed, no less by the Left than by the Right, that apartheid should not be brought to a precipitate end at the cost of ensuing chaos. Even the *New Statesman* was cautious at this time about comprehensive sanctions, arguing that 'if the West is to be asked to sacrifice economic interests and strategic rights it can only be with some clear proof that apartheid can be destroyed and replaced by a form of orderly government'.[96] The *Guardian* took a similar line.[97] *The Times*, on the other hand, was unequivocally opposed to sanctions, insisting that every 'legitimate chance' must be taken to hasten the end of apartheid, 'but a general application of sanctions is not one of them'.[98] It was in this context of uncertainty about, and opposition to economic sanctions that the Left came out more strongly than ever in favour of a complete ban on the sale of arms to South Africa.[99]

The future of arms sales to South Africa was one of the issues that deepened the divide of British opinion on South Africa along party lines. The arms sales debate became particularly heated in 1964 after Harold Wilson came to power with a promise to end all arms sales.[100] *The Times* tried to reduce the heat by calling for 'coexistence on common sense terms with bad neighbours'. *The Times* insisted that 'Repugnance for apartheid is shared by all three parties in Britain. It is not a Labour monopoly.' As far as *The Times* was concerned, 'The present regime in South Africa is an evil and sterile one, holding out no hope for

---

[92] *The Times*, in ILN, PRO 20, 'April Report', 1964. [93] *The Times*, 12 June 1964.
[94] *Spectator*, 26 June 1964. [95] *Guardian*, 13 June 1964.
[96] *New Statesman*, 17 April 1964. [97] *Guardian*, 13 June 1964.
[98] *The Times*, 21 April 1964. [99] See *Guardian*, 13 June 1964.
[100] T. Bale, '"A deplorable episode": South African arms and the statecraft of British social democracy', *Labour History Review* 62 (1997–8), pp. 22–40; J. W. Young, 'The Wilson government and arms to South Africa, 1964', *Journal of Contemporary British History*, 12 (1998), pp. 62–86.

posterity, white or black.'[101] The *Express* was even more critical of the arms ban, particularly the threatened cancellation of the sale of Buccaneer aircraft, arguing that Labour was 'acting with incredible irresponsibility'. The *Daily Express* doubted the value of the new Commonwealth and complained that the Labour government was seeking to 'ingratiate itself with African states like Tanzania where the Communists are so powerful that Britons are hounded out', or 'like Kenya where the Opposition has gone into "voluntary liquidation"... What sort of friends are these?'[102] The divisive debate over arms sales continued during the 1960s and regained public prominence when Edward Heath's Conservative government announced, soon after taking power in 1970, that it intended to sell the weapons needed by South Africa for naval defence.

Despite the fact that apartheid was ritually condemned by Left and Right alike in the 1960s, the British Right increasingly saw the choice in South Africa as being between apartheid and chaotic black rule. After the 1966 election in South Africa, there was certainly little hope that white English-speaking South Africans would ever regain power and succeed in promoting a more liberal multi-racial approach, one leading slowly to majority rule. According to *The Times*, 'The multi-racial gradualism of Smuts and Botha ... has been resoundingly rejected.' 'South Africa's tragic defiance of the twentieth century goes on.'[103] The *Economist*'s assessment of the election results was that the 'philosophy of white domination received its most comprehensive and enthusiastic endorsement to date', with the National Party for the first time producing 'evidence of significant support from the English-speaking population'.[104] By the mid-1960s, then, there was growing British awareness that apartheid was broadly supported by white South Africa, not just by Afrikaner Nationalists; and that unless white rule were overthrown, apartheid would have to be tolerated for years to come.

Even so, there remained little British sympathy either for apartheid or for its Nationalist protagonists. This was evident in the British reaction to Hendrik Verwoerd's assassination in September 1966, and in the subsequent rise of John Vorster. Few people in Britain were sorry to see the end of Verwoerd, even if they deplored the method of his demise. The cover of *Private Eye* showed four 'Zulu warriors' jumping for joy above the caption 'A NATION MOURNS'.[105] *The Times* noted that 'Dr. Verwoerd was probably more universally disliked than any other political figure in any country.'[106] British readers were once again reminded about Afrikaner Nationalist links with Nazi Germany and with Nazi ideology. Paul Johnson, for example, told readers of the *New Statesman* that Verwoerd had 'greatly admired' Hitler and was 'the chief architect of a

[101] *The Times* in ILN, PRO 20, 'November Report', 1964.
[102] *Express* in ILN, PRO 20, 'November Report', 1964.   [103] *The Times*, 1 April 1966.
[104] *Economist*, 2 April 1966.   [105] *Private Eye*, 17 Sept. 1966.
[106] *The Times*, 7 Sept. 1966.

Illustration 13.1 Dr Hendrik Verwoerd, prime minister of South Africa since 1958, was lucky to survive an assassination attempt in April 1960, but was killed in Cape Town in September 1966. The above illustration formed the cover of *Private Eye*, no. 124, 17 September 1966.

fundamentally evil system'.[107] Vorster was thought to be even worse. He had 'a terrible dossier', having 'belonged to the Ossewa Brandwag, which stood for the victory of Afrikaner nationalism through alliance with Hitler'. He had 'created one of the most inhuman police-states in the history of oppression'.[108] The *Economist* also mentioned Vorster's Nazi links and was hardly less harsh in its assessment: 'the choice of Mr Vorster seems to be almost deliberately provocative... South Africa can be expected to return to the cruder *wit baaskap* (white mastery) of Mr. Strijdom.'[109] There thus continued the association in

[107] *New Statesman*, 9 Sept. 1966. [108] *New Statesman*, 16 Nov. 1966.
[109] *Economist*, 17 Sept. 1966.

British minds of apartheid with Nazi-inspired Afrikaner nationalism, though this was tempered by the expectation that South Africa's 'system of racial tyranny combined with economic prosperity at home and quiet common sense in countries abroad' was likely to continue under Vorster.[110]

The question of whether British sportsmen should, in the 1960s and early 1970s, play against the all-white Springbok cricket and rugby teams highlighted the complex and contradictory nature of British attitudes towards South Africa. The 'D'Oliveira affair' brought the issue of sporting contacts to the fore in 1967. Early in the year the South African government announced that the English cricket team would not be welcome to tour South Africa if it included Basil D'Oliveira, a 'Coloured' South African who had moved to Britain precisely because his racial classification under apartheid prevented him from ever playing for the Springboks. The strong British reaction against D'Oliveira's exclusion came from two directions. The first was from those people, often on the Right, who supported sporting contacts with South Africa, but who deplored this South African attempt to impose apartheid on a British team. Nigel Lawson made this point in the *Spectator*: 'I've never believed in bringing politics into sport ... the main point is that the England selectors cannot respectably submit to dictation in their choice of team on any grounds.'[111] The second was from those others in Britain opposed in principle to apartheid. They were led at this time by David Sheppard, the former England cricket captain who had boycotted the 1960 Springbok tour, and who would later become bishop of Liverpool. After some ill-considered hesitation on the part of the England selectors, D'Oliveira was included in the team set to tour South Africa late 1968. Pretoria, however, made it clear that his inclusion was unacceptable, thus prompting England to cancel the tour. By then the story had gained great prominence in Britain, with respect both to the anti-apartheid campaign, and to Britain's commitment to non-racialism. After the cancellation of the tour, cricket commentator John Arlott would write in the *Guardian* that 'countless coloured children born in Britain of West Indian, Indian, Pakistani or African parents will now know that their British citizenship is not a fiction as far as cricket is concerned. It is as simple and important as that.'[112] Earlier on, there had been considerable support from other British quarters for the tour to proceed, from people who often simply wished to watch cricket. Some believed that Britain should learn to live with apartheid: 'Life is too short for us spectators to wait until the predictable voices, etc, are at last satisfied with the moral performance of the South African

---

[110] *Spectator*, 9 Sept. 1966.   [111] *Spectator*, 27 Jan. 1967.
[112] *Guardian*, quoted in B. Murray, 'D'Oliveira affair's shameful secret', *Mail & Guardian*, 12 Feb. 1999. See also Murray, 'The whole D'Oliveira affair', *Mail & Guardian*, 19 Feb. 1999; and Murray, 'Politics and cricket: the D'Oliveira affair of 1968', *Journal of Southern African Studies* 27, 4 (2001), pp. 667–84.

'Here, lad go and boo the cricketers while the gentleman and I talk business.'

Illustration 13.2. A young Peter Hain (subsequently a minister in Mr Blair's government), leading protester against the Springbok cricket tour of England, is despatched by Harold Wilson before the prime minister discusses trade relations with his opposite number, John Vorster. The cartoon reflects the belief of the Left that economic interests dictated British government policy. *Source: New Statesman*, 1 May 1970.

government (if ever that time should come).'[113] Some also hoped that cricket would help to 'build bridges', exert a liberalising influence on Afrikaners, and sustain contact with what remained of Smuts's 'loyal' white South Africa – which Springbok cricketers were felt to represent.[114] Pretoria's utterly unacceptable attitude towards D'Oliveira had, however, turned most British opinion against the tour.

Controversy over sporting contacts was renewed in 1969 and early in 1970 with the British protests against the Springbok rugby tour of Britain. The fact that the rugby Springboks were predominantly Afrikaners, and known to be Afrikanerdom's pride, increased the determination of some in Britain to see the tour cancelled. The strongest opposition naturally came from the Left. Under the front page headline 'APARTHEID IS NOT A GAME', the *New Statesman* stated simply that the tour 'should not be happening'. It pointed out that the Springbok side had been 'recruited on deliberately exclusive racial principles, and it comes here to bear witness for a racially exclusive way of life'; 'Far from breaking down prejudice, sporting contact tends to reinforce and spread it.'[115] Despite this opposition, the tour went ahead, supported by what the Left described as a 'hedonistic majority' in Britain who resented the Left's fight 'for a moral issue in the Dreyfusard tradition'.[116] The 'unhappy Springboks tour',[117] however, attracted significant protests, part of what was seen as the 'opening moves in a campaign to prevent South African cricketers from playing here in 1970'.[118]

The 'Stop the Seventy Tour' campaign gathered considerable force in Britain in 1969 and 1970. The Right defended the tour with the usual arguments, including the one that South Africa should not be singled out for isolation when sporting contacts were maintained with oppressive communist regimes such as the Soviet Union. The *Spectator* expressed the last point forcibly in a leading article in support of the tour: 'The oppression of one race by another is certainly evil (and all-too-widely practised, as it happens, outside South Africa too). So, and in the case of Russia even more so, is the oppression of a people by its rulers of the same race.' The 'anti-Springbok movement' was, the *Spectator* concluded, 'not based on reason at all'.[119] *The Times*, on the other hand, called for cancellation, arguing that 'to receive the South Africans here so soon after their boorish refusal to receive us there would be to condone their political meddling'.[120] Significant opposition to the tour also emanated from the Church – something that lent a powerful moral credibility to the campaign. In May 1970, it was reported that three organisations threatened the tour: 'The newest is the Bishop of Woolwich's "Fair Cricket" campaign, the oldest the Anti-Apartheid

[113] *Spectator*, 25 April 1969. [114] *The Times*, 23 Jan. 1969.
[115] *New Statesman*, 7 Nov. 1969. [116] *New Statesman*, 14 Nov. 1969.
[117] *The Times*, 2 Feb. 1970. [118] *New Statesman*, 7 Nov. 1969.
[119] *Spectator*, 2 May 1970. [120] *The Times*, 23 Jan. 1969.

Movement, the most feared the Stop the Seventy Tour Committee' led by Peter Hain.[121] Concerns that matches would be disrupted by protesters was only one of the reasons for cancelling the tour. The British home secretary, James Callaghan, argued (along with many others) that the tour would provoke racial discord or even an 'ugly clash' in many English cities, which would have been 'a setback to community relations in this country'. Indian and Pakistani leaders in Britain 'thought that a fair number of their people would have turned out to the anti-Springbok demonstrations – especially Indians from East Africa'.[122] Here, then, British attitudes towards South Africa did intersect directly with race relations in Britain and with the diasporic fallout from the end of empire.

No less controversial in 1970 was the question of arms sales to, and defence collaboration with South Africa. The unfolding of this controversy suggests that British tolerance for apartheid rule had grown significantly by the early 1970s as a consequence of a growing British acceptance of its apparent permanence. Other factors included British disillusionment with the Commonwealth, the lack of a credible multi-racial alternative to black majority rule or apartheid, and a continued British determination to sustain a world role and fight the Cold War. The Right emphasised the strategic importance of South Africa, portraying it as an indispensable Cold War ally, if an admittedly disreputable one. Sir Alec Douglas-Home, Britain's foreign secretary, referred in parliament to the 'vital sea routes round South Africa' and pointed to the need to strengthen South Africa as a naval ally.[123] In the same debate, Duncan Sandys sought to discount the significance of Commonwealth opposition to arms sales, complaining that 'many people cannot stomach the sanctimonious sermonising by Tanzania... which blatantly discriminates against its Asian inhabitants'.[124] The Liberal and Labour Parties, on the other hand, advanced an entirely different view. David Steele (Liberal) insisted that 'to sell arms to South Africa would be the biggest blunder since Suez'.[125] Press opinion was similarly divided. *The Times* insisted that 'Britain's security depends on a network of alliances, shared interests and friendships round the world', and that the morality of selling arms to South Africa 'need worry very few but those who see South Africa, not communism, as our real adversary'.[126] The *New Statesman* ridiculed the 'Dad's Navy' mentality of a Conservative government pursuing policies based on the 'naval strategy of the Second World War, the Russophobe reflexes of the Forties – and behind them a notion of great power status which belongs to the age of Admiral Fisher'.[127] Claims about South Africa's strategic significance,

---

[121] *New Society*, 14 May 1970. See also P. Hain, *Don't play with apartheid: the background to the 'Stop the 70 tour' campaign* (London, 1971).
[122] *New Society*, 28 May 1970. [123] HoC Deb., vol. 804, 49–62, 20 July 1970.
[124] HoC Deb., vol. 804, 51–2, 20 July 1970; Sandys had been secretary of state for Commonwealth relations, 1960–4.
[125] HoC Deb., vol. 804, 58, 20 July 1970. [126] *The Times*, 4 July 1970.
[127] *New Statesman*, 17 July 1970.

and about its geopolitical value as a Cold War ally, would nevertheless underpin and justify a British tolerance of apartheid in the early 1970s and right through to the end of the 1980s.

The demonisation of apartheid South Africa by the British Left, by the Church, and by the growing community of South Africans resident in Britain was, in the early 1970s, more than matched by the Right's defence of white rule in South Africa – a defence which urged tolerance of apartheid rule, even as it criticised apartheid policies. This demonisation was also counteracted by the renewed respectability conferred upon South Africa by its rapid economic growth and relative political stability in the late 1960s and early 1970s. In these years, Vorster even came to be seen, however improbably, as a moderate reformer – as the inheritor of Smuts's 'loyal Afrikaner' mantle. Such views were evident in *The Times*'s 1969 'Special report' on South Africa. Vorster, it reported, 'has broken with the reactionary wing of the Nationalist Party. This is the first time for a time – since . . . 1948 . . . – that there has been any forward movement in South African politics.' He was 'a very different kind of leader from his precursors'. *The Times* also expressed the hope – reminiscent of the thoughts expressed in 1910 about Afrikaner nationalism and South African racial policies – that 'Afrikanerdom, as it becomes more sure of itself, may become more forward and more outward looking.'[128] The *Spectator* expressed similar hopes in 1973, noting that there were 'emerging perceptible signs, if not yet of "the wind of change" reaching the Republic, at least a zephyr'.[129] The deplorably repressive nature of the apartheid state was acknowledged; but it was hoped that further economic growth would lead gradually to positive political change. There seemed, in any case, to be no point in trying to force the pace of change through outside pressure when Rhodesia had apparently proved the futility of sanctions. These views of *The Times* and *Spectator* – that the efforts of reformers within the apartheid regime should not be jeopardised by the application of sanctions, that economic growth would inevitably change South Africa for the better, and that any precipitate end to white rule would lead to anarchy – were widely accepted on the Right in Britain. This was true not only during the early 1970s, but also in the 1980s when they formed part of Margaret Thatcher's orthodoxy on South Africa.

Another key part of this cautious, conservative, and tolerant British approach to South Africa was an increasing acceptance of apartheid's premise that black South Africa was deeply divided along 'tribal' lines, that many Africans there were still primitive and prone to violence, and that these 'tribes' should be allowed to maintain their autonomy. This tendency to accept racial and ethnic difference as being irreducible was fuelled to some extent by the failure of

---

[128] *The Times*, 'South Africa: A special report', 27 Oct. 1969.
[129] *Spectator*, 24 March 1973.

'partnership' in Central Africa, and by ongoing ethnic conflicts elsewhere in Africa; and to a further extent by the growth of racial tensions within Britain itself, tensions exacerbated by the racial attitude of Enoch Powell and his devotees. In 1969 *The Times* reported in favourable terms on the development of 'Homelands' in South Africa.[130] By the 1970s, Zulu nationalism had become the archetypal example in British minds of South African 'tribalism', reinforced perhaps by British consciousness of the Zulu wars – so recently and powerfully reinserted into the public imagination by Cy Enfield's 1963 film 'Zulu'. In 1973, in the wake of large-scale strikes by Africans in Natal, the *Spectator* warned that 'The Zulus are getting going': 'Tribalism, the Afrikaner tribe may learn, is a dangerous concept to foster.'[131] The view that South Africa was beset by tribal divisions, and threatened by warlike Zulus, was again one that would persist until the end of the apartheid era.

Despite the existence of significant British opposition to the apartheid regime in the mid-1970s, it remains true that from 1962 to 1975 there developed in Britain a considerable body of opinion content to tolerate apartheid in the interests of sustaining white rule and stability there. This development was encouraged by the belief that the South African government was becoming more moderate, pragmatic, and reformist; and by the hope that economic growth would, in any case, gradually transform the country politically without the need for sanctions which might only damage British interests. Early in 1976, there were hopes in Britain that some sort of power-sharing constitution could be devised in South Africa which would give blacks a political voice without overthrowing white influence.[132] The first months of 1976 almost certainly, though, mark the high point of a British tolerance towards apartheid. Events in South Africa in June 1976 would, for many in Britain, demonstrate that a continuation of apartheid rule was more likely to provoke than to prevent South Africa's descent into disorder.

IV

The Soweto uprising in June 1976 shocked many people in Britain out of their tolerance or indifference. It also revived British support for a more active stance against Pretoria. But, as with Sharpeville, it was before long followed by a phase of forbearance, as relative calm returned to South Africa, and as Pretoria seemed to move gradually towards reform and made progress in resolving conflicts in neighbouring states, especially Zimbabwe. In the mid-1980s, though, violent unrest within South Africa would once again revive British opposition to apartheid. This proved to be the most intense and widespread opposition

---

[130] *The Times*, 'South Africa: A special report', 27 Oct. 1969.
[131] *Spectator*, 24 March 1973.   [132] See, for example, *Spectator*, 17 April 1976.

since Sharpeville, and it would be sustained during the remainder of the 1980s. British attitudes towards South Africa were, nevertheless, more polarised than ever in the 1980s, as Thatcher, her government, and her supporters strongly resisted aggressive action against Pretoria. This resistance, in turn, increased the tendency to condemn apartheid as a means of opposing Thatcherism more generally. British attitudes towards apartheid also remained tied to race relations within Britain, with racist elements closely identifying themselves with white South Africans, and opponents of racism rallying to the anti-apartheid cause. Deeply divided British attitudes about the future of white rule in South Africa would persist until the final end of apartheid rule in 1994.[133]

Pretoria's violent response to the Soweto uprising, and the graphic depictions of it in the British news media, drove home once more the violence and brutality required to sustain apartheid. Condemnation in the British press was widespread. According to *The Times*, Soweto showed that Pretoria was 'trying to do something that is manifestly impossible as well as immoral'.[134] The *Guardian* thought that Soweto 'shows a startling and ferocious capacity for violence lurking behind the formal boundaries of racial segregation'.[135] The *New Statesman* commented that 'South Africa stands starkly revealed as being today just as ruthless a police state as it ever was in Dr Verwoerd's time.' The manifold injustices, and the inherent instability of white rule – to say nothing of the South African government's aggressive representation of its views by manipulation of the media – were fully exposed in June 1976.[136]

Soweto did not, however, mark a return to attitudes prevalent in Britain at the time of Sharpeville. The *New Statesman* despaired at the change of British attitudes since 1960:

Few developments have been more depressing over the past decade than the way in which racial oppression in South Africa has come to be accepted by the world community as a fact of life – uncomfortable, no doubt, but something we must all learn to live with in an unemotional way. Sixteen years ago there was no doubting the universal sense of outrage – uniting Left and Right alike – that greeted the Sharpeville massacre . . . The days when the entire 'triple alliance' of the Labour movement could call for a consumers' boycott on South African goods and when Trevor Huddleston's *Naught for Your Comfort* could become overnight a runaway best-seller are now almost as if they had never been.[137]

The *New Statesman* perhaps overstated its case. But it remains true that British public pressure for aggressive measures against apartheid had subsided in the

---

[133] For an assessment of British policy towards South Africa in the Thatcher era see: J. F. Parks, 'Britain's South African foreign policy, 1979–1989: bilateralism and multilateralism' (unpublished PhD thesis, Keele University, 1997).
[134] *The Times*, 19 June 1976.   [135] *Guardian*, 21 June 1976.
[136] *New Statesman*, 25 June 1976. Media coverage of Soweto is the subject of a case-study in Sanders, *South Africa and the international media*, ch 7.
[137] *New Statesman*, 25 June 1976.

years prior to Soweto, and that public outrage was not nearly as strong and united in 1976 as it had been in 1960.

Still, this outrage was sufficient in the wake of Soweto to inspire some significant British actions against apartheid. James Callaghan's Labour government was spurred into backing, at long last, a mandatory UN embargo against arms sales to South Africa. In 1977 it also signed the 'Gleneagles Declaration' strictly limiting Commonwealth sporting contacts with South Africa. Moreover, it was after Soweto that British film and recording artists extended their bans on contacts with South Africa. The British reaction against apartheid also grew at this time in response to South Africa's military misadventures in Angola and Namibia; to the murder of Steve Biko and the violent suppression of opposition to apartheid; as well as to the evidence of National Party corruption and mismanagement which emerged with the 'Muldergate' scandal.[138] By the time of Vorster's resignation as prime minister in September 1978, apartheid South Africa was being widely criticised in Britain for its brutality and incompetence. As *The Times* recorded, 'The cruel and vicious system of apartheid is still in place, albeit, in a few respects, less rigid than before. Soweto and Steve Biko and the many other horrific manifestations of that system have changed it little'; Vorster 'leaves a country full of problems – increasing economic difficulties and an unworkable bantustan policy'.[139] Yet, however distasteful the British public may have found apartheid, there continued to be a widespread British resistance to efforts aimed at overthrowing white dominance in South Africa.[140]

Many people in Britain continued to hope that South Africa's system of government and race relations could somehow be reformed without a complete eclipse of white power. It was widely assumed that simple majority rule would mean a descent into chaos, so if in the late 1970s and early 1980s the white rulers of South Africa were about to embark upon the road to reform, no British action should be taken to impede their progress. This was the case, even when P. W. Botha – a man long well-known as South Africa's hard-line minister of defence – emerged as Vorster's successor. Some on the Left in Britain thought that no real positive change was likely to occur under Botha. The *New Statesman* called him 'a dangerous man' and suggested that 'the best that can be said is that South Africans of all races are in for a testing time'.[141] *The Times*, however, expressed the hope, one shared by many on Right, that he 'may blossom out both as a reformer at home and a man who can mend South Africa's fences with the Western world'.[142] There were also hopes in Britain that dominant

---

[138] *The Times*, 21 Sept. 1978.   [139] *The Times*, 21 Sept. 1978.
[140] O. Aluko, 'Britain and the conflict in southern Africa', *Round Table* no. 309 (1989), pp. 54–64; A. Payne, 'The international politics of the Gleneagles agreement', *Round Table* no. 320 (1991), pp. 417–30; L. Freeman, 'All but one: Britain, the Commonwealth and sanctions', in M. Orkin (ed.), *Sanctions against apartheid* (New York, 1989), pp. 142–56.
[141] *New Statesman*, 6 Oct. 1978.   [142] *The Times*, 30 Sept. 1978.

attitudes amongst the ruling Afrikaners were on the brink of a transformation, and that after Vorster's retirement 'a fresh beginning' might be made with the development of 'a new theory of plural societies' in South Africa.[143] The end of white rule and the emergence of a black-dominated government in Zimbabwe in 1980 raised British expectations that radical change of some sort was imminent South Africa. As *The Times* put it, 'how long before there is a revolution in which the oppressed black majority attempts to seize political power?'[144] *The Times*, however, thought Zimbabwe, with its constitutional safeguards protecting white interests, might provide a model for change in South Africa, though this would mean 'making a reality of the old formula . . . – a partnership of the races'.[145] The resolution of the conflict in Zimbabwe thus renewed a forlorn British hope that an alternative could be found both to apartheid and to straightforward black majority rule in South Africa.[146]

The British Right therefore gave favourable regard to the Botha regime's constitutional changes in 1983. These gave limited political rights to 'Coloured' and 'Indian' South Africans in a 'tricameral' parliament. As *The Times* put it, 'Botha's reforms . . . are in themselves tame, but they do at least mark a major and healthy psychological departure.'[147] These reforms encouraged British support for renewed sporting contact with South Africa. One hundred and eight Conservative MPs signed a motion supporting the English rugby tour of South Africa in 1984,[148] a tour that even *The Times* regarded as a premature relaxation of pressure on Pretoria.[149] British supporters of the tour despaired, however, when Dannie Craven – president of the South African Rugby Board – spoke admiringly of Hitler in a BBC television documentary in April 1985: 'Dr Craven did more harm to sporting ties with his country than a hundred Trevor Huddlestons.'[150] Such reminders of apartheid's links with Nazism merely sharpened the contrast between those people in Britain who were encouraged by P. W. Botha's reforms, and wished to see these rewarded by a normalisation of relations; and those others who urged more extensive sanctions in order to overthrow apartheid rule completely.

The deep division in British attitudes towards South Africa was especially evident in the response to P. W. Botha's controversial visit to London and Chequers in 1984. His purpose was to meet Britain's prime minister, the staunch Cold Warrior and dogmatic free-marketeer, Margaret Thatcher. Many on the Left and in the Church condemned a move that seemed certain to confer legitimacy and respectability upon the apartheid regime. The large-scale protests against his visit were considered to be a turning-point in British support for the

---

[143] *Listener*, 28 Sept. 1978.   [144] *The Times*, 5 July 1980.   [145] *The Times*, 18 April 1980.
[146] *The Times*, 19 Aug. 1980.   [147] *The Times*, 13 May 1983.
[148] HoC Deb., vol. 55, 838, 7 March 1984.   [149] *The Times*, 4 June 1984.
[150] *Spectator*, 14 April 1984.

Anti-Apartheid Movement, an organisation founded in 1959.[151] More than a few on the Right approved the visit as a means of encouraging and rewarding evolutionary reforms, the alternative being seen as a descent into tyranny, socialism, or merely chaos. The British response also revealed the persistence of old ideas about the link between apartheid and Nazism, and about white South Africans being loyal allies. One Labour MP reminded the House of Commons that during the Second World War Botha 'spoke out vividly in support of Hitler'.[152] Thatcher countered this by pointing out that 'many South Africans came and fought in the battle of Europe'.[153] The journalist Ronald Butt almost certainly spoke for much of the British Right when he argued that it was

> better to recognise and try to build on such improvements as are peacefully in prospect than to seek theoretical democracy at the price of cataclysm, especially with the example before us of other African states which have switched suddenly to universal suffrage and then exploited it for despotism.[154]

The case for supporting the Botha government's evolutionary reforms remained convincing enough for many in Britain in the 1980s, even if criticism of apartheid became more strident than ever from others.[155]

Beginning in 1985, developments within South Africa stimulated a dramatic increase in active British antagonism towards apartheid. For months in 1985 there were daily reports – in newspapers, on television, and on radio – of violent clashes between the South African government and its opponents of all races. 'Television is', wrote Paul Johnson in connection with South Africa, 'a gigantic magnifying glass which focuses and concentrates the spark of violence and conjures it into a fire.'[156] Pretoria's response was to ban, in November 1985, all news coverage of political unrest in South Africa. News of the violence in South Africa nevertheless continued, and it increased British support for anti-apartheid activities. There were new and more effective consumer boycotts of South African goods, protests against British businesses operating in South Africa, and demonstrations in Trafalgar Square, outside South Africa's London embassy. The British Left thought that the end of apartheid was near, redoubled its protest efforts, and called for tougher sanctions, arguing that sooner or later they would have 'a morale-sapping effect' on white South Africa.[157] In 1986, the *New Statesman* considered that 'the final civil war against white rule in southern Africa has started'.[158] By contrast, the British Right derided the growth of anti-apartheid activism, labelling it 'the protest flavour of the month'.[159] Reports of unrest in South Africa encouraged the British Right's belief that the

---

[151] *New Statesman*, 4 July 1986.   [152] HoC Deb., vol. 61, 161, Merlyn Rees, 5 June 1984.
[153] HoC Deb., vol. 61, 161, 5 June 1984.   [154] *The Times*, 17 May 1984.
[155] See *The Times*, 8 May 1984.   [156] *Spectator*, 2 Nov. 1985.
[157] *New Statesman*, 8 Aug. 1986.   [158] *New Statesman*, 1 Aug. 1986.
[159] *Sunday Telegraph* quoted in *New Statesman*, 4 July, 1986.

collapse of apartheid rule under the impact of external sanctions and domestic unrest would mean anarchy, communism, and white flight. Auberon Waugh warned that South Africa looked set to fall under the sway of 'frenzied, Marxist Zulus, given up to civil war, starvation and mass murder'.[160] For Paul Johnson, 'the current attempt to destroy the South African economy' was 'one of the most wicked things that has occurred in the world since the days of Hitler and Stalin'.[161] Divisions of British opinion thus became deeper than ever in 1985 and 1986.

British attitudes at this time were also influenced by the growth of international pressure against apartheid. Churches from around the English-speaking world, most with long-standing South African and British connections, were leading and vociferous critics.[162] They helped to amplify the calls for active opposition against Pretoria made by South African Anglican Church leaders such as Desmond Tutu. They also undermined the claims of the Botha regime and its apologists in Britain that the proponents of sanctions were communist-inspired revolutionaries.[163] The Commonwealth, with its own calls for action, played a similar role in lending legitimacy to the anti-apartheid cause: it was hardly plausible to argue that Canada and Australia were anxious to promote revolution or subvert Western interests.[164] For many in Britain, however, the Commonwealth had long since ceased to have any importance, its meddling in South African affairs being seen as further evidence that it was no more than an irritating imperial relic.[165] Some saw the globe-spanning Church in a similar light, its anti-apartheid activities confirming that it had lost its proper role. The main effect of international pressure against apartheid, then, was to intensify existing divisions of British opinion on South Africa.

Defiance of international pressure seems to have had attractions of its own for the British opponents of sanctions.[166] If Thatcher really did have significant British support for her opposition to Commonwealth sanctions, it must mean that a considerable number of people in Britain remained convinced in

---

[160] *Spectator*, 2 Nov. 1985.   [161] *Spectator*, 14 Sept. 1985.
[162] R. Pratt, *In good faith: Canadian churches against apartheid* (Waterloo, Canada, 1997).
[163] *Spectator*, 14 Sept. 1985.
[164] Commonwealth Eminent Persons Group on Southern Africa, *Mission to South Africa: The findings of the Commonwealth Eminent Persons Group on Southern Africa* (Harmondsworth, 1986). Commonwealth Committee of Foreign Ministers on Southern Africa, *South Africa: The sanctions report* (Harmondsworth, 1989).
[165] John Simpson noted that the Commonwealth 'has subsisted for years on the worthy fiction that there could be essential, underlying interests uniting 49 otherwise disparate nations': *Listener*, 14 Aug. 1986.
[166] According to Hugo Young, 'All that Mrs Thatcher felt about the Commonwealth was probably felt by a majority of the electorate. Opposing Commonwealth demands was a respectable way of aligning oneself with latent racialism at home': H. Young, *The Iron Lady: a biography of Margaret Thatcher* (London and New York, 1989), p. 484. For Thatcher's arguments against sanctions see *The Times*, 16 July 1986.

the 1980s that white rule should be sustained in South Africa at almost any cost. John Simpson, the diplomatic editor with BBC television news, thought that Thatcher's views 'were a mixture of standard right-wing Conservative sympathy for South Africa as an economic entity – well-run, successful, attracting black workers from outside countries – and irritability about the self-defeating nature of apartheid'.[167] Among right-wingers there was a widespread belief that apartheid should be reformed – but not if it meant an end to effective white control in South Africa, or damage to British economic interests, or led to Soviet expansion in southern Africa.[168]

Thatcher's personal and scornful view was that South African issues generated 'more hypocrisy and hyperbole than I heard on any other subject'. She was convinced that the only way forward was through a power-sharing constitution designed to sustain white influence. This is what lay behind her notorious assertion in 1987 that anyone who thought that the ANC was going to form the government in South Africa was 'living in cloud cuckoo land'.[169] The *New Statesman*'s blunt assessment was that: 'For Mrs Thatcher, South Africa is a "white" country and she gives every sign of hoping that events will keep it that way.'[170] She was also convinced that the ANC – through its increasingly effective internal and external pressure on Pretoria, and with its refusal to forgo violence – was the leading obstacle to a power-sharing constitution. Hence her outburst that the ANC was 'a typical terrorist organisation' on a par with the Palestinian Liberation Organisation and the Irish Republican Army.[171] Proponents of a power-sharing constitution also assumed that South Africa was deeply divided along tribal lines and that such a constitution would be backed by a substantial part of the black population if ANC influence were curtailed. Thatcher and much of the British Right saw Buthelezi and Inkatha (his Zulu nationalist party) as the most acceptable face of black power in South Africa. Inkatha's political ideology was conservative, even Thatcherite. Its celebration of Zulu identity reinforced the widespread British belief in Zulu 'tribalism', a belief continually renewed in the public imagination by a variety of means including film, and the influence of writers such as Laurens van der Post.[172] The British Right's fear of the ANC's socialism, its admiration for conservative Zulu nationalism, and its hopes for a power-sharing constitution underpinned

---

[167] *Listener*, 3 July 1986. [168] *Spectator*, 27 July 1985.
[169] M. Thatcher, *The Downing Street years* (London and New York, 1993), p. 487; A. Sampson, *Mandela: the authorised biography* (London, 1999), p. 342.
[170] *New Statesman*, 1 Aug. 1986. See also H. Young, 'Thatcher; the honorary citizen of South Africa', *Guardian*, 20 Aug. 1987, p. 23.
[171] *Guardian*, 19 Oct. 1987; Sampson, *Mandela*, p. 360.
[172] Van der Post could be seen as the leading 'loyal Afrikaner' of his day, as far as many in Britain were concerned. He had a disproportionately great influence on British opinion, not least in Downing St. Thatcher described him as 'my good friend ... who talks good sense about South Africa': Thatcher, *Downing Street years*, p. 521.

a British opposition to sanctions and support for white rule during the rest of the 1980s and into the 1990s.

The unwisdom of this stance on South Africa was self-evident to a growing number of British people in the late 1980s. British anti-apartheid activism may have been a means of taking a stand against the Thatcher government and of making a gesture against racism within Britain. But it was also obvious to anyone who followed the extensive British news coverage of South Africa that the maintenance of white power through the most violent and brutal suppression of apartheid's opponents was morally unjustifiable. This, more than anything else, inspired British support for boycotts and disinvestment, for the withdrawal from South Africa of British companies such as Barclays Bank,[173] and for anti-apartheid rallies.[174] It also stirred British interest in anti-apartheid music – most memorably 'Free Nelson Mandela', a song that reached the top ten in the British charts[175] – and anti-apartheid film, including Richard Attenborough's 'Cry Freedom', and the less mainstream 'Mapantsula'.[176] And it underpinned much of the popular British admiration for Mandela and support for gestures in his honour, including the famous '70th birthday concert' at Wembley in 1988.[177] The release of Mandela from prison in February 1990 was greeted with widespread joy in Britain and was seen on the Left as a vindication of active British efforts to promote radical reform in South Africa.[178] Thatcher, it was said – no doubt to her chagrin – had 'contributed absolutely nothing to the change'.[179]

For their part, Thatcher and her supporters thought that the British policy of not isolating South Africa had been 'proved right' by Mandela's release. They argued that F. W. de Klerk had only been able to push ahead with this and other reforms because he had not been pushed too far into a domestic political corner by international pressure.[180] They further argued that De Klerk's reformist hand needed to be strengthened by a rapid lifting of sanctions and resumption of international contacts: 'if Mr De Klerk does succeed in an orderly transition to a multiracial society it will be no thanks to those who have called and still call for an armed struggle and for the smashing of Pretoria'.[181] Behind these arguments lay the persistent conviction that white power and influence had to

---

[173] *New Statesman*, 8 Aug. 1986.
[174] S. Benton, 'Anti-Apartheid takes off', *New Statesman*, 4 July 1986, pp. 11–13.
[175] *New Statesman*, 10 June 1988.
[176] J. Lewis, 'The impact of the cultural and sport boycotts', in J. Hanlon (ed.), *South Africa: the sanctions report, documents and statistics* (London, 1990), pp. 210–21; P. Davis and D. Riesenfeld, *A viewer's guide for 'In darkest Hollywood: cinema and apartheid'* (Bloomington, IN, 1995), pp. 1–47.
[177] *New Statesman*, 10 June 1988; and *Guardian* 11 June 1988.
[178] *New Statesman*, 9 and 16 Feb. 1990.
[179] *New Statesman*, 9 Feb. 1990. For Thatcher's apologia for her South African policy, see *Downing Street years*, pp. 512–35.
[180] *The Times*, 3 Feb. 1990.   [181] *Spectator*, 10 Feb. 1990.

be sustained if South Africa were not to descend into anarchy, socialism, or both. Thatcher, it was said by the British Left, 'identifies so closely with South African whites as almost to feel one of them'.[182] After February 1990, many people on the Right in Britain continued to support the De Klerk government's aims, and, more generally, to sympathise with white South Africa.

Equally, others in Britain continued to oppose the British Right's stance on South Africa. The British Left strongly condemned the Thatcher government's early lifting of sanctions (calling it both 'immoral' and 'counterproductive'),[183] its excessive support for De Klerk ('no longer in control'),[184] and its backing of Buthelezi ('the artful Janus-faced manipulator and sponsor of murderous private armies').[185] Archbishop Trevor Huddleston, the president of the Anti-Apartheid Movement insisted, in February 1990, that 'it is vital that we maintain and intensify international pressure until apartheid is destroyed'.[186] The division of British opinion on South Africa was sharper than ever in 1990.

In the months that followed Mandela's release, developments in South Africa merely confirmed many long-established and conflicting British convictions about that country. Some saw further evidence of the cynicism, selfishness, and brutality of the country's Afrikaner rulers, of the inherent immorality of race-based rule and the perils of encouraging racial distinctions. Others found further proof that violence and anarchy would attend the collapse of white rule, with insurmountable 'tribal' divisions. Other developments, though, may have encouraged some modest adjustments in British attitudes. The collapse of the Soviet Union and the end of the Cold War made the ANC's socialist rhetoric and communist links seem less threatening. The same was true of the conciliatory and conservative pronouncements of ANC leaders, above all Mandela, who made frequent visits to Britain in this transition period. And yet, right up until the 1994 elections, there persisted a belief, widespread on the Right, that the end of white control would herald an explosion of inter-racial and inter-'tribal' violence. This belief was fuelled by the violent clashes between Africans, clashes often involving Inkatha-supporting Zulus. Under the headline 'Preparing for Civil War', William Rees-Mogg wrote in *The Times* in October 1993 that 'A unitary state probably means a civil war. The Zulu people would fight for their independence, probably successfully.'[187] In December 1993, a *Sunday Times* headline read 'Blood Set to Flow as Zulus Talk War'.[188] And in April 1994, little more than two weeks before the elections, the *Sunday Times* warned that 'South Africa prepared for civil war yesterday.'[189] British attitudes

---

[182] *New Statesman*, 16 Feb. 1990.   [183] *New Statesman*, 16 Feb. 1990.
[184] *New Statesman*, 9 Feb. 1990.   [185] *New Statesman*, 9 Feb. 1990.
[186] *The Times*, 3 Feb. 1990.
[187] *The Times*, 21 Oct. 1993, quoted in Sampson, *Mandela*, p. 470.
[188] *Sunday Times*, 19 Dec. 1993, quoted in Sampson, *Mandela*, p. 479.
[189] *Sunday Times*, 10 April 1994, quoted in Sampson, *Mandela*, p. 486.

towards South Africa were still divided on the very eve of the 'miracle' of the peaceful transition to democratic rule in 1994, with those who had been most tolerant of apartheid remaining pessimistic about the future, and those who had most strongly opposed white domination professing varying degrees of optimism.

To the great surprise of the doom-merchants in Britain, and to the great relief of the optimists, the April 1994 election was an amazing success as an exercise in peaceful, participatory democracy.[190] It was followed with considerable interest in Britain. British television viewers even watched a weather forecast for South Africa on the day the polls opened. The patience, goodwill, and camaraderie of South African voters was perhaps as important a demonstration as anything else of South Africa's potential for a harmonious multi-racial future. The *Guardian* felt that the holding of a free and fair election was 'a miracle of reality faced squarely'.[191] *The Times*, wishing to emphasise the role both of De Klerk and Mandela, labelled it 'A two-sainted miracle'.[192] The ANC's overwhelming success at the polls exploded the myths that South Africa was irreconcilably divided along 'tribal' lines and that whites could hold the balance of political power, given the right constitutional framework. John Simpson thought that blacks in South Africa had gained independence at 'precisely the time Britain once envisaged for its African colonies': South Africa was, as a consequence, unlikely 'to go the way of the rest of black Africa'.[193] The ANC's success, however, confirmed for some in Britain that South Africa might before long descend into the sort of one-party despotism familiar elsewhere in Africa. Peregrine Worsthorne suggested as much in the *Sunday Telegraph*. In 1963, he had given the apartheid regime its first big public relations break. In May 1994, he wrote: 'Black majority rule in South Africa should send a shudder round the world.'[194] Some on the British Right thus continued to expect the worst in South Africa under black rule even after Mandela took power. Still, it is probably fair to say that the 'miracle' of the peaceful transition in 1994, the relative peace and stability of South Africa since then, the success of the Truth and Reconciliation Commission, and the good government of the Mandela administration did much to win over a large majority in Britain to the view that South Africa was, after all, better off under the ANC than it been under the National Party. Without a doubt, relatively few people in Britain by the late 1990s regarded apartheid as being anything other than a monumental mistake; or thought of Mandela with anything but the greatest respect and admiration.

[190] *The Times* was generally optimistic about South Africa's future in April 1994, noting that the country 'is far better placed to thrive' than many others that emerged from minority rule: *The Times*, 26 April 1994.
[191] *Guardian*, 26 April 1994.
[192] Simon Jenkins, 'A two-sainted miracle', *The Times*, 27 April 1994, p. 16.
[193] *Spectator*, 30 April 1994.
[194] *Sunday Telegraph*, 1 May 1994, quoted in Sampson, *Mandela*, p. 494.

V

The rise, ebb, and resurgence of the British reaction against apartheid had complex and contradictory causes. The unfolding of events in South Africa – including, of course, the impact of apartheid policies there – obviously influenced British attitudes. The repression and resistance which accompanied apartheid's first phase was matched by the growth of British criticism of apartheid from 1948 to 1961. The Sharpeville massacre provoked an early peak in British antagonism towards South African racial policies. The relative peace and prosperity of South Africa in the years 1962 to 1975 corresponded to a period of declining British antagonism, even if some British critics were more active and strident than ever. The Soweto uprising and the township violence of the 1980s revived and extended British anti-apartheid activism, however resistant the British Right remained to overthrowing white rule in South Africa. To some extent, then, the trajectory of British attitudes towards apartheid simply reflected the course of the internal South African struggle against racial oppression. Nevertheless, this simple correlation cannot explain early strength and unity of British criticism; nor can it account for the deepening division of British opinion after the early 1960s.

The strong and united British reaction against apartheid in the years 1948 to 1961 arose from an unusual combination of factors. First, many British people were predisposed from the outset to condemn apartheid because it was identifying policy of the National Party – Afrikaner nationalists who were antagonistic towards South Africa's British connections and population, and who were associated with Nazism. Secondly, intimate cultural ties between Britain and South Africa ensured that British people were, from the start, fully appraised about the Nationalist government's attacks on the rights of black as well as white South Africans. Finally, the desire to protect Britain's prestige, influence, and interests in Africa and around the world – a desire in which the empire and Commonwealth loomed large – provided further reasons to reject apartheid. It damaged the moral authority of whites to rule anywhere in Africa, it challenged the British conception of multi-racial 'partnership', and it called into question the meaning and unity of the Commonwealth. In the circumstances of the 1950s and early 1960s, this meant that a broad spectrum of British opinion could unite in opposition to apartheid – those on the Left who favoured early black political emancipation, those stirred by religious or humanitarian impulses to seek justice and fair treatment for all in South Africa, and those on the Right who supported continued white rule on British lines.

Paradoxically, some of the same factors which generated the strength and unity of this early British reaction also helped to produce the deeply divided attitudes that emerged as South African, British, and international circumstances changed after the early 1960s. Several significant shifts occurred in the 1960s.

White English-speaking South Africans began to support the National Party in noteworthy numbers, with the result that apartheid came to be seen in Britain as being inseparable from white rule. Political unrest in South Africa subsided while its economy entered a period of dramatic growth. Racial tensions within Britain itself increased. 'Partnership' proved to be a failure in Africa, and British colonial rule came to an abrupt end. Many black African states descended into disorder. British illusions about the Commonwealth as a surrogate empire largely disappeared just as Britain began a painful reorientation towards Europe. These changes radically altered the context in which British people judged apartheid. The most significant result was the emergence in the 1960s of a new tolerance of apartheid by the British Right, tolerance that grew from attitudes and relationships previously engendering antagonism. The desire to protect British interests in Africa – which for many on the British Right had always meant supporting white rule there – would, by the mid-1960s, encourage a British tolerance or support for apartheid. Close cultural links with South Africa began, at that time, to inspire the British Right to identify more with white South Africans as a whole, rather than with opponents of apartheid. While the British Right's tolerance of apartheid grew, others in Britain became more antagonistic than ever towards apartheid. As in earlier years, the defence of Commonwealth unity, as well as of British prestige and interests in Africa, still demanded for some in Britain that apartheid should be actively opposed. Ever greater British antagonism towards apartheid also continued to be stimulated by close cultural links which raised British consciousness of conditions in South Africa. Furthermore, the National Party's repugnant ideology and old links with Nazism provoked, till the end, a strongly negative reaction, especially in those who wished to take a stand against racism in Britain. The early unity and later divisions of British attitudes towards apartheid were founded on a material and cultural relationship between Britain and South Africa which was strong and, in many ways, relatively constant. More remarkably, this unity and division were also founded on persistent, if contradictory British attitudes to nationalism and race, to democracy and human rights, and to Britain's needs and objectives in the wider world.

British attitudes towards apartheid were also shaped, united, and divided by party politics.[195] In the 1950s and early 1960s, the Labour and Conservative Parties were equally critical of South African racial policies, even though some of their motives and objectives differed. Signs of a split between these parties became evident in the 1950s, on the question of how best to encourage change in South Africa. But it was not until the mid-1960s that a serious division

---

[195] See P. Murphy, *Party politics and decolonisation: the Conservative Party and British colonial policy in tropical Africa, 1951–1964* (Oxford, 1995), pp. 132–3, 180, 206–7; and M. Clarke, *British external policy making in the 1990s* (London, 1992), pp. 217–21.

emerged, a division which widened in the decades that followed. For many on the British Left, anti-apartheid campaigning became 'a moral lodestone',[196] and a unifying focus of domestic political activity. Opposition to sanctions, defiance of the Left and of the Commonwealth, came to serve a comparable function for Conservatives. Each side's attitude towards South Africa encouraged the other to adopt a contrary stance. In this and in other ways, the various social, ethnic, and class cleavages at work in British party politics also had a role in shaping British attitudes towards apartheid. The sharp differences which developed in the 1970s and 1980s between the Conservative and Labour Parties on South Africa, persisted into the 1990s, reflecting and exacerbating the divisions of British opinion on the likely fate of the country after the fall of apartheid.

Some of these divisions still persist. The comparative success of the 'New South Africa', the popularity of Mandela as (ex-)president and as world statesman, the persistence and even revival of British cultural links with South Africa have meant that South Africa's existence has again become a source of pride for many people in Britain, just as it was in 1910 and in the Botha–Smuts years that followed. But, the disastrous impact of HIV/AIDS and the daunting problem of unemployment in South Africa have confirmed some of the dire prognostications of the British Right. More commonly, though, South Africa has come to be admired for demonstrating how reconciliation and a bold extension of political rights could overcome the most deep-seated and violent animosities, again as was true earlier in the twentieth century. Mandela became more highly regarded in Britain than almost anyone else: 'probably the most widely respected man in the world'.[197] In an astonishingly short space of time, South Africa has gone from being widely demonised in Britain for straying so far from British traditions of good government and fair play, to being paraded as an example of racial harmony and political reconciliation – a country which Britain should emulate in handling some of its own problems, whether in the racially divided cities of England, or the culturally divided north of Ireland. As a British Foreign Office minister commented during Mandela's visit to London in April 2001: 'South Africa continues to offer inspiration and hope to many in the world.'[198]

[196] *New Statesman*, 16 Feb. 1990.   [197] *Guardian*, 30 April 2001.
[198] Statement by Brian Wilson, 29 April 2001. Foreign and Commonwealth Office press release, www.fco.gov.uk.

Epilogue
The relationship restored: the return of the new South Africa to the Commonwealth, 1994

Whoever slipped 'Land of hope and glory' into the programme of music played at the inauguration of Nelson Mandela as president of South Africa can have had no idea of the anthem's message, no sense of political correctness, or else a wry sense of humour. For it was not merely the tune of this, the most unashamedly jingoistic of all British ceremonial music, that was played for the dignitaries assembling in the amphitheatre of Pretoria's Union Buildings on 10 May 1994. The South Africa Navy band (who, immaculately turned out in their summer whites, looked as though they could have stepped off a Royal Navy cruiser in 1910 to mark the establishment of the Union of South Africa) had their leading soloist sing the verse lyrics as well as the rousing chorus. Indeed, the event was very much one in the English social tradition: a day in the stewards' enclosure at the Henley royal regatta or a garden party at Buckingham Palace, the proceedings too well rehearsed, too much like a gathering of Edwardian high society, unconcerned by social realities carefully hidden from view by more than four terrible decades of apartheid social engineering. This resurgent Englishness effortlessly supplied alternative rituals long suppressed, much in the manner of Russian Orthodoxy which made itself available after the collapse of communism.

Mandela's inauguration was essentially an African independence ceremony, with South Africa playing host to representatives of 159 foreign states witnessing the last act of decolonisation on the African continent, a transfer of power in the classic mode to the charismatic leader of a successor regime.[1]

If the fall of the apartheid regime and the emergence of the 'new' South Africa was indeed a species of decolonisation, then the conceptual theories of African decolonisation should apply. Most British historians tend to opt for a judicious balance of metropolitan–domestic, colonial–nationalist, and international influences.[2] Internal economic constraints (which reduced available

---

[1] P. J. Henshaw, 'Land of hope and glory: Mandela's new South Africa', *Queen's Quarterly: A Canadian Review*, vol. 101 (Kingston, Ontario, 1994), pp. 439–50.

[2] This approach is generally characteristic of the contributions to J. M. Brown and W. R. Louis, eds., *The Oxford history of the British empire*, vol. IV: *The twentieth century* (Oxford, 1999), as well as

financial, military, and policing resources), and feasibility calculations about governability (and the preservation of future interests and prestige) in the face of nationalist resistance (or potential resistance), were clearly important in the British case. However, international considerations seem to carry the greatest explanatory power. These include: (1) the facilitating influence of foreign or neighbouring example, the impossibility of insulating territories from external modernising forces by the construction of ring-fences; (2) the over-riding importance of the Cold War, its context and imperatives; and (3) the importunate pressure of United Nations rulings and international criticism.[3] All these factors have a methodological applicability to the demise of apartheid. Some authorities have insisted that the old regime in South Africa was unconcerned about international opinion, but it is almost certain that the government was more influenced by it than it cared to admit. A profound structural economic crisis, marked by falling economic growth and capital formation, and the financial sanctions imposed by international bankers,[4] together with the fissiparity of internal politics, endemic *broedertwis* (fraternal strife), were highly significant in South Africa. Nevertheless, as O'Meara has been at pains to stress, 'external factors – sanctions, the looming inability to finance South Africa's external debt, military reverse in Angola, the collapse of the Soviet empire, the end of the Cold War, etc – were all likewise vital' to the evolving reconfiguration of power.[5]

This is not the place for a systematic account of the collapse of apartheid, or for authoritative statements about the relative significance of internal revolt and township activism as against external pressures and changing international contexts. But in explaining how the old regime had got to the point where it felt it had no alternative but to make its accommodation with the destabilisation threat from the African National Congress and the criticisms from outside, a number of interrelated political and cultural developments clearly need to be addressed. The breakaway of the Conservative (*Konserwatiewe*) Party in 1982 was a vital precondition, because it reduced internal strains within the National Party and allowed it to redefine things in a new way as a party no

---

of the latest books, J. Springhall, *Decolonization since 1945: the collapse of European overseas empires* (New York and Basingstoke, 2001), and L. J. Butler, *Britain and empire: adjusting to a post-imperial world* (London and New York, 2002).

[3] R. Hyam and W. R. Louis, eds., *The Conservative government and the end of empire, 1957–1964* (BDEEP, London, 2000), part 1, introd., pp. xlvi–xlvii and lxx–lxxii.

[4] R.W. Bethlehem, 'Economic restructuring in post-apartheid South Africa' in Alexander Johnston, S. Shezi, and G. Bradshaw, eds., *Constitution-making in the New South Africa* (London, 1993), pp. 138–53; D. O'Meara, *Forty lost years: the apartheid state and the politics of the National Party, 1948–1994* (Randburg and Athens, Ohio, 1996), pp. 354–60; South Africa's share of world gold production fell from 52 per cent in 1980 to 32.5 per cent in 1986 (p. 354).

[5] O'Meara, *Forty lost years*, p. 463.

longer yoked to Afrikaner nationalism as its sole political expression.[6] It placed the *verligte* ('enlightened') group in the ascendant. Nor should the power of religious revisionism and example be underestimated. The acceptable face of black leadership was first demonstrated in the churches. Without Archbishop Desmond Tutu there could have been no President Nelson Mandela. And if the theologians of the Dutch Reformed Churches were crucial to the evolution of apartheid they were equally instrumental in its collapse. In 1985 the NGK (Nederduitse Gereformeerde Kerk) of the Western Cape denied the supposed biblical justification for apartheid and the new Moderator of the NGK declared his church to be 'an open church . . . [which] cannot be closed to people of other cultures'. At Braamfontein in 1985 there was an interdenominational repudiation of apartheid by 150 theologians (the Kairos Document), and in 1990 Dutch Reformed Church leaders signified their public 'repentance' by the Rustenberg Declaration.[7] President F. W. de Klerk, a deeply religious Calvinist of the Gereformeerde Kerk (the smaller 'Dopper' church which had been the first to reject apartheid), appears to have been influenced by Dr Christian Beyers Naudé, once ostracised as the leading Afrikaner clerical critic of the regime, who was now adopted as part of De Klerk's negotiating team with the ANC in 1990. Apparently De Klerk believed that God had told him to dismantle apartheid.[8] Unfortunately, in offering good pragmatic advice about the proven unworkability of apartheid, the Almighty forgot to mention that it was also morally reprehensible – or so we must conclude from De Klerk's steadfast refusal to admit that it had been wrong, not simply a miscalculation.

If the spectacular collapse of communism in Soviet Russia and the fall of the Berlin Wall (1989) amounted to a revolutionary turning-point in the global geopolitical situation which made it impossible to justify apartheid any longer out of fear of black communism, geopolitical frustrations in the sub-continental arena provided a more positive motive for embracing reform. South Africa's hegemonic drive for a regional role was being fatally blocked by the need to reconcile this aim with the defence of a white-dominated state. Radical domestic changes were thus in part designed to secure the normalisation of external relations, in particular the claim to be the power-house and driving-force

---

[6] C. J. Louth, 'External pressures and internal changes in South Africa, 1976–1990' (Cambridge University MPhil dissertation, 1992); O'Meara, *Forty lost years*, pp. 306–16; H. Giliomee, '*Broedertwis*: intra-Afrikaner conflicts in the transition from apartheid, 1969–1991' in N. Etherington, ed, *Peace, politics and violence in the New South Africa* (London, 1992), pp. 162–95; Etherington's own contribution to this volume, 'Explaining the death throes of apartheid', pp. 102–20, is a lively survey of the general issues.

[7] Thus proving right Sir John Maud who had predicted in 1960 that Christianity was 'a much more serious long-term threat than Communism to white supremacy': see chapter 11, p. 264. The British Council of Churches, *The Kairos Document: a theological comment* (London, 1986); O'Meara, *Forty lost years*, pp. 336–7.

[8] W. de Klerk, *F. W. de Klerk: the man and his time* (Johannesburg, 1991).

behind regional economic development and co-operation, perhaps with aspirations around the Indian Ocean rim as well. Unsuccessful military engagements on South Africa's borders, in Angola and Mozambique, which were subject to escalating unpopularity at home, had effects rather like those which surrounded the involvement of the United States in Vietnam.[9]

A succession of British governments going back to Harold Macmillan's had publicly and strongly opposed the use of economic measures to bring about the end of apartheid. In 1960, Macmillan himself had spoken against the emerging British consumer boycott of South African goods, stating towards the end of his 'wind of change' speech that 'boycotts will never get you anywhere'. This dubious advice was ignored by growing numbers of people in Britain in subsequent decades. It was ignored also by people and governments around the world, to the extent that, in the mid-1980s Margaret Thatcher bitterly antagonised all other Commonwealth leaders with her obdurate opposition to sanctions. The British government did, nevertheless, impose a variety of sanctions in the 1980s. These included bans on the export of computers for use by the security forces, of nuclear technology, and of crude oil; bans on the imports of iron and steel, and of gold coins; as well as voluntary bans on new investment and on tourist promotion. The British government also became in the 1980s more amenable to sharing the Commonwealth line on the arms embargo. Britain had for many years limited arms sales. In 1960, the sight of British-made armoured cars spearheading the repression of black South Africans prompted the first restrictions on arms intended for internal use. Harold Wilson's government extended the embargo in 1964. Edward Heath's resumed the sale of arms for naval defence, thereby provoking a crisis in Commonwealth relations from 1970. Only after Labour's return to power in 1974 were British arms sales and overt defence collaboration finally and comprehensively banned.

In the transition period after 1990 the British government worked hard at the restoration of relations. It urged an early end to all Commonwealth sanctions against South Africa, despite the ANC's calls to the contrary. British trade and investment were promoted vigorously, and so successfully that Britain briefly regained its position as South Africa's largest trading partner, a position lost in the 1960s. In common with the rest of the Commonwealth, the British government waited until 1994 before lifting the ban on arms sales. It then began to assist the integration of the armies of liberation into the new South African National Defence Force, while at the same time actively encouraging the re-equipment of the Force with British weaponry. The British government also

---

[9] J. Barratt, 'Current constraints on South Africa's foreign policy and diplomacy', in Johnston, et al., eds., *Constitution-making in the New South Africa*, pp. 157–60; S. Chan, *Exporting apartheid: foreign policies in Southern Africa, 1978–1988* (London, 1990), pp. 91–113; R. Davies and D. O'Meara, 'Total strategy in Southern Africa: South African regional policy since 1978', *JSAS* vol. 11 (1985), pp. 183–211.

shared the Commonwealth's desire to bring the cultural boycott and 'people to people' sanctions to an early end. The Harare meeting of the Commonwealth heads of government agreed in October 1991 to a conditional lifting of the ban on sporting contacts with South Africa, a ban enshrined in the 1977 'Gleneagles Declaration on Apartheid in Sport'. Such contacts, particularly on the cricket and rugby fields, had provoked fierce and sometimes violent controversy since the 1960s. The Harare meeting called for South Africa's readmission to the International Cricket Council, and within weeks the Springboks were playing in India. The rugby Springboks toured Britain in 1992, the first such tour since 1969–70. Finally, and not insignificantly, Britain joined other Commonwealth countries in discreet diplomatic efforts to encourage South Africa to rejoin the Commonwealth. Less discreetly, Nelson Mandela was invited to the Harare meeting where he was treated by all, including the Queen, as a *de facto* head of state.[10]

The British government naturally welcomed warmly the return of South Africa to the Commonwealth in July 1994, marking it with due ceremony in Westminster Abbey in the following month. 'The Commonwealth without South Africa', declared prime minister John Major, 'was a bit like rice pudding without milk', and he called for a 'partnership in progress' between Britain and South Africa.[11] But why should the ANC have taken up the renewed hand of friendship? There was a formidable legacy of mistrust between the two. Although both sought the same general outcome, namely, abolition of apartheid and an end to white majority rule, they had seriously disagreed about the means, especially during the Thatcher era.[12] Fundamentally, however, the ANC was

---

[10] Commonwealth Committee of Foreign Ministers on South Africa, *South Africa: the Sanctions Report* (Harmondsworth, 1989); House of Commons, *Sixth report from the Foreign Affairs Committee, session 1985–1986, South Africa: observations by the government* (Cmnd 9925, London 1986), and *First report of the Foreign Affairs Committee, session 1990–1991, United Kingdom policy towards South Africa and the other states in the region: observations by the government* (Cm 1525, London, 1991); International Monetary Fund, *Direction of trade statistics yearbook* (Washington, 1999); L. Freeman, 'All but one: Britain, the Commonwealth and sanctions', in M. Orkin, ed., *Sanctions against apartheid* (New York, 1989); L. Freeman, *The ambiguous champion: Canada and South Africa in the Trudeau and Mulroney years* (Toronto, 1997); O. Aluko, 'Britain and the conflict in Southern Africa', *The Round Table: the Commonwealth Journal of International Affairs*, no. 309 (1989), pp. 54–64; 'Editorial: The Harare CHOGM and after', *The Round Table*, no 321 (1992), pp. 3–15.
[11] Quoted in S. A. Cardy, 'British foreign policy towards South Africa during the De Klerk era, 1989–1994' (Cambridge University MPhil dissertation, 1995), ch. 5, pp. 27–8.
[12] For British policy after 1979, see: M. Thatcher, *The Downing Street years* (London, 1993), pp. 512–35; D. Adamson, *The last empire: Britain and the Commonwealth, 1961–1988* (London, 1989), pp. 61–88; S. Chan, *The Commonwealth in world politics: a study of international action, 1965–1985* (London, 1988), pp. 35–46; Arnold Smith (with C. Sanger), *Stitches in time: the Commonwealth in world politics* (London, 1981), pp. 51–75, 204–44, on Rhodesia; J. Barber, '"An historical and persistent interest": Britain and South Africa', *International Affairs*, vol. 67 (1991), pp. 723–38; Michael Clarke, *British external policy-making in the 1990s* (London, 1992), pp. 217–21.

forced to accept pragmatic and co-operative relations with Britain, much as the National Party had been obliged to do in the past, simply because Britain's importance to South Africa was still great enough to determine that 'the national interest' must prevail over sectional sentiment. But magnanimously, too, the ANC reached back to pre-Thatcherite days, and remembered the clandestine help given by the Macmillan government to Nelson Mandela in the days of his freedom, to Oliver Tambo and the ANC, meeting in and moving through Bechuanaland by means of the MI6 'refugee pipeline' between 1960 and 1962.[13] Nelson Mandela in September 1994 recalled the encouragement Macmillan's 'wind of change' speech had given, repeating his admiration for it in the moving address he gave in Westminster Hall during his state visit to Britain in July 1996. Some of the ANC leadership, including Oliver Tambo, the president of the ANC, had always maintained that 'black South Africa never really left the Commonwealth', its departure having been improperly engineered by 'an illegal regime', a white minority government which had no right to make such a fundamental change to South Africa's constitutional and international status.[14] The very fact that Afrikanerdom disapproved of the Commonwealth, and dismissed it as an irrelevant relic, could only enhance its appeal to the ANC. In any case, the Commonwealth, like the British people – and both as distinct from the British government – had always appeared to be supportive.

Not even its most fervent advocates could reasonably argue that if the Commonwealth did not exist it would be necessary to invent it. But exist it did, and its population included one quarter of humanity and one-third of its states. It offered various cultural, sporting, professional, environmental, and educational links which were valued by its members.[15] It was no longer 'a white man's club', and had lost its 'British-centredness' through a process of becoming what has been called, rather awkwardly, 'de-Britannicised'. In the early 1990s, too, its potential was 'rediscovered' in Britain.[16]

So what specifically was it about the Commonwealth that South Africa's new government of national unity found attractive? As early as 1987 the Commonwealth secretary-general, Shridath Ramphal, had said that a free South Africa would be welcomed back. The Commonwealth Heads of Government Meeting

---

[13] Nelson Mandela, *Long walk to freedom: the autobiography* (London, 1994), pp. 364–5; T. Tlou, N. Parsons, and W. Henderson, *Seretse Khama, 1921–1980* (Braamfontein, 1995), pp. 200–2.

[14] Quoted by S. S. Ramphal, 'Canada and the Commonwealth: empires of the mind', *The Round Table*, no. 304, vol. 76 (1987), p. 431. For the views of an ANC activist towards the Commonwealth in the years 1960 to 1994 see Abdul S. Minty, 'South Africa and the Commonwealth: assessing the challenges ahead', in G. Mills and J. Stremlau, eds., *The Commonwealth in the 21st century* (Braamfontein, 1999), pp. 57–61.

[15] D. A. Low, *'The contraction of England': an inaugural lecture, 1984* (Cambridge, 1985), pp. 27–8; W. D. McIntyre, *The significance of the Commonwealth, 1965–1990* (London, 1991); Chan, *The Commonwealth in world politics*, esp. pp. 67–72.

[16] McIntyre, *The significance of the Commonwealth*, p. 5, and 'Commonwealth legacy', in Brown and Louis, eds., *The Oxford history of the British empire*, vol. IV, pp. 693–702.

in 1993 issued the formal invitation. Pariah states have to find a point of re-entry into the international community; the Commonwealth could provide this function, and rather obviously so as an organisation of which South Africa could be called 'a founder member'. Yet, remarkably, all South Africa's immediate neighbours (except Angola) had become or were seeking to become members: not just Lesotho, Botswana, Swaziland, and Zimbabwe, but also Namibia and Mozambique, with no previous connection with the British empire.[17]

Beyond this compelling if unexpected consideration, there were perhaps four possibilities which swayed the South African decision to rejoin the Commonwealth. (1) There was a good prospect of obtaining a privileged and generous share of Commonwealth aid, technical assistance, and educational opportunity; Canada and Australia since 1991 had given a disproportionate share of their attention to international aid for the southern African region. (2) There was the right to participate every two years in the Heads of Government meetings, a valuable but homely forum for international talks and with potential for networking contacts with fifty or so other governments well scattered about the globe; these meetings were in fact unique in bringing together so many world leaders for such long periods. (3) The Commonwealth had a value because of its record as a defender of cultural and human rights; Thabo Mbeki was anxious to reassure the Afrikaners, and urged the Commonwealth to send 'a clear and very important message that in much the same way as they took a position against apartheid, they would stand ready to act against any tendency in the new South Africa to deny people their rights'. (4) Finally, and probably by no means least, South Africa would through Commonwealth membership regain entry to the full range of international rugby and other sporting competitions (notably the Commonwealth Games, which were held every four years, alternately with the Olympics).[18]

Speaking in March 1994 in London, the South African ambassador, Kent Durr, had emphasised that the new South Africa shared the principled aspirations of the Commonwealth: 'a reformed South Africa is looking to rejoin a reformed Commonwealth. The Commonwealth, like us, finds it more productive to look forward than back.' He summed up as follows:

Joining the Commonwealth is not the *most* important priority in international relations for South Africa but it remains very important. It will mean a lot to many people in South Africa and it will definitely constitute a major normalization with the international community. It will be a forum from which we may derive many benefits and certainly the downside is nil and the costs are not prohibitive. The upside, I believe, is tremendous.[19]

---

[17] P. Vale, 'Foreign policy of a post-apartheid South Africa', in Johnston *et al.*, eds., *Constitution-making in South Africa*, p. 195.

[18] P. J. Henshaw, 'The Commonwealth and South Africa', in G. Mills, ed., *From pariah to participant: South Africa's evolving foreign relations* (Johannesburg, 1994), pp. 158–67.

[19] Kent Durr, 'South Africa and the Commonwealth', *The Round Table*, no. 330, vol. 83 (1994), pp. 169–73.

Commenting later in 1994, the Afrikaner historian, Professor O. Geyser, recalled that in 1961 'a close and historic link of true significance between South Africa and Britain was broken'.[20] Most observers were heartened by the restoration of that link, and shared the 'special sense of joy' expressed by the Commonwealth secretary-general, Emeka Anyaoku, upon South Africa's return to the Commonwealth, with all that this symbolised in terms of marking the definitive end of the evils of the apartheid era.[21] When Nelson Mandela came to Britain in the spring of 2001 it was a triumphant demonstration and celebration of what he called the 'unbreakable bonds' and 'long-established tie' of Anglo-South African friendship, of the restoration of that 'genuinely significant . . . special relationship, and its mutual benefits, which history has bound us in'.[22]

---

[20] O. Geyser, 'South Africa rejoins the Commonwealth', *The Round Table* no. 331, vol. 83 (1994), p. 325.
[21] Quoted by D. Ingram, 'Commonwealth update', ibid., p. 289.
[22] Magdalene College Archives, P/30/2, address by Nelson Mandela on the occasion of admission to an Honorary Fellowship, 2 May 2001; also the address in Trafalgar Square, London, at the Freedom Day Concert, 29 Apr. 2001. (Transcript by courtesy of the South African High Commission, supplied 5 July 2001.)

Select bibliography

I BRITISH GOVERNMENT AND OTHER ARCHIVES

1 *CABINET OFFICE AND PRIME MINISTER'S OFFICE* (PUBLIC RECORD OFFICE, KEW)

Cabinet Office registered files: CAB 21
Prime minister's letters to the Sovereign: CAB 41
Cabinet conclusions/minutes: CAB 23, CAB 128
Cabinet memoranda: CAB 37, CAB 129
Defence Committee: CAB 131
Commonwealth Prime Ministers' Meetings: CAB 133
Colonial Policy Committee: CAB 134
Prime minister's correspondence and papers: PREM 4 (1936–1945), PREM 8 (1945–1951), PREM 11 (1951–1964)

2 *GOVERNMENT DEPARTMENTS* (PUBLIC RECORD OFFICE, KEW)

(a) *Colonial Office*
Cape Colony (to 1910): CO 48
Natal (to 1910): CO 179
Orange River Colony (to 1910): CO 224
Transvaal (to 1910): CO 291
General Correspondence: CO 323
South Africa, high commissioner: CO 417
Supplementary secret correspondence: CO 537
Africa, correspondence: CO 847
Confidential print, Africa: CO 879
International Relations Dept: CO 936
Central Africa and Aden Dept: CO 1015
Southern Africa (from 1961): CO 1048

(b) *Dominions Office/Commonwealth Relations Office*
General correspondence: DO 9, DO 35
Confidential print: DO 116
Supplementary secret correspondence: DO 117
South Africa, high commissioner: DO 119
Private Office papers: DO 121

352   Select bibliography

South Africa, High Commission Territories (from 1960): DO 157
Southern Africa (from 1960): DO 180
Central Africa (from 1960): DO 183

(c) Foreign Office
Correspondence, political: FO 371

(d) Service Chiefs and Departments
Chiefs of Staff Committee
Minutes of meetings: DEFE 4
Registered files, general series: DEFE 7

Admiralty
Correspondence and papers: ADM 1
Record Office – cases: ADM 116
Board of Admiralty: ADM 167
First Sea Lord's papers: ADM 205
Intelligence Dept: ADM 231

War Office
Registered files, general series: WO 32

(e) Ministry of Supply
Atomic Energy Division: AB 16

(f) Treasury
Imperial and Foreign Division: T 220
Overseas Finance Division: T 236
Commonwealth and Foreign Division (from 1960): T 296

3 PRIVATE PAPERS

Asquith: Bodleian Library, Oxford
Batterbee: Rhodes House Library, Oxford
Bryce: Bodleian Library, Oxford
Sydney Buxton: Newtimber Place, Hassocks, Sussex
Campbell-Bannerman: British Library (Add. Mss.)
Churchill: Churchill College Archives Centre (CHAR)
Crewe: Cambridge University Library
Dilke: Bodleian Library, Oxford
Elgin: Broomhall, Dunfermline, Scotland
Herbert Gladstone: British Library (Add. Mss.)
Gordon Walker: Churchill College Archives Centre (GNWR)
Hankey: Churchill College Archives Centre (HNKY)
Lewis Harcourt: Bodleian Library, Oxford
Alan Lascelles: Churchill College Archives Centre (LASL)
Oliver Lyttelton: Churchill College Archives Centre (CHAN II)

Noel-Baker: Churchill College Archives Centre (NBKR)
Packer: Churchill College Archives Centre (PCKR)
Smuts: Cambridge University Library (microfilm)
Swinton: Churchill College Archives Centre (SWIN)

II SOUTH AFRICAN GOVERNMENT AND OTHER ARCHIVES

1 UNION AND STATE GOVERNMENT ARCHIVES

(a) South African National Archives (Government Records, Central Archives Depot, Pretoria)
Dept of External/Foreign Affairs: BTS
Dept of Information, London Office: ILN
London High Commission/Embassy: BLO
Governor-general's papers: GG
Prime minister's papers: PM
Accessions:
N. C. Havenga papers: A 38
J. E. Holloway papers: A 80
J. C. Smuts papers: A 1
C. T. te Water papers: A 78

(b) Cape Archives Depot (Cape Town)
T. E. Dönges papers: A 1646
A. L. Geyer papers: A 1890

(c) Natal Archives Depot (Government records, Pietermaritzburg)
Government House papers: GH
Interior Dept: CSO
Prime minister's papers: PM

(d) Transvaal Archives (Pretoria)
Photographic collection

2 OTHER DEPOSITS

Drum collection: Bailey's African History Archives, Lanseria, Johannesburg
P. Duncan papers: University of Cape Town (BC 294)
L. Egeland papers: Killie Campbell Africana Library, Durban
Hofmeyr papers: William Cullin Library, Johannesburg (A 1)
H. G. Lawrence papers: University of Cape Town (BC 640)
D. F. Malan papers: J. S. Gericke Library, Stellenbosch University
J. S. Marwick papers: Killie Campbell Africana Library, Durban
National Defence Force Archive, secretary for defence (DC): Pretoria
G. H. Nicholls papers: Killie Campbell Africana Library, Durban
L. Phillips papers: Barlow Rand Archives, Sandton, Johannesburg
Photographic collections: MuseumAfrika, Johannesburg
Press clippings file for *Argus* and *Cape Times*: University of Cape Town

C. J. Sibbett papers: University of Cape Town (BC 50)
Simon's Town Dockyard collection: Simon's Town Museum
Simon's Town Photographic collection: Simon's Town Museum
Royal Navy and South African Navy collections: South African Naval Museum, Simon's Town
J. C. Smuts collection: University of Cape Town (BC 714)
South African Institute of Race Relations papers: William Cullin Library, Johannesburg (AD 1788)
A. Thomas, Oral history of Simon's Town: University of Cape Town (BC 1004)
S. F. Waterson papers: University of Cape Town (BC 631)

III *COMMONWEALTH GOVERNMENTS' ARCHIVES*

1 *BOTSWANA NATIONAL ARCHIVES* (GABORONE)

Secretariat papers

2 *NATIONAL ARCHIVES OF CANADA* (OTTAWA)

Cabinet minutes and memoranda: RG 2
Dept of Defence: RG 24
Dept of External Affairs: RG 25
Dept of Finance: RG 19
Dept of Trade and Commerce: RG 20
Prime minister's papers: MG 26
N. Robertson papers: MG 30 E163

3 *LESOTHO GOVERNMENT ARCHIVES* (MASERU)

Proceedings of the Basutoland National Council, 1908–1958 (S 3/20/1–50)

4 *SWAZILAND NATIONAL ARCHIVES* (MBABANE)

Photographic collection
Resident commissioner's papers
Secretariat papers

IV *PUBLISHED PRIMARY SOURCES*

1 *UNITED KINGDOM: OFFICIAL PUBLICATIONS*

(a) Parliament
Debates, House of Commons; *Debates, House of Lords*; 1899–1994

(b) Command papers
Cd 2399   *South Africa: Report of the Native Affairs Commission* (1905) [Lagden Report]
Cd 3250   *Transvaal Letters Patent* (1906)

Select bibliography 355

Cd 3564 *Federation* [the Selborne Memorandum] (1907)
Cmd 7913 *Bechuanaland Protectorate: the succession to the chieftainship of the Bamangwato tribe* (1950)
Cmd 8354 *Reserves and liabilities, 1931 to 1945* (1951)
Cmd 8707 *Basutoland, the Bechuanaland Protectorate and Swaziland: a history of discussions with the Union of South Africa, 1909–1939* (1952)
Cmd 9520 *Exchange of Letters on defence matters between the Governments of the United Kingdom and the Union of South Africa* (1955) [the Simon's Town Agreement]
Cmnd 122 *United Kingdom balance of payments, 1946 to 1956* (1957)
Cmnd 399 *United Kingdom balance of payments, 1955 to 1957* (1958)
Cmnd 827 *Committee on the working of the monetary system* (1959) [the Radcliffe Committee]
Cmnd 1188 *United Kingdom balance of payments, 1957 to 1960* (1960)
Cmnd 1671 *United Kingdom balance of payments, 1959 to 1961* (1962)
Cmnd 9925 *Sixth Report from the Foreign Affairs Committee, session 1985–1986, South Africa: observations by the government* (1986)
Cm 1525 *First report of the Foreign Affairs Committee, session 1990–1991, United Kingdom policy towards South Africa and the other states in the region: observations by the government* (1991)

(c) Official serials
Bank of England, *Statistical Abstract* (London, starts 1970)
Bank of England, *Quarterly Bulletin* (London, starts 1960)
Commissioners of H. M. Customs and Excise, *Annual statement of the trade of the United Kingdom* [title varies] (London, 1947–72)
Parliament, *Accounts relating to the trade and navigation of the United Kingdom each month of the year* (London, 1931–1939)

2 UNION AND REPUBLIC OF SOUTH AFRICA

(a) Parliament
Debates, House of Assembly (Cape Town, 1924–1994)
Debates, Joint Sitting of House of Assembly and Senate (Cape Town, 1925–1956)
Debates, Senate (Cape Town, 1924–1980)

(b) Parliamentary reports
S.C. 9–1932 *Report of the Select Committee on the Gold Standard* (Cape Town, 1932)
U.G. 19–1952 *Negotiations regarding the transfer to the Union of South Africa of the Government of Basutoland, the Bechuanaland Protectorate and Swaziland, 1910–1939* (Pretoria, 1952)
U.G. 61–1955 *Summary of the Report of the Commission for the Socio-Economic Development of the Bantu Areas within the Union of South Africa* (Pretoria, 1955 [1956]) [Tomlinson Commission]

(c) Official serials
Department of Customs and Excise:
Annual statement of the Union of South Africa and the territory of South West Africa (Pretoria, 1931–54)
Annual statement of trade and shipping of the Union of South Africa (Pretoria, 1955–60)
Foreign trade statistics, 1961–1972 (Pretoria, 1962–73)

South African Reserve Bank:
Quarterly Bulletin of Statistics (Pretoria, 1949–1965)

Official publications:
Bureau of Census and Statistics, *Union statistics for fifty years: 1910–1960, Jubilee issue* (Pretoria, 1960)
Dept of Mines, *Mining statistics: summary of the data submitted to the government mining engineer by mines and works as defined by the Mines and Works Act No. 27 of 1956* (Pretoria, 1973)

3 CANADA

(a) Parliament
Debates, House of Commons (Ottawa, 1945–1961)

(b) Official serials
Dept of External Affairs: *Canada at the United Nations* [title varies] (Ottawa, 1947–1966)

4 INTERNATIONAL ORGANISATIONS

(a) Commonwealth Secretariat, London
Commonwealth Eminent Persons Group on South Africa, *Mission to South Africa: the findings of the Commonwealth Eminent Persons Group on South Africa* (Harmondsworth, 1986)
Commonwealth Committee of Foreign Ministers on Southern Africa, *South Africa: the sanctions report* (Harmondsworth, 1989)

(b) Bank for International Settlements, Basle
Annual Report (1970–1992)

(c) United Nations, New York
Yearbook of the United Nations (1947–94)
United Nations Weekly Bulletin [title varies] (1946–61)
United Nations Review (1954–1964)
Official Records of the General Assembly (1946–94)
General Assembly Debates
Trusteeship Committee Debates
Ad Hoc Political Committee Debates

5 NEWSPAPERS AND WEEKLY JOURNALS

(a) British
Economist
(Manchester) Guardian
Listener
New Society
New Statesman
Private Eye
Punch
Spectator
The Times

(b) South African
Argus
Die Burger
Cape Times
Drum
Fighting Talk
Forum
Johannesburg Star
Natal Mercury
Natal Witness
Optima
Press Digest (South African Jewish Board of Deputies)
Rand Daily Mail
South
Die Transvaler
Weekly Mail (*Mail & Guardian*)

V PRINCIPAL SECONDARY WORKS CITED

I BOOKS

Adam, H. and H. Giliomee, *Ethnic power mobilised: can South Africa change?* (New Haven, CT and London, 1979)

Ally, R. *Gold and empire: the Bank of England and South Africa's gold producers, 1886–1926* (Johannesburg, 1994)

Austin, D. *Britain and South Africa* (Oxford, 1966)

Bangura, Y. *Britain and Commonwealth Africa: the politics of economic relations, 1951–1975* (Manchester, 1983)

Barber, J. *South Africa's foreign policy, 1945–1970* (Oxford, 1973)
  South Africa in the twentieth century: a political history – in search of a nation state (Blackwell, Oxford, 1999)

Barber, J. and J. Barratt, *South Africa's foreign policy: the search for status and security, 1945–1988* (Cambridge, 1990)

Beinart, W. *Twentieth-century South Africa* (Oxford, 1994; 2nd edn, 2001)

Beinart, W. and S. Dubow, eds., *Segregation and apartheid in twentieth-century South Africa* (London and New York, 1995)

Benson, M. *Tshekedi Khama* (London, 1960)
  South Africa: the struggle for a birthright (Harmondsworth, 1966)

Benyon, J. *Proconsul and paramountcy in South Africa: the High Commission, British supremacy and the sub-continent, 1806–1910* (Pietermaritzburg, 1980)

Berridge, G. R. *Economic power in Anglo-South African diplomacy: Simonstown, Sharpeville and after* (London, 1981)
  South Africa, the colonial powers and 'African Defence': the rise and fall of a white entente, 1948–1960 (London, 1992)

Black, D. R. and J. Nauright, *Rugby and the South African nation: sport, culture, politics and power in the old and new South Africas* (Manchester, 1998)

Blake, R. *A history of Rhodesia* (London, 1977)

Bonner, P., P. Delius, and D. Posel, eds., *Apartheid's genesis, 1935–1962* (Braamfontein, 1993)

Boyce, D. G. *The crisis of British power: the imperial and naval papers of the Second Earl of Selborne, 1895–1910* (London, 1990)

Brotz, H. *The politics of South Africa: democracy and racial diversity* (Oxford, 1977)

Brown, J. M. and W. R. Louis, eds., *The Oxford history of the British empire*, vol. IV: *The twentieth century* (Oxford, 1999)

Bryce, J. *Impressions of South Africa* (3rd edn, London, 1899)

Butler, J. *South Africa: an empire with its colonies at home?* (Rhodes University lecture, Grahamstown, 1975)

Butler, R. A. *The art of the possible: the memoirs of Lord Butler* (London, 1971)

Cain, P. J. and A. G. Hopkins, *British imperialism, 1688–2000* (2nd edn, London, 2001) (1st edn, *1688–1990*, 2 vols, 1993)

Carter, G. M. *The politics of inequality: South Africa since 1948* (London, 1958)

Cell, J. W. *The highest stage of white supremacy: the origins of segregation in South Africa and the American South* (Cambridge, 1982)

Chan, S. *The Commonwealth in world politics: a study of international action, 1965–1985* (London, 1988)
  Exporting apartheid: foreign policies in Southern Africa, 1978–1988 (London, 1990)

Chanock, M. L. *Unconsummated Union: Britain, Rhodesia and South Africa, 1900–1945* (Manchester, 1977)

Clarke, M. *British external policy-making in the 1990s* (London, 1992)

Crush, J. *The struggle for Swazi labour, 1890–1920* (Kingston, 1987)

Davenport, T. R. H. *The Afrikaner Bond: the history of a South African political party, 1880–1911* (Cape Town, 1966)
  Senses in turmoil: an inaugural address at Rhodes University (Grahamstown, 1977)
  The birth of a new South Africa (Toronto and London, 1988)
  South Africa: a modern history (3rd edn, London 1987; 4th edn, 1991; 5th edn, with C. Saunders, 2001)

Davenport, T. R. H. with K. S. Hunt, *The right to the land* (Cape Town, 1974)

Davies, M. A. G. *Incorporation in the Union of South Africa or self-government? Southern Rhodesia's choice, 1922* (University of South Africa, communication C.58, Pretoria, 1965)

Davis, P. and D. Riesenfeld, *A viewer's guide for 'In darkest Hollywood': cinema and apartheid* (Bloomington, IN, 1995)

de Kiewiet, C. W. *The anatomy of South African misery* (Oxford, 1956)

de Klerk, W. F. W. *de Klerk; the man and his time* (Johannesburg, 1991)

de Kock, G. H. *A history of the South African Reserve Bank* (Pretoria, 1954)

Denoon, D. *A grand illusion: the failure of imperial policy in the Transvaal Colony during the period of reconstruction, 1900–1905* (London, 1973)

Douglas-Home, C. *Evelyn Baring: the last proconsul* (London, 1978)

Drummond, I. M. *British economic policy and the empire* (London, 1972)
 The floating pound and the sterling area, 1931–1939 (Cambridge, 1981)
 The gold standard and the international monetary system, 1900–1939 (London, 1987)

Dubow, S. *Racial segregation and the origins of apartheid in South Africa, 1919–1936* (Oxford, 1989)

Duminy, A. H. and W. R. Guest, eds., *Fitzpatrick, South African politician: selected papers, 1888–1906* (Johannesburg, 1976)

Dunbar Moodie, T. *The rise of Afrikanerdom: power, apartheid and the Afrikaner civil religion* (Berkeley, CA, 1975, 2nd edn 1980)

Dutfield, M. J. *A marriage of inconvenience: the persecution of Ruth and Seretse Khama* (London, 1990)

Engelenburg, F. V. *General Louis Botha* (London and Johannesburg, 1929)

Etherington, N. ed., *Peace, politics and violence in the New South Africa* (London, 1992)
 The Great Treks: the transformation of Southern Africa, 1815–1854 (London, 2001)

Evans, H. *Downing Street diary: the Macmillan years, 1957–1963* (London, 1981)

Fortune, C. *MCC in South Africa, 1964–1965* (London, 1965)

Frankel, S. H. *Investment and the return to equity capital in the South African gold mining industry, 1887–1965: an international comparison* (Oxford, 1967)

Fraser M. and A. Jeeves, eds., *All that glittered: selected correspondence of Lionel Phillips, 1890–1924* (Cape Town, 1977)

Freeman, L. *The ambiguous champion: Canada and South Africa in the Trudeau and Mulroney years* (Toronto, 1997)

Gann, L. H. *A history of Northern Rhodesia: early days to 1953* (London, 1964)

Geldenhuys, D. J. *South Africa's search for status and security since the Second World War* (Occasional Paper, South African Institute of International Affairs, Braamfontein, 1978)

Geyser, O. *Watershed for South Africa: London, 1961* (Durban, 1983)
 Jan Smuts and his international contemporaries (Johannesburg, 2001)

Gifford, P. and W. R. Louis, eds., *Britain and Germany in Africa: imperial rivalry and colonial rule* (New Haven, CT and London, 1967)

Goldsworthy, D. *Colonial issues in British politics, 1945–1961* (Oxford, 1971)
 ed., *The Conservative government and the end of empire, 1951–1957* (British Documents on the End of Empire Project, London, 1994)

Goosen, J. C. *South Africa's Navy: the first fifty years* (Cape Town, 1973)

Gordon Walker, P. C. *The Commonwealth* (London, 1962)

Select bibliography

Gregory, T. *Ernest Oppenheimer and the economic development of southern Africa* (Cape Town, 1962)

Griffiths, J. *Pages from memory* (London, 1969)

Grundlingh, A., A. Odendaal, and B. Spies, *Beyond the tryline: rugby and South African society* (Johannesburg, 1995)

Hailey, Lord. *The Republic of South Africa and the High Commission Territories* (London, 1963)

Hain, P. *Don't play with apartheid: the background to the 'Stop the 70 tour' campaign* (London, 1971)

Hancock, W. K. *Smuts*, vol. I: *The sanguine years, 1870–1919*; vol. II: *The fields of force, 1919–1950* (Cambridge, 1962, 1968)

Hancock, W. K. and J. van der Poel, eds., *Selections from the Smuts Papers* (7 vols., Cambridge, 1966–73)

Hanna, A. J. *The story of the Rhodesias and Nyasaland* (London, 1960)

Headlam, C. ed., *The Milner Papers: South Africa, 1897–1905* (2 vols., London, 1931, 1933)

Heard, K. A. *General elections in South Africa, 1943–1970* (Oxford, 1974)

Henry, J. A. *The first hundred years of the Standard Bank* (London, 1963)

Hofmeyr, J. H. *South Africa* (London, 1931)

Holland, R. F. *Britain and the Commonwealth alliance, 1918–1939* (London, 1981)
  European decolonization, 1945–1961: an introductory survey (London, 1985)

Horne, Alistair. *Macmillan*, vol. II: *1957–1986* (London, 1989)

Howe, S. *Anticolonialism in British politics: the Left and the end of empire* (Oxford, 1993)

Huddleston, T. *Naught for your comfort* (London, 1956)

Hunke, H. *Namibia: the strength of the powerless* (Rome, 1980)

Hyam, R. *Elgin and Churchill at the Colonial Office, 1905–1908* (London, 1968)
  The failure of South African expansion, 1908–1948 (London, 1972)
  Britain's imperial century, 1815–1914: a study of empire and expansion (London, 1st edn, 1976; 2nd edn, 1993; 3rd edn, 2002)
  ed., *The Labour government and the end of empire, 1945–1951*, 4 parts (British Documents on the End of Empire Project, London, 1992)

Hyam, R. and W. R. Louis, eds., *The Conservative government and the end of empire, 1957–1964*, 2 parts (British Documents on the End of Empire Project, London, 2000)

Hyam, R. and G. Martin, *Reappraisals in British imperial history* (London, 1975)

Johnston, A., S. Shezi, and G. Bradshaw, eds., *Constitution-making in the New South Africa* (Leicester/London, 1993)

Johnstone, F. *Class, race and gold: a study of class relations and racial discrimination in South Africa* (London, 1976)

Jones, S. and A. Muller, *The South African economy, 1910–1990* (London, 1992)

Karis, T. and G. M. Carter, *From protest to challenge: a documentary history of African politics in South Africa*, vols. II and III (Stanford, 1973, 1977)

Katzenellenbogen, S. E. *South Africa and Southern Mozambique: labour, railways and trade in the making of a relationship* (Manchester, 1982)

Kubicek, R. V. *Economic imperialism in theory and practice: the case of South African gold mining finance, 1886–1914* (Duke, NC, 1979)

Legum, C. and M. *South Africa: crisis for the West* (London, 1964)
Le May, G. H. L. *British supremacy in South Africa, 1899–1907* (Oxford, 1965)
Lewsen, P. *John X. Merriman: paradoxical South African statesman* (New Haven: Yale University Press and London, 1982)
  The South African constitution: euphoria and rejection (Raymond Dart Lecture, Johannesburg, 1982)
  ed., *Voices of protest: from segregation to apartheid* (Craighall, 1988)
Leys, C. *European politics in Southern Rhodesia* (Oxford, 1959)
Leys, C. and C. Pratt, eds., *A new deal in Central Africa* (London, 1960)
Lipton, M. *Capitalism and apartheid: South Africa, 1910–1985* (Aldershot, 1986)
Lonsdale, J. M. ed., *South Africa in question* (African Studies Centre, Cambridge, 1988)
Lowry, D., ed., *The South African War reappraised* (Manchester, 2000)
Lyttelton, O. *The memoirs of Lord Chandos* (London, 1962)
McIntyre, W. D. *The significance of the Commonwealth, 1965–1990* (London, 1991)
Macmillan, H. *Memoirs* vol. V: *Pointing the way, 1959–1961* (London, 1972)
Mandela, Nelson, *Long walk to freedom: the autobiography* (London, 1994)
Mansergh, N. *South Africa, 1906–1961: the price of magnanimity* (London, 1962)
Marais, J. S. *The fall of Kruger's republic* (Oxford, 1961)
Marks, S. ed., *The societies of Southern Africa in the nineteenth and twentieth centuries* (vol. XV, Collected Seminar Papers, 38: London, 1990)
Marks, S. and R. Rathbone, eds., *Industrialisation and social change in South Africa: African class formation, culture, and consciousness, 1870–1930* (London, 1982)
Martin, H. J. and N. D. Orpen, *South Africa at war: military and industrial organisation and operations in connection with the conduct of war, 1939–1945* (Cape Town, 1979)
Mason, P. *An essay on racial tension* (London, 1954)
Mawby, A. A. *Gold mining and politics – Johannesburg, 1900–1907: the origins of the old South Africa?* (2 vols., Lampeter, 2000)
Miller, J. D. B. *Survey of Commonwealth affairs: problems of expansion and attrition, 1953–1969* (Oxford, 1974)
Mills, G. ed., *From pariah to participant: South Africa's evolving foreign relations, 1990–1994* (Johannesburg, 1994)
Milner, Lord. *The nation and the empire: speeches and addresses* (London, 1913)
Morrah, D. *The royal family in Africa* (London, 1947)
Morris, J. *South African winter* (London, 1958)
Munger, E. S. *Afrikaner and African nationalism: South African parallels and parameters* (Oxford, 1967)
Murphy, P. *Party politics and decolonisation: the Conservative Party and British colonial policy in tropical Africa, 1951–1964* (Oxford, 1995)
Nasson, B. *The South African War, 1899–1902* (London, 1999)
Nauright, J. *Sport, culture and identities in South Africa* (Leicester/London, 1997)
Nixon, R. *Homelands, Harlem and Hollywood: South African culture and the world beyond* (London, 1994)
Nolutshungu, S. C. *South Africa in Africa: a study in ideology and foreign policy* (Manchester, 1975)
O'Meara, D. *'Volkskapitalisme': class, capital and ideology in the development of Afrikaner nationalism, 1934–1948* (Johannesburg and Cambridge, 1983)

Select bibliography

O'Meara, D. *Forty lost years: the apartheid state and the politics of the National Party, 1948–1994* (Randburg and Athens, OH, 1996)

Omissi, D. and A. Thompson, eds., *The impact of the South African War* (Basingstoke and New York, 2002)

Pachai, B. *The international aspects of the South African Indian question, 1860–1971* (Cape Town, 1971)

Pakenham, T. *The Boer War* (London and Johannesburg, 1979)

Palley, C. *The constitutional history and law of Southern Rhodesia, 1888–1965, with special reference to imperial control* (Oxford, 1966)

Pearce, R. D. ed., *Patrick Gordon Walker: political diaries, 1932–1971* (London, 1991)

Pienaar, S. *South Africa and international relations between the two world wars: the League of Nations dimension* (Johannesburg, 1987)

Porter, A. N. *Origins of the South African War: Joseph Chamberlain and the diplomacy of imperialism, 1895–1899* (Manchester, 1980)

Victorian shipping, business, and imperial policy: Donald Currie, the Castle Line and southern Africa (Woodbridge, Suffolk and New York, 1986)

Posel, D. *The making of apartheid, 1948–1961: conflict and compromise* (Oxford, 1991)

Pratt, R. *In good faith: Canadian churches against apartheid* (Waterloo, Canada, 1997)

Pyrah, G. B. *Imperial policy and South Africa, 1902–1910* (Oxford, 1955)

Randall, P. *Little England on the veld: the private school system in South Africa* (Johannesburg, 1982)

Redcliffe-Maud, J. *Experiences of an optimist: memoirs* (London, 1981)

Reddy, E. and F. Meer, *Passive resistance, 1946: a selection of documents* (Durban, 1996)

Redfern, J. *Ruth and Seretse: 'a very disreputable transaction'* (London, 1955)

Rich, P. B. *Race and empire in British politics* (Cambridge, 2nd edn, 1990)

Robinson, K. *The dilemmas of trusteeship: aspects of British colonial policy between the wars* (Oxford, 1965)

Robinson, R. E. and J. Gallagher, *Africa and the Victorians: the official mind of imperialism* (London, 1961)

Rotberg, R. I. *The rise of nationalism in Central Africa: the making of Malawi and Zambia, 1873–1964* (Cambridge, MA, 1966)

Rotberg, R. and J. Barratt, eds., *Conflict and compromise in South Africa* (Cape Town, 1980)

Saker, H. *The South African flag controversy* (Oxford, 1980)

Sampson, A. *Mandela: the authorised biography* (London, 1999)

Sanders, J. *South Africa and the international media, 1972–1979: a struggle for representation* (London, 2000)

Saunders, C. *The making of the South African past: major historians on race and class* (Cape Town and Johannesburg, 1988)

Sayers, R. S. *Financial policy, 1939–1945* (London, 1956)

The Bank of England, 1891–1944 (2 vols., Cambridge, 1976)

Schreuder, D. M. *Gladstone and Kruger: Liberal government and colonial 'Home Rule', 1880–1885* (Oxford, 1969)

The scramble for Southern Africa, 1877–1895: the politics of Partition reappraised (Cambridge, 1980)

Schrire, R. ed., *South Africa: public policy perspectives* (Cape Town, 1983)

Seegers, A. *The military and the making of modern South Africa* (London, 1996)
Seldon, A. *Churchill's Indian summer: the Conservative government, 1951–1955* (London, 1981)
Seligmann, M. *Rivalry in Southern Africa, 1893–1899: the transformation of German colonial policy* (London, 1998)
Sillery, A. *Botswana: a short political history* (London, 1974)
Smith, Arnold, with C. Sanger, *Stitches in time: the Commonwealth in world politics* (London, 1981)
Smith, Iain R. *The origins of the South African War, 1899–1902* (London, 1996)
[Smuts J. C.], *Eeuw van Onrecht/A century of wrong* (issued by F. W. Reitz, 1899/London, 1900)
Smuts, J. C. *Wartime speeches: a compilation of public utterances in Gt Britain* (London, 1917)
  Greater South Africa/Plans for a better world: speeches (Johannesburg, 1940/ London, 1942)
Spence, J. E. *The strategic significance of Southern Africa* (London, 1978)
Strange, S. *Sterling and British policy: a political study of an international currency in decline* (London, 1971)
Streak, M. *Lord Milner's immigration policy for the Transvaal, 1897–1905* (Johannesburg: Rand Afrikaans University, 1969)
Stultz, N. *Afrikaner politics in South Africa, 1934–1948* (Berkeley, CA, 1974)
Tatz, C. M. *Shadow and substance in South Africa: a study in land and franchise policies affecting Africans, 1910–1960* (Pietermaritzburg: Natal University Press, 1962)
Thatcher, M. *The Downing Street years* (London and New York, 1993)
Thompson, L. M. *The unification of South Africa, 1902–1910* (Oxford, 1960)
Thompson, L. M. and J. Butler, eds., *Change in contemporary South Africa* (Berkeley, CA, 1975)
Thompson, P. *Natalians first: separatism in South Africa, 1909–1961* (Johannesburg, 1990)
Tlou, T., N. Parsons, and W. Henderson, *Seretse Khama, 1921–1980* (Braamfontein, 1995)
Torrance, D. E. *The strange death of the Liberal empire: Lord Selborne in South Africa* (Liverpool, 1996)
Tunstall, W. C. B. *The Commonwealth and regional defence* (London, 1959)
van den Heever, C. M. *General J. B. M. Hertzog* (Johannesburg, 1946)
van der Merwe, N. J. *Marthinus Theunis Steyn* (2 vols., Bloemfontein, 1921)
van der Poel, J. *Railway and customs policies in South Africa, 1885–1910* (London, 1933)
Vatcher, W. H., jr, *White laager: the rise of Afrikaner nationalism* (London, 1965)
Walker, E. A. *Lord de Villiers and his times: South Africa, 1842–1914* (London, 1925)
  A history of Southern Africa (1st edn, London, 1957; 3rd edn, 1968)
Warwick, P. ed., *The South African War: the Anglo-Boer War, 1899–1902* (London, 1980)
Watts, R. L. *New federations: experiments in the Commonwealth* (Oxford, 1966)
Welensky, R. *Welensky's 4000 days: the life and death of the Federation of Rhodesia and Nyasaland* (London, 1964)
Welsh, F. *A history of South Africa* (London, 1998)

Wilson, J. *CB: a life of Sir Henry Campbell-Bannerman* (London, 1973)
Wilson, M. and L. M. Thompson, eds., *The Oxford history of South Africa* vol. II: *South Africa, 1870–1966* (Oxford, 1971)
Wirgman, A. T. *Storm and sunshine in South Africa, with some personal and historical reminiscences* (London, 1922)
Wood, J. R. T. *The Welensky papers: a history of the Federation of Rhodesia and Nyasaland* (Durban, 1983)
Worden, N. *The making of modern South Africa: conquest, segregation and apartheid* (Oxford: Blackwell, 1994)
Young, H. *The Iron Lady: a biography of Margaret Thatcher* (London and New York, 1989)

2 JOURNAL ARTICLES AND CHAPTERS IN BOOKS

The following abbreviations are used:

HJ   *Historical Journal*
JAH   *Journal of African History*
JICH   *Journal of Imperial and Commonwealth History*
JSAS   *Journal of Southern African Studies*
RT   *Round Table: the Commonwealth Journal of International Affairs*
SAHJ   *South African Historical Journal*

Aluko, O. 'Britain and the conflict in Southern Africa', *RT* no. 309 (1989), pp. 54–64
Atmore, A. and S. Marks, 'The imperial factor in South Africa', *JAH* vol. 3 (1974), pp. 105–39
Bale, T. ' "A deplorable episode": South African arms and the statecraft of British social democracy', *Labour History Review* vol. 62 (1997–8), pp. 22–40
Barber, J. ' "An historical and persistent interest": Britain and South Africa', *International Affairs* vol. 67 (1991), pp. 723–38
Benyon, J. ' "Main show or side-show"? Natal and the South African War', *JICH* vol. 27 (1999), pp. 27–58
  ' "Intermediate" imperialism and the test of empire: Milner's "excentric" high commission in South Africa' in D. Lowry, ed., *The South African War reappraised* (Manchester, 2000), pp. 84–103
Berridge, G. R. and J. E. Spence, 'South Africa and the Simonstown agreements' in J. W. Young, ed., *The foreign policy of Churchill's peacetime administration, 1951–1955* (Leicester/London, 1988), pp. 181–205
Booth, A. R. 'Lord Selborne and the British Protectorates, 1908–1910', *JAH* vol. 10 (1969), pp. 133–48
Brownell, F. G. 'British immigration to South Africa, 1946–1970', *Argief-Jaarboek vir Suid-Afrikaanse Geskiedenis/Archives Yearbook*, 48th year, vol. I (Pretoria, 1985), pp. 1–192
Bundy, C. 'The emergence and decline of a South African peasantry', *African Affairs* vol. 71 (1972), pp. 369–88
Butler, J. 'The German factor in Anglo-Transvaal relations' in P. Gifford and W. R. Louis, eds., *Britain and Germany in Africa: imperial rivalry and colonial rule* (New Haven, CT and London, 1967), pp. 179–214
  'The gold mines and labour supply: a review article', *SAHJ* no. 18 (1986), pp. 93–7

Crowder, M., 'Tshekedi Khama and opposition to the British administration of the Bechuanaland Protectorate, 1926–1936', *JAH* vol. 26 (1985), pp. 193–214
  'Tshekedi Khama, Smuts, and South-West Africa', *Journal of Modern African Studies* vol. 25 (1987), pp. 25–42
  'Professor Macmillan goes on safari: the British government observer team and the crisis over the Seretse Khama marriage, 1951' in H. Macmillan and S. Marks, eds., *Africa and empire: W. M. Macmillan, historian and social critic* (Aldershot, 1989), pp. 254–78
Cuthbertson, G. and A. Jeeves, 'The many-sided struggle for Southern Africa, 1899–1902', *SAHJ* no. 41 (1999), pp. 2–21
Davenport, T. R. H. 'The South African Rebellion, 1914', *English Historical Review* vol. 78 (1963), pp. 73–94
  'The tiger in the grass', *SAHJ* no. 9 (1977), pp. 3–12
Davies, R. and D. O'Meara, 'Total strategy in Southern Africa: South African regional policy since 1978', *JSAS* vol. 11 (1985), pp. 183–211
Denoon, D. 'The Transvaal labour crisis, 1901–1906', *JAH* vol. 8 (1967), pp. 481–94
  '"Capitalist influence" and the Transvaal government during the Crown Colony period, 1900–1906', *HJ* vol. 11 (1968), pp. 301–31
Drus, E. 'Select documents from the Chamberlain Papers concerning Anglo-Transvaal relations, 1896–1899', *Bulletin of the Institute for Historical Research* vol. 27 (1954), pp. 157–89
Dubow, S. 'Afrikaner nationalism, apartheid and the conceptualisation of race', *JAH* vol. 33 (1992), pp. 209–37
  'Colonial nationalism: the Milner Kindergarten and the rise of "South Africanism", 1902–1910', *History Workshop Journal* vol. 43 (1997), pp. 53–85
Dugard, C. J. R. 'The Simonstown Agreement: South Africa, Britain and the United Nations', *South African Law Journal* vol. 85 (1968), pp. 142–56
Durr, K. 'South Africa and the Commonwealth', *RT* no. 330 (1994), pp. 169–73
du Toit, A. 'Political control and personal morality' in R. Schrire, ed., *South Africa: public policy perspectives* (Cape Town, 1983), pp. 54–83
  'No chosen people: the myth of the Calvinist origins of Afrikaner nationalism and racial ideology', *American Historical Review* vol. 88 (1983), pp. 920–52
Eidelberg, P. G. 'The breakdown of the 1922 Lourenço Marques port and railway negotiations', *SAHJ* no. 8 (1976), pp. 104–18
Fedorowich, K. 'Anglicisation and the politicisation of British immigration to South Africa, 1899–1929', *JICH* vol. 19 (1991), pp. 222–46
Feinberg, H. 'The 1913 Natives Land Act in South Africa: politics, race and segregation in the early twentieth century', *International Journal of African Historical Studies* vol. 26 (1993), pp. 65–109
Frankel, S. H. and H. Herzfeld, 'An analysis of the growth of the national income of the Union in the period of prosperity before the war', *South African Journal of Economics* vol. 12 (1944), pp. 112–38
Franklin, N. N. 'South Africa's balance of payments and the sterling area, 1939–1950', *Economic Journal* vol. 61 (1951), pp. 290–309
Freeman, L. 'All but one: Britain, the Commonwealth and sanctions' in M. Orkin, ed., *Sanctions against apartheid* (New York, 1989), pp. 417–30

Garson, N. G. 'The Swaziland question and a road to the sea, 1887–1895', *Argief-Jaarboek vir Suid-Afrikaanse Geskiedenis/Archives Yearbook for South African History* 20th year, vol. 2, part 2 (Pretoria, 1957), pp. 263–434
  'British imperialism and the coming of the Anglo-Boer War', *South African Journal of Economics* vol. 30 (1962), pp. 140–53
  '*Het Volk:* the Botha–Smuts party in the Transvaal, 1904–1911', *HJ* vol. 9 (1966), pp. 101–32
  'South Africa and World War I', *JICH* vol. 8 (1980), pp. 68–85
Geldenhuys, D. J. 'The politics of race: a study of the impact of South Africa's general election of 1948 on Anglo-South African relations', *Journal for Contemporary History / Joernaal vir die Eietydse Geskiedenis* vol. 4 (Bloemfontein, 1979), pp. 1–21
Geyser, O. 'South Africa rejoins the Commonwealth', *RT* no. 331 (1994)
Gifford, P. 'Misconceived dominion: the creation and disintegration of the Federation of British Central Africa' in P. Gifford and W. R. Louis, eds., *The transfer of power in Africa: decolonisation, 1940–1960* (New Haven, CT, 1982), pp. 387–416
Gilbert, B. B. 'The grant of Responsible Government to the Transvaal: more notes on a myth', *HJ* vol. 10 (1967), pp. 457–9
Goldsworthy, D. 'Britain and the international critics of British colonialism, 1951–1956', *Journal of Commonwealth and Comparative Politics*, vol. 29 (1991), pp. 1–24
Gupta, P. S. 'Imperialism and the Labour government of 1945–51', in J. Winter, ed., *The working class in modern British history: essays in honour of Henry Pelling* (Cambridge, 1983)
Gurney, C. 'When the boycott began to bite', *History Today* vol. 49, 6 (1999), pp. 32–4
Hancock, W. K. 'Literacy and numeracy and some South African elections', *Australian Journal of Science* vol. 28 (1965), pp. 114–19
Hattingh, J. L. and H. O. Terblanche. 'Suid-Afrikaanse kroniek, 1971–1972', *SAHJ* no. 9 (1977), pp. 80–119
Hayes, F. 'South Africa's departure from the Commonwealth, 1960–1961', *International History Review* vol. 2 (1980), pp. 453–84
Henshaw, P. J. 'Land of hope and glory: Mandela's New South Africa', *Queen's Quarterly: A Canadian Review*, vol. 101 (1994) pp. 439–50
  'The Commonwealth and South Africa' in G. Mills, ed., *From pariah to participant: South Africa's evolving foreign relations* (Johannesburg, 1994), pp. 158–67
  'The "key to South Africa" in the 1890s: Delagoa Bay and the origins of the South African War', *JSAS* vol. 24 (1998), pp. 527–44
Hexham, I. 'Dutch Calvinism and the development of Afrikaner nationalism', *African Affairs* vol. 79 (1980), pp. 195–208
Hummel, H. C. 'Sir Charles Coghlan: some reflections on his political attitudes and style', *SAHJ* no. 8 (1976), pp. 59–79
Hyam, R. 'Africa and the Labour government, 1945–1951', *JICH* vol. 16 (1988), pp. 148–72
  'The primacy of geopolitics: the dynamics of British imperial policy, 1763–1963', *JICH* vol. 27 (1999), pp. 27–52
  'South Africa, Cambridge, and Commonwealth history', Smuts Distinguished Lecture on the 50th anniversary of the death of Smuts, delivered Nov. 2000, Cambridge, *RT* no. 360 (2001), pp. 401–14

Jackson, A. 'Tshekedi, Bechuanaland, and the Central African Federation', *SAHJ* no. 40 (1999), pp. 202–22

Jeeves, A. 'Rand capitalists and the coming of the South African War, 1896–1899', *Historical Papers* (1973), pp. 61–83

'Control of migratory labour in the South African gold mines in the era of Kruger and Milner', *JSAS* vol. 2 (1975), pp. 3–29

Kantor, B. 'The evolution of monetary policy in South Africa', in M. Kooy, ed., *Studies in economics and economic history: essays in honour of Professor H. M. Robertson* (London, 1972)

Krozewski, G. 'Sterling, the "minor territories" and the end of formal empire, 1939–1958', *Economic History Review* vol. 46 (1993), pp. 239–65

Lambert, J. 'South African British? Or Dominion South Africans? The evolution of an identity in the 1910s and 1920s', *SAHJ* no. 43 (2000), pp. 197–222

Lawrie, G. G. 'The Simonstown Agreement: South Africa, Britain and the Commonwealth', *South African Law Journal* vol. 85 (1968), pp. 157–77

Legassick, M. 'British hegemony and the origins of segregation in South Africa, 1901–1914' in W. Beinart and S. Dubow, eds., *Segregation and apartheid in twentieth-century South Africa* (London, 1995), pp. 43–59

Lewis, J. 'The impact of the cultural and sports boycotts' in J. Hanlon, ed., *South Africa: the sanctions report, documents and statistics* (London, 1990)

Lipton, M. 'British arms for South Africa', *The World Today* vol. 26 (1970), pp. 427–34

Lloyd, L. '"A most auspicious beginning": the 1946 General Assembly and the question of the treatment of Indians in South Africa', *Review of International Studies* vol. 16 (1990), pp. 131–53

'"A family quarrel": the development of the dispute over Indians in South Africa', *HJ* vol. 34 (1991), pp. 703–25

McCormack, R. L. 'Airlines and empires: Great Britain and the "scramble for Africa", 1919–1932', *Canadian Journal of African Studies* vol. 10 (1976), pp. 87–106

'Man with a mission: Oswald Pirow and South African Airways, 1933–1939', *JAH* vol. 20 (1979), pp. 543–57

Makin, M. 'Britain, South Africa and the Commonwealth in 1960: the "winds of change" reassessed', *Historia* (*Historiese Genootskap van Suid-Afrika/Historical Association of South Africa*) vol. 41 (Pretoria, 1996), pp. 74–88

Marks, S. 'Scrambling for South Africa: a review article', *JAH* vol. 23 (1982), pp. 97–113

'Southern and Central Africa, 1886–1910' in R. Oliver and G. N. Sanderson, eds., *Cambridge history of Africa*, vol. VI: *1870–1905* (Cambridge, 1985), ch. 7

'Southern Africa' in J. M. Brown and W. R. Louis, eds., *The Oxford history of the British empire*, vol. IV: *The twentieth century* (Oxford, 1999), ch. 24

'White masculinity: Jan Smuts, race and the South African War', Raleigh Lecture on History, 2000, *Proceedings of the British Academy* vol. 111 (2001), pp. 199–223

Marks, S. and A. Atmore, 'The imperial factor in South Africa', *JICH* vol. 3 (1974), pp. 105–39

Marks, S. and S. Trapido, 'Lord Milner and the South African state', *History Workshop Journal* vol. 8 (1979), pp. 50–80

'Lord Milner and the state reconsidered' in M. Twaddle, ed., *Imperialism, the state and the Third World* (London, 1992), pp. 80–94

Martin, G. W. 'The Canadian analogy in South African Union', *SAHJ* no. 8 (1976), pp. 40–59
Martin, W. G. 'South versus Southern Africa in the inter-war period', *JSAS* vol. 16 (1990), pp. 112–38
Mayall, J. 'The South African crisis: the major external factors' in S. Johnson, ed., *South Africa: no turning back* (London, 1988)
Mendelsohn, R. 'Blainey and the Jameson Raid: the debate renewed', *JSAS* vol. 6 (1980), pp. 156–70
Minty, A. S. 'South Africa and the Commonwealth: assessing the challenges ahead' in G. Mills and J. Stremlau, eds., *The Commonwealth in the twenty-first century* (Braamfontein, 1999), pp. 57–61
Murray, B. 'Politics and cricket: the D'Oliveira affair of 1968', *JSAS* vol. 27 (2001), pp. 667–84
Nasson, B. 'War opinion in South Africa in 1914', *JICH* vol. 23 (1995) pp. 248–76
O'Meara, D. 'The Afrikaner Broederbond: class vanguard of Afrikaner nationalism 1927–1948', *JSAS* vol. 3 (1976), pp. 156–86
Ovendale, R. 'The South African policy of the British Labour government, 1947–1951', *International Affairs* vol. 59 (1983), pp. 41–58
  'Macmillan and the wind of change in Africa, 1957–1960', *HJ* vol. 38 (1995), pp. 455–77
Parsons, N. 'The impact of Seretse Khama on British public opinion, 1948–1956 and 1978', *Immigrants and Minorities* vol. 12 (1993), pp. 195–219
Payne, A. 'The international politics of the Gleneagles Agreement', *RT* no. 320 (1991), pp. 417–30
Phimister, I. 'Secondary industrialisation in southern Africa: the 1948 Customs Agreement between Southern Rhodesia and South Africa', *JSAS* vol. 17 (1991), pp. 430–42
  'Unscrambling the scramble for Southern Africa: the Jameson Raid and the South African War revisited', *SAHJ*, no. 28 (1993), pp. 203–20
Pirow, O. 'How far is the Union interested in the continent of Africa?', *Journal of the Royal African Society* vol. 144 (1937), pp. 317–20
Porter, A. N. 'Lord Salisbury, Mr Chamberlain and South Africa, 1895–1899', *JICH* vol. 1 (1972), pp. 3–26
  'The South African War (1899–1902): context and motive reconsidered', *JAH* vol. 31, 1 (1990), pp. 43–57
  'The South African War and the historians', *African Affairs* vol. 99 (2000), pp. 633–48
Posel, D. 'Does size matter? The apartheid state's power of penetration' in H. Judin and I. Vladislavić, eds., *'blank': architecture, apartheid and after* (Rotterdam, 1998), pp. 237–47
Rich, P. B. 'The impact of South Africa's segregationist and apartheid ideology on British racial thought', *New Community* vol. 13 (1986) pp. 1–17
Richardson, P. and J. J. Van-Helten, 'The gold mining industry of the Transvaal, 1886–1899' in P. Warwick, ed., *The South African War, 1899–1902* (London, 1980), pp. 18–36
Ritner, S. R. 'The Dutch Reformed Church and apartheid', *Journal of Contemporary History* vol. 2 (1967), pp. 17–36
Robertson, H. M. 'Can industry afford to break the economic link?', *Optima* vol. 10 (Johannesburg, 1960), pp. 123–35

Robinson, R. E. 'Sir Andrew Cohen: proconsul of African nationalism (1909–68)', in L. H. Gann and P. Duignan (eds.), *African proconsuls: European governors in Africa* (Stanford, CA, 1978)
  'The moral disarmament of African empire, 1919–1947', *JICH* vol. 8 (1980), pp. 86–106
Rotberg, R. I. 'The federal movement in East and Central Africa, 1889–1953', *Journal of Commonwealth Political Studies* vol. 2 (1964), pp. 141–60
Salomon, L. 'The economic background to the revival of Afrikaner nationalism' in J. Butler, ed., *Boston University Papers in African History* vol. I (1964), pp. 219–42
Saunders, C. 'Historians and apartheid' in J. M. Lonsdale, ed., *South Africa in question* (African Studies Centre, Cambridge, 1988), pp. 13–32
  'The history of South Africa's foreign policy', *SAHJ* no. 23 (1990), pp. 147–54
Seiler, J. 'South African perspectives and responses to external pressure', *Journal of Modern African Studies* vol. 13 (1975), pp. 447–68
Smith, H. '*Apartheid*, Sharpeville and "impartiality": the reporting of South Africa on BBC television, 1948–1961, *Historical Journal of Film, Radio and Television* vol. 13 (1993), pp. 251–98
Smith, I. R. 'The origins of the South African War (1899–1902): a reappraisal', *SAHJ* no. 22 (1990), pp. 24–60
  'Joseph Chamberlain and the Jameson Raid', in E. J. Carruthers, ed., *The Jameson Raid: a centennial retrospective* (Houghton, Johannesburg, 1996)
  'Jan Smuts and the South African War', *SAHJ* no. 41 (1999), pp. 172–95
Spence, J. E. 'British policy towards the High Commission Territories', *Journal of Modern African Studies* vol. 2 (1964), pp. 221–46
  'Southern Africa in the Cold War: ideological and geopolitical factors in the struggle for supremacy', *History Today* vol. 49, 2 (1999), pp. 43–9
Spence, J. E. and G. R. Berridge, 'Simonstown', *Contemporary Record* vol. 2 (1988), pp. 181–205
Stadler, A. W. 'The Afrikaner in opposition, 1910–1948', *Journal of Commonwealth Political Studies* vol. 7 (1969), pp. 204–15
Stokes, E. T. 'Milnerism', *HJ* vol. 5 (1962), pp. 47–60
Swanson, M. W. 'The urban origins of separate development', *Race and Class* vol. 10 (1968), pp. 31–40
  'The sanitation syndrome: bubonic plague and urban native policy in the Cape Colony, 1900–1909', *JAH* vol. 18 (1977), pp. 387–410
Thompson, L. M. 'The compromise of Union', in *Oxford history of South Africa*, vol. II, ch. 7, pp. 325–64
Thornton, R. 'The potentials of boundaries in South Africa: steps towards a theory of social edge' in R. Werbner and T. Ranger, eds., *Post-colonial identities in Africa* (London, 1996), pp. 136–61
Torrance, D. E. 'Britain, South Africa and the High Commission Territories: an old controversy revisited', *HJ* vol. 41 (1998), pp. 751–72
Trapido, S. 'The origins of the Cape franchise qualifications of 1853', *JAH* vol. 5 (1964), pp. 37–54
  'Landlord and tenant in a colonial economy: the Transvaal, 1880–1910', *JSAS* vol. 5 (1978), pp. 26–58
Turrell, R. V. ' "Finance . . . the governor of the imperial engine": Hobson and the case of Rothschild and Rhodes', *JSAS* vol. 13 (1987), pp. 417–32

Van-Helten, J. J. 'Empire and high finance: South Africa and the international gold standard, 1890–1914', *JAH* vol. 23 (1982), pp. 529–48
Warhurst, P. R. 'Rhodesia–South African relations, 1900–1923', *SAHJ* no. 3 (1971), pp. 93–108
  'Smuts and Africa: a study in sub-imperialism', *SAHJ* no. 16 (1984), pp. 82–100
Welsh, D. 'Urbanisation and the solidarity of Afrikaner nationalism', *Journal of Modern African Studies* vol. 7 (1969), pp. 265–76
  'The politics of white supremacy' in L. M. Thompson and J. Butler, eds., *Change in contemporary South Africa* (Berkeley, CA, 1975), pp. 51–78
Wetherell, H. I. 'Britain and Rhodesian expansionism: imperial collusion or empirical carelessness?', *Rhodesian History* vol. 8 (Salisbury, 1977) pp. 115–28
  'Settler expansionism in Central Africa: the imperial response of 1931 and subsequent implications', *African Affairs* vol. 78 (1979), pp. 210–27
White, W. B. 'The United Party and the 1948 general election', *Journal for Contemporary History/Joernaal vir die Eietydse Geskiedenis* vol. 17 (1992), pp. 73–97
Wickens, P. L. 'The Natives Land Act of 1913: a cautionary essay on simple explanations of complex change', *South African Journal of Economics* vol. 49 (1981), pp. 105–29
Wilson, F. 'Farming, 1866–1966' in M. Wilson and L. M. Thompson, eds., *The Oxford history of South Africa*, vol. II: *South Africa, 1870–1966* (Oxford, 1971), pp. 104–71
  'Southern Africa' in M. Crowder, ed., *The Cambridge history of Africa*, vol. VIII: *c. 1940–1975* (Cambridge, 1984), ch. 6
Wolpe, H. 'Capitalism and cheap labour power in South Africa, from segregation to apartheid', *Economy and Society* vol. 1 (1972), pp. 425–56
Worrall, D. J. 'Afrikaner nationalism' in C. Potholm and R. Dale, eds., *Southern Africa in perspective* (New York, 1972), pp. 19–30
Young, J. W. 'The Wilson government and arms to South Africa, 1964', *Journal of Contemporary British History* vol. 12 (1998), pp. 62–86

V UNPUBLISHED DISSERTATIONS/THESES

Cardy, S. 'British foreign policy towards South Africa during the De Klerk era, 1989–1994' (MPhil, Cambridge, 1995)
Edgecombe, D. R. 'The influence of the Aborigines Protection Society on British policy towards black African and Cape Coloured affairs in South Africa, 1886–1910' (PhD, Cambridge, 1976)
Feigen, M. A. 'The power of Proteus: Great Britain, South Africa, and the Simonstown Agreements, 1948–1955' (MPhil, Cambridge, 1985)
Geldenhuys, D. J. 'The effects of South Africa's racial policy on Anglo-South African relations, 1945–1961' (PhD, Cambridge, 1977)
Griffiths, H. 'A study of British opinion on the problems and policies of the Union of South Africa, from the end of the Second World War until South Africa's withdrawal from the Commonwealth' (MSc, London, 1962)
Henshaw, P. J. 'South Africa's external relations with Britain and the Commonwealth, 1945–1956' (PhD, Cambridge, 1989)
Hudson, R. F. 'The British origins of South African segregation' (PhD, Cambridge, 2000)

Jeeves, A. 'The Rand capitalists and Transvaal politics, 1892–1899' (PhD, Queen's University, Kingston, 1971)

Kirstein, J. 'Some foundations of Afrikaner nationalism' (Hons. research essay, Cape Town, 1956)

Louth, C. J. 'External pressures and internal changes in South Africa, 1976–1990' (MPhil, Cambridge, 1992)

Mawby, A. A. 'The political behaviour of the British population of the Transvaal, 1902–1907' (PhD, Witwatersrand, Johannesburg, 1969)

Parks, J. F. 'Britain's South African foreign policy, 1979–1989: bilateralism and multilateralism' (PhD, Keele, 1997)

Peberdy, S. 'Selecting immigrants: nationalism and national identity in South Africa's immigration policies, 1910–1998' (PhD, Queen's University, Kingston, 1999)

Quarrington, D. 'The transfer issue: Britain's relations with South Africa over the High Commission Territories, 1948–1961' (MA in Area Studies, SOAS, London, 1992)

Reeves, L. A. 'The Anglo-South African relationship before and after World War II' (MPhil, Cambridge, 1985)

Robinson, R. E. 'The Trust in British Central African policy, 1889–1939' (PhD, Cambridge, 1950)

Wetherell, H. I. 'The Rhodesias and amalgamation: settler sub-imperialism and the imperial response, 1914–1948' (PhD, Rhodesia, 1977)

Index

Abdul Rahman, Tunku 265–6
Aborigines Protection Society 79, 101
Abubakar Tafawa Balewa 262, 265–6, 268–9
Acheson, Dean 6
Addison, Lord 149–50, 184
African Defence Organisation 16, 138, 231, 235, 244, 246, 250–1
African interests and attitudes 58, 77–101, 103, 174, 186, 201
  in Rhodesia 214, 220–1
African National Congress 7, 278, 279, 294, 338, 344, 348
Afrikaans 31, 275, 277
Afrikaner Party 20, 133, 309
Afrikaner people
  in civil service 7, 25, 112
  nationalist identity 6, 18, 19, 230, 233, 256, 281, 308
  views of Britain 273–306
  see also Broederbond
Alexander, A. V. 236–7, 239, 250, 252
Alexander, Field-Marshal Lord 243, 246
Altham, E. 45
Amery, L. S. 105–7, 112–13, 114, 200
Anglo-American Corporation 302
Anglo-Boer Wars
  1880–1881 2
  1899–1902 9, 19, 37–54
  concentration camps 65, 278, 280, 305
Angola 332, 344, 346, 349
Anti-Apartheid Movement 334, 338
Anyaoku, Emeka 350
apartheid
  British reactions to 33, 116, 155, 229, 307–42, 346; Africa Bureau 194, 222
  end of 16, 343–7
  ideology 11, 16, 21
  origins 34
Arlott, John 325
arms sales and embargoes 35, 253, 321, 322, 328–9, 332, 346

army (South African) 14, 25, 27, 28, 242, 276, 346
Asiatic Land Tenure and Indian Representation Act (1946) 151
Asquith, H. H. 60, 68, 83, 86
Athlone, Lord 107
Attenborough, Richard 337
Attlee, C. R. 132, 178, 181, 184, 187, 189, 200, 204, 206, 215–17, 221, 225, 233, 236–7, 240–1
Australia 34, 76, 82, 105, 118, 128, 252, 349
Ayub Khan, M. 265, 267, 270

Balfour, A. J. 69
Ballinger, W. 293
Bandaranaike, Mrs S. R. D. 265–6, 268
Bangwato people 168, 170–3, 193–4
Bank of England 48, 123, 129–33, 136–7, 140, 143, 163, 263
Bantu Education Act (1953) 289–90, 315
Bantustans 21, 25, 101, 109, 116, 319, 330
Barber, J. 75
Baring, Sir Evelyn 32, 33, 107, 116, 135–6, 137, 173–4, 178, 184–5, 194, 225, 255
Basutoland (Lesotho) 2, 77–101, 196
  see also High Commission Territories
Bathoen, Chief 97
Baxter, G. H. 186, 187, 204–7, 210–12, 215, 218–19
  Baxter Report 206, 210, 213, 215, 219, 224
Bechuanaland (Botswana) 77–101, 166, 168–96, 293
  see also High Commission Territories
Beetham, E. B. 192
Beira 111
Benson, A. E. T. 205, 225
Berridge, G. R. 230–3, 242–3, 249–52, 256
Bevan, Aneurin 157, 184, 254
Beyers, General C. F. 19, 71–2, 174
Biko, Steve 332
Bismarck, Otto von 6, 77

Index

Bloemfontein 52, 297
Booth, A. R. 77, 86, 87
Boshoff, Ds G. J. J. 260
Botha, Louis 10, 19, 27, 32, 57, 66, 74, 76, 97–8, 99, 106, 296, 323
Botha, P. W. 253, 332–4
Botswana *see* Bechuanaland
boy scout movement 15, 23
British South Africa Company 110
British South Africans 14, 18, 31, 73, 174, 279, 285, 308, 323
broadcasting 283–5, 317, 334, 339
Brockway, A. Fenner 182–3, 195
Broederbond, Afrikaner 16, 23–4, 227
Brook, Sir Norman 180, 187
Brookes, Dr E. H. 79
Bryce, James 68, 78
Buchanan, J. N. 169
Bullock, H. L. 190
Bureau of State Security (BOSS) 25
Burger, Schalk 71, 72
Burns, John 67
Buthelezi, Mangosuthu (Gatsha) 336–8
Butler, R. A. 269
Butt, R. 334
Buxton, Lord 107
bywoners 12

Cabinet decision-making (British) 6
  Anglo-Boer War (1899–1902) 47
  Central African Federation 213–14, 216, 217–18, 221–2
  general relations with South Africa 17 (Sept 1950), 208, 259 (Apr 1951)
  Seretse Khama 176, 179–80, 181 (June 1950)
  Simon's Town 238, 249
  South Africa Act (1909) 83
  South African 'Indians' 151
  Southern Rhodesia (1921) 110–12
  South-West Africa 149, 156
  transfer of High Commission Territories 108
  Transvaal constitution (1906) 58–64
  United Nations issues 158
Calata, J. 280
Callaghan, James 239, 328, 332
Campbell-Bannerman, Sir Henry 57–64, 74
Canada 42, 73, 76, 120, 128, 159, 199, 239, 252, 275, 349
Cape native franchise *see* franchise rights
Cape route to the East 1, 8, 28, 37, 43, 46–7, 53, 231–3, 250, 328
Cape Town 44, 297
Carnarvon, Lord 79, 87

Carrington, Lord 65
Catto, Lord 131–2
Central African Federation 18, 110, 116, 163, 191, 194, 198–229, 255–6, 286, 288, 330
Chamberlain, Austen 47
Chamberlain, Joseph 9, 38, 40, 51, 68, 73
Chinese labour 10, 61, 66, 68–9, 74, 84
churches (UK) 290, 327–9, 333–5
Churchill, Sir Winston 28, 59, 62, 65–7, 68, 76, 81, 92, 102–3, 182, 184, 208, 217, 241, 243–4, 246, 257, 287
Citizenship Act (1949) 284, 310
Clark, Sir (W) Arthur (W) 190–2, 194, 225, 228
Clark, Sir William 107, 108
Clifford, B. E. H. 112
Cohen, Sir Andrew 175–6, 179, 198, 201–19, 233–4, 258
Colby, Sir Geoffrey 225
Cold War 8, 194, 224, 231, 255, 263, 305, 320, 328, 338, 344
  see also communism
Collins, Canon John 290, 295
colour bar 82, 168, 204, 293, 303
  see also apartheid
'Coloured' people (Cape) 15, 23, 26, 77, 82, 139, 238, 247–9, 252, 277–8, 280, 284, 289, 291, 294, 297, 302, 312–13, 315, 325, 333
Commonwealth 17, 30, 57, 107, 115, 118, 129, 133, 134, 138, 147, 149–53, 154, 159–60, 163, 165, 185, 211, 230–3, 252, 259, 286, 300, 320, 335, 341
  Prime Ministers' Meeting, 1960 261
  Prime Ministers' Meeting, 1961 254, 264–70, 302
  South Africa's departure (1961) 19, 21, 35, 142, 145, 260–272, 273, 302–3
  South Africa's return (1994) 346–50
communism 16, 17, 182–3, 195, 235, 259, 264, 289, 310, 343, 345
  see also Cold War
Conradie, J. M. 108
Conservative Party (South Africa: Konserwatiewe Party) 20, 344
Conservative Party (UK) 157, 190, 269, 287, 317, 318, 321, 333, 341
Constantine, Leary 183
copper 32, 211, 220, 228
Corner House Group (mining) 9
Coupland, Sir Reginald 169
Courts of Appeal 34, 275–6, 284
Cranborne, Lord *see* Salisbury, 5th Marquess

Index

Craven, Dannie   333
Creech Jones, A.   175–6, 177, 179, 202–4
Crewe, Lord   80–101, 102–3
  Crewe Circular (1909)   170
cricket   15, 227, 277, 318, 325–7, 347
Criminal Law Amendment Bill (1953)   313
Crowder, M.   197
Crush, J.   101
cultural links and issues   14–16, 274, 277, 296–8, 305, 314
currency (Rand)   306
Curtis, Lionel   107
customs revenue   18, 41, 195, 227, 347

Davenport, T. R. H.   26, 58, 72
decolonisation (British)   167, 198, 209–10, 272, 275, 286, 289, 298, 320, 339, 341, 343–4
defence issues   16, 44, 230–53, 276
de Kiewiet, C. W.   113, 116
de Klerk, F. W.   337–8, 339, 345
Delagoa Bay   30, 39, 42–53, 111
de la Rey, J. H.   19, 71
Democratic Party (Rhodesia)   227
Denoon, D. J.   58, 65, 69
de Villiers, Sir Henry   90, 93
de Wet, Gen. C. R.   19, 72
diamond mining   2, 13
Diefenbaker, J.   262–3, 264, 267, 268, 270
Dilke, Sir Charles   82
Dixon, Sir Pierson   163
d'Oliveira, Basil   325
Dönges, Dr T. Eben   134, 135, 139, 292
Drakensberg Boys' Choir   16
Driberg, Tom   154, 195
Dubow, S.   26
Dugdale, J.   155, 287
Dunbar Moodie, T. *see* Moodie, T. Dunbar
du Plessis, P. T.   108
du Plessis, W. C.   301
Durban   31, 44, 82, 240, 243, 251, 297, 303
Durr, Kent   349
Dutch Reformed Churches   23–5, 73, 227, 345
Dutfield, M. J.   196
du Toit, C. L. de Wet   240, 242
du Toit, J. D.   73

East Africa High Commission   201, 207
Eccles, Sir David   164
economic links and issues   13–14, 118–45, 224, 272, 275, 276, 305, 344
Eden, Sir Anthony   231, 244, 246, 247–9, 257, 294–5

education   2, 15, 73, 277, 289–90, 305
  Christian National   23, 26, 290
Edward VIII, King *see* Windsor, duke of
Egeland, L.   173, 187
elections (South African)   22
  1907 (Transvaal)   65, 69–70, 74
  1915   19
  1924   112
  1929   75, 106
  1948   75, 116, 133, 282, 309
  1966   323
  1994   338–9
Elgin, Lord (9th Earl)   59, 60, 66, 68, 81
Enfield, Cy   330
Erasmus, F. C.   234, 237–9, 242, 247, 251, 291
expansionist issues ('Greater South Africa')   18, 28, 31, 33, 99, 102, 200, 208–12, 224–9, 256
exports (South African)   13, 119, 120, 125

farming interests (white)   74, 108, 126–7
federalism   2, 30, 76, 198, 207
Federasie van Afrikaanse Kultuurverenigings (FAK)   23–4
Federation of Rhodesia and Nysasland *see* Central African Federation
film   330, 332, 336–7
flag controversies   21, 112, 276, 291–2, 316
Flett, M. T.   136
Foot, Dingle M.   183
Foot, Sir Hugh   192
Forsyth, D.   173
franchise rights   21, 23, 74, 79, 80–2, 285, 291
freemasonry   15

Gaitskell, Hugh   134, 294
Ganspan   251
George VI, King: royal tour (1947)   278–81
Gereformeerde (Dopper) Kerk   345
German policy   19, 46–9
  Anglo-German Convention (1898)   46, 49, 54
Germond, J. D. A.   192
Geyer, A. L.   241
Geyser, O.   102, 350
Gladstone, Lord (Herbert)   94
Gladstone, W. E.   2, 69
Gleneagles Declaration   332, 347
gold   2, 9, 12, 13, 37–9, 48, 107, 118–45, 230, 263, 344
gold loan (1948)   132
gold standard (SA)   120, 126

Index

Gold Coast (Ghana)   160, 164, 257, 269, 286, 293
Goodenough, K. M.   225
Gordon Walker, P. C.   17–18, 31, 35, 154, 156–7, 175, 178, 181–90, 203, 204–17, 238, 240, 254, 270
Gorell Barnes, W. L.   219, 221
Graaff, Sir de Villiers   170
Graham, Sir Fred   61, 72
Great Trek   1, 305
'Greater South Africa' *see* expansionist issues
Grey, Sir Edward   68
Greyling, J. C.   293
Griffiths, James   156–7, 189, 204–6, 211, 213–17, 227, 254
Group Areas Act (1950)   312
Guiana, British   166
Gupta, P. S.   224

Hailey, Lord   150
Hailsham, Lord (Quintin Hogg)   182
Hain, Peter   326, 328
Hall, G.   148
Hancock, Sir Keith   28, 75
Harcourt, L. V.   71, 86, 98, 107
Hardie, Keir   82
Harlech, Lord (W. Ormsby-Gore)   107, 200
Harragin, Sir Walter   176–8, 179–80, 187
Havenga, N. C.   112, 126, 127, 128, 133, 137, 138, 244–5, 250–1, 309
Heath, Edward,   323, 346
Heathcoat Amory, D.   140, 259
Hertzog, General J. B. M.   19, 21, 30, 72, 99, 106, 112–14, 127, 128
Het Volk (Party)   11, 20, 69–70, 74, 76, 97
Hicks Beach, Sir Michael   51
High Commission Territories   12, 17, 31, 102–17, 136, 194–6, 222, 231, 242, 255, 260, 286
   see also Basutoland, Bechuanaland, Swaziland
historiography   3–13, 77, 106, 250
   see also individual names
HIV/AIDS   342
Hofmeyr, J. H.   32, 106
'Hoggenheimer' (cartoon character)   281
Holyoake, K. J.   265–6
Home, Lord (Sir Alec Douglas-Home, 1963)   138, 141, 161–2, 163–4, 259, 269–70, 319, 328
homelands *see* bantustans
Hopkinson, H. L.   220–1

Hopwood, Sir Francis   103
Huddleston, Fr Trevor   290, 295, 315, 331, 333–4, 338
Hudson, R. S.   175, 177, 194, 221
Huggins, Sir Godfrey   204, 206, 208, 215, 218–19
humanitarian tradition *see* trusteeship

immigration
   Afrikaner into Rhodesia   206, 208, 211–12, 224–8
   British   10, 21, 54, 284
Immorality Act (1950)   170
indentured labour *see* Chinese labour
Indian government policy   150
   see also Nehru, J.
'Indians' in South Africa   11, 15, 31, 74, 83–4, 146, 150, 159, 277–8, 279–80, 294, 299, 302, 333
industrial policies   12
   see also gold, diamond mining, mining industry
influx control   25
Inkatha   336, 338
International Court of Justice   155–6
investment, foreign   14, 39, 120
Ireland (Eire)   107, 128, 252, 336
Isandhlwana (1879)   1
Ismay, Lord   191–3, 216–20, 241

Jabavu, J. T.   82, 84
Jacottet, Revd E.   86
jam   119, 134
Jameson, L. S. and Jameson Raid   3, 40, 76
Jarrett, C. J.   244
Jeffries, Sir Charles   254
Jewish South Africans   9, 278, 281
Johannesburg   2, 68, 70, 208, 290, 297, 303, 315
Johnson, Paul   323, 334–5
Johnstone, F. A.   12
Jones, A. Creech *see* Creech Jones, A.
Jones, Sir Roderick   115
Just, H. W.   68, 73

Kairos Document   345
Keith, A. B.   67
Kennedy, Sir John   208, 225
Kenya   7, 30, 32, 103, 111, 147, 174, 194, 208–10, 288, 293, 323
Kenyatta, Jomo   170
Kerr, P.   105
Kgama (Khama) III   80, 84, 94, 98, 172, 191
Kgamane, Rasebolai *see* Rasebolai, Kgamane

Khama, Ruth (Williams) 168, 176–7, 179–80, 185, 188, 192
Khama, Seretse 18, 34, 149, 156, 168–97, 216, 228, 255–6, 287, 311
Khama, Tshekedi 113, 149, 169–97
Kilmuir, Lord 270
Kimberley, Lord 44, 79
Konserwatiewe Party *see* Conservative Party (South African)
Krishna Menon, V. K. 183, 184
Krozewski, G. 140
Kruger, President Paul 2, 37–54, 61, 253
KwaZulu *see* Zulu people

Labour Party (British) 183, 193, 222–3, 287–8, 294–6, 298, 306, 316, 321, 328, 331, 341
Labour Party (South Africa) 23, 69–70
Lagden (Native Affairs) Report (1905) 33, 79
Lambert, H. C. M. 48
land
  Land Bank 11
  settlement schemes 54
  territorial division and segregation 32, 108
  see also Natives Land Act (1913)
Lane, E. F. C. 105
Lawson, Nigel 325
League of Nations mandates 148, 159
legal system 25
Legassick, M. 25
Le May, G. H. L. 58, 75
Lesotho 2, 349
  see also Basutoland
Le Rougetel, Sir John 190, 225, 245, 247, 257
Letsie, Chief 84, 94
Lewis, W. A. 183, 222
Leyds, Dr W. J. 61
Liberal Party (British) 54, 65, 328
Liesching, Sir Percivale 173–5, 187, 189, 194, 203, 217–19, 239, 247, 254, 258
Limpopo River 17, 200, 225, 255, 288, 292
Lipson, D. L. 190
Listowel, Lord 153
Little, K. 222
Lloyd, Selwyn 162, 163–4, 259
Lloyd, Sir Thomas 213, 225
Lloyd George, D. 59, 65
Lobatsi 185
Loreburn, Lord 62, 68
Lourenço Marques 46, 111
Louw, E. H. 134, 135, 138, 159, 247, 251, 261–72

Lyttelton, A. 54, 58–64 (Lyttelton Constitution, 1905)
Lyttelton, Oliver (Lord Chandos) 216–19, 221, 223

MacDonald, J. R. 82
MacDonald, M. 107
McGrigor, Sir Rhoderick 242
Machtig, Sir Eric 153
McIntosh, Phean 170
Mackinder, Sir Halford 8
Macleod, Iain 162, 163, 259
Macmillan, Harold 6, 16, 34, 139–40, 162–5, 246, 258–72, 298–9, 317, 346, 348
Macmillan, W. M. 190, 197
McNeil, Hector 155, 184
Mafeking 176–7
Major, John 347
Majuba Hill 2
Malan, Group Captain A. G. ('Sailor') 312
Malan, Dr D. F. 19, 22–3, 25, 116, 127, 133, 154, 173, 195, 219, 234, 242, 250, 257–8, 280, 283, 286
Mandela, Nelson ii, xi, 15, 279, 290, 299, 304, 321, 337, 338, 339, 342, 343, 345, 347–8, 350
Marks, Shula 3, 8, 12
Maud, Sir John (Redcliffe-) 6, 36, 254, 256, 260–1, 263–4, 270–2, 319, 345
Mawby, A. 70
Mbeki, Thabo 349
Merriman, J. X. 83, 91
Menzies, Sir Robert 265, 267
Meyer, Dr P. 23
Mfecane 1
Michell, Sir Lewis 111
migrant labour 101
  see also Witwatersrand Native Labour Association
Millin, S. G. 59, 285
Milner, Lord (Alfred) 6, 9, 10, 38, 39–56, 65, 69, 73, 74, 107
mining industry 5, 9, 12, 40, 61, 120, 127
  see also diamond mining, gold
missions and missionaries 15, 79, 86, 98, 168, 222, 280, 289, 315
Montgomery, Field-Marshal Lord 299
Moodie, T. Dunbar 22, 25
Morley, John 59, 62–3
Morris, James (Jan) 316
Morrison, H. S. 184
Mozambique 103, 110, 346, 349
Muldergate scandal 332

Index

Naicker, Dr G. M. 301
Namibia 332, 349
  see also South-West Africa
Natal 31, 76, 80, 92, 97, 243, 285
national anthem 276, 280, 292, 316
National Party 7, 16, 20, 22–3, 33, 133–45, 152, 231, 251, 280, 309
Natives Land Act (1913) 28, 108, 114
Naudé, Ds C. Beyers 345
navy (South African) 245, 248, 251, 343
Nazi influences 8, 19, 257, 308, 309–11, 314, 315–16, 318, 323, 333–5, 340–1
Nederduits Gereformeerde Kerk (NGK) 345
Nehru, Jawarhalal 262, 264, 266–9
Nel, M. D. C. de Wet 25
New Zealand 15, 118, 128, 149, 159, 297
Newfoundland 199
newspapers *see* press opinion
Ngamiland 108
Nicolson, Harold 5, 316
Nkrumah, Dr K. 220, 265–6, 267–8
Nkumbula, H. 221
Noel-Baker, P. J. 154, 171–6, 178–81, 202–3, 236
nuclear issues 224, 230, 289, 346
Nyasaland 111, 201, 216, 218

Okovango River 108
O'Meara, D. 11, 12, 19, 344
Oppenheimer, H. 302, 304
Orange Free State/Orange River Colony 52, 64, 67–8, 134
Orangia Unie 20, 76
Ormsby-Gore, Sir W. *see* Harlech, Lord
Ossewa Brandwag (OB) 23–4, 32, 280, 324
Ottawa Agreements (1932) 127

Pakenham, Lord 239
Palmerston, Lord 5
Pan-Africanist Congress (PAC) 302
pass laws 25
Patterson, Revd L. 169
Pearce, Dr R. D. 197
Perham, Dame Margery 9, 10, 107, 183, 194, 222
Pethick-Lawrence, Lord 151
Pilkington, Dr R. 169
Pirow, Oswald 32, 106, 200, 280
Platts-Mills, J. 311
police policy 25, 292, 303
population 14–16, 26, 277, 308
Portuguese empire 46, 111, 115, 126
Powell, (J.) Enoch 330
Poynton, Sir (A.) Hilton 224

press opinion (newspapers and journals) 40, 51, 168, 182, 277
  Argus (Cape) 294, 299
  Bantu World 186, 287
  Bloemfontein Post 74
  Die Burger 240, 287, 294, 299, 304
  Cape Times 15
  Daily Despatch 302
  Daily Express 193, 323
  Daily Mail 318
  Daily Telegraph 193, 321
  Drum 302
  Economist 137, 313, 319, 323–5
  Fighting Talk 288, 301
  Imvo Zabantsundu 77, 187, 297, 301
  Johannesburg Star 168, 280, 301, 303
  Kerkblad 302
  Manchester Guardian 175, 183, 193, 309, 313, 321–2, 325, 331, 339
  Natal Mercury 15, 288
  New Statesman 310, 313, 317, 321–4, 327, 331–2, 334–6
  Observer 310, 321
  Pretoria News 15
  Private Eye 323
  Rand Daily Mail 287, 299
  Round Table 107
  Spectator 310, 313, 315, 319, 322, 325, 327–8, 329–30
  Sunday Telegraph 321, 339
  Sunday Times 315, 338
  The Times 183, 193, 309, 313–16, 317, 321–3, 327–30, 331, 333, 338–9
  Die Transvaler 280, 282, 287, 289, 293, 294
  Tribune 309
  Volksblad 289
pressure groups (British) 5, 101, 115
  see also under titles
Pretoria 2, 69–70, 103, 343
Privy Council, Judicial Committee *see* Courts of Appeal
Progressive Party 300
Prohibition of Mixed Marriages Act (1949) 170, 172
Promotion of Bantu Self-Government Act (1959) 25
Purified National Party 20, 127, 234

Queen Elizabeth II 279, 347

race issues 146–67, 182, 183, 194, 219
  see also apartheid
railways 11, 18, 32, 41, 42, 105, 108–11, 227
Ramphal, Shridath 348

Rasebolai, Kgamane   191, 196
Reddingsdaadbond (RDB)   23–4
Redmayne, M.   269
Republic, declaration of (1961)   18, 143
republican movement   21, 27, 72, 74, 285, 292, 300–2
Rees-Mogg, W.   338
Reeves, Bishop Ambrose   290
Rheinallt Jones, D.   187
Rhodes, Cecil   40, 79
Rhodesia, Northern   201, 209, 211–12, 216, 227
  see also Central African Federation
Rhodesia, Southern   30, 53, 77, 97, 110–12, 174, 200–29, 293, 304, 320
  see also Central African Federation
Ripon, Lord   68, 99
Rivonia trial (1962)   305, 321
Robinson, Sir J. B.   11, 70
royal tour (1947)   278–81, 297
Rubusana, Revd W.   82, 84
rugby   15–16, 169, 227, 277, 291, 296–8, 314, 327–8, 333, 347, 349
Rumbold, (H.) A. (F.)   240–1
Rustenberg Declaration   345

Sackville-West, V.   316
Sadie, J. L.   26
Salisbury (Harare)   208, 214
Salisbury, Lord (3rd Marquess)   42–3
Salisbury, Lord (5th Marquess)   31, 51, 192, 220–2, 313
sanctions   16, 21, 145, 166, 322, 329, 335, 344
Sandys, Duncan   270, 328–33
Schapera, I.   177
Schreiner, W. P.   82
Scott, Revd Michael   155
Seaja, Nchocho   222
Sebele, Chief   94–5
Seely, J. E. B.   81–2, 92, 93
segregation   22, 33
  see also apartheid
Seiler, J.   32
Sekgoma II   170, 172, 191
Selborne, Lord   7, 30, 42, 45–6, 51, 54, 60, 72, 88–90, 101
sexual issues   34, 68, 168–71, 176, 186
Sharpeville shootings (1960)   140, 142, 163, 260, 304, 317, 319, 330–1, 340
Sheppard, David (Bishop)   325
Shinwell, E.   214, 239–41
Sillery, A.   187, 193
Simon's Town   12, 17, 18, 44, 46, 160, 165, 230–53, 255–6, 276, 288, 291–2

Simpson, John   335, 336, 339
Slachtersnek (Slagters Nek)   71
Smuts, General (Field-Marshal) Jan C.
  before 1914 (Transvaal government)   10, 11, 27–8, 57–75, 76, 98, 296
  1914–1924 (prime minister, 1919–1924)   19, 30
  1924–1948 (prime minister, 1939–1948)   28–9, 75, 126, 128–33, 273
  Britain and Commonwealth, relations with   2, 31, 148–54, 234, 236, 276, 282, 308
  expansionist policies   33, 103–7, 110–12, 114–16, 200, 227
  racial policies   171, 184, 323
Sobhuza II, Ngwenyama of Swaziland   114, 186
Solomon, Sir Richard   66, 69
South African Airways   32
South African National Convention (1908)   82–9
South African Party (SAP)   11, 20, 74, 126
South African War *see* Anglo-Boer Wars (1899–1902)
South-West Africa   6, 18, 19, 23, 27, 46, 71, 103, 146–50, 223, 300
  see also Namibia
Soweto uprising (1976)   321, 330–2, 340
Spence, J. E.   231–3, 242–3, 249–52
Spender, J. A.   5
sport   15–16, 227, 277, 296–8, 332, 347
  see also cricket, rugby
Springbok Legion   279
Springbok teams   15, 296, 302, 314, 318, 325
Stanley, Sir Herbert   107, 110
Statute of Westminster (1931)   114
Steele, David   328
Stellenbosch   24, 72, 315
Stephenson, Sir Hugh   319
sterling area   17, 118–45, 276
Steyn, M. T.   71–2
Strauss, J. G. N.   170
Strijdom, J. G.   106, 138, 159, 227, 234, 245, 257, 291, 297, 324
Suez Crisis (1956)   159, 271, 293–4, 317, 328
Suid-Afrikaanse Nasionale Lewensmaatskappy (SANLAM)   23
Swaziland   28, 33, 34, 77–101, 107, 195
  see also High Commission Territories
Swinton, Lord   221–2, 224, 242, 244, 246, 250

Tambo, Oliver   348
Tanganyika (Tanzania)   27, 103, 162, 174, 323, 328

Index

Thatcher, Margaret 145, 305, 329, 331, 333, 335–6, 337 346
Thomas, J. H. 107, 113, 114
Thomas, J. P. L. (Lord Cilcennin) 241, 245–6
Thompson, L. M. 77
Tomlinson Commission report (1955 [1956]) 32, 108–9, 228
Torch Commando 285
Torrance, D. 13, 100
township violence (1980s) 340, 344
Transvaal (South African Republic) 1, 2, 10, 38–56, 57–75, 98, 126, 208
Transkei 90
Trapido, S. 10–11
treason trials 315
Treasury policy (UK) 131–3, 134, 139–40, 163, 263
trusteeship (British) 12, 28, 79–101, 103, 107, 117, 200, 210, 235
Truth and Reconciliation Commission 339
Tutu, Archbishop Desmond 335, 345

Uitlanders in Transvaal 2, 39, 48, 73
Union of South Africa, creation and constitution (1909) 11, 27, 77–101, 102, 275, 284, 312
  Schedule (South Africa Act, section 151) 30, 78, 86–94, 95, 100, 114, 195
Unionist Party 11
United Nations 139, 146, 258–9, 260–1, 288, 344
United Party 20, 133, 153, 235, 277, 300
United States of America 78, 81, 183, 237, 274, 289
uranium 17, 138, 149, 156, 196, 230, 235
urbanisation 22, 33

van Biljon, P. 34
van der Post, Laurens 336
van Rensburg, H. 23
van Rensburg, J. F. 19, 71
van Rooy, J. C. 23
Vereeniging, Treaty of (1902) 71
verligtes 345
Verwoerd, Dr H. F. 32, 139, 140–3, 159, 165, 258–9, 260–72, 280, 293, 301, 323–4
Vorster, B. J. 23, 323–5, 329, 332
Vorster, Dr J. D. 23

Walker, E. A. 75
Waugh, Auberon 335
Welensky, Sir Roy 201–5, 215–16, 219
Wernher-Beit Co. 9, 40–1, 50
West Indies Federation 201
West Ridgeway, Sir Joseph 64, 66–7, 70
Wheare, K. C. 207
Whyte, Q. 187
Williams, Ruth see Khama, Ruth
Willink, H. U. 59
Wilson, Harold 322, 326, 346
Windsor, duke of (King Edward VIII) 170, 171, 175, 178, 192
Wirgman, Archdeacon A. 2
Witwatersrand 2, 69–70
Witwatersrand Native Labour Association (WNLA) 10, 11
Wolseley, Field-Marshal Lord 45
women 65, 168, 169–71, 174, 188, 280, 287, 294, 305
World War, First 19, 27, 71, 106, 110, 148
World War, Second 28, 106, 128, 144, 151, 248, 273, 302, 308
Worsthorne, Peregrine 321

Xuma, Dr A. B. 186, 279

Younger, K. G. 156–7

Zambesi River 45, 103, 224, 225
Zambia see Rhodesia, Northern
Zimbabwe 305, 330, 333
  see also Rhodesia, Southern
Zoutpansberg 98
Zulu people 1, 76–7, 80, 97, 323, 330, 335, 336, 338–9
Zuma, Dr A. B. see Xuma, Dr A. B.

Printed in Great Britain
by Amazon